D1589995

The Right Honorable Thomas, Sixth Lord Fairfax, Baron of Cameron, and Proprietor of the Northern Neck. Portrait by Sir Joshua Reynolds in the possession of Alexandria-Washington Lodge No. 22, A.F.&A.M., Alexandria, Virginia. Used with permission. Photo by Marler Studios.

Fairfax County, Virginia
A History

By

Nan Netherton
Donald Sweig
Janice Artemel
Patricia Hickin
Patrick Reed

Fairfax County Board of Supervisors
Fairfax, Virginia
1978

Contents

Illustrations

1840-1870

1870-1925

1925-1976

Tables and Graphs

1649-1800

Preface

In July 1974, as plans were being made for the observance of our nation's bicentennial, the Fairfax County Board of Supervisors authorized and funded a proposal for the writing of the first authoritative, book-length Fairfax County history. The project was placed under the Office of Comprehensive Planning's ongoing history program. An advisory panel was selected, including historians, local citizens, and county officials.

Five authors were engaged to research and write the text. Donald Sweig was responsible for the period from 1649-1800; Janice Artemel, 1800-1840; Patricia Hickin, 1840-1870; Patrick Reed, 1870-1925; and Nan Netherton, 1925-1976. Each author was selected for his or her academic training, interest and proven ability to research, interpret, and write independently. Each was free to carry out the task in whatever manner seemed best and to reach conclusions which the facts warranted. The reference materials were from primary sources as time permitted, and footnotes and bibliographies are included.

Emphasis throughout the book has been on public life as revealed in public and private records and publications. To a lesser extent descriptions of domestic life are presented, derived from letters and diaries, from newspapers and other published sources. The authors have endeavored to give insights by analyzing the significance of particular events and trends and to place them in perspective. Because of the large amount of research material available on the county, time and space did not permit everything to be included here. Maps and other illustrations have been carefully chosen to amplify the text.

The completion of this project would have been impossible without the cooperation and assistance of numerous people. The members of the Advisory Panel and the Fairfax County History Commission demonstrated continued support and cooperation. The research assistants spent countless hours providing the authors with documentation for the book. The assistants were Kathleen Boyle, Margaret Windisch, Marty Feldkamp, Brenda Shackleford Butler, and Lynda McConnell.

Staffs at many repositories rendered valuable assistance. The record rooms at the Fairfax, Loudoun, and Arlington County courthouses and the Alexandria city hall; the Virginiana collections at the Fairfax, Arlington, and Alexandria libraries; the Military History Research Collection at Carlisle Barracks, Pennsylvania; and the Friends Historical Library at Swarthmore College, Swarthmore, Pennsylvania, were rich sources of research materials. So, also, were the collections at the National Archives, the Library of Congress, and the Alderman Library at the University of Virginia. John Castellani, librarian at Mount Vernon, and Bennie Brown, librarian at Gunston Hall, were very helpful, as were the staff members at the Virginia State Library, particularly in the Archives Division, and the staff at the Virginia Historical Society. Grateful acknowledgment is given to the Fairfax County Division of Mapping and Graphics and the Office of Public Affairs for their invaluable assistance and consultation, particularly Jeannie Brendler.

Many individuals read portions of the manuscript or provided historical materials. They included Joyce Travis Aument, Joseph Beard, Ernest Cassara, Thomas P. Chapman, Jr., Carol Compton, Elizabeth David, Dorothea de Wilde, Henry Douglas, Lee Farrow, Mary Fraser, Herman Friis, Robert Gamble, Richard W. Griffin, Frederick Gutheim, Alvaine Hamilton, Trudy Hanmer, Betsy Ross Hinkle, James Hoofnagle, Priscilla Howe, Jane E.P.W. Hustvedt, Mary Isom, Clement Jacobs, Bess and Peter Johnson, William Leary, Anne Lewis, Jay Linard, Richard Little, Jen and Boris Mandrovsky, Ellen McAllister, Verna McFeaters, Susan Melville, George Milner, Beth Mitchell, Emily Monk, James T. Moore, Robert Morgan Moxham, Agnes Mullins, Ross Netherton, Ilah Osborn, Josephine Pacheco, Jean Packard, Ida Patton, Virginia Peters, Kirk Reed, Constance Ring, Harva Sheeler, Susan Smith, Vivian Smith, Edith Sprouse, Richard Stephenson, Suzanne Stromberg, Constance and Mayo Stuntz, Carolyn Sung, Beth Sundquist, Julie Terry, Robert Truax, Dory Twitchell, Emily Walcher, James Walker, W. T. Woodson and Tony Wrenn.

Special appreciation goes to Robin Pedlar and other secretaries in the Office of Comprehensive Planning who assisted with the preparation of several thousand pages of manuscript for review and publication. Sandra Costich was the copy editor and Gloria Matthews, the artist and book designer.

Nan Netherton
Project Director

Captain John Smith's Map of Virginia. Reproduced from an engraving originally published in 1624. Library of Congress.

Introduction

The Potomac Meeting Place

Today, Fairfax County, Virginia, a "second tier" suburb of the nation's capital, provides homes for more than half a million people, a large portion of whom work outside the borders of the county in the office complexes of Washington and Arlington. It is a county of subdivisions, townhouses, and apartments. It is a county of government workers, of professional, white and blue collar workers, of housewives, and of children. And hence it is a county of shopping centers, schools and parks, a county whose zooming population turns country lanes into country roads, where farm and forest give way not only to new homes and commercial and industrial complexes, but to super highways and airport runways.

Fairfax County lies in the northeastern corner of Virginia, in the Tidewater-Piedmont transition zone of the Potomac River watershed. Its elevation above sea level ranges from five feet along the river shore to 518 feet at Tysons Corner. Modern Fairfax County includes 399 square miles of land and 11.4 square miles of water surface within its boundaries. It is roughly rectangular in shape, bounded on the northwest by Loudoun County, on the northeast and southeast by the Potomac River and Alexandria (opposite Maryland and the District of Columbia), and on the southwest by Prince William County.

The major bays and streams, proceeding north up the Potomac from the Occoquan, are Belmont Bay, Pohick Bay, Accotink Creek, Dogue Bay, Little Hunting Creek, Great Hunting Creek, Four Mile Run, Spout Run, Donaldson Run, Pimmit Run, Scotts Run, and Difficult Run. As a source of water, a mode of transportation and a dominant element of the landscape, the Potomac River has always played a major role in the county's history.

The temperate climate is humid and mild winters reflect both the sheltering influence of the Appalachian Mountains to the west and the relatively close proximity of the Atlantic Ocean to the east. The frost-free season lasts about 200 days, long enough for the maturing of a wide variety of field crops, vegetables, and fruits. The ground is generally frozen only to shallow depths.

Fairfax County's forests and streams have offered habitats for a rich variety of fish and wildlife, both because of their location in the border zone between northern and southern species, and because the Potomac River basin for centuries has served as flyway and seasonal habitat for migratory wildlife. Additionally, the river itself has provided a meeting place for salt water and fresh water marine life at the Little Falls of the Potomac, and at the mouths of its tributary streams.

Throughout its history, Fairfax County's fortunes have been strongly influenced by the presence of the Potomac, and a geological feature known as the "Fall Line." Created by erosion of the soft Cretaceous rock of the coastal plain where it meets the harder crystalline rock of the Piedmont, the Fall Line is an escarpment which stood as a temporary barrier to river navigation until it was overcome by the canal engineers of the eighteenth century. Below the Fall Line, the Potomac is broad and placid, rich in marine life, and hospitable to both planters on the shore and travelers on the river as its bays and inlets offered sites for boat landings and its tributaries provided avenues to the Piedmont.

When Captain John Smith sailed up the Potomac River in 1608 with a small party of English explorers, he observed and described many of these natural features. A few Indian villages, which Smith mapped, lay along the waterways within what were later to become Fairfax County's boundaries. Reminders of these native inhabitants linger today in names like Dogue and Pohick, Accotink and Occoquan. Smith and his party went as far north as the head of navigation, the Little Falls of the Potomac, where he reported finding fish in more plentiful quantities and varieties than any of them had ever before seen.[1]

The Indians in the area at the time of Smith's visit were no doubt representative of both northern and southern cultures. A group of Susquehannocks (Iroquois) came down a distance of two days' journey to see him, at his request. They had with them hatchets, knives, and other commodities obtained through trade with the French.

Watercourses served as highways in those times: they were main routes for the Indians and for the traders and settlers who came later. All were able to move easily back and forth between the shores of presentday Maryland and Virginia. Thus, the Necostins, also known as

1. Captain John Smith, *The Generall Historie of Virginia, New England and the Summer Isles* (London: Printed by I.D. and I.H. for Michael Sparkes, 1624. Facsimile edition printed in Italy for the World Publishing Company, 1966), pp. 56-63.

Nacotchtanks or Anacostins (Algonquins), lived at the mouth of the Anacostia River on the Maryland side and also on Analostan (now Theodore Roosevelt Island) off the Virginia shore. The Dogues (also spelled Doag, Toag and Taux) lived on Mason Neck, once called Dogue's Neck, and on an island off Mason Neck which has eroded away since Smith's day. Dogues also lived on the Maryland side of the Potomac. These two separate tribes were once part of the Powhatan Confederacy but by Smith's time were beginning to ally themselves with the Iroquois from the north. The local villages were Tauxenent on the Occoquan; Namassingakent on Dogue Run; Assomeck below Great Hunting Creek; and Nameroughquena on Analostan Island; there were also settlements at Pimmit Run, and at Pohick, Accotink and Little Hunting creeks.[2]

With the coming of later Englishmen, who followed Smith, the Indian presence gradually but steadily waned. The English brought new diseases, more lethal weapons, and an insatiable greed for what had once been Indian land. They also brought a firm determination to impose their order on the new land.[3]

2. For detailed information on the history of Indians prior to the first settlement by the white man in Fairfax County, see: William M. Gardner, Stephen J. Gluckman, Ellis E. McDowell, and Charles W. McNett, Jr., "A Report of Excavation at the Stout Site," *Bulletin of the Archaeological Society of Virginia*, 24 (1970) 133-40; C.B. Rose, Jr., *Arlington County, Virginia : A History*, (Arlington, Va.: Arlington Historical Society, 1976), pp. 9-13; Ben C. McCary, *Indians in Seventeenth Century Virginia*, (Williamsburg, Va.: 350th Anniversary Celebration Corporation, 1958) p. 1; E.R. Reynolds, "Ossuary at Accotink, Virginia," *Abstracts of Transactions of the Anthropological Society of Washington, D.C.* (Washington, D.C., 1880-1881) pp. 92-94; Robert L. Stephenson, *The Prehistoric People of Accokeek Creek* (Accokeek, Md.: Alice Ferguson Foundation, 1959), pp. 16-17; J.R. Swanton, *The Indians Tribes of North America*, Smithsonian Institution Bureau of American Ethnology Bulletin 145 (Washington, D.C.: Smithsonian Institution Press, 1952), pp. 68, 70.

3. William Waller Hening, ed. *The Statutes at Large: Being a Collection of all the Laws of Virginia*, 13 vols. (Originally printed in Richmond, Va. 1823. Reprint Charlottesville; University Press of Virginia, 1969), 1:iv, 114-18, 143-44, 175.

Stone projectile points representing a small portion of the cultural remains of possibly eighteen different societies present in Fairfax County during the past 12,000 years. Photo by Bernie Boston.

1649 — 1800

Donald Sweig

A Note About Dates

In 1582, Pope Gregory XIII proclaimed a new calendar known as the Gregorian calendar. The Julian calendar in use before this date figured the year as slightly shorter than it is. The cumulative result by 1582 was that the dates of the equinoxes were behind by ten full days. The Gregorian calendar solved this by removing those ten days; 5 October 1582 became 15 October 1582. The new year began on January 1, and an extra day was added to every fourth year (making it a leap year) to prevent the cumulative error in the future. By 1600 most of Europe had adopted the new calendar, but not England. The problem was further complicated by the English continuing to reckon their new year from 25 March. Thus, for example, 30 January 1649 on the Gregorian calendar in use on the Continent was held as 20 January 1648 in England. This dichotomy continued until the British Parliament adopted the Gregorian calendar in 1752.

For the historian, dates are a tool of the trade, and this difference in the calendar can cause serious misunderstandings. If an action was taken by a county court on 10 January 1740, and a subsequent action taken 10 April 1741, it could appear that there was a lapse of one year and three months between the actions, when in fact, due to the March commencement of the English calendar year, the lapse was only three months.

For this reason, many dates in English history for the first three months of the year and between the years 1582 and 1752 are written in the following form: 10 January 1740/41. As the American colonies were in every respect part of the British Empire, this calendar problem is of real concern here. This work shall maintain the English month date (which was ten days behind the Continent) and write the year with a slash: 15 February 1739/40 should be read 15 February 1739 old style, and 25 February 1740 according to the new style calendar.

I

Before It Was Fairfax

The Proprietary

During the colonial period the Northern Neck of Virginia, including all of what is now Fairfax County, was held as a proprietary. This vast domain of over five million acres was given to a group of English noblemen, with control eventually coming to rest in the Fairfax family. Even though many of the people and events involved in the proprietary seem far removed from Fairfax County, both the persons and policies of the proprietors had a marked effect on the development of Fairfax, both before and after it was organized as a county. A short history of the proprietary will serve as a backdrop against which to place the people and events involved in the development of Fairfax County.

In September 1649 King Charles II of England granted to seven Englishmen all Virginia between the Rappahannock and Potomac rivers as a proprietary. The extent of the grant was hardly recognized by either the king or the grantees. Most of it had never even been mapped. The owners of the proprietary patent, or grant, were to possess, within the proprietary, all the rights of an English court baron. "They could build towns, Castles and forts, could create and endow colleges and schools, and were to enjoy the patronage of churches." They could "give, grant, or by any other way or means sell or alienate lands within the proprietary." Such lands sold or leased were to be held by any lawful tenure, rendering and paying rents and other lawful reservations to the proprietors.[1]

Until 1660 the proprietary had little real meaning as Charles II, due to political struggles in England, was a king without a kingdom. Even

---

1. Douglas Southall Freeman, *George Washington: A Biography,* (New York: Charles Scribner's Sons, 1948), 1:451.

after his return to the English throne in 1660, the proprietors thought little of their grant. Meanwhile, as early as the 1650s, the Virginia government at Jamestown had been granting land in what was to become Fairfax County. Eventually, Thomas, second Lord Culpeper, came into control of five of the six remaining shares of the proprietary, and in 1690, Culpeper's daughter, Catherine, married Thomas, fifth Lord Fairfax. It was their son Thomas, sixth Lord Fairfax, who came to control all six shares of the proprietary in 1719.

In 1732, the year in which the first attempts were made to create Fairfax County, Lord Fairfax took active control of his Virginia lands. The incident which occasioned this action was the death of Robert "King" Carter, Fairfax's land agent in Virginia. Fairfax now arranged to have his cousin William Fairfax appointed Collector of Customs for South Potomac River, Virginia; at the same time he made William his land agent. In 1735 Lord Fairfax himself came to Virginia.

As early as 1660 the Virginia government at Jamestown had been hostile toward the proprietary and the proprietors. They were, after all, losing control over a significant portion of Virginia, a fact they resented. They tried more than once (with no luck) to have the king annul the patent; they tried (with no success) to buy out the proprietors; the best they could do was to get some concessions when the proprietary grant was renewed. By 1735 this feud between the Virginia government and Lord Fairfax, who now held all the shares in the proprietary, was still not settled. The specific issue at this time was the southern and western boundaries of the proprietary, and Lord Fairfax came to Virginia to see about a survey to settle the matter. The survey was duly made, and in 1737 Lord Fairfax returned to England to argue his case before the privy council. Before leaving, however, he rode over much of his domain and set aside for himself a tract of 12,588 acres near Great Falls, in what was to become Fairfax County. At about the same time, William Fairfax began to acquire the land in Fairfax County near Mount Vernon where he would build his mansion and establish the estate called Belvoir. By 1741 William had finished and moved into his new house.

In 1745 Lord Fairfax came back to Virginia, having won his claim to the most extensive boundaries for the proprietary in exchange for certain land concessions to the Virginia authorities. Virginia had won political control over the proprietary and its inhabitants in the seventeenth century. Lord Fairfax lived at Belvoir until he moved to Frederick County in 1761.

Lord Fairfax died in Virginia in 1781; with his death, the proprietary effectively ceased to exist. All the land which had been granted by Lord Fairfax remained in the hands of the grantees; the remainder of ungranted land came under the control of the new Commonwealth of

Weights and measures bearing the inscription "The County of Fairfax 1744." These may have been procured by Lord Fairfax, for the new county named in his honor, while he was in England. Alexandria-Washington Lodge No. 22, A.F. & A.M., Alexandria, Virginia. Photo by Anthony Hathaway. Used with permission.

Virginia. As we shall see, however, from the inception of the county in 1742 until the turn of the nineteenth century, the Fairfax family exercised powerful influence on the affairs of Fairfax County. Until the time of the Revolution, they were, even before the Washingtons, the first family of Fairfax County.[2]

2. A fuller treatment of the Fairfax proprietary may be found in Kenton Kilmer and Donald Sweig, *The Fairfax Family in Fairfax County*, (Fairfax, Virginia: Fairfax County Office of Comprehensive Planning, 1975).

The Evolution of the Counties

Prior to 1649, the entire Northern Neck had been designated by the Assembly as one large county called Northumberland. As the population grew and spread north and west, new counties were created. In 1653 Westmoreland County was erected, comprising the majority of the northern portion of Northumberland. Stafford County was then created from the northern portion of Westmoreland in 1664. In each case, the new county encompassed the area between its southern border and the Potomac River. What is now Fairfax County was, therefore, first in Northumberland, then Westmoreland, and from 1664 to 1730, Stafford.

It was more than sixty years later before the growth of population created demand for another new county in the Northern Neck. In 1726 there was a proposal to create a new county from the northern portion of Stafford County; it was to be called Hartford County. This proposal was rejected by the Assembly at Williamsburg.[1]

Four years later, when a new county was created from northern Stafford, a new procedure was used.

> Throughout the seventeenth century the practice of the Assembly was to create counties as they were necessary and to require the county courts to divide them into parishes; but in 1730 it began itself to assume the function of creating parishes also. What is most interesting about the new policy is that henceforth the organization of the parish preceded the organization of the county, and so reversed the old practice.[2]

This pattern was to prevail for all of the Northern Neck counties. The Assembly would first create a new parish and then a new county whose boundaries were coterminus with those of the parish. In this manner, Hamilton Parish became Prince William County, Truro Parish became Fairfax County, and Cameron Parish developed into Loudoun County.

On 9 July 1730, the Assembly passed two bills: the first, which took effect 1 January 1730/31, created Hamilton Parish in the northern portion of Stafford County, and the second, which used the same boundaries, created Prince William County on 25 March 1731. (This was New Year's day by the English calendar.)[3] The year following the creation of Prince William County, the Assembly continuing the new policy of creating parishes prior to counties, docked the northern portion of Hamilton Parish to form the parish of Truro. The new parish was to be

---

1. Fairfax Harrison, *Landmarks of Old Prince William* (Berryville, Virginia: Chesapeake Book Co., 1964), pp. 311-12 (hereafter cited as Harrison, *Landmarks*].
2. Ibid., p. 281.
3. Ibid., p. 312.

everything north of "the river Ockoquan, and Bull Run (a branch thereof) and a course from thence to the Indian Thoroughfare [Ashby's Gap] of the Blue Ridge of Mountains."[4]

Although in 1732 the Assembly would go no further than to create a new parish, already, by that date, there were attempts to divide Prince William County.

24 May 1732

Ordered, That the Propositions from the Counties of *Prince William* and *Spotsylvania,* for Dividing the said Counties, be referr'd to the Consideration of the new Session of the Assembly.[5]

By 1736 it had been decided to make such a division:

2 September 1736

Resolved, That the County of Prince William be divided and made Two distinct Counties.[6]

On 9 November 1738 the House was asked to receive a petition from residents of Prince William to divide the county. The Assembly refused to receive this petition.[7]

Finally, 28 May 1740:

Resolved, That the proposition from Prince William, for dividing that County, in the same Manner, as the Parishes of Truro and Hamilton, in the said County, are divided, is reasonable.[8]

Further action on the division was delayed by the absence of Governor Gooch from 1740 until 1742.

By 1741 William Fairfax had moved to Belvoir on the Potomac and was elected a burgess for Prince William County to the Assembly of February 1741-42. Fairfax Harrison asserts that William Fairfax "went to Williamsburg with a mandate to bring about the long-pending separation into two counties."[9] In any event, the County of Fairfax was created by

---

4. William Waller Hening, *The Statutes at Large: Being a Collection of All the Laws of Virginia . . .,* 13 vol. (New York: R. & W. & 6. Bartow, 1823) 4:367.

5. H.R. McIlwaine, ed., *Journals of the House of Burgesses of Virginia* (Richmond: 1909-1910), p. 124.

6. Ibid., p. 284.

7. Ibid., p. 333.

8. Ibid., p. 405.

9. Harrison, *Landmarks,* pp. 318-20.

legislation introduced in May 1742, effective the following December. The dividing line was the same as that which separated Hamilton and Truro parishes; a line up Occoquan River and Bull Run, and "from the head of the main branch of Bull Run, by a straight course to . . ." Ashby's Gap in the Blue Ridge. The decision was approved by the council and governor, and it became law 19 June 1742.[10]

The new county was most likely named for Thomas, sixth Lord Fairfax, proprietor of the Northern Neck. In order to help assure the stability of the government of the new county, many of the men who had been officials in Prince William and who were living in what was then Fairfax, were appointed to positions in Fairfax County. The following men were appointed to the county court of Fairfax; William Fairfax (Presiding Justice), John Colvill, Richard Osborne, Jeremiah Bronaugh, Lewis Elzey, William Payne, Thomas Pearson, and John Minor. All of these men were from the Prince William Court. Also appointed were: William Henry Terrett, John Gregg, Gerard Alexander, Edward Barry, Daniel Jenings, and Thomas Arbuthnot. William Fairfax was appointed county lieutenant; Lewis Elzey was made sheriff; Catesby Cocke, who had been county court clerk in Prince William, became the first clerk in Fairfax. The government in Williamsburg had placed all the effective power in Fairfax County in the hands of men who were a known quantity; the county lieutenant, sheriff, clerk, and the quorum of the county court had all held office in Prince William County.[11]

The Council also "ordered that the Court House of Fairfax County be built at a place called Springfield, situated between the New Church and Ox Roads, in the Branches of Difficult Run, Hunting Creek and Accotink."[12]Springfield (in the area of what is now Tyson's Corner) was a 1,429 acre tract of land owned by William Fairfax. It drew its name from Wolf Trap Branch of Difficult Run, Scotts Run, Pimmit Run, and the Long and Bear branches of Accotink all having their sources there.[13]

Considering that what is now Loudoun County was then part of Fairfax, Springfield was a good central location; that was important for the roads were very few and the major means of travel was by horseback. The justices had to travel to the courthouse for the meeting of the county court and few men had any desire to ride any farther than necessary. The first meeting of the Fairfax County Court was held on 16 December 1742.[14] This meeting could have taken place in a newly or partially completed courthouse at Springfield, although there is no cer-

10. Ibid.
11. Ibid.
12. Ibid.
13. Ibid.
14. Fairfax County Deed Book, B-1, p.368.

tainty that it was not held at the home of William Fairfax, or of Catesby Cocke, nearer to the Occoquan.

Fairfax County was now an operating reality; it had a county court, perhaps a courthouse, and county officers. The people living there had not only created the demand for the new county, but cleared some primitive roads, and erected three church buildings of the Anglican establishment. The warehouses on the Potomac received the tobacco grown on the small farms and great plantations. Clustered around the warehouse at Great Hunting Creek were the houses of factors for Scottish merchants; these were the beginnings of Alexandria. Some men lived on and worked their own land, but much of the labor was provided by tenants, white indentured servants, and black slaves.

Fairfax County at 1742

The Land

What is now Fairfax County was settled and titled to the land taken by the same breed of men and for the same basic reason as the rest of Virginia: profit. Whatever may be said of other British North American colonies, Virginia was colonized by investors and speculators, or by agents for such men. Soon after the initial settlers at Jamestown discovered that there were no gold mines, they began to lay claim to what was to be the real wealth in the virgin wilderness: the land. A man was socially and economically ranked by the land he held. Many prominent Virginians held title to huge land grants, far more than they could ever farm or develop in any way. As land in the southern Virginia tidewater became scarce, the speculators moved west into the piedmont, and north into the Northern Neck. The main concern of the proprietors of the Northern Neck was the financial return from the quitrents on the land. Therefore, large tracts were handed out, and the only real restriction was the ability of the grantee to pay the quitrent. The Carters, Lees, Fitzhughs, and others patented or took grants on large areas in Fairfax County. In order to take firm title to a colonial land patent, a person was required to "seat and plant" on his land within three years. This requirement could be met either by building a hut to live in and keeping a couple of pigs, or by clearing an acre of ground. In either case, a prosperous landowner could, and often did, simply settle an indentured servant or a few slaves on the land to fulfill the seating and planting requirements.

Little can be said with certainty of the early patents and settlers in Fairfax County. It is not possible to know who was the first man to live here, or to be certain who had the first land patent.

Robert Moxham, who has conducted extensive and careful investigations of early land patents in Fairfax County, places the first patent north of the Occoquan River as 2,109 acres at the confluence of the Occoquan and Potomac rivers: "Doggs Island." This patent was granted to Robert Turney on 8 July 1651.[1]

By 1655 all the land on the northwest shore of the Occoquan up to the falls had been claimed. In September 1653, Thomas Speake patented 1,000 acres at the mouth of Pohick Creek,[2] and in 1654, Margaret Brent took a patent of 700 acres on the Potomac, in the Great Hunting Creek basin. This was the first land patented up the Potomac as far as Great Hunting Creek, and encompassed most of what is now downtown Alexandria. As the Brents at this time lived at Aquia Creek, the perfection of her patent implies that she seated or planted the land. This was most likely accomplished by a tenant who may have been the first English resident of Fairfax County.[3]

During the period from 1649 to 1680 there was a great conflict over who had the right to make grants in the Northern Neck. Technically, by the patent from Charles II in 1649, the land belonged to the proprietors. The colonial government in Jamestown, however, continued to issue patents along the Potomac and elsewhere in the Neck. "From 1651 to 1679 nearly a hundred colonial patents were given, conveying rights to many thousands of acres of the Potomac waterfront from the Occoquan River to Great Falls."[4]

Many of these early patents were obtained for speculative purposes. Some were sold; others were escheated for want of seating. Many were simply abandoned and the land was subsequently regranted. As if all this were not enough confusion, boundaries were often overlapped, either intentionally or by mistake. For example, even though Margaret Brent had a valid claim to the 700 acres she patented in 1654, in 1669 the colonial government granted to Robert Howsing 6,000 acres which included Brent's 700 acres. Additionally, the landmarks of the surveyors were often inexact, or worse yet, perishable; a rock or tree was often used as a marker. An outrageous, though typical, example comes from a letter of George Washington, who was a licensed surveyor, writing to Bryan Fairfax in reference to a tract of land which Fairfax had once obtained for Washington.

> I was unable, with the assistance of several of the Neighbours thereabouts, to survey the lines, or more than one corner of the tract. There was also a corner to the Land lately belonging

1. Robert M. Moxham, *The Colonial Plantations of George Mason* (Springfield, Virginia: Colonial Press, 1974), p. 4.

2. Ibid., pp. 4-5.

3. Robert M. Moxham, *The Great Hunting Creek Land Grants* (Springfield, Virginia: Colonial Press, 1974), pp. 6-7. (hereinafter cited as Moxham, *Hunting Creek*).

4. Ibid., p.6.

to the Earl of Tankerville, and at the end of the first course after leaving the run (where it was supposed the upper corner tree thereon formerly stood). From this, well known corner, neither line tree nor corner tree could be found; the next, called for by the Deed, was a white oak on the bridge branch.[5]

The point of all this is that with both the colonial government at Jamestown and the proprietors granting land, with previously granted land being regranted, with inaccurate metes and bounds, not to mention deliberate fraud, the early land grants in Fairfax County, as elsewhere, are less than clear. The courts were kept busy for many years sorting all this out, and this is precisely what makes tracing the earliest patents so very difficult.

It is possible to say that the earliest grants were speculation pure and simple. (In this regard, whatever one may think of twentieth-century land speculators and developers, there is ample precedent for their actions from their seventeenth-century predecessors.) It has been mentioned that the earliest resident of Fairfax was probably a tenant on Margaret Brent's 700 acres at Great Hunting Creek. Moxham is of the opinion that most of the seatings and plantings prior to 1680 or 1690 were by tenants and slaves. About 1690, the owners of the land began to come here to live, and as the tenants, many of whom were indentured servants, obtained their freedom, they patented land of their own and settled on it.

Of special note in this regard is the 21,996-acre tract named Ravensworth that is listed in the Northern Neck grant book as being granted to William Fitzhugh 1 October 1694.[6] This property was originally granted to John Matthews on 28 April 1684, and sold to William Fitzhugh in August 1685.[7] By April 1686 Fitzhugh made reference to the late shipment of tobacco from "my Plantation . . . so far above me . . ." which Fairfax Harrison takes to mean Ravensworth.[8] The following month, May 1686, Fitzhugh was hoping to settle Huguenots on the Ravensworth tract:

> For the french Protestants I have convenient and good Land enough to seat 150 or 200 fam'lys upon one Dividend wch contains 21,996 acres, which I will either sell them in fee at £ 17 sterling for every hundred acres, or else lease it to them for three lives paying 20 shillings p. annum for every hundred

5. J.C. Fitzpatrick, ed., *The Writings of George Washington from the Original Manuscript Sources, 1745-1799* (Washington: United States Government Printing Office, 1932-1940), 37:440.

6. In his will (1701), William Fitzhugh bequeathed the 21,996 acres in Fairfax County to his two elder sons William and Henry. The descendents of William eventually settled in Fairfax County and gave the tract its longstanding name: Ravensworth. Harrison, *Landmarks*, p. 189.

7. Ibid., pp 187-89.

8. Ibid.

acres, and they may have the liberty of renewing one two or three lives at any time, paying for each life to be renewed one year's Rent, without demanding any fine or other consideration for their first purchase; and will engage to find them with bread and meat for the first year, meat at 2s 6d p. hundred and corn at 2s 6d p. bushel, for as many soever as comes in if it be three or four hundred people, and all other necessarys for their money at the Country market price. The Land I offer to Sell or lease is scituate in this county, lyes within a mile and a half of Potomac River, and of two bold navigable creeks, is principal good land and is more proper for frenchmen, because more naturally inclined to vines, than yours or any about our neighbourhood; and will engage to naturalize every Soul of them at 3 p. head without any more or other matter of charge or trouble to them, whereby the heirs will be capacitated to inherit the father's purchase.[9]

By July 1690, Fitzhugh was still concerned about his large tract in Fairfax and still seeking tenants to settle there. In a letter of 10 July 1690, he made reference to "the absolute securing my great tract of 21,996 Acres which I have now got Deeds for, as good as the Proprietors by their Attorney Coll [colonel] Ludwell do or can give . . . ."[10] He continued,

And now [I] do intend to settle it with Tennants for three lives, allowing to each Tennant 200 acres, paying twenty shillings a year or a hhd Tob [a hogshead of tobacco] without any manner or fine and to renew a life or lives at any time paying one year rent for each life so renewed to perpetuity, which is almost as good as giving them the land in fee simple, and should be ready to supply each Tennant with corn, provisions and nails for the first year, they repaying me again at the crop according to the market rate.[11]

Apparently, some Huguenots were settled on Fitzhugh's lands in Fairfax County. In 1701 the second George Mason writing to Governor Nicholson noted that "the ffrench [sic] Refugees is most of them gone to Maryland."[12] Owing to the loss of the 1690 grant for the Ravensworth tract, Fitzhugh was obliged to take out another grant on the same land 1 October 1694.[13] Fitzhugh's experience, both with regard to getting clear title to the land and with regard to the tenants, is typical of the earliest years of what is now Fairfax County.

9. Ibid.
10. *Virginia Magazine of History and Biography* 3 (July 1895): p. 8.
11. Ibid.
12. Harrison, *Landmarks*, p. 189.
13. Ibid., p. 195.

Table I indicates the land grants in Great Hunting Creek Basin and on Mason Neck from 1651 to 1710, as determined by Moxham.

The table reflects land grants only in two areas of Fairfax County; similar information is not available for other areas in Fairfax.

Other land grant information is available, however, on a statistical basis from the Northern Neck grant books. They provide us with an overview of land grant trends and patterns in Fairfax County. It is worth emphasizing that initially Fairfax County also encompassed what is now Arlington County, Loudoun County, and the cities of Alexandria and Falls Church.

The "great land boom" in Fairfax County occurred during the period from 1720 to 1732. Beginning with the earliest known grant in the county in 1654, the subsequent 46 years witnessed only 37 land grants. Also, whereas between 1700 and 1720, 79 grants were recorded, during the following ten years from 1720 to 1730, the number of recorded grants more than doubled to 163. Due to the death of Robert Carter, proprietary land agent in 1732, grants were only made and recorded for about sixty days in 1732. Nevertheless, the years 1730, 1731, and the 60 days of 1732 evidenced 173 grants, which is more than the preceding decade, over twice the number of grants made between 1700 and 1720, and over four times the total number during the 46 years prior to 1700. Clearly, the granting of lands in Fairfax County centered around the years 1729 to 1732. When the land grants were resumed in 1737, only 48 grants were recorded in three years.

The reasons for this pattern may be found in speculation and proximity. Prince William County was founded in 1730, and there was soon pressure for a new county. Remembering that there was only a little over three months between the creation of Hamilton parish and the coterminus county of Prince William in 1730, when the Assembly in 1732 created the parish of Truro, many men undoubtedly felt that the creation of the new county could not be far behind. As the creation of a new county would encourage settlers and raise land values, the land speculators saw this as an opportunity to turn a handsome profit. On two days, 29 June and 30 June, 1731, George Carter took grants for 6,243 acres, and his brother Landon Carter took grants for 15,419. Both George and Landon were sons of Robert Carter, who had himself patented over 11,000 acres in 1727, and nearly 19,000 in 1729. The Carters were land-hungry speculators on a grand scale, but were not the only ones by any means. For example, a neighbor of Carter's from Lancaster County, Charles Burgess, took over 20,000 acres in 1731. This brings us to another point; namely, that many of the large land speculators were absentee landlords. These men took advantage of their wealth and social position in more settled counties to get large land grants in Fairfax. Although the large land holdings of the great specula-

Table I

Name	Location	Date	Number of Acres	Moxham's Reference
Robert Turney	Mason Neck	8 July 1651		P2: 16
John Jenkin	Mason Neck	1653	1,000	P3: 80
Gervais Dodson	Mason Neck	1653	1,300	P3: 82
Thomas Speake	Mason Neck	11 Sept. 1653	1,000	P3: 68
Richard Boren	Mason Neck	1654	650	P3: 325
Miles Cary	Mason Neck	1654	3,000	P3: 285
John Motrom	Mason Neck	1654	3,609[1]	P3: 306
Margaret Brent	G.H.C.B.	6 Sept. 1654	700	P3: 275
John Drayton	Mason Neck	25 Nov. 1654	2,000	P3: 313
Newberry	Mason Neck	ca. 1657	?	P4: 118
John Gosnell	Mason Neck	1657	500	P4: 118
Peeter Smith	Mason Neck	1657	500	P4: 117
Thomas Molton	Mason Neck	1657	500	P4: 119
James Cloughton	G.H.C.B.	5 June 1658	500	P4: 156
Richard Bushrod	Mason Neck	1660	2,000[2]	P4: 450
Richard Normansell and Martin Scarlett	Mason Neck	1666	2,550	P4: 323
William Boren	Mason Neck	5 June 1666	1,000	— —
George Brent	G.H.C.B.	7 Nov. 1667	1,143	P6: 625
John Matthews	G.H.C.B.	2 July 1669	1,567	P6: 238
Robert Howsing	G.H.C.B.	21 Oct. 1669	6,000[3]	P6: 262
John James	Mason Neck	20 July 1670	500	NS: 146
William Travers	Mason Neck	22 March 1678	780	P6: 622
John Carr and John Simpson	G.H.C.B.	20 Nov. 1678	627	P6: 621
William Fitzhugh	G.H.C.B.	1 Oct. 1694	21,996[4]	N2: 14
John Matthews	G.H.C.B.	13 Oct. 1694	2,466	N2: 39
William Sherwood	Mason Neck	14 Sept. 1696	670	N2: 253
John Ball	Mason Neck	8 March 1699	300	N2: 311
William Strutfield	G.H.C.B.	21 Jan. 1705	534	N3: 121
John Waugh	Mason Neck	26 July 1706	298	N3: 132
Giles Tillett	Mason Neck	4 Dec. 1706	198	N3: 145
John West, Thomas Pearson, William Harrison	G.H.C.B.	23 Dec. 1706	4,639	N3: 153
Thomas Pearson	G.H.C.B.	2 Sept. 1709	660	N3: 225
William Going and Thomas Evans	Mason Neck	23 Nov. 1714	124	N5: 8
John Todd	G.H.C.B.	23 Jan. 1715	236	N5: 47
Alexander Scott and William Harrison	G.H.C.B.	24 Jan. 1715	1,340	N5: 48
William Darell	G.H.C.B.	21 Nov. 1715	714	N5: 105[5]

1. Moxham's note: "Includes Turney's 2,109 acres, Jenkins 1,000 acres and an added 500 acres."

2. Moxham's note: "Includes Speake's 1,000 acres and 1,000 acres additional."

3. This, illegally, included Margaret Brents' 700 acres.

4. This, as noted in the text, was the third patent or grant for the same piece of land issued in 1685, 1690, and 1694.

5. This table is a composite taken from Moxham, *The Colonial Plantations of George Mason*, and *The Great Hunting Creek Land Grants*.

tors seem spectacular, the majority of land grants made between 1720 and 1732 in Fairfax were in smaller tracts of between 200 and 500 acres. The men who took these smaller grants filled out land ownership and provided population increase in Fairfax County. The second of the major reasons for the land boom at this time in Fairfax was proximity.

Court days were a big event in eighteenth-century Virginia. The justices, important men in the county, and many others would meet at the courthouse to conduct county business and private business, and to socialize. The county court of Stafford County met at the town of Stafford which is below Aquia Creek. It is a long way from Aquia to Fairfax, and men who came to court had little opportunity to look over the virgin land in the upper Northern Neck. In 1730 when Prince William County was created, the courthouse for the new county was placed on Occoquan River. There is some conjecture as to whether the actual location was on the upper or lower side of the river, and for our purposes it is inconsequential. It was on the Occoquan at the site of the ferry, approximately where Route 1 now crosses the Occoquan. From this location it would have been far easier to ride north to examine the unspoiled lands in what was to become Fairfax County. In all likelihood the men who came to court did just this and staked claims on pieces of this land for themselves. This would explain the great proliferation of land grants between 1729 and 1732; the proximity of the fresh land and the hope for profit when a new county (Fairfax) was created spurred the land fever.

Upon the death of Robert Carter in 1732, Lord Fairfax appointed his cousin William Fairfax as agent for the proprietary. William, however, did not have authority to issue land grants in the name of the proprietor, Lord Fairfax. By the time such authority was granted in 1739, Lord Fairfax had "set aside for his own use" 12,588 acres on the Potomac near the Great Falls, as he felt there were mineral deposits there. The tract was officially surveyed by John Warner and granted to Lord Fairfax in 1739. In the same year William Fairfax granted an adjacent 5,560 acres to John Colville, who transferred the tract to William Fairfax in January 1740/41. This may have been an attempt by William to circumvent the policies of his cousin, the proprietor. Lord Fairfax had been displeased at the policies of Carter, especially Carter's grants of large tracts to himself and his sons. This was partially the reason that William Fairfax did not have the power to grant lands until 1739. At that time he promptly granted himself 5,500 acres, disguising the grant by putting it in Colville's name first and then acquiring the property from Colville. Further evidence of such land manipulation is apparent from the lands granted to Catesby Cocke in 1739. Cocke had been trained in Williamsburg, being the son of a secretary of state. In 1728 he became clerk in Stafford County, in 1730 he was transferred to the clerkship in Prince William, and in 1742 became the first clerk in Fairfax. In 1739 he lived near the Prince William courthouse on the Occoquan.[14] By social standing, as a clerk and son of a secretary of state, Cocke would have been a social peer of William Fairfax. Additionally, Cocke lived near the site where William was acquiring lands for Belvoir. It seems more than coincidental that, soon after William Fairfax had acquired the power to grant land, Cocke on seven successive days in May 1739, acquired 13,089 acres of land in eighteen separate grants. Cocke was obviously in a position to know the land, and was probably a friend of the land agent. In yet another strategic move, Cocke acquired 5,985 acres on 13 April 1742, only a short time before legislation was introduced creating Fairfax County. As this legislation was introduced by William Fairfax, who was then living at Belvoir, it seems more than coincidental. Eighteenth-century Virginians were men determined to carve a private fortune and personal security from the American wilderness, and land ownership seemed to be the road to both those goals.

The question then becomes how many of the men who took land grants in Fairfax around 1730 actually came and lived there. Demographic information for the eighteenth century is seldom available, and inexact when it is. The tithing lists for both the parish and county are the only sources of such information before 1782. The Truro Parish vestry book gives the tithables for 1733 at 681. From this it may be calculated that the total population was approximately 2,043 persons, male and female, black and white. Table II will indicate approximate population profiles in Truro Parish from 1733 until 1742.[15]

The figures in Table II indicate a fairly steady rate of growth during the decade before the actual formation of Fairfax County in 1742. The total number of tithables, which reflects this growth, is fairly reliable as the figures were actually counted by a parish official. On the other hand, due to the method of calculation, the percentages of the total population represented by whites and slaves remains constant, and it is unlikely that this was the case. With the large number of navigable waterways bordering and penetrating the county, there would have been excellent opportunities to unload slaves directly from the ships. It is possible, and perhaps even probable, to suggest that the total number of slaves was higher than the table reflects. This means that the percentage of the total

---

14. Harrison, *Landmarks*, pp. 155, 321.

15. The method used for these demographic calculations follows. There exists for 1749 a detailed tithing list prepared by the Reverend Doctor Green. From that list it is possible to determine that the number of black tithables, male and female, was approximately forty-five percent of the total number of tithables, which counted only white males. Thus, applying these percentages to the 1733 Truro Parish tithing figure of 681, we get 374.5 white tithables, males only, and 306.54 black tithables, male and female. Governor Dinwiddie estimated that the total number of whites was four times the white tithables, and the total number of blacks twice the black tithables. Thus, for 1733, we calculate 374.5x4=1,498 white inhabitants and 306.45x2=612 black inhabitants.

Table II

Year	Tithables	Total Whites	Total Blacks	Population Total
1733	681	1,498	612	2,110
1734	676	1,487	608	2,095
1735	732	1,610	658	2,268
1736	818	1,799	736	2,535
1737	880	1,936	792	2,728
1738	1,013	2,228	911	3,139
1739	1,002	2,204	901	3,105
1740	1,166	2,565	1,049	3,614
1741	1,124	2,472	1,011	3,483
1742	1,331	2,928	1,197	4,125

population which was slave would have been higher than the table indicates. Also, as many slaves would have been imported who were under age sixteen, the total number of blacks in the area would have been larger, as slaves under age sixteen were not counted.

It is simply not possible to be more explicit about the number and composition of the population of Fairfax County during the early years. It is possible to say that the population grew steadily and that probably the proportion of Negro slaves was a third or more of the total population.

Roads 1742

In today's complex urban society with a network of roads and highways, a dependable maintenance system and elaborate traffic control for those roads, it is difficult to imagine a society in which formal roads did not exist. It is equally difficult to imagine the land now covered with roads to be without any, although Fairfax County in 1742 was very much this way. To try to understand the situation it is well to look at the subject of eighteenth-century roads in general. G.M. Trevelyan described a road of Georgian England as:

> not a metalled surface of definite limits hedged off from the rest of the world and maintained by an army of special functionaries paid from the public purse. It was an open track through the fields or over the common; its borders were metaphysical for it was in law a right of way from one village to another; and if, as usually happened after bad weather, the customary track was foundrous, passengers had the right to take their beasts over the edge of the neighbouring field, even if it were under corn.[16]

16. Harrison, *Landmarks*, p. 444.

It may be safely said that, as in other matters, Virginians conceived of roads in the English model and made little, if any, attempt to improve upon that model. The most common method of traveling was on horseback. Likewise, walking or driving animals allowed the users of the road to go around ruts, holes, and mud.

To this chaotic situation the Virginians, at least tidewater Virginians, added their own peculiar apathy, because the real highways, the highways upon which the houses were built, and upon which the imports and exports flowed, existed when the Englishmen arrived. These highways were the rivers. It was for good reason that Mount Vernon, Gunston Hall, and Belvoir were built on the banks of the Potomac. Similarly, the towns of Alexandria and Colchester were located on the Potomac and the Occoquan, and tobacco warehouses were built on the Occoquan, at Hunting Creek, and at Pimmit Run. Even small rivers and creeks were useful as eighteenth-century ships displaced less water, and the water level in the rivers and creeks was greater than it is in the twentieth-century. The energy needed to move goods also favored the rivers, for only on the water could the power of the wind be harnessed to move man and his wares.

The result of all this was that not only were eighteenth-century roads terrible, but that Fairfax County had little need of them. As civilization spread inland, the roads built usually led to the water, and the other roads connected the churches and the courthouse. As the roads developed, they frequently followed old Indian or animal trails or the line of least resistance along the top of natural ridges.

The best available evidence of early roads in Fairfax County is a map drawn between 1745 and 1748. Using this map as a guide, one may locate and trace the early and important roads in Fairfax County.[17]

One of the oldest roads in northern Virginia was the Potomac Path. It was originally an Indian trail running along the natural ridge between the Potomac and the Rappahannock. Beginning at the ferry crossing on the Occoquan, the Potomac Path ran to Great Hunting Creek, the present site of Alexandria. Located on this road and indicated on the map is the original Truro Parish church of 1733. Between Pohick Creek and Accotink Creek, a road branches off which runs closer to the Potomac. Created to better serve the Potomac plantations, this road, not the original Indian trail, became the Potomac Path, later U.S. Route 1. The western road running parallel to the Potomac Path followed the Indian trail and was known as the "back road," now Telegraph Road. Branching off the Potomac Path just past Accotink was the Ravensworth Rolling Road which dated from the seventeenth century. From the 22,000-acre

17. Fairfax Harrison, "A Map of Fairfax County in 1748," *Virginia Magazine of History and Biography* 36 (April 1928): 180-82.

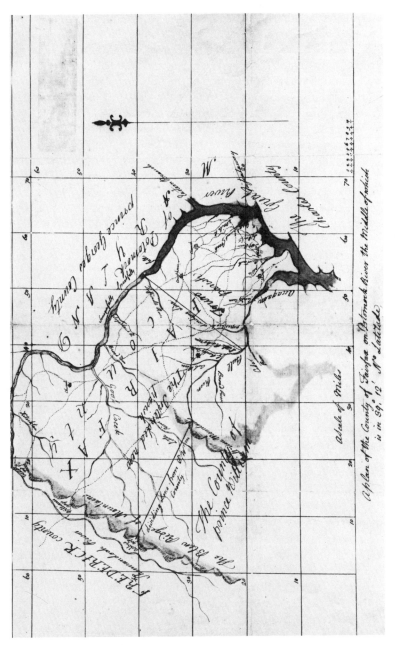

Map of Fairfax County c. 1745-1748, perhaps by Daniel Jennings. Library of Congress.

Ravensworth plantation of the Fitzhughs, it ran to Pohick Creek, and, as the name suggests, enabled casks of tobacco to be rolled from Ravensworth to the warehouse on Pohick. By 1748, the rolling road had been extended in a fork to the Upper or Falls Church of Truro Parish, and on to the Fairfax courthouse. The road from the north side of Hunting Creek to the Falls Church was a continuation of the Potomac Path and followed the eastern ridge of the county. From the Falls Church this eastern ridge road may be followed to the courthouse, then along the river, and crossing Goose Creek, on to Vestals Gap. There is also shown a road intersecting the ridge road just below the Falls Church and running to the river; this was the origin of Lee Highway. At the river, the road from the church joins the one from Hunting Creek near what is now Key Bridge and where in 1748 there was a ferry.

From the Occoquan ferry, the road leading west was known as Ox Road or Middle Ridge Road. As originally laid out in 1729 by Robert "King" Carter, Ox Road ran from Occoquan to the Frying Pan Copper Mine on the Horse Pen Branch of Broad Run. Just below Popes Head Creek Ox Road joined "Walter Griffin's Rolling Road" which crossed Little Rocky Run and continued on to Williams Gap in the Blue Ridge.

Of the remaining roads on the 1745 map, that from the courthouse to Williams Gap Road served as access from the back country to the court. It has apparently disappeared from the modern road system. The road from Hunting Creek to the juncture below Popes Head follows the general pattern of the present-day Braddock Road, but there is no firm evidence to indicate a relationship. Finally, the road from Ox Road to the courthouse was surely built to provide access to the court. It runs approximately along the path of Route 123. [18]

Not all roads are depicted on the 1745 map. For example, the map shows neither the roads from the Potomac Path to Belvoir nor to Mount Vernon. The map, however, makes clear the functions of roads in Fairfax County before there were towns and population centers: they connected churches, the courthouse, the warehouses on the water courses, and provided access to the Shenandoah Valley through gaps in the Blue Ridge Mountains.

The cash crop and the major source of economic growth in Virginia during the colonial era was tobacco. While the first residents of what was to become Fairfax County may have been tenants and have had little purpose on the land except to make good the patent, it is safe to assume that when the first settlers came here to engage in an economically profitable enterprise, they grew tobacco.

Tobacco was in every way the economic base of both Fairfax County and Virginia. It was the major export crop and also served as a

18. Ibid.

MB BJG I∘P CJG
DM LW BF ST
GM GM G∘M GM

Marks used to identify tobacco casks of some Fairfax County planters. From left to right, top to bottom: Marmaduke Beckwith, Benjamin Grayson, John Peake, Charles Green (Minister of Truro Parish), Daniel McCarty, Lawrence Washington, Bryan Fairfax, Sampson Turley, George Mason—Dogue Plantation, George Mason—Pohick Plantation, George Mason—Rent tobacco Remarked (collected from others as rent for land, repacked by Mason and marked with his brand), George Mason—Hallowing Plantation. Marks courtesy of Beth Mitchell.

medium of exchange. Civil and ecclesiastical officials were paid in tobacco; fines, assessments, and tithes were levied in tobacco. But this situation created some major problems. In order to protect the market, there had to be some control over the quality of the tobacco exported. If the quality of the tobacco were bad or inconsistent, it would have an adverse effect on the market price. Various tobacco inspection systems were adopted prior to 1730; before that date, however, the planter could sell his tobacco from his own wharf directly to the ships for export. In 1730, through the long and diligent efforts of Governor Gooch, the tobacco regulations were amended with public inspection warehouses to be established at locations selected by the Assembly. The first location selected by the Assembly for Fairfax (then Prince William County) was at "Great Hunting Creek, Upon Broadwater's land." The warehouse, however, was actually built on Simon Pearson's land on, or near, a small inlet known as Ralph's Gut. There had apparently been private warehouses located at the same site prior to 1730.

Once the Assembly had selected the site for the warehouse, the owner of the land was ordered to build the warehouses and rent them to the inspectors. If the owner refused, the warehouses were to be erected at public expense. A planter paid for each hogshead of tobacco inspected; this fee paid the rent on the warehouse and the salaries of the inspectors. The purpose of the inspection was to be sure that the tobacco was clean, contained no dirt or sand, was of general good quality, and was neatly packed into the hogshead. All bad or "trash" tobacco was burned at the warehouse by the inspectors. The owner of such tobacco suffered from the loss due to the burning. After the tobacco was inspected, it was weighed, and the hogshead was stamped with the name of the warehouse, the inspectors, and the weight. The planter would then receive an "inspectors note." The note would acknowledge receipt of a certain number of pounds of tobacco at a given warehouse, and would be signed and sealed by the inspectors; it promised to deliver that amount of tobacco to the bearer upon demand. Tobacco notes circulated and were legal tender in Virginia. The 1730 Tobacco Act provided:

> That during the continuation of this act, all public, county and parish levies, quit-rents, secretary's clerks, sherifs, surveiors, and other officers fees, paible in tobacco, shall be paid and satisfied by . . . inspectors notes . . . [and] nothing shall be accounted a lawful tender, to discharge any debt, contract, or duty, paiable in tobacco, unless paiment of the same be tendred in inspectors notes.[19]

This procedure provided a solution for several practical problems. It eliminated the problem of hauling around hundreds of pounds of tobacco to pay a debt. Likewise, it prevented payment in bad tobacco and thereby guaranteed the value of the payment. The idea, of course, was that eventually the inspectors' notes would end up in the hands of a merchant or ship captain who would then present them at the warehouse and take possession of the tobacco for export.

The first tobacco warehouse in Fairfax, constructed in 1732 on Simon Pearson's land, was "at the foot of what was afterwards Oronoko Street," in Alexandria.[20] In May 1732, Lewis Elzey and John Awbry were appointed inspectors for this warehouse.[21] A second warehouse was authorized to be built on the land of Dennis McCarty at the mouth of the Pohick, with Edward Barry and Francis Awbry designated as inspectors.[22] The salary for the inspectors was set at thirty pounds per annum at Hunting Creek, and thirty-five pounds at Pohick.[23] It is not clear why the Assembly set a higher rate for Pohick than for Hunting Creek; perhaps it was felt that more tobacco would be inspected there. In any event, the quantity of tobacco inspected at Pohick was so small that the Assembly in 1734 repealed the designation of Pohick as an inspection warehouse and established a replacement "at the copper mine landing upon Occoquan."[24]

A third warehouse was eventually established in 1742 on the lands of Thomas Lee at the little falls of the Potomac. It was Lee's hope that a warehouse on this site would serve the plantations to be established

19. Hening, *Statutes*, 4: 256.
20. Harrison, *Landmarks*, p. 414
21. Beth Mitchell, "Tobacco Inspectors." Unpublished research report. Fairfax, Virginia, 1975.
22. Harrison, *Landmarks*, p. 424; Beth Mitchell, "Tobacco Inspectors."
23. Hening, *Statutes*, 4:536.
24. Harrison, *Landmarks*, p. 424.

above the falls, but happenstance and Lee's own efforts prevented the bringing to fruition of his plans. First, the large "manor" land grants of the Fairfaxes were located just above Lee's land and acted as a barrier to development in this region. Secondly, Lee alienated the powerful Carter family by deliberately taking patents on land which he knew Robert "King" Carter had intended as an ore dock, and then he refused to share any commercial advantages at the Falls with the Scots merchants who were later to found Alexandria. The result was more opposition than even Lee, a man of no small means, could encompass, and the warehouse was not built at the falls site until 1742.[25]

Other than warehouses, the only other enterprise in what was to become Fairfax County which could be called commercial prior to 1742 was the Frying Pan Copper Mine of the Carters. Even though the commercial importance of the mine was negligible, the mining operations exerted an effect on other areas of development in the county.

The Carters discovered on the Frying Pan Branch of Broad Run a deposit of green sandstone which they took to be a deposit of copper ore. The land upon which the ore was found was patented by Robin Carter in October 1728. Subsequently, in March 1728/29, Robert "King" Carter, his sons Robin and Charles, and Robert's son-in-law Mann Page of Rosewell entered into a contract to exploit the ore deposit for their mutual benefit. Carter had first planned to load the ore onto ships near the little falls of the Potomac. Thomas Lee patented all the available land along the river to block Carter and, as a consequence, not only angered Carter, but forced him to transport the ore to the Occoquan. On the north bank of the Occoquan, near the falls, Carter illegally patented land and built a wharf to load the ore. The Occoquan warehouse was established in 1734 at "the copper mine landing." To transport the ore to the Occoquan, Carter enlarged and extended an Indian trail, the original Ox Road, from the mine to the landing on the Occoquan. "The Frying Pan Company, as it was now called, bodied up in all some 27,000 acres of land, including the tract at the Occoquan and a half-way station on the Ox Road, at the springs of Pope's Head."[26] Some Cornish miners were imported and the operation began. The Carters expected great returns from the operation:

> A Person skilled in these things who before our faces hath extracted out of some of the best of the oar [sic], a fourth, near a third, of good solid Copper, which whets up our Humours to be as Vigorous as we can in making Search into this Piece of Land.[27]

25. Ibid., pp. 422, 147-49.
26. Ibid., pp. 422-23.
27. Ibid.

However, "the more conservative assayers of London and Bristol were unable to report so favorably on the samples of ore submitted to them." Harrison asserts that the Carters realized the uselessness of the ore even before the death of "King" Carter in August 1732. In all, the operation took less than four years, and its major accomplishment was not increasing the supply of copper, but rather the construction of both the Ox Road and the landing and wharf on the Occoquan.

It is, therefore, possible to say that by 1742 much of the land in Fairfax County had been granted or patented, with much of the land held by absentee landlords for speculators. Of the total population of about 4,000, a third or more were Negro slaves, and a considerable portion of the whites were most likely indentured servants. Roads developed connecting the churches, the courthouse, and the commercial centers on the water courses. The major commercial sites in 1742 were the tobacco warehouses on the Occoquan, at the little falls of the Potomac, and most importantly, at the mouth of Great Hunting Creek. Around the warehouse at Hunting Creek were the houses of a small number of Scots merchants who later founded Alexandria. From these beginnings developed the prosperous town of Alexandria, the society in which George Washington, George Mason, and Bryan Fairfax lived and worked, and finally and eventually the county we know today.

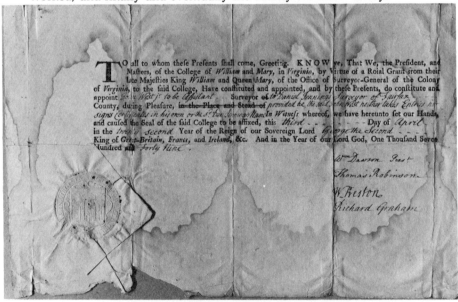

Certificate appointing John West, Jr. as Assistant Surveyor to Daniel Jennings, Surveyor of Fairfax County. This was issued by and bears the colonial seal of the College of William and Mary in Virginia at Williamsburg, which licensed all surveyors in Virginia. George Washington received his surveyor's license from the College in 1749, the same year in which this certificate was issued. Earl Gregg Swem Library, The College of William and Mary in Virginia. Used with permission.

It was, as we shall see, a middle class society governed for the most part by its upper classes.

Richard Hofstader,
America at 1750

II

The Growth and Development of Fairfax County

By 1800 the County of Fairfax had changed markedly from what it was in 1742. The land area had been reduced by almost 60 percent with the cession of Loudoun in 1757, and of Alexandria City and Alexandria County in 1798, to form the new District of Columbia. Yet the population had increased threefold. The towns of Alexandria and Colchester had been founded, the former prospering to become a major seaport and commercial center, and the latter well on its way to extinction. The courthouse had been moved twice, roads were established, mills built, and the economy had grown and flourished.

There had, of course, been the American Revolution and the founding of the new nation. In both these efforts Fairfax County provided the single most important participant: General, and later President, George Washington. Similarly, while supported by many others, George Mason sounded the clarion call for human rights in civilized society with the Virginia Declaration of Rights, and his insistence upon a bill of rights to accompany the new federal constitution. Mason's efforts helped provide the first ten amendments to the United States Constitution; to this day they protect the liberties which most Americans so cherish.

Perhaps never again did Fairfax County attain the self-contained economic strength and the claim to national recognition which it had in the late eighteenth century. With the cession of Alexandria City and Alexandria County, the exhaustion of its soils from the cultivation of too much tobacco, and the death of its two most prominent figures, Mason in 1792 and Washington in 1799, the county was on the doorstep of the economic and demographic decline which it suffered in the early nineteenth century. The decline, however, was in the future and it first remains to investigate the growth of this flourishing society on the banks of the Potomac.

Population

Much can be determined about a geographical area, or a human society, by the fluctuations in and composition of the population. Growth in population usually means economic prosperity, and demographic decline may indicate economic or political change or depression.

Similarly, whatever may be said for soil, climate, and the like, one of the major differences apparent to a stranger between eighteenth-century Fairfax County, Virginia, and, for example, a county in Pennsylvania, was the large number of blacks in Fairfax and the absence of the same in the north.

As has been noted, population information for eighteenth-century Virginia is scarce and inexact. As the county and parish were both financed by a poll tax (there was no other tax until 1777 when the newly formed Commonwealth of Virginia instituted a land tax), it was necessary each year to determine the number of tithables for both parish and county. These are recorded in the parish vestry book and the county court minute book, and there was an actual census in 1782.

Between 1742 and 1748 the boundaries of Fairfax County and Truro Parish were the same. In 1748 Cameron Parish was separated from Truro, encompassing the area later to become Loudoun County; but until 1757 both parishes were part of Fairfax County. For this reason the tithing enumeration in the county court minute books offers the best source of information to determine the population of Fairfax County between 1742 and 1800. There are, however, a number of minute books missing; therefore, a complete picture is not possible. Also, the tithing figure in the minute books is only for white adult males and black adult males and females. Therefore, the total population must be calculated and this leaves a high margin for error. Nonetheless, if the error is constant, it is possible to get a picture of the changes in population in Fairfax County.

After 1782 the population figures may again be calculated by using information from the newly instituted personal property tax return required by the Commonwealth. These returns were not submitted by individuals, but were taken as a census might be by the enumerator and again listed as white and black tithables, for the poll tax was continued.

As the court minute books are missing from 1742 until 1749, the only source of population information for the first years of Fairfax County continues to be the Truro Parish vestry book from which the population may be calculated. (See Table III.)

In perspective; the population increased in six years from 4,125 in 1742 to 5,167 in 1748, an increase of 25 percent; or to go back even further to 1733 when the earliest records for Truro Parish are available,

Table III

Year	Tithables	Total Whites	Total Blacks	Total Population
1742	1,331	2,982	1,197	4,125
1743	1,372	3,018	1,234	4,252
1744	1,476	3,247	1,328	4,575
1745	1,550	3,410	1,395	4,805
1746	1,669	3,671	1,502	5,173
1747	1,745	3,839	1,570	5,409
1748	1,667	3,667	1,500	5,167

the population had increased from 2,110 in that year to 5,167 in 1748, an increase of 3,057 or 144 percent.

In 1749 two significant events occurred which are useful in understanding the population profile at that date. First, tithables that year were listed for both the new parish of Cameron, which was to become Loudoun County, and for Truro Parish which would remain Fairfax County. The totals were 1,240 for Truro Parish, and 707 for Cameron Parish. This information helps to determine where the people were living in Fairfax County in 1749. (See Table IV.)

Table IV

	Tithables	Total Whites	Total Blacks	Total Population	% of Total Population	Total County Population
Truro Parish	1,240	2,728	1,116	3,844	64%	
Cameron Parish	707	1,555	636	2,191	36%	
						6,035

This also indicates that only 36 percent of the people living in Fairfax County in 1749 were living north or west of Difficult Run, which was the parish line. This is not surprising because people usually settled near the rivers first and then spread inland. Regrettably, in light of later developments, these figures will not allow us to determine the percentage of slaves in each parish. Based on later information, it is safe to speculate that the percentage of slaves would have been markedly lower in the new parish which became Loudoun County.

The second event which occurred in 1749 was that the Reverend Mr. Charles Green, minister of Truro Parish, made an enumerated list of the tithables for both parishes. Green's list makes the total of white tithables 1,123, and of black tithables 904, for a total of 2,207. (The discrepancy between Green's figures and the Truro Parish vestry book cannot be explained. His list is, however, very important for it allows an analysis to be made of the population at that date.)

Analysis of Green's list indicates that the total population was about 6,260 persons of all ages, black and white. Of these, 4,452 or 71 percent were white, while 1,808 or 28.88 percent were slave. Of the total 1,123 adult white males, 189 or 16.82 percent owned all the slaves. It is evident then that a small percentage of the population, 189 males, owned nearly 30 percent of the total population. Further, it is possible to determine *how* the slaves were held. That is to say, were there a large number of slaveholders with two or three slaves such as one might use on a small farm, or were most of the slaves held in large groups such as great plantations would require? Was Fairfax County in 1749 a land of large plantations run with slave labor, or was it composed of small farms where the slaves would labor alongside their white masters?

Nearly 24 percent of the slave owners held only one or two slaves, and over 61 percent of the slave owners owned six or fewer slaves. That 61 percent, however, held only 26 percent of the slaves. On the other hand, twenty-one men or 11 percent of the slave owners held over 30 percent of the slaves in groups of between twenty and forty slaves each. An additional four men owned nearly 16 percent of the slaves in groups of over forty slaves each. This means that 13 percent of the slave owners held 45 percent of the slaves. Fairfax County was also a land of great plantations run with slave labor.[1] (Table V indicates statistical data on how the slaves were held, and Table VI the names of those men who owned over twenty slaves each.)

A careful look at the twenty-five men who owned over twenty slaves includes virtually all the important men in Fairfax County: Fairfax, Washington, Mason, Alexander, Fitzhugh, Broadwater, Lee, and others. Eight of the twenty-five men owning twenty or more slaves were either justices or vestrymen. The four largest slaveowners, Lee, Washington, Colvill, and Fitzhugh held some of the earliest land patents in Fairfax County: 1719, 1674, 1734, and 1686, respectively.

Nothing could be more illustrative of the social and governmental structure of an eighteenth-century Virginia county—in this case, Fairfax County. The oldest landowners owned the most slaves; and these were the very men who because they were justices or vestrymen ruled Fairfax County. The three largest slaveholders owned 234 slaves, over 28 percent of the total number of slaves held in lots of over twenty.

---

1. Library of Congress, Washington, D.C., Manuscript Division, Fairfax County Lists of Tithables for 1749. (AC. 1808.) The Green list is for tithables only, which of course means that only blacks over age 16 were counted. To determine the total number of slaves, the tithable number was multiplied by two. This method causes certain problems. The list will indicate which men owned one, two, four, six, etc,, total slaves. In other words, while the general formula of multiplying tithable blacks by two to obtain total slave population will work for the overall picture, it does not allow us to determine how many of those listed with one tithable slave actually owned one, and how many actually owned two slaves. For this study, the formula has been strictly applied with full knowledge of the possible distortion of data in the lower figures.

Table V

Number of slaves	2*	4	6	8	10	12	14	16	18	20	40 or more
Number of owners with a given number of slaves	44	40	33	12	14	9	4	4	4	21	4
Total number of slaves in each group	88	160	198	96	140	108	56	64	72	538	288
Percentage of slave owners with "X" number of slaves	23.3	21.2	17.5	6.5	7.4	4.8	2.1	2.1	2.1	11.1	2.1
Percentage of tithable whites with "X" number of slaves	3.9	3.6	2.9	1.0	1.2	0.8	0.3	0.3	0.3	1.9	0.3
Percentage of total number of slaves held in each group	4.9	8.9	11.0	5.4	7.7	6.0	3.1	3.5	4.0	29.7	15.9

*The number of slaves has been calculated by doubling the number of the tithing list of 1749. Other calculations were made using the calculated number of slaves, not the number on the tithing list.

Of additional interest is that ten of the twenty-five slaveholders with over twenty slaves were absentee landlords; that is, they did not live in Fairfax County. These ten men owned 306 slaves or 37 percent of the slaves held in large groups. The classic example of absentee landlordism in Fairfax County was the Fitzhugh family. They not only owned the 22,000-acre Ravensworth patent, by far the largest single land patent in Fairfax County, but they also owned 166 slaves, the largest single slaveholding in the county. None of the Fitzhughs lived in Fairfax County. (Of the four Fitzhughs on Green's list, three are listed as residents of Stafford County and one as a resident of Westmoreland County.)

It is safe to say that in 1749 Fairfax County was dominated by slave labor, that the majority of the slaves were held in groups of over twenty slaves by the old established families, and that the large slaveholders governed the county. Further, much land and many of the

Table VI

Name	Number of Slaves	Other Information
Robert Carter, Jr.	20*	Westmoreland County
Elisha Hall	20	Quaker, Upper parish
John Graham	20	County Court Clerk
James Steptoe, Jr.	20	Westmoreland County
Hugh West	20	Vestryman
Charles Broadwater	22	Vestryman—County Court Justice
George Mason	22	
Will Newton, Jr.	22	Westmoreland County
John Woodbridge, Jr.	22	Richmond
Berman, heirs	22	
Gerard Alexander	24	Justice
Abr. Barnes	24	Vestryman
Daniel McCarty	24	
Catesby Cocke	28	Justice
Gedney Clark	28	Barbadoes. Clark was the brother-in-law of William Fairfax.
Aylets, heirs	28	Westmoreland County
Thomas, Lord Fairfax	30	Proprietor of Northern Neck
Daniel French, Jr.	30	Justice
William Fitzhugh, Jr.	36	Westmoreland County
William Fitzhugh, Jr.	38	Stafford County
Henry Fitzhugh, Jr.	38	Stafford County
Fitzhugh, heirs	54	Stafford County
Lawrence Washington	54	Justice (of Mount Vernon)
John Colvil	58	Justice, former Vestryman
Thomas Lee, Jr.	122	

Total: 826

*The number of slaves is double that of tithable slaves on Green's 1749 list.

slaves were held by men who lived outside of Fairfax County. It was a slave empire in the classic sense.

In general, the population continued to increase in Fairfax County until 1800, with a temporary general decrease during the late 1780s and early 1790s, and occasional sharp changes in population due to major changes in the boundaries of the county. (See Table VII). By 1756 the total population had increased to 7,628, an increase of 85 percent since the founding of the county in 1742.

Then in 1757, when Loudoun County was created from the northern and western section of Fairfax, the population dropped to 4,283, slightly more than it had been in 1742. After 1757, however, the area of Fairfax was less than half of what it had been in 1742. The cession of Loudoun again makes it possible to determine where the majority of people lived in Fairfax County in 1756. Of the 7,628 persons in Fairfax, 3,345 or 44

Table VII

			Total	Total	Percent	Total	Percent
Date	Source	Tithables	Population	Black	Black	Whites	White
1749	Rev. Green	2,027	6,260	1,808	28.88	4,452	71.11
1750	Minute Book	1,795	5,564	1,615	28.88	3,949	71.11
1751	Minute Book	1,983	6.146	1,784	28.88	4,362	71.11
1752	Minute Book	2,028	6,286	1,825	28.88	4,461	71.11
1753	Minute Book	2,233	6,921	2,009	28.88	4,912	71.11
1754	Minute Book	2,472	7,662	2,224	28.88	5,438	71.11
1755							
1756	Minute Book	2,461	7,628	2,214	28.88	5,414	71.11
1757	Minute Book	1,382	4,283	1,243	28.88	3,040	71.11
1758	Minute Book	1,416	4,389	1,274	28.88	3,115	71.11
1759							
1760	Minute Book	1,609	4,987	1,448	28.88	3,539	71.11
1761	Minute Book	1,647	5,105	1,482	28.88	3,623	71.11
1762	Minute Book	1,686	5,226	1,517	28.88	3,709	71.11
1763	Minute Book	1,807	5,601	1,626	28.88	3,975	71.11
1764							
1765							
1766							
1767							
1768	Minute Book	2,242	6,949	2,017	28.88	4,932	71.11
1769	Minute Book	2,295	7,114	2,065	28.88	5,049	71.11
1770	Minute Book	2,385	7,393	2,146	28.88	5,247	71.11
1771	Minute Book	2,508	7,774	2,257	28.88	5,517	71.11
1772	Minute Book	2,619	8,118	2,357	28.88	5,761	71.11
1773	Minute Book	2,681	8,310	2,412	28.88	5,898	71.11

White Tithables x 4 = Total

Whites

Black Tithables x 2 = Total Black

percent lived north and west of Difficult Run. The majority of the population still lived close to the Potomac River.

By 1768 the population had risen to 6,949, an increase of 62 percent in eleven years. By 1773, on the eve of the Revolution, the population of Fairfax stood at 8,310, an increase of nearly 20 percent since 1768, and of nearly 95 percent in the sixteen years since Loudoun was ceded in 1757. Fairfax County was a very rapidly growing area.

There are no population figures available for Fairfax County during the years encompassing the American Revolutionary War, 1773-1782.[2] By 1782 information is again available from the newly instituted personal property tax return which is useful in determining both the numbers of blacks and whites, and where the population was concentrated in the county. (See Table VIII). In addition, for the year 1782, there exists the first and only extant census of Fairfax County during the eighteenth century.[3] For this one year it is possible to determine something of the composition of the population.

2. The county court minute books for these years are missing.
3. The library of the Mount Vernon Ladies Association of the Union. Photographic copy of original manuscript, courtesy John Castellani, Librarian.

Table VIII

Date	FAIRFAX PARISH DISTRICT				TRURO PARISH DISTRICT				COUNTY TOTAL
	White male over 16	Slaves over 16	Slaves under 16	Total whites x 4 plus blacks	White male over 16	Slaves over 16	Slaves under 16	Total whites x 4 plus blacks	
1782†	928* (Total county white tithables for this year.)								7,271
1783	1,231 (Total county white tithables for this year.)								8,576
1784	667	968	930	4,566	567	862	937	4,067	8,633
1785	769	957	913	4,946	523	796	862	3,750	8,696
1786	776	1,005	974	5,083	546	854	915	3,953	9,036
1787**					539	855	906	3,917	
			[Estimated slaves under 16]				[Estimated slaves under 16]		
1788	657	930	(930)	4,488	537	830	(830)	3,808	8,296
1789	635	962	(962)	4,464	576	837	(837)	3,978	8,442
1790	634	981	(981)	4,498	567	817	(817)	3,902	8,400
1791	641	1,001	(1,001)	4,566	584	810	(810)	3,956	8,522
1792	608	995	(995)	4,422	591	823	(823)	4,010	8,432
1793	629	1,013	(1,013)	4,542	574	835	(835)	3,966	8,508
1794	634	996	(996)	4,528	615	911	(911)	4,282	8,810
1795	636	1,027	(1,027)	4,596	616	916	(916)	4,296	8,892
1796	611	1,068				935	Incomplete Data		
1797	617	1,079	(1,079)	4,626	650	840	(840)	4,280	8,906
Alexandria	788	368	(368)	3,888	(8,906 + 3,888 = Fx. & Alex. total of				12,794
1798	594	953	(953)	4,282	549	998	998	4,192	8,474
From Loudoun	593	831	(831)	4,034	(4,034 + 8,474 = Fx. & Loudoun total of	549	998	(998)	4,192	12,508
1799	779	1,212	(1,212)	5,540	839	1,539	(1,539)	6,434	11,974
1800					799	1,525			

†Figures for 1782 and after are from personal property tax lists.
*This number is low. Total whites should be 5,154 and white tithables = c. 1,288. 928 x 4 = 3,712 whites + 3,559 blacks = 7,721 total.
**Decrease in white population figure after 1786 is due to deletion of white males 16 to 21, and in 1789 and after, of only counting blacks below 16 down to age 12. There also seems to have been an actual population decrease, whites and blacks, in addition to the information above.

The total population of Fairfax County in 1782 was 8,763, of which 5,154 were white and 3,609 black. The percentage of blacks had risen from 28 percent of the population in 1749 to 41 percent in 1782, and the distribution of slaves had changed. Whereas in 1749 only four men had owned over forty slaves, and the slaves owned by these men were only 15 percent of the total number of slaves, by 1782 there were nine owners of over forty slaves, and these slaves accounted for over 23 percent of the total number of slaves. The major slave owners, with one exception, were all old established powerful families in Fairfax County. The largest slaveholder was George Washington with 188 slaves. He was followed by George Mason with 128 slaves; William Fitzhugh with 122 slaves; Penelope French and B. Dulany with 102 slaves; Thomas Fitzhugh with 91 slaves; Philip Lee with 82 slaves; Alexander Henderson with 72 slaves; Eleanor Custis with 65 slaves; and John Carlyle with 49 slaves.[4] Also, the percentage of the white population owning slaves had increased from 4 percent in 1748 to 7.9 percent in 1782; by the later year 300 whites owned under 10 slaves, 77 owned between 10 and 20 slaves, and 22 owned between 20 and 40 slaves.

The evidence that Fairfax County was becoming increasingly a slave society seems conclusive. The total number of slaves had risen from 1,808 in 1749 to 3,609 in 1782; the percentage of slaves in the total population had risen from 28.85 percent to 41 percent; the number of slave owners had increased from 189 to 408; the percentage of the white population owning slaves had risen from 4 percent to 7.9 percent; and the number of slave owners with more than 40 slaves had more than doubled from 4 in 1749 to 9 in 1782. Most important, the most powerful men in Fairfax County, George Washington, George Mason, Thomas and William Fitzhugh, were the largest slave owners. [5] This increase in the number of slaves, and the percentage of the total

4. Any attempt to arrive at slave holdings for eighteenth-century Fairfax County must be undertaken very cautiously. The numbers given here are those from the 1782 listing. The list was, however, taken by several different men in different areas of the county, and each man would list for a given slave owner only those slaves held in his particular district. For example, George Mason appears on the list of Martin Cockburn as having in his household nine whites and owning ninety slaves; on Charles Little's list, Mason has six whites and thirty-eight slaves. The most probable explanation is that the ninety slaves were at Gunston Hall and the thirty-eight on another piece of Mason land in Fairfax. Even this would not take into account slaves which a Fairfax resident may have held elsewhere. The figures themselves are in need of interpretation: does the number given include all slaves or only tithable slaves? If a man hired slaves from another (a common practice), under whose name would these slaves appear? The question is more than academic, for while Washington in 1782 is listed with 188 slaves, by 1786 his own listing of slaves numbers 216. Even for a man of Washington's means, an increase of 28 slaves in four years seems high, but not impossible. In 1786 Washington specified his slaves by age, so we know his figure of 216 is inclusive; the listing for 1782, however, does not specify which slaves were counted and it is unclear whether the apparent increase of 28 slaves in four years was in fact an increase or only a result from different slaves being counted.

5. The degree to which Fairfax County, the Commonwealth of Virginia, and all of America accepted Negro slavery is clearly illustrated by George Washington (perhaps the most important man in America in 1782) being the largest slaveholder in the county in which he lived. Indeed, far from being a political liability, being a large slaveholder was a decided political advantage.

population which was slave, is a safe indicator of economic prosperity and growth in Fairfax County, as slaves were expensive property requiring large capital investment. While the white population only increased 15 percent from 4,452 in 1744 to 5,154 in 1782, the slave population nearly doubled from 1,808 in 1749 to 3,609 in 1782. Clearly, slave labor had an increasingly important effect on the economy of Fairfax County during the mid-eighteenth century.

By 1786 the population of Fairfax had reached approximately 9,000, which was a high point until 1798 when more land area was encompassed within the county boundaries. From 1786 on, the general population trend was down; this anticipated the severe decline of the early nineteenth century. By 1798 the population had fallen to about 8,400, but in this same year, a section of Loudoun between Difficult Run and the current Loudoun-Fairfax line was returned to Fairfax County. This boosted the total population to 12,508. Even so, during the following year, 1799, the population had fallen to 11,974, and this trend continued for nearly 30 years.

During the entire period from 1742 to 1800, the population in Fairfax County increased, except after 1786 when the population began to decline. There was, of course, a sudden drop in population when Loudoun became a separate county in 1757; there was also an immediate increase when part of Loudoun again became Fairfax County in 1798.

Black slave labor was an important economic and demographic factor in Fairfax County during the entire eighteenth century. The number of blacks increased steadily and rapidly, much more rapidly in fact than did the white population. A large portion of the slaves was held in large groups; the owners of the largest parcels of slaves were leaders in the county or absentee landlords. Slaveholding was presumably profitable and definitely prestigious in Fairfax County during the eighteenth century.

Major Changes During the Eighteenth Century

The Creation of Cameron Parish

When Fairfax County was created in 1742 the land area it encompassed was exactly the same as that of the previously established Truro Parish. All of what is now Fairfax, Loudoun, and Arlington counties, and Alexandria City was originally one parish, Truro, and one county, Fairfax. It was not long, however, before this vast area began to be subdivided into smaller units of various kinds.

The first action taken was to establish Cameron Parish in 1748. Cameron Parish was defined as all of Truro Parish north of Difficult Run "to the head thereof, and from thence by a line to the head of Popeshead run," down Popeshead to where it empties into Bull Run. [1] This action just about divided in half what had been Truro Parish, but both parishes were still in Fairfax County.

The Courthouse Moves to Alexandria

The same session of the House of Burgesses which created Cameron Parish also authorized the town of Alexandria. [2] By 1752 the inhabitants of Alexandria were petitioning the government at Williamsburg to move the Fairfax County courthouse to Alexandria. The old courthouse, then in use for ten years, needed repairs, and the Alexandrians offered to build a new courthouse by subscription, thereby saving the county government any expense by the move. On 10 March 1752 the Committee on Propositions and Grievances of the House of Burgesses rejected a petition from Fairfax residents in opposition to moving the courthouse to Alexandria. Twelve days later, 23 March, the Governor's Council read the petition proposing the move and gave notice to the justices of the Fairfax Court "to signify their objection against such removal, if they have any, by the 25th of next month."

No objection was recorded from the Fairfax Court, and accordingly, 25 April 1752 the Council "ordered that the court house and prison be removed . . . to the town of Alexandria." [3] Governor Dinwiddie thereupon issued his proclamation adjourning "the County Court of Fairfax to the Town of Alexandria on Potomac," on the "third Tuesday" of May 1752. [4] The court was definitely in Alexandria by 19 May 1752, for on that day the minute book notes: "At a Court held at the Court House in Alexandria May the 19th, 1752 . . . A Proclamation from his Honour the Governor as also a writ to adjourn the Court from the former Courthouse [5] of this County, and to hold pleas in the Town of Alexandria being read were ordered to be recorded." [6] The new courthouse "stood on the east side of the Market Square, facing Fairfax Street between Cameron and King, nearly opposite the Carlyle House." Seen in retrospect, the movement of the courthouse to Alexandria was a practical move. There were more people living in the southern part of the county near the Potomac and the Occoquan; also, Alexandria was fast becoming the commercial center of the county. It is not unlikely, had the petition to move the courthouse been rejected, that the aggressive Scots in Alexandria might have petitioned that the southern portion of Fairfax County be docked to form a separate county.

1. Harrison, *Landmarks*, pp. 288-89.
2. Ibid.
3. Ibid.
4. Fairfax County Deed Book, C-1, 1,314.
5. The former courthouse was at the "place called Springfield" near what is now Tysons Corner.
6. Fairfax County Court Order Book, 1749-1752, p. 191.

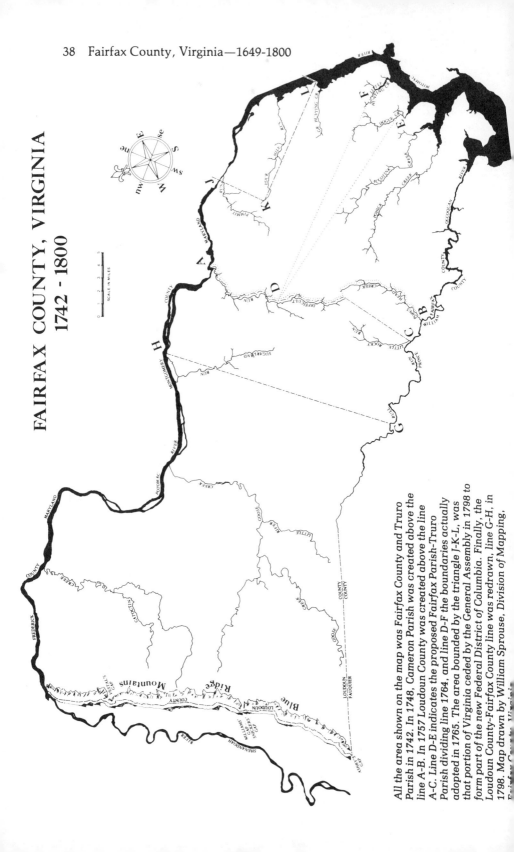

FAIRFAX COUNTY, VIRGINIA
1742 - 1800

SCALE IN MILES

All the area shown on the map was Fairfax County and Truro
Parish in 1742. In 1748, Cameron Parish was created above the
line A-B. In 1757 Loudoun County was created above the line
A-C. Line D-E indicates the proposed Fairfax Parish-Truro
Parish dividing line 1764, and line D-F the boundaries actually
adopted in 1765. The area bounded by the triangle J-K-L, was
that portion of Virginia ceded by the General Assembly in 1798 to
form part of the new Federal District of Columbia. Finally, the
Loudoun County-Fairfax County line was redrawn, line G-H, in
1798. Map drawn by William Sprouse, Division of Mapping,
Fairfax County, Virginia.

The Creation of Loudoun County

The objections to moving the courthouse to Alexandria undoubtedly came from inhabitants of both Cameron Parish and the upper end of Truro Parish, because they would have to travel the far greater distance to Alexandria to conduct court business. It is, therefore, not surprising that in October 1754 the residents of Cameron Parish petitioned the burgesses to form a new county. The petition was deferred, then further postponed, and finally a bill was passed, only to be disallowed by the Council. Finally, in April 1757, a bill was introduced which became law 8 June 1757. The new county did not include all of Cameron Parish for the dividing line between Fairfax and Loudoun was defined as "Difficult run, which falls into Potowmack river and by a line to be run from the head of the said run a straight course to the mouth of Rocky run."[7]

Fairfax County had been docked of over 50 percent of its land area, but lost only about 40 percent of its population. The number of tithables in Fairfax County in 1756 is given as 2,461.[8] The following year after the loss of Loudoun, the tithables in Fairfax were down to 1,382,[9] which means that about 1,079 were in Loudoun.[10]

Fairfax Parish

It has been suggested that had the courthouse not been moved to Alexandria in 1752, the residents in that area might have petitioned for a separate county. This is not idle speculation for, as has been shown, the losers in the courthouse battle, i.e., the upper inhabitants of Fairfax County, soon succeeded in creating a county of their own. In like manner the growing concentration of population in and about Alexandria soon led to a local demand for a new parish.

The first application for a separate parish was made to the burgesses in 1761, but it was not until 1764 that a new parish was formed. The new Fairfax Parish was to be all of Truro Parish north of a line "by Doeg Creek, from the mouth thereof to Mr. George Washington's mill and from thence by a straight line to the plantation of John Munroe" and by a straight line to the Loudoun-Fairfax line. The problem with this solution was that it gave two-thirds of the tithables in the county to the new parish, including some of the largest slave owners such as George Washington. A protest was made with the burgesses, and a new line was offered which was also rejected by Truro Parish; finally, an agreement was reached in May 1765. The boundary which was accepted ran "from the mouth of Little Hunting Creek up the same to the forks thereof; thence up the meanders of the South branch thereof to the Gum Spring thereon; from thence by a straight line to the ford of Dogue run where

---

7. Harrison, *Landmarks*, p. 326.
8. Fairfax County Court Order Book, 1756-1763, I, pp. 33-42.
9. Ibid., p. 178.
10. This figure is for tithables only.

the back road from Colchester crosses the said run and from thence by a straight line to the forks of Difficult [run]."[11]

As the Anglican establishment was an important aspect of local government during most of the eighteenth century, it is useful to discuss briefly the location of the churches in both parishes. When Truro Parish was created in 1732 the Overwharton chapel stood just above Occoquan River; this became the parish church of Truro Parish and was first called Occoquan Church until the name was changed to Pohick in 1737. In 1767 a new Pohick Church was established which was closer to Mount Vernon than its predecessor. The parish began to use the new church in 1772; it still stands and is in use.

The Falls or "upper church" was established by Truro Parish in 1733 at the crossroads of the road which ran atop the natural ridge from Alexandria to Difficult, and the road to the ferry at Little Falls. It was from this latter road that the church derived its name, and the present city took the name of the church. Richard Blackburn built the first church on this site, and the vestry book specifies it as being "forty foot in length, two and twenty feet wide, and thirteen foot pitch, to be weather boarded, covered, and all the inside work performed" for "thirty three thousand and five hundred pounds of tobacco."[12] Additions were made to the original wooden church in 1750, and by 1763 Truro Parish had decided to build a brick church at the same site. The Falls Church was in the new Fairfax Parish created in 1765, and so that parish completed construction of the still-surviving brick Falls Church in 1769.

The first church built in what is now Loudoun was "the Chapell above Goose Creek" which Francis Awbrey constructed between 1733 and 1735. In 1745 a fourth church was built by the Truro Vestry " on the lands of Willoughby Newton" at Rocky Run. This is the site of present-day Centreville.

Six years later, in 1751, the ambitious Scots at Alexandria erected a church with funds raised by holding a lottery. By 1753 the Reverend Green, minister for Truro Parish, was instructed to preach every third Sunday at Belhaven (Alexandria). This church also became part of Fairfax Parish in 1765, and by 1772 the new brick structure known as Christ Church was completed to replace the original wooden Alexandria church.

Finally, in 1766, Truro Vestry arranged to have a church built "on the middle Ridge near the Ox Road," to be constructed by Edward Payne. It was known as Payne's Church. Payne was paid £579 "Virginia Currency" for his efforts, and the construction details were set forth in the most exact detail in the vestry book.

11. Harrison, *Landmarks*, pp. 290-91.
12. *Minutes of the Vestry, Truro Parish, Virginia, 1732-1785* (Lorton, Va.; Pohick Church, 1974) pp. 3-4. (hereinafter cited as *Vestry Book*)

The said Edward Payne doth undertake and agree to build and finish in a Workmanlike manner a Church on the Ox Road, to be placed agreeable to an order of the said Vestry, of the following Dementions & according to the annex Plan, to wit, Fifty three and a half feet in length, and thirty feet in breadth in the Clear, the Walls to be built of good bricks well burnt, of the ordinary size, that is nine Inches long, four and an half Inches broad, and three Inches thick the outside bricks to be laid with mortar, two thirds lime and one third Sand, the inside Bricks to be laid with mortar half lime and half Sand. The Corners of the House, the Windows & Doors, to be of rubbed brick. The arches and Pediment heads of the Doors & Windows to be of bricks rubbed gauged and set in Putty.

The Doors to be made of Pine Plank, two Inches thick moulded and raised Pannells on both sides.

The Sashes to be made of Pine Plank, one Inch and three quarters thick, and to have Sixteen lights in each square Sash, of the best crown-Glass, twelve Inches by ten. The Window & Door Cases to be made with double Archatraves.

*The floors and Gallery to be framed with good Oak, the Roof to be framed with good Poplar, and the Scantling to be of a size and proper Proportion to the Building.

The Roof to be covered with Inch pine Plank, cyphered and capt, one and an half Inches, And to be Shingled with good Cypress Shingles, twenty Inches in length and to show six Inches.

The floors to be laid with Pine plank, one and an half Inch thick, the Iles to be laid with Brick Tyle, the Pews to be wainscotted with Pine plank, an Inch and an half thick, double work on each side of the framing and raised pannel on one side.

To have an Altar Piece sixteen feet high & twelve feet wide, and done with wainscot after the Ionic order. The floor of the Communion place to be raised twelve Inches higher than the floor of the house with handrails and Banisters of black Walnut.

The Pulpit, Canopy, and reading Desks to be of black walnut, Wainscoted with proper Cornish.

The Gallery to be supported by Collums turned & fluted, to come out as far as the second Window at the West end of the Church, to have a Wainscoted front, and to have four Seats raised one behind and above another. The whole to be done and finished by the first Day of October in the Year one thousand seven hundred and sixty eight, in a Sufficient and workmanlike manner agreeable to the Plan aforesaid.[13]

13. Ibid., pp. 96-97. The churches are discussed in more detail in Harrison, *Landmarks*, pp. 286-88, 290-91, from which this account is taken.

The Courthouse Moves "Into the woods"

In 1789, the Virginia Assembly passed an act of cession making Virginia land available for the erection of the new national capital provided for in Article I, section 8 of the United States Constitution. The loss of Alexandria, and with it the Fairfax Court House, to the new federal government therefore became a very real possibility. Additionally, by 1788 the courthouse built in Alexandria had fallen into such a sad state of disrepair that the court ordered the sheriff to give notice of the intention to levy tobacco either to repair the existing courthouse or to build a new one. [14]

George Mason took this opportunity to object to the proposed levy on the grounds that the Virginia Declaration of Rights had removed from the county courts the right of taxation. As the Virginia Declaration of Rights had by that time been in effect for twelve years, Mason's action may be seen as a political move. The vote on the issue was close with twelve justices (Mason, Chas. Alexander, Martin Cockburn, Rich. Chichester, David Arell, Chas. Little, William Payne, Chas. Broadwater, Roger West, Wm. Lyles, Wm. Herbert and Thomas Gunnell) objecting that the court had no such power, and ten justices (Robt. Adam, Geo. Gilpin, John Moss, David Stuart, James Wren, Rich. Conway, John Fitzgerald, Wm. Brown, Benj. Dulany, and John Potts) asserting that the court could levy tobacco. On the same day a "Remonstrance against Levying Tobacco or money for the Purpose of Building or Repairing a Courthouse in the Town of Alexandria" signed by "a number of inhabitants" was produced and read in court. [15] The court applied to the Assembly for power to levy the tobacco.

On 4 December 1789, the Assembly settled both the issue of moving the courthouse and of the levying of tobacco by passing "An Act For Altering The Place of Holding Courts In The County of Fairfax." This directed the Fairfax Court "in the usual manner to levy" a sufficient sum to erect a new courthouse. Further, the act directed that the court purchase two acres of ground and that they build a courthouse, prison, pillory and stocks; the ground purchased was to be "on the lands of William Fitzhugh [Ravensworth] or on the lands of any other person, within one mile of the Cross Roads, at Price's Ordinary . . . ." [16]

There is no way of telling whether the Assembly acted in response to a request from the Fairfax Court or whether with prescient insight foresaw the loss of Alexandria to the federal government and, therefore, realized that Fairfax County would need a new courthouse. It is, however, worthy of note that a petition was presented to the Assembly on

14. Fairfax County Court Order Book, 1788-1792, 1:80.
15. Ibid., pp. 84-85.
16. Hening, *Statutes*, 13:79.

12 November 1789, and another on 14 November, objecting to the removal of the courthouse from Alexandria "into the woods...." The petition further asserted that the removal of the courthouse from Alexandria "is so pregnant with impolicy, inconvenience and injustice, and so opposite to the true intent of the Country, that we feel ourselves called upon by every social duty to arrest as far as in our power the completion of a Project so replete with mischief...." The petition of 14 November was signed by about 350 Fairfax residents and that of 12 November by about 100 citizens, not the lease of whom was George Washington, who by this time was President of the United States. (It seems a humorous example of historical irony that "The Father of His Country" could not keep the courthouse in Alexandria.) Among the other signatories on the 12 November petition were a number of leading citizens: Jas. Wren, Lund Washington, Wm. Triplett, Benj. Dulany, Robert Boggess, Thos. Herbert, and William Hartshorne.[17]

In any event, the actions of the Fairfax Court in carrying this act into effect may be seen as an example of eighteenth-century bureaucracy.

The court first postponed action from the February 1790 meeting to the April 1790 session, at which time the action to levy tobacco was again postponed "because There is Reason to Apprehend a Situation Cannot be Had and Obtained w/in one Mile of the Cross Roads at Prices Ordinary." Chas. Broadwater, Chas. Little, Wm. Payne, John Moss, and Benj. Dulany were appointed "to view the situation" and ascertain if there were indeed a suitable two acres of ground within one mile of Price's Ordinary on which to build the new courthouse.[18] Not surprisingly, the "commissioners" found that there was not a suitable two-acre tract within one mile of the specified intersection. Undaunted, some members of the court felt that they should proceed to levy the tobacco for building the courthouse anyway, even if there were no place to build it. The commissioners, however, were also justices, and they being "of a contrary opinion . . . the motion for Levying Tobacco was lost."[19] Consequently, on 15 November 1790, the Fairfax Court "considering the bad state of the present Courthouse it being unfit to transact business at this time . . ." agreed to accept the offer of the town of Alexandria "of the new courthouse over the Markett on the Courthouse lott . . . ."[20] Thus things were to remain for eight years.

The location set by the Assembly for the new courthouse "within one mile of the Cross Roads at Prices Ordinary" has long eluded students of Fairfax County history. Harrison placed the location of Prices on what is

17. Virginia State Library, Legislative Petitions, Fairfax County, 12 November 1789, 14 November 1789.

18. Fairfax County Court Order Book, 1789-1791, p. 69; 1788-1792, II, p. 290.

19. The details of the commission report are in the Fairfax County Court Order Book, 1788-1791, II, 17 May 1790, p. 291.

20. Ibid., p. 357.

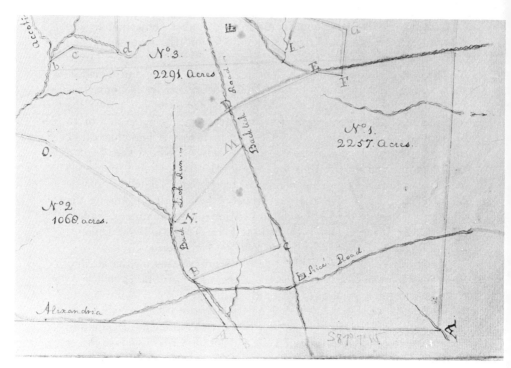

Plat showing location of Price's Ordinary in 1797. The road labeled "Alexandria Road" on the plat corresponds to what is now Braddock Road. Plat in Fairfax County Deed Book, A-2, page 186. Photo by Bernie Boston.

now Braddock Road at the intersection of either Guinea Road or Rolling Road. A careful examination of the facts will prove this is not possible, and that a far better case can be made for the intersection of Braddock Road with Backlick Road.

A 1797 plat prepared for a deed case shows Prices at the intersection of what would later become Backlick and Braddock.[21] Taken by itself this is not conclusive; but the other available evidence both supports the notation on the map and shows that Prices could not have been at Guinea or Rolling Roads. The commissioners appointed to select the courthouse site in 1789 reported:

> We accordingly proceeded to lay off the mile beginning at the centre of the cross roads at Price's and run northeasterly course nearly with the road . . . and we found our distance of one (1) mile from Price's to be one chain short of the place of Benoni Price said to be where the Ravensworth line crosses the road.

21. Fairfax County Deed Book, A-2, p. 186.

The report agrees with the map in placing Price's at a crossroads. Further, Braddock Road now runs approximately northeast toward Alexandria. The distance along Braddock Road from the intersection with Backlick is within 100 feet of where the old Ravensworth line crossed the road as measured and reported by the commissioners in 1789. By the same process, proceeding one mile northeast from Braddock and Guinea, or Braddock and Rolling Road, brings one nowhere near where the Ravensworth line crosses the road. The commissioners report supported by the 1797 plat indicates that Price's Ordinary was at, or very near, the present intersection of Braddock and Backlick.

Price's was, of course, a well-known eighteenth-century landmark in Fairfax County. Not only was it used as a guide to the location of the proposed new courthouse, but it was also where the overseers of the poor held their meetings and where the general Fairfax County meeting for adoption of the federal constitution was held.

Finally, in 1798, the Assembly acted to remedy two situations. Prodded by some discontented residents of Loudoun County, the Assembly first restored to Fairfax County all of Loudoun County which lay between the 1757 Fairfax-Loudoun line and a new boundary, "a line drawn from the mouth of Sugar Land run to Carter's Mill on Bull run," which is the current Fairfax-Loudoun boundary. Having increased the land area of Fairfax County, the Assembly ordered the Fairfax Court to settle upon a new site for holding court "at or near the centre . . . having regard to that part of Loudoun hereby added to the said County of Fairfax."[22] The site selected by the court was on two acres of land belonging to Richard Radcliff on Ox Road. This is the site upon which the Fairfax County courthouse has stood for 177 years. The first meeting of the court in the new building was held on 21 April 1800.

In February 1801 the federal government took jurisdiction over that portion of Fairfax County which was to be included in the new District of Columbia—that is, all of Arlington County and much of what is now Alexandria City. Undoubtedly, many residents of Fairfax County in 1801 felt special pride that a section of their land had been chosen for the national capital. Aside from its probable economic advantages, it was in the tradition of service to the new nation. For not only had Fairfax County provided the commanding general for the Continental Army and the first president of the United States, but it now gave land for the seat of the new government.

22. Harrison, *Landmarks*, pp. 325-26, 329.

III

Daily Life in Fairfax County
in the Eighteenth Century

Having a general overview of the ebb and flow of the population in
Fairfax County prior to 1800, and having discussed the major changes in
boundaries of the county, its parishes, and the locations of the churches
and the courthouse, we may now investigate what it was like to live in the
county in the eighteenth century.

The major sources of information of life in Fairfax County during
the eighteenth century are the county court record books and the Truro
Parish vestry book, which, of course, between 1748 and 1757 and after
1765 did not represent the entire county. These sources tell only what
was done, or ordered to be done; they relate none of the debate or issues
surrounding the decisions. The simple knowledge that there was no
newspaper in Fairfax or Alexandria says much about the pace of life and
the concerns of the citizens, and provides an explanation for the lack of
detail of everyday life of that time. It is possible, however, to get a
general picture of life in those times, decade by decade.

The 1740s

The court minute books prior to 1749 are lost or destroyed, so the
only documented information is the parish vestry book. The Reverend
Mr. Charles Green was the minister for Truro Parish during all of the
1740s. In 1742, the parish levy was twenty-four pounds of tobacco for
each tithable in the parish. This was sufficient for paying the salary of
16,640 pounds of tobacco to the Reverend Mr. Green; for keeping "a
poor child" and "a poor man;" as well as for "maintaining Mary Brown"
and "keeping Saml. Russell." The child was allotted 300 pounds of
tobacco; Russell and Brown 500 pounds each: they were poor indeed.[1]

1. *Vestry Book*, pp. 36-37.

On 21 July 1743, the County Court ordered the vestry to divide the parish into precincts so that the land might be processioned. Processioning involved two men of the parish walking the boundaries of each parcel of land in each precinct. It was done with the owners of the land, and the purpose was to see that the boundaries were understood and agreed upon. This was one of the important civil functions of the parish. Accordingly, the vestry divided the county into nineteen precincts, some of which were not processioned as no freeholders lived there. For example, there was no freeholder in the precinct "Between William's gap, Ashby's gap [in the Blue Ridge], the County line, & Goose Creek to the Beaver dam & back to the Gap . . . ." Two male freeholders were to procession all the lands in each precinct. In addition to the usual expenditures for clerks and sextons at the various churches, and for building repair, there were five people on the parish "welfare list" for 1743. The levy was twenty-five pounds of tobo. (tobacco) per poll.[2]

During 1744 there was some excitement in the county regarding the vestry. On Monday the eighth of February, the sheriff, William Payne, came to the vestry house and said that pursuant to an act of the legislature he had dissolved the current vestry and held elections for new vestrymen. The Reverend Mr. Green noted at this point in the vestry book "(one of the causes assigned for the dissolution of the Vestry was that several of them were illiterate—there was but one of them illiterate, namely Edward Emons [Emms] who was re-elected. C.G. [Charles Green])."

The newly elected vestrymen were:

Capt. John West	Capt. Richard Osborn
Capt. Lewis Elzey	Mr. Daniel French
Mr. John Sturman	Mr. Edward Emons [Emms]
Capt. John Minor	Mr. Robert Boggess
Mr. Hugh West	Colo. John Colvill
Mr. Andrew Hutchinson	Mr. Charles Broadwater.

The new vestrymen all took an oath provided for in "an act for the further security of his Majesty's person & Government & of the succession to the Crown in the heirs of the late Princess Sophia being protestants & for extinguishing the hopes of the pretended Prince of Wales & his open & secret abettors . . . ." They then subscribed the test and were sworn as vestrymen.[3] The Assembly also ordered the justices of

2. Ibid., p. 38-41.

3. Ibid., pp. 42-44. The test oath was one of the strictures applied by the Anglican Establishment against Roman Catholics and other nonconformists such as the Quakers and the Puritans. The oath had its origin in the political and religious turmoil of seventeenth and eighteenth century England. The

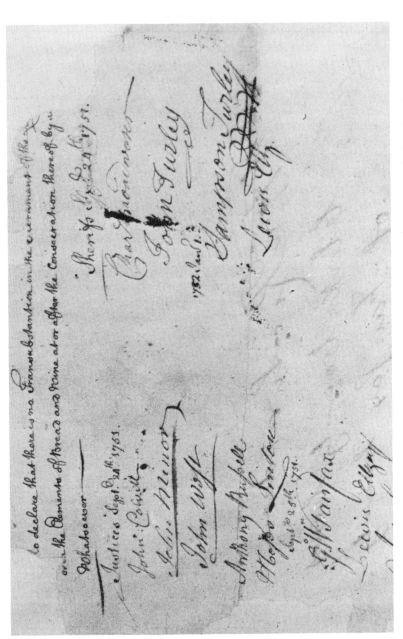

The test oath signed by justices of the Fairfax County Court in 1751. The full text reads: "I do declare that there is no Transubstantion [sic.] in the Sacrament of the Lords Supper, or in the Elements of Bread and Wine at or after the Consecration thereof by any person Whatsoever." Used with permission of James Hoofnagle, Clerk of the Circuit Court, Fairfax County, Virginia. Photo by Bernie Boston.

Fairfax and Prince William counties to levy sufficient funds to contract with and pay Mrs. Ann Mason for maintaining a ferry across the Occoquan River.[4] The Masons had maintained a ferry at this location since 1684,[5] and the action of the Assembly was motivated by the refusal of the justices of both counties after 1742 to levy funds for this purpose.[6] The ferry was a public one maintained at public expense.

During the remainder of the 1740s, the levy ranged between nineteen and twenty-seven pounds of tobacco per poll, and the vestry's expenses were more or less consistent. Rocky Run Church was finished in 1746, and Reverend Mr. Green was ordered to preach there eight times a year. In 1746 an orphan, Alexander Roe, was bound to Richard Nelson who was to teach the boy to be a shoemaker, and to read and write. This is the first evidence of a craftsman in Fairfax County, and as neither Alexandria nor Colchester yet existed as towns, there is no way of telling where Nelson practiced his trade.[7] Most likely he would have worked in his home, and it may have been near the courthouse as that was the central gathering point in the county.

In 1749 the first county court records became available, enabling one to get a more detailed picture of life in Fairfax County. Much of the information in the record books is repetitive, listing the same basic information with different names or different amounts of money for each year. Therefore, after discussing 1749 in as much detail as possible, the specifics for subsequent years will be mentioned only when they seem important. First, 1749 was the year in which the Reverend Mr. Green made his enumerated census of the tithables in both parishes. The town of Alexandria was also founded that year.

principle of ending such turmoil by forcing conformity to the Church of England dated back to the Acts of Supremacy and Uniformity in the reign of Elizabeth I. In 1661, shortly after the restoration of Charles II, a "test" (receiving the communion of the Church of England) was imposed and was aimed at nonconformists as well as Roman Catholics. Subsequently, Charles II used his dispensing power to remove the stricture on nonconformists. This was the immediate cause for the test act of 1672, the full title of which was "An act for preventing dangers which may happen from popish recusants" and required denial of transubstantiation. The act applied to all persons filling any civil or military office. In this capacity, the test act forced James, Duke of York (the brother of Charles II), later King James II to resign his post as Lord High Admiral. Following the popish plot furor of 1678, a new test act was passed which extended to peers and members of the House of Commons. Finally, under the English Bill of Rights (1684), the oath was even applied to the monarch who held the English throne. The American colonies inherited from England the general pattern of the relations of church and state, and this included the test oath. The oath is long and carefully worded to avoid any exceptions. It required the person taking the oath to swear "there is not any transubstantiation . . ." and that "the invocation or adoration of the Virgin Mary or any other saint and the sacrifice of the mass" were "superstitious and idolatrous." "Test Acts," Encyclopedia Britannica, 1911, 26:665. New Catholic Encyclopedia, 1967, 10:598; 12:332, 693.

4. Hening, Statutes, 5:252.

5. Ibid., 3: 21.

6. Ibid., 5: 252.

7. Vestry Book, pp. 45-56.

There were 1,947 tithables in Fairfax County in 1749, and they were levied at four pounds of tobacco per poll. This figure seems very low in light of the levies for future years and of the general level of parish levies. The vestry book does not list the tithables or levy per poll for that year. There may have been some confusion within the vestry as Cameron Parish had been formed 10 June 1749, and the vestrymen had the job of liquidating the assets of the old parish so that they could be divided among the two new parishes; these included the church plate, and the glebe land. The glebe was land purchased by the vestry and given to the minister as part of his living. The glebe lands of the original Truro Parish were just south of the Long Branch of Accotink and just north of what is now Telegraph Road.

The total county budget for 1749 was 7,788 pounds of tobacco. That was the amount of the levy; a good deal more appears to have been spent. The major expenditures were:

John Hamilton Gt. Dep. Kings Attorney	2,000 lbs of tobacco
John Graham Clerk	1,260 lbs of tobacco
Lewis Elzey Gt. Sherif [sic]	1,260 lbs of tobacco
Geo. Mason For Occoquan Ferry	1,600 lbs of tobacco
Thomas Evans for Ferry over Goose Creek	1,000 lbs of tobacco
Garrard Trammell for finding water for the court	600 lbs of tobacco
Hugh West—For Ballance of the prison	2,100 lbs of tobacco

The sheriff was also allowed 6 percent (401 pounds of tobacco) for his service in collecting the levy.[8] A sizeable portion of the budget went to paying bounty on wolves: 100 pounds of tobacco were paid for an old wolf's head, and 50 pounds for a young wolf's head. Nine men collected bounty on eleven old wolves' heads, and three men brought in 15 young wolves' heads, for a total of 1,850 pounds of tobacco. The court also paid 3,534 pounds of tobacco for "sundry defalcations in Crows and Squirrels." Crows, squirrels, and wolves were considered undesirable as they ate the crops and were a menace to humans and livestock.

Among other officials in the county during 1749 were John West and Thomas Harrison, inspectors of pork, beef, flour, fur, and turpentine, and the inspectors at the various tobacco warehouses. Only one license was granted on 22 June 1749 to Elisha Hall to operate an ordinary, but it is very difficult to believe that there was only one ordinary in Fairfax County at that time. Even at this early date, it seems reasonable to assume that C. Vann Woodward's characterization of the citizenry below the Potomac as having "a regional propensity for living it up" would have applied, and ordinaries would have been logical places to "live it up."

8. Fairfax County Court Order Book, 1749-1754, pp. 47-48.

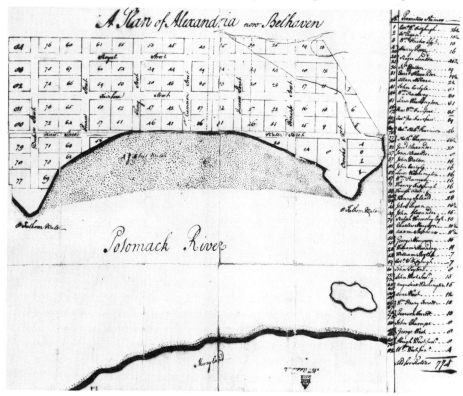

Plan of the town of Alexandria drawn by George Washington, indicating the purchasers of each town lot. Library of Congress.

Not surprisingly, the court minute books contain numerous references to crimes and punishments. Up to a point, such matters are interesting in themselves; however, they are more important for what they tell us of the activities of the citizens and the concerns of the court. Five cases of assault and battery were listed for 1749, but no judgments were recorded. Five women, most likely indentured servants, were brought before the court for having bastard children. Mary Lot was sentenced to serve one year, which probably meant that she was to serve her master one extra year, and this would clearly mark her as a servant. Rebeckah Davis was sentenced to fifty lashes or a fine of 500 "lbs." of tobacco. Margaret Webster was similarly sentenced to twenty-five lashes. The lashes were commonly administered by the sheriff at the public whipping post, on the bare back and "well laid on." The object of such punishment was public humiliation as well as the physical pain of a whipping, and women were equally treated in this regard.

Thomas Lewis was brought before the court "for not keeping the road in repair between Ravensworth and the Ox Road." The freeholders and tithables who lived on the land adjacent to a given road were responsible for keeping that road in repair. This was attended to with some degree of laxity, and the court records are replete with offenders.[9]

Finally, on 29 September 1749, the court "ordered that a Seale Be Provided for This County & that John Colville, John Carlyle & Geo. Mason consider of the same & send for it to be Paid for By the County." This is the first, last, and only reference to a seal in the court records during the eighteenth century.[10]

The 1750s

Before considering this decade as a whole, a number of interesting comparisons can be made by looking at the county and parish accounts for 1750. The county levy for 1750 was based on 1,795 tithables at 12 pounds per poll for a total of 21,540 pounds of tobacco; the parish levy was on only 1,221 tithables at 32 pounds per poll for a total of 39,072 pounds of tobacco (in fact, the total parish revenues for 1750 were 42,157 pounds of tobacco). The difference in the number of tithables can be rectified easily: Fairfax County encompassed both Truro and Cameron parishes. What is significant is that Truro Parish, which was less than half of Fairfax County, needed nearly twice the operating budget of the county. Nothing could more clearly illustrate both the importance of the civil function of the parish and the full realization of the meaning of an established church. For every pound of tobacco a man had to pay to the county, he had to pay three pounds to the parish.

The reasons for this situation are readily apparent. The county had only four paid officials: clerk, sheriff, king's attorney, and jailer. Their combined salaries were only 5,614 pounds of tobacco. On the other hand, the Reverend Mr. Green's salary alone was 16,640 pounds of tobacco. In addition, the vestry maintained a clerk and sexton at each church; their combined salaries were 3,520 pounds of tobacco. Add these salaries to Green's salary and the result is 20,160 pounds of tobacco, nearly four times the amount paid to the county officials.

The other major expense of the vestry was the maintenance on the churches and the vestry house. By 1749 there were three churches: Pohick, Falls, and Rocky Run in Truro Parish. The vestry house was a fourth building. The county only had to maintain the courthouse (probably less expensive than one church) and a jail. The vestry simply had more capital outlay. In fact, the county budget for 1750 was higher

---

9. In order to avoid the circumstance of having five or ten footnotes in every paragraph where specific information is listed, it may be assumed that the reference is to the Fairfax County Court Order or Minute Book for the year in question. All other sources will be footnoted.

10. Fairfax County Court Order Book, 1749-1754, p. 40. This is a tantalizing lead, but it has never been proven whether a seal was ever procured for the county. A yearly accounting by the court continued for the next 14 years, but there was no mention of a seal. The matter may have simply been forgotten.

Table IX

Fairfax County Court Levy	26 December 1750
Levy	Pounds of Tobacco
Clerk of this Court by law	1,260
Sherif "County"	1,260
Mr Secretary Nelson by account	128
Jn Hamilton Gt Dep Kings Attorney	2,000
Clerk for a called court on Oden & Dial	160
Ditto for Ditto on Simon Bailey	160
Clerk for Record book	72
To William West by account	260
Geo Mason for Occoquan Ferry till next March	1,600
Chas Broadwater for an inquest on a dead body	133
Robt Wills Constable for summoning an inquest	40
Garrad Trammell for cleaning the Court House finding Water &tc	600
Edward Payne by account as Goaler	1,094
Ditto by Account	1,600
William Elzey by Account	40
Joseph Shelton, Wm Barton & Jonathan Ray for the addition to the Courthouse to be left in the Sherifs hands until the work is completed	9,500
Wm Barton for work done on Courthouse	200
Sherif for collecting the DeFalcations in Crows & Squirrels	200
Wm Pearle for 1 old wolf	100
John Ratcliff for 2 old wolf & 5 young ones	450
Henry Brown for 1 old wolf & 5 young ones	350
Edward Payne "	100
John Emmitt by Account	150
	22,617

By Depositum in the Sherif Hands Last Year	1,125	
"Defalcations in Crows & Squirrels	1,739	
	2,864	- 2,864
		19,753
To Sherif 6% for collection		1,185
"Allowance of 6% " "1739 Tobacco		103
"Depositum to be accounted for next year		499
		21,540

1795 Tithables at 12 Lbs/Poll

than normal because of the 9,500 pounds of tobacco being set aside for an addition to the courthouse. In 1751 when no such expenditure was incurred, the county court only collected 7 pounds per poll for a total of 13,881[11] (which would not even have paid Reverend Green's salary), while in the same year, the parish levy was 41,650 pounds of tobacco or 34 pounds per poll.[12]

11. Fairfax County Court Minute Book, 1749-1754, pp. 178-79.
12. Vestry Book, p. 62.

This situation would have been especially unpleasant for a Roman Catholic, a Quaker, or other "nonconformist," for everyone had to pay the parish levy. The county and parish budgets for 1750 reproduced in Tables IX and X allow a comparison to be made.

The 1750s were a time of major change and many problems for the vestry of Truro Parish. As it was necessary to sell the former glebe and divide the proceeds with Cameron parish, the land was advertised and

Table X

*At a Vestry held for Truro Parish October the 8th 1750
Present the Reverd. Mr. Charles Green Minister

Mr. Hugh West
Mr. James Hamilton
Mr. William Payne
Mr. Charles Broadwater
Mr. Abraham Barnes
Mr. William Peake
Mr. Thomas Wren
Mr. Robert Boggess
&
Mr. John West

Truro Parish Dr.

To the Revd. Mr. Charles Green for his Salary & Cask 16640
To John Barry Clerk at Pohick Church 1000
To John Wybird Dainty Clerk at upper Church 1000
To William Henry Terrett Clerk of the Vestry 500
To Philip Howel sexton at Pohick Church 560
To Mary Bennit Sexton at Upper Church 460
To Majr. Lawrence Washington for 27 Levys overcharged last year . . 567
To Colo. William Fairfax for 6 Levys overcharged 126
To George Taylor for 3 Levys overcharged. 63
To James Hamilton for 1 Levy overcharged 21
To Doctor John Robertson P. account. 240
To Doctor John Hunter P. account 1040
To John Graham P. account 206
To Sarah Brookshire for keeping Susana Williams 745
To Walter Taylor for keeping John Murrah 3 months & 20 Days. 330
To John Keen for maintaining a poor Child 500
To Joseph Boling for keeping a poor Child 500
To Cameron Parish for their proportion of the Clerks & Sextons
     Salarys. 527
To Drummond Wheeler for his relief 400
To William Kidwel for burying a poor man 200
To John Hollis for burying a poor man 250
To Mr. Charles Broadwater for an addition to the Upper Church . . 12000
To Mr. Charles Broadwater for making a Door to the Desk & hinges . . 50
To 6 PCt. for collecting 36730 lb. tobo 2203
To a Depo. in the Collectors hands 139
                                                                                    42157

*Contra Cr.
                                                                               lb. tobo.
By Mr. Hugh West. 3085
By 1221 Titheables at 32 lb. tobo. P. poll 39072
                                                                                    42157

sold at public auction to William Ramsay, an Alexandria merchant, for "Fifty pounds Current Money." The vestry then proceeded to buy 167 acres of land adjoining the old glebe to serve as the new glebe. This land was purchased from the Reverend Mr. Green for 13,500 pounds of tobacco, and of course, continued to be his to use so long as he was the minister for the parish. Later that same month, June 1752, the vestry agreed to "Receive Proposals for building on the glebe including a dwelling house . . . in the Clear about Twelve hundred feet to be one Storie with a Cellar below and Convenient Rooms and Closets as the Ground will allow." Agreement was reached with Thomas Waite to build the house for 425 pounds of "Current money" and the Reverend Mr. Green agreed to build the other buildings.

The parish budget for 1752 provided for 34,049 pounds of tobacco "To be sold by the Churchwardens for Cash towards building on the Glebe." This raised the parish levy to a whopping 63,669 pounds of tobacco, or fifty pounds per poll which was to be the highest rate of the decade. (The county levy for 1752 was only 36,504 pounds, or eighteen pounds per poll; this included 16,000 pounds to build a bridge.)

By 1754 severe problems regarding a building for the glebe were becoming apparent. Even though Waite had agreed to fulfill his contract within two years, that is by October 1754, in June 1754 the vestry sent a letter to Waite informing him that Daniel McCarty, Hugh West, and George Mason had inspected the work and found that the bricks "are done very bad & not fit to be used . . .," and that what had been done must "be pulled down & done with good brick." They also felt "none of the bricks of the two first kilns were fit to be put into the Walls of the Glebe House."

Whatever Waite's reaction, it is apparent that the vestry intended Green to have a brick and not a frame house, and that there probably were no bricks available for purchase because Waite was making his own.

When the vestry met in June 1755, they agreed to pay Waite "thirty nine pounds thirteen Shillings" as a final installment on the first half of the payment for the house. George Mason would not sign the order until his "Dissents" from this action were entered into the record. At the November 1758 meeting of the vestry, Waite was put on notice that if he had not completed the work by 1 July 1759, the vestry would find other workmen to finish the job. Apparently he did not finish the work, and in November 1759 the vestry moved to find other workmen. One may wonder where the Reverend Mr. Green was living in the meantime.

Procrastination of the sort exhibited by Waite did not seem to be unusual, for even though the parish was divided in 1749, it was 1752 before the old glebe lands were sold. Similarly, while the vestry purchased the new glebe lands at the same time as they sold the old, 1752, Green was not paid his 13,500 pounds of tobacco for two years.

Although the vestry had to cope with the problem of the house, it kept about its regular functions of building and maintaining churches, caring for the poor and orphans, burying the indigent, and bringing moral misdemeanors before the county court. Cases of Sabbath breaking, drunkeness, fornication, adultery, bastardy, public swearing, and the like, were all matters in which the vestry acted as the local police and brought the offender to heel before the court.

An interesting item is included in the entry for the June 1755 meeting of the vestry: "Ordered that the churchwarden give notice for the impotent people of this parish to appear at the Vestry the second Monday in May & also for any person who will undertake to board them." This was an open invitation for the poor and helpless to present themselves for assistance. Likewise at the last meeting of the decade on 12 November 1759, the vestry ordered the church wardens to spend 400 pounds of tobacco for "Eliz. Palmer towards the support of her child a Lame Idiot."[13]

For Fairfax County as a whole, the 1750s were a time of rapid growth and major change. The population rose from 5,564 in 1750 to 7,628 in 1756, an increase of almost 40 percent in six years. The courthouse was moved to Alexandria in 1752, as the community began to be the center not only of government but also of commerce, and even of population for Fairfax County. From 1749 on, the history of Fairfax County is very much the history of the town of Alexandria; and the creation of Loudoun County from northwestern Fairfax in 1757 acknowledged the shift of Fairfax affairs to the town on the Potomac.

Even though much road building took place in Fairfax County during the 1750s as a natural result of an increase in population and trade, it is nearly impossible to trace with any degree of exactness the growth of the road system. Apparently, anyone could build a private road on his own property; on the other hand, an order was necessary from the county court to build a public road. A petition could be presented to the court requesting a road; an individual could come into court and make such a request; or the court could act on its own. The usual procedure was for the court to appoint "viewers" to examine the proposed site and route of the new road. If they returned a favorable report, the individual would be allowed to build the road, or the tithables on the land near the new road would be ordered to clear or "turn" the road and to keep it in repair. Road work was part of the obligation which tithables owed the county, and there was no expense to the county in creating a new road, i.e., the tithables were not paid for their work.

Roads and bridges were built throughout the county with much activity around Alexandria. Perhaps the greatest number of new roads built were in the outer reaches of what is now Loudoun County. The problem with ascertaining just where the roads were built should become

13. The 1750s are covered in *Vestry Book*, pp. 57-80.

apparent from the following entry in the county court minute book. It was reported by the viewers "that there may be a better way than the old Road made by leaving the Country road at the plantation of John Ford & going through the said plantation along a path formerly a mill road into the Ox road at the Wolf Pit hill . . . ."[14] Assuming it is possible to determine the location of the "old road, "the plantation of John Ford," and "Wolf Pit hill, "it might be possible to ascertain the route of the proposed road "along a path formerly a mill road." On another occasion a road was ordered to be viewed "from the lower part of the Island on Potomack River belonging to John Trammell to the place [what place?] where he is erecting his house."[15] The only answer to a problem of this sort is to ascertain who owned every piece of land in Fairfax County, and where on that land he had, or might have had, a house, barn, mill, or other structure. Worse yet, many road reports used landmarks as guides which have long since disappeared: the old oak, the giant poplar, the large rock. There is obviously no way of tracing roads using such landmarks as guides. It is possible to say that many new roads were built in all parts of the county, and that the county court was much concerned not only with new roads, but also with the failure of the persons responsible for maintenance of old roads.

Two bridges were built in the county during the 1750s. A petition was presented to the court 21 May 1752 for a bridge over Broad Run; the court ordered that John Carlyle, William Ramsay and Charles Broadwater "agree with workmen to build the said bridge." The county budget set at the November 1752 court provided 16,000 pounds of tobacco for the Broad Run Bridge, and in August of the following year, the sheriff was ordered to sell this tobacco for cash. At the same court, Stephen Lewis, John Hough, and Francis Hough were ordered to view the bridge over Broad Run, while at the November 1753 court Charles Broadwater was ordered to pay John Tramell for building Broad Run Bridge, and Tramell, in turn, was ordered to "clear a road over Broad Run Bridge."

By the May court 1754, Broadwater had still not paid Tramell, for he was again ordered to pay for building the bridge, and the sheriff, Daniel McCarty, was ordered to sell enough tobacco as was necessary to raise £100 "with the money in the hands of the said Broadwater." The bridge was apparently built for £100; just how much tobacco this was is hard to say. The 1752 levy allotted 16,000 pounds for the bridge, and the 1753 levy 10,000 pounds for the same purpose. It is not clear whether the 10,000 pounds of 1753 was in addition to the 16,000 pounds of 1752, or simply what remained of the larger amount. By 1759, Broadwater and Gunnell were working with the Loudoun Court to repair the Broad Run Bridge.

14. Fairfax County Court Minute Book, 1756-1763, 1:361.
15. Ibid., 1754-1756, 2:384.

A bridge was also built over Cub Run in 1754 by Jacob Remey for 2,650 pounds of tobacco. The previous year, 1753, the inhabitants of Alexandria were exempted from road work for one year so that they could "clear the streets and public landings."

It is constantly necessary to remember that in 1750 Fairfax County was mostly wilderness. There may have been much land under cultivation, but there was more forest than field. The town of Alexandria was tiny and had been literally chopped out of the woods. Most of the road work in Alexandria was undoubtedly just to keep pace with the growth of new vegetation in the area already cleared. By way of general observation, Richard Hofstadter has noted that in 1750 a mariner approaching the North American coastline could smell the pine trees 180 nautical miles out at sea. Fairfax County, like all of America in 1750, was very much a wilderness society.

Some other projects paid for during the 1750s were a wharf costing 22,000 pounds in 1754;[16] the repair of the bridge over Difficult Run costing 80 pounds in 1755;[17] a "whipping post & stocks & also a ducking stool for punishing offenders" in Alexandria;[18] and "fenc[ing] in the Court House Lott w/Post & rails levelling the lott & building a necessary house." In an interesting entry in the record book, the sheriff was ordered to have a bar erected around the clerk's table in the court because "the papers lying on the table are frequently mixed and confused and many times thrown down by persons crowding in & throwing their hats & gloves on the said table . . . ."[19]

In one of the last sessions held in the old courthouse, 8 February 1752, several petitions were presented to the court: two involved the sale of the glebe lands of Truro Parish; one asked for fairs to be kept in Alexandria; one from John Posey requested permission to operate a ferry from his house over the Potomac; and finally a petition against moving the courthouse to Alexandria. As has been explained, the glebe was eventually sold. Later that same month, the Assembly enacted a statute authorizing fairs to be held in Alexandria twice each year. In November 1753 the court authorized John Posey to operate a ferry from his lands to Charles County, Maryland.[20]

The first recorded meeting held at the new courthouse in Alexandria was on 19 May 1752. At this meeting, the sheriff, Charles Broadwater, protested "against all damages that may happen for want of a sufficient prison." This was a rather *pro forma* procedure, many sheriffs entering a similar protest. In this case, however, there may have been a real

16. Ibid., 1754-1756, 1:164.
17. Ibid., 2:423.
18. Ibid., 1749-1754, 182.
19. Ibid., 1756-1763, 1:42.
20. Hening, *Statutes*, VI, 27 February 1752.

problem, for the court had just moved to Alexandria on rather short notice, and the jail may not have been finished. This would seem to be the case, as a month later, 18 June 1752, the court ordered the sheriff "to remove the prisoners in his custody to the former prison for the greater safety . . . ." As Broadwater lived near the old courthouse and prison, this was surely a felicitous arrangement for him.

The county levies for the 1750s ran from 7 pounds per poll in 1751, to 19 pounds per poll in 1752. The total levy varied widely from 13,881 pounds in 1751 and 14,160 pounds in 1758, to 42,427 pounds in 1753 and 44,496 pounds in 1754. Surprisingly, the levy did not increase drastically when Loudoun was docked in 1757; the levy set in November 1757 was 13 pounds per poll (down from 14 in 1756), and 10 pounds per poll in 1758.

The value of tobacco in terms of specie or other currency is difficult to determine for a number of reasons. The value of the specie fluctuated widely with its availability; both English and Spanish coins circulated widely. In general, there was a great shortage of currency of all kinds, which is why the Virginians used tobacco as a medium of exchange. The value of tobacco for 1750 can be approximated because it was then that the court ordered that all those not working in tobacco could pay their levy at the rate of 12 shillings, 6 pence per 100 pounds of tobacco. This would put the levy at 1 shilling, 6 pence per poll, and make the entire levy for 1750 worth £134,125. The Reverend Green was paid 16,000 pounds or £100 per year, and this was also the cost of the Broad Run Bridge.[21]

The conversion from tobacco to currency was never certain, for both the value of tobacco and currency varied widely, and tobacco was sold at auction. Some indication of the value of specie may be obtained from the rates set by the county court for ordinaries in 1750. (See Table XI.) The rate schedule covered everything from the various kinds of beverages to a night's lodging to stabling and fodder for a horse, the latter two items each being 6d. a night. Interestingly, whereas the rate set for the levy was 12s. 6d. per 100 pounds of tobacco, the rate of exchange at the ordinary was 10s. per hundred pounds, which gave the ordinary owner an advantage over the county in tobacco exchange.

The court licensed seven ordinaries in 1750, eight in 1751, seven in 1752, seven in 1753, five in 1754, six in 1756, seven in 1758, and five in

---

21. The following calculations are helpful here: 12s. 6d. = 150d. 100 pounds of tobacco equals 150 pence. By multiplying the value of 100 pounds of tobacco (150d.) by .12 (the levy of 12 pounds of tobacco for 1750) we get 150 x .12 = 18d. or 1s., 6d. For larger sums, we know, for example, that the price paid for Broad Run Bridge was £100, and that 16,000 pounds of tobacco were levied for that purpose. Therefore, since we know 100 pounds of tobacco equal 150d., for all numbers over 1,000 pounds of tobacco, we first divide by 100, and then multiply by 150 to determine the net worth in pence of that amount of tobacco. That figure can then be divided by 240 to get the number of £ sterling or by 12 to get the number of shillings.

Table XI

1750

Liquor Rates

Rum the Gallon	10s
Nantz Brandy"	10s
Va. Peach Brandy"	6s
Apple Brandy"	5s
New England Rum"	2/6
Arrach the Qt made into Punch w/Fruit	10s
Whiskey the Gallon	4s
Red Wine the Qt	3s
White Wine"	3s
Madera Wine"	2/6
Fyal & Other Low Wines"	1/3
English Strong Beer"	1/3
Va Strong Beer	4d pena
Cider the Quart Bottled	4d
Otherwise	3d
Qt of Rum Punck w/Loaf Sugar	1/3
w/Brown Sugar	1 shilling
A Hot Diet w/small Beer or Cyder	1s
" w/o "	10d
Cold " "	6d
Corn or Oats the Gallon	4d
Stableage & Fodder 24 Hr for a Horse	6d
Pasturage 24 Hr	4d
A Nights Lodging w/Clean Sheets	6d

Ordered that the several & Respective Ordinary Do Sell & take at the aforesaid Rates in Money or Tobacco at the Rate of 10s% & that they do not Presume to Demand More of any Person Whatsoever

1759; the average being about six or seven ordinaries in the county, including Alexandria and Colchester, at any one time.

There were 188 cases of assault and battery during the 1750s, and an even 100 cases of women brought before the court for having bastard children. In some of these latter cases the fathers were specified, and the women were sometimes sentenced. These sentences were usually fines of 500 pounds (of tobacco), 25 or 50 lashes, one year's additional service to her master, or a combination of these fines. Two of the women were servants: "Elizabeth Turner a servant woman belonging to John Floyd, and Mary Gwin a servant of Joseph Moxley." Both women were sentenced to serve their masters for one additional year, and Turner was also given "twenty five lashes on her bare back well laid on."[22]

22. Fairfax County Court Order Book, 1754-1756, 1:92,163. Women convicted of having bastard children were required by colonial statute to pay 15 to the church wardens, presumably for the support of the child. Elizabeth Turner was whipped not as punishment for having a bastard child, but rather because of her inability to pay the fine; presumably, this is also the case with the other women who were whipped. Regardless of the motivation, the whipping of the women is a clear reminder of the harsh, practical nature of justice in colonial America.

There were five cases of fornication: Thos. Lewis with Eliz. Harris; Col. John Colvill with Mary Carny; Wyat William with Isabel Sankstone; Michael Melton and Martha Evans; Simon Pearson. There were three cases of adultery: John McDaniel with Margaret Gooding; Wm. May with his housekeeper; Joseph Cash with Joseph Hith's wife. There were a number of cases of retailing spirits without a license, but only two robberies or burglaries: John Briggs and Samuel Cudozier were brought before the court for taking "7 Guineys" and some other property from Henry Awbrey, and Samuel Gray for breaking into the clerk's office.

The more serious crimes were tried at the court in Williamsburg, but they were usually brought before the county court first. An example of such a case was that of Daniel Foot who was charged with "assaulting & ravishing Ann Shiel." Foot was put in jail in Fairfax "til he shall be removed to the Publick Goal in Wmbg [Williamsburg]."

Little can be said of industry and trade in Fairfax County during the 1750s. Not only is information scarce, but also there was little industry to speak of. By 1759, John Ballendine had erected on the south side of the Occoquan, in Prince William County, an iron furnace, a forge, water grist mills, bolting mills, saw mills, and numerous buildings.[23] There is no record of such activity north of the Occoquan, and presumably Ballendine supplied both Colchester and Alexandria with finished lumber for construction. The town of Alexandria had a shipyard by 1759, although the extent of shipbuilding cannot be determined.[24]

On 28 June 1750, the court granted Edward Garret permission to build a mill on Beaver Dam Branch of Goose Creek. This is the earliest evidence of a water grist mill in Fairfax County. The same year Stephen Lewis petitioned to erect a mill on Difficult Run; the following year Lewis's case was still before the court with the additional petition of William Fairfax and Edward Masterson to erect mills on the same waterway. Similarly, Daniel Thomas petitioned for a mill on Popes Head Run in November 1753, and John Hough was given permission to build a mill in June 1755 on his land "in the Gap on Short Hills."

It was just about this time that Alexandria which had earlier made a great effort in regard to exporting wheat and flour, and had exhausted the supply of grain in the northern Virginia Tidewater and Piedmont began to divert wheat from the Shenandoah Valley to her merchants on the Potomac. Presumably, some of the Fairfax farmers, by 1760, were beginning to grow wheat instead of tobacco.[25]

23. Harrison, *Landmarks*, p. 428.
24. Ibid., p. 416.
25. Ibid., pp. 407-9.

Other occupations were being practiced by Fairfax residents and they often had orphan apprentices. Some examples are:

John Sumers, cordwainer
Edmund Linton, carpenter
Manasseh Lyles, carpenter and cordwainer
James Connell, joyner [sic]
Nathaniel Popejoy, cordwainer
Lee Massey, attorney.

In retrospect, the 1750s witnessed the loss of Loudoun County, the first real growth in Alexandria, an increase in population, the expansion in the number of roads, and the removal of the courthouse from "the place called Springfield" to Alexandria. The county had changed markedly in ten years, and the concentration of population, wealth, and power along the river was beginning to make itself felt.

Before proceeding with the 1760s, it is worthwhile relating an interesting and quixotic series of events witnessed by the citizens of Fairfax County, and more specifically of Alexandria, in the spring of 1755. If the events were not quixotic then, they have certainly become so in later recapitulation.

The story really began a year earlier in 1754 when upon hearing that the French were building fortifications on the Ohio River, which was then claimed by Virginia, Governor Dinwiddie sent twenty-two-year-old George Washington with some colonial militia to build a fort at the forks of the Ohio. When Washington arrived, he found that the French were already at work fortifying the forks. He retreated down river, but in July 1754 was forced to surrender to the French. Washington and his men were allowed to return home if they would carry the message that Ohio belonged to France. Dinwiddie then asked the London government for help, and they responded by sending General Edward Braddock and about one thousand British regulars to fight the French in Ohio.

The troops sent to Alexandria were Sir Peter Halkett's 44th Regiment of Foot and Colonel Thomas Dunbar's 48th Regiment of Foot, each consisting of about 500 men whose number Braddock hoped to increase with colonial militia. They arrived in Alexandria in mid-March aboard thirteen transport and three ordinance ships, and after disembarking, made camp outside of town. When Braddock arrived in late March he made his headquarters in Alexandria at the home of the merchant John Carlyle. It was while he was at Carlyle's house that Braddock had a meeting with five colonial governors: William Shirley of Massachusetts, Robert Dinwiddie of Virginia, James DeLancey of New York, Robert Morris of Pennyslvania, and Horatio Sharpe of Maryland. Sharpe had earlier invited the governors to meet at Annapolis, with Braddock and Dinwiddie traveling to the Maryland capital. However, when the other governors could not attend at that time, Braddock had postponed the meeting until 14 April and changed the place to Alexandria.

The main topic of discussion at the meeting was the instructions given to Braddock before leaving England, that he should have the governors persuade their respective legislatures to appropriate money for a common fund to help finance the cost of defending the colonies from the French and Indians. Such an intercolonial funding scheme had been proposed by Benjamin Franklin the year before at the Albany conference, but it met with a very cool reception from the colonial legislatures which were in no mood to give up control of the purse. With this experience fresh in mind, the governors told Braddock "that such a Fund can never be established in the Colonies without the aid of Parliament." Braddock in turn informed the ministry of the governors' feelings and added "I cannot but take the liberty to represent to you the necessity of laying a tax upon all his Majesty's dominions in America . . . for reimbursing the great sums . . . advanced . . . in this important crisis."[26]

Aside from raising money, Braddock's major responsibility in America was to raise troops to supplement his regulars in fighting the French. In this too he was less than successful for, while hoping to raise a considerable force of colonials and Indians in Virginia, he finally set off with only 8 Indians and about 1,200 militia to supplement his own troops. In the end, the forces set out in two groups, traveling by different routes to reach the Ohio. Dunbar's regiment, apparently accompanied by Braddock, left on Saturday 12 April marching up the river to a point opposite Rock Creek and then crossing into Maryland; this makes Braddock's march through Fairfax County all of three or four miles. Halkett's regiment left in sections from 9 April to 26 April and marched from Alexandria to the old courthouse the first day, and to Sugarland Run the second. From there they proceeded westward. If Braddock had any plans to return to or through Fairfax, they never materialized, for his

---

26. It is upon this point that later interpretation of Braddock's mission becomes quixotic. It has been maintained that this comment of Braddock's in 1755 led to the Stamp Act ten years later and by steady steps to the American Revolution. What this position fails to take into account is that by 1765 there was not only a new ministry but also a new king. Further, that the financial realities resulting from the Seven Years War, which lay *ahead* in 1755, were entirely different than the financial situation in 1755. By 1765, the ministry was faced with an enormous debt which rendered the financial assistance of the colonies not only desirable, but mandatory. Also, the Stamp Act was only one of a number of methods used by the ministry at the later date to help reduce their debt. The idea of raising money by a direct tax in America was too obvious to assume that Braddock was the only, or even the first, man to put it forward. The five governors had as much as told Braddock this when they mentioned that they could not raise money "without the aid of Parliament." The aid which they sought would logically have taken the form of a direct revenue tax such as the Stamp Act. The single most important evidence of the lack of importance of Braddock's comment in 1755, however, was that no tax was enacted by the Parliament, and no further action was taken by either the ministry or the colonial governors for ten years. The assertion that Braddock was responsible for either the Stamp Act or the principle which motivated the act cannot be supported with the available evidence. Braddock's suggestion was too obvious both in 1755 and ten years later to assume it was unique to him.

lack of success in Fairfax turned into disaster in Ohio. On 9 July the French ambushed the English, killing Braddock and killing or wounding over 900 of his men.

It is doubtful if Alexandria missed Braddock or his men. John Carlyle, writing to his brother in August 1755, expressed "our great joy [when] they marched from hence [Alexandria]." Carlyle further described the man who had lived in his home for a month as "a man (if I am a Judge) of week [sic] understanding, positive, & very indolent, Slave to his passions, women & wine, as great an Epicure as could be in his eating, tho a brave man."

The 1760s

The 1760s continued to be a time of growth in Fairfax County, especially for the town of Alexandria with the population continuing to increase, though not so rapidly as in the 1750s. Whereas, in the four years between 1750 and 1754, the population increased by 2,098 persons (from 5,564 to 7,662); between 1760 and 1768, a period of eight years, the population grew by only 1,962 persons (4,987 to 6,949).

The county levy varied widely from six pounds per poll in 1768, for a total of only 13,452 pounds of tobacco, to twenty-six pounds per poll in 1763 for a total of 46,982 and 48,854 pounds of tobacco, respectively, in those years. The cause for such a dramatic rise in the county revenues was the construction of a new prison; it was to be two stories, thirty-six-feet long, twenty-feet wide, and was to be paid for in two annual installments.[27] The "workmen" agreed with for this construction was William Ramsay of Alexandria. Ramsay was a prominent merchant and a "gentleman"; as such, it is quite certain that he did not do the work himself, but had others do it for him. He may, therefore, have been the first building contractor in Fairfax County. Ramsay owned twenty slaves in 1782, and although it is not possible to say how many, if any, slaves he owned in 1763, the prison was very likely built by black slave labor. In December 1763 Ramsay was given permission "to burn the bricks for the new prison to be built on the Courthouse lot," which is yet another reminder that building materials in the eighteenth century had to be made, as they could not be bought. It also virtually assures us that there was no brickyard in the county at this time. Ramsay was paid 28,000 pounds of tobacco in both 1763 and 1764 for a total of 56,000 pounds for the prison. This is almost exactly three times the total county budget in 1760 of 18,848 pounds of tobacco. That a two-story brick building 36 feet by 20 feet should cost triple the average annual levy is some measure of either how very little county government did in eighteenth-century

27. Fairfax County Court Order Book, 1763-1765, A, p. 45.

Virginia, or how little was paid for out of general taxation. The sheriff, for example, was paid only 1,250 pounds of tobacco, but he collected much more than this in fees which were paid by individuals and not by the general levy; likewise, the expense of public tobacco warehouses was borne by the users. For 1760, 1761, and 1762, the levy each year provided 2,000 pounds of tobacco to George Mason for "keeping Occoquan ferry"; after 1762 there is no further allotment of public tobacco to Mason for the ferry.

Additional work was done on the courthouse in 1765: the old brick in the foundation was replaced with new, the wooden floor was replaced, the windows were newly glazed, the plaster was mended, the shutters were whitewashed, and a new door and table were provided for the jury room. [28]The name of the workmen and the price paid are not known as the order book for the last half of 1765 is missing.

The commission of peace for 1762 listed the following men as justices of the county court:

21 Dec 1762

Justices at Common Law & Chancery

Geo Wm Fairfax	Robt Adam
Lewis Ellzey	John Hunter
John West	Rich Sanford
Daniel McCarty	Wm Payne
John Carlyle	Benj Grayson
Wm Ramsay	John West Jr
Chas Broadwater	Bryan Fairfax
Thos Colville	Sampson Darrell
Townshend Dade	Wm Adams
Henry Gunnel	Edw Blackburn
Marmaduke Beckwith	Hector Ross

By 1764, however, John Hunter was reported dead, and several others had not acted as magistrates in the county for several years: Thomas Colvill, Henry Gunnell, Marmaduke Beckwith, Richard Sandford, Townshend Dade, and Sampson Darrell. "As the business of the county absolutely requires more justices," the court recommended to the governor that George Washington, Lee Massey, Daniel French, Harry Piper, John Muir, Chas. Alexander, and Robt. Alexander be added to the court. [29]

The interrelationship of church and state is again apparent in the text of the oath required of all civil officials as recorded in the 1764

28. Ibid., B, 84, 20 March 1765.
29. Ibid., 21 November 1764, p. 60.

Fairfax County Order Book. Each man was required to "declare that there is not transubstantiation in the sacrament of the Lords Supper, or in the elements of bread & wine, at or after consecration thereof, by any person whatsoever," further "that I will be conformable to the doctine & discipline of the Church of England as by law established."

The major activity taking place in Fairfax during this decade was ecclesiastical reorganization and change. Beginning with a holdover of a problem from the previous decade, by 1760 Thomas Waite had not satisfactorily finished the glebe house which he had agreed in 1752 to have completed within two years. The vestry had paid Waite all but £ 100 of the money for the house, but even so, in 1760 they contracted with William Buckland, the craftsman of Gunston Hall, to finish the work for £ 93 2s. In October 1762 George Washington was chosen a vestryman; in 1764 he was appointed a justice to the county court. These events mark the beginning of Washington's active participation in the public affairs of Fairfax County.

For the first half of the decade, the parish levy was between twenty and thirty-two pounds per poll, a figure which was more than double the normal county levy; for 1764 it rose to thirty-two pounds per poll (the same year that the county levy was at its highest, twenty-six pounds per poll) in order to build the new prison. During this same year, 1764, the parish was divided and the Parish of Fairfax was created from the northern half of Truro. The boundaries, however, were not finally set until May 1765.

Washington was quite active in the matter of the new parish and in establishing the boundary between the parishes. The first division placed him in the new Fairfax Parish, as did the second, and even though both of these boundaries were refused and protested by Truro Parish, Washington was elected to the new Fairfax vestry 28 March 1765. He was the fifth most popular candidate, receiving fewer votes than John West, Charles Alexander, William Payne, and John Dalton. When the third and final boundary between the parishes was adopted by the Assembly in May 1765, Washington was again in Truro. Accordingly, he was elected to the Truro vestry 25 July 1765, receiving more votes than anyone except George Mason, and Edward Payne. The selection of Washington to serve on the Truro vestry twice, and the Fairfax vestry once in a period of four years is a safe indicator of his social position in Fairfax County. The only time the parishioners were given the opportunity to choose vestrymen was when a new vestry was selected due to a parish division; at other times, vacancies on the vestry were filled by vote of the remaining vestrymen. Washington's first election to the vestry in 1762, was by vote of the vestrymen only, and is an indication of his secure position with the ruling elite, as represented by the vestrymen. His election three years later, first to the Fairfax vestry and then in four months to the

Truro vestry, is clear evidence of respect and trust from his neighbors and fellow parishioners throughout the county. That he received a larger percentage of votes for the Truro vestry which was centered more closely on Mount Vernon is understandable. In this light, not only is Washington's appointment to the Fairfax court in 1764 not surprising, but his subsequent choice as vestryman at two independent elections in different areas of the county also illustrates that the appointed officials of county government were more than acceptable to the citizens. Further, Washington's activities regarding the disputed boundary between the parishes are testimony of his acceptance of the responsibility placed upon him. At both of the vestry elections in 1765 he made a careful list of the candidates for election in each parish and the number of votes received by each, thereby proving that Fairfax Parish had received more tithables in the original division and that the boundary should be moved. He also prepared a map, probably late in 1765, which indicates clearly the new boundary line and a number of houses on each side of the line. Although there is little doubt that Washington preferred to be in Truro Parish, his taking time to make the election lists and to draw the map are indicative of his concern with parish affairs in general.

The parish division reduced the tithables in Truro from 1,879 in 1764 to 962 in 1765 and nearly doubled the levy to a whopping sixty pounds per poll. When the Reverend Mr. Green died late in 1764, Truro Parish found itself with no minister and less than half of its former tithables. Undaunted, in 1766 the vestry selected Lee Massey to be its new minister. As Massey was at that time still a layman, the vestry wrote to the Bishop of London and to Francis Fauquier, Governor of Virginia, informing them that they wished to have Massey as the minister for Truro, and requesting his ordination by the bishop and appointment by the governor. While there is no reason to doubt that Massey was a man of good character and that the vestry both needed and desired him to serve as minister, the matter seemed to be very much an affair of business. The letter to Fauquier mentions that Massey "has an Intention of entering into holy Orders, provided he can have a Certainty of this Parish;" in other words, he wanted a guarantee of the living afforded by the parish. The vestry agreed to hold the position of minister open until Massey should return from ordination in England. They could not, however, be assured that they would still have the authority to offer the position to Massey, so they asked the governor "to favour him with an Induction or Presentation to this Parish, in case he returns after the Expiration of our right. . . ."

In the meantime the vestry paid the Reverend James Scott 8,632 pounds of tobacco for twenty-six sermons, or 332 pounds per sermon.

By May 1767 the vestry book notes, "Present The Revd. Lee Massey Minister." The book is strangely silent as to whether Massey did indeed

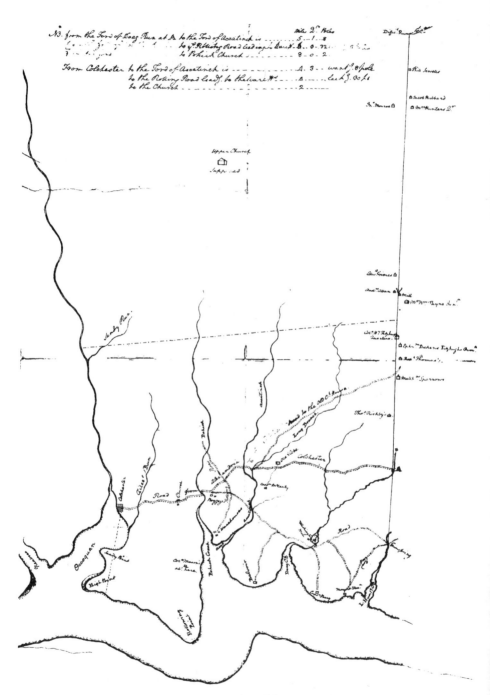

Map drawn by George Washington probably between June 1765 and February 1766, indicating major roads and land owners. Library of Congress.

go to England for ordination, or whether he simply assumed the mantle of minister without ordination. In any event he was minister and the parish levy, set in November 1767, provided for his salary "for the 14th of Janry 1767, to the 14th of Janry 1768. . ." the sum of 17,200 pounds of tobacco, also 4,000 pounds "in Lieu of a Glebe." In 1766, they also undertook to build a new church on the Ox Road. Edward Payne agreed to build the church for £579 Virginia currency, and it was henceforth known as Payne's church.

With the division of the parish, it was again necessary to sell the glebe lands and church plate. Accordingly, both were sold "at Publick Vendue" on 22 May 1767 to Daniel McCarty who paid £322 Virginia currency for 385½ acres of glebe land and £26 for the church plate. McCarty gave the plate for the use of the parish.

It was decided to build a new church in 1767; this was the Pohick Church which is still standing. This new structure was closer to Mount Vernon than the original church building nearer to Gunston Hall. There was a controversy over the location for the new church with Washington and Mason each taking an active role and opposite points of view. Mason, contending for a new building at the old location, pleaded that this was the church of their ancestors and should not be abandoned. It was reported that his eloquence upon this occasion was such that everyone was sure he would carry his point. "Washington then rose," in the words of Jared Sparks, "and drew from his pocket a roll of paper, containing an exact survey of Truro Parish, on which was marked the site of the old church, the proposed site of the new one, and the place where each parishioner resided." Reportedly, the map was persuasive, and the church was built at the new location nearer Mount Vernon. Whether or not this story is true (a map conforming to that described by Sparks is not known to exist), there doubtless was controversy over the location for the new church. For this occasion, Washington may have used the map which he prepared in 1765 to show the new parish boundary.

Daniel French "undertook to Build the Church for the sum of Eight hundred Seventy and seven pounds [£ 877] Current Money of Virginia . . . ." It was to be a handsome and well-constructed building 66 feet by 45½ feet, and the construction details were extremely specific. The bricks were to be "well burnt" and 9 by 4½ by 3 inches; the walls were to be three bricks thick down to the water table and "two and a half afterwards"; even the composition of the mortar was specified; no detail was omitted down to "a Communion Table of black walnut" and orders for "The Apostles Creed, the Lords Prayer, and the ten Commandments to be neatly Painted on the Alter-piece in black letters."[31] French further

---

30. *Vestry Book*, pp. 94-97.
31. The construction details are in *Vestry Book*, pp. 115-17.

agreed "to build two Horse-Blocks with each two flight of Steps;[32] to fix six benches for the People to sit on under the Trees; and to clear and remove all the Rubbish and litter from off the church Lott, so as to fit it for the Reception of the Congregation." Such care may be ascribed to two factors: sad experience with improper workmanship in the past; and a genuine desire to have the new church as splendid and pleasant as possible. After all, this church would be attended by Washington and Mason; the two men were vestrymen, had helped draw up the specifications, and both were well acquainted with the finer points of architecture.

Meanwhile, the Fairfax Parish vestry held its first meeting 26 August 1765; the vestrymen were:

John West	Edward Duling
William Payne	Richard Sandford
William Adams	David French
John Dalton	Thomas Shaw
Thomas Wren	Townshend Dade

The levy for the new parish was on 1,013 tithables at forty-seven pounds per poll, which the vestry valued at £ 476, eleven shillings sterling. At this rate the total levy of tobacco was 47,611 pounds of tobacco, or one pound sterling per hundred pounds of tobacco, which would make tobacco worth about five pounds per shilling. In December 1765 Townshend Dade was appointed minister for the new parish and a clapboard vestry house was ordered to be built sixteen feet square with an inside chimney and plank floor, at the Falls Church.

A year later the tithe per poll was raised to sixty-five pounds of tobacco, about half of which was for building two new brick churches, one at the Falls Church and one at Alexandria. The vestry met again on New Year's day 1767 when James Wren produced a plan for a brick church sixty feet by forty feet and agreed to build the new Falls Church for £ 300 15s. This was agreed to by the vestry who, at the same time, contracted to pay James Parsons £ 600 for a brick church, built to Wren's plans, at Alexandria. In May of the same year, the vestry was petitioned by "sundry inhabitants" for an addition to the Alexandria church, which Parsons agreed to undertake in consideration of being allowed to sell ten pews "for his benefit."[33] The vestry further specified that "no one is to be permitted to be a purchaser but Inhabi-

---

32. A horse-block was "A small platform, usually of stone, ascended by 3 or 4 steps, for convenience in mounting a horse"; Oxford English Dictionary, 5: 398.

33. For background on the sale of church pews see Pohick Church.

tants of this parish or that pay taxes in the same." As the new church had been built, and the upkeep would be paid for with parish taxes, the vestry was not content to allow someone who did not live in the parish to purchase a pew and occupy a church for which others had paid. With the parish levy for 1767 at forty-seven pounds per poll, and sixty pounds per poll in 1768, the inhabitants of the parish might well, and with reason, have objected to outsiders buying pews in a parish church. This was especially true in an important colonial port town such as Alexandria where wealthy merchants from other towns or colonies might have purchased a pew for those Sundays when they were in Alexandria.

In the last year of the decade, the vestry accepted the completed Falls Church from James Wren and expressed satisfaction with his work. In July 1769, they reached agreement with the Reverend Townshend Dade to purchase the 400 acres upon which Dade then lived for £800, to be used as the parish glebe. However, by December they were again advertising for glebe lands, and it is not apparent why they did not purchase Dade's land. In May 1770, the vestry agreed to purchase over 400 acres from Daniel Jennings at 15s. per acre.[34]

All four tobacco inspection warehouses continued to operate, closely regulated and inspected by the court. As tobacco was the medium of exchange, and with obligations payable in tobacco notes rather than the tobacco itself (What would the Reverend Mr. Green have done with 16,000 pounds of tobacco?), it becomes clear why the inspection warehouses were of such importance. If enough inferior tobacco got through to cast serious doubt on the value of the tobacco notes, the entire economic foundation of the times would have come apart. As it was, the highly fluctuating value of tobacco on the market caused the notes to be received unenthusiastically by some. For this reason, as time passed, more of the county and parish obligations were paid in Virginia currency rather than tobacco notes.

A larger number of orphans were apprenticed to craftsmen in the 1760 s than ever before, indicating the expanding number of trades being practiced in Fairfax County:

Thomas Bench, tight cooper	John Cannon, sadler
Thomas Halbert, tight cooper	Dorson Vallandingham, tight cooper
James McCleod, Taylor [sic]	John Crook, tight cooper
William Sewall, baker	Thos. Fleming, ship carpenter
Timothy Lyon, weaver	Nicholas Garrett, shoemaker
Thos. West, cordwainer	Thos. Dowdle, tight cooper
John Seale, shipwright	John Bolling, shoemaker
Wm. Mundy, joiner	Robt. Adams, mariner
& house carpenter	Joseph Hannah, weaver

34. "Fairfax Parish Vestry Book," entries for 26 August 1765 through 17 May 1770 (Alexandria, Virginia: Christ Church).

Three ordinaries were licensed by the court in 1760; five in 1761; eight in 1762; four in 1763; six in 1764; three in 1765; and seven in 1769.

Fairfax County Ordinary Licenses Granted 1760-1769

Name	Location	Year of License
Chas. Taylor	Colchester	1760
James Brown	Pohick	1761
Wm. Linton	Colchester	1761
David Young	Alexandria	1761
Michael Grater	Alexandria	1762
David Sexton	Colchester	1762
John Conner	Cameron	1763
Thos. Saunders	Ferry in Alex.	1763
(Saunders was also appointed Ferrykeeper in 1763.)		
Daniel Bush	Alexandria	1764
Pearse [sic] Bayley	Colchester	1764
Richard Arrell	Alexandria	1764-1765
Elizah Williams	Browns Ordinary	1765
Chas. Turner	Alexandria	1769
Henry Barnum	Old Courthouse	1769
William Courts	Colchester	1769
John Lomax	Alexandria	1769

It is not surprising that most of the ordinaries were either in Alexandria or Colchester, for as centers of trade and commerce they were the natural gathering places of the people. Among the licenses issued without a specified location was one to Ann Mason in 1760 which she most likely operated in conjunction with the ferry over likely the Occoquan. Similarly, the presence of an ordinary at the old courthouse indicates that this had not ceased to be a gathering place for residents of the upper part of the county.[35]

Assault and battery again led the list of the most frequent crimes of the forty-six cases in the court records for the 1760s. Additionally, there were eight cases of stealing, most of which were punished by whipping at the public whipping post;[36] Catherine Sutteran was put in jail for "madness";[37] and there were two cases of passing counterfeit money: Robert Boggess was accused and acquitted of passing a counterfeit £ 3 bill, and Blanch Flower Duncan of passing three £5 bills.[38]

35. The list given above was surely not inclusive of all the ordinaries in Fairfax County in the 1760s. The court record books are missing for 1765-1768, and there appear to be omissions in the records. For whatever reason, the list above cannot be considered to be complete.

36. Fairfax County Court Order Book, 1756-1763, II, pp. 632, 615, 522, A, 15, B, 162, 78, II, 630, A, 51.

37. Ibid., II, 782.

38. Ibid., II, 631, 797.

JOHN SMITH TRAINER.

Y,
ated

To be *R E N T E D*, *in* ALEXANDRIA,
THE GEORGE TAVERN. There are
three Fire Places below Stairs, a very good
Bar, and fix Rooms above; a Kitchen adjoining, with two good Rooms below and above,
a Dining Room 24 Feet by 18, a Room of the
fame Dimenfions above it, in which is a very good
London BILLIARD TABLE. There are alfo, a
Garden, Stable, Smoke-houfe, &c.

Any Perfon inclining to Rent the fame for a
Term of Years, may know the Terms and Time,
by applying to the Subfcriber, (or in his Abfence
to Mrs. *Ramfay*) and enter on the Premiffes in
good Order.

WILLIAM RAMSAY.

Alexandria, Jan. 30. 1760.

THERE is at the Plantation of *William Ranter*

Advertisement for the George Tavern, from Maryland Gazette, 6 March 1760.

A number of other criminal matters brought before the court are of
interest for what they tell us of the temper of the eighteenth century.
Hugh West, a justice, was fined by the court "for misbehaving to the
clerk by cursing him in the execution of his office before the court"[39];
Catherine Ramsay was brought before the court and charged with being
"a person of Lewd life & a disturber of the peace."[40] In a somewhat
humorous incident, John Hurst, Jr., was presented by the grand
jury "for behaving in an indecent manner on Sunday the 17th instant at
the Falls Church by bringing a mare to his stallion in presence of part of
the congregation in time of service."[41]

Francis Dade may, however, hold the honor of being the most
obstreperous man brought before the court. Dade, an attorney licensed
to practice before the Fairfax court, had accepted 11s. 3d. to plead a case
for William Greenwood in February 1769. When summoned by the
sheriff to come plead his case, Dade replied "that he would not come &
that the court might kiss his Arse." The justices thereby ordered Dade
brought before the court by the sheriff, and told Dade either to defend
Greenwood or refund the money. Dade refused to do either and left the
court.[42] Then in May 1769, he was again before the court

39. Ibid., II, 625.
40. Ibid., II, 490.
41. Ibid., II, 782.
42. Fairfax County Court Order Book, 1768-1770, p. 99.

for verbally abusing the justices in a public ordinary; he had called them "partial sons of bitches [and said] that he would have their ears cropt & he would turn them out of commission." Unwilling to leave well enough alone, Dade showed up in court drunk, "grossly abused Sampson Darrel [the sheriff] in open Court," and was fined £5.

Among other criminal charges were nine cases of retailing liquors without a license; one case of fornication and adultery involving Simon Pearson and Pelitiah Graffort in 1769; and three additional cases of adultery in 1768 involving Joseph Watson, Cecilia Trig, and again, Simon Pearson. Pearson was virtually a habitual offender having been charged with adultery in 1759, 1761, and 1768. There were also thirty-two cases of bastardy, of which two specified that the child was a mulatto. This means, of course, that the father was either a black or mulatto slave, and the mother white as a slave woman would not have been brought into court.

The 1770s

With the 1770 s Fairfax County entered upon its last six and one-half years as part of the British colonial empire. The court records are missing from 1774 to 1783, so that the actions of the court during the war years are unknown. The Revolution, however, left Virginia county government largely unaltered, so there is little reason to think that the routine functions of the court changed a great deal. What little military action there was in Fairfax County was under the control of the committee of safety, whose records are also missing.

For the vestry, which enjoyed its last full decade of existence under the establishment, the major items of concern were the new churches. The new Pohick Church was by far the most important church in the parish, and was attended by the most affluent, influential citizens. The enormous amount of care expended on making every detail of the church as fine as possible, at no small expense, surely resulted in a richly ornamental, finely finished, and beautiful building. This expense was reflected in 1770 when the highest levy in the entire history of the parish was set: an unheard-of eighty pounds per poll, for a total levy of 90,480 pounds of tobacco, of which 56,330 pounds were for the new church. The following year, 1771, the levy dropped slightly to seventy pounds per poll for a total of 85,960 pounds of tobacco. However, for both years, this was over six times the rate of the county court levy. The new church sufficiently was finished in time for the vestry meeting 5 June 1772, by which time the altar had been embossed in gold leaf; "Presented to this Parish by the Honrble. George Wm. Fairfax and George Washington Esqrs." The altar was obviously a gift from these leading citizens. Also at this first meeting in the new sanctuary, the vestry made arrangements for the sale of the pews in the new church. This was an important matter: the

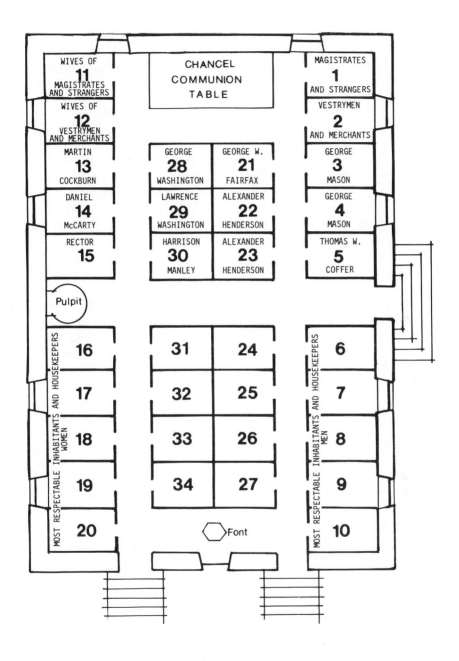

WIVES OF
11
MAGISTRATES
AND STRANGERS

WIVES OF
12
VESTRYMEN
AND MERCHANTS

MARTIN
13
COCKBURN

DANIEL
14
McCARTY

RECTOR
15

CHANCEL
COMMUNION
TABLE

MAGISTRATES
1
AND STRANGERS

VESTRYMEN
2
AND MERCHANTS

GEORGE
3
MASON

GEORGE
4
MASON

THOMAS W.
5
COFFER

GEORGE
28
WASHINGTON

LAWRENCE
29
WASHINGTON

HARRISON
30
MANLEY

GEORGE W.
21
FAIRFAX

ALEXANDER
22
HENDERSON

ALEXANDER
23
HENDERSON

Pulpit

MOST RESPECTABLE INHABITANTS AND HOUSEKEEPERS WOMEN

16

17

18

19

20

31

32

33

34

24

25

26

27

MOST RESPECTABLE INHABITANTS AND HOUSEKEEPERS MEN

6

7

8

9

10

Font

Plan of Pohick Church, c. 1770, from a measured drawing by Glenn Brown. Redrawn by Gloria Matthews, Fairfax County Office of Comprehensive Planning.

pews sold at high prices, and actual deeds were executed from the vestry to the purchaser, for the purchasing of a pew was not only a mark of social standing, but an affirmation of support for the parish and vestry. The six most important pews were those in front of the cross aisle and between the two side aisles.

The two front pews in the center section next to the communion table went to the two most important county residents, George William Fairfax and George Washington, at £16 each. The two pews in the center behind Fairfax's were both sold to Alexander Henderson, the prominent and wealthy Colchester merchant for £13, and £13 10s., respectively, with the two center pews behind Washington's and adjoining Hendersons' purchased by Lund Washington for £13 10s., and by Harrison Manley at £15 10s. George Mason purchased two pews on the south wall for £14 11s. 8d. each; this would seem to indicate that Mason was the sixth most important citizen in the county as he was not among those to purchase center pews. On the other hand, the pews were sold at auction and he may have felt less affluent than some of the others. He may also have resented the fact that the new church was closer to Mount Vernon than to Gunston Hall. The remaining pews were sold to Thomas Withers Coffer for £14 13s.; Martin Cockburn for £15 10s.; and Daniel McCarty for £15 10s. Pew number fifteen was not sold, there being no buyer available, and it was, therefore, reserved for the use of the rector and his family. The sale of the pews was a sizable financial recovery for the parish. A total of £162 6s. 4d. was collected, which represented nearly twenty percent of the entire £876 cost of the new church. The six pews in the center front were on the floor level; those on the side, such as Mason's, were raised above the aisles. This prompted Fairfax and Henderson to request permission, on behalf of themselves and the three other owners of the center pews, to raise their pews, at their own expense, to the same height as those on the side. The vestry agreed, and then raised the eight center rear pews at the expense of the parish—an object lesson in social consciousness in colonial Virginia. With the church paid for, the levy fell to 49 pounds per poll in 1772. In 1774, the year that the active Revolution really started in Fairfax County, the levy fell to twenty-six pounds per poll, and by 1779 it fell to twelve pounds per poll, a striking contrast with the eighty pounds per poll of 1770. [43]

For Fairfax Parish, the new Christ Church at Alexandria was the issue of most concern. At the meeting in May 1772, the vestry asked James Parsons if he would finish the church in Alexandria. When Parsons refused to answer, the vestry advertised in the papers for a worker to complete the building and granted the job to the lowest bidder. The work would be paid for by selling the pews which had previously

43. *Vestry Book*, pp. 120-47.

been allotted for sale by Parsons. John Carlyle, Jr., agreed to finish the church by Christmas 1772 for £ 220. He too was late; the vestry pronounced the church finished "in workmanlike manner" in February 1773.

At the same May 1772 meeting, the ten pews formerly given to Parsons were sold at auction with the terms specified as £ 15 cash and the remainder to be paid in six months. The pews were sold for a total revenue of £ 298 10s., which was almost half of the original price of £ 600 promised to Parsons. The pews were purchased by:

	£	s.
John Muir	£ 36	5s.
John West, Jr.	£ 33	0s.
Thomas Fleming	£ 21	5s.
John Carlyle	£ 30	0s.
William Ramsay	£ 33	0s.
John Dalton	£ 30	10s.
Robert Alexander	£ 30	10s.
Robert Adam	£ 30	0s.
Townshend Dade	£ 28	0s.
George Washington	£ 36	10s.

The purchase of a pew by Washington is of more than passing interest. So far as is known, he did not pay taxes in Fairfax Parish and, therefore, should not have been allowed to purchase a pew; he already owned a pew at Pohick, the church he had worked to have placed near Mount Vernon; he paid five shillings more for his pew in Christ Church than any other man, thereby asserting his social position. With the exception of Dade, the parish minister, the other pews were purchased by prominent Alexandria merchants.

The vestry continued its ambitious building campaign in 1773 by arranging for construction of a number of buildings on the glebe; these included:

a dwelling house	42 by 28 feet
a kitchen	20 by 16 feet
dairy	12 feet square
meathouse	12 feet square
barn	32 by 20 feet
stable	24 by 16 feet
a fenced garden	100 feet square

The following year they added a sixteen-by-ten-foot hen house "of hewed [sic] logs covered with the best shingles."

The details of the operation of the parishes in Fairfax County have been given here because the parish represented an important organizational and controlling force in the lives of the people. The vast majority of an individual's tax obligation was to the parish vestry which exerted day-to-day control over a person's life, and the secular ruling elite, such as George Washington, discharged his social obligation by serving on the vestry, while giving his approval to the establishment by purchasing one or more pews. In a society which saw organized religion as the cement that held society together by protecting and enforcing the public virtue, the parish as the local representation of that controlling stabilizing force was of great importance in the lives of the people. The minister as the local parish officer of the establishment was, at least in Fairfax County, well provided for. The buildings on the glebe were for the use of the minister as was the glebe land, over 500 acres in Fairfax Parish. He could, and often did, rent this land to tenants as a supplement to his annual salary of 17,500 pounds of tobacco (about £44 at 5 shillings per hundred pounds).

The general taxation to support the establishment, the handsome churches, and the minister's comfortable lifestyle were a constant irritation to various dissenting religious groups. In October 1776, when the Assembly of the newly formed Commonwealth of Virginia not only freed the dissenters from paying the parish levy but also suspended the use of levy money for ministers' salaries, it dealt the vestries a mortal blow.

Acting in conformity with the new law, and at the same time bringing to an end the general support of Anglican ministers in Fairfax County, the Truro vestry made its last payment to the Reverend Lee Massey in November 1776: 17,280 pounds of tobacco for the year 1776. Similarly, in March 1777, the Fairfax Parish vestry paid the Reverend Townshend Dade 3,600 pounds of tobacco for the period from October 1776 to January 1777. These were the last payments to ministers in Fairfax County under the establishment.

This evidently had an effect upon Townshend Dade, for by August 1777 the vestry was inquiring why he neglected his duties as minister for the parish. By November 1777, eight vestrymen visited Dade and asked if he would resign the glebe "as he fails to do his duty as a minister." Witnesses were asked to appear to testify against Dade in February 1778. In June of that year he resigned, and the vestry took possession of the glebe and collected the rents of the tenants on the glebe land. After some confusion, David Griffith was chosen in February 1779 to succeed Dade as minister for Fairfax Parish.[44]

To the twentieth-century reader recitation of budgets and salaries being paid in tobacco and occasionally in pounds sterling and shillings is confusing at best and it may be worthwhile realizing that the entire currency situation was less than clear even to men of the eighteenth

---

44. Fairfax Parish Vestry Book, 26 November 1770 through 17 February 1779.

century. An entry from the records of the Fairfax Parish vestry for 1775 reveals the various types of currency circulating in Fairfax County on the eve of the Revolution, and the necessity of local men to establish a value for them:

> That the churchwardens discharge the several cash debts this day assessed in dollars, silver or Paper at six shillings, half Johannes of nine penny weight at forty eight shillings, English Guineas at twenty eight shillings, Spanish Pistols of four penny weight, six grains at twenty two shillings.[45]

This entry points out that monetary exchange was unstable, although one should not overlook that Alexandria was an important port where money of many countries was available and that the monetary action cited above was taken by the vestry of Fairfax Parish, which included Alexandria.

For the four years from 1770 to 1773, court records show that the levy ran between thirteen pounds per poll in 1770, to seven pounds per poll in 1772, and back up to sixteen pounds per poll in 1773. In the latter year, the county court provided £45 for the "Trustees of the Rd from Vestals & William Gaps leading to Alex. & Colchestr." This is a matter of considerable importance. The roads in Virginia were maintained by free labor service from the tithables along a given road. This task took men from their private labors and was never popular. As the trade of Colchester and Alexandria expanded, the roads to the Shenandoah Valley via William's and Vestal's gaps were more widely traveled. They were especially used by the wagons which brought grain and other products to the river towns. These wagons, however, put more strain on the roads, and required better roads in the first place. The result was an outcry from the tithables who had to maintain the roads and a simultaneous plea from Alexandria to provide proper roads for the trade upon which her economic development depended.

The Assembly in 1772 responded by providing for Fairfax, Loudoun, Berkeley, and Frederick county courts to levy a special annual tax to be turned over to trustees who would in turn use the money to improve and maintain the roads. The trustees for Fairfax were Bryan Fairfax, William Ramsay, Alexander Henderson, and Edward Payne. The total sum specified for the four counties to provide the trustees was £175 yearly,

45. The silver dollars referred to were the Spanish-milled dollar or eight real piece, frequently called "pieces of eight," which circulated widely in the colonies. The paper dollar is puzzling. The author could find no known paper dollar at this date. A half Johannes was a gold Portuguese coin. English guineas and Spanish pistoles were also gold. The entry is further confusing because it is not known whether the shilling to which the other coins were reckoned were English or Virginia shillings. English shillings would have been a more stable currency, but were scarcer. Further, the English guinea was equal to twenty-one shillings; yet here it is valued at forty-eight shillings, which could indicate reference to inflated Virginia currency.

and £ 45 was the share of Fairfax County in 1773. This arrangement was the beginning of the turnpike concept in northern Virginia; although no fees were charged at this time, the continuing problem and need for transportation resulted in the construction of Little River Turnpike, Middle Turnpike, Georgetown Leesburg Turnpike, and a toll road from Alexandria to Georgetown after the turn of the century.[46]

It is interesting to note as time progressed more of both county and parish expenditures were expressed in currency, as with the £45 for the road and £876 for the new church, and less were accounted for in terms of pounds of tobacco, although levies continued to be payable in tobacco.

By June 1773 there was a smallpox epidemic in Alexandria, and the June court empowered John Carlyle, William Ramsay, and Robert Adams to take whatever measures were necessary to stop the spread, and if necessary, to grant licenses to innoculate against the disease, a reminder of the threat which such an outbreak posed in the eighteenth century. As all three men appointed to deal with the problem were residents of Alexandria, the court probably reasoned that they would be especially interested in keeping the disease under control and in any event would stay with their families in their homes in Alexandria. By appointing justices who resided in Alexandria to cope with the problem, the court relieved those justices who lived elsewhere in the county of the necessity of coming to court in Alexandria and exposing themselves to the disease.

A number of mills were petitioned for or built between 1770 and 1773.

George Simpson	Wolf Run	May 1771
Charles Alexander	————	August 1771
William Carlin	Four Mile Run	August 1772
Moses Simpson	Sandy Run	August 1772
Thomas Lewis	Wolf Trap Run	March 1773

The court also acted "on the motion of Geo. Washington Gt. proprietor of a mill in this co. it is ordered to be recorded that he makes his flour w/a brand having the following letters G. WASHINGTON."[47] It is often forgotten that Washington was primarily, at least in his mind, a businessman. Even by 1772 he was a powerful man in Fairfax County: at one and the same time a large and prosperous land and slave owner, the proprietor of a mill, a trustee of the town of Alexandria, a justice of the county court, a member of the parish vestry, a Fairfax County burgess to the House of Burgesses, and a land speculator in the Ohio country.

---

46. Harrison, *Landmarks*, pp. 561-82.
47. Fairfax County Court Order Book, 1772-1774, p. 158.

Nonetheless, in August 1770 the Fairfax court required that both he and George Mason give security for keeping ferries at their respective landings in Fairfax County.

As if to compete with the new Pohick Church and the new wall around the prison, the court ordered what amounted to a flurry of construction in relation to the four tobacco warehouses. On 20 March 1771, "John Carlyle proprietor of Hunting Creek warehouse & Wm. Bayly proprietor of Colchester warehouse" as well as "the inspectors at the Falls and Pohick Warehouses" were required to "erect brick funnels to burn the trash tobacco."[48] A mere six months later, 17 September 1771, the inspectors at Hunting Creek warehouse reported that in the last year they had inspected 1,117 hogsheads of tobacco, and that the present warehouse would only hold 350 hogsheads; the court ordered the proprietor, John Carlyle, to build an additional warehouse to hold 400 more hogsheads. Similarly, the inspectors at Colchester reported inspection of 1,540 hogsheads with a warehouse fit to hold 600. As the proprietor, William Bayly, refused to construct a new warehouse to hold 420 additional hogsheads, Hector Ross and Alexander Henderson were ordered by the court to have the warehouse built and report to the court. The larger inspection and warehouse at Colchester is significant evidence that Alexandria had begun to give more attention to wheat, flour, and other commercial enterprises than to tobacco. This may have saved the town, for with the end of the tobacco boom in later eighteenth century, a town such as Colchester, built almost solely on that staple, was doomed. The plan presented by Carlyle for the new warehouse at Hunting Creek was for a building 70 by 28 feet. Carlyle, however, acting as agent for Sybil West the proprietor, refused to build the new structure, and the court ordered George Washington and John West to have the work done. The following year, 1772, the firm of Taylor and Thornton supplied Hunting Creek warehouse with weights costing £9 3s. 4d.

Three ordinary licenses were issued in 1770, seven in 1771, six in 1772, and four in 1773.

A brief look at the criminals brought before the court will complete the available data for the 1770s. There were ten women brought before the court in 1770 for bastardy, and one in 1772. The court had one case of fornication in 1771 (Margaret House with her husband's servant, James McManning); two in 1772 (John Dowdall and Magdalene Jenkins, and Ann Hughes with George Athy); and one in 1773 (Henry Boggess with

---

48. As the tobacco was brought in and inspected, any which did not pass inspection was burned by the inspectors. The owner of the tobacco had no control over this procedure, and he was not reimbursed for the tobacco.

Mary West). There were additional cases of adultery: a schoolmaster, Peter Robinson, with Christian Goldsborough, and Thomas Hutch with Mornacha Hayle. There were forty-six cases of assault and battery in the four years from 1770 to 1773. Surprisingly, the number of cases of selling liquor without a license increased to fifteen in 1770 alone, while the entire decade of the 1760s had occasioned only nine incidents of this sort. Finally, there were seven cases of thefts of different kinds: May Saviners stole a goose; Robert Brook, a rifle; Samuel Johnson, two geese; Franklin Perry, a shovelful of meal from "tolson mill"; Bennett McCarling, a linen shirt and silk handkerchief; and Philip Langfitt, a hog.

In retrospect, Fairfax County had undergone enormous change from its founding in 1742 until the time that the county's two major statesmen were preparing to make their entrance onto the national and international stage: George Washington as the "Father of His Country", and George Mason as the father of constitutional protection of liberties for the citizens of the new nation. During these thirty odd years, the land area of the county was reduced by more than half with the formation of Loudoun County in 1757; even so the population had more than doubled from 4,125 in 1742 to 8,310 in 1773. The towns of Alexandria and Colchester had come into being and flourished, with the former claiming the county courthouse. There were now two parishes and five active churches, including the splendid new edifice at Pohick.

Fairfax County had grown from a sparsely populated wilderness to an affluent colonial society with limitless possibilities for growth and development ahead. Whatever may be said of the political grievances of the American colonists, Fairfax County, along with the rest of British North America, had grown and prospered under colonial rule. They were soon to try their hand at going it alone, but first they had to forcibly cut the lifeline with Great Britain.

*What do we mean by the Revolution? The War? That was no
part of the Revolution; it was only an effect and consequence of it.
The Revolution was in the minds of the people, and this was
effected, from 1760 to 1775, in the course of fifteen years before a
drop of blood was shed at Lexington.*

John Adams to Thomas Jefferson, 1815

IV

The Effect of Fairfax County
on the American Revolution

No stirring campaign or major military battle of the Revolutionary
War was fought in Fairfax County. In a practical day-to-day sense, the
lives of the common people were disturbed little by the war. This is of
course, a relative matter; undoubtedly there were inconveniences and
shortages occasioned by the nonimportation and the hostilities. There
were extra financial burdens due to the necessity of military
preparations, not to mention the constant fear that the British army
would land there. The Potomac provided a ready avenue for the
powerful British fleet, as Washington, Mason, and many others fully
realized, and Alexandria was an inviting target for such a maneuver.
However, it simply never happened, and in that sense, the Revolutionary
War had little effect on Fairfax County. On the other hand, the men who
lived in Fairfax County had a profound effect upon the American
Revolution and the Revolutionary War. Perhaps the single most
important military figure of the war was General George Washington,
Commander of the Continental Army. Washington was, of course, both
a resident and a leading citizen of Fairfax. However, if John Adams, who
was not exactly a disinterested bystander, is to be believed, the real
Revolution was not effected by the army, but was with the people before
1775, and certainly before 4 July 1776.

When the Revolution is defined in these terms, Fairfax County
takes a commanding position not only in Virginia, but also in all of British

North America, which was later to become the United States. Not only did Fairfax County produce an intellectual giant in George Mason, but the freeholders of the county supported Mason and Washington and endorsed their far-reaching proposals and documents hammered out at Gunston Hall, Mount Vernon, and in county meetings in Alexandria. George Washington, although less given to revolutionary documents than his friend Mason, had a full understanding of the course of events, and it was to Bryan Fairfax, virtually a lifelong resident of Fairfax, that Washington most clearly described his feelings on the Revolution. Indeed, if it were not for the letters from Washington to Fairfax, we would know little of how Washington felt about the basic issues during those critical days in 1774. If the war had little effect on the county, the county had a marked effect on the Revolution; and the Revolution in this sense begins in the early 1760s, as John Adams clearly remembered.

Britain came out of the Seven Years War (the French and Indian War) in 1763 with a vast new colonial empire, including not only colonies on the Atlantic coast, but also Canada and the Mississippi Valley. She also came out of the war with an enormous debt, £ 122,603,336 in 1763 which increased to £ 129,586,789 in 1764. It became necessary to station 10,000 British regulars on the western frontier to protect the British colonists against the hostile French and Indians. The cost of maintaining these troops was over £ 200,000 a year, with total military expenditures for the colonies of over £ 350,000, which, not unreasonably, the British Government felt the colonists should help to pay. As the total receipts from the royal customs in the colonies was only £ 1,800 per year (due to inefficient customs officers and massive American smuggling), the government in London felt new measures were needed. One of the men chosen to solve this problem was George Grenville, and of the measures he took, the first of which we need to take notice is the Stamp Act passed by Parliament 22 March 1765 and set to take effect 1 November 1765. The act required a revenue stamp varying from two pence to £ 10 for almost every kind of paper document: newspapers, cards, dice, university degrees, court orders, customs clearance papers, and many more. The colonists reacted with civil disobedience and a flat refusal to accept the revenue stamps. In many ports they intimidated the royal customs officers into issuing ships' clearance papers without the stamps. The royal governor in Virginia, Francis Fauquier, provided each ship with a signed statement that no stamps were available, which may account for the lack of violence in the port of Alexandria. Also in most colonies, Virginia included, the courts were closed as legal papers required stamps.[1] It was here that

1. Edmund S. Morgan and Helen M. Morgan, *The Stamp Act Crises* (Chapel Hill: University of North Carolina Press, 1953), pp. 21-23, 57, 70, 160, 172-73, 178 (hereinafter cited as Morgan, *Stamp Act*).

George Mason first took an active role in the Revolutionary struggle. As the courts were closed, and Mason foresaw their being closed for months or perhaps even years, it was not possible for landlords to take tenants to court for nonpayment of land rentals. On 23 December 1765, Mason therefore, drew up and sent to Washington a "Scheme for Replevying Goods and Distress for Rent," whereby landlords could collect rents from uncooperative or improvident tenants without using stamped legal documents. [2] The substance of Mason's scheme is unimportant, but the scheme itself is notable for it marks Mason's active participation in the colonial resistance to parliamentary authority; as the Revolution wore on, Mason drafted many more significant documents.

In 1765 George Washington also took his first stand with the colonial position. He realized full well that with any interference in trade between Britain and the colonies, such as taxes on exports and imports, British manufacturers would soon feel the commercial disadvantage. He went on to note that if the courts were closed due to the Stamp Act and if British merchants could not sue for debts owed them "the Merchants of G. Britain trading to the Colonies will not be among the last to wish for a Repeal of it."[3]

It was not necessary for Washington to introduce Mason's scheme in the House of Burgesses, for the Stamp Act was repealed 4 March 1766. As Washington had foreseen, the British merchants had pressured Parliament for a repeal; then a group of London merchants published an open letter in several colonial newspapers admonishing the colonists for their civil disobedience and warning them how closely they had come to punitive measures at the hands of Parliament. Mason was evidently outraged, for he penned a vitriolic seven-page reply to the London merchants which very neatly summed up the American position; as such, his reply deserves to be considered in detail. Before proceeding with this consideration, however, having accepted Adams's premise that the Revolution preceded the war, and further, having said that the contributions of Fairfax County to the Revolution were primarily intellectual, attention should be given to the intellectual position of the colonists in order to have a guide or basis to interpret the writings of Mason, Washington, and Bryan Fairfax.

In October 1774, George Washington was in Philadelphia attending the Continental Congress, and was, therefore, in intimate contact with delegates from the other colonies and in a position to know their feelings. Writing from Philadelphia he observed, "I think I can announce it as a

2. Robert A. Rutland, ed., *The Papers of George Mason* (Chapel Hill: University of North Carolina Press, 1970), 1:60-65 (hereinafter cited as Rutland, *Papers*).

3. John C. Fitzpatrick, ed., *The Writings of George Washington from the Original Manuscript Sources* (Washington: United States Government Printing Office, 1931-1944), 2:426 (hereinafter cited as Fitzpatrick, *Writings*).

fact, that it is not the wish or interest of that government [the colony of Massachusetts] or any other on this continent, separately or collectively, to set up for independency."[4] Judging from other sources, this seems a fair and accurate assessment of the situation. The colonists saw themselves as Englishmen entitled to all the rights of Englishmen, and to the protection of the time-honored British constitution. This constitution was not a written document, but was represented by the common law and parliamentary law, which were in harmony with natural law and equity, all of which were embodied in the legislature of England (the king, lords, and commons in Parliament assembled). The Americans felt fortunate to have inherited such a constitution, which they saw as " 'the best model of Government that can be found by Mortals' "; few Americans felt any need to repudiate their English heritage of liberty which they saw as anchored firmly in both English history and natural law. [5] This constitution they conceived of as being balanced, and that balance was protected by the unification of king, lords, and commons in Parliament. The king was power and prerogative, the people a unified group representing liberty, and the nobles or lords acted as a balance to keep either power or liberty from going astray. These three social orders (not to be confused with the legislative, executive, and judiciary of our own federal system) comprised all of society, for the benefit of all. [6] This entire conception was intellectually buttressed by the colonists with the use, albeit selective, of classical authors, a glorified English past (dating to Anglo-Saxon times), and actual experience.

The colonists believed they saw this perfect constitution being destroyed by corruption from within. Totally unaware of or unwilling to recognize the very real and complex problems being faced by the ministry, problems which required effective remedies, the colonists saw ministerial attempts to deal with financial problems and to get programs through Parliament by political maneuvering as tyranny, and corruption of the legislature by placemen and pensioners. They saw a ministerial conspiracy to destroy the original, first, and fundamental principles of the constitution. This was evident to them not only by the actions of the ministry, but also by evidence of wealth, luxury , and venality in Britain itself. The colonists saw America as the last bastion of virtue, and "they revolted not against the English constitution but on behalf of it."[7]

4. Ibid., 3:245.

5. Gordon S. Wood, *The Creation of the American Republic, 1776-1787* (Chapel Hill: University of North Carolina Press, 1969), ch. 1 and specifically p. 10 (hereinafter cited as Wood, *Creation*).

6. Ibid., pp. 18-19.

7. Ibid., p. 10. This entire background is fully discussed in Wood, *Creation*; Morgan, *Stamp Act*; and by Bernard Bailyn, *The Ideological Origins of the American Revolution* (Cambridge: Harvard University Press, 1967) (hereinafter cited as Bailyn, *Origins*). The summary given here is severely limited and simplified due to lack of space, and the original sources take on a greatly expanded meaning when the background is more fully understood.

Such a position did not come about all at once, nor was it equally clear even to all colonial patriots at any one time. The development of this idea of a conspiracy, and its acceptance by a sufficient number of colonists to make the bid for independence seem necessary, or even possible, was the Revolution to which John Adams referred as taking place "in the minds of the people."

The specific question in 1765 regarding the Stamp Act was the issue of taxation and representation. The colonists, the ministry, and the Parliament were in agreement that an Englishman could not legally be taxed without either his consent or that of his duly elected representative. The colonists claimed, however, that they could only be taxed by their own colonial legislature which they elected and not by the British Parliament in which they had no representation. The ministry replied that the colonists, indeed all Englishmen, were *virtually* represented in Parliament, for each member sat for all Englishmen and not only those who had elected him. They pointed out that " 'Nine-Tenths of the People of *Britain*' " did not choose representatives to the House of Commons; that Manchester, Birmingham, and other trading centers sent no representatives to Parliament, yet they were Englishmen represented in and taxed by Parliament. Such a position, which the "colonists never decisively repudiated," depended upon the concept that all Englishmen were a single people "with one definable interest." What the Americans rejected was that they had such a unity of interest with Britain; they noted "the disparity of interests between mother country and Colonies" and " 'we are not, and from our local situation never can be *represented*'" in Parliament. [8] The colonists also insisted that all those in England, including members of Parliament, were equally affected by Parliamentary taxation, while the Parliament could tax the colonies all they wanted and affect no one in Britain at all.

There was also the widely misunderstood issue of internal taxation and external taxation. The colonists flatly denied the Parliamentary right to lay an internal tax to raise a revenue in the colonies. They would, at least in 1765, accept customs duties designed to regulate trade (which some called external taxation), provided it did not raise a revenue. They pointed out that the annual customs duties for the last thirty years had been about £2,000 per year, which cost £7,600 to collect, for a net loss of £5,600.[9] Such duties were clearly for regulating trade, not raising a revenue; yet the need to raise a revenue in America was exactly the problem which faced the ministry. The matter was left unresolved, although neither the ministry, the Parliament, nor the colonists were fully aware of the lack of resolution.

8. Wood, *Creation*, pp. 173-77.
9. Morgan, *Stamp Act*, p. 85.

Before repealing the Stamp Act, the Parliament passed a Declaratory Act giving themselves " 'full power and authority to make laws and statutes of sufficient force and validity to bind the colonies and people of America . . . in all cases whatsoever.' " Any specific reference to taxation had been expressly left out by the ministry. However, due to machinations during the Parliamentary debate, the Parliament was left with the clear impression that "in all cases whatsoever" included taxation. The colonists interpreted the lack of specific reference to taxation as meaning Parliament lacked such right. This dichotomy of views was of the utmost importance, for the Parliament proceeded to pass other duties designed to raise a revenue, which the colonists saw as a ministerial conspiracy "seeking by gradual degrees to enslave them." The British for their part saw each instance of resistance to revenue acts as further evidence of "the Americans inching their way toward independence." In a sense there was a conspiracy, for the Rockingham Ministry which had engineered the Declaratory Act was aware of this dual interpretation of the act by Parliament and colonists, and in hopes of avoiding an open confrontation had allowed the misunderstanding to go unresolved. Thus, "The English were encouraged to believe that the Americans were seeking independence in large stages and the Americans to think that the English were trying to enslave them by slow and insensible degrees."[10] This was also part of the Revolution referred to by John Adams.

Mason's 1766 letter to the London Merchants reflected many facets of the American position, often explicitly spelled out. The letter also warned the merchants that the Americans would not tolerate what they saw as tyranny and oppression, and it began in a satirical manner by putting the merchants firmly in their place, noting that the British were always treating the colonists in the "authoritative Style of a Master to a School-Boy."

> We have, with infinite Difficulty and fatigue got you excused this one time; pray be a good boy for the future; do what your Papa and Mamma bid you, and hasten to return them your most grateful Acknowledgements for condescending to let you keep what is your own; and then all your Acquaintance will love you, and praise you, and give you pretty things; and if you shou[l]d, at any Time hereafter, happen to transgress, your Friends will all beg for you, and be Security for your good Behavior . . . Is not this a little ridiculous, when applyed to three Millions of as loyal and useful Subjects as any in the British Dominions, who have been only contending for their Birth-right . . . .

10. Ibid., pp. 290-91.

Proceeding to the substance of the matter that "We do not deny the supreme Authority of Great Britain over her Colonys," Mason contradicted himself, for "supreme Authority" would include the right of taxation; and that the colonists most emphatically did deny! He went on to the provision of the Stamp Act which allowed violations of the navigation acts to be tried in admiralty courts and complained of the "odious Distinction" made between native and colonial Englishmen by depriving the Americans "of the ancient Tryal, by a jury of our Equals." Further, he continued, such an accused man could be taken a "Thousand Miles" from his home to be tried before a judge who was a "creature of the Ministry." The admiralty courts had only a judge and no juries; they were, however, instituted not to usurp the rights of colonists, but because the colonial juries refused to convict violators of the customs laws. As the American admiralty courts were often bribed or intimidated by merchants and mobs, the new legislation allowed the cases to be transferred to the court at Halifax, Nova Scotia. It might have appeared to Mason that this was a clear violation of their rights as Englishmen; however, the ministry had the practical responsibility of enforcing the customs and navigation laws, and the Americans did frequently act like intransigent children.

Mason then expanded upon the theme of the rights of Englishmen and ministerial corruption, cautioning the English merchants that the precedents set in the colonies might be used at a future time to infringe on civil liberties at home. And then he reminded them that they were all, Englishmen and colonists alike, "descended from the same Stock . . . nurtured in the same Principles of Freedom." "We are," he continued, in every respect the same people they were "only not yet debauched by Wealth, Luxury, Venality, and Corruption."[11] Perhaps more perceptive than many of his peers, Mason expressed, a full ten years before the Declaration of Independence, in unmistakable terms, the American claim to the ancient right of Englishmen (as he and others perceived them), and the colonists' sincere belief that wealth, luxury, corruption, and conspiracy were threatening the liberties not only of Americans but also of Englishmen in the homeland. His references to wealth, luxury, conspiracy, and corruption may seem mere rhetoric and propaganda, but to George Mason and others, they were as real as air and sunlight.

His letter continues by warning the merchants of the interdependence of the colonies and the mother country for markets and credit, and that no form of compulsion will effect anything other than a serious disruption of trade and more resistance in the colonies: "Such another experiment as the Stamp-Act wou[l]d produce a general Revolt in

11. Rutland, *Papers*, pp. 65-73.

America." Mason's letter makes it abundantly clear that he, and presumably others in Fairfax County, were well aware of the situation very early in the game: for George Mason, the Revolution had already begun in 1767.

Although in the summer of 1767 Parliament passed the Townshend Revenue Act which placed a duty not only on tea but also on glass, lead, and painters' colors, neither Mason nor Washington appear to have had any serious reaction until April 1769. Similarly, Washington does not emerge as having been particularly active in the proceedings of the House of Burgesses in 1768 when that body protested the duties to king and Parliament. By 1769, the merchants of Philadelphia and Annapolis had formed nonimportation associations to boycott British goods. (It is interesting to note the lack of any problem with the dutiable items at Alexandria, which was a major colonial port. One may suppose that the items were landed and the duties paid.) Copies of these Associations were sent to both Washington and Mason by their mutual friend Dr. David Ross of Bladensburg in early 1769. On 5 April 1769, Washington and Mason exchanged letters regarding the Associations. Washington, not knowing Mason had also received a copy of the Associations formation from Dr. Ross, sent his copy to Mason with a letter both warmly endorsing the concept of nonimportation, "how far then their attention to our rights and priveledges is to be awakened or alarmed by starving their Trade and Manufacturers, remains to be tryed," reflecting on the added difficulties of implementing nonimportation in the plantation economy of Virginia, and asking for Mason's advice on implementation. Mason answered the same day, returning Washington's copy of the Associations, commenting on the difficulty of such a plan in Virginia and, dropping the first hint at nonexportation, he noted that it would be useful to inform the ministry that until the grievances were redressed, the colonists might withold their exports, especially tobacco "by which the Revennue wou'd lose fifty times more than all their Oppression cou'd raise here." [12] Mason again wrote Washington on 23 April 1769 with suggestions for a few changes in the Associations. Washington inserted the changes in his copy of the draft and took it to Williamsburg for the meeting of the House of Burgesses. [13] Unfortunately, before Washington could present the draft to the House, Governor Botetourt dissolved the Assembly; the members then retired to the Raleigh Tavern and unofficially continued their meeting. A committee was appointed to prepare a nonimportation paper, and Washington not only served on this committee, but probably acted as chairman; the agreement adopted closely resembled the draft taken to Williamsburg by Washington.[14]

12. Ibid., pp. 94-100.
13. Ibid., pp. 95, 102.
14. William J. Van Schreevan, comp., and Robert L. Scribner, ed., *Revolutionary Virginia: The*

Once again, both Mason and Washington were active in the conflict between America and the mother country, yet there was a conservatism about their activity. Both men were members of the planter aristocracy with a deep respect for property and a concern (almost a preoccupation) with trade, commerce, and property rights. Mason's entry into the conflict, the replevying scheme of 1765, was not an impassioned document grounded in the rights of man; it was a device to enable members of Mason's social and economic class to collect rents on their land. His letter of 1766 to the London merchants was strongly buttressed with the interdependence of America and Britain in matters of trade and commerce, as was his reply to Washington regarding nonimportation in 1769. Even in later years as his Revolutionary activity increased, his radicalism never reached that of Patrick Henry, nor did his philosophy ever attain the broad-based Enlightenment humanitarianism of Thomas Jefferson. Ironically, it was to be Mason who provided the framework for the foundation of the new government in Virginia, contributing more than Jefferson himself. Similarly, Mason and Patrick Henry were to be allied in 1788 in trying to defeat ratification of the new federal constitution. But government, after all, is more a practical than a philosophical matter, and a stable government is most desirable to those who have the most to lose—men of property.

Washington was even more conservative, more property minded, and less inclined to philosophize than Mason. His comments on the Stamp Act, his lack of comment on the Townshend duties, and his reflections upon nonimportation in 1769 are all strongly, indeed exclusively, based on benefits, liabilities, and interdependence in regard to trade and commerce. [15] There is no indication from the writings of George Washington from 1766 to 1769 that he was concerned with natural law, equity, or the rights of man, but rather in redressing what he felt to be violations of his rights by economic sanction against Britain. In time, Washington came to believe sincerely that there was a ministerial conspiracy to enslave the colonies, and he did not hesitate to act to defeat it; but even then his thought was behind that of the more liberal and radical thinkers. It should be noted that property was a very important matter in the eighteenth century, perhaps even more than it is today. Neither Mason nor Washington were professional politicians; they were plantation owners primarily concerned with getting this year's crop in the ground, and last year's crop to market. Their activities as patriots

Road to Independence. Vol. I, Forming Thunderclouds and the First Convention, 1763-1774: A Documentary Record, (Charlottesville: University Press of Virginia, 1973), p. 73 (hereinafter cited as Van Schreevan, *Revolutionary Virginia*).

15. For evidence of Washington's preoccupation with property, see Fitzpatrick, *Writings* 3:425-26, 466, and Rutland, *Papers*, 1: 96-98.

were seen by them as obligations they owed their fellow citizens, not as a chance for personal advancement.

Beginning in 1770, Mason took an increasingly more radical position in the developing conflict. The Virginia nonimportation agreement of 1769 was widely disregarded and less effective than had been hoped.[16] On 7 June 1770 Mason wrote to Richard Henry Lee in regard to strengthening the Association in Virginia; in this letter Mason first mentioned what was to be his most radical, and as regards the Revolution, his most far-reaching idea. Both merchants and their customers were ignoring the nonimportation agreement and Mason hoped to bring this practice to a halt. He suggested that "the Sense of Shame and the Fear of Reproach" be "inculcated and enforced in the strongest Manner" by publishing the names of "such Persons as purchase or import Goods contrary to the Association" so that such people could be "stigmatized as Enemys to their Country." He continued that the merchants could be brought into line by getting the "principal People" to cease trading with those who imported goods "contrary to the Tenor of the Association." The proper way to carry out such a plan was to appoint a committee in each county to examine such matters and to ask the merchants to produce the invoices covering the shipments of imports. If any violators were found, the committee should request the merchants to return the goods to the exporter. If the merchants refused, "inform them of the Consequences, & proceed to publish an account of their conduct." Mason emphasized this was to be done Without any Manner of Violence," but surely he must have realized that intimidation and violence would be the result of such publication of names. It was on this very point that his radicalism was most extreme; it was, however, radicalism directed not at the ministry, but at his fellow Virginians: directed at other men whose civil rights were equal to his own. He saw this clearly and attempted to defend his position.

The objection was "ill founded," he wrote, that such measures would be "infringing the rights of others, while we are contending for Liberty ourselves." Each member of the society was "Duty Bound" to contribute to the good of the whole; "every inferior consideration, as well as the Inconvenience to a few Individuals, must give place to it."[17] Another nonimportation agreement was effected in 1770, and the language of the second paragraph of that document, providing for the publishing of the names of violators, is remarkably similar (almost verbatim) to sections of Mason's letter to Lee.[18] There can be no question that the letter inspired the resolution. Why did Mason make such

16. Rutland, *Papers*, 1:120.
17. Ibid., pp. 116-20.
18. Ibid., pp. 120-25.

suggestions to Lee rather than to Washington? Both Lee and Washington were members of the House, but it would seem to have been more natural for Mason to have made his suggestions to his friend at Mount Vernon, unless Mason knew Lee to be the author of the 1769 Association. Perhaps Washington did not favor such a proposal. For the present, the question must remain unanswered.

The 1770 Association was printed as a broadside bearing 164 printed signatures, with at least seven copies of the broadside making their way back to Fairfax County. Washington may well have brought them with him when he left Williamsburg on 23 June, the day after the Association was agreed to. There is some doubt, however, as to whether the broadside could have been printed so quickly. In any event, by 28 July he had them in hand for his diary entry, for that day notes that he "went up to Alexandria with the Association papers." Below the printed signatures on the broadsides Washington wrote a subscription pledging the inhabitants of Fairfax County to abide by the terms of the Association. The copies were then circulated in various parts of the county and signed by 333 county residents. No other Virginia county followed this procedure, once again indicating the radical trend of Fairfax County in Revolutionary matters within the colony.

From the signatures it is possible to determine where in Fairfax County each broadside was signed. One was signed in Alexandria for it bears the signatures of John Carlyle, John Dalton, John West, and William Ramsay, all of whom lived in the town. George Mason's signature on this copy indicates it was probably signed at the courthouse, as Mason was a justice. Another broadside bears the names of Hector Ross, Peter Wagener, and Peirce [sic] Bayley, indicating it was signed in Colchester; one was signed near the juncture of the Ox Road and Colchester Road; and two others were signed on the roads between Colchester and Alexandria. Yet another was signed along what is now Route 7 between the Falls Church and the old courthouse site. Finally, one was circulated in that part of Fairfax which is now Arlington County. Whether Washington was responsible for this circulation of the broadside is problematical. The subscriptions are written in his hand; however, in the light of later developments, the principle of getting everyone to commit themselves was to be a favorite tactic of Mason, and it is not unlikely that on this occasion he may have suggested the idea to his friend at Mount Vernon.[19]

There was no further activity in Fairfax, nor further action taken by Mason or Washington regarding the Association until July 1771,

19. The seven copies of the broadside are in the Library of Congress, Manuscript Collections. Six of the seven are in the Washington Papers, and the seventh is in the Peter Force Papers. A careful search has failed to produce any other copies of this broadside with or without the Fairfax subscription.

although there is reason to believe that it was not enforced at either Alexandria or Colchester. In a letter to an unknown recipient in December 1770, Mason remarked that the nonimportation associations were "in a very languid State," and that most people were waiting to see what Parliament would do about "redressing American Grievances."[20] It would seem then that publishing names was ineffectual, or even impossible, unless a significant majority of the people supported the Association in the first place. Apparently this problem existed in all the colonies, for Mason makes note of the associations being "drawn up in a Hurry" and upon the "erronious Principle" that it would produce a unified effort which would result in a "Stagnation in Trade" and force the Parliament to repeal the duties. He continued in a vein that reads like a testimonial of American loyalty: the Americans, he wrote, had no intentions of "throwing off their Dependence" or challenging the sovereignty of Great Britain; we have "the warmest Affection for the present Royal Family; the strongest Attachment to the British Government & Constitution." Having "experienced its' Blessings" they preferred it to "any that does or ever did exist."[21]

The *Virginia Gazette* of 18 July 1771 printed a letter from "the committee of the associators in Fairfax county" to Peyton Randolph, moderator of the Virginia nonimportation Association. Alexander Henderson, a Colchester merchant, and William Balmain, an Alexandria merchant, had presented themselves at a metting of the committee complaining that other merchants were violating both "the spirit and the letter" of the Association. In consequence, Henderson and Balmain made a "public declaration" that they intended to do likewise, excepting only tea and other dutied articles. The merchants also invited the committee to examine the invoices of two cargoes of imported goods which had just arrived consigned to Henderson and Balmain. The committee (Mason, Washington, Peter Wagener, John West, and John Dalton) had found that Henderson and Balmain were conforming to the Association, and the letter was requesting Randolph to convene a meeting of "a sufficient number of the associators" to attempt to remedy the situation.[22] Nothing could be more illustrative, than this letter, of the ineffectiveness of the colonial boycott effort, unless it was the subsequent repeal of the Association in the summer of 1772, "except as to the Article of Tea."[23]

For all practical purposes, after the summer of 1771, the Revolutionary spirit cooled in Fairfax County. The correspondence of

20. Rutland, *Papers*, 1:127.

21. Ibid., pp. 127-30. It seems doubtful, in light of later scholarship, whether such a government and constitution ever existed outside the minds of Mason and other colonial patriots. There can be little doubt, however, that the Association of 1770 had little effect in either Britain or Virginia.

22. Ibid., pp. 132-33.

23. Van Schreevan, *Revolutionary Virginia*, 1:85.

Washington and Mason contains no further reference to nonimportation, ministerial conspiracy, or the rights of Englishmen until the late spring of 1774. In the meantime, both men conducted much private business, buying goods in England, selling tobacco, carrying on land transactions, and Mason composed his will: all most unrevolutionary activities.

Then it happened. On the night of 16 December 1773 a group of Boston patriots disguised as Indians threw 340 chests of tea, belonging to the British East India Company, into the waters of Boston Harbor. This wanton destruction of private property "goaded the long-suffering Parliament to harsh retaliation."[24] On 31 March 1774, Parliament passed the Boston Port Act which effectively closed the harbor of Boston and threatened to bankrupt and ruin that commercial city. By the middle of May 1774, the news of the Port Bill reached Williamsburg. Mason arrived there soon after on private business and said that the whole town was talking about "the Boston affair." It was on this occasion that Mason met Patrick Henry. Greatly impressed with Henry's oratorical ability, Mason described him as "the most powerful speaker I ever heard." His general opinion of Henry was equally flattering, calling him "the first man upon this continent, as well in abilities as public virtues." Thomas Jefferson agreed with Mason as to Henry's prominence as a speaker, but felt Henry had intellectual limitations.

Serious reaction to the events in Boston first occurred in Fairfax County during July 1774. By 5 July, the residents had pledged £273 in specie, 38 barrels of flour, and 150 bushels of wheat "for the benefit and relief of those (the industrious poor of the town of Boston) who by the late cruel act of Parliament are deprived of their daily labour and bread . . . to keep up that manly spirit that has made them dear to every American, through the envy of an arbitrary Parliament . . . ."[25] Nine days later, on 14 July, George Washington and Charles Broadwater were chosen at a Fairfax County meeting to be the county representatives at the convention in August 1774 of the now dissolved House of Burgesses. Washington had desired Bryan Fairfax or George Mason to be elected with him as he felt "Major Broadwater, though a good man, might do as well in the discharge of his domestic concerns, as in the capacity of a legislator."[26]

Fairfax had written to Washington on 3 July 1774 that he had been forced to decline to stand for election "chiefly because I thought I could not give Satisfaction in general upon this Occasion," adding that he

24. Benjamin Woods Labaree, *The Boston Tea Party* (London: Oxford University Press, 1966), p. viii; Arthur Meier Schlesinger, "Political Mobs and the American Revolution," *Proceedings of the American Philosophical Society*, vol. 99, no. 4, p. 244.

25. *Virginia Gazette* (Rind ed.), 25 August 1774; Peter Force, ed., *American Archives*, 5 vols. (Washington, D.C.: M. St. Clair Clarke and Peter Force, 1837), 1:517.

26. Fitzpatrick, *Writings*, 3:227.

opposed violent measures now and felt the proper course of action was to petition the Parliament for a repeal of the duties. Fairfax stressed that such a petition should be "unaccompanied with any Threats or Claims," and that any plan for nonimportation would be an "arduous Undertaking" which once begun should be "strictly kept." He continued that few in Alexandria shared his opinion.[27]

Replying the following day, Washington offered the American position: they had petitioned before; there was a "regular, systematic plan" to "fix the right and practice of taxation upon us"; Parliament had begun an attack upon the property and liberty of the people of Boston, and this was "as clear as the sun in its meridian brightness . . . . " He felt, however, it was "inconceivable" that they should refuse payment of just debts to British merchants.[28] Washington's revolutionary ideals were tempered by an unyielding respect for property.

On Sunday afternoon, 17 July, Mason rode to Mount Vernon to meet with Washington, and surely the topic of conversation was a series of resolves being readied for a general meeting of freeholders which was scheduled for the following day at the courthouse in Alexandria. Mason spent the night at Mount Vernon, and the next day he and Washington rode into town. The resolves which they took with them were intended to be the county's instructions for its two delegates to the convention. The existing manuscript of the resolves is in Mason's handwriting;[29] the style and language are also his; but the ideas represent a consensus of both the two men and the citizens.[30] The committee which the inhabitants of Fairfax County had selected to draw up resolutions met on 18 July to revise and correct these resolutions before the general meeting which followed at the courthouse the same day. At this "general Meeting of the Freeholders and Inhabitants of the County of Fairfax" the Fairfax County Resolves were adopted, along with a resolution ordering the proceedings transmitted "to the printers at Williamsburg." At this same meeting, Washington, Mason, and twenty-three others were appointed to "be a Committee for this county: that they, or a majority of them on any emergency, have power to call a general meeting, and to concert and adopt such measures as may be thought most expedient and necessary."[31] The name of Bryan Fairfax is conspicuously absent from this committee. As Washington had wanted him to stand for election for burgess and apparently felt he would be elected, it is highly unlikely that he was not considered desirable—or capable for service on this occasion; indeed, it is surprising that Fairfax did not even attend this important meeting.

27. Stanislaus Murry Hamilton, ed., *Letters to Washington and Accompanying Papers,* 5 vols. (Boston: Houghton, Mifflin and Company, 1901), 5:19 (hereinafter cited as Hamilton, *Letters*).

28. Fitzpatrick, *Writings,* p. 227.

29. Washington Papers, Library of Congress, series IV, vol. 13, 18 July 1774.

30. Rutland, *Papers,* 1:199-201.

31. Ibid., Force, *Archives,* pp. 601-2.

Writing to Washington on 17 July, the day before the meeting, Fairfax asked to be excused in order that his business not suffer; however, he asked that the letter which contained some criticism of the proposed resolves be read at the meeting.[32] One can only conjecture about Fairfax's motives on this occasion. It is most likely that he wanted to avoid being placed in a position of treason to the crown by attending any such revolutionary assembly or by serving on any committee which might similarly embarrass him. Lord Fairfax, Bryan's cousin, who was a justice of the peace in Frederick County, had resigned his post for just this reason.

In the 17 July letter, Fairfax revealed not only a clear understanding of the basic difference in ideological position between himself and Washington, but he also developed a line of reasoning based upon his position. He observed that the committee and those who supported the resolves and other revolutionary activity were convinced that "there is a regular System for enforcing the principle of Taxation." "This," he continued, "is the very point on which our difference in opinion is founded." Those who believed there was a ministerial conspiracy would side with the resolves and those who did not see such a conspiracy would see the resolves as premature. Fairfax then pointed out:

> An Englishman however clear he may be in Opinion as to the Rights of Taxation ought to consider the Motives from which an Opposition in America arises. He ought to consider that it springs from virtuous, tho' (as he may think) erroneous principles. In like Manner the Americans ought to consider the Majority of the english Parliament, or a great part, as acting from honest tho' erroneous principles.

If Parliament believed it had a right to impose the duty on tea, Fairfax asked, could it avoid taking notice of what had happened at Boston? Indeed, Parliament might find itself bound to protect British trade, with no further design to enforce the principle of taxation. Fairfax noted that there were several reasons why Parliament had not repealed the tea tax, and that given a "decent opportunity," it might still do so. "If this is the Case," he continued, "we deprive ourselves by hasty Resolutions of what we can never Recover. It will be too late hereafter to petition. We must effect what we desire by compulsion. This must be the Work of years." Continuing, he said that there may be corruption in Parliament, as well as men with unjust designs. He advised, however, with an eye to the next Parliament, "we ought to gain the Affections of those who mean well."

This was a more neutral position based on an implicit identification with and trust in British government, rather than a conservatism based

32. Hamilton, *Letters*, pp. 22-29.

on protection of property; Fairfax was taking a position against faction, discord, and strife. He observed that mild behavior contributed to a reconciliation in any dispute, and that the spectators are always on the side of moderation. The very inconsistency of his recommendations for action underlined his stand for moderation. How else could he write that he wished no resolves had been entered into, but as most of the colonies and the counties in Virginia were doing so, "perhaps it would be prudent in this county to join also, as the Colonies ought to be unanimous," and to follow this with "it becomes good Subjects to submit to the Constitution of their Country"? [33] This was neither an American nor British position, but an attempt to be as conciliatory as possible. The colonists were, however, not in a conciliatory frame of mind. Fairfax then took issue with specific points in the resolves. He objected to the "Expression then in one of our Resolves . . . that is, a Hint to the King that if his Majesty will not comply, there lies but one Appeal." The specific phrase to which Fairfax was making reference is in the twenty-third resolve as adopted by the meeting: "from our Sovereign there can be but one Appeal." He further objected to "a Resolve which ought to be the most objected to," and he was referring to the colonists' rejection of the authority of Parliament. This is in the third resolve as adopted, although Fairfax refers to it specifically as "I hope some Alteration will be made in the 2^d Resolve." [34]

The general position of historians as to the genesis of the Fairfax Resolves has been, as stated earlier, that they are mostly the work of Mason, and that they were hammered out or "whipped into shape" by Mason and Washington at Mount Vernon on 17 July. But Fairfax wrote to Washington on 17 July, and he made specific reference to exact language used in the twenty-third resolve, and to the contents of what he called the second, and what later became the third resolve. This means that either he was present with Mason and Washington on the seventeenth, which seems unlikely as he wrote Washington that day, or that the content of the resolves was known by him before the seventeenth; otherwise, he could not have made such specific objections. That the resolves were substantially worked out before the seventeenth is further substantiated by a letter from Washington to his brother, 11 July, a full week before the meeting of the eighteenth. He makes reference to a meeting being held "last Tuesday." As the eleventh was a Monday, this puts the meeting "last Tuesday" on 5 July. At this meeting they "appointed a Committee to frame such Resolves as we thought the Circumstances of the County would permit us to go into & have appointed the 18th for a day of Meeting to deliberate on them." It is, of course, possible, if not probable, that George Mason was on that committee, and he was most

33. Ibid.
34. Ibid.

The Parliament from Prescription have a Right to make
Laws binding on the Colonies, except those imposing Taxes.
From Prescription the Americans are exempted from Taxation.
Let us stand upon good Ground in our Opposition, otherwise many
upon Reflection may desert the Cause. Therefore I hope some Alteration
will be made in the 2.ᵈ Resolve; or that Nothing under this Head will
be mentioned. These, Sir, I have made some Objections as it
appeared incumbent on me to do, and hope that you will cause
this Letter to be read as containing my Sentiments on this important Occasion.

I am with great Respect & Regard,

Sir Yr. most obed.ᵗ Serv.ᵗ

Bryan Fairfax.

July the 17:ᵗʰ
1774.

The final page of the letter from
Bryan Fairfax to George
Washington, 17 July 1774
expressing Fairfax's objections to
the Fairfax Resolves. The final
sentence of the first paragraph
makes plain that the substance of
the Resolves had been worked out
prior to 17 July, the day on which
Mason and Washington have been
credited with composing the
Resolves at Mount Vernon.
Manuscript Division, Library of
Congress, Washington, D.C.

likely the major author of the resolves. It is not possible to say who wrote the resolves, or when they were written; in light of Fairfax's letter, however, it seems certain that regardless of what Mason and Washington did and said on the seventeenth, Fairfax also had a copy of the resolves by that time. It seems unlikely that Mason would have given a copy to Fairfax, for they appear not to have been correspondents; however, Fairfax could have gotten a copy from his friend Washington, or from a member of the committee appointed on 5 July, if indeed he was not a member. This means that the resolves were written before the seventeenth and that they were in fact a consensus of the sentiments not only of Mason and Washington, but also of at least the ruling elite of Fairfax County; certainly they were not worked out in substance by Mason and Washington at Mount Vernon on 17 July.

Washington answered Fairfax's letter on 20 July, explaining that he had not read the 17 July letter to the meeting as Fairfax had requested, but rather had shown it to the committee, none of whom were disposed to adopt Fairfax's sentiments. In fact, one member had advised him not to read it as it was "repugnant to the very principle we were contending for." In attempting to reply to Fairfax in reference to the resolves, Washington again reiterated the American position: Parliament was acting with "great rapidity" to pass acts "to enforce their tyrannical system," and the government was pursuing a regular plan to overthrow "our" constitutional rights and liberties at the expense of law and justice; we object not to the tax, but to the principle of taxation; his Majesty had been petitioned before." Furthermore, Washington wrote, the various acts respecting Massachusetts were "self evident proofs" of a "fixed and uniform plan to tax us." If, on the other hand, the colonies were to petition for repeal of the tax, they would be tacitly admitting the right of Parliament to tax, for a petition is asking a favor, "and not claiming a right, which, by the law of nature and our constitution" they were entitled to.[35]

Fairfax again wrote to Washington on 5 August, mentioning that he had spoken with Mr. Williamson,[36] Mr. Dalton,[37] and Mr. Henderson[38] who told him that there were many at the courthouse on 18 July who

---

35. Fitzpatrick, *Writings*, 3:230-34. Washington's justification by the "law of nature" and the rights guaranteed by "our constitution" were among the keystones of the American Whig ideology. They were Englishmen and, as such, entitled to the protection of the British constitution. That constitution, it was felt, was firmly supported by natural law: the way things naturally should be, and were, until the ministers corrupted it.

36. Washington had mentioned that Williamson was the only member of the committee to share the feelings expressed by Fairfax in the letter of 17 July. The list of committee members given in Force, *Archives*, 1: 601-2, does not list a Mr. Williamson.

37. John Dalton, an Alexandria merchant, was to be very active in 1776 in obtaining a fleet of small ships to defend Alexandria. Dalton is listed by Force as a member of the committee; why he did not support the Fairfax letter on 18 July is also a mystery.

38. Alexander Henderson was a colonial merchant from Colchester.

opposed the resolves in part, but were reluctant to speak. The general consensus of these men was that the Bostonians should pay for the tea, and that until that was done, Parliament had no choice but to close the port. Fairfax then proceeded to attack the assertion that the Parliament had no right to make laws binding on the colonies, by pointing out that until recently the colonies always accepted the acts of Parliament respecting America. Specifically, he noted that when he first heard George Mason speak against a proposed Parliamentary tax on land in America, and although Mason had opposed the tax on many grounds,

> I did not hear him make one objection as to the Right of Parliament. When I came afterwards to hear the Right called in Question I recollected the Conversation, and was surprised that I had not heard a Man of his understanding and readiness to find fault with every thing irregular, take Notice of it; . . . yet it is a proof that the Idea of the Parliament having no Right to make any Laws for us had not ever entered into his Mind before.[39]

Similarly, he noted the inconsistency of Richard Henry Lee, who, while now denying the right of Parliament, had in the past acted as a justice of the peace aboard ship, under the authority of an act of Parliament which gave him the power to do so.[40]

Washington answered on 24 August, and he made no attempt to defend his position or to change Fairfax's mind. His only comment was that he was convinced of the evil of Parliament and of the correct actions of the colonies.[41] If Washington and Mason saw a conspiracy which did not exist and believed in a constitution which might not have existed, Bryan Fairfax clearly failed to see a revolution in process. John Adams more than once referred to the American Revolution as "this radical change in the principles, opinions, sentiments, and affections of the people."[42] The change in Mason's attitude toward Parliamentary taxation was a clear case in point. Mason, like all American patriots, was forced to make a transformation, a transition, and "to distinguish fundamentals from institutions and from the actions of government so that they might serve as limits and controls."[43] Mason was experiencing, participating in, and effecting the Revolution, a Revolution which Fairfax failed to perceive. Whatever may be said about the ideological positions of Washington, Mason, and Fairfax, about their conservatism or radicalism, about the validity of the grounds for their respective beliefs and actions, the American Revolution, which was the change and

---

39. Hamilton, *Letters*, p. 34.
40. Ibid.
41. Fitzpatrick, *Writings*, 3:237.
42. Bailyn, *Origins*, p. 160.
43. Ibid., p. 181.

Bryan, Eighth Lord Fairfax, of
Belvoir, Towlston Grange, and
Mount Eagle. Rector of Fairfax
Parish 1790-1792. Portrait owned
by Mrs. Charles Baird, Jr. Photo:
Virginia State Library.

transition of those positions, beliefs, and actions, was in every sense a
clear reality.

Apparently, the Fairfax County Committee did not send the resolves
to Williamsburg to be printed in the *Virginia Gazette*, but waited and
allowed Washington to carry them with him when he went to attend the
convention. The *Virginia Gazette* for 21 July and 28 July 1774 reported
having received resolves from thirteen counties and a list of elected
burgesses for twelve counties; in neither case was Fairfax County on the
list.[44]

The Fairfax Resolves were intended to convey the "sense" of the
citizens of the County of Fairfax at the first Virginia Convention held on
1 August 1774; similar resolves exist for thirty other Virginia counties.
The Fairfax Resolves, however, are of special importance as they are by
far the "lengthiest and most detailed of all the proposals submitted to the
convention."[45] They are equal in form and superior in content to the
Albermarle County Resolves, which have been attributed to Thomas

44. *Virginia Gazette* (Rind ed.), 21 July, 28 July 1774.
45. Van Schreevan, *Revolutionary Virginia*, 1:110.

Jefferson, although the felicitous phrases and bold humanitarian stance of Jefferson are missing in the Fairfax document.

Taking the form of twenty-four separate resolutions and beginning always with the single word "Resolved," the Fairfax Resolves set forth several far-reaching and radical proposals: the twelfth resolve showed no lack of courage or firmness and called for a congress "to consist of Deputies from all the Colonies, to concert a general and uniform Plan for the Defense and Preservation of our common Rights." The twenty-third resolve went even further and, adopting the very language to which Bryan Fairfax objected, asserted that if redress were not forthcoming by petitioning "his Majesty" then "from our Sovereign there can be but one Appeal," namely, war. The twentieth resolve reiterated the provision of the 1770 nonimportation Association that a committee in each county should "publish by Advertisements . . . a List of the Names of those" who violated the Association so "that such Traitors to their Country may be publickly known and detested." No other Virginia county was prepared to go so far as Fairfax did in these three resolves, and in this sense, Fairfax helped to lead Virginia into independence. The Virginia Convention meeting in August 1774 did adopt an Association as Fairfax and other counties had recommended, and it further adopted the Fairfax proposal for publishing the names of violators in the "Gazettes." [46] The Continental Association subsequently adopted these matters in October 1774.[47] With the genesis of the publishing idea traceable to George Mason in 1770, both Mason and the Fairfax Resolves emerge as influential at the Virginia Convention and the Continental Congress; the latter, as well as the appeal to arms (both called for in the Resolves) were not long in coming.

What is perhaps most useful about the resolves is what they can tell us about how Mason, Washington, the Fairfax Committee, and the Fairfax freeholders felt about the dispute: how they saw themselves, and the political world in which they lived. The first resolve began on a very interesting note by declaring that Virginia was not a "conquered Country" and that "if it was, that the present Inhabitants are the Descendants not of the Conquered, but of the Conquerors." This contains implicit references to William the Conqueror whose descendants all the way down to George III claimed their sovereignty at least partly on the basis of the conquest. The Virginians were perhaps also justifying their treatment of the American.Indian and surely the existence of Negro slavery. (The slaves, after all, had been captured and conquered in Africa.)

---

46. Ibid. pp. 230-34.
47. Henry Steele Commager, *Documents of American History*, 6th ed. (New York: Appleton-Century-Crofts, 1958), p. 84.

The second resolve is both an assertion of the right of being governed only by elected representatives, and a denial, therefore, of the concept of virtual representation as applied to the American representation in the British Parliament. As the third resolve denies in many respects the authority of Parliament in America, and as Bryan Fairfax had objected to this denial which he claimed was in the "2^{d} Resolve," it is possible that the present second resolve was added as a result of Fairfax's comment to solidify and justify the position taken in the third. The third resolve admits, however, that the principle of Parliament regulating colonial trade "hath proved its utility." When taken along with the eleventh resolve that after a proper redress of grievances "if the Destruction of the Tea at Boston be regarded as an Invasion of private Property, we shall be willing to contribute towards paying the East India Company the Value," this reflects a rather conservative attitude and a clear respect for private property. Washington's strong respect for property may have prevailed here; also, Alexandria was an important colonial port which had prospered under the British regulations, and its citizens were not about to justify the passion of the mob against private property. The fifth resolve made reference to "the first principles of the Constitution" and "natural Rights of Mankind"; the ninth asserted that there is a "premeditated Design and System formed and pursued by the British Ministry, to introduce an arbitrary Government into his Majesty's American Dominions."[48] Here was a clear statement of American whiggism: the constitution, natural law, and ministerial conspiracy. Indeed, at almost the very same time, a hundred miles away in Albemarle County, Thomas Jefferson was writing "a series of oppressions, begun at a distinguished period, and pursued unalterably thro' every change of ministers, too plainly prove a deliberate systematical plan of reducing us to slavery."[49] The Fairfax Resolves both stated the opinion and the ideological position of those who drew it, and pointed the way for the future: Continental Congress, appeal to arms, enforcement of nonimportation. Surely, Bryan Fairfax was correct in saying that not everyone approved of these measures, and perhaps even more people disapproved than ever dared speak. The majority, one may assume, did approve of such proposals; besides, revolutionary principles are seldom carried by conciliation.

The Virginia Convention, meeting in August 1774, authorized each county to establish an independent militia company, independent, that is,

48. All citations for the Fairfax Resolves are in Rutland, *Papers*, 1:201-9; Rutland in turn used the manuscript in Mason's hand in the Washington Papers at the Library of Congress. The matter of the influence of John Locke on the author of the Fairfax Resolves cannot be taken up here, but should not be disregarded. A careful study of Locke's *Second Treatise of Government* and a comparison with the Fairfax Resolves will show many similarities.

49. Julian P. Boyd, *The Papers of Thomas Jefferson*, 1:125. It will also be found fruitful to study Jefferson's "Summary View" from which this quotation was taken. It reveals more of the American Whig position expressed in the Fairfax Resolves. The "Summary View" may be found in Boyd, 1:121-35.

of the royal governor. Accordingly, 21 September 1774, at a county meeting, Fairfax County formed "The Fairfax Independent Company of Volunteers"; the color and style of the uniform was specified; each man was to have "a good Fire-lock and Bayonet, Sling Cartouch-Box and Tomahawk." Gunpowder, lead and gunflints were to be kept at hand.[50] The resolution justified the company by referring in the first paragraph to "this Time of extreme Danger, with the Indian Enemy in our Country . . . ," and that the company was "to defend . . . the legal prerogatives of our Sovereign King George the third. . . . "[51] The Indians referred to were involved in warfare on the frontier several hundred miles west of Fairfax, and the king's prerogatives, which the company was pledged to defend, were conveniently qualified by the word "legal."

During early January 1775, Washington drilled the Fairfax Company at Alexandria, where it became apparent that there was a need for better arms and more ammunition. The Fairfax Committee of Safety then passed a resolution recommending a "contribution" of "three Shillings per poll" to be paid by or for every tithable person in the county to the sheriff who was to render this, with a list of persons who refused to pay, to the committee.[52] This action of the Fairfax Committee is the first recorded instance in which a county "arrogated to itself the power to levy and collect a tax."[53] This is especially interesting in view of the position taken by the colonists that they could only be taxed by their duly *elected* representatives. Nonetheless, Fairfax County was again taking the lead in radical Revolutionary action. A second resolution, noting that a well-regulated militia was necessary for a stable society and that such a militia would relieve the mother country of the necessity of taxing to provide protection "and render it unnecessary to keep Standing Armies among us—ever dangerous to liberty," provided that the inhabitants of the county from age sixteen to fifty should form themselves into companies of sixty-eight men and to select for each company a captain, two lieutenants, an ensign, four sergeants, four corporals, and one drummer."[54] Writing to Washington, 6 February 1775, Mason enclosed a copy of the "Fairfax County Militia Plan 'for embodying the People,' " which used basically the same language as the January resolution, and which Mason intended to be circulated among the citizens of the county and signed as an indication of their acceptance.[55] Mason, who was always speaking and writing about liberty, was determined that every-

50. Rutland, *Papers*, pp. 210-11.

51. Ibid.

52. *Virginia Gazette* (Rind ed.), 2 February 1775.

53. Van Schreevan, *Revolutionary Virginia*, 2:242.

54. The text of this resolution given in Rutland, 1:212, is incomplete, omitting the sentence "to form themselves into companies of 68 men," which leaves one wondering why the county inhabitants were choosing the officers.

55. Rutland, *Papers*, pp. 20-22.

one should enjoy and exercise his liberty as he and others desired. The enforcement provision of the Fairfax Resolves and this Militia Plan of 6 February 1775, were both designed to seek out and force people to take a stand on important issues, and to show them the error of their ways should they make the wrong choice.

As it would take some time to collect the "contribution" for ammunition, Mason and Washington advanced the money to the county so the powder could be ordered. Apparently, there was some misunderstanding as to the amount of powder ordered, for writing to Washington 17 February 1775, Mason mentioned that he could not understand how Mr. Harper could have ordered twice the amount of powder necessary for Fairfax County.[56] As the order was placed in writing, Mason felt that if the writing could have been misinterpreted, they should pay for all the powder; if not, they should only pay for what was ordered.[57] He also requested that he might be allowed to pay for the powder in ten days, after he had collected the "tytheables" as many of these would be paid in "Paper Dollars and Pensilvania [sic] Money, which from Mr. Harper's connections to the Northward, may suit him as well, or perhaps better than Gold. . . ."[58]

There was also some question as to when, and by whom, the money should be collected. Mason mentioned that rather than wait for the sheriff to collect the money for the powder, he would have his son collect it; this was on 17 February. Washington must have been very displeased and answered quickly, for the next day, 18 February, Mason again wrote Washington and defended his plan by observing that the sheriff would not collect the money until late summer and would get a commission for doing so. By having his son collect the money now, they would get it sooner and save the commission.[59] As Washington had written Bryan Fairfax twice that all debts owed in Great Britain must be paid, one may speculate that he objected to Mason's plan because the sheriff would lose his commission in the process; Washington was, after all, a man with a high respect for property, debts, and financial obligations. On 8 March 1775, Mason again wrote to Washington noting, "We make but a poor Hand of collecting; very few pay, tho' every body promises, except Mr. Hartshorn, of Alexandria;[60] who flatly refused: his Conscience I suppose wou'd not suffer him to be concerned

---

56. Harper was a Quaker merchant at Alexandria who had ordered the powder from Philadelphia on the personal credit of Mason and Washington.

57. Rutland, *Papers*, pp. 220-22.

58. Ibid.

59. Ibid., pp. 223-26.

60. Hartshorn was a Quaker merchant in Alexandria and a member of the Fairfax Committee of Safety. How he could serve on that committee and not contribute to the powder, and why Harper, the Quaker merchant who ordered the gunpowder, did not suffer similarly the dictates of conscience is impossible to say.

in paying for the Instruments of Death."[61] In any event, Mason's son collected the money by 17 April 1775 and accounted for it on that date.[62]

Nicholas Cresswell, an Englishman who was traveling in the colonies and became stranded, left a different picture of Fairfax County in late 1774 and early 1775. Cresswell arrived at Alexandria 19 October 1774 and noted everything was in "utmost confusion": that committees were inspecting into the character and conduct of every tradesman to prevent them from buying British manufactures or selling tea, and that "some of them have been tarred and feathered, others had their property burnt and destroyed by the populace."[63] Fifteen days later, he saw the independent company exercise and an "Effigy of Lord North . . . shot at, then carried in great parade into town and burnt."[64] His next entry, 24 November, mentions large quantities of high quality wheat being brought down to Alexandria and that this sold for "from 2/9 to 4/6 sterling, per bushel."[65]

Over the next four months Cresswell's impression was that everything was in confusion due to a preoccupation with committees and politics; in February 1775 he complained that "the rascals seize all Foreign letters" and the following month he recorded a review of the independent companies by George Washington. (The uniform colors, blue and buff, and red and blue, were those provided for in the Fairfax Committee Militia Resolution of 21 September 1774.) In conclusion, Cresswell pictured the militia "in all about 150 men, and make a formidable appearance."[66] If Cresswell is to be believed, the various resolves and plans of the Fairfax Committee were being carried out; the militia companies were formed, equipped, and drilled; and the citizens were avid to ferret out the traitors in their midst.

During the middle months of 1775 when there are few records of activity within the county, both Washington and Mason were primarily occupied with personal business. The *Virginia Gazette*, 12 May 1775,

61. Rutland, *Papers*, pp. 224-26.

62. Ibid., p. 228. The young Mason collected from 509 persons at 35d. per poll, for a total of £74 13s. Mason and his son then paid for their own "tytheables," including sixty-four slaves, in the amount of £ 9 12s., for a grand total of £84 5s. (This was paid in Virginia currency.) Mason deducted £ 52 8s. as part payment of his advance to pay for powder and sent Washington £31 17s., which when added to the £20 11s. which Washington owed for 137 "tytheables," gave Washington an equal reimbursement on the money advanced for powder of £52 8s.

63. *The Journal of Nicholas Cresswell 1774-1777*, (London: Jonathan Cape, Ltd., 1925) (hereinafter cited as Cresswell, *Journal*).

64. Ibid., p. 46.

65. Ibid., p. 47. Remembering that on 5 July 1774 the residents of Fairfax County had pledged 150 bushels of wheat to be sent to Boston, and using Cresswell's prices as a guide, it is possible to compute the value of that wheat as between £20 12s. 6d. and £33 15s. sterling. The true value of this would depend on the price of a loaf of bread, a pair of shoes, or some other common everyday commodity at that time. Some comparison can be made by realizing that between 1763 and 1786, an average artisan would earn between £25 and £30 sterling per year, approximately the value of the 150 bushels of wheat, and a laborer for the same year about £5 sterling plus room and board.

66. Ibid., pp. 51, 57-59.

carried an advertisement placed by Washington for two runaway men servants (white), and twenty dollar reward for the return of each. [67]

Mason wrote to his London tobacco factor, William Lee, on 20 May 1775 that he had shipped one hundred hogsheads of tobacco, over 50,000 pounds, with Captain Edward Browne, Lee's business partner, aboard the ship *Adventure*. He requested Lee to insure this for eleven pounds sterling per hogshead.[68]

This placed Mason in a rather ironic light, for while a strong supporter for nonimportation, nonexportation, and coercion to achieve compliance with these measures, he was now frantically hurrying to get his tobacco shipped and sold before the legal date which prohibited him from doing so, even to the point of insuring it for an inflated and false value. As Lee explained in a letter of 13 July 1775, he had insured Mason's tobacco for £1,145 in case of loss, but that "I cannot flatter you with the prospect of gaining as much by its safe arrival."[69] Like Mason, other Virginia planters were dumping their tobacco on the London market, and consequently, the price did not rise as Mason had expected.

In view of Mason's forceful statements to Richard Henry Lee in 1770 regarding violation of the nonimportation Association, his own actions in 1775 place him in a hypocritical and self-serving position. He had assured Lee that "every Member of Society is in Duty bound to contribute to the Safety & Good of the Whole . . . every inferior Consideration, as well as the Inconvenience to a few Individuals, must give place to it." Further "all such persons have imported goods contrary to the Association, have done it with eyes open . . . *with a view to private gain, which deserves no countenance from the public* . . . [emphasis added]. Unquestionably Mason understood that the whole idea behind nonexportation was to dry up the supply of those colonial products upon which the British merchants made their profit, and *nothing* qualified as well as tobacco. He could not have misunderstood that his sale of tobacco only contradicted, as he expressed it, "the Tenor of the Association." That he was willing to do this only points up the conflict between private interest and public good, and casts Mason as a very human being faced with difficult decisions to make. In this case, his decision was less than true wisdom.

By June 1775, Washington had been appointed commander-in-chief of the Continental Army and wrote the officers of the Fairfax Militia bidding farewell to them and their companies;[70] the officers answered expressing high regard and affection for the general.[71]

67. *Virginia Gazette* (Purdie ed.) 12 May 1775.
68. Rutland, *Papers*, pp. 234-35.
69. Ibid., p. 240.
70. Force, *Archives*, 2:1031.
71. Ibid., p. 1607. A letter signed by James Hendricks, George Gilpin, and Robert H. Harrison.

George Mason of Gunston Hall. By Dominic Boudet, c. 1811, after John Hesselius, c. 1750. Photo by Charles Baptie.

While Washington was in New England commanding the Continental Army, he left supervision of his Mount Vernon plantation to his cousin Lund Washington. Writing to the General in September 1775, Lund Washington reported, "our Committee has made choice of their militia officers [West, McCarty, Broadwater, Harrison, Gilpin, Triplett]";[72] this was a change from the prior policy of having the men elect the officers.

Throughout the summer and fall of 1775 Mason was active in various capacities with Revolutionary business. He served on the Fairfax Committee, was elected to the 1775 Virginia Convention in place of Washington, where he served on several committees and was appointed to the Virginia Committee of Safety. In a letter to John Hancock, president of the Continental Congress in November 1775, Mason and five other members of the Fairfax committee of correspondence pointed out the critical need for salt (it was used as a preservative as well as a condiment), urged the congress to make every effort to import salt "this winter," and requested a lifting of the ban on exportation of "County-produce" in return for importation of salt.[73] The congress responded 15 December 1775 by passing a resolution permitting George Meade and Co., a Philadelphia merchant, to export from Virginia produce equal to the value of salt imported, and to deliver the salt to the committee of safety. The same day the letter was written to Hancock, Mason also wrote to the Maryland Committee of Safety to inform them of information received from General Washington "that Majr. Connely [sic] and two others were in jail in Frederick Town [Frederick, Maryland]" and that Connolly had with him a commission from General Gage to raise a force of Indians who would march with him in the spring toward Alexandria where Connolly would be met by Lord Dunmore.[74]

Cresswell, in October 1775, pictured the people in Alexandria as cursing the king and all things English, and being "ripe for a revolt," also noting that Virginians and Marylanders in general were in great debt to British merchants and felt that a revolt would solve the problem. The following day he wrote, "Understand I am suspected of being what they call a Tory (that is a Friend to my Country) and am threatened with Tar and Feathers, Imprisonment the D---l [devil] knows what. Curse the Scoundrels." His journal entry of 6 November pictures meaningless, senseless mob action and hysteria among the populace; the day "being the anniversary of the Gunpowder Plot . . ., effigies of the pope, Lord

---

72. Letter from Lund Washington to George Washington 29 September 1775 (Mount Vernon Library. Courtesy John Castellani, Librarian).

73. Rutland, *Papers*, pp. 239-40, 242, 249, 252, 257-58; the signatures were those of John Dalton, Wm. Ramsay, John Carlyle, John Muir, and James Kirk.

74. Rutland, *Papers*, pp. 258-59; Major John Connolly was a loyalist with knowledge of frontier conditions along the Ohio. Connolly and the other two were remanded to the jurisdiction of the Continental Congress and jailed in Philadelphia.

North, Massachusetts Governor Barnard and Lt. Governor Hutchinson, and the devil were carried through town with fifes and drums and then cast into the flames."[75] The inclusion of the pope would lead us to believe that Cresswell's account was reasonably accurate as fear of a popish plot was a bugbear which for over a century had sent Englishmen into wild, uncontrollable hysteria, not to mention that neither the pope nor the gunpowder plot had anything to do with the issue between Britain and the colonies in 1775. The committee of safety met on 29 January 1776 to choose officers for the new militia. Cresswell noted, "they are 21 in number, the first men in the county and had two bowls of toddy, but could not find the cash to pay for it."[76] The number of committee members being twenty-one indicates that Fairfax was complying with the Virginia law of July 1775, setting the number of all committees of safety in the state at twenty-one, for the original Fairfax committee had twenty-five members.

George Mason was most likely among those who were at this meeting, for two days later, 31 January 1776, Mason and John Dalton wrote to the Maryland Council of Safety that they had been "empowered and directed" by the Committee of Safety "to build two row gallies, one to carry a twenty-four and the other an eighteen-pounder, and provide three arm'd cutters for the protection of Potomac River. . . ."[77] They also asked for the cooperation of the Maryland Council in adopting a similar plan to protect the river. By early February 1776, Mason and Dalton were busily engaged in assembling a small fleet to protect towns and estates along the lower Potomac. By 15 March, they had purchased three sloops, the largest of which was *The American Congress*, a vessel of about 110 tons, mounting fourteen carriage guns (six and four pounders), and manned by a crew of ninety men. The other two ships were about half that size, from forty to fifty tons, each mounting eight, three, and four pounders. Supplying powder was still a major problem. Mason and Dalton wrote to the Maryland council in March 1776 requesting the loan of ten barrels of powder for *The American Congress*, pending the arrival of the twenty barrels they had ordered in Philadelphia. Conveniently, the powder from Maryland and that from Philadelphia arrived at the same time, so the loan was immediately repaid. By 2 April, Mason was able to write Washington that they had on hand twenty barrels of powder, a ton of shot, and some small arms for the marines on board *The American Congress*. In this same letter Mason mentioned that in spite of lengthy plans and negotiations with

75. Cresswell, *Journal*, pp. 127-28.

76. Ibid., pp. 130-37.

77. John Dalton was an Alexandria merchant who had been on the Committee of Safety since 1774 and was a prime mover in the business of protecting Alexandria and the Potomac River.

Maryland, it was still not possible to place effective batteries to protect the Potomac.[78]

Since October 1775, Lund Washington had been discussing the matter of shore batteries and other measures for securing the Potomac, in his correspondence. Mason, Lund, General Washington, and many others were in agreement that some protection was needed; the question was what and where? What they were looking for was a place in the river where the channel was narrow and/or shallow enough to permit it to be blocked. An early suggestion was a battery at lower Cedar Point, but the water was found to be sixteen or eighteen fathoms deep, with a strong tide; Indian Head on the Maryland side was similarly rejected.[79] It was decided that the river should be sounded and measured, and in early November, Captain Conway of the Maryland Militia and John West from Fairfax set out to do the job. They hoped that the channel might be blocked by sinking three ships; the site below Quantico proposed by George Washington was found to be unsuitable.[80] Lund eventually decided that nothing could or would be done either to block the channel or to erect batteries; the only practical plan was a battery at Indian Head, and no one seemed interested in getting it established. He feared that "we must defend our plantations on the Potomac with our muskets, I believe the gentlemen are ready and willing to turn out and defend any mans property, but the common people are hellishly frightened."[81]

By early 1776, the boisterous spirit of previous months waned: The Alexandrians expected to have the British burn the town and yet would do nothing to prevent it. Most of the militia had gone to Williamsburg and taken their weapons with them, so the remainder in Alexandria exercised with clubs as their only arms. Lund's letter of 31 January 1776 reported that a rumor of five large ships had put the city in a panic, caused the women and children to leave Alexandria and "stowg themselves into every little Hut they can get, out of the reach of the Enemys canon as they think," and that every wagon, cart, and pack horse was engaged in moving goods out of town. He concluded by writing that he expected the five large ships "will prove to be 5 oister Boats."[82] Cresswell indicated there was a general confusion, that the militia numbered about 700 men, and new recruits were being offered ten

78. Rutland, *Papers*, pp. 259-65.

79. Letter from Lund Washington to George Washington, 29 October 1775 (Mount Vernon Library. Courtesy John Castellani, Librarian).

80. Letter from Lund Washington to George Washington, 5 November 1775 (Mount Vernon Library. Courtesy John Castellani, Librarian).

81. Letters from Lund Washington to George Washington, 14 November 1775; 3 December 1775; 17 December 1775 (Mount Vernon Library. Courtesy John Castellani, Librarian).

82. Letters from Lund Washington to George Washington, 17 January 1776; 31 January 1776 (Mount Vernon Library. Courtesy John Castellani, Librarian).

dollars advance and forty shillings a month, but that they still had few arms. He noted that he did not dare to say he would like to go to England or he would be put in jail.[83]

The British did not burn the town, or even get the chance to, and by the late summer of 1776, the Alexandrians had recovered their senses and their courage and were making preparation to protect themselves. The row-gallies were patrolling the Potomac, one of them getting involved in an interesting episode. On 23 July 1776, the row-galley *Protector* was proceeding up the Potomac, the English fleet having gone up river before them. Upon sighting the fleet, it was decided to wait and try to slip past the British under cover of darkness. The *Protector* proceeded back down river about a half mile, and the crew, seven in number, went to the Maryland shore in two rowboats. One rowboat was hidden in the marsh and the larger one staked well up on the beach. Some thirty or forty Maryland militia met them on the shore where they observed the British land on the Virginia shore, burn a house, and return to their ships. By this time the number of Maryland militia had increased to three or four hundred. Finally, a British row-galley and a schooner tender made for the Maryland shore. When they were within range, they fired on the Marylanders who, instead of returning the fire, ran for the woods with their commanding officer yelling "Come back!" The officer then followed them into the woods. The British seized and destroyed the larger rowboat. A period of charges and countercharges followed between the Marylanders and the crew of the *Protector*. Eventually, the captain and three other officers of the *Protector* had affidavits published in the *Virginia Gazette* describing their version of the incident.[84]

The fleet encountered by the *Protector* was part of Lord Dunmore's forces which had conducted raids along the Potomac during the summer of 1776, raids which so alarmed the residents of Alexandria that they fortified the town. As all the available cannon were either in use or pledged to the continental army, Mason wrote to John Hancock requesting the Continental Congress to allow the Fairfax Committee to purchase cannon from "Messr. Hughes's of Frederick County, Maryland"; Hughes was under contract to sell all the cannon they produced to the continental army. Mason added that if the price was more than £35 Virginia currency per ton (the amount allowed by the committee for cannon), the residents of Alexandria would make up the difference themselves. Subsequently, Alexandria built two shore batteries containing sixteen cannon and formed an artillery company to man them.[85]

---

83. Cresswell, *Journal*, pp. 140-49.
84. *Virginia Gazette* (Purdie ed.), 6 September 1776.
85. Rutland, *Papers*, pp. 316-17.

The British did not molest Alexandria, nor any other place in Fairfax County, in any serious way, although in April 1781 a British warship anchored off Mount Vernon. The sloop-of-war *Savage*, commanded by Captain Richard Graves, took a number of Washington's slaves from the Mount Vernon plantation. Lund's account to the General listed three old men, an overseer, a bricklayer, a horseler [*sic* (hostler)], a weaver, six young men, two young women, and two boys, about seventeen in all; five men and both women were later recovered by Washington. The worst of it was that Lund went on board the *Savage*, took refreshment to the British, and tried to bargain for the return of the slaves. About a week after the incident, the Marquis de Lafayette wrote to Washington from Alexandria as to "how unhappy I have been" to hear of Lund's actions. "This being done by the gentleman [Lund] who, in some measure, represents you at your house" Lafayette continued, "will certainly have a bad effect, and contrasts with spirited answers from some neighbors, that had their houses burnt accordingly." One can only imagine Washington's reaction upon receiving this letter. He was a proud man who may have been expected to disapprove of Lund's actions on principle; but to have no less a person than Lafayette first bring it to his attention, and then to suggest that Lund's actions had brought disgrace to the General's house and "contrasts with spirited answers" of Washington's neighbors was sure to anger this patient but sensitive man. Washington's letter to Lund was surprisingly restrained, but left no doubt whatsoever that the General was most displeased by his cousin's handling of the situation. Obviously still smarting from Lafayette's remarks, Washington said he would have preferred "they had burnt my House." He told Lund," you ought to have considered yourself as my representative, and . . . reflected on the bad example of communicating with the enemy." His remonstration with and censure of Lund, however, went even further:

> To go on board their Vessels; Carry them refreshments; commune with a parcel of plundering Scoundrels, and request a favor by asking the surrender of My Negroes, was exceedingly ill-judged, and 'tis to be feared, will be unhappy in its consequences, as it will be a precedent for others, and may become a subject of animadversion.

Washington's position was certainly uncomfortable. After six long years of war, with many private sacrifices, here was Lund Washington, the General's cousin and overseer, dealing with the British to save a few slaves and the General's house. Whatever Lund's motives, it did present a very bad example. Washington was not above criticism by others at the time, and his reaction to the situation is understandable.[86]

86. Fitzpatrick, *Writings*, 22:14-15; and Jared Sparks, ed., *Correspondence of the American Revolution being Letters of Eminent Men to George Washington* . . . (Boston: Little, Brown and Co., 1853), 2:295.

Meanwhile, in Williamsburg, George Mason made what was to be his, and through him, Fairfax County's most significant contribution to the American Revolution. In fact, it was perhaps the most significant contribution made by any single Virginian to the Revolution in Virginia, Thomas Jefferson and George Washington not excepted; for Mason was primary author of the Virginia Declaration of Rights and the Virginia Constitution of 1776. These two documents provided the *modus operandi* for the government of the newly formed Commonwealth of Virginia. Jefferson asserted, even before the fact, that the establishment of a new form of government was "the whole object of the present controversy." When seen in this light, the contribution of George Mason, sent to the convention by the freeholders of Fairfax County, assumes new proportions.

The wheels of independence were set on their final course 10 May 1776 when the Continental Congress passed a resolution advising the colonies to adopt new governments where non existed "sufficient to the exigencies of their affairs." Five days later, 15 May, a resolution was passed instructing the Virginia delegates at the Continental Congress to propose a declaration of independence separating the colonies from Great Britain. At the same time the convention appointed a committee to prepare a declaration of rights and a plan of government; whatever may be said in favor of 4 July 1776, these three actions, one in Philadelphia and two in Williamsburg on 15 May were the real declarations of independence.[87] Mason, who had been ill, arrived in Williamsburg 18 May and was immediately appointed to the committee to draw up the declaration of rights and the constitution. By 24 May, Edmund Pendleton was able to write Jefferson that the documents were being prepared and that "Colo. Mason seems to have the Ascendancy in the great work."[88]

Mason's Declaration of Rights was probably ready for the committee by 24 May, and the revised committee draft was read to the convention 27 May; the draft submitted by Mason was in its essential points adopted by the convention 12 June 1776. The Declaration of Rights drafted by Mason, and to a lesser degree that adopted by the convention, was not only an enumeration of specific individual and collective rights which the government must respect, but was an all-encompassing political and philosophical catechism. In its formation, Mason, as Jefferson was to do in the preamble to the Declaration of Independence, set forth the natural, indefeasible rights of all mankind,

87. Wood, *Creation* p. 131-132; and Boyd, *Papers*, 1:290-91. The 15 May 1776 Virginia resolution calling for independence was introduced in the Continental Congress by Richard Henry Lee on 7 June and resulted in the appointment of a committee to draw up a formal declaration. The result was Jefferson's Declaration of Independence, which after minor modification by the committee and the Congress, was passed 4 July 1776.

88. Boyd, *Papers*, 1:296.

inherent in each individual by virtue of his very existence. There can be little doubt that most of the ideas expressed by Mason, and later by Jefferson, were the common intellectual heritage of that group of eighteenth-century men known as "Whigs"; both Mason's draft and the final adopted text of the Declaration owed much to the writings of Locke, Montesquieu, and such political writings as *Cato's Letters*. Mason's opening manifesto for humanity was felt by the more conservative members of the convention to present ambiguities and dangers in a slave-holding society. Therefore, certain words and phrases were added or changed to reflect the slaveholder's views. The most significant of these changes was to insert "when they enter into a state of society" into the first declaration that men could not be deprived of life, liberty, property, and happiness. It was then a simple matter to justify the holding of Negro slaves on the grounds that they were not part of society.[89]

At the same time he was drafting the Declaration of Rights, or soon after, Mason set to work on a constitution for Virginia. The whole idea of a written constitution was both new and fundamental to Englishmen, even American Englishmen.[90] A written constitution would restrain and control the government which operated under it; this was a concept very clear to George Mason who set down those fundamental principles by which he and his colleagues felt a government should itself be governed.[91] Such fundamental principles once embodied in a written constitution would prevent any part of the new government from encroaching upon the rights of the people. Mason's draft of the constitution was probably finished by 10 June; the final document as revised and adopted by the convention 29 June 1776 was a compromise, being much less than Jefferson and Madison would have wished and much altered both by the committee and the convention, but the basic framework of the document was the work of Mason. This constitution was to serve Virginia until 1830.[92] A preamble written by Jefferson was added to the text of the constitution itself, and between the two sections was inserted "By which several Acts of Misrule, the Government of this Country, as formerly exercised under the Crown of Great Britain is totally dissolved." The Commonwealth of Virginia had declared its independence.

89. Rutland, *Papers*, 1:274-91. Both Mason and the Convention were greatly influenced by John Locke's *Second Treatise of Civil Government* for all of the declarations. In particular, the phrase "when they enter into a state of society" was almost, if not exactly, verbatim from Locke, and the logic is Locke's throughout.

90. The question of a constitution as fundamental law is clearly set out in Wood, *Creation* pp. 273-82.

91. The fundamental principles owed much to Locke. As Mason was obviously very familiar with Locke's *Second Treatise* he could have borrowed the idea of "standing laws" governing the government from the *Second Treatise*. Also, Mason's choice that Virginia should be a Commonwealth was certainly a debt owed to Locke.

92. The substance and evolution of the Constitution of 1776 are fully discussed in Rutland, 1:295-310, and Boyd, 1:329-86. For this reason it is not developed here.

Mason presumably stayed in Williamsburg long enough to help elect Patrick Henry the first governor of the new commonwealth, and served on a committee to design a great seal; he then returned to his home in Fairfax County. Nothing he did in the future was to equal his contributions in the spring and summer of 1776, and no other representative of Fairfax County influenced the Revolution in Virginia to the extent he did. Indeed, if the Revolution is taken to be the change in the minds and hearts of the people as John Adams asserted, then even George Washington's contribution to the Revolution as a whole did not equal that of George Mason. In all events, it is safe to say that through the efforts of both Mason and Washington the influence of Fairfax County on the Revolution was paramount in Virginia and significant on the whole.

The Virginia Declaration of Rights, in the handwriting of its author, George Mason. Library of Congress.

V

Fairfax County and the New Nation

When the Virginia Convention, 29 June 1776, declared independence of the government of Great Britain and adopted a constitution for the new Commonwealth of Virginia, they left the forms of county government, the county court, and the vestry intact. The Virginia Declaration of Rights adopted earlier the same month, however, set the basis for serious dissent from the authority of both the county court and the vestry regarding taxation.[1] Although attempts by Mason, Jefferson, and Madison for complete disestablishment failed in 1776, these three champions of religious liberty succeeded in December 1776 in getting past the legislature a bill exempting religious dissenters from contributing to the established church.[2] The dissenters were, however, required to contribute toward obligations which the vestry had contracted before January 1777, and to continue to contribute towards those functions of the vestry which pertained to poor relief.

The Truro Parish vestry book makes no mention of this action, but either the accounts or the budget of the vestry appear to reflect it. The levy for 1776 was 40,110 pounds of tobacco, and the parish expenses included 17,280 pounds for the salary of the minister, 500 pounds for the clerk of the vestry, and a variety of charges for the churches. The

---

1. Rutland, *Papers of George Mason*, 1:304, 309, 287-89. The significance of Fairfax County's George Mason being the author of the Declaration of Rights, and the major author of the constitution is too complicated to discuss here. The specific sections of the Declaration that tended to undermine court taxation and vestry authority in general are: No. 6, that men "cannot be taxed or deprived of their property for publick uses without their own consent or that of their Representative so elected" (the justices of the county courts were, of course, appointed); and No. 16, "That Religion . . . can be directed only by reason and conviction, not by force or violence; and therefor, all men are equally entitled to the free exercise of religion, according to the dictates of conscience." Such sentiments were, of course, anathema to any established church, and fatal to the civil responsibilities of the vestry in Virginia.

2. Rutland, *Papers*, 1:318-19; and Boyd, *Papers*, 1:532, 534; 2:547.

account for 1777, on the other hand, was only 2,340 pounds of tobacco and £ 54 2s. sterling. The 1777 account did not include a minister's salary or any other church expenses with the exception of 500 pounds of tobacco for a clerk, whose services would have been required to administer poor relief. The levy was lowered accordingly from thirty pounds per poll in 1776 to fifteen pounds per poll in 1777, and to twelve pounds per poll in 1779. Interestingly, the number of tithables was 1,337 for 1776; 1,316 for 1777; and 1,357 for 1779; so what was collected in 1777 and after was for the poor only and was levied on all the tithables.[3] Similarly, the Fairfax Parish levy declined after 1777, being thirteen pounds per poll in 1780, twenty pounds in 1781, twenty-two pounds in 1782, and fourteen pounds in 1784. The vestry meetings were now held only once a year. Just how the parishes provided for ecclesiastical expenditures is not clear.

Although total disestablishment failed in 1776, Jefferson's great bill to effect this action stood waiting in the wings and was finally pushed through the legislature by Madison and Mason at the 1785/86 session. This utterly extinguished any and all civil authority of the vestry for the bill provided "That no man shall be compelled to frequent or support any religious worship, place, or ministry whatsoever, nor shall be enforced, restrained, molested, or burthened in his body or goods . . ."[4] This could have come as no surprise to the vestries in Fairfax County, for the Fairfax Parish in April 1785, a full nine months before the Bill for Establishing Religious Freedom passed the legislature, held "a meeting of the Minister and Vestry of the Protestant Episcopal Church in Fairfax Parish"; likewise, the Truro vestry held its last meeting as a civil body in January 1785.

The same Assembly which enacted the bill for religious freedom, also passed other legislation which stripped the vestries of all civil duties, and provided that the county courts should divide each county into districts and that three overseers of the poor should be elected in each district. The Fairfax County Court in March 1786 set the two districts for Fairfax County as the Parish of Truro and the Parish of Fairfax, and ordered elections for three overseers of the poor in each district, the

3. *Vestry Book*, pp. 142-47.

4. Hening, *Statutes*, 12:84-86. Fairfax Harrison in his chapter "The Parishes and Their Churches" in *Landmarks of Old Prince William* notes "In the eighteenth century the Virginia parishes were working symbols of an ancient race inheritance," pp. 299-300. While allowances may be made for the fifty years since Harrison wrote, the use of the term "race" in this context is unfortunate. Surely Harrison knew (*Landmarks*, p. 301, notes 4 and 5) that the civil functions of the parish had originated in Tudor England and before that, in different form, in the Roman Catholic establishment in England and had nothing whatsoever to do with "race inheritance." One may contrast Harrison's somewhat nostalgic reflection on the demise of the parish with the comment of Thomas Jefferson to James Madison (16 December 1786) on the passage of the bill for religious freedom which had brought about the extinction of the parish in Virginia, "In fact it is comfortable to see the standard of reason at length erected, after so many ages during which the human mind has been held in vassalage by kings, priests and nobles; and it is honorable for us [Virginia] to have produced the first legislature who has had the courage to declare that the reason of man may be trusted with the formation of his own opinion." (Boyd, 10:604.)

election for Truro to be held 4 April 1786, and for Fairfax, 5 April 1786.[5] William Deneale was to supervise the election in Truro and James Wren in Fairfax. The results of the first election inTruro are unknown, and the election in Fairfax Parish was less than conclusive. The three men elected were John Moss, James Wren, and Richard Ratcliff; Moss and Wren refused to serve, and Ratcliff was ineligible as he was a subsheriff. The court, therefore, ordered a new election held on 28 April 1786. The county levy for that year provided for £137 for the overseers of the poor in Fairfax District, nothing being allotted for Truro.

The first meeting of the overseers of the poor for Truro District (formerly Truro Parish) was held on 28 May 1787 and a total of £158 4s. was recorded as being expended to help nineteen persons. While now a purely civil body, the overseers, as if from habit, held this first meeting at Pohick.[6] The following year, 1788, the meeting was again at Pohick, and nineteen persons were again provided for at a total cost of £95 6d. From the entry for this year it is possible to determine how the overseers obtained money to help the poor; it was collected as a county levy, but separate from the levy of the county court. In 1788 the sheriff was instructed to collect three pounds of tobacco or six shillings for each of the 3,801 tithables in the county for that year.[7]

The following year, 1789, the overseers for both districts met in September at Price's Ordinary where the total expenditure for the poor was set at £337 5s. 6d., which was eighteen pounds of tobacco or 2s. 3d. for each of the 2,993 tithables in the county, including Alexandria. Peter Wagener, Thomazen Ellzey, John Moss, and George Minor were each paid one dollar for attending the meeting in 1789.[8]

The exclusion of Alexandria from the county levy for maintenance of the poor in 1789 may have been the result of a petition sent to the Assembly in November 1787. There were, in fact, two petitions from Fairfax County bearing not only on the poorhouse, but also on the general competition between town and country folk in the county on several issues.

The first petition was sent by people objecting to the current administration of the poorhouse, and to Alexandria in general, noting that as Alexandria was in the upper (Fairfax) district, and as the overseers elected for the lower (Truro) district had refused to serve, that the three men elected for the upper district had to serve all the poor in the whole

---

5. Fairfax County Court Minute Book, 1783-1788, p. 189.

6. Truro Parish Vestry Book (Manuscript Division, Library of Congress, Washington, D.C.), p. 192. The records of the overseers of the poor, first for Truro District and later for both Truro and Fairfax districts, are at the end of the Truro Vestry Book. The page numbers given here refer to the page numbers in the bound positive photostatic copy of the vestry book at the Library of Congress. These page numbers may or may not correspond to the page numbers in the original vestry book which was not available for use.

7. Ibid., p. 193.

8. Ibid., p. 198-203.

county. This appears to have been the case because the overseers' refusal to serve in Truro District was admitted in the other petition. For those sending the first petition, however, this was meant only as an introduction, for they went on to complain that two of the three overseers in the upper district were Alexandria men and, therefore, (for reasons not explained in the petition) the poor in the lower district were not cared for. Additionally, this petition charged that instead of locating the poorhouse near the center of the county, the overseers had "at a great Expence [sic]" provided a poorhouse close to Alexandria and the river where supplies were "much dearer" and where there was "want of ground" to grow vegetables for their own support. Finally, the petition noted that the poor were "maintained in such idleness, Ease and Plenty, as cannot continually fail to increase their Number." It went on to complain that the county court had also "illegally, wantonly & oppressively" levied thirty thousand pounds of tobacco for no specific purpose, and that this was done because as the levy was a poll tax and as the town of Alexandria had fewer tithables (meaning perhaps slaves), the burden fell unequally on the country folk. The petition concluded by supporting the request of Alexandria for a separate delegate to the Assembly and by asking the Assembly to provide Alexandria with a separate poorhouse. This petition was signed by 617 Fairfax inhabitants; a counterpetition was signed by about 190 inhabitants, many of them Alexandrians, making this a major issue in the county.[9]

The counterpetition affirmed that a plantation had been rented, both near Alexandria and on the river, "for the purposes of a Poor House" at £12 per year which the petitioners were "pursuaded is as low a rent as the same plantation . . . in the most remote and interior part of the county . . . ." Further, that those in the poorhouse "have always raised for themselves . . . an abundance of garden vegetables and roots and have also been employed (as far as they were able) in fishing and picking oakum."[10] They went on to declare that there were no unnecessary poor in the poorhouse, and that the high levy the previous year was for "a stock of bedding, cloathing, tools, and utensils for the use of the Poor House on its being first set on foot . . . ." Finally, they denied that Alexandria had ever petitioned for a separate delegate to the Assembly.

9. Both petitions may be found in Virginia State Library, Fairfax County Legislative Petition, 24 November 1787. In the same box with the petitions are two notices or affidavits, one from Dixon the publisher of the *Virginia Gazette*, and the other from "Aug. Davis" pointing out that notices had been published for four successive weeks in their newspapers, and that this petition would be presented to the General Assembly. To Dixon's affidavit is appended the note, "Sir, the charge of advertising is nine Shillings. [signed] George Mason, Esq."

10. Picking oakum involved untwisting old rope to get the loose hemp fibers which were then used as ship caulking. There is an unsubstantiated story that the Alexandria poorhouse, or the overseers, made a nice profit from this activity. As Alexandria was a major seaport which would occasion both a generous supply of old rope and a genuine need for ship caulking, the story seems at least plausible.

Besides the casual interest aroused by the specific complaints in these petitions, they show a definite dichotomy of opinion between what may be seen as a town and country faction within Fairfax County, with important implications. The plantation owners represented the old society built on land, and as such may be seen as conservative. They were feeling the pinch as the price of tobacco declined, and as their old exhausted land produced less than before. The aggressive Alexandrians represented a threat, for the economic prosperity of Alexandria was booming and was based on trade (in wheat and *not* tobacco), shipping, and commerce. In the wording of the "country" petition, the general dislike of Alexandria and its control, (both real and imagined) of Fairfax County is clearly evident. The location of the poorhouse was a convenient cover for the real issue of who was going to control Fairfax County, and the "country" folk, apparently feeling they were no match for the Alexandrians, were proposing to solve the problem by trying to exclude Alexandria from county politics. The exclusion of Alexandria tithables from the 1789 poorhouse levy would seem to indicate that Alexandria did set up its own poorhouse, for otherwise it would hardly have been excused from the levy, and that in this respect the conservative element held sway.

On the same day, 24 November 1787, another petition was presented to the legislature complaining of yet another injustice brought upon the inhabitants of the county by Alexandria; this time the subject was roads. By an act of 1772, at the request of Alexandria, the roads from the town to the Blue Ridge were to be maintained by special county levies administered by appointed road commissioners. This act was renewed in 1785 and a provision added to install turnpike gates and collect tolls in order to raise additional revenue. By the same act, Fairfax and the other counties involved were to levy a special tax of £60 a year for three years for the benefit of the roads.[11]

Tolls on the roads from the Blue Ridge and from Georgetown to Alexandria in 1785 were:[12]

	Shillings	Pence
Coach or four-wheeled riding carriage	1s.	3d.
Two-wheeled chaise or chair		8d.
Loaded wagon	1s.	
Loaded cart		6d.
Unloaded wagon	1s.	
Empty cart		6d.

If the toll was paid going into town,
it was not collected on the return trip.

11. Hening, *Statutes*, 12:75.
12. Ibid., p. 76.

The tolls were collected without regard to the distance traveled, and this was among the complaints in the 1787 petition signed by 635 Fairfax residents. The whole purpose of the tolls, the commissioners, the levies, and the roads was to facilitate commercial travel for the town of Alexandria. Not surprisingly, the county residents resented having to do free road work and to pay a special levy to maintain roads for the benefit of people at the ends of the road, that is, at the valley and Alexandria. The petition complained that all this trouble was for two roads only and the road to Colchester mentioned in the 1772 act had been entirely neglected; that the new toll roads were in reality the old main roads to town; that all the smaller roads joined the main road and therefore, anyone wishing to go to town now had to pay a toll. This was even more galling as everyone had to go to town sooner or later, as it was the commercial center and the courthouse was there. Most of the tariff was being paid by county residents for the benefit of the Alexandria merchants and nonresidents. In this case, even though the town conflict with the county was evident, the petitioners did have a valid case; at least the Assembly felt they did, for on 2 December 1787 an act was passed amending the earlier acts and providing some relief for the local residents. By the terms of this amended act, any county resident who lived on or near the toll road could use it free, without toll, providing that the distance traveled on the toll road was less than one quarter of a mile, and that they obtain a certificate signed by two justices of the county court. A final amendment was made to the 1785 act, by dropping the £ 60 levy for the maintenance of the roads. There is no way of knowing to what extent this remedied the problem, but it is safe to assume that anyone living up in the county would still have to pay tolls and would still resent the free work required on the roads. It is also safe to assume that the town-country rivalry continued, perhaps unabated.

As early as 1781 there was a petition sent to the Assembly remonstrating against the county court and the Alexandria justices in particular. This petition has not been found. However, the petition of November 1782 in reply from seven Fairfax justices throws much light on the contents of the lost petition and of the state of the county at that date. The lost petition maintained that the justices were "not the Representatives of the People at Large, nor amenable to them," and the justices replied that this "we admit." They went on to say they were amenable to the governor who "may order a new commission & leave out whom he pleases."[13] This later argument is especially ironic in light of a later opinion of this same court on the same subject.

Two years and four months after presentation of the petition, 22 March 1785, the Fairfax Court refused to receive a new commission of

13. Fairfax County Legislative Petition, 20 November 1782, Virginia State Library (hereinafter cited as Petition).

the peace from Governor Benjamin Harrison. Among the reasons given for this refusal was that by receiving it they would "afford a dangerous precedent . . . that the Justices derive their office entirely from the list [commission] . . .," and that ". . . by leaving out any Justice's name he would thence forward be deprived of his office [!] . . ."; only one justice, George Gilpin, signed both the 1782 petition and this 1785 order of the court. The 1785 action of the Fairfax Court went on to say that this was notoriously practiced under the former government, "and that exercise of such a power is altogether illegal giving to the Executive Department of the State an undue & dangerous influence over the Courts of Justice directly contrary to the Declaration of Rights & to the Fundamental principles of our free government."[14] Although this may seem to be infallible and commonplace logic in the twentieth century, it represented a very radical position for 1785, especially when expressed by the assembled justices of a Virginia county court. On the one hand, the entire concept of fundamental principles as expressed in the Declaration of Rights was a mainspring of the American Revolution; on the other hand, the court was looking forward to the independence of the judiciary from the executive which would emerge in 1787 at Philadelphia.[15]

The 1782 petition from the Fairfax justices went on to make further points. They made reference to the former petition being "pregnant with fears, suspicions & jealousies of the Town Justices, & insinuates their being linked together in party interest & sinister views . . . ." They were accused of oppressing the people by appointing land commissioners "who have romantick & exorbitant notions of the value of Land." The petition points out that of the fifteen justices who appointed the land commissioners, only four were from the town. They also answered the charge that they had levied thirty thousand pounds of tobacco "unjustly Illegally & unnecessarily" by saying that an addition had to be made to the prison in 1779 and further that in January 1781, when the levy was laid, "The Court-House was found in a ruinous condition, the windows were Broken, there were no doors, & the roof leaked so, that when it rained one could not Stand dry in the House, The Plaistering too was gone, the laths rotten, & not a Table or Bench in the Jurors Rooms." This situation was rendered totally impossible as the men appointed to oversee the repair work were under the burden of advancing the money from their own funds as "the workmen . . . would not trust the County" and "no Tradesmen would credit the County." The justices concluded their case by saying "we never knew it was Illegal to levy Tobacco for the reparation of the Public Buildings when necessary"; this had been the

14. Fairfax County Court Order Book, 1783-1788, p. 114.
15. The precedents set in the earlier English struggle between the Crown (not exactly an executive) and the courts have not been ignored. However, it does seem that in this case, the Fairfax County Court was looking forward and not backward for the justification of its position.

practice in the past, and "If therefore we have err'd it is from Precedent."[16]

It seems difficult to believe that the courthouse could have been in as bad a condition as the justices claimed. However, as there was only the clerk at the court on a full-time basis, and as the war was still going on, it is possible that the building had fallen into serious disrepair. If so, no wonder neither workmen nor tradesmen would trust or credit the county. This was also far from being the last occasion on which the court would hear that it was illegal to levy tobacco. The matter was to be brought up later, specifically by George Mason in 1789. Mason, a justice himself, "objected that the court had no legal authority to levy on the inhabitants of the county any money or tobacco for any purpose whatsoever." He based his objection on the Virginia Declaration of Rights, the issue being, as previously mentioned, that taxation was limited to elected representatives and the justices were appointed. As for the matter of precedent, the court very soon took a new and opposite position on an issue that had formerly been firmly anchored in precedent; this was all part of the Revolution.

The elixir of republicanism permeated all phases of life and government in the late eighteenth century, and was a strong force in Fairfax County. In November 1783 a petition, signed by about 60 Fairfax citizens, was presented to the Assembly requesting that the residents in the county be allowed every two years to elect freeholders to care for the poor; the petitioners felt that having the churchwardens care for the poor was "inconsistent with the Principles of Republican Government," and "unconstitutional." Further, that by allowing for election of those caring for the poor that "these unfortunate people" would be "more Constitutionally provided for." Surely, the poor did not care how they were provided for, only that they were fed, clothed, and housed. Were the petitioners extremists or indulging in meaningless rhetoric? All indications suggest that they were genuinely concerned that all aspects of their life be conducted in a constitutional and "republican" manner. Republicanism was, and is, a very contagious and uncontrollable phenomenon.

To an ever increasing degree, the growth and power in late eighteenth century Fairfax centered in and revolved around the town of Alexandria; the major roads went to Alexandria, the commerce of the town was booming, and a very real resentment developed in the upper parts of the county toward the Alexandrians, as is evident from the legislative petitions.

16. Petition, 20 November 1782.

In October 1779 a petition was presented to the Assembly from "The Merchants, Adventurers to Sea, in the town of Alexandria." The petition requested that a naval office for the inspection and registry of incoming and outgoing ships be located at Alexandria, as almost all the vessels on the Potomac were owned by merchants in Alexandria or Colchester, and as almost all foreign vessels came to one or the other of these ports.[17] By 1780 the inclusion of Colchester was a formal courtesy; the ships came to Alexandria. Alexandria got its naval office, and 1780 was the busiest year of the war for the town.[18] Hooe and Harrison, Alexandria merchants, owned nine vessels with a value of £14,700 sterling. Disregarding the British blockade, they dispatched ten loaded ships in 1780. Also in 1780, the Amsterdam firm of John Neufville and Sons sent sixteen ships to Alexandria. Paradoxically, even in 1781 when the depreciation of paper money in Virginia was very severe, being 400 to 1 in July and 1,000 to 1 in December, the Alexandria merchants survived by establishing credit with Philadelphia and Baltimore merchants.

Perhaps the most important factor in the ability of Alexandria to survive this financial crisis was that the merchants in that town did not rely on tobacco for a commercial mainstay, but on wheat and flour. So secure was Alexandria's commercial position that her chief commercial rivals were completely outside of the state: Baltimore and Philadelphia. As early as 1782 a petition was sent to the Assembly asking for that body to help encourage trade and commerce in Virginia. The petition noted that Virginia was behind the northern states in trade and that merchants were needed in Virginia. The petitioners pointed out that Maryland had a clear commercial advantage because her duties were lower; they requested that the Assembly lower the Virginia duties so that the commonwealth's merchants could compete with those of other states. The petition was signed by about 100 "Inhabitants of the County of Fairfax", but many of the signatures were those of prominent Alexandria merchants: Wm. Ramsay, Robert Adam, Robt. Hooe, John Fitzgerald, John Muir, Dennis Ramsay, and Wm. Hartshorne, to mention only a few of the more well known. This was clearly an attempt of Alexandria to compete with Baltimore for the Chesapeake trade in the first of the post-war years.[19]

The backbone of Alexandria's trade was wheat and flour, an enterprise which she had entered in the 1760s. Nonetheless, the flour milled at Alexandria was inferior to that of Baltimore and Philadelphia, and the northern cities attracted the commerce of those wishing to

17. Legislative Petitions, Alexandria city, 25 October 1779, Virginia State Library.

18. Much of the following information has been taken from John Stoessel, "The Port of Alexandria: Virginia in the Eighteenth Century" (unpublished M.A. diss., Catholic University of America, 1969) (hereinafter cited as Stoessel, "Port of Alexandria").

19. Fairfax County Legislative Petition, 27 May 1782, Virginia State Library.

pay more for the farmer's wheat. A vicious circle soon developed as some of the best Virginia wheat went to northern markets, further degrading the milled products of Alexandria. The Alexandria merchants, seeing their business eroding before their eyes, petitioned the Assembly for stricter flour inspection in Virginia.

In spite of the rise of Baltimore and the competition of Philadelphia, the foresighted Washington and Jefferson still hoped to make the Potomac a prosperous commercial river and with it Alexandria the premier port on the eastern seaboard. Washington had been interested in the trade of the Ohio Country since the early 1770s, prompting Jefferson to write to the General in March 1784 that the trade of the Ohio and Mississippi "is nearer to Alexandria than New York by 730 miles, and is interrupted by one portage only." "Nature has declared in favour of the Patowmac [sic]" he continued, "and through that channel offers to pour into our lap the whole commerce of the Western world."[20] This was a noble dream and a practical and realistic prospect to Jefferson and Washington. Both men saw Alexandria as a great trading and commercial center. The problem was to make the Potomac fully navigable to its headwaters, and with this very purpose in mind, Jefferson had turned to the one man who had any hope of effecting it: George Washington. Washington did not disappoint the man from Monticello, for at the October session of the Virginia Assembly, he pushed through a charter for the Patowmack Company to open the upper Potomac to navigation. The company was organized at a meeting in Alexandria on 17 May 1785, George Washington being elected president.[21] At the same session, the Assembly passed the Virginia Port Bill which made Alexandria the only official port of entry on the Potomac.

During the 1780s Alexandria was described as being "alive with carpenters and bricklayers." The Italian Count Luigi Castiglioni, traveling through Alexandria in 1785, portrayed it as a town of 300 houses and 3,000 residents. By 1788, Brissot de Warville observed that while thirty or forty years before there were only two houses, the town now planned to surpass Baltimore with "servants in silk stockings and their masters in boots." Convinced of the natural advantage of their harbor, notes de Warville, the Alexandrians "are building on all sides, they have set up superb wharves and raised vast warehouses." Streets were extended and as befitted a future great center, were built 66-feet wide, and Washington Street 100-feet wide.[22]

20. Boyd, *Papers*, 7:26.
21. Harrison, *Landmarks*, pp. 543-44.
22. Ibid., pp. 408-9; and Stoessel, "Port of Alexandria," pp. 59-60.

In 1785 the Alexandria Academy was founded and a year later chartered by the Assembly. Motivated by the population increase and the plentiful supply of grain, brewing and distillery establishments sprang up and developed. A bit farther up the river, across from Georgetown, there may have been a tobacco finishing factory.

The *Virginia Journal and Alexandria Advertizer* began publication on 5 February 1784; it was the first newspaper in Fairfax County. For the first four and one-half years it was published weekly, each Thursday, and contained four pages (actually one large sheet printed on both sides and folded) with three columns per page. The publisher was George Richards and Company, who printed many items of casual interest reflecting on the growth of the town. Each issue listed the ships which entered and cleared at the naval office in Alexandria. From 25 March to 23 September 1784 a total of 85 ships entered at Alexandria, of which more than 60 had come from North American ports (Philadelphia, 11; Boston, 9; New York, 5; Baltimore, 12; Eastern Shore, 16; Norfolk, 3; Gloucester, 3; James River, 1; Charleston, 2; Georgetown, 1), whereas the remainder arrived from the Caribbean (Bermuda, Antigua, Martinique) or European ports (London, Glasgow, Lisbon, Ireland). Of the outgoing 58 ships during the same period, 27 went to American ports, eight to the Caribbean, and 22 to Europe (London, 4; Amsterdam, 6; Leghorn, 2; Belfast, 3; Hamburg and Cadiz, one each; and others). Alexandria was clearly a busy port with ships covering the major maritime routes, and presumably exporting large quantities of wheat and flour to foreign markets.[23]

There was a large and growing number of merchants advertising in the *Gazette*, most of whom sold an assortment of general merchandise. The *Gazette* served as the news sheet for all of northern Virginia and even western Virginia. It was quite common for ads to appear from Loudoun, Prince William, Fauquier and other counties. For example, on 17 December 1784 there was a notice of the sale in Frederick County of "About Fifty valuable SLAVES, consisting of men, women, and children, late the property of the Right Hon. Thomas Lord Fairfax." Most of the notices, however, were from the town itself or Fairfax County. There were many notices of land to be sold or rented, both in Alexandria and in the county, and some idea of miscellaneous business establishments in and about Alexandria. On 6 October 1785 a notice appeared of the opening of "The Alexandria Inn and Coffee House"; on 4 January 1787 another coffee house run by Nicholas Hannah; on 4 December 1788 "Evan McLean, At the Sign of the Orange Tree, on Harpers Wharf, Begs leave to inform his friends and the public that he has opened an Oyster

23. *The Virginia Journal and Alexandria Advertiser*, 25 March-23 September 1784; 6 January, 6 October 1785; 5 January 1786; 4 January 1787; 5 February, 4 December 1788, 26 March 1789; and *The Virginia Gazette and Alexandria Advertiser*, 3 September 1789.

ROYAL GIFT,

And the

Knight of Malta,

Two valuable imported Jack Asses,

WILL cover mares and jennies, at Mount-Vernon the ensuing spring, for three guineas the season, and two shillings and six-pence to the groom, for his care of, and attention to the females.—The first is of the most valuable race in the kingdom of Spain; the other of the best breed in the island of Malta.——ROYAL GIFT (now seven years old) has increased in size, since he covered last season.—— The KNIGHT of MALTA will be five years old this spring, about 14 hands high, most beautifully formed for an afs, and extremely light, active and sprightly:——Comparatively speaking resembling a fine courier.

Thefe two JACKS feem as if defigned for different purposes, but equally valuable.——The first, by his weight and great strength, to get mules for the flow and heavy draught.—The other by his activity and sprightliness, for quicker movements.——The value of mules, on account of their strength, longevity, hardiness and cheap keeping, is too well known to need defcription.

The money is to be paid before the mares or jennies are taken away, as no accounts will be kept.— Good pafture, well enclofed, will be provided at half a dollar per week, for the convenience of thofe who may incline to leave their mares or jennies, and every reafonable care will be taken of them; but they will not be infured against thefts, efcapes or accidents.

JOHN FAIRFAX, Manager.

Mount Vernon, March 12, 1789.

I WILL SELL

That Beautiful Seat,

WHERE I NOW LIVE,

Lying on Holmes's Run, *four miles from Alexandria.* It contains 60 acres of LAND, 30 are low ground

Advertisement for imported Jack Asses at Mount Vernon from The Virginia Gazette and Alexandria Advertiser, 26 March 1789.

House"; and in the same issue, William Page announced a "Merchants Coffeehouse . . . being furnished with most of the Eastern, Northern, and Southern News-Papers, likewise the Philadelphia Price-Current . . . hop[ing] to render this institution useful to the Merchants of Alexandria in Particular, and the Public in general." There was a brickyard "about a mile from the courthouse," with "a case or wall built for burning bricks . . ."; also a theatre and a Masonic Lodge. By 1788 the *Gazette* was published biweekly on Tuesday and Thursday, and in 1789 the name was changed to *The Virginia Gazette and Alexandria Advertiser*, which was printed by Samuel Hanson and Thomas Bond. The same year the "Academy" opened a second English school.[24]

Amidst all this commercial and cultural activity there were frequent reminders of the agrarian reality that was eighteenth-century Fairfax County. The 26 March issue of the *Gazette* published the following notice:

ROYAL GIFT

and the

Knight of Malta

Two valuable and imported Jack Asses, will cover mares and jennies, at Mount Vernon the ensuing spring, for three guineas the season, and two shilling and six pence to the groom, for his care of and attention to the females.

John Fairfax, Manager

By 1789, Alexandria was ready to receive its commercial crown, and even more was in the offing.

Commerce and Constitution

Commercial rivalry was long standing, between Virginia and Maryland, with much of the controversy arising over the Potomac River. By the charter of 1632 the southern boundary of Maryland was placed along the southern bank of the Potomac, which left the river and a small amount of Virginia shoreline, under the control of Maryland; on the other hand, at the point where the Potomac emptied into the Chesapeake, it was bounded on both sides by Virginia land. There was, therefore, constant controversy over taxation and regulation of traffic on the river. In an effort to work out the problems, the Virginia

---

24. Even though there was no newspaper in Alexandria with "Gazette" in the title until 1789, for general reference in the text hereafter, we shall use *Gazette* to avoid confusion. The full title of the newspaper will be given each time it changes up to 1800.

Assembly in June 1784 appointed four commissioners (George Mason, James Madison, Alexander Henderson, and Edmund Randolph) to meet with representatives from Maryland. Nothing happened for nearly a year, during which time no one bothered to notify the commissioners of their appointment. As it turned out, the Maryland commissioners were to meet with the Virginians at Alexandria in March 1785. Two or three days prior to the meeting, Mason received a letter from the Marylanders saying they would stop at Gunston Hall enroute to Alexandria; this was the first notice which Mason had either of the meeting or of his appointment as a commissioner. Mason, Henderson, and the Marylanders waited in vain at Henderson's Alexandria home for Randolph and Madison, finally adjourning to nearby Mount Vernon. The fact was that no one had sent Randolph and Madison a copy of the Assembly resolution which not only appointed them commissioners but also gave them power to act and told them what action was necessary. By chance, Washington, who significantly was not a commissioner, had at Mount Vernon a copy of a similar resolution affecting Pennsylvania which gave any two commissioners power to act. The Assembly resolution regarding Maryland required three commissioners, but not knowing this, Mason and Henderson proceeded to work out an agreement with the gentlemen from Maryland. Had he been notified more properly, Mason might have declined to serve (as he did at the more important Annapolis conference in late 1786), but as much out of hospitality toward the Marylanders as anything else, he could hardly have deserted when only he and Henderson were available, and thus he was drawn into the matter.[25]

The Mount Vernon conference did evolve into a similar meeting at Annapolis in September 1786, finally culminating in the federal convention at Philadelphia in May 1787. Mason was then sixty-two years old and might have been expected to decline an appointment to a convention in Philadelphia, a city he had never visited and which, if he attended, would involve him in the longest journey of his lifetime. However, when he and his neighbor among others, were appointed to represent Virginia, Mason consented to go. Four months later, September 1787, Mason and Washington had parted over the proposed constitution: Washington pledged to work for its ratification, and Mason was avidly against it. Mason, in fact, walked out of the convention and refused to sign the document. James Madison wrote Jefferson that Mason left Philadelphia "in an exceeding ill humour indeed," adding "His conduct has given great umbrage to the County of Fairfax, and particularly to the Town of Alexandria."[26]

25. Rutland, *Papers of George Mason*, 2:812-14, 826-27, 835-38; 3:885-87.
26. Boyd, *Papers*, 12:280.

The Constitution was first printed in the Alexandria Gazette on 13 September 1787, and reprinted several times thereafter. A couple of weeks later a notice appeared that the freeholders of Alexandria were requested to meet to appoint a committee to meet with the freeholders of Fairfax County at "Price's old Field" for the purpose of instructing their delegates to the Assembly," on a subject of the highest importance to their Existance and well being as a people." The result of this meeting was a strongly worded instruction to the Fairfax delegates to the Assembly, George Mason and David Stuart, that the freeholders of Fairfax supported the proposed new government, favored its adoption and wishes for the Assembly to call a convention to undertake ratification. This could only have been a bitter sentiment to Mason, a sentiment made even worse by the appointment of a committee of twenty county residents and nine Alexandrians to carry the instructions throughout the county so that the freeholders could individually sign.[27]

Beginning in late October, every issue of the Gazette carried at least one article on the constitution. The first was a three-column speech delivered in Philadelphia supporting ratification; following this was the first of a series "On the Federal Government" which remarked on the nonhereditary nature of the president and congress, "Our President bears no resemblance to a King" and the Senate "no Similitude to Nobles"; it was signed "An American Citizen." Later issues examined the various sections of the proposed constitution, one at a time. Not only was the constitution warmly endorsed, but Mason and his objections were held up to criticism and, if possible, ridicule. In late November a letter appeared over the signature "BRUTUS" setting forth Mason's objections in detail, and ending with the opinion that such objections were more "calculated . . . to alarm the fears of the people" than to achieve any good purpose. Further, Brutus declared, it would be "doubtful whether they were the production of Col. Mason's abilities," if his authority were not provable from other sources. Brutus appeared several more times with much the same message, being joined in the following issue by "Philanthropus" who also defended the constitution and criticized Mason.

The local sentiment was so strongly for ratification and against Mason that he was not elected to represent Fairfax County at the ratifying convention in Richmond in June 1788; the Fairfax delegates were David Stuart, Federalist friend of Washington, and Charles Simms

27. The Virginia Journal and Alexandria Advertizer, 13 September, 27 September, 11 October 1787. The committee consisted of Charles Broadwater, George Gilpin, Charles Little, William Payne, John Harper, Lund Washington, James Wren, John Moss, Thomas Pollard, Elisha C. Dick, William Thompson, Roger West, William Deneal [sic], Peter Wagener, Daniel McCarty, George Minor, and Thomas West, Esquires, also the Rev. David Griffith, Jeremiah Moore, and William Waters, "in the County," and William Hunter, Jun. [Mayor of Alexandria], Robert T. Hooe, William Hartshorne, James Keith, William Brown, William Herbert, Charles Simms, David Arell, and John Fitzgerald, Esquires, from Alexandria.

of Alexandria. Mason was encouraged to run in Stafford where anti-Federalist sentiment was stronger, and he made his contribution to the convention as a delegate from that county. The following June when news arrived of the ratification of the constitution, there were celebrations in Alexandria. Washington wrote of the "rejoicing in a place, the inhabitants of which are *ALL* Federal," noting that the "cannon roared and the town was illuminated."

Political sentiments aside, the Alexandrians had good reason to rejoice for it was already rumored that the new nation's capital might be located on the Potomac. Spurred on by such hopes, a group of Alexandria merchants served on a committee to make known the advantages of the Potomac for the federal city. There could only have been the greatest of rejoicing when in July 1790 the residence bill passed the new congress in New York, providing for the national capital on the Potomac. Indeed, Alexandria was included in the new federal district. Surely, many Alexandrians felt their city would be chosen for the capital, and Washington himself is said to have favored it, except for his being "confined to a choice on the east side of the Potomac."[28] The prospects for Alexandria, still part of Fairfax County, never seemed brighter, and prosperity for Alexandria would mean prosperity for all of Fairfax County. So it seemed in 1790.

Federalist Fairfax

It would seem at first glance that few in Fairfax County would have been dissatisfied with the economic and political progress of the county. There was, however, a serious crack or even a gaping hole in an old and formidable political bulwark in the county. George Washington and George Mason had been among the most important and most influential men in Fairfax County for over twenty years. Unquestionably, in 1790 they were *the* two outstanding citizens. They had served together as vestrymen for Truro Parish, and both attended Pohick Church; they had sat together on the bench of the county court; they had acted together in the closest concert to serve the county, the commonwealth, and the nation in the Revolution. Indeed, they *were* the Revolution for the county; and they were very good friends. In regard to the 1769 and 1770 nonimportation Association, the Fairfax Resolves, the move for independence, and on many other issues, Washington and Mason stood together and represented the gentry in Fairfax County. Certainly their combined opinions carried much weight with the lesser people in the county.

It was the opinion of the Marquis de Chastellux that the Revolution in Virginia was a process of "popular trust" by the uninformed masses "in

---

28. Stoessel, "Port of Alexandria," pp. 65-66.

'a small number of virtuous and enlightened citizens.' "[29] For Fairfax County, Washington and Mason were the most influential of the virtuous and enlightened citizens to whom the people had learned to turn for guidance. But now, Washington and Mason were political foes, having parted company over the issue of the constitution. For two men as important as Washington and Mason in the affairs of Fairfax County, men who had formerly stood so closely together, to differ so widely in opinion, to disagree so vehemently on an issue of such fundamental importance as the new federal constitution must have had a serious effect upon the social fabric of Fairfax County. Regrettably, little if any of the controversy can be known in any detail; however, it is certainly more than coincidence that on 17 August 1789 the justices of the Fairfax Court each "solemnly made oath that he would support the Constitution of the United States," and that on the same day George Mason, in a letter written at Gunston Hall to the Fairfax Court, resigned his office as justice of the peace in Fairfax County, an office he had held for over forty years since 1749.[30] Such action on Mason's part was surely motivated by his unwillingness to take an oath to support a constitution in which he could not in good conscience believe. In March 1790, Virginia Governor Beverley Randolph sent Mason a commission appointing him to the United States Senate. Mason refused the position, informing Governor Randolph that his action was necessitated by "my present State of Health (if I had no other Objection). . . ." Lund Washington, writing his cousin George on 28 April 1790, mentioned that Mason had considered it an insult and "D---n'd impudence to send him a Commission to act under a Government that he never had subscribed to, but had openly opposed & condemnd."[31] A man as important and visible as George Mason must have had many in Fairfax County who looked to him for leadership and who, with him or because of him, shared in his disillusionment. In this spirit, Mason prepared a petition for removal of the Fairfax courthouse from Alexandria (a move opposed by Washington), which was presented to the Assembly 3 November 1789. The editor of Mason's papers maintains that "A feud between George Mason and his 'country-party' adherents against the Alexandria town leaders had certainly been building since the autumn of 1787—first over ratification of the constitution and later over tax matters and turnpikes."[32] If the town of Alexandria was rejoicing over the new constitution and, by 1790, at being included in the new District of Columbia, it is at least possible, if

29. H. Trevor Colbourn, *The Lamp of Experience* (Chapel Hill: University of North Carolina Press, 1965), pp. 3-4.

30. Fairfax County Court Order Book, 1788-1792, 1:174-75.

31. Rutland, *Papers*, 3:1, 191-92.

32. Ibid., pp. 1, 184.

not probable, that many of the "country party" in Fairfax County were rejoicing because of the removal of Alexandria from the political affairs of the county.

_____

On 21 September 1784 the Fairfax Court, complying with an act of the Assembly, appointed Richard Chichester, George Gilpin, Charles Little, John Gibson, James Wren, and William Payne to take a list of the number of white persons, dwelling houses, and other buildings in Fairfax County. The returns showed that there were 3,687 whites, 594 dwelling houses, and 1,652 other buildings in the county. Doubtless many of these buildings were slave quarters, and some parallels between the number of slaves and the number of buildings owned can be made for some of the largest slaveowners.[33]

	Number of Slaves	Number of Other
George Washington	188	21
William Fitzhugh	122	22
George Mason	128	30
Alexander Henderson	72	25

In like manner, information from the personal property tax lists for 1782 will give some idea of the character of Fairfax County at that date.

Whites	928	(males over 21 only)
Blacks	3,559	(males and females, all ages)
Cattle	8,110	
Horses	3,091	
Wheels	140	(this is the total number of wheels on all the vehicles in the county)
Billiard tables	1	
Stud horses	23	(from 1783 list)
Ordinary licenses	9	

Ordinary Owners:
Samuel Bayly
James Collins
William Duvall
John Graham
Michael Gretter
John Lomax
Francis Summers
William Ware
John Wise   (owner of the billiard table)

33. Photographic copy of original manuscript. Library, Mount Vernon Ladies Association of the Union. (Courtesy John Castellani, Librarian.)

Similar information is available for every year after 1782. Because there are only small variations, we shall not reproduce it here.[34]

In spite of the war, the county court appears to have continued operating in a somewhat normal fashion. The county levies ran from a low of five pounds of tobacco per poll in 1783, to a high of thirty-one pounds per poll in 1785. The expenditures for these years were very similar to those of earlier years. Much of the remainder of courthouse business for the 1780s centers, in one way or another, around the courthouse, the courthouse lot, or the jail. In 1784, as a result of a petition of some Alexandria residents, they were allowed to erect a "markethouse" on the courthouse lot. Reporting on a court-ordered inspection of the jail in 1786, the inspectors found it "so filthy & uncleanly" as to "endanger the lives of those whose misfortunes subject them to confinement." Accordingly, the sheriff was ordered to keep the jail "more decent and cleanly." In 1788, Jacob Berry was given permission to erect "scales for the purpose of weighing hogs on the courthouse lot." It is unclear just how or why a markethouse and hog scale were allowed on the courthouse property, and as the records mention nothing about renting the lot, the assumption is that no rent was charged. If anything, these two incidents serve to exemplify the quasi-official nature of the atmosphere at the courthouse. Four men were authorized by the court to build mills during the 1780s; Amos Fox in 1786 on Difficult Run, Thomas Pollard in 1787 on Grants Castle Branch, Thomas Herbert in 1788 on Holmes Run, and Hepburn and Dundas in 1788 on Backlick. The extent and location of mills in Fairfax County during the entire eighteenth century is unclear. If Alexandria was rivaling Philadelphia and Baltimore in flour export, then, of necessity, milling was a major enterprise in the county. Yet the county records indicate fewer mills than would appear to be necessary to support such trade. It seems fair to conclude that the county court records are by no means a complete record of the number or location of mills in Fairfax County.

The large number of apprentices bound by the court in the 1780s sheds considerable light on the development and sophistication of Fairfax County, especially when compared to similar lists for earlier periods.

John Chew - joiner	Jacob Hineman - butler[35]
Chas. Hall - ship carpenter	Lewis Weston - ship carpenter
Michael Clark - cooper	David Shaon - house carpenter
John Longdon - taylor [sic]	Philip Conn - house carpenter
Washer Blunt - blockmaker	Richard Weightman - taylor [sic]

34. Fairfax County Personal Property Tax, 1782. Virginia State Library.

35. This man may or may not have been a butler in the twentieth-century definition. The eighteenth-century usage of this word described one who "has charge of the wine cellar and dispenses the liquor." *Oxford English Dictionary,* 1214. The word may carry a meaning which has been lost with time. It is, nonetheless, an interesting occupation to which to apprentice a thirteen-year-old boy.

John Elton - joiner
Edward Ramsay - joiner
Hugh Gibney - bricklayer
John Vernon - wheelwright; miller
Jacob Bond - house carpenter
Wm. Duvall - taylor [sic]
Robt. McDougal - taylor [sic]
French Simpson - seaman
Joseph Brownels - joiner
David Penticost - house carpenter
Wm. Trares - blacksmith
Thomas Jacobs - taylor [sic]
John Stuart - cabinetmaker
Thomas Mitchum - bricklayer
Robt. Findley - millright
Oliver Price - sadler
Wm. Jones - taylor [sic]

Beal Howard - butcher
Michael Sreiber - baker
Michael Reynolds - hatter
Andrew Jamison - baker
Geo. Hill - cooper
Peter Wilk - baker
Daniel McCallistre - millwright
Wm. Wright - stone mason
Aaron Hews - hatter
Anderson and Jamison - bakers
Edward Servis - blacksmith
John Smith - butcher
James Sillett - shoemaker
Wm. Rick - tanner
Samuel Shannon - tailor
Barten Martin - shoemaker

There are now two bricklayers, and a stone mason; a sadler, a cabinetmaker, two hatters, five bakers, and a butler. This information represents only those men practicing trades to which children were apprenticed and when taken with the available information on the growth of Alexandria, evidences that at least part of Fairfax County was not a backward agrarian wilderness, but a vigorously growing and flourishing society.

An interesting note reflecting on the level of sophistication in Alexandria from as early as 1781 is available from the correspondence of Thomas Jefferson. On 27 February 1781, Jefferson, who was then Governor of Virginia, wrote to John Fitzgerald, an Alexandria merchant, that "Messrs. Amable & Alex. Long of Alexandria advertised a Copy of the Encyclopedie for sale,"[36] which Jefferson subsequently purchased from Fitzgerald for the use of the commonwealth. It seems significant that in 1781, before there was even a newspaper in Alexandria, a merchant in that town felt he had a market for the Encyclopedie.

The usual number of crimes are mentioned in the court record book for the period: one case of bastardy, one of fornication, three of adultery, seventy-six cases of assault and battery, and one of retailing spirits without a license. Whatever economic or cultural developments there were, they did little, if anything, to temper the quality of justice dispensed by the court. On 24 June 1786, Michael Dulany was brought before the court for "behaving in a disorderly & riotous manner on Whitsun Monday last . . . "; Dulany was sentenced to 30 lashes at the

36. Boyd, Papers, 5:15, 311-12.

public whipping post on the back well laid on." For all of the nostalgic ruminations of later generations on the eighteenth century, it was a time of hard life, and perhaps was often lacking in the subtle refinements to which those later generations became accustomed.

The End of an Era

In January 1790, Fairfax County began its first full decade as a constituent part of the United States under the federal constitution. When the residence bill was passed in July of that year, Alexandria reacted with enthusiasm, for the future of the town seemed assured by the location of the new national capital on the Potomac. Surely some of the residents of the Fairfax County "backcountry" were also pleased by this turn of events; with the federal city on their doorstep, the county's prosperity also looked bright, and with Fairfax's leading citizen George Washington now leading the new republic, Fairfax County had reason to be proud of its contributions to the new nation.

Ironically, Fairfax County's second most eminent citizen, George Mason, continued to be an avowed foe of both the constitution and the new government. Mason, also at odds with the town of Alexandria, and leader of the emerging "Country party" in the county, expressed the sentiments of many in the county who were undoubtedly less than optimistic about the future.

> The Alexandrians, as usual, are very much bouyed up, on the Occasion, [location of the capital city on the Potomac] and think their Fortunes made for ever; altho' it is evident, to any cool impartial sensible Man, that if the Inland Navigation of Potomack & Shanandoe is effectually compleated, & the Seat of the Federal Government fixed near the Harbour of the Eastern Branch [Anacostia River], Alexandria must become a deserted Village.[37]

Whether Mason was really concerned about the fate of Alexandria, or was simply looking for any excuse to criticize the Alexandrians, and was reluctant to admit the possibility of even greater prosperity for the town, the history of Fairfax County in the 1790s again centers on Alexandria.

Thomas Jefferson arrived in Alexandria on the evening of 10 March 1790; he was on his way from Monticello to New York to serve as George Washington's Secretary of State. Jefferson came up through Colchester and probably took the Kings Highway to Alexandria. He failed to stop and see his friend George Mason at Gunston Hall, although both men wished to visit and discuss the new government. It was snowing heavily in Alexandria that day, and the following morning Jefferson noted in a letter "the snow is so deep I cannot get from the house to the stable. . . ."

37. Rutland, *Papers*, 3:1227.

Upon his arrival in Alexandria he was met by a number of citizens, and a public dinner was held in his honor at Wises' Tavern, where Will Hunter, Mayor of Alexandria, presented an address of welcome from the town, and Jefferson made a reply; doubtless, he was made aware of the hopes of the citizens that the national capital might be located there.[38] Later, when he was intimately involved in the negotiations for the location of the national capital, Jefferson's stop in Alexandria may have helped to bolster his instinctive preference for a site on the Potomac. Fearing he might have trouble on the road, the snow was, by his own report, eighteen inches deep, he sent his phaeton to New York by water, and left Alexandria by stage for Philadelphia.[39]

Alexandria continued to grow rapidly throughout the decade to the turn of the century. By 1800 there were two newspapers in the town and

38. Address of Welcome From the Mayor of Alexandria [to Jefferson]:

Alexandria the 10th of March 1790

SIR

You have returned to your native Country. Permit us the inhabitants of Alexandria to join with the rest of our fellow citizens in the warmest congratulations to you on that happy event. As a commercial town, we feel ourselves particularly indebted to you for the indulgencies which your enlightened representations to the Court of France have secured to our trade. You have freed commerce from its shackles, and destroyed the first essay made in this Country towards establishing a Monopoly. But we assure you that these events, though more recent, are not more deeply impressed on our minds, than the whole tenor of your conduct when we were struggling in the sacred cause of freedom. A sense of the benefits we have already derived from your talents and virtue, in the various offices you have filled, induces us to entertain the most auspicious hopes from your arrival at this crisis; when a constitution newly adopted, and which is to decide the fate of republican forms of Government, is commencing its operations; and when subjects of the highest importance to the Union must necessarily be discussed. That you, Sir, in every walk of life may meet with the reward of your meritorious services and fulfill the high expectations of a free and republican people is our sincere wish.

In behalf of the Citizens of Alexandria

WILL. HUNTER, JR. MAYOR

[Jefferson's] Response to the Address of Welcome

Alexandria, Mar. 11, 1790

SIR

Accept my sincere thanks for yourself and the worthy citizens of Alexandria, for their kind congratulations on my return to my native country.

I am happy to learn that they have felt benefit from the encouragements to our commerce which have been given by an allied nation. But truth and candor oblige me at the same time to declare you are indebted for those encouragements solely to the friendly dispositions of that nation which has shown itself ready on every occasion to adopt all arrangements which might strengthen our ties of mutual interest and friendship.

Convinced that the republican is the only form of government which is not eternally at open or secret war with the rights of mankind, my prayers and efforts shall be cordially contributed to the support of that we have so happily established. It is indeed an animating thought that, while we are securing the rights of ourselves and our posterity, we are pointing out the way to struggling nations who wish, like us, to emerge from their tyrannies also. Heaven help their struggles, and lead them, as it has done us, triumphantly thro' them.

Accept, Sir, for yourself and the citizens of Alexandria the homage of my thanks for their civilities, & the assurance of those sentiments of respect & attachment with which I have the honor to be, Sir, your most obedient and most humble servt.,

TH: JEFFERSON

Boyd, *Papers*, 16:222-25.

39. Dumas Malone, *Jefferson and the Rights of Man* (Boston: Little Brown and Co., 1951), p. 254.

two more had been lost along the way. *The Virginia Journal and Alexandria Advertiser*, begun in 1784, had ceased publication in 1789, being taken over and renamed *The Virginia Gazette and Alexandria Advertiser* that same year; this continued until November 1793 when it too discontinued publication. In the meantime, in November 1792, *The Columbian Mirror and Alexandria Gazette* began and continued publication until 1800. So, for the year between November 1792 and November 1793, Alexandria had two newspapers; after April 1797 with the publication of *The Times* and the *District of Columbia Daily Advertiser*, there were again two newspapers in the town. The Alexandria newspapers of the 1790s show a clear development from the eighteenth-century style, to what was to become the nineteenth-century form. While continuing to have only four pages, the number of columns per page increased from three to four, and the issues per week were increased from two to three (Tuesday, Thursday, and Saturday) as early as 1794. The advertisements also took on a more commercial appearance, differing from the more straightforward approach of earlier times.

By 1790 Jenckes, Windsor and Company were among many merchants advertising general merchandise and such luxuries as "an elegant PHAETON . . . and a few neat painted FREE-MASONS APRONS." In the same year, Hepburn and Dundas, who had been granted permission to erect a mill in 1788, now offered it for rent. It was described as "situated on Back-Lick and Indian Runs, about 6-miles from Alexandria, and 1½ miles from Prices Tavern." The house was four floors and thirty feet square; its recommendation "both for merchant and county work . . . " suggests that Fairfax County mills were grinding grain both for local consumption, and on commercial account for export.[40] As the mill was being rented so soon after construction and advertised with "works entirely new," it may have been built with the intention of renting it, indicating a prosperous market for flour.

The following year, 1791, Gilbert Harrow notified the public that he "continues," at a new location, to teach English, Latin, Greek, French, writing, arithmetic, bookkeeping, geography, geometry, trigonometry, navigation, astronomy, gauging, algebra, conic sections, fluxions, fortification, gunnery, and land surveying. For the "Classical Scholars," he offered ancient and modern history, composition in English, Latin and French, and lectures on natural history, natural and moral philosophy and logic. He also owned a telescope "of power sufficient to discover the Satellites of Jupiter, Saturn's Rings, etc. [sic]. . . ."[41]

Among the events of special note in 1792 was the establishment of the Bank of Alexandria on 23 November, making it the first bank in

40. *The Virginia Gazette and Alexandria Advertiser*, 7 January 1790.
41. Ibid., 13 January 1791.

Virginia. By 1794 the total assets of the bank were $357,636.74; they rose to $851,356.08 by 1800. Also in 1792, there was an unusually large number of notices of land for sale on "long credit," as well as many lots and houses in Alexandria for sale or rent. On 9 February 1792, under the heading "Vive Le President!" was inserted a notice for a ball to be held on 13 February "in celebration of the BIRTH OF THE PRESIDENT OF THE UNITED STATES."

By 1793 the paper was full of notices indicating expansion and growth. The first available issue of the *Gazette* for that year, 14 March, printed a notice of James Wilson offering to sell "A KILN OF BRICKS', about 100,000 and some stone." John Beatty and Henry Walker informed the public that they had opened a "Biscuit baking business"; Henry Piercy advertised an "Earthen Ware Manufactory"; and John Kerr advertised mild ale, table beer, and whisky for sale "at his Brewery and distillery in Alexandria." There were also two notices relating to education: the Alexandria Academy needed "A teacher . . . to take charge of the Mathematical school. . . ," and "H. Wilbar, Late Master of the Steine House Academy, Brighthelmston," opened a new academy offering English, writing, arithmetic, and bookkeeping, at two dollars per month, "Pens and Ink Included." With the federal city now under construction across the river, the Alexandria paper printed advertisements of land for sale in "Washington City" as well as plans of the proposed seat of government. When *The Columbian Mirror and Alexandria Gazette* made its appearance in November 1792, it was printed Wednesday and Saturday of every week by Ellis Price "at the East End of the Market-House." This could conceivably have been the same market house erected on the courthouse lot in 1784. The general development of the early 1790s continued on through the decade: more merchants and more complicated and sophisticated enterprises; much land for sale or rent in the county, in town, and across the river in Washington city; and more general development of the area. By way of random example, in 1793 the *Gazette* carried a notice of a lottery "for the improvement of the Federal City," 50,000 tickets at seven dollars each for a total of 350,000 dollars. The grand prize was to be a "superb hotel" valued at $50,000.

By 1794 one might see an advertisement for "the Alexandria Book store," or notice of "McMann & Sittler, Coppersmiths & Tinmen," from whom one might purchase kettles and pans of numerous variety, including tin plates and dishes, bake pans, tin ovens, sheet iron stoves, scales and weights, gutters and spouts, as well as "stills of all sizes." John Beale operated a "copper and Tin Manufactory" as did James Jobson; John Kitten advertised as a "Tailor & Habit-Maker," and Charles Jones "Coach and Chair Maker." In 1795 there was a public notice for men to carry the mail between Baltimore and Alexandria. Such men were required to meet the following schedule: From 1 April until 1 November,

mol alarming nature. It
not only with the Creeks,
evitable. The fale of the
d States will be totally de-
t, inltead of a reduction of
on of hoftil ies with the
inftead of peace—and the
lars by the inability of the
ands, will be the fruits of
reculations of a few indivi-
s bufinefs is indifpenfable ;
ietefh the tranquility of the
among the peculiar guar-
ice, are concerned in it,
ations, and their country's
G. U. S.

RLESTON, Jan. 2 4.
gia, which difpofes of the
ts that it fhall be granted
s called the Georgia Com-
James Gunn, Matthew
nd their offociates, for the
aid in fpecie, bank bills of
ts for the years 91, 92,
e governor, the prefident
houfe of reprefentatives :
in the treafury previous
ander to be paid on or be-
r next : whenever the laft
or is to fign the grant.
d out of this tract for the
and to be granted as the

d the Georgia Miffifippi
d to Nicholas Long, Tho-
n, and Thomas Cumming
of 155,000 dollars, pay-
ollars to be depofited in
act ; the remainder on or
next.
led the Upper Miffifippi
John B. Scott, John C.
en, 35,000 dollars, pay-
revions to paffing the act ;
ie firft day of November

d the Tenneffee Company
x. Mathias Maher, and
ollars; 12,000 dollars to
ander on or before the firft

eorgia Miffifippi company
pper Miffifippi company,
the Tenneffee Company,
the citizens of the ftate.

is in a charming fituation. What if the Algerines were
to conftitute him their Dey, and then oblige him to declare war againft his other domeftics ?

Fitzgerald's Night
" Which either makes him or undoes him quite !"

.'is not in Mortals to command fuccefs !
But h'll do more—endeavor to deferve it.

" Ufe the Player's well ; for they are the abftract and
brief Chronicle of the times !"

The meeting of a very refpectable fraternity on this evening,
has induced Mr. Fitzgerald to affix his Beneft for
Monday next, with the agreeable hope of enjoying the
full patronage of a kind public.

On Monday Evening March 2,
A new Prelude never yet performed, entitled
JONATHAN
IN JAMAICA ; OR THE CREDULOUS YANKEE.

Jonathan,	Mr. Fitzgerald.
Fingercafh,	Mr. Smith.
Acid,	Mr. Kedey.
And Capt. O'Donnavan,	Mr. M'Grath.
Louifa,	Mifs Marfhall.

The Comedy of THE
RECRUITING OFFICER.

Captain Plume,	Mr. Andrews.
Sergeant Kite,	Mr. M'Grath.
Juftice Balance,	Mr. Smith.
Worthy,	Mr. Kedey.
Bullock,	Mr. Fitzgerald.
Recruits, Conftable,	by Affiftants.
And Captain Brazen,	Mr. Fitzgerald.
Melinda,	Mrs. Kedey.
Rofe,	Mrs. M'Grath.
Lucy,	Mrs. Moore.
And Sylvia,	Mrs. Decker.

Collins' Siege of TROY,
by Mr. Fitzgerald.

The celebrated Scotch Song of Bonny Jem of Aberdeen—
by Mifs Marfhall.

The FRENCH ANATOMIST :

IS hereby given
I ed from the p
longer confidere
the houfe ; the b
ufual under the
charged with the

A. N
RETURN t
the public
have received in
refpectfully infor
now opening a
Water ftreets, fo
which the Eighte
Morhoufe expect
in the Flour and
nity of offering h
pleafe to favour
tion line or oth
George Young
and will conduct
Alexandria.
Feb. 12, 1705

GA
A CHOICE
ry ufeful ;
perfectly frefh ;
rowfat Peas, Gr
Savoy, Drumhe
Turnip, Stone di
Orange Carrot, e
early Cucumber,
four forts, Spinna
JO
Alexandria. Fe

Vice Confulfhip o
29 Pluviofe, i
indivifible, (1
ALL the G
of the Sc
(that has been acc
r4th inftant in th
Magazines of the
red to give a copy
ful of the faid R
prices of their dei
turned to them.
The American

Advertisement for plays to be performed at Alexandria in The Virginia Gazette and
Alexandria Advertiser, 28 February 1795.

leave Baltimore every Monday, Wednesday, and Friday mornings and arrive in Alexandria the same day by six in the evening; leave Alexandria Tuesday, Thursday and Saturday mornings to arrive in Baltimore by half past four in the afternoon. From November until April the schedule was roughly the same, except that the rider only had to go from Baltimore to Georgetown the same day and then to Alexandria the next morning. There was an often repeated advertisement for "Imported Garden Seeds . . . at Mr. Swoope's store . . ." and frequent notices of plays and theatrical presentations of various kinds. *The Columbian Mirror*, 28 February 1796, gave notice, with much ado, a full column long, of "A new Prelude never yet performed, entitled *Jonathan in Jamaica*; or the credulous Yankee." This was to be followed by a new comedy *"The Recruiting Officer,"* and the evening would conclude with *"The French Anatomist*; or Sham Doctor." Tickets were to be had "at the usual places," indicating that the theatre was a regular feature of Alexandria's cultural life.

The Alexandria Town Council, among other duties, regulated the quality of bread sold in the town.[42] The standard price of a loaf of bread being three pennies, the council stipulated the weight of a loaf in relation to the price of wheat. The loaf had to weigh 23 ounces when flour was at 22 to 25 shillings per barrel and varied as follows.

Weight of loaf	Price of flour per barrel
21 ounces	25-27 shillings
19	28-31
17	32-35
15	36-39
14	40-44
13	45-48
12	49-52
11	53-57
9½	63-67
9	68-72
8½	73-77
8	78-82
7½	83-86
7	87-90

This allowed for almost a fourfold increase in the price of flour, and if the price actually fluctuated that widely, then the economic conditions were less stable than might appear from other sources. This action may also be seen as careful regulation of business in a society which we are often told

42. *The Columbian Mirror and Alexandria Gazette*, 29 February 1796.

was weaned on the "free enterprise" system; the evidence of regulation in the sale of not only bread, but tobacco, pork, and beef, and control of the erection of mills and roads indicates that free enterprise, as it is often interpreted in the twentieth century, did not exist in the eighteenth.

There was definitely a proliferation of business enterprises of all sorts in Alexandria in the 1790s, as evidenced in both the manufacturing and retailing operations. Alexandria was an important commercial town, and the prospect of the national capital across the Potomac combined with hopes of opening the navigation of that river inland promised much future growth. As most of this growth had taken place in a period of about twenty years, and as the growth certainly occasioned a change in priorities, it is understandable that some of the "country" residents of Fairfax felt their way of life threatened. When George Mason died in the autumn of 1792, a certain amount of the open conflict between the town and the county probably subsided. Mason had been the acknowledged leader of the "anti-town" faction and the most literate thinker in the county, surpassing even Washington.

The overseers of the poor met at Price's Ordinary in September 1790 and presented bills amounting to £258 14s. 11d. for the relief of about 36 poor persons. This was a meeting of the overseers for both districts of the county, a procedure which continued henceforth to determine the amount expended and the number of poor living in the entire county. (The overseers for this year were Peter Wagener, John Moss, George Minor, Simon Summers, Thomazin Ellzey, and Richard Simpson.) By 1796 the bill for the poor had risen to £ 306 14s. 4¾d., and while the total amount was stated in pounds, shillings, and pence, the assessment per poll was set at 32 cents. The following year, when the meeting was held at James Wren's tavern, the sum for the poor was 319 dollars and 23 cents. This is one of the very first instances of the term dollars being used in the public record, a full twenty years after the declared independence from Great Britain. Two years later in 1799, the expenditures for the poor had apparently increased over six times to $1,919.72, an increase which appears to be unexplainable. However, the rate per poll had risen only twelve cents, from 32 cents in 1796 to 44 cents in 1799. It is also possible to calculate, using the number of tithables and the per poll rate of 32 cents, that the total assessment of £306 14s. 4¾d. for 1796 was equal to $1,022.40. What, therefore, needs to be explained is not the high figure for 1799, but the $319.23 for 1797.

Throughout all the controversy concerning Alexandria, the turnpike, the national capital, and the new United States Constitution, the Fairfax County Court went about its business of governing the county, albeit with some controversy among the justices, and between the justices and the citizens. The county levy ran from six pounds of tobacco per poll in 1790, to eleven pounds in 1792. In 1797, along with those of the overseers of the poor, all the expenditures for the county were expressed in dollars and cents; the county budget for 1797 was $913.29, and the tax rate was 21 cents per poll. This is the first county budget expressed in familiar money terms.

Fairfax County Levy, 23 November 1797[43]

Lewis Summers, Deputy Sheriff	$ 45.82
Robert Moss, " "	16.87
Simon Thomas, Jailer	232.46[44]
John Moss, Sheriff	73.20
Peter Wagener, Clerk	127.84
John Thomas, for two record books	20.00
George, for half the cost of a stove for the courthouse	9.20
[To the sheriff for collecting $801.64 to 6%]	48.12
Fraction remaining in Sheriffs hands	63.29
	$913.29

4,349 Tithables at 21 cents each.

In December 1791 and again in January 1792, the court was petitioned and granted permission for a "general innoculation of the smallpox" as there was an infection of that disease which threatened to spread. In December 1797 the court allowed the sheriff 30 cents per day for maintaining prisoners in the county jail; this was probably 30 cents per day for all the prisoners and included "1¼ lbs. of fresh meat & 1¼ lbs. of good wheat bread made of fine flour each day." It also was "ordered that a copy of this order be stuk [sic] up in each apartment of the goal." At this same December 1797 session of the court, the jailer, Simon Thomas. was charged with not giving the prisoners the proper allowance of food and with "extorting illegal fees from prisoners." John Moss, the sheriff, was called into court to explain "his neglect of supervising the jailor"; finally, in January 1798, the jailer was ordered to furnish fires for the prisoners in cold weather.

By the spring of 1798, that portion of Loudoun County between the former and the present county line had been returned to Fairfax County, and the commissioners, Charles Little, David Stuart, William Payne, James Wren, and Geo. Minor, were about the business of erecting a

43. Fairfax County Court Order Book, 1797-1798, 23 November 1797.

44. This amount may include the allotment for the maintenance of the prisoners. It also must be remembered that officials who appear to earn less than the jailer, i.e., the sheriff and the clerk, also received fees for their services such as the $48.12 to the sheriff for collecting the levy. In reality the clerk and sheriff both earned much more than the jailer.

courthouse "on the lands of Richard Ratcliffe," which is where the courthouse still stands. The court provided that the courthouse be 40 feet by 30 feet, "with a 12 [foot] portico [,] one gaol [jail] 40 x 20 with 3 rooms on the 1st floor & 2 on the 2nd with an addition to the back below of a room 15 x 10 [,] one clerks office 24 x 18 to be arched or covered with slate or tile & one gaolers house 24 x 18 with stocks [,] pillory & whipping post."[45]

There is no evidence that there was any unusual activity respecting the tobacco warehouses during the 1790s. The court continued to regulate the tobacco inspections with Colchester, Alexandria, and Falls warehouses specifically mentioned in the court minute book. (It would be most interesting to know if the local lands, which had now been farmed for over 100 years, still gave a good yield of tobacco and if the majority of the tobacco brought to the warehouses was grown in Fairfax or elsewhere.)

In 1705 the Assembly authorized the trustees of the roads from the valley to Alexandria to erect turnpike gates and collect tolls. This arrangement was apparently used on three roads in the county: the road which passed the Falls Church, the road which later became Little River Turnpike, and a road from Alexandria to Georgetown. The toll receipt book for "Turnpike Gate No. Two" on one of these roads for the period 20 August 1792 to 14 July 1793 lists the name of each person to pass the gate, whether he was driving a carriage, riding chair, wagon, or cart, and lists the fee paid; the book records 1,186 vehicles passing the gate during

Table XII

	Carriages	Chairs	Wagons	Carts
August 20-31, 1792	6	11	13	10
September 1792	10	31	39	13
October 1792	27	25	32	17
November 1792	18	22	103	14
December 1792	4	7	95	18
January 1793	3	1	80	19
February 1793	0	3	22	3
March 1793	1	2	75	9
April-May 1793[46]	7	11	154	15
June 1793	17	10	150	9
July 1-15, 1793	5	7	63	5
Totals	98	130	826	132

45. Fairfax County Order Book, 1797-1798, 22 May 1798, p. 10.

46. April and May 1793 have been counted together of necessity, as a page appears to be missing from the book on which was kept the records for 27 April through 15 May 1793.

The Washington Family by Edward Savage, c. 1796. Left to right: George Washington Parke Custis, George Washington, Eleanor Custis, Martha Washington; in background on right, perhaps William Lee, Washington's bodyservant. National Gallery of Art.

this period and the revenue collected at £ 60 8s. Table XII indicates the number of each type of vehicle to pass the gate for each month covered by the receipt book.[47] Several things become evident at once. The most numerous type of vehicle on the road was the wagon; there were, in fact, over six times as many wagons as any other form of traffic. And, of course, wagon traffic was the very issue that most annoyed the Fairfax tithables who had to keep the roads in repair, for the wagons put excessive wear on the road and brought little direct benefit to the local residents. The number of wagons indicates the importance of this commerce to the city of Alexandria; on January 7 and 8, 1793, twenty-five wagons passed this toll gate and they are all entered in the book as belonging to a stranger, perhaps a caravan of goods from the valley on its way to the port of Alexandria. The seasonal variation in the number of wagons is of interest, but the variance cannot be accounted for. [47]

Turnpike gate number two was most likely either on the road to Falls Church or on the road from Alexandria to Georgetown. As it

47. Fairfax County Court Records, item no. 14, Account Book kept by Joseph Birch, Keeper of Turnpike Number 2, from 20 August 1792 to 15 July 1793, Fairfax County Court Records, Earl Gregg Swem Library, The College of William and Mary in Virginia.

happens, President George Washington is listed in this toll book twice: the first time 9 October 1792 when he paid for three carriages, and the second time 13 April 1793 when he paid for one carriage; on both occasions the president was leaving his home to return to his official residence in Philadelphia.[48] There is a great deal to be understood about the eighteenth century from the fact that Washington, who was not only the premier citizen of Fairfax County but also President of the United States, paid one shilling and three pence for the privilege of using the road from Alexandria to Georgetown as would any other citizen. He did not travel with a small army, such as would accompany a European king or later American presidents, and it was not necessary to protect his person or to impress the local inhabitants with such an array. For him to have acted, or to have been treated in any other manner, would have betrayed the principles for which he had fought in the Revolution.

There were at least two other major accomplishments regarding the roads in Fairfax County during the 1790s. The earliest private turnpike charter in Virginia was granted in 1796 to the "President, Manager, and Company of the Fairfax and Loudoun Turnpike Road." The road itself was not built until after 1800, and then it was done by another company.[49] Nevertheless, the beginning of the turnpike system in Virginia was in Fairfax County with this 1796 charter. The second major event was the 1797 opening of the first bridge to span the Potomac; it was located at the Little Falls. Built by a Maryland-chartered company, it was first known as Falls Bridge and later by its still familiar name, Chain Bridge;[50] the important matter is that Fairfax County was the southern terminus of this important bridge.

The continual problem of locating other roads in the county is evident from this extract from the court minute book for 15 February 1790:

> We the . . . subscribers . . . viewed the road from the Little Falls Road to the Great Falls road as follows viz, Beginning at or near Mr. Thrifts Gate opposite his house than a direct course thro' the said Thrifts Turnip Patch to the top of a hill in his old field thence along that ridge til it intersects the Great Falls road at or near the corner of John Jackson's fence . . . .

There is no way to determine the location of Thrift's gate, Thrift's turnip patch, or John Jackson's fence. In 1790 these were real landmarks, probably known to most county residents, and in that context they served the purpose of laying out a new road. For our purpose in trying to locate that road, they are totally useless. The same may be said of a

---

48. Fitzpatrick, *Writings* 32:175-77 (7 October 1792), pp. 418-19 (13 April 1793).
49. Harrison, *Landmarks*, p. 564.
50. Ibid., p. 566.

Gunston Hall, home of George Mason, river front. Photo by Charles Baptie.

particularly graphic example from 19 June 1796: that a road was to be "opened from [the] white oak 150 yards below [the] red house thence to a parcel of rocks & along a parcel of broken bushes. . . . " We shall have to be content for the present with the knowledge that new roads were built throughout the county from about 1730 on, and that the county court designated when and where such roads were to be built.

Soon after the Fairfax Court occupied the present courthouse in April 1800, the federal government took possession of that portion of Fairfax County which now comprises Arlington County and much of Alexandria City. It seems somehow appropriate that the death of George Washington on 14 December 1799 coincided so closely with the occupation of the new Fairfax courthouse, and that in point of time it was so near the end of the eighteenth century. His death marked the end of an era. Washington, who had been so important to Fairfax County, represented the old order which was now past; and the new courthouse would be associated with the future. But things would never be the same, and perhaps never again would Fairfax County assume the position of national importance which it held in the late eighteenth century.

1800 — 1840

Janice Artemel

I

The Population and Economy
of Fairfax County

The final decade of the eighteenth century was the end of an era, the closing period after the war years which culminated with the death of George Washington in 1799. His death was symbolic of changes in both Fairfax County and the nation as a whole. It has been said that the national election of 1800 was also a revolutionary turning point in American history with the election of Thomas Jefferson and the transfer of power from one set of partisans to another. The election "gave impetus to the dogma of local sovereignty that would set the stage for the sectional conflict of mid-century; it turned the direction of growth toward the limitless West . . . and it loosed in America the humanistic forces that would ultimately endow the common man with worth and dignity."[1]

For several decades after the turn of the century, there was significant change in the population of Fairfax County. This change was in both actual numbers and composition and was due to some basic factors, including the loss of Alexandria in 1801 to the Federal District and to changes in the agricultural and economic patterns of the country and nation as a whole.

In general, there was a decline in the total population of the county after 1800, as can be seen in Table I. The most dramatic loss occurred between 1810 and 1830; between 1830 and 1840 there was a slight increase in the population. Fairfax County's population was heaviest in Fairfax Parish, which was the northeastern half of the political juris-diction. This concentration remains so in present times. Fairfax Parish included the developing town of Falls Church, which a contemporary

---

1. Charles M. Wiltse, *The New Nation, 1800-1845* (New York: Hill and Wang, 1961), p. 1 (hereinafter cited as Wiltse, *The New Nation*).

mapmaker simply called Wren's after Col. James Wren's tavern which was situated near the crossroads of the routes from either Alexandria, Georgetown, or the Falls Bridge (Chain Bridge) to either the new county courthouse or Loudoun County and Leesburg.[2] Population also grew during this period at Fairfax Court House, incorporated as Providence in 1805, and at the town of Centreville.[3] The 1820 census is grouped into five areas for enumeration: Centreville, Providence, Truro Parish, Fairfax Parish, and Colchester. By the nineteenth century, however, Colchester was rapidly losing population, while its neighbor Occoquan in Prince William County was gaining.[4]

A scientific analysis of the composition of the population is difficult because of the irregularity in the recording of population statistics.[5] Some records were lost after the War of 1812, and even though a federal census has been compiled regularly since 1790, methods of reporting and recording are constantly changing. For example, during the years after the Revolution when the political jurisdictions which had been created by the Church of England were retained, the population was listed by parish. More recently, however, population was noted by political units.

Alexandria should be included in a discussion of Fairfax County, since historically it was a geographic, political, economic and social focal point of the county. Even though it was not technically a political part of the county after 1801, it remained a center for the county residents.

As shown in Table I, the total population of Fairfax County in 1810 was 13,111, of which 6,626 constituted the total white population, and 7,028 black, both free and slave. The population of Alexandria (See Table II) for the same time period was 7,227, of which 4,903 were white, 1,488 black slave, and 836 were listed as "others not taxed," which may indicate that they were, at least in part, free blacks as well as Indians and foreigners. These figures serve to demonstrate the basic economic pattern of the predominantly rural county, the urban and commercial flavor of Alexandria, as well as the nature of the slavery system in Virginia. Despite the fact that wealth was concentrated in Alexandria due to the numerous profitable economic enterprises centered there, the ratio of slaves to whites was about 1 to 4 in the city, while the ratio in the rural

2. Jonathan Lovette, "Sketch and Table of Distances" (1801). Copy in the Falls Church Public Library. An especially prepared version of this map is located in *Falls Church: History of a Virginia Village* by Tony P. Wrenn, (Falls Church, Va.: Historical Commission of the City of Falls Church, 1972), p. 9.

3. U.S. Decennial Census, 1790, 1810, 1820, 1830, 1840, National Archives, Washington, D.C. (Microcopy at Fairfax County Public Library.)

4. Edith Moore Sprouse, *Colchester: Colonial Port on the Potomac* (Fairfax, Virginia: Fairfax County Office of Comprehensive Planning, 1975), pp. 104-11.

5. Methods had not yet become standardized for census taking, and the questions asked and the categories created had been in constant flux since the first federal census. There is no extant census for the year 1800.

Table I
Population of Fairfax County
1790-1840

	White	Black		Total
		Slave	Free	Population
1790				
Male	—	—	—	—
Female	—	—	—	—
Total	—	—	—	12,320*
1810				
Male	3,269	—	—	—
Female	3,357	—	—	—
Total	6,626	6,485	543	13,654**
1820				
Male	3,057	2,140	497	5,702
Female	3,092	2,285	243	5,620
Total	6,149	4,433	740	11,322**
1830				
Male	2,467	2,047	146	4,660
Female	2,426	1,955	165	4,546
Total	4,893	4,002	311	9,206**
1840				
Male	2,645	1,713	211	4,569
Female	2,794	1,738	237	4,769
Total	5,439	3,451	448	9,338**

SOURCE: United States Decennial Census, 1790, 1810, 1820, 1830, 1840,
National Archives, Washington, D.C.
*Includes population of Alexandria
**Does not include population of Alexandria

county was nearly 1 to 1, even though the economic circumstances in farming areas of northern Virginia would not indicate an ability to support a slave system. One note should be inserted here concerning the number of blacks, both free and slave. The laws of Virginia made it extremely difficult for free blacks legally to remain in the county between 1806 and the Civil War, a fact that was equally true in Alexandria.[6] This means that the population figures for blacks during these years should be viewed with a certain amount of skepticism, as they most likely are low. Not only would there be more free blacks than are listed, but also some whites may have listed freed blacks as slaves, since there were legal difficulties in remaining free in the state.

6. See Ch. 4, herein for legal difficulties encountered by blacks in this period.

Table II
Population of Alexandria
1790-1830

| | White | Black | | Total |
		Slave	Free*	Population
1790				
Male	1,214	—	—	—
Female	939	—	—	—
Total	2,153	543	52	2,748
1810				
Male	2,525	—	—	—
Female	2,378	—	—	—
Total	4,903	1,488	836	7,227
1820				
Male	2,667	606	461	3,734
Female	2,948	802	707	4,457
Total	5,615	1,408	1,168	8,191
1830				
Male	2,712	565	462	3,739
Female	2,969	816	739	4,524
Total	5,681	1,381	1,201	8,263

SOURCE: United States Decennial Census, 1790, 1810, 1820, 1830, National Archives, Washington, D.C.
*Category also includes Indians, the number not specified, if any.

Fairfax County population declined between 1810 and 1830, but the number of persons residing in Alexandria increased dramatically between 1810 and 1820, with the growth of the Federal District and the anticipated benefits to Alexandria. In addition, the number of "others not taxed" grew by nearly half. The slave population, however, dropped slightly in this time period. The years between 1820 and 1830 were not good for Alexandria with the economic depression in the early part of the decade having a decided effect on the economy of Alexandria. In addition, there was fear created by the yellow fever outbreak of 1821, and some persons left the city. The number of persons contracting and dying from the disease was much less than the number from the epidemics of yellow fever in 1800, 1802, 1803, and 1804, when nearly half the population of 6,000 left the city, and more than 200 died.[7]

7. Wyndham B. Blanton, *Medicine in Virginia in the Nineteenth Century* (Richmond: Garrett & Massie, 1933), p. 236. Blanton is citing the description by Elisha Cullen Dick in *Medical Repository*, 7(1804):190; 8(1805)18.

Migration was a major factor in the population decline and underlying reason for the migration was the depletion of the soil after generations of tobacco planters had given little thought to methods of productivity. As a consequence, the tobacco yield lessened tremendously. In conjunction with this factor, trade embargoes with European nations in the early nineteenth century made it difficult to sell tobacco. These two reasons, plus the dwindling size of farms as land was divided again and again among successive generations, made tobacco farming increasingly unprofitable.

At the same time there was the beckoning call of life in the West, especially to the frontiers of Kentucky and Ohio. During these early decades of the nineteenth century, therefore, many leading families of Fairfax County and Alexandria began the legendary westward migration. It is quite easy to trace the direct migration of Fairfax County persons to counties of Kentucky or Ohio, and then to follow them on to Missouri a few years later. A large number of settlers from the county, including old families named Darne, Wren, Blackburn, Davis, and Broadwater settled Callaway County, Missouri.[8]

One of the early families to leave the county was that of William and Nancy Jones who followed George Rogers Clark to Kentucky after their marriage in 1785.[9] According to family tradition, their son John Jones, born 9 September 1786, was the first white boy born in what is now Louisville, Kentucky. Mrs. Jones was a granddaughter of Col. Thomas Wren, an early resident and vestryman of Truro Parish, who held large amounts of land in Fairfax and Loudoun counties.

Another early emigrant was the Reverend William Talbott who was in Pike County, Ohio, before 1801.[10] Reverend Talbott was a grandson of Col. John West, a member of the Virginia House of Burgesses.

The most westward movement, however, occurred in later decades. Ann Trammell, who married John S. Cartwright, moved to Dandridge, Jefferson County, Tennessee, in 1816, and William John Trammell was in Knoxville, Tennessee, by 1816.[11] Both were grandchildren of "Gentleman" John Trammell, Sr., who was a large landowner in Fairfax. Several of the children of Col. James Wren went as Methodist missionaries to Shelby County, Kentucky, after the Honorable Simon Adams, son of Col. William Adams of Fairfax County, settled in Shelby County with his wife Catherine Wren in 1786.[12]

Added to this outward flow of persons to the West was the attraction of the towns and cities in the developing nation. Some persons were

8. Melvin Lee Steadman, Jr., *Falls Church: By Fence and Fireside* (Falls Church, Va.: Falls Church Public Library, 1964), p. 47 (hereinafter cited as Steadman, *Falls Church*).

9. Ibid., p. 512.

10. Ibid., p. 461.

11. Ibid. p. 442.

12. Ibid. p. 225.

attracted to the life as a trader or craftsman in Alexandria, Washington, or Georgetown, if not the larger cities of Philadelphia, New York, or Boston. A contemporary writer passing through Richmond in 1825 remarked: "Many of the citizens of Alexandria have quit that city and come to this place with a view of bettering their fortunes."[13]

This was not only a time of change for the white population, but it also included the black population in a different manner. It had become increasingly popular after the War of Independence to free slaves when the owner died, thereby increasing the number of free blacks. In consequence of this, a law restricting manumission was enacted.

It was apparent to the legislators in Richmond that a law prohibiting manumission would cause a reaction among the many who were vigorously advocating freedom for slavery. So, a law with later amendments was enacted in Virginia, beginning 1 May 1806, with varying degrees of enforcement, specifying that freed slaves from Virginia could not remain within the state more than twelve months after freedom.[14] Thus we have a situation, as shown in Table I, where the slave population of Fairfax County was nearly halved between 1810 and 1840, from 6,485 to only 3,451. The free black population also declined in the same period.

This means that the freed black men and women went elsewhere. Those with skills or a trade, mainly those few who had been house servants, went to the cities and found work there. Certain occupations became traditional for blacks, such as barbers, coopers, carpenters, and gardeners, especially since they were prohibited from some occupations such as teaching. It is said that in some cities, such as Richmond, nearly all barbers were black.[15] Some blacks used the fine skills they had learned on the plantation and became apprentices to craftsmen or were hired as personal or body servants. Others without skills were hired as laborers on construction projects.

Some free blacks lived with Indians, intermarried, and had children who were labeled "mustecs" or "mustizo."[16] In this region the Doegs were known for their intermixture with blacks. Other free blacks who were able to obtain papers permitting them to stay within the county married and lived with slaves. It was especially advantageous for a freed black man to live with a slave woman: he could remain free while the wife was still fed and clothed by her master.[17] However, any children born of a slave mother were slaves. Probably the most common solution to the

---

13. Anne Newport Royall, *Sketches of History, Life and Manners in the United States* (1826; reprint ed., New York: Johnson Reprint Corp., 1970), p. 120 (hereinafter cited as Royall, *Sketches of History*).

14. Fairfax County Will Book, U-1, p. 185.

15. John H. Russell, *The Free Negro in Virginia* (1913, reprinted ed., New York: Dover Publications, 1969), p. 150 (hereinafter cited as Russell, *The Free Negro in Virginia*).

16. Ibid., p. 72.

17. Ibid., p. 132.

Richard Bland Lee. An early portrait, painted about 1790 and later copied by his great granddaughter, Alice Matilda Reading, from the original miniature. Virginia Historical Society.

problem of subsistence was to hire oneself out, by the job or for a limited amount of time. In fact, some persons sold themselves back into slavery when financial matters were pressing.

The expanding free black population was viewed as a problem when the tobacco-based economy which had supported and required large numbers of slaves no longer existed in the county. Slaves began to be freed in larger numbers by the first and second decade of the nineteenth century.[18]

There was a steady decline in the slave population of Fairfax County. The free black population also declined, but only after rising to a high of 740 in 1820. This number dropped to 311 in 1830, undoubtedly because of restrictive state laws and their increased enforcement in the county court.

However, this was by no means the end of slave trading in the region, for although importation of slaves into Virginia and the United

18. See the Fairfax County Will Books for the many instances, including those of Sarah Jones, Fairfax County Will Book, L, p. 53; Hannah Adams, Fairfax County Will Book N, p. 81; and Elizabeth Lee Jones, Ibid., with four pages of instructions on slave disposition, admitted 21 February 1823. See also Ch. 4 herein.

States stopped in 1808, there was an increased demand for slaves in states to the south where cotton was replacing tobacco as a dominant export. Certainly some Fairfax residents found that slaves could bring higher prices and could relieve the distressed conditions found on their own farms. Such circumstances have been particularly described concerning the general decline of Sully Plantation in Fairfax County which had been built by Richard Bland Lee.[19] By 1835 Sully was a liability, and the heirs to the property agreed to sell the farm and to sell or hire the remaining slaves in the deep South either through a private agent or through the slave market in Alexandria.[20] The farm's administrator, Henry T. Harrison, wrote on 22 June 1835, "You will please bear in mind the southern expedition and see if it will be possible to get any or all of those negroes off, the sooner arrangements are made, the better." [21]

When one sees that the population dropped from a high of 13,111 in 1810 to a low of 9,206 in 1830, a loss of 3,805 persons in a 20-year span, the tremendous migration out of the county can be realized. Of that number the greatest loss in the white population occurred between 1820 and 1830. This was a period of great westward expansion, symbolized by the election of Andrew Jackson in 1824 and the financial depression which followed later in the cotton states.

The slave population had diminished earlier (between 1810 and 1820) when one-third of the slaves left Fairfax County. By 1830 land was selling at a loss, and people began to farm on smaller plots than the earlier tobacco planters had, and with more attention to diversified crops and improvement of the exhausted soil with the application of fertilizers, gypsum, and lime.[22]

Added to the new interest in farming and the consequent move back to the county by some former residents, new immigrants came to the county during the 1830s from Europe primarily to work on roads and bridges. Most of them stayed. Emphasis should not be placed on the topic of immigration at this period, however, because even though the population increased, it did so without disturbing the character of the population, as shown in Figure 1. Analysis by age group does indicate that the society remained as it was: dominated by couples with large families. In 1840, 3,295 persons out of a total of 9,370 were engaged in agriculture; only 77 were in manufacture and trade; and 18 persons claimed to be in the learned professions or to be engineers.[23]

19. Robert S. Gamble, Sully: The Biography of a House (Chantilly, Va.: Sully Foundation, Ltd., 1973), pp. 65-67 (hereinafter cited as Gamble, Sully).

20. Ibid., p. 65.

21. Henry T. Harrison to George W. Hunter, 22 June 1835, Hunter Papers, Sully Foundation, Ltd., Chantilly, Va.

22. Numerous advertisements placed in the Alexandria Gazette and National Intelligencer confirm this when it is stated that an estate is for sale and a paragraph describes how well the soil can be improved with clover, plaster, or gypsum. See Ch. 2 for specific examples.

23. U.S. Decennial Census, 1840.

Figure 1

POPULATION PYRAMID
FAIRFAX COUNTY, 1830-1840

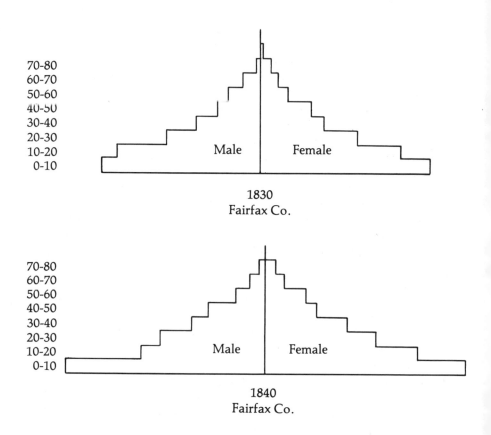

1830
Fairfax Co.

1840
Fairfax Co.

SOURCE: United States Decennial Census, 1830, 1840, National Archives,
Washington, D.C.

Economy

The colonial pattern of large land holdings began to disappear after the beginning of the nineteenth century. This was an evolutionary development lasting perhaps fifty years. Agricultural productivity did decrease because of soil exhaustion, and it became more difficult to maintain the previously high standard of living at those plantations without diversified crops or interests. Maintaining an old way of life became critical for the children of large landholders who had been raised as gentlemen or ladies of the tobacco plantation. When they received an inheritance, it was often found that by the time their family's land was divided among them (since primogeniture law was abolished), and with declining crop yields, they were barely able to exist at a fraction of their old way of life.

Ravensworth serves as a good example of the division of a large estate; an enormous holding of 21,996 acres, it was granted to William Fitzhugh in 1694 by the proprietors of the Northern Neck of Virginia.[24] The property stretched from Fairfax Courthouse to what is now Shirley Highway south of Little River Turnpike.[25] In 1701 it was divided between William Fitzhugh's two sons, William and Henry. Neither son lived on the property, and it was not until William Fitzhugh, Jr., of Chatham, great-grandson of the original William Fitzhugh, built the house at Ravensworth after the Revolution that a Fitzhugh resided on the land. By this time he occupied the southern moiety of approximately 9,000 acres. Colonel Henry Fitzhugh of Bedford owned the northern section of 12,585 acres.[26]

Land division began at this point, for when Col. Henry Fitzhugh died, his share of the estate was divided among his five sons, Nicholas, Richard, Mordecai, Battaile, and Giles.[27] Each son still received a sizeable parcel, averaging over 2,000 acres each. This was a real beginning to the dissolution of Ravensworth, because these sons, in turn, sold portions of their inheritance.

The other half of the original 21,996 acres belonging to William Fitzhugh was divided upon his death in 1809 between his son and daughters, Ann Randolph Craik and Mary Lee Custis, according to the terms of his will.[28] Each daughter received approximately 800 acres of the Ravensworth tract. His son William Henry Fitzhugh received the remainder, more than 7,000 acres, which he occupied until his own death

24. Northern Neck Book 2, p. 14 (Virginia State Library, Richmond); also in *Proceedings in Land Causes, Dumfries District Court, Prince William County*, Book 1789-1973, p. 395.

25. "Ravensworth", *Yearbook of the Historical Society of Fairfax County, Virginia, Inc.*, 3 (1954):15, (based on material gathered by Courtland Davis and Mrs. John Alexander).

26. Ibid., p. 20.

27. Fairfax County Deed Book A-2, p. 187.

28. Fairfax County Will Book J, p. 244.

Ann Randolph Fitzhugh, the wife of William Fitzhugh of Chatham and Ravensworth. Portrait by John Hesselius. Photo courtesy of Mr. and Mrs. A. Smith Bowman. Museum of Early Southern Decorative Arts, Winston-Salem, N.C.

William Fitzhugh of Chatham. First resident owner of the vast Ravensworth estate in Fairfax County and builder of the first family residence there. He was the great grandson of the original patentee, William Fitzhugh, who received 21,996 acres from the Proprietors of the Northern Neck in 1694. Portrait by John Hesselius. Photo courtesy of Mr. and Mrs. A. Smith Bowman. Museum of Early Southern Decorative Arts, Winston-Salem, N.C.

in 1830. According to his instructions, 1,300 acres were inherited by his adopted daughter Mary Caroline Goldsborough, and the remainder went to his wife to be held in trust for his sister, Mary Lee Custis, and his niece, Mary Randolph Custis, who later married General Robert E. Lee.[29] Her inheritance was divided among her children in 1874.[30]

Another factor which must be considered as contributing to the breakup of the large landholdings (which we know as plantations) is that Fairfax County never saw the large number of extremely wealthy planters firmly established in the county. There were the once-wealthy Washingtons, Lees, Masons, and Fitzhughs, but these families also had economic difficulties. Many of the original landholders in the county had come in the early eighteenth century from Stafford or King George counties of Virginia where there generally was little tradition of an established authoritarian slaveholding class.[31] Rather, there were large numbers of land grants in Fairfax County in the early and mid-eighteenth century.[32] Over fifty have been located for the years between 1700 and 1798 on Great Hunting Creek and its tributaries. The amount of land granted never approached the enormous amount received by William Fitzhugh in 1694; it generally ranged below 500 acres.[33] A perusal of the deed records indicates that these lands in turn were divided and leased on a life basis to other newcomers, usually second-generation Americans, with payment in hogsheads of tobacco. However, by the time this way of life began to establish itself and create a "typical" southern plantation culture, economic and political events changed the course of events.

Some large landholders sold their land to a single member of the family or to a faithful tenant farmer. They then left Fairfax County and migrated to bounty land in Kentucky or on the Ohio River which had been granted to them during the Revolutionary War. From the time of the Revolution, we find increasing numbers of Fairfax County residents migrating west to the newly created states where they were encouraged to settle.[34] Some fortunate persons disposed of their unproductive land at a profit. By the 1830s and 1840s, however, some farms were completely abandoned; by the early 1840s, much of the land in Fairfax County was no longer under cultivation.[35] The Alexandria *Gazette* and other news-

29. Fairfax County Will Book Q, p. 57.

30. Fairfax County Deed Book R-4, p. 464.

31. Fairfax Harrison, *Landmarks of Old Prince William* (Berryville, Va.: Chesapeake Book Company, 1964), p. 157 (hereinafter cited as Harrison, *Landmarks*).

32. Robert Morgan Moxham, *The Great Hunting Creek Land Grants*, (North Springfield, Va.:, Colonial Press, 1974), pp. 15-16.

33. The average amount of land granted the fifty-one individuals cited by Moxham in *The Great Hunting Creek Land Grants* between 1700 and 1798 is 448.88 acres.

34. For numerous examples of the legal encouragement, see Hening's *Statutes*, 10:445; 11:87, 282-287, 296; and 12: 38, 39, 395, 510, 789, and 790.

35. Richard H. Abbott, "Yankee Farmers in Northern Virginia, 1840-1860," *Virginia Magazine of History and Biography* (January 1968).

Sully. The home of Richard Bland Lee and his wife, Elizabeth Collins Lee, as it probably appeared when constructed in 1795. Sketch by Gloria Matthews. Fairfax County Office of Comprehensive Planning.

papers of the region reveal the exceptional number of farms for sale in the county during this period; many were being sold as a last resort by court sale to settle outstanding debts at the death of the owner.

Sully, the former plantation of Richard Bland Lee, was among those experiencing severe economic difficulties and was sold at public auction on 1 September 1838. The purchaser was William Swartwout, a speculator, who paid $8,950 for the house, outbuildings, and 750 acres.[36] These were years of severe economic depression, and Swartwout died in 1841 in financial ruin with three mortgages totaling more than $20,000 on Sully.[37] Again, the court ordered a public auction to be held, and the sale notice was placed in newspapers of Alexandria, Washington, and Winchester, as well as those in Swarthwout's home town, Poughkeepsie, New York.[38]

Some very wealthy families (such as the Fitzhughs) were able to retain some of their land; others survived for the time being: John Mason on Analostan Island, the Lewises on Woodlawn Plantation, and George Washington Parke Custis on Washington Forest, the large 1,200 acre tract originally owned by George Washington on Four Mile Run.[39] However, both Custis' land and Mason's island were economically diversified and the natural endowments of the sites utilized, as the following discussion explains.

Mason built a large plantation which was entirely self-sufficient, and he was also interested in alternate methods of cultivation as an active member of the Columbia Agricultural Society of Washington.[40] However, even on the island where wild life was abundant and farm produce sufficient, profit came to John Mason by the operation of a ferry from Georgetown, creating easy access to the Virginia shore before the construction of the Aqueduct Bridge.

The plantation system was doomed, however, with the advent of cities as trade and commercial centers, and with the consequent changes in labor, trade, and production. Consequently, the Mason family was forced to sell the island in 1833, and Washington Forest was subdivided many times in ensuing years. This development had been foreseen by the newly immigrated Scotsman Thomas H. Palmer in 1814 when he stated in a letter to a friend in Philadelphia: "The whole system of Virginia agriculture, with perhaps a few exceptions, is fundamentally and radically wrong. The farms, or plantations, as they are called, are generally

36. Lee's Committee v. Robertson, *Fairfax County Chancery Causes*, Final No. 59 (198).
37. Thompson v. Swartwout, *Fairfax Chancery Causes*. Final No. 93 (4). A complete discussion of the financial problems surrounding the Sully Plantation is well documented in Gamble, *Sully*, Ch. 4.
38. Alexandria *Gazette*, 10 September 1842 (hereinafter cited as *Gazette*); and Gamble, *Sully*, p. 73.
39. Charles W. Stetson, "George Washington's Woods on Four Mile Run," *Records of the Columbia Historical Society*, 35-36 (Washington, D.C., 1935): p. 179.
40. Mary E. Curry, "Theodore Roosevelt Island: A Broken Link to Early Washington, D.C. History", *Records of the Columbia Historical Society*, 48 (1971-72): p. 20 (hereinafter cited as Curry, "Theodore Roosevelt Island").

very extensive, and the quantity of land under cultivation far beyond the means of the cultivator.. The land consequently in a few years becomes literally good for nothing and more woodland must be cleared for future operations . . .[41]

Some individuals were advocating reform in farming methods in the late eighteenth and early nineteenth centuries. George Washington was quite aware of the experiments being conducted to develop methods of cultivation which would improve the fertility of the soil, and he experimented with the methods being promoted through the many agricultural societies. As discussed in the publication on Green Spring Farm, west of Alexandria, farmers of Fairfax County were shifting to a wider variety of foodstuffs to meet the demand for agricultural produce within the nation.[42] Washington's experience at Mount Vernon was probably typical of his neighbors' when wheat was gradually introduced as a substitute for tobacco and "the increasing number of cattle accounted for the introduction of mangel-wurzels, turnips, and other root crops in the rotation. The soil building virtues of peas were discovered. Beef cattle grew in increasing numbers, . . . orchards and vineyards were planted more widely."[43] Washington uniquely left a carefully documented study of the results of his agricultural experiments. His brother-in-law, Fielding Lewis, advocated the application of lime to the soil.

John Alexander Binns of Loudoun County had applied gypsum to the soil and very early in the century had advocated deep plowing, his influence making that county one of the most productive in the state. Binns also drew the attention of Thomas Jefferson who noted his achievements in 1803 when writing to Sir John Sinclair, the head of the English Board of Agriculture, and to Mr. William Strickland, also a member of that Board.[44]

The advertisements in the Alexandria *Gazette* of land for sale, even in the early 1800s, indicate an awareness of the improvements that could be realized in agricultural production by the use of "plaister" (gypsum). One such was placed by Augustine Fitzhugh in an advertisement of land for sale on Little River Turnpike in 1815: "the soil is of the kind which can easily be improved by Clover, and from experiments which have been made in the neighborhood of it, there is no doubt but the plaister of paris will act on it most powerfully."[45]

It is clear that some residents of Fairfax County followed the advice of Binns and adopted methods and products that might improve the

41. John Cook Wyllie, ed., "Observations Made During a Short Residence in Virginia," *Virginia Magazine of History and Biography*, 76, no. 4 (October 1968): 387.

42. Ross and Nan Netherton, *Green Spring Farm, Fairfax County, Virginia,* (Fairfax, Va.: Fairfax Office of Comprehensive Planning, 1970), pp. 7-10.

43. Frederick Gutheim, *The Potomac* (New York: Grosset & Dunlap, 1968), p. 98.

44. Rodney H. True, "John Binns of Loudoun," *William and Mary Quarterly*, 2, no. 1 (January 1922): 20.

45. Alexandria *Advertiser and Gazette*, 26 September 1815.

productivity of the land and their own circumstances. In the account of the estate of William Darrell there is a notation that plaster was purchased from B. Hartshorne, a merchant in Alexandria, on 4 April 1803 for £2.9.[46] The following year on 19 March 1804 "plaister of paris" was purchased by I. Iram for 2. Its appreciated use was also indicated in a letter by Richard Bland Lee of Sully in 1802: "Finding the Plaister highly beneficial I have for two years past used it largely."[47] This point is further borne out in a publication by Avery O. Craven who says that from 1800 to 1820, the use of gypsum in soil made enormous changes in agricultural life.[48]

A list of the hundreds of agricultural publications distributed between 1790 and 1830 was compiled by E.G. Swem and published in 1913 by the Virginia State Library in Richmond. One of the most significant publications of the early nineteenth century was that by Edmund Ruffin, *Essay on Calcareous Manures* which emphasized the significance of the use of marle in worn-out lands.[49] In 1833 he founded the *Farmer's Register*, a monthly journal designed to disseminate his ideas on agricultural development. In 1843 an agricultural journal entitled *Farmer's Intelligencer* was edited and published in Fairfax County by J.D. Hitt. The subject matter was designed to inform the farmer of political as well as agricultural matters, as the first issue 21 October 1843 advocated a revision of the Virginia constitution for a more economical and simplified court procedure.

There were agricultural societies active at the time which served to disseminate information on new experiments in agricultural productivity. One such society was the Columbia Agricultural Society of Washington, while other groups were active in Fairfax and Loudoun counties and in Alexandria. These organizations had begun by 1773 in Williamsburg.[50] G.W. Parke Custis was particularly active in promoting the success of experiments in agriculture and even submitted a sample for exhibition to the *National Intelligencer*.

John Mason of Analostan Island was deeply involved in the promotion of the Columbia Agricultural Society and in the application of methods advocated for cultivation of the island.[51] In 1809 letters were sent around to promote interest in the society with the stated purpose "to improve

46. Fairfax County Will Book J, p. 205.

47. Richard Bland Lee to Zaccheus Collins, 5 June 1802, Richard Bland Lee Collection, Library of Congress, Manuscripts Division, Washington, D.C.

48. Avery O. Craven, *Soil Exhaustion as a Factor in the Agricultural History of Virginia and Maryland, 1606-1806* (Urbana: University of Illinois Press, 1925).

49. Edmund Ruffin, *Essay on Calcareous Manures* (Petersburg, Va.: J. W. Campbell, 1832).

50. R.B. Davis, *Intellectual Life in Jefferson's Virginia* (Chapel Hill: University of North Carolina Press, 1964), p. 167.

51. Curry, "Theodore Roosevelt Island," p. 20.

agriculture and to encourage domestic manufactures."[52] The following notice was placed in the newspapers of Washington and reprinted in the Richmond *Inquirer*.

AMERICAN MANUFACTURES.

In addition to the improvements displayed at Mr. Custis's, we have the pleasure to announce to our readers an agricultural and manufacturing experiment, perhaps not before attempted in this country. Gen. Mason, of this town, has manufactured a piece of nankeen, from cotton raised on his estate in this district, very little inferior to that imported from India. The public spirited exertions of Gen. Mason, in this particular, as well as in many others, entitled him to the thanks of his country. It is well known that the seed of the true nankeen cotton is to be found in many parts of the southern states; and if it was cultivated carefully and separately from the common cotton, there is no doubt but as handsome nankeen might be made in this country as in India. The experiment is certainly worthy of the attention of cotton planters. Specimens of Gen. Mason's nankeen may be seen at this office . . . . Washington Fed. [53]

By the early 1800s the farmers were no longer depending on tobacco, and in fact, there is little evidence of much tobacco being grown here at that time. However, all indications are that the estate of William Darrell was typical of the more prosperous farmer.[54] In 1809 wheat was sold from his estate to I. Stump and D. Ricketts for $260.24, and in 1808 the following products were sold:

126½ barrels of long corn
14½ barrels of short corn
12 bushels of potatoes
1100 lbs rye straw
1400 lbs hay for fodder
30 bushels rye
12 bushels oats
2¾ bushels flax seed
12 bushels turnips.

Not only was there a development of diversified crops, but efforts were also made in crop rotation and in the planting of clovers and grasses between other crops. The following advertisement placed in the Alexandria *Gazette* in 1801 by Richard Bland Lee testifies to the general

52. Ibid., p. 21.
53. *Richmond Inquirer*, 28 April 1809.
54. Fairfax County Will Book J, p. 205.

acceptance of the improvement that could be realized by the changing farming methods.

A Farm For Sale

I will sell the farm on which I reside, situate in the County of Fairfax and state of Virginia 25 miles from the cities of Washington and Alexandria and containing about 1000 acres. Of this tract between five and 600 acres are cleared and the remainder in excellent timber. A never-failing stream runs through the center of the tract.

There are 30 acres of best Timothy Meadows, in complete order, and 10 acres of mowable clover. There are 300 bearing Apple trees of excellent quality for cyder and 200 young grafted trees of the best kind of table fruit.

There has also been lately planted an orchard of about 1200 peach trees. The whole tract, wood-land and cleared, is enclosed by new and substantial fences and divided into convenient fields. The soil is particularly adapted to grass.

. . . A Garden of two acres containing the most valuable fruits and plants and a spacious yard are enclosed in a durable manner.

There are good stables and carriage house, with every necessary house for labourers, the latter with brick or stone chimnies. There is an old Barn of the common kind, but the greater part of the materials to build a new barn on the most approved Pennsylvania plan and all the materials to build a large stone dairy are collected . . . .

. . . . There are eighty acres of growing wheat, fifty of which in fallow land prepared in the best manner, and all promising a large crop; and forty acres of Rye . . . .

Richard Bland Lee[55]

Inventories of estates during this period indicate that there was wide-spread ownership of "patent plows" and a diversified economy with cows and sheep valued highly, along with stocks of corn and wheat.

The estate inventory of James Wren who died in 1815 indicates that he was using a variety of new inventions intended to increase farm productivity, including patent plows, the type not specified.[56] The inventory and sale of William Moss's estate in 1835 points out that by

---

55. Alexandria *Advertiser and Gazette*, 9 February 1801.
56. Fairfax County Will Book S, p. 275. Among the farming equipment are listed a wheat fan, 3 harrows, and 4 barshear plows. Another inventory of the period, that of Hannah Adams, Fairfax County Will Book N, p. 81, includes a triangle harrow, a cultivator, a plow and swingletrees, barshear plows, and a wheat fan.

that time the Fairfax County farmer was aware of the availability of labor-saving equipment, and he used it.[57]

Farm animals were well established in the region by the eighteenth century, including dairy cattle, sheep, mules, and hogs. The William Fitzhugh estate inventory listed farm animals on his Backlick, Centre, and Pohick farms, with 167 sheep and 67 hogs in 1808.[58] Indeed, bacon was an item on most inventories of the period, and the William Moss inventory listed over 700 pounds of bacon.[59]

Merino sheep were especially of interest in the county for the wool they produced. William Jarvis, representing the United States in Lisbon, exported thousands of the coveted animals to the United States during Napoleon's entry into Spain.[60] G.W.Parke Custis raised them at his Arlington estate, and Francis Lightfoot Lee of Sully advertised in 1816 the sale of 200 sheep, "one fourth full bred, the rest mixed merinos, all in perfect health and fine order."[61]

The economy of the entire United States suffered with the trade embargoes during the years before the War of 1812, and the war itself was painful for a newly developing nation. By the time many of the "old" families of the county were financially able to recover enough to initiate changes in their agricultural practices, others were better situated to intensively cultivate smaller plots, without the hindrance of a "plantation mentality." This problem occurred at Sully, in addition to personal problems encountered by the Lees. As has been indicated, land values dropped drastically in these years, and settlers from other regions gradually began to migrate to this area attracted by the minimal land prices.

It must not be assumed that all families suffered through this period, however, for some never left and were able to do quite well through the early nineteenth century as the following will of a later James Wren indicates. "I also desire and request that my said wife will carry on the farm and conduct it in every particular as I am in the habit of doing—as seeding clover seed and sowing plaister—and farming the land in a farmer-like manner . . ."[62] He had purchased the land known as Mt. Rocky in the 1830s and had apparently prospered, for his estate was valued at $6,666.61 at his death.[63]

---

57. Fairfax County Will Book S, pp. 7-18. For a more complete description of the Moss family as farmers in the county see Netherton, *Green Spring Farm*, pp. 3-35.

58. Fairfax County Will Book J, p. 285.

59. Fairfax County Will Book S, p. 7.

60. Wiltse, *The New Nation*, p. 53.

61. Alexandria *Advertiser and Gazette*, 8 October 1816.

62. Fairfax County Will Book U, p. 137.

63. At least 46 acres and 54 poles were purchased for $10 an acre, as noted in Fairfax County Deed Book D-3 p. 38. For division of the Mt. Rocky estate, see Fairfax County Deed Book C-4, p. 208.

II

Commerce and Industrial Development

Washington, D.C. became the political center of the nation after the Capitol and White House were built, but it took some time for the Federal District to be more than a provincial capital. Georgetown, on the banks of the Potomac River, gradually increased in influence as goods and services were needed for the developing capital. Traffic increased on the Potomac as legislators came in and out of the city during periods when Congress was in session. But as Washington was developing, Alexandria was struggling to continue the prosperity she had enjoyed during the final years of the eighteenth century before becoming part of the Federal District in 1801.

By 1800 there were several banks, tobacco warehouses, and bread and biscuit bakeries, especially those catering to the needs of the hundreds of ships that came into her port each year. In addition, there were breweries, as well as significant numbers of craftsmen such as silversmiths, who were well known throughout the region. There were thirty-four licensed inns in Alexandria in 1800, and conditions were so difficult in Washington that Gadsby's Hotel in Alexandria was the preferred place to stay until accommodations of equal comfort could be offered in the new capital. In addition, since there was no theater in Washington until after 1800, persons accustomed to such entertainment often came to Alexandria to eat at Gadsby's and then attend a performance at Liberty Hall in the evening.

The *Columbian Mirror and Alexandria Gazette* for the year 1800 advertised the many advantages offered the resident and visitor in the town, including two breweries. The Potomac Brewery made ale, strong, table, and small beer;[1] the Alexandria Brewery also sold strong, table,

1. *Columbian Mirror and Alexandria Gazette,* 11 January 1800

and small beer. A new tavern was opened by Peter Heiskill with "the sign of General Washington on Horseback" and was on the stage line to Georgetown, Baltimore, and Philadelphia, leaving every morning, and another arriving in the evening.[2] Mrs. West's Company of Comedians arrived in the fall with a great deal of publicity, and the Alexandria Theatre opened on 1 November 1800, with both a tragedy, "The Count of Narbonne" and a farce, "The Citizen."[3]

Transportation across the Potomac was often difficult and limited to the use of ferries. There was a ferry from Georgetown to Analostan Island which was linked to the Virginia shore by a causeway constructed by the Mason family. Steamboats and ferries also operated between Washington and Alexandria.[4] By 1808, the charter of the Washington Bridge Company was obtained by an Act of Congress, passed 5 February 1808. This bridge, called Long Bridge, was contracted to the Mandeville Brothers of Alexandria and built by immigrant Irish laborers, finished in 1809.

Despite the fact that Alexandria was part of the Federal District in the first half of the nineteenth century, it remained a commercial and cultural center for Fairfax County. It had been part of Fairfax County until the land was ceded by the state of Virginia; and the county courthouse had been located there for nearly fifty years. Geographically, it remained apart from the city of Washington and Georgetown because of the Potomac which constituted a physical barrier. In addition, being a seaport, Alexandria depended considerably on the decline and rise of the country's agricultural circumstances. Even though the political center of Fairfax County was now at the new courthouse in Providence, commercial activity followed the roads and turnpikes which were beginning to be built through the county, most of which provided relatively easy access to Alexandria. Undoubtedly, Fairfax County residents traveled to Alexandria for what goods and services were needed depending on larger cities like Baltimore, Philadelphia, or New York only on rare occasions. Travel to these more distant cities was quite difficult due to the general lack of comfortable inland transport between them, and a trip would be contemplated only rarely, even by those of a financially privileged position.

However, personal goods were still desired from Philadelphia by those who could afford the "finest." There was a general feeling that the craftsmanship of the furniture and silver was of a higher quality than that

2. Ibid., 14 January 1800.

3. Ibid., 28 October 1800.

4. One such ferry was operated by W.H.Washington and Philip Alexander in 1803 to transfer men and horses from Alexander's Island to Commissioner's Wharf in Washington City, as advertised in the local newspapers.

made locally. After the Revolution when British goods were no longer imported, furniture made in Philadelphia and New York reached a high level of workmanship.[5]

The Stabler-Leadbeater Apothecary Shop of Alexandria, which today operates as a museum, has in its records the many requests from Fairfax and Loudoun County residents for goods it stocked. In the nineteenth century the store carried farming materials as well as drugs.[6]

Alexandria was the commercial center for Fairfax County, and this is readily apparent in the county records. As an example, in the William Darrell estate there are notations for sundries of A.C. Cassenove, plaster of B. Hartshorn, plaister of paris of I. Iram, sundries medium of E. Stabler, among many others.[7] The above list makes it obvious that the people in the county relied on ordinary shops to stock the everyday supplies they needed.

During the first ten years of separation from Virginia, Alexandria almost doubled in size from its 2,748 population in 1790. Despite the increase in population, however, the city began to decline as a regional trading center about 1799. This was because of the looming danger to American and Alexandria vessels by French privateers and men-of-war. Between 1792 and 1801, for example, twenty or more Alexandria vessels were captured.[8]

In 1807, the total exports of Alexandria reached $1,181,862.[9] After the Embargo Act of 1807 and the ensuing War of 1812, Alexandria again began to prosper despite major setbacks by periodic depressions, a major fire in 1827 when 53 houses burned, and occasional epidemics of cholera and yellow fever. Joseph Martin in his *Gazetteer* of 1835 summarized the trade from its port as follows: "Alexandria carries extensive trade in flour, tobacco, sumack, lumber, etc. with the southern states, the West Indies, and Europe."[10] He further stated that in 1831, 206,294 barrels and 6,001 half barrels of flour were exported from this point. In addition, exports to foreign ports were significant, but not in comparison to those at the beginning of the nineteenth century. In 1829 total exports reached $687,259; in 1830 they dipped to $628,142; and in 1831 they rose again to $864,484.

5. Personal interview, J.B. Marshall (Alexandria, Virginia, May 1976). Also see Gamble, *Sully*, pp. 42-44, for description of Lee family purchases in Philadelphia.

6. Interview with Donald Slough (Stabler-Leadbeater Shop, Alexandria, Virginia, May 1976).

7. Fairfax County Will Book J, p. 205.

8. Roy Martin Rothgeb, Jr., "An Analysis of the Rise, Decline, and Possible Determinants of Redevelopment of the Seaport of Alexandria, Virginia" (MBA thesis, City College of the City of New York, 1957), p. 15. (Copy in the City of Alexandria Public Library.) (Hereinafter cited as Rothgeb, "An Analysis of the Rise.")

9. Joseph Martin, *A New and Comprehensive Gazetteer of Virginia and the District of Columbia* (Charlottesville, Va.: Joseph Martin, Mosely and Tompkins, Printers, 1835, p. 478 (hereinafter cited as Martin, *Gazetteer*).

10. Ibid.

The largest Alexandria ship of this early period was the *Lydia*, formerly of Bath, Maine, which registered 465 tons and was commanded by Captain Caleb Heath, transferred to the Alexandria registry in 1815. Next in size was the 342-ton ship *Potomac* of Captain John Brooks.[11] The remainder of the shipping consisted largely of brigs, brigantines, and schooners under 100 tons. The peak of shipping during the nineteenth century was the year 1840, during which time sixty-four foreign vessels entered the port bringing 9,911 tons of cargo, and 196 ships cleared carrying 16,725 tons of cargo.[12] In that year there were thirty-nine ships registered for foreign voyages, the biggest of which was the 677-ton ship *General Washington* and the second largest was the 209-ton bark *Archibald Gracie.*[13]

While Alexandria continued as a commercial center for the United States and Virginia, as well as for Fairfax County, it was in small towns such as Centreville that everyday business was conducted for residents of the county. Centreville and Fairfax Court House (Providence) were on the stage lines and eventually found themselves on the major improved roads within the area. When turnpikes were constructed, tolls were collected at these points, often at local taverns. As Eugenia B. Smith noted, "During the first half of the nineteenth century, town activity continued to center around the tavern at the sign of the eagle, and passenger coaches stopped at the stable lot as well as the freight wagons hauling cargo between Alexandria and Warrenton or the Shenandoah Valley."[14] By the 1830s, the mail coach service passed through Centreville three times a week on a route from Washington, D.C. to the Culpeper County Courthouse. Providence was the seat of government for Fairfax County, and this fact alone made it a local trading center.

Banking

Modern banks, as we know them, did not exist in America before the Revolution and the first institution to exercise the functions of discount, deposit, and issue was planned and put into operation by Robert Morris in 1781 "for the purpose of giving financial aid to the Continental Army."[15] The establishment of the First Bank of the United States in 1781 created much interest among the merchants of Virginia, especially in Richmond, together with other nearby towns. Together, they submitted

11. Brian Brown, "Days of Sail in Alexandria," *Yearbook of the Alexandria Association* (1957), p. 43.

12. Rothgeb, "An Analysis of the Rise," p. 24.

13. Brown, "Days of Sail in Alexandria," p. 45.

14. Eugenia B. Smith, *Centreville, Virginia: Its History and Architecture* (Fairfax: Fairfax County Office of Comprehensive Planning, 1973), p. 45.

15. George T. Starnes, *Sixty Years of Branch Banking in Virginia* (New York: Macmillan Company, 1931), p. 18 (hereinafter cited as Starnes, *Sixty Years of Branch Banking*).

To the General Assembly of Virginia,

THE PETITION OF THE CITIZENS OF THE COUNTY O:

Respectfully shews that your petitioners are desirous of recall-
ing the attention of the Legislature to the subject of sundry memorials and petitions, presented to the last session of the General Assembly, from several counties both to the eastward & westward of the Blue Ridge—it
was then represented to the General Assembly, to be an object of primary importance to the interest & prosperity of that rich, populous and extensive tract of country, bordering on the river Potomac, that it should
participate in the advantages resulting from the establishment of the Bank of Virginia, that from the existing
organization of the Bank and its offices, that portion of the state, would be wholly excluded from such participation, that the only adequate market, on the southern shore of the Potomac for the produce of the many
important and flourishing counties in that quarter of the state, was the town of Alexandria, it was further
represented that the town of Alexandria, was in a situation to employ, very beneficially to your petitioners
and with great advantage to the proprietors of the Bank, any additional banking capital that might be allotted
to the establishment of a Branch of the Bank of Virginia, in that part of the county of Fairfax, in the immediate ... ... more full exposition of the principle & facts urged in support of this

YOUR petitioners therefore humbly pray that an act may be passed for establishing an Office of the
Bank of Virginia, for the purposes of Discount & Deposit, in that part of the county of Fairfax adjacent to
the town of Alexandria ; and for increasing the capital stock of that Bank to such an amount as may enable
the president and directors to establish the said office upon a footing adequate to the occasion.

Petition of Fairfax County Residents to the General Assembly of Virginia for a branch of the Bank of Virginia in 1805. Virginia State Library.

a petition for the establishment of a branch bank in Richmond. Many other petitions were submitted, but the Bank of the United States had many enemies in Virginia, especially James Madison and Thomas Jefferson. The majority of the people in Virginia were engaged in agricultural ventures and had learned from experience to fear all commercial institutions offering the slightest possibility of developing into a monopoly.

By 1792, however, the merchants of Alexandria had lobbied so successfully that the Bank of Alexandria was the first banking institution chartered by the General Assembly of Virginia, and was the second bank chartered south of Philadelphia.[16] Its purpose was to assist Alexandria in her competition with Baltimore for an important part of Virginia's trade. Even Jefferson changed his previously stated position to say that it was not wrong to encourage Alexandria, because "it is a rival in the very heart of Baltimore."[17] The Maryland legislature had chartered the Bank of Maryland on 10 December 1790.

The capital of the Bank of Alexandria was $150,000, divided into 750 shares of $200 each.[18] The immediate success of this bank which was supported so strongly by the merchants is shown by the fact that within two years its stock sold at one hundred percent above par.[19] To meet the demands for loans and discounts, it became necessary to increase the capital to $500,000 by 1800, and by this time it had a circulation of over a quarter of a million dollars and loans and discounts of over $500,000.[20]

16. Ibid.
17. Thomas Jefferson, Jefferson's Works, Ford ed. 4:19.
18. Hening, Statutes, 16:592.
19. Nile's Register, supplement to vol. 9, (Baltimore, Md.), p. 156.
Calendar of Virginia State Papers, 9:290.
20. Calendar of Virginia State Papers, 9:290.

No. *791.* —

John Wise & John Summy is entitled to One Share of Augmented Stock in the Bank of Alexandria, transferable at the said Bank by the said

John Wise & John Summy

or their Attorney

WITNESS *the Seal of the President, Directors, and Company of the Bank of Alexandria, the Fifth day of July 1796 —*

By order of the Board — W Herbert pres:

Bank of Alexandria stock was issued and this particular certificate, dated 1796, was purchased by William Herbert. Copy courtesy of Alexandria Coin Sales.

So much jealously developed over the monopoly of the banks which had been chartered by the legislature that during the year 1804 it was impossible to get a charter except by lobbying. Hence, the citizens of Alexandria did not wait for the General Assembly, but organized the unincorporated Bank of Potomac in 1804 and adopted bodily the articles of association of the Union Bank of Baltimore.[21]

Of major importance to Virginia at this time, when Alexandria was part of the Federal District, was the granting of a charter for the Bank of Virginia by the Virginia State Legislature on 30 January 1804. In accordance with this charter, the Bank of Virginia was to be located in Richmond, with branches at Norfolk, Fredericksburg, and Petersburg. Fairfax County submitted petitions to the State Legislature for a branch of the Bank of Virginia in the county on 6 December 1805.[22] Two copies of this broadside have been located with more than 100 signatures of local residents in favor of a branch bank within the county. It was not granted, however, and so, even in 1812, the nearest branch was in Winchester. Undoubtedly, most of the banking of Fairfax County residents was done in the banks of Alexandria. By 1806 the currency of the Alexandria banks was in circulation as far north as Philadelphia.[23]

According to the county court order books, in 1817 there were notes from the chartered banks of Virginia, the Bank of Virginia, and Farmer's

21. Starnes, *Sixty Years of Branch Banking*, p. 36.

22. Petition to the General Assembly of Virginia for a branch bank of the Bank of Virginia in Fairfax County, December 6, 1805, in Broadsides, Virginia State Library, Richmond. Among the signatures are Francis Sangster, Charles Simms, Lee Massey, Martin Cockburn, George Triplett, John Reardon, and John W. Ashton.

23. Charles E. Howe, "The Financial Institutions of Washington City in its Early Days," *Records of the Columbia Historical Society*, vol. 7-8, (Washington, D.C. 1905), p. 8.

Bank of Virginia circulated in the county, as well as those from all the chartered banks of the District of Columbia (including Alexandria), the city of Baltimore, and the city of Annapolis.[24]

During the period of financial distress after the War of 1812 there was a shortage of coins, so private and business scrip, or "shin-plasters", as they were called, were issued to serve as currency. These were typeset and locally printed.[25] Charles Affleck has located such scrip issued during the 1818 financial crisis in 2-3-4-5-6¼-8-10-12½-25-, and 50-cent denominations, with similar issues printed in 1837. Bank notes have been located for six banks of Alexandria in existence before 1840. These include the Bank of Alexandria, Farmer's Bank of Alexandria, Franklin Bank of Alexandria, Bank of Potomac, Mechanics Bank of Alexandria, and Merchant's Bank of Alexandria, although there were other banks in existence during this period. None, however, has been in continuous operation until the present time. Some, including the Bank of Alexandria, reopened after failure in the 1830s or 1840s with new capital, but with the same or similar names that are recognizable today.[26]

Industry

During the early decades of the nineteenth century, the industrial revolution began to have a profound effect on northeastern towns and cities, and the efforts of another war with England caused a reevaluation of the dependence on a European market for export and import. Fairfax County planters and farmers began to shift their attention away from tobacco to other crops in the latter half of the eighteenth century, and other economic changes developed.

Since there was a gradual change to producing grains, especially wheat and corn, one of the first noticeable developments in the economy was in the number and operation of merchant milling establishments. During the time of self-sufficient plantation life, milling was often done on the

---

24. Fairfax County Court Order Book, 20 January 1817.

25. Charles J. Affleck, *The Obsolete Paper Money of Virginia,* 2ed. (Virginia Numismatic Association, 1968).

26. Disruptions in trade and a developing economy created a situation whereby many kinds of money were in use in Fairfax County in the early decades of the nineteenth century. Since the majority of trade was with Spain and Portugal in these years, it follows that payment for these goods must have been in currency of those nations. That some of this money came to Fairfax County is evidenced by the following transaction recorded in Fairfax County Deed Book E-2, pp. 289-91:

between Nicholas Fitzhugh and Sarah his wife of the Town and County of Alexandria in the District of Columbia, of the one part, David Stuart, of the County of Fairfax, in the State of Virginia, of the other part . . . in Consideration of the sum of thirteen thousand eight hundred and fifty four Spanish milled dollars and fifteen cents . . . a tract of land . . . upon Accotinque Run in the said County of Fairfax . . . eight hundred and thirty one acres and a quarter . . . part of that Tract of land known by the name of Ravensworth . . . .

premises, or by one mill for several large farms within a small geographic area (the neighborhood mill). However, "merchant milling became increasingly important in Northern Virginia's economy during the last half of the eighteenth century and continued to provide the area's major means of earning credits in the markets of other regions until the centers of wheat production and flourmilling shifted westward in the 1830s and 1840s."[27]

Merchant mills were sometimes built by the owners of large plantations as an additional activity which, it was hoped, could augment the income from general farming and the sale of tobacco and wheat. Washington's mill on Dogue Creek and Carter's mill on Catharpin Creek were early attempts for this purpose. However, since little money passed into a miller's hands (he was generally paid in some other commodity), it was not often a profitable enterprise.

Flour inspection was enforced at ports, and beginning in 1772, flour sold in casks or barrels had to be marked by a brand showing the quality of the flour or meal, the name of the owner of the mill, the name of the inspector, and gross and net weights. Flour inspectors were appointed in Alexandria, Fredericksburg, and Occoquan mills for northern Virginia, those being the leading centers at the time. By 1819 there were additional inspectors assigned to Colchester and Dumfries.[28] In 1801 Daniel Douglass was reappointed flour inspector for the port at Alexandria by the Fairfax County Court. In ensuing years, this appointment was subject to approval by the Federal District and Congress.

One of the most important factors in the development of a milling industry was the availability and construction of a transportation system. River transport had been traditional in northern Virginia; this area was infamous among travelers, especially Europeans, for the poor quality of its roads and inattention to comfort in carriages and wagons. Tobacco plantations normally were near navigable water courses or had developed a system of rolling roads for the transport of hogsheads of tobacco to port towns. But these rolling roads were not meant for the comfort of the traveler, nor maintained for heavy wagon use. Thus, initially, the grain farmer had to rely on existing roads which were highly inadequate for his needs. As long as good roads were lacking, inland mills were restricted to serving local areas. In Fairfax County, early mills were primarily located on navigable watercourses until the development of the several improved turnpikes in the early decades of the nineteenth century. Some of the inland mills survived simply because it was difficult and expensive to transport large bags or barrels of grain, and if the

    27. Ross D. Netherton, *Colvin Run Mill*, (Fairfax Va.: Office of Comprehensive Planning, 1976), p. 6 (hereinafter cited as Netherton, *Colvin Run Mill*). *Stat.* 18 (1796)
    28. 2 *Stat.* 18 (1796); 2 Shepherd, *Code of 1819*, ch. 222, sec. 10.

farmer could have the milling done close to home or along the way to market, he could save money in transportation costs.

Some of the mills of the nineteenth century for which documentation exists include those on the Potomac and its tributaries. A major mill of some renown was the Patterson Mill at Pimmit Run and the Little Falls of the Potomac, next to Chain Bridge. It enjoyed a choice location by the bridge, on the tidewater of the Potomac, and only three miles from Washington and Georgetown. In the 1820s, the Georgetown-Leesburg Turnpike led past the mill's door, and this was a factor advertised when an announcement was made of its availability for sale.[29] Patterson's Mill was the repository of State Department documents for one night during the War of 1812. These documents included the Declaration of Independence, "the laws, a secret journal of Congress and the correspondence of General Washington," according to Stephen Pleasanton, a State Department auditor for many years. Pleasanton was the person responsible for the preservation of these documents, and he had them put into coarse linen bags and carried by ordinary cart to the grist mill on Pimmit Run in 1814.[30]

Several mills were constructed to take advantage of the anticipated canal traffic. One such mill was erected in 1821 at the Little Falls by Leonidas H. Johns; it was introduced as Canal Mills in the *Intelligencer*.[31] Another mill was erected in Matildaville at Great Falls when this town was incorporated in 1790.

Not all grist mills were on the Potomac; many more were inland on tributaries of that river, often close to the developing turnpikes or connecting roads. Nelson's Old Mill was on Kirby Road, and two mills were sold to William Nelson in 1825 by William Adams. The lower and older mill was on Little Pimmit Run close to the confluence with Big Pimmit. It is said that Dolley Madison passed by this mill in her flight from the British in 1814.

Arlington Mill was built in 1836 by George Washington Parke Custis, grandson of Martha Washington, and it was still serving as an ice plant a century later.[32] It was located on Columbia Pike, west of Four Mile Run, and when the railroad was built from Alexandria to Leesburg, it followed the valley of Four Mile Run along the border of the large tract inherited by Custis from George Washington. Another mill was Barcroft Mill on Holmes Run south of Columbia Pike and the present dam of Lake Barcroft; it was purchased in 1824 by Robert J. Taylor.[33]

29. *Daily National Intelligencer*, 29 December 1821.
30. Allen C. Clark, "The Old Mills," *Records of the Columbia Historical Society*, vol. 31-32 (Washington, D.C. 1930), p. 111 (hereinafter cited as Clark, "The Old Mills").
31. *Daily National Intelligencer*, 21 December 1821.
32. Arlington County Deed Book W-2, p. 184.
33. Clark, "The Old Mills," p. 113.

Colvin Run Mill. The mill, now restored, functioned primarily as a merchants mill, serving the farmers of the region by grinding their grains for market as well as for local use. Sketch by Gloria Matthews. Fairfax County Office of Comprehensive Planning.

Another mill, a reproduction of which is now known as Washington's grist mill, was built to replace a mill built by George Washington in 1770. Washington selected a spot farther down Dogue Creek than his father's 1735 mill location as the better site for a mill to serve his own and his neighbor's needs. It was provided with the best machinery obtainable and the flour and meal were of excellent quality, usually being exported directly from the mill to the West Indies. When the attempt at merchant milling did not prove profitable, it is thought that Washington set up a bakery and attempted to sell ship biscuits.[34]

Still another mill was located on Colvin Run and what was called Eastern Ridge Road. This has been purchased and restored by the Fairfax County Park Authority. It is now called Colvin Run Mill, but for many years it was known as Carper's Mill, built and operated by Philip Carper in 1811.[35] Like other mills around it, Carper's Mill served the farmers in the region by grinding their corn and wheat; but as a merchant miller, he also purchased grain, processed it, and sold the flour and meal to suppliers and exporters. After the construction of Little River Turnpike, much of the Shenandoah Valley traffic was diverted from Ridge Road, leaving this mill off the main thoroughfare. Despite numerous petitions by Georgetown and Alexandria merchants who wanted a direct link to

34. L.M. Mitchell, "Old Mills in the Centreville Area," *Yearbook of the Historical Society of Fairfax County, Virginia, Inc.,* vol. 6, (1958-59), p. 27.
35. Netherton, *Colvin Run Mill,* p. 16.

the agricultural interests of Leesburg and the Shenandoah Valley, the fortunes of this mill did not recover even when John Powell purchased the mill from Philip Carper in 1842, and as an active politician of Fairfax County was successful in connecting the mill with the Falls Bridge Turnpike (later the Georgetown-Leesburg Turnpike).[36]

Fairfax County is fortunate to have a neighborhood mill of the early nineteenth century still standing and in good repair on the west bank of Piney Branch. This mill stands on land which was owned by Edward Payne, a justice of the Fairfax County Court, and builder of Payne's Church. It was called Hope Park Mill, being on the Hope Park plantation of Payne and later Dr. David Stuart.[37] The mill was a small local operation, probably used by the plantation owner and neighbors. John Barnes, Sr., purchased the Hope Park Mill from the Stuart estate in 1837, and after years of disuse it was put into operation again as a local milling establishment called Barnes' Mill.[38] The name changed again in 1896 when it was called Robey's Mill after J. Frank Robey who purchased the mill and operated it profitably for a decade.[39]

Joseph Martin recorded that the growth of Occoquan in Prince William County in 1835 included an extensive flour mill grinding 150 barrels of flour a day, owned and operated by John Irwin and John H. Janney. The Alexandria *Gazette* advertised Occoquan Mills in 1800 under the name of Isaac McPherson.[40] The principal trade was with Fairfax County, made convenient with a bridge over the river and being on the mail route from Washington. By 1835, however, the estuary of the Occoquan was gradually silting up, and eventually sea-going vessels could not reach the mills. Thus, even though improvements were made for river navigation, the town never regained its prominence.

County records document many requests from residents to dam a stream in order to build a water grist mill. Not all requests were granted, usually because the dam would infringe on a neighbor's land and water rights. Daniel McCarty Chichester applied in 1801 for permission to construct a water grist mill on the long branch of Accotink Creek.[41] In 1810 the Douglas family, William, William L., and John, asked permission from the court to dam a site on Holmes Run for a water grist mill;[42] John Douglas came again in May of the same year for permission to erect a mill and dam for a "cotton machine."[43]

36. Ibid., p. 18. *Landmarks*, p. 570.

37. Fairfax County Deed Book Q-1, pp. 145-49.

38. Martin Petersilia and Russell Wright, "Hope Park and Hope Park Mill" (Office of Comprehensive Planning, Fairfax, Virginia, December 1972), p. 146.

39. Ibid.

40. *Columbian Mirror and Alexandria Gazette*, 11 January 1800.

41. Fairfax County Order Book, 21 September 1801.

42. Ibid., 19 April 1810.

43. Ibid., 21 May 1810.

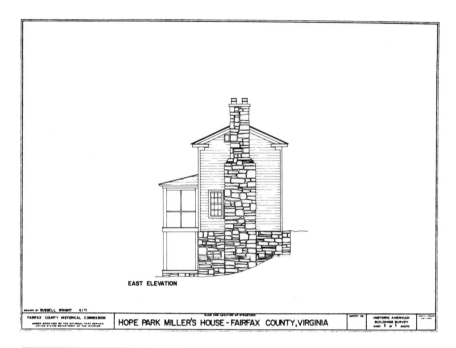

EAST ELEVATION

DRAWN BY RUSSELL WRIGHT 4/71

FAIRFAX COUNTY HISTORICAL COMMISSION
UNDER DIRECTION OF THE NATIONAL PARK SERVICE
UNITED STATES DEPARTMENT OF THE INTERIOR

HOPE PARK MILLER'S HOUSE - FAIRFAX COUNTY, VIRGINIA

HISTORIC AMERICAN
BUILDINGS SURVEY
SHEET 2 OF 3 SHEETS

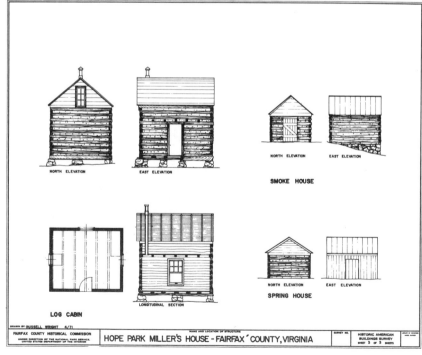

NORTH ELEVATION   EAST ELEVATION

NORTH ELEVATION   EAST ELEVATION

SMOKE HOUSE

LOG CABIN

LONGITUDINAL SECTION

NORTH ELEVATION   EAST ELEVATION

SPRING HOUSE

DRAWN BY RUSSELL WRIGHT 4/71

FAIRFAX COUNTY HISTORICAL COMMISSION
UNDER DIRECTION OF THE NATIONAL PARK SERVICE
UNITED STATES DEPARTMENT OF THE INTERIOR

HOPE PARK MILLER'S HOUSE - FAIRFAX COUNTY, VIRGINIA

HISTORIC AMERICAN
BUILDINGS SURVEY
SHEET 3 OF 3 SHEETS

SOUTH ELEVATION   SCALE 1/4"=1'0"

NEW CONSTRUCTION (c.1960)

DRAWN BY RUSSELL WRIGHT   4/71
FAIRFAX COUNTY HISTORICAL COMMISSION
UNDER DIRECTION OF THE NATIONAL PARK SERVICE
UNITED STATES DEPARTMENT OF THE INTERIOR
HOPE PARK MILLER'S HOUSE - FAIRFAX COUNTY, VIRGINIA
HISTORIC AMERICAN
BUILDINGS SURVEY
SHEET 2 OF 3 SHEETS

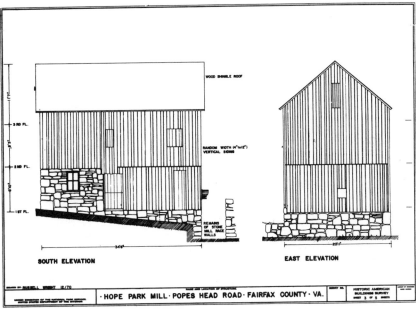

SOUTH ELEVATION   EAST ELEVATION

·HOPE PARK MILL· POPES HEAD ROAD· FAIRFAX COUNTY· VA.
HISTORIC AMERICAN
BUILDINGS SURVEY

*Hope Park Mill and miller's house were built about 1820 and comprise one of the few
mill complexes in the country which has survived with most of its outbuildings and
original wooden machinery. Measured drawings by Russell Wright. Historic
American Buildings Survey. (Scale of drawings as reduced, one inch equals twenty
and a half feet).*

Alexandria was the chief market for Virginia produce of the Potomac basin for at least a hundred years before the introduction of railroads into this region. In the first fifteen years of the nineteenth century, Alexandria exports averaged $1,114,000 annually, a considerable sum and eight times the Georgetown exports for the same years.[44] These figures vary considerably from year to year due principally to international trade interruptions. Alexandria exports were small in 1808 and 1809, as were all American exports because of Jefferson's Embargo and Non-Intercourse Act, and they were practically nonexistent in 1814 when the total export was $2,500 because of the British blockade during the War of 1812. The largest export from Alexandria during this time span was in 1811 when it was nearly $2,000,000. Exports were also large after the War of 1812 was over. However, the total exports from Alexandria the year before the Trade Embargo Act reached $1,181,862.[45]

These number seem even more significant when one realizes that the first decade of the nineteenth century was a dangerous time on the sea when American vessels were captured by French privateers, the cargo confiscated, and the crew imprisoned. In addition, British ships were taking American sailors captive and forcing them to work on the British ships as sailors.[46]

The main exports from Alexandria and northern Virginia to Europe during the early nineteenth century were grain and flour. About 97 percent of the total exports from Alexandria were domestic exports, not re-exports of foreign goods, for during the 1790s the demand in Europe was for flour, wheat, and corn. During the Napoleonic period, Alexandria flourished because of the European demand for breadstuffs which could be exported from its ports. From 1801 to 1805, Alexandria exported to foreign countries 1,154,778 barrels of flour, 323,920 bushels of wheat, and 592,954 bushels of corn.[47]

A major factor in the economic growth of the port was the completion of the locks and opening of the canal around Great Falls on the Virginia side by the Patowmack Canal Company in February 1802. This made it much easier to bring produce from the upper Potomac valley to the Alexandria market and port. Exports of flour and wheat from the city in 1802 nearly doubled those of 1801 and continued to grow the following year. A major portion of this growth can be attributed to the use of the canal by farmers in the western counties.

From 1801 to 1815, Portugal was the best market for exports from Alexandria, taking 57 percent of the corn, 54 percent of the wheat, and 27 percent of the flour. Spain took 27 percent of the wheat and 24 percent

44. Arthur G. Peterson, "The Alexandria Market Prior to the Civil War," *William and Mary Quarterly*, Series II, vol. 12 (April 1932), p. 105 (hereinafter cited as "The Alexandria Market").
45. Brown, "Days of Sail in Alexandria," p. 8.
46. Rothgeb, "An Analysis of the Rise," p. 15.
47. Peterson, "The Alexandria Market," p. 105.

of the corn, while the West Indies imported one-third of all flour exports with 35 percent of the corn and a small amount of wheat. England took 10 percent of the flour and wheat and one percent of the corn.[48] Most of the agricultural products arriving for export at the port came from the fifteen northern Virginia counties and some from Maryland and what is now northeastern West Virginia.

The Alexandria *Herald* reported in 1817 that flour inspections at the port from June 1816 to June 1817 were of 209,000 barrels, a considerable amount and a sharp increase from the previous war years. Domestic exports to other east coast ports were also significant. Grain and grain products, preserved meat products, tobacco, and some forest products went to the northern states from Alexandria. The years from 1836-1838 were not good ones in the export trade. This can be attributed to the general business depression and the poor crops of the late 1830s. The peak of shipping during the nineteenth century from the Alexandria port was in 1840, during which time 64 foreign vessels entered the port bringing 9,911 tons of cargo, and 106 vessels cleared carrying 16,725 tons of cargo.[49]

However, not all mills were grist mills in Fairfax County during this time period, as might be inferred from the earlier discussion. Wool and cotton mills were quite active, and sawmills were located in some of the smaller communities of the county. Patterson Mills, already noted as a significant grist mill at Little Falls, was a well-known wool factory, being a two-story stone building of sufficient size to contain machinery to manufacture blankets and cloth. The blankets made at Patterson's Mill in the 1830s were prized because of their wearability.[50]

The cotton and wool manufactury in Occoquan was also well known and patronized by Fairfax residents. This cotton factory was one of the first in the state and by 1835 was running 1,000 spindles.[51] Cotton manufacture continued on a smaller scale at some existing self-sufficient plantations, such as that of John Mason on Analostan Island in the Potomac where nearly everything needed for home consumption was produced on the island, even cotton.[52]

Domestic manufacture had been greatly encouraged by many, one such advocate being George Washington. In an address to Congress in April 1789, he encouraged the cultivation of flax, cotton and hemp, as well as the raising of sheep for wool, with the ultimate idea of the manufacture of articles by machine.[53] There was an attempt to raise

48. Ibid.
49. Rothgeb, "An Analysis of the Rise," p. 24.
50. Clark, "The Old Mills," p. 111.
51. Martin, *Gazetteer*, p. 481.
52. James F. Duhamel, "Analostan Island," *Records of the Columbia Historical Society*, vol. 35-36 (Washington, D.C. 1935), p. 138 (hereinafter cited as Duhamel, "Analostan Island").
53. J.C. Fitzpatrick, ed., *The Writings of Washington from the Original Manuscript Sources, 1745-1799*, (Washington, D.C.: United States Government Printing Office, 1932-1940), 30:296-308.

Silver trophy awarded to
William Foote of Hayfield, a
magistrate of the Fairfax
County Court, in April 1809
at one of the annual sheep
shearing contests held by
George Washington Parke
Custis at Arlington House.
Photo courtesy of the George
Washington Bicentennial
Center, Alexandria.

merino sheep in this area, and it was moderately successful in the early nineteenth century. George Washington Parke Custis followed in this endeavor, and as the idea gained greater acceptance, he wrote the following to the *National Intelligencer* concerning the Washington Woolen Factory and domestic manufactures.

> The formation of companies for the purpose of fowarding this truely beneficial system has taken place in many parts of the Union, since last spring—with much success in the North and with very partial prospect of encouragement southwardly. With the exception of Charleston [S.C.] most of the other companies have been but moderately patronized and seem unlikely to succeed. Whether these companies have been founded on too extensive a scale or whether the disposition of the inhabitants in those parts of the country are unfriendly to these institutions, is not for me to determine—very certain it is that the laudable and patriotic views of the promoters of these institutions are, at present much paralyzed, by the apathy of their fellow-citizens, and the enthusiasm in favor of domestic economy, seems subsiding to its former level. . . .[54]

General Mason, along with G.W.P. Custis, was very active in promoting these experiments and displayed the results widely, receiving much

54. *National Intelligencer,* 24 February 1809.

publicity in the newspapers, as in the earlier passage on General Mason's nankeen cotton.

Certainly the careful work of these men, among others, was heeded, and thus the *National Intelligencer* advertised that the Domestic Manufacture Company of Alexandria had been established and that books of subscription would be opened 1 December 1809.[55] The price was two dollars per share payable at the time of subscribing. Commissioners included G. Deneale, Hugh Smith, John Longdon, John M'Kinney, and James Irwin.

Concurrent with the development of the milling industry was the growth of a body of skilled craftsmen and a working class free to move about the region. As small trading centers developed, persons displaced by the disappearance of large tobacco plantations went into business for themselves. One of the primary needs was for general mercantile stores. By 1835 there were three such shops in Centreville, one in Pleasant Valley, three in Fairfax Court House, as well as stores in Matildaville and Turberville. Undoubtedly, others sprang up within the county, especially along transportation routes and at crossroads. The itinerant peddler was probably quite common, and at least two persons obtained licenses in order that they might retail goods within the county: Thomas W. Master paid $20 for a one-year period in 1803,[56] and Asher F. Scranton was given a one-year license to sell tin in 1825.[57]

The developing system of improved roadways also encouraged the number of taverns and their influence within the county. Every town and crossroads had at least one tavern or ordinary, and they not only served as hotels and restaurants for travelers, but also as social and communication centers which often held public sales.

The farmer was in need of other workers, especially the blacksmith, who was often located at crossroads such as Centreville, Pleasant Valley, and Falls Church. At least two names are in the records as blacksmiths of the period: James Sangster whose blacksmith shop was operating in 1810,[58] and Hugh Beard who had a blacksmith shop at the crossroads on Middle Turnpike in 1835.[59]

Transportation was very important to the county resident then as now, and the wheelwright and wagonmaker were essential craftsmen. Hugh Piper was known as both a wheelwright and a wagonmaker in the first decade of the nineteenth century, and John Earnshaw was noted as a wheelwright in 1817 in the county record books.[60]

55. Ibid., 27 November 1809.
56. Fairfax County Court Order Book, 21 February 1803.
57. Ibid., 17 October 1825.
58. Ibid., 21 May 1810.
59. Ibid., 20 July 1835.
60. Ibid., 17 October 1817, p. 258.

Skilled craftsmen most often found their way to the larger towns and cities. Richard Going was a weaver and both Enoch Hansbrough and Geo. Williams were "taylors" in 1800 and 1822, respectively.[61] Many of the craftsmen coming to Alexandria and other larger towns were freed slaves who had been taught a craft or trade on the plantation, and upon their manumission went where public opinion was more favorable toward them. Anne Royall, during her travels in the United States, made a special note of the large numbers of blacks and mulattos working in Alexandria in 1824.[62] In that city there were cabinetmakers and silversmiths of some reknown, in addition to those persons (black and white) in the service trades. Alexandria had enjoyed a reputation for fine silversmithing in the eighteenth century. Until the advent of machine fabrication, all work was done by hand, with objects stamped or molded by hand or hammered from solid silver disks. Among those artisans whose work survives today are James Adam from the late eighteenth century and John Adam who worked in Alexandria until about 1829. John Adam is credited with several tea services and silverware, but also a pair of sunglasses, now in the collection of the Mount Vernon Ladies Association of the Union.[63]

Benjamin Barton, Sr., arrived in Alexandria on 4 December 1801, and set up as a watchmaker-silversmith until his death in 1816. His sons Thomas and Benjamin Barton, Jr., took over the business after their father's death, with Benjamin, Jr. continuing in Alexandria until at least 1841.[64] Charles A. Burnett worked from 1785 to 1849 in both Alexandria and Georgetown. A good deal of his work survives today in the Washington area. He is credited with making a snuff box for James Madison which is now in the Yale University Art Gallery, and there are two salt spoons inscribed "Presidents House" in the White House Collection.[65] John Gaither was another smith working in Alexandria during this period. He reportedly made a set of drinking cups owned by George Washington. Adam Lynn worked in Alexandria from 1795 to 1835. One of the earliest known smiths in the region was Mordecai Miller (1763); still another was William A. Williams, who also had a shop in Washington. John Duffey made the small silverbladed mason's trowel for George Washington's use when the cornerstone of the Capitol was laid.[66]

61. Ibid., 18 March 1800; 17 September 1822.

62. Royall, Sketches of History.

63. Corcoran Gallery of Art, "A Century of Alexandria, District of Columbia & Georgetown Silver, 1750-1850: Exhibition Catalog," (Washington, D.C.: Associates of The Corcoran Gallery of Art, 1966), p. 8 (hereinafter cited as Corcoran Gallery of Art Catalog).

64. Ibid., p. 11.; interview with Mrs. Mayo Stuntz, a descendant of the Barton family, 1975.

65. Corcoran Gallery of Art Catalog, pp. 13-14.

66. The trowel is now the property of the Alexandria-Washington Lodge No. 22, A.F. and A.M. Useful reference works are George Barton Cutton, Silversmiths of Virginia (Richmond, Va.: The Dietz Press, 1952), and Worth Bailey, "Silversmiths of Alexandria," Antiques Magazine (February 1945).

Most of the silversmiths came to Alexandria in the late eighteenth century before that city was part of the Federal District. Business was good, and most silversmiths remained in Alexandria through the early decades of the nineteenth century, some even for two generations, like the Adams, Bartons, Duffeys, Galts, and Griffiths, or some formed partnerships with existing smiths. Before 1850, Virginia had more silversmiths than any other state south of the Mason-Dixon line; they numbered over 400, with the earliest noted smith setting up business in 1694.[67] During the nineteenth century, however, Richmond, Georgetown, and Baltimore provided competition as business and commercial centers.

Those persons in Fairfax County able to purchase silver did so, sometimes from the craftsmen in Alexandria, although Philadelphia silver still had a special appeal.[68] Silver played an important role in the life of the wealthier resident and was prized by individual piece. The wills of the county recount many individual pieces that were given to favorite persons, such as James Wren's request in his will that a soup ladle be given to Virlinda McGruder, daughter of his friend Daniel McGruder, and six silver tablespoons to a favorite grandchild, Verlinda Wren.[69]

The cabinetmakers of Alexandria did not confine themselves to the manufacture of just one item, but were skilled in many aspects of woodworking and fine carpentry. John Muir was well known, until his death in 1815, as a cabinetmaker and manufacturer of fine chairs, said to be equal to those made in Baltimore and Philadelphia. However, even in the nineteenth century, there remained a certain degree of snobbery connected with the purchase of fine furniture, and those able to do so often purchased their chairs and tables in Philadelphia or New York.[70]

Joseph Spear was in Alexandria by 1811, specializing in cabinets, but later making musical instruments and coffins. Evidently he prospered in the latter, for by 1815 he had acquired a hearse, but still repaired "sophas."[71] John Sellers made a fine piano exhibited at the Smithsonian Institution; after 1810 he had a musical instrument business. Other cabinet makers, such as Maurice Spillawn in 1813 and John B. Hammet in 1815, went into the business of upholstery and paperhanging. By 1831 the cabinetmakers felt that their needs would be better met by the formation of a cabinetmaker's union, a fact advertised in the Alexandria *Gazette* of 11 November 1831. Shopowners employing cabinetmakers hotly debated this matter in subsequent issues of the *Gazette*.

67. Cutton, *Silversmiths of Virginia*, p. xxi.
68. Interview with Emily Monk regarding Lyceum Exhibition on Silversmiths of Alexandria, June 1976.
69. Fairfax County Will Book K, p. 363.
70. See description in Gamble, *Sully*, on purchases by the Lee family in Philadelphia.
71. Dorothy Holcombe Kabler, "Early Cabinet Makers," *Yearbook of the Alexandria Association, Alexandria, Virginia* (1957), p. 78.

III

Internal Improvements

Toward the end of the eighteenth century, the toll roads movement, then at its height in England, made its appearance in America. The first charter to a toll road company in the colonies was granted by the Virginia legislature in 1772, and what was probably the first toll road in the nation was established in 1785 by Virginia between Alexandria and Snicker's Gap in Loudoun County. By 1808 there were three such roads in the state.[1] Albert Gallatin, Jefferson's Secretary of the Treasury, had proposed a system of internal improvements in 1808 with canals and roads joining the nation together, to be financed by a bonus to be paid the government by the Second Bank of the United States and by government bank stock dividends.[2] This plan, however, was never realized during Jefferson's administration.

Almost all internal road improvement in Virginia to this time had been confined to improving Indian trails, joining new settlements to their neighbors, or turning old packhorse paths into crude wagon roads. Since the first settlements clung to the coasts and rivers, early travel was largely confined to the waterways.

In the first decade of the nineteenth century, however, Virginia turned her attention to internal improvements. The period from 1801 to 1861 was characterized by state activity encouraged by the popular demand of its residents. Albert Gallatin and Thomas Jefferson had aroused public interest in good roads, and Fairfax County residents, most with friends

1. Albert Gallatin, Letter from the Secretary of the Treasury, in the *Writings of Albert Gallatin*, Henry Adams, ed., 1879, reprinted in Alvin F. Harlam, *Old Towpaths: The Story of the American Canal Era*, Port Washington, N.Y.; Kennikat Press, Inc., 1926.
See discussion of Albert Gallatin's contribution to America's efforts in road and canal building in *Bridges, Canals & Tunnels* by David Jacobs and Anthony Neville, Robert M. Vogel consultant. American Heritage Publishing Co., Inc. in association with the Smithsonian Institution, New York, New York, 1968, pp. 9-11.
2. Wiltse, *The New Nation*, p. 58.

Samuel Love. One of the original commissioners for the Fairfax and Loudoun Turnpike Company, along with Richard Bland Lee, his friend and neighbor. Miniature by Robert Field, painted about 1800 when Love was about 45. Watercolor on ivory. National Collection of Fine Arts.

and relatives who had "gone west," realized the importance of roads for better communication and closer commercial ties between east and west. The National Road already reached toward the Ohio River from Cumberland on the headwaters of the Potomac. When a proposal was made to construct a turnpike from Alexandria to the Little River, Richard Bland Lee readily endorsed the idea. Recalling the success of the toll road between Philadelphia and Lancaster, Pennsylvania, he requested Zaccheus Collins to send him a copy of the statute authorizing the Pennsylvania turnpike. "In the convening legislature of Virginia an attempt will be made by me to obtain a law incorporating a company of subscribers for making a turnpike road from Alexandria toward Winchester."[3] On 26 December 1795, the Assembly passed the law creating the "Company of the Fairfax and Loudoun Turnpike Road."[4] Lee, with his neighbor Samuel Love, was named one of the company's commissioners. This road ultimately became known as Little River Turnpike. Thus, people within the county saw the need for better roads, especially to encourage trade, as the economic picture changed.

3. Richard Bland Lee to Zaccheus Collins, Collins Papers, 29 October 1795, Library of Congress, Manuscripts Division, Washington, D.C.
4. Shepherd, *Statues at Large*, 1:378-88.

Virginia met this popular demand by encouraging the building of turnpikes and bridges by private companies. These accomplished a great deal, but were hampered by insufficient capital. Only a few persons were farsighted enough and could put together sufficient money to initiate a risky road-building project. The state then became a partner in many of these enterprises. On 5 February 1816, the Board of Public Works was established by an Act of the General Assembly and was endowed with all the stocks held in the state bank and in the various turnpike and canal companies.[5] Before the Board was formally authorized, however, numerous studies were undertaken to determine the necessity of such an enterprise and the condition of the existing facilities for transportation. One general statement speaks for the initiative of the men who undertook this project: it was determined that it would be extremely difficult to construct roads over much of the state, and some would have to be paved; both facts would increase the cost.[6] However, they went ahead and a fund was created "by law to be denominated" 'The Fund for Internal Improvement.' "[7] For the next fifty years, the Board of Public Works had charge of all the internal improvements made by the state, subject to the laws of the General Assembly. The board was similar to modern state highway and transportation departments.[8]

In 1817 the Virginia Assembly passed a general law under which turnpike companies were to operate and build roads. These specifications included such details as the road should be sixty feet wide, eighteen feet of this to be covered with gravel or stone, and summer roads on each side were to be cleared for use between May 1 and October 31. Tollgates were to be erected on every five miles of the road, and tolls could be charged to all travelers except troops of the state and the United States. The rate of the tolls was to be printed and affixed to every tollgate; milestones were to be erected to enable travelers to calculate their mileage; and scales for weighing wagons were to be placed at the tollgate.[9]

The Little River Turnpike subscription books were opened in 1803 in Alexandria by William Hartshorne and J.T. Ricketts;[10] this followed the work pioneered by Richard Bland Lee and the Fairfax and Loudoun Turnpike Road. There was an artificial bed of pounded or broken stone, a vast improvement over the usual muddy roads. The road was completed from Duke Street in Alexandria to the Little River at Aldie by

5. Virginia State Board of Public Works, *Reports*, 1815-1816, (Richmond, Va.: Virginia State Library), p. 54.

6. Ibid., pp. 1-40.

7. Ibid., p. 54.

8. *Historic American Highways* (Washington, D.C.: American Association of State Highway Officials), p. 47.

9. Revised Code of the Laws of Virginia . . . (Richmond, Virginia, 1817): 211.

10. *Alexandria Advertiser and Gazette*, 31 August 1876.

Claudius Crozet. Born in
France in 1789, this engineer-
planner devoted the greater
part of his life to establish
internal improvements in his
adopted state of Virginia.
During his period of service,
in part as the state's
principal engineer, great
arteries of transportation
including highways, canals,
and railroads were built
throughout Fairfax County,
Northern Virginia, and the
state. Portrait by William
Garl Brown, Virginia
Military Institute.

1806. This was a distance of approximately thirty-four miles, with
wooden or stone bridges across the many streams that traversed the
route. After the Virginia State Board of Public Works was organized and
purchased 125½ shares in the Little River Turnpike Company (worth
$12,550) in 1815, the tolls collected for the year ending 31 December
1816, were $24,937.96, a sum that was greater than expected.[11] A letter
from Josiah Thompson, treasurer of Little River Turnpike Company, to
Bernard Peyton in Alexandria, dated 20 November 1817, indicates that
the total amount received in tolls from 11 October 1806 to 1 January 1817
was $101,791.26½.[12]

The early years seem to have been the most profitable for this
turnpike, for tolls collected diminished in ensuing years, undoubtedly
because of competing turnpikes and "improved" roads. In 1824 the tolls
received were $15,970.10, and $14,498.29 in 1825![13] Later years saw the
annual toll ranging from $10,000 to $18,000, depending primarily on the
crop production for that year. A report of the principal engineer
Claudius Crozet in 1826 indicated that the turnpike had been inspected

11. Virginia State Board of Public Works, pt. 2, 1818, p. 5.

12. Ibid., p. 13.

13. Virginia State Board of Public Works Annual *Report* (1826) pp. 204, 30, respectively.

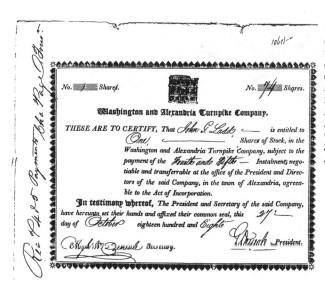

Washington & Alexandria Turnpike Company was organized in 1808 and issued stock certificates to its subscribers. The original road was from Long Bridge on the Potomac to Alexandria, following what is now Henry Street. Copy courtesy of Alexandria Coin Sales.

from Alexandria to where it met the Fauquier Turnpike, and it had been repaved with small broken stones, or "M'Adamized" for fifteen miles when it was said that "it will now be one of the best roads in the United States."[14] Five percent of the revenue was given to its stockholders; this was a considerable amount. The financial success of the turnpike has been credited to its efficient management by its Quaker President, Phineas Janney, especially in its early years.[15]

When Washington began to grow, a company for the construction of a turnpike to that city was organized in Alexandria in 1808 by Jonah Thompson, Thomas Swann, Charles Alexander, Edmund J. Lee, Jacob Hoffman, Cuthbert Powell, and John Mandeville.[16] The Washington and Alexandria Turnpike Company opened the road from Long Bridge, which was called Bridgepoint on Alexander's Island, to the town of Alexandria. This is roughly what is now called Henry Street, runs parallel to the Potomac, and ultimately was extended into the present Jefferson Davis Highway, or Route 1. As incorporated by an Act of Congress on 21 April 1808, this turnpike was not to be less than thirty nor more than one hundred feet wide between Alexandria and Bridge Point opposite Washington. In addition, this company had the power to erect a bridge across Four Mile Run and to collect tolls from persons using it.[17]

14. Ibid., p. 30.

15. Harrison, *Landmarks*, p. 565.

16. *Gazette*, 31 August 1876.

17. James R. Caton, *Legislative Chronicles of the City of Alexandria* (Alexandria, Va.: Newell Cole Co., 1933), p. 133.

This part of the Washington and Alexandria Turnpike met with another road built at the same time which joined with Little River Turnpike in Annandale and was called Columbia Turnpike Road (still designated Columbia Pike) via "Baily's Crossroads."[18]

To the north, a road was built in 1809 from the ferry landing across from Analostan Island to the Alexandria-Washington Road through George Washington Parke Custis' land in Virginia, and on to Columbia Turnpike. This road is sometimes referred to as John Mason's Alexandria Turnpike.[19]

In 1813, William Robinson, Charles Lee, Charles Alexander, Thomas Swann, Robert Conway, and Philip R. Fendall organized a company to construct a turnpike road from Alexandria to Leesburg, and this was incorporated by an Act of Congress 13 July 1813 "to construct a turnpike from the corner of Washington and Pendleton Streets to Leesburg." The tolls were: "for each head of sheep, five cents, each head of hogs, five cents, every horse or mule and driver, three cents, and every stage or wagon and two horses, ten cents.[20]

This project was not begun until 1818, and by the 1828 Board of Public Works report it was being improved with the assistance of Virginia and called Middle Turnpike. The road was to extend from Alexandria to Difficult Run "in the direction of Leesburg: its length will be 16½ miles. It is expected to be met by another turnpike five miles long, branching off from the Leesburg Turnpike. Thus, a very direct road will be formed from Alexandria to Leesburg."[21] The engineer's report indicated that the road was direct and fairly level, "not to exceed three degrees," but a concern was for the road bed, which necessitated a stone capping, greatly adding to the cost. In a further discussion of the advantages of such a road, the potential of Alexandria as a market and shipping center was favored over Georgetown.

> The whole country in the direction of Leesburg is greatly interested in this road, Alexandria offering to it an excellent shipping and its best market; but, the condition of the present road . . . is frequently so bad that waggons are often prevented from traveling it . . . .
>
> As to its probable revenue, it depends upon so many variable elements . . .: on the one hand, the influence of the turnpike will extend beyond Leesburg to the county of Jefferson; on the other, it is confined by the Little River Turnpike on the south side, and, when the canal along the Potowmac shall have been made, the Georgetown market

18. Harrison, *Landmarks*, p. 569.
19. Shepherd 2 *Stat.* 539 (1808).
20. Caton, *Legislative Chronicles of the City of Alexandria*, p. 133.
21. Virginia State Board of Public Works (1828), p. 504.

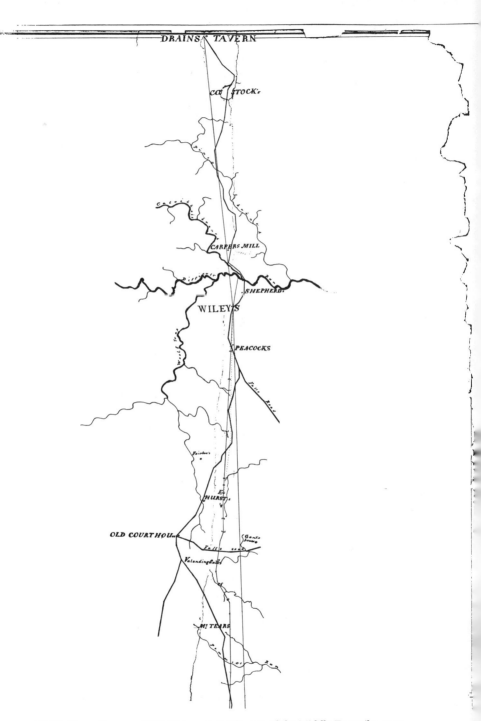

Middle Turnpike map, 1827. This surveyor's map of the Middle Turnpike, now Leesburg Pike, shows the road which ran from Alexandria to Difficult Run, where it was met by another road from Leesburg. Some of the landmarks noted on the map can be located today. National Archives.

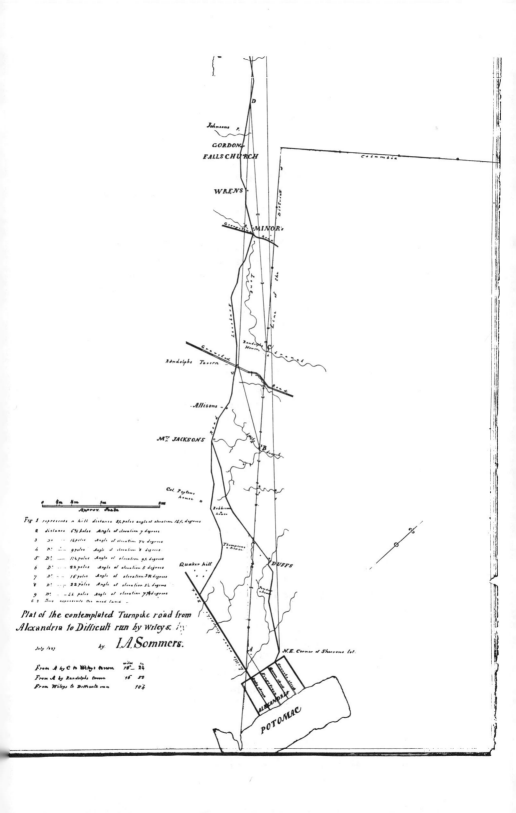

Johnsons F.

GORDON-
FALLSCHURCH

Columbia

WRENS

Gen.e L. MINOR's

Randolphe Tavern

Randolphe House

Allisons

M.t JACKSONS

Col. Payton
house

Robinson
house

Thompsons
House

Quaker hill

DUFFS

Fig 1 represents a hill distance 2¼ poles angle of elevation 14½ degrees

2   distance 6¾ poles   Angle of elevation 7 degrees
3   D.o   14 poles   Angle of elevation 7½ degrees
4   D.o   9 poles   Angle of elevation 8 degrees
5   D.o   11¾ poles   Angle of elevation 9½ degrees
6   D.o   22 poles   Angle of elevation 5 degrees
7   D.o   16 poles   Angle of elevation 5¼ degrees
8   D.o   22 poles   Angle of elevation 5½ degrees
9   D.o   44 poles   Angle of elevation 7¾ degrees

C.3   this represents the mead land

Plat of the contemplated Turnpike road from
Alexandria to Difficult run by Wileys.

July 1827   by   I. A. Sommers.

N.E. Corner of Sharons lot.

ALEXANDRIA

POTOMAC

From A by C to Wileys town   miles   18 _ 24
From A by Randolphs town   16   50
From Wileys to Difficult run   10¼

revived, there will also be a competition in that direction, which can be counteracted only by conducting the land trade to Alexandria by as good a road as practicable. There the advantage of an immediate shipping may continue to operate in favor of its market; whereas, by way of Georgetown, an additional expense of transportation must be incurred; so that if a good road be opened, it will be found simpler to go at once to Alexandria, than to use the canal, with the disadvantage of a double translation of the produce."[22]

Middle Turnpike, or the Alexandria-Leesburg Turnpike, had a direct effect on the future development of the town of Falls Church and today intersects the town as Broad Street and continues through the county as Leesburg Pike (Route 7). However, the road was not completed until after 1838 when Congress finally came to the relief of the company and authorized a lottery to ensure sufficient funds to complete the work on the road.

The Little River Turnpike bypassed the important trading center of Centreville, much to the distress of its inhabitants, as well as others between Alexandria and Warrenton. Thus the Fauquier-Alexandria Turnpike was planned and incorporated in 1808 by Alexandria merchants.[23] The plan was to build an all-weather road between Alexandria and the farmland in Fauquier and Culpeper counties. By 1810, an Act of the Virginia Assembly appointed directors in Alexandria, the District of Columbia, and Fairfax, Prince William, Fauquier, Shenandoah, Frederick, and Loudoun counties, and the turnpike became generally known as the Warrenton Turnpike. The directors in Fairfax County were George Summers, William Moss, and Humphrey Peake. By 1812, Humphrey Peake was president of the board of directors.[24] This turnpike was to be built from Warrenton through Buckland to intersect with Little River Turnpike at Fairfax Court House, a distance of twenty-eight and one-half miles. The road was to be twenty feet wide, except between Warrenton and Buckland where it was to be sixteen and one-half feet wide. There were to be two side roads, each eleven feet wide. The road was completed as far as Buckland in 1815, and was macadamized from Fairfax Court House to Buckland in 1824, including the stone bridge over Bull Run. The entire turnpike was completed by 23 December 1827 at an approximate cost of $2,000 a mile.[25] This turnpike was well traveled, but like most turnpike companies it failed to make profit for its investors who often had difficulty raising money to make

22. Ibid.
23. Shepherd 3 *Stat.*, pp. 379-85 (1808).
24. *Gazette*, 9 January 1812.
25. Virginia State Board of Public Works (1826-27), pp. 26-27, 195-97.

simple road and bridge repairs. By 1828, an act authorized $30,000 to be raised by lottery to improve the road.[26]

Similar efforts were made by other private subscribers in Fairfax County during this period of road building, but all suffered financial distress as tolls could not cover the high maintenance costs that accrued. Among these other turnpikes, there was Fairfax Turnpike, which was maintained by Virginia from 1824 to 1852, and Falls Bridge Turnpike Company, which was surveyed periodically between 1820 and 1852 by the Board of Public Works of Virginia. In 1811 the Occoquan Turnpike Company was chartered; this rang the death knell for the town of Colchester when the bridge across the Occoquan was built to the north at Occoquan Mills leaving Colchester with only a ferry to cross the river.[27]

An important adjunct to the turnpike construction was the building of bridges across the many streams and rivers of northern Virginia. Small wooden or stone bridges often were swept away during periods of flooding. This constituted a major expense for the turnpike companies, for if they were not repaired quickly, traffic was diverted to a competing road and the tolls collected were reduced. Residents of the area using the roads sometimes undertook the construction of these bridges, as did William Lane, Jr., who was allowed $328.33 by the county court in 1800 for building a bridge over Flat Lick Run.[28]

Of even more importance were the bridges over the larger rivers, especially the Potomac. These took superior engineering skill and even then were subject to periodic destruction. The first bridge that was constructed at the location of the present Chain Bridge, or at Little Falls on the Potomac, was a covered timber structure designed by Timothy Palmer of Newburyport, Massachusetts, and built in 1797 by the Georgetown Potomac Bridge Company. This company issued 400 shares of stock at $200 each. The bridge collapsed in 1804 from a combination of weathering and the heavy loads it supported; in particular, the herds of cattle being driven to Georgetown auction markets.[29] Another bridge was immediately constructed, designed by Theodore Burr, a successful bridge engineer, on the principle of the "Burr truss" which consisted of wooden arches carried by a wooden truss. This bridge cost $80,000, but was carried away within six months. The original Chain Bridge was built in 1805 with a span of 128 feet. It was suspended from chains with four-and-a-half-foot links anchored in stone abutments. The oak flooring on this bridge was washed away in 1810, and an Act of Congress in 1811 permitted the Georgetown Potomac Company to assess its stockholders for funds to rebuild the bridge. The third bridge lasted until 1852, but

26. Virginia State Board of Public Works (1828), p. 580.
27. Sprouse, Colchester: Colonial Port on the Potomac, p. 108.
28. Fairfax County Court Order Book, 21 April 1800.
29. See account in Harrison, Landmarks, p. 578.

Chain Bridge. The first bridge built with chains was erected in 1805 below the Little Falls of the Potomac River after a patent design of James E. Finley of Uniontown, Pennsylvania. Chain Bridge was the third bridge at the site, the first having been constructed in 1797. Patterson Mills are shown beside the span. United States Commission on Fine Arts.

private ownership ended in 1833. Bitter complaints had been raised over the high tolls, such as twenty-five cents for a horse.[30] Consequently, Congress appropriated $150,000 to permit the Georgetown Board of Aldermen and the Georgetown Common Council to purchase and operate the bridge as a municipal facility and to abolish the tolls.

Also of major importance in connecting the newly constructed turnpikes with markets of Washington and Georgetown was the Long Bridge, which was financed by the Washington Bridge Company by selling 200 shares of stock at $100 each.[31] The tolls charged included three cents a head for swine and sheep, and one dollar for stages and coaches. This bridge was closed periodically, first during the War of 1812 when in August 1814 the British invaders of Washington set the Washington end of the bridge on fire to frustrate an attack from the south, and the American forces burned the Virginia side to prevent pursuit. The fires were extinguished before they spread to the center. The structure lasted until a flood in 1831; Congress then purchased the franchise, abolished the tolls, and appropriated $200,000 for a new bridge. The new bridge was completed in 1835 and cost only $114,000. Transportation across this bridge was advertised in the Alexandria papers. The ads stated that a hack left every morning from "Gordon's" at 9:00 o'clock for the bridge and returned at 10:30. It again left in the afternoon at 3:00 and returned at 4:30. The fare was 50 cents, free of toll on the bridge. At that time it was referred to as "Washington Bridge."[32]

The Aqueduct Bridge was constructed in 1843 by the Alexandria Canal, Railroad and Bridge Company to bring the C&O Canal over the Potomac to connect with a canal in Alexandria. The conduit for the canal rested on stone piers covered with woodwork. Over this was a roadway for "persons, vehicles and animals." The aqueduct was finished and officially opened on 4 July, 1843.

Several ferries furnished service to other popular locations either before the construction of a convenient bridge, or when service was discontinued because of repairs to an existing bridge. One of the first ferry services began at Little Falls in 1738 and probably continued until a permanent structure was built crossing the Potomac at this location. One of the most financially successful was the ferry from Georgetown to Rosslyn via Mason's Analostan Island; it ran until 1868.[33] According to James F. Duhamel, this ferry was quite a source of profit to Mason's

30. Robert L. Taylor, "The History of the Potomac Bridges in the Washington Area," *The Arlington Historical Magazine*, 1 (October 1957):43.

31. Ibid., p. 46.

32. *Gazette*, 29 April 1809.

33. Fred A. Emery, "Washington's Historic Bridges," Records of the *Columbia Historical Society*, 39 (1938):51.

plantation on the island, and its revenue only diminished after Aqueduct Bridge was finished. In addition, before Long Bridge was built, Duhamel estimates that the annual revenue from the ferry was more than $1,400.[34] Two boats were required here: one for "the conveyance of waggons, carriages, etc., and the other for the purpose of carrying horses and footmen." In 1802, the county court authorized this ferry to be operated by James G. Smith and provided that two able ferrymen were to be constantly ready to manage the boats.[35]

Another important ferry was the one from the Seventh Street wharves in Washington to Alexandria. Despite regular steamboat service and the improvement of the bridges across the Potomac, this ferry was used until 1889.

An important form of transportation in early America was the stagecoach which ran on regular runs between towns carrying passengers, mail, and news for persons away from major cities. In fact, the stageline, in many ways, was the antecedent of the railroad. One such stageline was that of "Extra Billy" Smith, as William Smith, (later to be governor of Virginia) was known. By 1830, he had consolidated a number of local stagelines into a single through route from Alexandria, Virginia, to Salem, North Carolina, and connecting there with stagelines to the south and southwest.[36]

Until 1815, when steamboats began to appear on the Potomac, the only route south was on the "Potomac Path," and it was this route that was used by the mail-carrying stage traveling south. The mail left Alexandria before dawn and reached Fredericksburg by night, making "fifty miles in sixteen hours."[37] This, said one passenger, was "the only public conveyance to the southward. It is a covered wagon, open at the front, with four horses; and although it was intensely cold, I was obliged to take my seat by the driver in order to secure a view of the country during the remainder of the day."[38] The trip was a tedious one, the condition of the roads generally poor. Eleven or more persons crowded into one stage made traveling difficult; and if the group was not congenial, the trip became a disaster and was described as such. By the time steamboat service had begun on the Potomac, it seems to have been well utilized for the boat trip as far as Potomac Creek took eight hours, which was half as long as the stage.

34. Duhamel, "Analostan Island," p. 139.
35. Fairfax County Court Order Book, 21 March 1802.
36. Marshall Andrews, "History of Railroads in Fairfax County," *Yearbook of the Historical Society of Fairfax County, Virginia*, 3(1954):30.
37. Harrison, *Landmarks*, p. 450.
38. Ibid.

Water Transport and the Potomac Canal

There was an historical precedent for the preference for river transport in Virginia, given the settlement pattern, topography, and natural resources, especially the many streams and rivers. Thus, even though settlement patterns began to change and people moved inland and westward, water transportation was still desirable.

George Washington was very active in promoting the use of rivers for transportation. He wrote extensively on the subject, in private and as a member of the House of Burgesses. He felt that canals should be constructed on both the James and Potomac rivers for the purpose of opening navigation on them as far as practicable in order to open communication with the west.

As early as 1769 it was "Ordered that Leave be given to bring in a Bill for clearing and making navigable the River Potowmack from the Great Falls of the said River, up to Fort Cumberland; and that Mr. Richard Henry Lee and Mr. Washington do prepare and bring in the same.[39] Reports were made by these men to the House of Burgesses on 8 December 1769, 13 December 1769, and 14 December 1769 until finally on Wednesday, 18 March 1772, a petition was presented which authorized public development of canals to circumvent the falls on the Potomac River.[40]

Soon after, John Ballendine of Fairfax County was circulating his "Proposals for opening the navigation and the rivers James and Potomac and was seeking subscribers."[41] A meeting was held at Georgetown on 10 October 1774 attended by Washington, Thomas Johnson, and other prominent men who subscribed large sums to the plan of Ballendine's to clear the Potomac. Washington subscribed £500 Virginia currency with about £8,000 in various currencies being subscribed at this meeting.[42] On 22 December 1774, an announcement was placed in the *Virginia Gazette* discussing the approval of the trustees to hire fifty slaves to cut the canals around the several falls of the river. However, with the advent of the Revolutionary War, these projects were delayed until 1784 when the Patowmack Company was organized.

In the wartime years, emigration to the western states increased, and thus a convenient route east and west was of great concern to many prominent persons, including George Washington, Thomas Jefferson, and James Madison. The legislatures of Maryland and Virginia discussed their mutual problems in this concern. On 5 January 1785 the Virginia

---

39. Journals of the House of Burgesses, 1766-1769. (December 5, 1769) p. 225.

40. Hening, *Statutes*, 3:573.

41. Mrs. Corra Bacon-Foster, *Patomac Route to the West* (Washington: Columbia Historical Society, 1912), p. 25.

42. Ibid., p. 27.

Great seal of the Patowmack Company. Organized in 1785, the company pioneered in an effort to use rivers and canals to transport goods from inland areas of the country to the ports of the region. The company operated with limited success until the acquisition in 1828 by the Chesapeake and Ohio Canal company. From Corra Bacon-Foster, The Patomac Route to the West. Used with permission of the Columbia Historical Society.

Assembly finally enacted laws, as did the Maryland Assembly, which formally established the Patowmack Company. Subcription books were opened in Virginia at Richmond, Alexandria, and Winchester, and in Maryland at Annapolis, Frederick, and Georgetown, to be closed by 10 May 1785. In January 1785, the General Assembly of Virginia passed an act giving Washington and his heirs fifty shares in the Patowmack Company.[43]

Finally on 17 May 1785, a meeting was held in Alexandria to organize the company. Four hundred three shares had been subscribed to at this time, 135 of them in Alexandria. George Washington was elected president, and Thomas Johnson, Thomas Sim Lee, James Fitzgerald, and George Gilpin were elected directors of the Patowmack Company. There were ninety-seven unsold shares, and these were sold in the Alexandria store of William Hartshorne, treasurer of the company. A number of Fairfax County residents were shareholders in the company. Eighty-seven of these shares were taken by three firms in Amsterdam, Holland, probably influenced by Louis Casenove, their American agent.[44]

There was now some difficulty in finding a chief engineer for the canal. The work required untried skills, and there being no canals in America, few engineers understood the mechanical principles involved. Finally, however, James Rumsey was appointed the first superintendent. His pay was to be £200 Virginia currency per year, "inclusive of all expenses he may incur." Mr. Richardson Stewart was appointed assistant manager at

---

43. Ibid., pp. 53, 56.
44. For a list of the subscribers see Bacon-Foster, *Patomac Route to the West*, pp. 59, 62.

a salary of £125 Virginia currency. The rations for the laborers were to be: one pound of salt port, or 1¼ pounds of slat beef, or 1½ pounds of fresh beef or mutton; 1½ pounds of flour or bread; and three gills of rum per day.[45]

The engineering work was of the greatest scientific and mechanical interest, and articles were published in all the major scientific journals describing the various phases of the project.[46] Indicative of this interest was the fact that the 402 shares, amounting to £40,300, were subscribed to so readily.

Three different groups of men were ultimately utilized as laborers on the canal. Indentured Irish servants were used, as well as hired men, both of whom were seen as being unsatisfactory. Finally, it was resolved to hire black slaves for £20 Virginia currency per year, with clothing and rations. By 1786, work was proceeding at Shenandoah, Seneca, and Great Falls.

> From the Alexandria Gazette of the 1st January we hear that several servants who had been purchased to work on the Potowmack Navigation lately ran away, but being soon after apprehended, were sentenced to have their heads & eyebrows shaved, which operation was immediately executed, and is to be continued every week during the time of their servitude, or until their behaviour evinces that they are brought to a sense of their duty. This notice, it is expected, will sufficiently apprize the country should they again make a similar attempt.
>
> These indented Irish servants, Wm. Fee (shaved), James Nevin, Francis Cacy, Arthur Mullin (shaved), Thos. Moore, James Mannay, Hugh Taylor, Rob't Meighan, Taylor took a variety of clothes with him, among them a super fine green cloth coat with brightbuttons. £60 reward for all or £10 for each.
>
> [10 July 1786] Four more Irish servants & a woman belonging to a neighboring planter, claims to have married Taylor, she wore a crimson frieze clothe cloak, a blue petticoat & a white furred hat, (all stolen) £100 reward for all or £20 for each.[47]

The first annual report of the company reported the expected progress, but by the second year the financial difficulties that were to arise began to assert themselves with delinquent assessments as unexpected expenses continually arose. However, the removal of rocks and other obstructions

45. Ibid., p. 63.
46. One such article was written by Tobias Lear, a director of the Company, entitled "Observations on the River Patowmack and the Country Contiguous, &c" in *New York Magazine of Literary Repository*, vol. 5 (1794).
47. Bacon-Foster, *Patomac Route to the West*, pp. 72, 73.

in the Potomac River channel began, and even by August 1785, four "flat boats" and two "sets of hands" numbering fifty men each performed the initial work. Narrow passageways were blasted through the solid rock formations to provide sufficient depth. Five short canals were constructed skirting the major river falls where a channel could not be made. Work began on locks at Great Falls in 1793, and by 1802 the Potomac river and canal navigation system was substantially completed.

Not all labor problems were determined by the difficult construction, as C. Myers' letter to the governor in 1796 indicated; "I am here the Engineer for the Potomack Company. A variety of characters are employed, who of course are not of the best description. Riots and quarrels are now becoming so frequent that the exercise of legal power has become absolutely necessary, not only to cheque, but to secure offenders of the public peace . . . . "[48]

Land speculation was great along the river with high anticipation of the great wealth to be derived from the canal. In 1790 the Virginia Assembly issued a charter for a town named Matildaville, which was to be forty acres at the Great Falls in the possession of Bryan Fairfax. The trustees were George Gilpin, Albert Russell, Josiah Clapham, Richard Bland Lee, Levin Powell, and Samuel Love. The Patowmack Company headquarters was located at Matildaville from 1785 to 1799; there it maintained a large warehouse, forge, grist mill, sawmill, shops, superintendent's residence, barracks for the laborers, and boarding houses.

The longest of the five canals was more than two miles in length and located on the Maryland side of the river at Little Falls. At Great Falls, on the Virginia side, a canal three-quarters of a mile long with five lift locks was constructed. A third short canal was built around Seneca Falls, and the fourth and fifth near and above Harper's Ferry.

Gondolas carrying furs, whiskey, flour, and lumber followed this route from western Maryland to Georgetown. The gondola was a flat-bottomed boat, fifty- to seventy-five feet long and six- to nine feet wide. Even when loaded, it only drew one foot of water and was propelled by poles with the help of the river currents. During 1807, $15,000 was collected in tolls. The boating season was limited to about two months a year (the periods of high water), and it was necessary to spend much time and money on the continuous clearing of obstructions.

Alexandria had taken a lively interest in the development of the canal; unfortunately, "almost as soon as trade began to come down the river, it was found that Georgetown reaped the advantage, because many of the boats, especially in stormy times were afraid to venture out into the wide and deep water between Georgetown and Alexandria."[49] Accordingly, in

48. *Calendar of the Virginia State Papers*, vol. 8 (31 May 1796): 372.
49. *Gazette*, 30 August 1876.

Table IV

A TABLE Shewing the amount of Tolls received by the Potomac Company in each year, from the 1st August, 1799, to the 1st August, 1817, together with the number of boats and tonnage employed, and the produce and merchandize transported, with the estimated value of the same during that period.

Years	Boats	Tonnage	Flour	Whiskey	Tobacco	Iron	Articles of Produce Estimated	Return Goods Estimated	Amount of Tolls Received	Total Estimated Value
							Dolls. cts.	Dolls. cts.	Dolls. cts.	Dolls. cts.
1800	296	1,643	16,584	84	25		2,950	7,851 00	2,133 58	129,414 00
1801	413	2,993	28,209	619 1-2	100	187 1-2	14,060	6,180 00	4,210 19	328,445 32
2	305	1,952	17,250	379	5	238 1-2	27,233 50	000 00	3,479 63	163,916 00
3	493	5,549	45,055	257	32	480 1-2	3,936 00	10,386 00	9,353 93	345,472 82
4	426	3,823	39,350	578	8	88	3,250 00	7,514 00	7,665 58	284,040 60
5	405	3,208	28,507	436	11	137	32,975 18	7,486 00	5,213 24	340,334 18
6	203	1,226	19,079	459	5	20 1-2	3,553 40	4,998 00	2,123 69	86,790 40
7	573	8,155	85,248	971	20	35	11,796 00	7,314 00	15,080 42	551,896 47
8	508	5,994	48,463	1,535	3	13	10,532 47	7,613 00	9,924 27	337,007 47
9	603	6,767	40,039	1,527	37	494	8,537 00	11,510 00	9,094 89	305,628 00
10	568	5,374	40,757	1,080	13	191 1-2	5,703 00	000 00	7,915 85	318,237 62
11	1300	16,350	118,222	3,768	27	200	6,810 00	6,000 00	22,542 89	925,074 80
12	613	9,214	55,829	3,143	6	360	1,694 00	7,319 75	11,471 37	515,525 75
13	623	7,916	55,902	3,464	11	252	1,899 00	6,119 32	11,816 22	423,340 32
14	596	5,987	38,769	2,684	18	361	675 60	5,314 12	9,109 82	312,093 72
15	613	6,354	47,183	4,616	9	314	2,075 00	5,211 15	9,789 57	489,498 15
16	550	6,132	35,918	1,774	29	419	9,291 65	6,371 35	7,501 52	357,661 00
17	856	8,197	57,662	1,385	10	335	4,094 00	14,000 00	13,948 23	787,994 00
		106,834 1-2	818,026	28,759 1-2	369	4,126 1-2	151,065 80	121,187 69	162,379 95	7,002,370 62

True Statement from the Books.

Jos. Brewer, Tr. P. Co.

order to avoid both the open water and the Long Bridge, the Common Council of Alexandria in 1811 applied for and obtained the right to cut a canal from the Potomac, opposite Georgetown, around the west end of the causeway from Mason's Island to the western shore of the river, and into the arm of the river that passes around the western side of that Island, "and along the west side of Alexander's peninsula and through any points of land between Mason's Island and Alexandria." However, the war with Great Britain came, and the work was abandoned.

It can be seen from the chart (page 207) reprinted from the Board of Public Works Reports that from 1 August 1799 to 1 August 1817, the highest amount in annual tolls received was in 1811: $22,542.89. That year an unusually large amount of flour was transported, 118,222 barrels, when 1,300 boats passed with a tonnage of 16,350. By 1814, Virginia had purchased seventy shares in the Patowmack Company; these were transferred to the Board of Public Works upon its inception. The total amount of expenditures from 1784 to 1818 was $650,000, and the tolls collected from August 1799 to August 1817 were $162,379.95.

Financial affairs did not improve as expenditures continued to rise, and so in 1821, a joint committee appointed by the Virginia and Maryland legislatures to examine the affairs of the Patowmack Company recommended that its charter be revoked. Some men envisioned a continuous canal 360 miles in length connecting the tidewater of the Potomac with the navigable waters of the Ohio River at Pittsburgh. The route of the canal, its dimensions, and probable cost were carefully studied, and in June 1828, the Chespeake and Ohio Canal Company was organized with a capital stock of $3,000,000. Soon afterward, the old Patowmack Company turned over all its charter rights and privileges along the Potomac Valley to the new company. On 4 July 1828, President John Quincy Adams turned the first spade of earth near Little Falls.

All three segments of the District of Columbia were stockholders; Alexandria and Georgetown subscribed to $250,000 each, and Washington City to $1,000,000 in capital stock. In 1876 the event was described:

> During the darkest period of the existence of our old town, when everything was at a standstill, and the progress of the town so slow that in ten years the population increased but 25 souls, when the town had been just ravaged by fire; and when without hope at home, the faces of all young Alexandrians turned for their future towards the great West, the town determined to embark in a great effort to regain its trade. . . . The money to pay the subscription had been borrowed in guilders from a company of Holland merchants and the United States had agreed the payment of the

The Winchester and Alexandria Mail Stage. Before railroad
lines crossed the county in the 1850s all overland
transportation depended on horses traveling over roads that
were often in deplorable condition. Among the major routes
crossing the county were those leading from Alexandria to
the farms of the Valley of Virginia. Virginia Historical Society.

debt. . . . The people soon became restive under the tax . . .
it grew to be a common saying that the town was 'mortgaged
to the Dutch' and the Holland debt was the grievance of the
day. Finally Congress assumed the debt. [50]

In 1830, Alexandria embarked alone on the construction of the
Alexandria Canal from the terminus of the C&O Canal at Georgetown.
Alexandria needed to bridge the Potomac with an aqueduct over which
horse-drawn barges could pass onto a seven-mile lateral canal to the
wharves. On 26 May 1830, Congress passed an act granting a charter to
the Alexandria Canal Company. The subscribers included John Roberts,
Phinneas Janney, Robert I. Taylor, Thompson F. Mason, Hugh Smith,
Anthony C. Cazenove, Wm. H. Miller, Charles Bennett, Edmund J. Lee,
Colin Auld, Henry Daingerfield, George Brent, and Jonathan Butcher.

"The town at once subscribed for $50,000 of stock and on the 4th of
July 1831, a procession, civic and military, headed by a plow on wheels,
moved to the place selected for the purpose and John Roberts, Mayor of
the town, broke ground for the canal, G.W.P. Custis delivering one of
his characteristic orations in honor of the event."[51] That Alexandria
could and would embark again on a risky financial venture was aided
this time by the fact that the C&O Canal was completed from Rock
Creek at Georgetown to Seneca, despite numerous labor problems and
disease. The people were jubilant over the prospects of the financial gains
for their towns.

The aqueduct was finished and officially opened on 4 July 1843, and
several manufacturers contracted with the directors of the C&O Canal
for use of "waste" water for propelling mills. The following five months
saw the completion of the Alexandria Canal, which was formally opened
2 December 1843.

50. *Gazette*, 29 August 1876.
51. *Gazette*, 1 September 1876.

IV

Black Population in Fairfax County

The legislative reforms which led to an election reform with universal white male suffrage instigated little discussion in local publications when compared to the slavery controversy which existed from the time of the Revolution through the early decades of the nineteenth century. Early travelers wrote that local men deplored the institution of slavery, but continued to keep their own slaves. As Elias Pym Fordham wrote in his travel diary of 1817, "almost all of them [Virginians] deplore the existence of slavery; though they think it must be continued, now it is introduced . . . but they (that is the young men) draw the dirks, which they usually wear. . . . ."[1] When Anne Newport Royall wrote of her stay in Alexandria and the surrounding county she said that "the slaves of this place bear every mark of good treatment; they look happy and are comfortably clothed, though not half so fine or richly dressed; indeed the white people of this place lack a great deal of being dressed equal to the blacks of Huntsville [Alabama] or Lexington."[2]

There are many cases in the courts, including Fairfax County courts, where blacks sought to be freed or to certify their freedom, but laws were enacted to make it more difficult for the slave to obtain his freedom. In 1798, an act excluded abolition society members, but not slaveholders, from juries hearing freedom suits.[3] This law combined with the fact that freedom suits were almost always prosecuted in the county courts "where the common county justices preside, and those justices often considerable slaveholders; under these circumstances the claimant must appear as

---

1. Elias Pym Fordham, *Personal Narrative of Travels in Virginia, Maryland* . . . (Cleveland: Arthur H. Clark Co., 1906).
2. Royall, *Sketches of History*, p. 104.
3. Shepherd, 1 *Stat.* (2 December 1795) 363-65; 2 *Stat.* (25 January 1798) 77-79.

clear as the sun at noon before it would be admitted for tryal." This "destroyed almost every suggestion of hope that any person . . . can obtain liberty by due process of law."[4]

Gabriel's Insurrection was an attempted slave revolt organized near Richmond which was planned to affect the entire state. This uprising, thwarted at the last moment, plus the revolt in Santo Domingo, Haiti, caused a strong reaction against liberalization of the laws among many, but brought the problem to the forefront for many others. By 1803 the southern abolition societies had nearly disappeared, and further expansion of schools established for black children was discouraged.

There were contrary forces working in Fairfax County, however, which did not make it typical of the entire state. Large slaveholders were common in Fairfax County, but not to the extent found in more prosperous counties in the state. By the early nineteenth century, the Quakers and Methodist Society were quite active in this region, encouraging the education and sometimes emancipation of slaves. Particularly influential was the Adams family, who had been converted by Bishop Asbury in his travels, and who preached at the Fairfax Chapel between 1798 and 1810. Mrs. Ann Lawyer Adams is said to have been particularly active in converting others, and her husband Col. William Adams, who died in 1809, gave freedom to over twenty slaves. Typical of others within the county, and incurring the wrath of some, was Col. James Wren, architect of the Falls Church, Christ Church, and the Fairfax County Courthouse, who once was a very active churchman and served on the vestry for more than twenty years. Colonel Wren was also a convert to Methodism, and two of his daughters married men in the Adams family who were active Methodist ministers. Sarah Wren, his wife, made provisions for some of her slaves to be freed when they came of age and were educated, and freed all her slaves after her death.[5] It has been argued that persons such as Sarah Wren and William Adams had nothing to lose by freeing their slaves after their death, since they were able to use their services during their own lifetime, and those freed were often old. This is true in some cases, but in the instance of Sarah Wren her former slaves had accumulated enough money so that they were able to purchase some of their mistress' household items and personal goods from her estate. This probably means that the former slaves had been allowed to earn and to keep their wages, while still technically slaves.

Other persons who were kept as slaves within the county were able to enjoy at least a semblance of a normal life and live as a family group. This is noted in the inventory of William Fitzhugh's estate where a

4. George Drinker to Joseph Bringhurst, 10 December 1804; Petition from Alexandria Abolition Society to the Virginia General Assembly, 1796, Pennsylvania Society for Promoting the Abolition of Slavery Papers, Historical Society of Pennsylvania, Philadelphia.

5. Fairfax County Will Book M-1, p. 312.

good number of the total 232 slaves were listed by family group. That is, the name of the person, his age, and that of wife and children were grouped together, with the value of the entire family noted:

Ben Douglas	age 30	. . . . .$350
Scharlotte	35	 250
Sintha	14	250
Lucy	6	150
Franky	2	100

$1,100. [6]

Most of those listed as a family group had a last name, an unusual practice, and some were listed with their occupations such as smith, carpenter, cook, or tanner.

The law of 1806 forbidding any freed slave to remain in Virginia more than twelve months was later amended to permit local courts to give manumitted slaves permission to continue to live in Virginia if they had performed some act of "extraordinary merit," or if they were persons of "good character, sober, peaceable, orderly and industrious." These amendments of 1815 and 1837 stood throughout the antebellum years.[7] The initial statute of 1806, however, caused a reaction in other states where freed slaves were apt to go and these other states followed by enacting similar laws, such as those found in Maryland, Kentucky, and Delaware. Within twenty-five years, Ohio, Indiana, Illinois, Missouri, North Carolina, and Tennessee had passed similar laws. The result was, of course, that a freed slave had no place to go except to the north or to the far west, if he or she could find a way to get there.

Some slaves did not wait for their masters to offer freedom, or for the courts to certify their liberty; they bought it with their own hard work. Many slaves bought their liberty with money they earned while hiring their own time. George Drinker explained the decline of slavery in the Northern Neck as partly the result of the "practice among lenient slaveholders of setting a moderate value on the time of slaves and suffering them to hire out at the best terms they could get."[8]

The Common Council of Alexandria passed a bill in 1806 which would "prevent migration of free negroes and mulattoes, into the corporation of Alexandria and to prescribe the mode of registering the same and to enforce the payment of their capitation tax."[9] This bill was

6. Fairfax County Will Book J-1, p. 285.
7. Virginia Laws, 1815, ch. 24; Ibid., 1836-37, ch. 70.
8. George Drinker to J. Bringhurst Papers, Historical Society of Pennsylvania, Philadelphia.
9. Gazette, 19 February 1806.

obviously passed by those in Alexandria who feared that the urban atmosphere might be attractive to persons hiding from the strict Virginia law, while still finding work. The *Gazette* almost daily carried advertisements of businesses offering employment opportunities for blacks, even though of a menial nature.

The Fairfax County court records quite effectively recount the varying moods of the white citizens in the judgments brought before the court. Many advertisements were placed in the local newspapers, including the Alexandria *Gazette*, for runaway slaves; the rewards ranged from ten to one hundred dollars, depending on the economic situation of the times and the value of the slave to the holder. Because a slave was apprehended did not mean that he would be returned to his owner, as the records point out.

In 1800, a runaway, or even a free man, was often returned to the former owner at the court's expense. For instance, when "John Bell, a free mulatto, was committed to the gaol of this county, on suspicion of being a runaway being this day brought before the court and on hearing it is ordered that he do return to the state of Maryland and that the gaoler charge the expense of his keeping to the county."[10] At the same time, if the black man could not or did not produce the right papers, and no one claimed the person as a slave, he was liable for court costs. "James Conner, Gaoler, brought before the court a negro man slave named Will who was committed to the gaol of this County as a runaway and the said negro having remained in for upwards of two months and no person appearing to claim him, and it appearing to the court that he has been advertised according to law, it is the opinion of the court that he ought to be hired out for the payment of his gaol fees at a sum not less than 20% per month."[11] By 1807, the same situation could apply to a black man only suspected of being a runaway, accruing prison fees of $24.05 in two months. In such a situation the jailer was "ordered that he hire the said negro immediately at public auction for the shortest time that any person will pay the amount aforesaid and that the said negro was hired to Wm. Payne for one year for the amount aforesaid."[12] After this man's year of servitude was over, the problem was usually the payment of prison fees, often a considerable sum for the times. If the fees were paid, the man was freed. Money was the key, and if the black was able to earn and keep ready cash, then he usually would have a chance to remain free. Some whites did leave sums of money to their slaves in their wills, as did Sarah Wren.[13]

10. Fairfax County Court Order Book, 17 June 1800.

11. Ibid., 21 July 1800.

12. Ibid., 22 January 1807.

13. Fairfax County Will Book L-1, p. 53.

Elizabeth Lee Jones, sister of Thomas ap Catesby Jones, set all her slaves free by the terms of her will of 1822. The will is interesting in its four pages of explicit instructions as to the disposition of the slaves in order that they remain free forever. She entrusted the matter to the American Colonization Society of which Bushrod Washington was one of the leaders.[14]

Most were not so fortunate, however, such as Peter Vevet "who was committed to the jail of this county by warrant under the hand of Geo. Summers under suspicion of being a foreign imported slave being this day brought before the court and examined. It is ordered that the jailer hire him out to some humane and discreet person for the best price that can be obtained for three months or until such time as the court shall take some further order respecting the said Peter Vevet."[15] A slave who found the opportunity to run away often found that his situation could be worsened, as in the case of a man called "negro Tom" who was held in Fairfax County jail as a runaway in 1826. It was judged that his value was only $35, and since he had come from King George County, it was "ordered that the jailer of this county sell the said negro Tom . . . and report the amount of sales to the court."[16] Women were sold as well as men: an advertisement in 1838 was placed on the front door of the court house for one month (as required by law) describing a "negro woman Sally" who was suspected of being a runaway. No response was given to the advertisement and the woman was sold.[17]

In 1822 all free negroes and mulattoes who were delinquent in their taxes were hired out by the sheriff of the county "for as long a time as will raise the taxes being respectively due by them."[18] Thus, manumission was no guarantee that a former slave would remain free. When a former slave found it difficult to raise money to buy the necessities of life, or wanted to purchase his own wife, husband, or child, he (or she) might hire himself out for a certain period, often for a number of years, in order to raise the necessary cash. And being freed was not a simple thing. Once a will was probated, the case would have to be approved by the court, and the necessary documents prepared which the black had to carry with him. All blacks were suspected of being slaves. It was up to the free black to provide proof.

Many blacks went through the difficulties of a court proceeding and the expense of an attorney in order to obtain recognition of their freedom or to seek an injunction against someone illegally holding their children.

14. Fairfax County Will Book, U-1, p. 185.
15. Fairfax County Court Order Book June 1801.
16. Ibid., 15 September 1826.
17. Ibid., 18 June 1838.
18. Ibid., 19 June 1822.

In 1825 a free black woman named Nelly Gaskins was granted a ruling again John Lewis who was holding her three children.[19]

An act passed in 1837 brought about the following interesting decision:

> On hearing the petition of Dennis Comer a free man of colour for permission to remain in the county of Fairfax it appearing to the satisfaction of the court that the acting justices of the peace for the county Fairfax have been first duly summoned and that a majority of them were actually present and satisfactory proof having been made to them that the applicant is a person of good character, peaceable, orderly and industrious and not addicted to drunkeness, gaming or other vice, and it further appearing that notice of said application has been posted at the front door of the courthouse of said county for upwards of two months immediately preceding said application, and three-quarters of the justices concurring, it is ordered to be entered of record that the said Dennis Comer, the Petitioner, is of the character and description required by an Act of the General Assembly of Virginia passed in the 22nd day of March 1837, entitled, An Act amending the laws concerning emancipated slaves, free negroes and mulattoes, and that permission is hereby granted him, the said Dennis Comer to remain within the commonwealth and reside within the county of Fairfax during the good pleasure of the court and further that it be entered of record that the attending attorney of the Commonwealth was present in court and represented the interests of the Commonwealth in the case.[20]

It is interesting to contrast the above tedious recitation to a court decision of 1807 "on the motion of Sambo, a free black man. It appearing to the court that he is a person of honest reputation and demeanor. License is granted him to keep and carry fire arms according to law."[21]

Public whipping was the usual punishment for stealing, whether the person was black or white, with the usual number being "39 lashes on bare back well laid on at the public whipping post." Whites committing offenses against blacks were also punished, as in the case of "J. Weir who stands charged for stabbing a negro man named Dennis, the property of _____ Edwards . . . . It is the unanimous opinion by the court that he be burnt in the hand in open court and receive 39 lashes on his bare back well laid on at the public whipping post."[22]

19. Ibid., 20 June 1825.
20. Ibid., 19 June 1837.
21. Ibid., 21 September 1807.
22. Ibid., 22 October 1822.

In 1840, Fairfax County experienced an insurrection documented in the following court record:

> At a court for the county of Fairfax the 12th day of March 1840 for the trial of negroes Alfred, Spencer, Taylor, Dennis and Henry, charged with rebellion and insurrection. This day came as well the attorney for the commonwealth as Bernard Hooe and Henry M. Thomas counsel for the prisoners and thereupon the said prisoners yesterday and pleaded not guilty, being again led to the bar in custody of the sheriff of this county and the court after hearing the evidence and the arguments of counsel, it is the opinion of the court that the prisoners Alfred and Spencer are guilty of willfully and maliciously assaulting and beating John Ashford, Stephen B. Jones and Frances P. Ashford with intent in so doing to kill the said . . . as charged in the warrant, and that the prisoners Henry, Dennis and Taylor are not guilty of the offence as charged. It is therefore ordered by the court that the said Alfred and Spencer be taken to the jail from whence they came and there safely to be kept until the 3rd Friday in April next and then to be removed from the said jail to the place of public execution and between the hours of 12 noon and 2 o'clock of the same day to be hanged by the neck until they be dead, and that the sheriff of this county carry this judgement of the court into execution.[23]

The problem for most free blacks was to find a way to support themselves and their families. A few were successful in staying in their old locality, if welcomed, but most migrated to the cities which encircled the South and became centers of free black population. Since the Quakers and Methodists had been active in offering religious instruction to free blacks, there were numerous black ministers, especially in the early nineteenth century.[24] Bishop William Meade of the Anglican church was one who provided religious education to blacks in Alexandria and Fairfax County as late as 1813 and 1814.[25] At this time it was also the practice to worship together in the same chapel, and in the Fairfax Circuit of the Methodist Society there were 300 white members and 47 blacks. By 1812, however, the number had risen to 337 whites and 229 blacks.[26]

John Davis, a teacher who traveled through Fairfax County and tutored local children, wrote of his visit to Pohick Church while he was

---

23. Ibid., 12 March 1840.

24. Probably the earliest black preacher in Fairfax County was Harry Hoosier, who is recorded as giving a sermon in 1781 at the Fairfax Chapel. Francis Asbury, *The Journal of the Rev. Francis Asbury*, 3 vols. (New York: Bangs & Mason, 1821). vol. 1 p. 328.

25. Ibid., 3 vols.

26. Steadman, *Falls Church*, pp. 103-4.

employed as a tutor in Occoquan: "Of the congregation of Powheek Church, about one half was composed of white people, and the other of negroes . . . . After church, I asked Parson Wems his opinion of the piety of the blacks. 'Sir,' said he, 'no people in this country prize the Sabbath more seriously than the trampled-upon negroes. They are swift to hear, they seem to hear as for their lives. They are wakeful, serious, reverent, and attentive in God's house; Oh! it is sweet preaching when people are desirous of hearing!'"[27]

However, the reality was that it was difficult to find work, and even with an education, most blacks were "toilers" at jobs such as barbers, coopers, carpenters, mechanics, bricklayers, painters, tanners, gardeners, bakers, and body and personal servants.[28] These were professions or skills learned on the plantation and could be performed with ease, if the person could find an employer and retain his freedom. Usually, however, the free black man labored on roads and bridges, performing the lowest level of work. And even in that, there was often competition with the Irish or German immigrant, with the black often losing his place to the European.

The majority of the white population retained ingrained prejudices. The opinion of the local residents of free blacks and mulattoes was reflected in the writings of Anne Royall, an outspoken social critic and newspaperwoman, who commented on her first impression of Alexandria in 1824:

> Having been whirled here in the night, I had no opportunity of seeing the city. Upon going to the window next morning, which faces the street, and market square, I was shocked at a sight entirely new to me. The street and market-square presented groups of men, women and children, every shade of colour, from the fairest white, down to the deepest black . . . . White and black people I had been accustomed to see, and a few mulattoes, but such a multifarious mixture, bursting upon the sight at once, was as novel as it was unexpected. Some of these were about half-white, some almost white, leaving it difficult to distinguish where the one ends, and the other begins. To one unaccustomed to see human nature in this guise, it excites feelings of horror and disgust. It has something in it so contrary to nature, something which seems never to have entered into her scheme, to see a man neither black nor white, with blue eyes, and a woolly head, has something in it at which the mind

---

27. John Davis, *Travels of Four Years and a Half in the United States of America*, (Bristol: R. Edwards, Printer, 1803), p. 48.
28. Russell, *The Free Negro in Virginia*, p. 150.

recoils. It appears that these people, instead of abolishing slavery, are gradually not only becoming slaves themselves, but changing color.[29]

The place of slavery in antebellum Fairfax County was generally the same as that found in other areas of the state. Slaveholding was a financial matter and, to a large extent, was the basis of the cash reserve of the owner and his family. As Joseph Packard recalled:

> The slaves formed a large portion of the wealth of the rich and were almost the same as bonds, for they were readily converted into cash on occasion. Hence a man who had such property had good credit with the merchants. The planter could get what supplies he needed year by year, sending down what he had to spare from the farm, and being credited for the rest, and charged from twelve to twenty percent more for interest. This might go on for years unless either the merchant or the farmer should die. In that case the sale of a slave or a family or two of slaves would settle the matter. The planters were not used to paying their debts until they died . . . .[30]

This manner of economic settlement in Fairfax County is documented in the accounts of the estate sales in Fairfax County will books. The will of William Fitzhugh made just such a provision when it was specified that one-third of the slaves in his estate were to be set aside to "pay debts."[31]

29. Royall, *Sketches of History*, p. 100.

30. Joseph Packard, *Recollections of a Long Life*, ed. Thomas J. Packard (Washington: Byron S. Adams, 1902) p. 108.

31. Fairfax County Will Book J-1, p. 244.

V

Providence and the New Courthouse

In 1798 the Virginia General Assembly directed that the Fairfax County Courthouse be relocated in a place more central to the county than Alexandria. Various groups within the county had been debating the most desirable location for almost ten years, but now that it was known that Alexandria would become part of the District of Columbia, a site had to be chosen.[1] The present location of the county courthouse was selected and purchased from Richard Ratcliffe for one dollar.[2] The debate for the past decade had centered on several issues, including the location. Businessmen in the vicinity of the courthouse would be assured of an increase in business, and traffic on the roads would increase. Some felt that an inland location would isolate the court. Justices had to travel to the courthouse, and in inclement weather a man might decide that the trip would be too difficult. There constantly was difficulty in getting the justices to attend all court sessions. They were not paid and the civic duty proved wearisome at times.[3]

By 1798 the decision was made to locate the courthouse at the crossroads of the present Little River Turnpike and Ox Road. The following notice was placed in the Alexandria *Gazette*:

The Fairfax County Court House Commissioners have fixed on Thursday, the 28th instant, for letting out the

1. For documents relating to the debate over location of the courthouse, see the Charles Simms Papers, Peter Force Collection, vol. 3 Library of Congress, Manuscripts Division, Washington, D.C. (hereinafter cited as Force Collection).

2. Ross D. Netherton and Ruby W. Waldeck, *The Fairfax County Courthouse* (Fairfax, Va.: Office of Comprehensive Planning, 1977).

3. For a discussion of the duties and responsibilities of the county court magistrate, see Albert Ogden Porter, *County Government in Virginia: A Legislative History, 1607-1904* (New York: Columbia University Press, 1947).

erection of the necessary PUBLIC BUILDINGS to the lowest
bidder. As they have adopted the plan exhibited by Mr.
Wren. Those workmen who mean to attend at Mr. Earps
store, may have a sight of the plan and the manner in which
the work is to be finished, by application at the Clerk's office.

Charles Little, D. Stuart, W. Payne,
J. Wren, C. Minor.[4]

The building was completed by 1800 as the following court record
notes:

At a meeting of the courthouse on the 27th day of
January 1800. Present Charles Little, David Stuart, William
Payne, James Wren and George Minor, Gentlemen Commis-
sioners

We, the said Commissioners, appointed by an Order of
May Court, 1798, for the purpose of superintending the
erection of the necessary public buildings for holding of the
courts—having met on this day to receive the said buildings
from the persons with whom we had contracted to build
them, do report that we have examined and find them to be
executed agreeable to contract. They are therefore accepted
by us, on behalf of the county . . . .[5]

The four acres that had been purchased from Richard Ratcliffe were
the site for the courthouse, jail, clerk's office, a brick tavern, kitchen,
stable, and a storehouse.[6] The first court session was held in the new
building on 21 April 1800.[7]

The courthouse complex gradually became the center of activity for
the county, and in 1805 the town of Providence was incorporated at the
site of the courthouse, including fourteen acres of land surrounding it,
again the property of Richard Ratcliffe.[8] The trustees of the newly
created town were Charles Little, William Payne, Richard Bland Lee,
John Jackson, John C. Hunter, Richard Coleman, Daniel McCarty
Chichester, Henry Gunnell, Jr., Marmaduke B. Beckwith, Daniel Lewis,
Francis Coffer, David Stuart, William Middleton, and Richard Fitzhugh.
This location was ideal, being at the junction of Little River Turnpike and
Ox Road and providing relatively easy access to most parts of the
county.

4. *Alexandria Advertiser and Gazette*, 21 June 1798.
5. Fairfax County Deed Book, B-2, pp. 503-4.
6. Ibid.
7. Fairfax County Court Order Book, 1799-1800, p. 509.
8. 3 *Stat.* p. 177.

Fairfax County Courthouse as completed in 1800. It was constructed according to the plan of James Wren, a magistrate of the court and former sheriff of the county. Thirty years earlier, Wren had designed the three major churches of the county, Pohick, Christ, and the Falls Church. Sketch by Gloria Matthews. Fairfax County of Comprehensive Planning.

Of course, all official business took place at Providence, and as time went on the population grew and the services offered were expanded. Attorneys generally took a room in the hotel near the courthouse and used that as their office, advertising their services in the Alexandria *Gazette*. In 1835, for instance, Archibald Henderson, Jr.'s advertisement read "Attorney at Law, will practice in the Superior and Inferior Courts of Fairfax and Loudoun Counties" and that he was located in "the Hotel of William D. Wilcoxon at Fairfax Courthouse." In the same year, George W. Hunter, Jr., Attorney at Law, announced his office at Allison's Tavern at Fairfax Courthouse. [9]

The town of Providence was generally called Fairfax Court House, until it was incorporated as the Town of Fairfax in 1875. The number of public buildings gradually increased as a jail was constructed in 1800, and a clerk's office was built with "proper iron grating for the windows."[10] The land surrounding the courthouse was leveled and a fence erected around the property. By December it was deemed necessary

9. *Gazette*, 10 January 1835.

10. Fairfax County Court Order Book, 18 March 1800.

to create legislation to forbid sellers or retailers of liquors to set up booths on the public lot.[11] "English" or other grass was planted. In 1803 a plan was presented to the court for a poorhouse; one was erected, and land was set aside for its use. Gallows were erected at "Race Field" on the east side of a house occupied by Patrick McCarty on land owned by Richard Ratcliffe.[12] The county jail was destroyed by fire in 1809 and a temporary jail was established in Centreville.[13] The new jail was built in the following year at a cost of $2,486.[14]

Grand jury indictments were returned in 1810 for a number of serious crimes including illegal tolls exacted on the Little River Turnpike by Henry Padgett, John Powell, and William Crump. Thirty-four persons did not vote in the previous election for a representative to the General Assembly; these persons included Lawrence Lewis, William Foote, Bushrod Washington, Jr., William Millan, Lee Massey, John and Thomas McIntosh, Caleb Strong, George Triplett, J. Love, and Daniel McCarty.[15] The punishment was a fine, although this law was seldom enforced.[16]

In general, however, the cases presented before the county justices were often an indication of the tenor of the times and of a personal nature, as the following examples relate.

John Hugely appeared before the court with two witnesses who testified that the upper part of his left ear had been bitten off in a fight.[17]

William Johnston was accused of stealing one linen shirt, 50c; one pair pantaloons, 50c; one shawl, 75c; one pair of stockings; 25c. He was found guilty and sentenced to ten lashes at the public whipping post.[18] There were gambling offenses, and Ralph Hodgkin was accused of operating a shuffle board in 1803.[19] John Bickler was charged with unlawful gaming, keeping a disorderly house, and retailing liquors without a license in 1809.[20]

James Massey was found guilty of horse stealing in 1820 and was sentenced to five years in the public jail and penitentiary house in a solitary cell and kept on a "low and coarse diet" for half of the time.[21] The severity of his punishment indicates how seriously horse stealing was viewed at the time. On the other hand, Lee Pumeroy was ordered to

11. Ibid., 15 December 1800.
12. Ibid., 19 December 1803.
13. Ibid., 18 December 1809.
14. Ibid., 19 February 1810.
15. Ibid., 18 June 1810.
16. Porter, County Government in Virginia, p. 170.
17. Fairfax County Court Order Book, 21 March 1803.
18. Fairfax County Court Order Book, 18 June 1810.
19. Ibid., 22 March 1803.
20. Ibid., 21 June 1809.
21. Ibid., 23 May 1820.

support the child begotten by Betsy Tillett, she charging him with being the father. The child, Washington Tillett, alias Pumeroy, five years old, was apprenticed to Lee Pumeroy who was to teach him the "art and mystery of farming and reading, writing and arithmetic," according to law.[22]

The justices of the county court traditionally were a self-perpetuating body; they recommended new members to the governor and simply ratified their appointment. These men served for life, and since Fairfax County was a large county, those living near the courthouse were generally those most frequently in attendance at the monthly court meetings. Thus, attendance was frequently so poor that a remedy was sought in 1807 for the continuing dilemma. The 19 June 1807 court meeting decided that on the next court date that the "several justices of the peace for this county" shall meet "to recommend so many proper persons to act as justices of the peace as may be deemed necessary to remedy the evils aforesaid, and that such of the magistrates as can and do not attend be requested to signify their intention either to continue and do business or resign their respective offices."[23] When a majority of the justices finally appeared, it was decided that there was not a sufficient number of justices to do the business of the county "with convenience and dispatch." Therefore, John C. Hunter, John C. Scott, Daniel McCarty Chichester, Joseph Powell, Edward Dulin, James L. Triplett, John F. Ricketts, and George Mason were all recommended to the governor as justices of the peace or to be added to the commission of the peace for the county.[24] The governor, however, did not approve all of the above men and commissioned some of them, an act which brought about the anger of the justices. A letter signifying such was submitted to the governor on 21 March 1808.[25] Finally, in 1810, the remaining persons from the original list of 1807 were again submitted to the governor with the names of John C. Scott, Daniel M. Chichester, James Power, Edward Dulin, and George Mason recommended to fill vacancies and to provide magistrates in parts of the county where deficiencies existed.[26] The other men from the original list were already serving on the bench.

22. Ibid., 20 April 1809.
23. Ibid., 19 June 1807.
24. Ibid., 17 August 1807.
25. Ibid., 15 February 1808.
26. Ibid., 21 May 1810.

VI

The War of 1812

Early nineteenth-century Virginians took an active but distant interest in the conflicts of the European nations, generally tending to favor the British. Between 1792 and 1801 French privateers and men-of-war had captured twenty or more Alexandria vessels.[1] However, when Britain found itself in strained circumstances and began to confiscate American ships on the Atlantic, opinion began to change. Thus, to be captured by the British and to labor on their ships as seamen was an increasing hardship and danger not anticipated by those favoring Great Britain in the War of 1812.

Many Virginians naturally were outraged when the British frigate *Leopard* attacked the American cruiser *Chesapeake* off Cape Henry in the Hampton Roads area of the state. Militia volunteers quickly organized and were ready to fight. The following broadside is probably typical of many which were circulating after this event: "The citizens of Alexandria have declared their sentiments in the hostile attack of the British ship *Leopard*, on the American frigate *Chesapeake* in the annexed resolutions. We shall be happy to cooperate with you in promoting the public safety if future events should render it necessary." This was signed in Alexandria on 3 July 1807.[2]

Jefferson was opposed to war over this episode, and he continued to advocate his philosophy that economic sanctions were the proper course for the nation to follow. However, after the Embargo Act of 1807 was passed by Congress, local planters and businessmen from Alexandria found the economic picture bleak. All exports from America were prohibited, and various articles of British manufacture were refused

---

1. Rothgeb, "An Analysis of the Rise," p. 15.
2. Broadside No. 3175, Alexandria, 3 July 1807. Duke University, Durham, North Carolina.

entrance. Tobacco, wheat, and corn were all major exports from this region, and when no market could be found for these goods, local residents found their already depressed situation worsened. Alexandria's exports dwindled to a fraction of the prosperity enjoyed by that city at the turn of the century. Even though the Embargo Act was repealed in 1809 after severe criticism, Alexandria was not to regain much of its former trade until 1840, and this success was short-lived with the advent of the railroad and alternate trade routes to other ports from the interior of the country.

When Congress finally declared war on Great Britain in 1812, ostensibly for commercial reasons, neither the war nor President Madison were popular with local residents. It is sometimes thought that this war did not affect the local residents significantly, but even though the fighting was not centered here, there still was much activity surrounding it which had a profound effect on the citizens of the county and Alexandria. Not the least of these was the fact that many of the local men were members of militia units which were used during the conflict.

When it seemed likely that the British were coming to attack Washington, an idea initially denied by Madison's closest cabinet advisors,[3] Colonel George Minor of Fairfax County, in charge of the 10th Virginia Militia, was ordered to Washington from Falls Church in Fairfax County on 23 August 1814.[4] Because the attack was so unexpected, few of the 700-man regiment came armed. When in Washington, Minor went with the regimental surgeon, Dr. Peake, to President Madison and to Secretary Armstrong, and they agreed to supply arms and ammunition for the regiment the next day. After sleeping the night in the Capitol, the regiment went to the supply headquarters and again encountered delays. Bureaucratic confusion reigned in all areas, and the group was not called to the first fight at Bladensburg.[5]

Meanwhile the army's baggage wagons went across the Long Bridge into Virginia, carrying government documents and the army's stockpiles. It has been said that Governor Barbour of Virginia proclaimed this day "the proudest day which Virginia has seen since the foundation of the commonwealth."[6] Some go on to state that so many turned out for the defense of Virginia against a possible British invasion that facilities were totally inadequate. In reality and in retrospect, it seems as if the problem was not in the lack of adequate facilities, but in confusion as to the British plan, bureaucratic difficulties, and personal conflict among the leaders of the nation and of its official defensive groups.

3. Wiltse, *The New Nation*, p. 48; Walter Lord, *The Dawn's Early Light* (New York: W.W. Norton & Company, Inc., 1972), p. 24 (hereinafter cited as Lord, *The Dawn's Early Light*).

4. Lord, *The Dawn's Early Light*, p. 98.

5. Ibid., p. 108.

6. Virginius Dabney, *Virginia, the New Dominion* (Garden City: Doubleday & Co.), 1971, p. 207.

Minor's militia of 700 armed Virginians was finally used to bolster the effort in Washington under Gen. Walter Smith. However, the administration leaders were scattered in northern Virginia. Much of our knowledge of what happened during these crucial days comes from the Mordecai Booth report, which is a detailed narrative of the proceedings and engagements from 22 August to 10 September 1814, when the powder was removed from the naval magazine by Booth under orders from Commodore Thomas Tingey of the Washington Naval Yard.[7] It was taken to the farm of Daniel Dulany near the Falls Church. Booth relates that on 23 August he met Colonel Minor of the Fairfax Militia, each of them going the opposite direction. That night, when the regiment was camping in the Capitol, Booth was staying at Wren's Tavern close to the Falls Church and within one mile of the Dulany farm. He stayed there again on the 24th after a safe retreat from the Capitol, just before its burning. The wagon loads of gun powder from the navy magazine were guarded by six persons from Colonel Minor's regiment, until they could be deposited at the Dulany farm.

On the 24th, Booth wrote the following to Tingey: "Desirous of having the powder delivered and under guard, I was on my horse at the dawn of day, and ordered the waggons to gear up, and follow me on getting to the Farm, I found Seventy five barrels of Powder had been deposited—the Barn in which it was, open, and much out of order—I went to the House of Mr. — Bennett 'a respectable Citizen,' recommended by Col. Minor, in whom I might confide, for its care he Agreed to have my orders attended to, and to have collected a competent guard." On the 25th he continued, "I returned to Wrens, and very soon Serjeant Maj Forrest arrived to take Charge of the Powder; he had with him a guard of 20 to 24 Men and Boys . . . . The troop of Fairfax Dragoons commanded by Capt. George Graham had arrived—many of the most respectable gentlemen of the County was with him—such a quantity of Powder being in so public a place, appeared to excite great alarm."[8] However, no better place could be agreed upon to store the powder, and it remained in the barn until between the 6th and 10th of September 1814, when one hundred fifty barrels of powder were taken back to Washington from Fairfax County.

In the meantime, President Madison and his entourage, including Attorney General Rush, headed toward Salona, near Little Falls, where the President expected to meet his wife. Secretary of State Monroe went to Wiley's Tavern near Great Falls on Difficult Run. Secretary of the Navy William Jones and Dolley Madison, with others, were struggling through the crowded roads to Salona. Mrs. Madison, writing of the

---

7. Mordecai Booth, "Report on Removal of Powder from the Washington Navy Yard to Falls Church, 1814," microcopy (Washington, D.C.: National Archives).
8. Ibid., no p. nos.

events of these traumatic days said: "I should be ready at a moment's warning to enter my carriage and leave the city . . . . I am accordingly ready; I have pressed as many cabinet papers into trunks to fill one carriage; our private property must be sacrificed, as it is impossible to procure wagons for its transportation . . . . Two messengers covered with dust, come to bid me fly [August 24] . . . . At this late hour, a wagon has been procured; I have had it filled with the plate and most valuable portable articles belonging to the house . . . ."[9] She crossed over into Virginia the next day where she spent the night of the 25th at Rokeby, home of Mrs. Madison's friend, Matilda Lee Love, instead of arriving at Salona where the President had expected to meet her.

Madison, Rush, and General John Mason rode to Wren's Tavern at the Falls Church, and from there the president went to the Minor home, finally arriving at Salona where he spent the night with the Maffitt family, not knowing that his wife was a mile away at Rokeby. The next morning Madison went back to Wren's Tavern to look for his wife. Returning to Salona, he learned that Mrs. Madison and the Jones and Carroll families had gone by on their way to Wiley's Tavern near Difficult Run. President Madison and Attorney General Rush followed and took refuge from a "hurricane" in a house at the "Crossroads," five miles from the Little Falls Bridge.[10] At midnight the president went to Conn's Ferry above Great Falls, and at dawn he crossed the river into Montgomery County, Maryland. Mrs. Madison stayed at Wiley's Tavern until the President sent her word that Washington was safe.

During the excitement of the flight of the officials from Washington, other activities were taking place that were of consequence to the county in economic terms, and many county residents were armed and ready in other commands, including Captain Nicholas Darne who was a hero of this war and involved in the fighting in Baltimore. Robert Darne was also called and served under his father-in-law, John Wren, in the Fairfax Militia.[11] During the fighting in Washington, General Robert Young brought reinforcements from Fairfax County.[12]

On 25 August, the Reverend James Muir of Alexandria along with Dr. Dick Johnathon Swift and William Swann came to Dr. James Ewell's house near the Capitol in Washington where Admiral Cockburn and General Ross were making their headquarters.[13] They came carrying a

9. Dolley Madison to Lucy Todd, *Life and Letters of Dolley Madison.* Allen Culling Clark, ed. (W.F. Roberts, 1914).

10. Ellen Anderson, "Salona," (Fairfax, Va.: Office of Comprehensive Planning, forthcoming).

11. Steadman, *Falls Church,* p. 47.

12. Lord, *The Dawn's Early Light,* p. 193.

13. James Ewell, *The Medical Companion,* (1807; 3rd ed. owned by Mrs. Nora Lamborne, Alexandria, Va. Extracted by permission from the Historic Alexandria Foundation, P.O. Box 524, Alexandria, Va.), p. 677.

white flag and said that Alexandria was completely defenseless—what surrender terms could they expect? The following account describes the meeting as seen by Dr. Ewell.

> The terror struck into the good people of our city, by the capture and conflagration as aforesaid, rolled on in such conflomorating floods to Alexandria, that, by the time it reached that place, it had acquired a swell of mountainous horrors, that appear to have entirely prostrated the spirits of the Alexandrians. Men, women and children in that defenceless place saw nothing, in their frightened fancies, but the sudden and total destruction of their rising city, by the British army then at Washington, and the British squadron, under captain Gordon, coming up the river.
> In this alarming situation, they very wisely determined to throw themselves on the generosity of the enemy, and supplicate security for their town, on the humble conditions of capitulation. As men in the time of their troubles seem naturally to look for a blessing through the ministration of the godly, the Alexandrians selected four of their citizens distinguished for piety and morals, as Drs. Muir and Dick, and Messrs. Johnathon Swift and Wm. Swann. They arrived during the dreadful tornado which we experienced on that memorable day and as I happened to be sitting in my diningroom with Admiral Cockburn, when these delegates presented themselves, I had a fair opportunity to hear every word that passed on this occasion. Soon as they communicated to the admiral the object of their mission, he replied, with the brevity that characterized him, 'Gentlemen, I have nothing to say, until you first tell me whether captain Gordon is in sight of Alexandria.
> The reply was, that captain Gordon was not in sight of Alexandria.
> 'Well, then, gentlemen', continued he, 'I am ready to negotiate with you. And now, all I have to say is, that we want provisions, and must have them. But let me tell you, that for every article we take, you shall be allowed a fair price.'
> Upon this they very soon retired. [14]

The same situation was reported by William Chamberlayne in a letter to his wife. He further added, "A deputation from Alexandria waited on the British Commander who recd for answer that persons not found in arms, shd. be respected in their persons and property. [h]e sayd that he wanted flour & wd. have it, but he wd. pay a fair price for it . . . ."[15]

---

14. Ibid.
15. "Letters of William Chamberlayne," *William and Mary Quarterly*, 8 (1928):33.

This was, as stated, even before there was any sight of a British squadron on Potomac, but Alexandrians were most anxious to avoid a conflict in their own city. However, they were not alone, because the people of Georgetown were also attempting to surrender.[16]

In the meantime, there was a real danger to Alexandria, for after leaving Fort Washington, which had deliberately destroyed its own ammunition, the way was opened to Alexandria, and a small boat came toward the frigate *Seahorse*, the flagship of the expedition of forces on the Potomac under Captain James Gordon. About 10 A.M. on the 24th, three of Alexandria's leading citizens came bearing a white flag and asked to see Captain Gordon.[17] Gordon Swift, spokesman for the group, began by saying that they hoped Captain Gordon would show respect for the city of Alexandria. Gordon replied that he planned to respect all shops and houses, but planned to seize all ships and cargo waiting for export. Swift thought that unfair. It seemed as if the major concern of the commerce-minded Alexandrians was that someone might try to rescue them from British control, and that shooting would ensue. Alexandrians felt unprepared for their town to be the site of a major battle, since they knew that Brig. General John P. Hungerford's 1,400-member Virginia militia, hurrying toward them, was just 24 miles away. The committee sent a resolution to General Hungerford asking him to stay away as Alexandria had no military force to protect itself and intended to surrender at its own discretion.[18]

By 7 P.M. Captain Gordon's squadron was anchored two miles away, but the vessel *Aetna* continued up to the city. Consequently, the city again renewed its apprehension and a Committee of Vigilance sent businessman William Wilson to Gordon asking to be left alone. Captain Gordon refused.[19]

By Monday, 29 August 1814, the British squadron came opposite the town and asked for:

1. all naval stores, public or private
2. all scuttled vessels
3. all goods intended for export
4. all goods sent out of town since 19 August 1814, to be retrieved and given up.[20]

Naturally the town leaders balked at such an extensive list of demands, but the only concession given by the British was that of not raising and

16. Lord, *The Dawn's Early Light*, p. 182.
17. Ibid., p. 198.
18. Ibid., p. 199.
19. Ibid.
20. Ibid. The account of this event is well described in this book, compiled from American and British military and governmental records and personal letters from the involved parties. There also is some correspondence related to this in the Charles Simms Papers, Library of Congress.

Johnny Bull and the Alexandrians. British demands at Alexandria and the local response during the War of 1812. Virginia State Library.

delivering vessels at the bottom of the river because it would be too lengthy and difficult a task.

Thus, for the next three days, until 31 August, the crew loaded the three vessels with goods from the Alexandria warehouses, principally tobacco, flour, cotton, wine, and sugar. But the owners were not allowed "a fair price."[21] In general there was no overt friction between the town fathers and the British seamen, but Mayor Simms might be cited for overstating the case when he wrote to his wife; "It is impossible that men could behave better than the British behaved while the town was in their hands."[22]

Alexandrians were still in danger of witnessing a fight on their territory, however, since by 29 August General Hungerford was still hurrying toward the city, ignoring their request to leave them to their own resources. At the last minute, only three miles from the city of Alexandria, Hungerford received new orders from Washington which left him with fewer men, and he was therefore prevented from "saving" a town that did not wish to be saved.

21. This event was also described by Henry Adams, *History of the United States, 1801-1817*, (New York: Charles Scribner's Sons, 1904) 8:157-58. There also are three articles on the subject by Thomas Lamond in *Gazette*, 27, 28, 29 August 1962.

22. Charles Simms Papers, Library of Congress.

Another incident occurred that might have upset the "Alexandria plan." It is related by Mayor Simms in letters to his wife Nancy.[23] Two American naval officers, Commodore David Porter and Captain John O. Creighton, were near Alexandria when they heard that some British officers were dining at Tripplett's Hotel. In the hopes of seizing them by surprise, Porter and Creighton came into town by horseback, but the officers had been warned and they escaped. Excited by this, the two American officers rode to the waterfront where they saw a young British midshipman, John West Fraser, who was supervising the loading of the captured ships. Creighton seized Fraser by his tie and tried to carry off the young man, but the midshipman's tie broke, and he escaped aboard the ship. Danger ensued from this careless action because the alarm gun was sounded, the *Seahorse* hoisted a signal to prepare for battle, and the guns were again focused on the city. Mayor Simms wrote an apology to the offended British, while a delegation went to the *Seahorse* carrying official regrets: The town had no control over the perpetrators of the outrage, it should not be held responsible for the actions of the officers, and it would take steps to see that such a thing would not happen again. Thus, Alexandria again had relieved itself of a fight.[24]

By 2 September 1814, the British had finished their job in Alexandria and left empty warehouses; they took with them 21 vessels, 13,786 barrels of flour, 757 hogsheads of tobacco, and tons of cotton, tar, beef, and sugar, as well as other merchandise valued at $100,000. And not a shot was fired.

It was said that Fairfax County and Alexandria were the scenes of much excitement but little action during the War of 1812. It would be better to say that although little gunshot was spent the economic loss was tremendous: it was in part the county's goods that were filling up the bulging warehouses in Alexandria, waiting for an opportunity to ship them abroad.

Not only was the loss to the merchants high, but apparently the personal expense was considerable if one wanted to escape the misery of military duty. Captain Nicholas Darne of the Fairfax Militia wrote to his wife on 10 September 1814 from Baltimore, "you may inform Brother Robert that he is detailed for duty and I think he had better come on as quick as possible and make some arrangement to get a substitute at this place. Substitutes is Very high, Eighty dollars for three months . . ."[25] Evidently "brother Robert" did come, for he is cited as serving under John Wren.

23. Ibid.
24. Lord, *The Dawn's Early Light*, pp. 200-201.
25. Steadman, *Falls Church*, p. 296.

VII

Social and Cultural Life

Religion

Through the revolutionary times of the eighteenth century the dominant religious force in Fairfax County had been the Church of England. In 1785 the state legislature broke all ties with the church, relieved the vestries from all responsibility for the poor and orphans, and gave this responsibility to the local government. This act also paved the way for the establishment of alternate religious groups and philosophies.

There probably had been more exposure in Fairfax County to various religious beliefs than in most areas of the state due to its location: for example, the Quakers in Pennsylvania, Catholics in Maryland, and early Scotch-Irish Presbyterians who settled in Alexandria as merchants. The fact that these groups were present in the county before the disestablishment is noted on the list of tithables made by the Reverend Charles Green in 1748/9. There are many persons noted as "Quaker, of Upper or Lower Parish," or as "Papist," or as "Presbyterian."[1]

The Quakers had been established in what is now Loudoun County since the mid-eighteenth century, and their influence was felt very early in the northern sections of Fairfax County, since that area was included in the "Fairfax Society." Residents of the county often owned land in both counties, with boundaries less distinct than now and migration common between the two units. Most certainly there was dialogue between neighbors with differing philosophies. Education was a chief concern of the Quakers and they established schools and gave these schools their main support.[2]

---

1. Rev. Charles Green, Truro Vestry, List of Tithables, 1748/9. (Washington, D.C.: Library of Congress).

2. William Cook Dunlap, *Quaker Education in Baltimore and Virginia*, (Philadelphia: 1936).

The Methodists also have an early history in Fairfax County. They were assisted by the active Reverend William (Billy) Watters, who was born near Chesterbrook where he later had a farm. He is credited with being the first native-born itinerant Methodist preacher in America, and his wife, Sarah Adams, daughter of Colonel William Adams and Ann Lawyer Adams, is credited with being influential in the conversion of numerous local families. The women in and near the Adams family were strong individuals; they declared their intentions and stood firm, whether it was for religion, education, abolition, or for women to manage their own affairs. Whether it was the missionary spirit or simply a developing sense of independence, women such as Sarah Adams Watters, Sarah Jones Wren, Hannah Wren Adams, Kitty Hughes Payne, and others, all of whom were related and had converted to Methodism in the late eighteenth century, were extraordinary for their time and have left their mark in the court order books and in wills and other official documents of the county.[3]

There were many early Methodist preachers, but the first noted black Methodist minister was Harry Hoosier, who preached his first sermon on record in 1781 at the Fairfax Chapel near the Falls Church.[4] For a time in the early nineteenth century, the Methodists were using the old Falls Church and Pohick Church, both of which had fallen into disuse after the disestablishment.

Baptists were also active in the county, especially through the efforts of Jeremiah Moore, who was one of the early itinerant Baptist preachers of Fairfax County. He owned land in the Difficult Run area and preached at the Difficult Run Church until 1800, at the Frying Pan Church and at Back Lick, in addition to being one of the founders of the First Baptist Church in Alexandria in 1803. He was a supporter of the Ketocton Association meeting of 1797, at which a plan of gradual emancipation was prepared. Jeremiah Moore died in 1815 at his home "Moorefield," a present-day landmark in the county near Vienna.[5]

The Presbyterians were successful in Alexandria with the large numbers of Scotch settlers there. The Old Meeting House was built in 1772 by John Carlyle, who also constructed much of the Christ Church in Alexandria. However, a regular building was not erected in the county until 1846 when the Lewinsville Presbyterian Church was established.

---

3. Her husband, William Watters, mentions her numerous times in *A Short Account . . .* by William Watters and S. Snowden (Alexandria, Va., 1806). Copy in the Library of Congress, Rare Books, Washington, D.C. The wills of these women are unusual in that they specify that women are individuals, with rights apart from their fathers or husbands. Hannah Wren Adams's will (Fairfax County Will Book N, p. 81) even names her niece Kitty Hughes as executrix of her will, and Betsy Adams a witness to the will.

4. Asbury, *The Journal of the Rev. Francis Asbury*, p. 282.

5. Thomas V. DiBacco, *Moorefield: Home of Early Baptist Preacher Jeremiah Moore*, (Fairfax, Va.: Division of Planning, 1971) pp. 8, 18-19.

The Roman Catholic church was also late in coming into the county, even though St. Mary's Church was established in Alexandria in 1778 with a building erected in 1796. However, there were Catholics residing in the county as early as 1748, and there were a number of Irish settlers by the early 1800s.[6] In 1838, two Catholic families living in Fairfax, the Hammills and the Cunninghams, donated a tract of land to the Diocese of Richmond for a church and cemetery. However, work did not begin on the church until the late 1850s when there was an increased demand from Irish immigrants who had settled near Fairfax Station, and a mission, St. Mary's, was established by the Alexandria church.[7]

Education

The early nineteenth century saw the growth of a number of private academies throughout the county. These private schools were often opened by persons of a definite religious affiliation; they offered courses appropriate to the philosophy of the denomination. For instance, with the establishment of strong Quaker communities in Alexandria and Loudoun County, Virginia, there were a number of classes being offered especially for them.

The Alexandria *Gazette* was one place where teachers new to the region could announce their availability and specialty; it was also a good place for a town or family to place an advertisement for a tutor or instructor. One such advertisement was placed stating: "A Tutor Wanted—A salary of $200 will be given to an elderly gentleman of good moral habits who will undertake the tuition of twelve boys in a private family. It will be required that he has a perfect knowledge of the English language and the different branches of Mathematics." Signed, "Benj. Dulany".[8] Benjamin Dulany had a town house in Alexandria and home on Shuter's Hill, but the advertisement does not indicate where the tutor was expected to reside. Some wealthy families kept the children on the rural estate, much to the displeasure of many young men and women.[9]

"Old Tracy" Thomas Tracy from Dublin had been a tutor to the Custis children at Mount Vernon and Abingdon and continued in this capacity at Hope Park with the children of John Parke Custis after Custis widow, Eleanor Calvert Custis, married Dr. David Stuart.[10] He had been

6. Thomas Tracy was one of the early residents of the county from Dublin. He was a tutor to the children of the Custis and Stuart families, later willing his property, Mt. Erin, to his nephew who left Ireland for his inheritance.

7. Jeanne Rodrigues with William Hammond, *St. Mary's Fairfax Station, Virginia*: The Beginnings and Growth of a Community (Fairfax Station, Va.: St. Mary's Church, 1975), p. 7.

8. *Gazette*, 3 January 1815.

9. See Petersilia and Wright "Hope Park" for difficulties expressed by Custis and Stuart children concerning life in the interior of the county, when they longed to remain in the bustle of the town or city.

10 *Virginia Gazette and Weekly Advertiser* (Richmond, Va.) 6 December 1783, carried a notice of their marriage on 20 November 1783 in Fairfax County.

a music teacher, but also was able to offer a more complete education to the Custis and Stuart children and to the slave children who attended classes at the Hope Park plantation, separated in different buildings.[11]

An Englishman, John Davis, wrote an interesting book on his travels through the United States between 1798 and 1802 as he accepted temporary teaching positions in various regions. For instance, he stayed a short time in Occoquan, Prince William County, and described his initial meeting with his new employer as follows: "Our agreement was soon made. Quakers are men of few words. Friend Ellicott engaged me to educate his children for a quarter of a year. He wanted them taught reading, writing and arithmetic. Delightful task! As to Latin, or French, he considered the study of either language an abuse of time; and very calmly desired me not to say another word about it . . . ."[12] Thus, the Quakers' emphasis on the basics of education was quite contrary to the traditional education of a "Virginia gentleman." John Davis was also employed in the Frying Pan region of the county for a short time before his return to England.

One early school set up in the interior of the county was described by Ellen Lightfoot Lynch who attended the school from 1836 to 1850 with her sisters Mary Ann and Jane. A substantial log building was built for this purpose in 1780 and it remained until the Civil War. This building was constructed with wooden pegs and shuttered windows. There was a shingled gable roof which was covered with moss by the time Mrs. Lynch attended the school. The logs were kept whitewashed, and at the back of the one large room was a fieldstone fireplace. The teacher sat on a raised platform in the middle of the room.[13]

The one-room schoolhouse educated the children of the farming community in the elementary subjects of reading, writing, and arithmetic. In the schools attended by students who were needed as seasonal workers on the farm, class attendance was sporadic and dictated by the limits imposed by weather, planting and harvest times, and economic circumstances. Beyond the fundamentals of education that the teacher in such a situation was able to provide, those children whose families were financially secure often attended a boarding school in Alexandria, lived with relatives, or were able to locate a regional academy within a reasonable distance of home. There were many academies in Alexandria, some quite short-lived, and other schools were opened in towns such as Centreville. A comprehensive education was offered to boarding students at schools such as the one operated by William Maffitt, the Presbyterian minister, at Salona near Little Falls.[14]

11. Petersilia and Wright, "Hope Park," pp. 109-110, manuscript.
12. Davis, *Travels in America*, p. 27.
13. Steadman, *Falls Church*, pp. 128-29.
14. Anderson, "Salona." no page nos.

William Brent, Jr., opened a similar school at Sully in 1825 and advertised it in the *National Intelligencer* as having a healthy inland situation, surrounded by fine fruit and water, in full view of the mountains.[15] "The course of instruction will be liberal, and will comprise Reading, Writing, Grammar, Composition, Geography, the use of the Globes, Civil History, the Elements of Natural Philosophy, and Chemistry, Arithmetic, Algebra, Geometry, the Latin and French, Belle-Lettres, Logic and Ethics." The charge for the ten-month scholastic year was $250, which included board, bed, and washing. This school operated through 1834, when Brent again announced the opening of his "seminary."

The desire for an education was by no means restricted to the wealthy, and there was a conscientious effort to provide a basic education for the poor. With the disestablishment of the position of the Church of England after the Revolution and its responsibility for the lower economic groups, the new government of Virginia established the county position of Overseer of the Poor. But people did not see the general need for a state or locally supported school; education had been considered a responsibility of the family, just as food and shelter were.[16] The first general state school law was initiated in 1796 which was to provide a system of public schools.[17] Public schools were seen as poor schools with permissive law and not compulsory, depending on the decision of the county residents and the action of the county court. It was up to the poorer people of the county to convince the court that there should be a tax for this purpose. Thus, since the court was generally made up of those men from wealthier circumstances, very little action was taken along these lines.[18]

The establishment of general education in the county came in 1810 when the Literary Fund was founded. This was state supported by funds set aside for the encouragement of learning and for providing schools for the poor in any part of the state.[19] In 1819 the Assembly voted that when the income of the fund reached $45,000 a year, it was to be distributed among the counties of the state on the basis of the white population for the education of poor white children. Initially, the income was used only for paying the wages of teachers, but this was amended in 1829 when 10 percent of the county allotment could be used for buildings, provided that the parents paid three-fifths of the cost, 5 percent could be used for the purpose of buying books, and $100 could go toward paying the

15. *National Intelligencer*, 20 September 1825.
16. Porter, *County Government in Virginia*, p. 217.
17. 2 *Stat.* 3.
18. Porter, *County Government in Virginia*, p. 219.
19. Acts of Assembly, 1809-1810, ch. 14.

teacher, if the parents contributed an equal amount.[20] The teacher was paid four cents per day for each poor child who was entered by the county commissioners, although there could be other pay if other children were in attendance at the school, but this was a matter between the teacher and the parents, except for the $100 from the Literary Fund.

The Alexandria Academy was established in 1786 as a free school, especially for the education of the poor. Prominent citizens contributed to the support of this school, and George Washington, among others, gave fifty pounds a year to an academy "for the sons of widows." In his will he bequeathed $4,000 (20 shares of the Bank of Alexandria) toward support of a free school. The Female Free School opened in Alexandria in 1812, endowed by Bartholomew Dandridge and taught by Mrs. FitzJohn Porter.

In 1840, the federal census listed Fairfax County as having two universities or colleges with 16 students; one academy with 20 students, six primary schools with 245 students and 57 scholars at public charge. However, out of a total population of 9,370, only 28 were noted as "over 20, white, able to read and write." This was an incredibly small number and is open to speculation, given the number of schools operating.[21]

The education of girls was often the same as that of boys, often in the same classroom, until the basic skills were learned. However, there was a tendency to let girls then learn the "womanly arts" while boys went on to a more formal education in science and mathematics. However, this was not always the case, and there is an interesting series of letters from an anonymous "Junius" in the March 1800 issues of the Alexandria *Gazette* entitled "Open Letter to Young Ladies of Alexandria," where "Junius" states that young ladies need to "improve [their] minds" and to "assert their rights and remove the great objection to female education by showing you that you are capable of as high improvements as our sex [male] . . . ."[22] The reaction to this series of rather lengthy letters is not known, but it may not be a coincidence that at the same time there were advertisements in the paper announcing the opening of an "Academy for Young Ladies," which was "opened by Mr. William Black, educated at the University of Glasgow and Edinburg." The courses of instruction would include, "reading, writing, arithmetic, English grammar, composition and letter writing, geography and the use of the Globe, and French."[23] There is no mention that the young ladies would also learn any of the sciences.

In the same year we find John Livingstone stating that "from this day I purpose to begin teaching from 12 to 2 o'clock every day, for the

20. Acts of Assembly, 1828-1829, ch. 14.
21. U.S. Decennial Census, 1840, microcopy, (Washington: D.C.: National Archives).
22. 1-11 March 1800, *Alexandria Advertiser and Gazette.*
23. Ibid.; also 11 January 1800.

accomodation of such young Ladies as may be otherwise engaged during the rest of the day."[24] However, the idea of a profession for women was not even proposed in an item placed by Elisha C. Dick reading: "I will take one or two young gentlemen to the study of medicine."[25]

By the time Martin's *Gazetteer* was published in 1835, there were boarding schools in Alexandria for girls and boys, free schools for both sexes, thirty other schools unspecified as to nature, and the Protestant Episcopal Seminary and the Episcopal High School.[26] Some private academies were permanent and more well known than others, such as the Alexandria Academy established by Dr. James Muir, pastor of the Presbyterian Meeting House in Alexandria. A Board of Guardians of the Free Schools had been created in 1811, and Dr. Muir taught a school for young ladies during these years. After Dr. Muir's death, the Reverend Elias Harrison assumed the position of head of the board. Benjamin Hallowell was an active member of the board.

Hallowell came to Alexandria from Maryland where he had been an instructor in Quaker academies. In 1824 he began a course of lectures on "Chemistry, Natural Philosophy and Astronomy," probably to make known his abilities. The school filled slowly, with only four students at first. The initial fee was $6 a quarter, or $10 a quarter if mathematics were included. If board were included, the charge was $30 a quarter. Despite his later success, he had many problems. His main problem was that people paid very slowly;[27] luckily, however, he said that creditors were easy on him. At this same time, Hallowell's wife Margaret opened a school for girls, with the girls also attending his lectures and supplementary classes from Eliza Porter's and Rachel Waugh's schools. Hallowell, like most schoolmasters, was forced by economic circumstances to seek private tutoring in order to meet his expenses.

Hallowell, a Quaker, was also interested in the conditions of and the opportunities for blacks. In 1827, a Benevolent Society was formed in Alexandria with Hallowell as secretary. The object of the Society was to render assistance to freed slaves. Samuel M. Janney, George Drucker, Abijah Janney, Townsend Waugh, Presley Jacobs, Thomas Preston, Daniel Cawood, among others, were members. They were active, working openly until the Nat Turner rebellion in 1831. In those few short years, with an objective of not interfering with slavery but securing the slaves their own rights, a few blacks were freed and hired by the state of Maryland. These policies did not hinder the success

24. Ibid., 5 June 1800.
25. Ibid.
26. Martin, *Gazetteer*, p. 478.
27. Benjamin Hallowell, *Autobiography*, 2nd ed. (Philadelphia: Friend's Book Association, 1884), p. 100.

Benjamin Hallowell. opened a school in Alexandria in 1824. He was one of the founders of the Lyceum, an author, first president of the Alexandria Water Company, and first president of the Maryland Agricultural College. Portrait by John Singleton Copley. Print courtesy Colby College Library.

of the Hallowell school, and by 1833 there were more than 100 scholars.[28] The fame of the school increased, and in 1835 there were boarders from fourteen states, as well as students from South America, Cuba, and England.

Hallowell and Dr. Harrison founded the Lyceum in 1834. Hallowell was elected the first president and delivered the first lecture, the subject being vegetable physiology.[29] That such a lecture would attract an audience indicates the nature of the local economy: it was a farming area with great interest in methods of productivity. His boarding students all attended the Lyceum meetings; it was part of their education. The lectures were given once a week on literary and scientific subjects, followed by debate. In spite of the lack of inspiring titles for many of these public lectures, the Lyceum was well attended and attracted many significant and well-known public figures as guest lecturers. Political and religious subjects were barred.

Another well known school was St. John's Academy which was run by William F. and Richard Carne in 1833. Students from this school were known by the regular drilling done on the streets of Alexandria.[30] The Virginia Theological Seminary was founded in 1823 in Alexandria as part of the general attempt to revive the earlier significance of the Protestant Episcopal Church. As successful as the seminary was, this denomination never regained its former domination of the social and cultural life in the communities it served. Local government took over these functions, and by the 1820s other religious groups had filled the vacuum left by its disestablishment in the immediate post-revolutionary period.

Centreville Academy opened on 2 January 1806 under the Reverend Mr. Snyder. Annual tuition was $25 for geography classes, $20 for mathematics, and $14 for reading, writing and arithmetic.[31] It was also expected that a small contribution would be made for "attention to the firewood." The advertisement of its opening in the Gazette indicated that the school would place particular attention on the morals of its students both in and out of school. Nearly twenty years later, William Brent's Academy at Sully had the same objective to "attend to the morals, manners and progress of all my pupils . . . ."[32] By 1808 the General Assembly of Virginia had incorporated the Centreville Academy and appointed as trustees prominent citizens in the vicinity including David Stuart, George Graham, Humphrey Peake, John C. Hunter, Thomas Blackburne, Charles Tyler, Jr., Francis Adams, Newton Keene, Alexander Waugh, Edmund Denny, Spencer Ball, Charles J. Love,

28. Ibid., p. 115.
29. Ibid., p. 128.
30. "Mrs. Perry's Scrapbook," [n.d.], (copy located in Alexandria, Va. Public Library).
31. Gazette, 2 January 1806.
32. National Intelligencer, 20 September 1825.

Richard B. Lee, William Lane, Jr., Coleman Brown and John Hening.[33] Evidently the school was still functioning in 1815 when an advertisement was placed in the Alexandria *Gazette*[34] with F. Snyder as instructor. The hope at this time was to draw students from outlying regions by reminding potential customers of the healthy climate in Centreville, as opposed to that in Alexandria and Washington City.[35]

Health

The Philadelphia Medical Society advertised in the *Gazette* on 15 March 1800 that a medal would be given for the best dissertation on "the effects of the following medicines on the human body, especially upon the _____, viz, Hyocyamus niger (Black henbane), Datura stramoncum (Thorn apple), Conium maculatum (Hemlock), Camfor, Amber, musk, Digitalis perpurea (foxglove), Scilla maritima (squill), Rhododendrum maximum (mountain laurel) and the principal preparation of lead. By order of the Society, Benjamin S. Barton, John Moore, George Lee." It is not noted whether any local persons did write the requested dissertation, but there were doctors practicing in Alexandria, who had been well educated at European universities, especially in Edinburgh.

One apparently outstanding physician who took up residence in Alexandria near the turn of the century was Dr. John Richards, who had studied "physic, surgery and midwifery" at the University of Glasgow and Edinburgh.[36] Dr. Richards remained in Alexandria for a number of years, as noted by references to him in the *Gazette*, and became active in the maintenance of the health of its residents, rich and poor.

Another such advertisement was placed by Doctor T. Flloyd who was prepared to practice "physic" and who had studied midwifery in London.[37] His specialty was listed as the diseases of women and children, without a note as to why they were grouped together and men excluded.

Doctors very often were called on to both diagnose the problem and provide the medication. Doctor Flloyd also operated T.C. Flloyd's New Medicine Store. Other doctors were not so specific, such as Doctor Hamilton who advertised that he was available "to receive families."[38]

There were periodic epidemics in Alexandria from various causes, including the relatively mild influenza which prevailed in 1802 and 1815,

33. Eugenia B. Smith, *Centreville, Virginia; Its History and Architecture* (Fairfax, Va.: Office of Comprehensive Planning, 1973), p. 39.

34. *Gazette*, 24 January 1815.

35. Benjamin Hallowell in his *Autobiography* effectively recounts the difficulties of living in Alexandria and the many areas that seemed to breed disease.

36. *Gazette*, 11 January 1800

37. Ibid., 17 July 1800.

38. Ibid., 2 October 1800.

to yellow fever, small pox, cholera, and others.[39] The year 1803 was a particularly bad one in Alexandria for 200 died from yellow fever.[40] Nearly one-half the population of 6,000 left the city. It was said that this epidemic of yellow fever came from oysters. The epidemic was described by Dr. Elisha C. Dick in *The Medical Repository.*[41] The same situation in 1821 was much less severe. It began near the wharf, and nearly fifty persons died.[42] Cholera ravaged the city in 1832.

Despite attempts to control small pox, there were outbreaks of it, especially among the poor. The following notice was placed in the newspaper for the notice of all: *"Smallpox,* exists in a small tenement of Alexandria in neighborhood of Ezra Kenzies' tanyard. Vaccine Infection supply available." Signed, Wm. A. Dangerfield, H.P. Dangerfield, Wm. Washington, John Richards, Thomas Semmes, Archibald B. Dick, Elisha C. Dick.[43] By this time (1808) there was vaccine, but a continual effort had to be made to convince people of themerits of its use.

Physicians were available to the poor through the Alexandria Dispensary which was administered by the Common Council of the city. The council provided health services to the families in the poor house, especially that of wives and children. The rules and regulations as noted in 1805 were that there would be four attending physicians and one apothecary elected annually.[44] They were in attendance every Monday, Wednesday and Friday, and daily, August through November. In that year Henry Rose, Elisha C. Dick, W.H. Washington, and Thomas Semms were elected as physicians to the Alexandria Dispensary; the Apothecary was Jesse Talbot. It was also noted that the attending physicians would make home visits if necessary.

There were constant admonitions to the citizens of the city of Alexandria that sanitation was an issue which had to be dealt with, especially in the hot summer months. At the Board of Health meeting on 2 August 1811 it was announced that there would be an inspection and cleaning of the gutters, alleys, and privies in the city. They made quick lime available for the inhabitants to use to prevent disease, particularly in the warm season.[45] There were doctors in the outlying areas of the county, however, and by 1835, Martin's *Gazetteer* lists three doctors as residing in Centreville, and two at Fairfax Court House.

Dentists were also available and advertised their services through the newspapers. Those advertisements ranged from those found in 1803

39. Blanton, *Medicine in Virginia*, p. 236.

40. Alex. J. Wedderburn, "Alexandria, Virginia, Souvenier Sesquicentennial, 1899," (copy located in Alexandria, Va. Public Library).

41. Elisha C. Dick, *The Medical Repository* New York, 1797-1824., 7:190, 8:18.

42. Blanton, *Medicine in Virginia*, p. 236.

43. *Gazette,* 16 December 1808.

44. *Gazette,* 7 September 1805.

45. *Gazette,* 10 August 1811 (Board of Health meeting held 2 August 1811).

when "T. Bruff, Dentist," coming from Washington, "will furnish customers with the best dentifrice and excellent brushes."[46] There is an earlier note on 20 June 1792 in the estate account of John Parke Custis (managed by David Stuart): "Doctor Kennedy for two tooth brushes . . . 0.1.0."[47] Perhaps furnishing Dr. Bruff, Dentist, with his customers, was Dr. Fendall, who advertised on 22 March 1803 as an operator upon teeth, with an office in a room of Gadsby's Tavern.[48]

Social Life

Entertainment available to county residents was generally of two types: that provided in the home and that found in larger communities, especially Alexandria. There were also many sources of amusement at taverns, churches, fairs, court days, political rallies, and militia displays.

Plantation life, with sparsely settled areas, generated a form of entertainment seldom found today: that is, family members and guests entertaining each other by means of conversation, discussion, gossip, music, and dance. Those estates on waterways found transport easier than those in the interior of the county, and thus there was less social life for those in homes such as Sully and Hope Park. Elizabeth Lee wrote to her brother Zaccheus Collins, "I am, my Brother, the most shut up lonesome creature thee can possibly picture, nor do I see human being save my family weeks together."[49] This sentiment was shared by the Custis children and Dr. David Stuart's own children while at Hope Park, and on one occasion Ann Calvert Stuart wrote to her friend Elizabeth Lee, "We spent two weeks very charmingly in the City Washington . . . . We had some difficulty in leaving, so many were the regrets expressed on our coming to be buried in this dismal place—some did not scruple to say."[50] Despite these complaints, since extended families often lived together, and very often three generations were in one house, or perhaps a brother or sister and their spouses and children, entertainment could often be found under one roof.[51] In addition, house guests generally were not for the afternoon or "overnight." When an individual or families took the trouble to travel, they generally prepared to stay a few weeks or occasionally months. Travel from Philadelphia took two weeks by packet, and an overland route was rarely contemplated because of the rough terrain and poor roads. Most persons were not as isolated as the

46. *Gazette*, 22 February 1803.
47. Fairfax County Will Book G-1, p. 472.
48. *Gazette*, 22 March 1803.
49. Elizabeth Lee to Zaccheus Collins, 29 May 1810, Parker Papers, Historical Society of Pennsylvania. Quoted in Gamble, *Sully*, p. 51.
50. Ann Calvert Stuart to Mrs. Richard Bland Lee, (n.d.), Elizabeth Collins Lee Papers, Virginia Historical Society, Richmond.
51. The Lee Family very often had brothers or sisters living in Sully with them for a time. See Gamble, *Sully*.

Lees at Sully and Stuarts at Hope Park, who later moved to more hospitable locations. Plantation life tested the resourcefulness of the women, since they were the ones who were the most often alone. The men of the household generally traveled to court sessions and on business. Letters, therefore, such as those between Mrs. Lee and Mrs. Stuart, gave a means to express feelings of boredom. In the days before the telephone, feelings of resentment and anguish because of having no one with whom to converse must have been common.

In social life, however, conversation was an art that was learned and greatly appreciated. Music also, among the fortunate, was a form of expression which could be shared. Women were often noted for their ability on an instrument or their singing voice, as was Frances Parke Lewis of Woodlawn who was known for her voice and harp playing.[52] A scene was described by Mrs. Lewis at Woodlawn which might be taken as typical of her class. "The music might well have continued far into the night . . . . [A gentleman] who plays very well on the violin & sings well, Captn Mackay, on the flute, & Parke, the Harp—they harmonize very agreeably . . . we sat up until half past one at night, & thought it was only 10 . . . ."[53]

The education of a woman among the wealthier families aimed to produce an amusing and gentle hostess, one who could entertain the most exalted statesman and at the same time manage a plantation and bear numerous children. Dancing lessons were very popular, and the advertisements in the Alexandria *Gazette* during the first decades of the nineteenth century found more space given to dancing schools than to academic courses offered. The estate account of John Parke Custis gives ample space to the payment of a dancing master and music tutor known as "old Tracey."[54] Parke Lewis of Woodlawn was described by her future husband, Edward G.W. Butler, as "indeed an elegant and accomplished woman, as an evidence of which is perfectly genteel, remarkably amiable, very prudent, entirely unassuming and insistent in her endeavors to please those around her."[55]

Fox hunting was an active sport in Fairfax County through the early decades of the nineteenth century. In 1828, a farmer noted that at least three hunts were located in this county: the Fairfax Hunt, the Centreville Hunt, and the Washington Hunt.[56] Several dogs were noted as being exceptionally good, and one of them, Juno, even had an obituary written

---

52. Meredith Johnson, "A Day at Woodlawn with the Lewises," *Yearbook of the Historical Society of Fairfax County, Virginia, Inc.* 4 (1955): 22 (hereinafter cited as Johnson, "A Day at Woodlawn").

53. Ibid., p. 23.

54. Fairfax County Will Book G-1, p. 472.

55. Johnson, "A Day at Woodlawn", p. 17.

56. Edward F. Howrey, "Foxhunting in Fairfax County," *Yearbook of the Historical Society of Fairfax County, Virginia, Inc.*, 2 (1952-53):30.

about her: "Died, on the 25th ult. in Fairfax County, old Juno, for many seasons the favourite leader of the Washington pack of fox hounds . . . ."[57] One account of a two-day hunt at Ravensworth was published in 1830:

> Messrs. Terret's Chichester's, and Darnes's hounds met at the Pines on New Years day to hunt Ravensworth and the neighboring grounds; and a more beautiful district for that delightful sport is not to be found. The country is cleared and open, with here and there a copse of wood, or pine thicket, and little or no fencing for miles.
> From the number and respectability of the field of well mounted horsemen, and the number, beauty, and condition of the hounds, it is evident that fox hunting has lost none of its charms in Fairfax County. Twenty-one horsemen and twenty-one couple of hounds were at the place agreed upon, at the appointed hour . . . .
> The writer will not speak of the welcome which awaits the stranger's arrival in Fairfax County; nor the ample board and ample bowl;—they are in keeping with the good days of lang syne.[58]

On the other hand, those citizens who were able to travel to Alexandria, or who had a town house there were able to take advantage of a wide variety of activities designed to entertain. The Alexandria Theatre was well known and drew its audience also from Washington City, which had no theater in the early years of its existence. The fall season in 1800 began with a tragedy, "The Count of Narbonne," and a farce, "The Citizen," both presented on the same evening. Musicals and comedies were also performed in successive weeks.[59] Mrs. West's Company of Comedians was greatly heralded in the newspaper and presumably well attended.[60] Both vocal and instrumental concerts were held at the "New Theatre."

Taverns, inns, and ordinaries also provided entertainment such as concerts by traveling musicians, fetes of magic, or even "wondrous displays" such as those now seen in a sideshow. One such exhibition was displayed in 1803 at an Alexandria tavern: "A CURIOSITY—The Learned Pig—to be seen at Mr. Charles M'Knight's THE SPREAD EAGLE, corner of King and Royal Streets. The sagacity of this Pig is equal, if not superior, to any animal ever exhibited in America; the proprietor will therefore avoid a puffing advertisement; and only state what the Pig actually performs . . . . He reads printing and writing,

57. Ibid., p. 31.
58. *American Turf Register*, February 1830.
59. *Gazette*, 11 November 1800.
60. Ibid., 28 October 1800.

spells, tells the time of day, . . . the date of the year, the day of the month, distinguishes colors, . . . will add, subtract, multiply and divide . . . . Any person may draw a card from a pack, and keep it concealed, and the Pig, without hesitation, will discover it. The Price of Admittance—25 Cents."[61]

Perhaps the most famous of all taverns was Gadsby's Tavern in Alexandria where presidents were entertained, including Washington, Adams, Jefferson, and Madison, and where welcoming toasts were given to visiting dignitaries from Europe. Until the White House was finished, and even later, official receptions were held at Gadsby's, since there was no appropriate place in Washington City at that time, and such was its reputation that an occasional reference was made by a visiting European that this was as fine a tavern as any to be found in England. A reception took place in 1801 when the guests of the establishment were Thomas Jefferson, Aaron Burr, and members of Jefferson's cabinet. The following newspaper excerpt describes the event well.

PRESIDENTIAL FESTIVAL

On Saturday last, the President of the United States, at the invitation of the citizens of Alexandria, partook of an elegant entertainment at Gadsby's Hotel, specially provided for the Occasion; to which were invited the Vice-President, the Heads of Departments, General Wilkinson and his Aid.

An escort of two troops of cavalry received the President on the western side of the George-Town ferry—At the vicinity of Alexandria, he was saluted by Captain Janney's volunteer company of riflemen, and on his entrance into the town received the usual military salutations from Col. DENEALE'S militia. A numerous levee occupied the intervening space between the time of his arrival and the hour of dining. Political distinctions, on this occasion, totally disappeared; Republicans and Federalists alike pressed forward to honor the man who was the choice of the nation, and to testify their belief in the political aphorism, *that an absolute acquiescence in the decisions of the majority is the vital principle of republics.* Order and convivial harmony preserved their entire ascendance throughout the arrangements of the day. The following selection of toasts were drank, and followed respectively by the discharge of cannon.

[Toasts were given for principles ensured by the Bill of Rights and to the memories of Washington and Franklin].[62]

Taverns served many purposes. Not only were eating, drinking, and sleeping quarters provided for the traveler, but there were also places where traveling merchants could set up temporary offices. Music and

61. *Gazette,* 14 April 1801.
62. Ibid., 16 March 1801.

Dranesville Tavern. Typical of local wayside inns of the period, this building was constructed of logs about 1830 as an accommodation for drovers and other travelers along the Alexandria-Leesburg Turnpike. The logs were covered with clapboards in the 1850s. Sketch by Gloria Matthews. Fairfax County Office of Comprehensive Planning.

dance lessons were given there; tutors gave lessons; auctions were held; and meetings convened in its rooms. The stage line coaches left from the Eagle Tavern in Alexandria, and mail was delivered and held there. Most estate sales were held in taverns or ordinaries throughout the county, and slaves were sometimes sold in taverns at advertised sales.[63]

The list of taverns and ordinaries that could be found at any one time in Fairfax County is quite long. Fees were fixed and had to be posted for the convenience of the traveler, although it is known that the traveler was sometimes overcharged.[64]

One form of entertainment for those able to read was the daily newspaper. A perusal of the *Gazette* for any one day gives much for discussion, not always of a serious nature, and some newspapers were known for their attention to the "gossip" of the day. The *Gazette* was filled with news of a local, national, and international nature, local advertisements, legal notices, announcements of meetings to be held, or already held. Medical discussions were often included on the subject of a cure to a common ailment, sometimes in the form of an advertisement for a particular medicine.

The newspaper was often used as a public forum for the airing of complaints. One very interesting example was the public complaint filed by Harriot McCue against her husband Henry McCue in 1800.

63. See numerous examples through first decades in the nineteenth century, *Gazette*.
64. Anne Royall relates an instance of her stay at a nearby inn when she was obliged to pay excessive rates. See Royall *Sketches of History*, p. 98.

NOTICE: I Harriot McCue, would wish to inform the public, that this Henry McCue . . . cannot charge me with leaving him without his desire. For before seven evidences he swore that if I did no leave the house, he would murder me; and likewise before these seven people, told me to go and look for board, and he would pay as far as three dollars and a half per week. I daresay that Mr. McCue wanted me away for some other convenience; for Mr. McCue has left my bed for three or four months at a time; and for nine months I don't believe that he has lodged seven weeks at home, and that at different times; and when he would be going out of a night, and I happened to ask him where he was going, his answer would be, Go to hell. You damned bitch, what is it your business? Now if any hardworking and industrious wife, and the mother of several children, that has been married to him three and twenty years, I don't know . . . in my own house, a mistress of his (as is reported) tore my cap off my head and choaked me, and he stood by and laffed at it; and I at the time went down on my knees and begged him for mercy's sake to give me some trifle and let me go where I could be some comfort . . . . Poor old man, I pity his weakness . . . . Well, I have now said as much as injured innocence wishes, and not liking to be troublesome to the printer, I will conclude.[65]

Ten years later the following notice appeared.

CAUTION:My wife Harriot having left my house, and separated herself from me, I hereby give this public notice, that I will not discharge any debt or debts which she may contract, nor in any manner be bound for any of her transactions or contracts. Signed Henry McCue, April 30, 1810.[66]

However, when his will was recorded in 1811, he bequeathed: "Unto my beloved wife Harriet Margaret McCue . . . . all my real and personal estate."[67]

65. *Gazette,* 4 November 1800.
66. Ibid., 30 April 1810.
67. Alexandria Will Book, 13 August 1811, p. 86.

1840 — 1870

Patricia Hickin

Rejuvenation, Occupation, and Reconstruction

Perhaps the most momentous and traumatic years in the history of Fairfax County were the three decades between 1840 and 1870. At the beginning of the period almost everyone who traveled within the bounds of the county described it as a "desolate" area; by 1860 news of the county's agricultural revival had spread up and down the entire Eastern seaboard. Five years later, after four years of war, Fairfax again was virtually prostrate; another five years and its farmers had made it into one of the most productive counties of the state.

This section seeks to tell the story of the people of Fairfax as they tried to understand and to deal with a variety of technological, economic, political, and social changes in times of peace and of war and in the aftermath of war. During these years, Fairfax citizens saw the first rail and telegraph lines cross the county; they learned to cope with cook stoves and sewing machines, commercial fertilizers and steam mills. They witnessed the reversal of population trends, as Northerners and Europeans discovered the attractions of Fairfax lands; and they learned to take advantage of new markets and of improvements in agricultural practices.

In thirty fleeting years, they saw their local government functioning under three successive state constitutions and watched the painful adoption of yet a fourth. They saw county offices become elective for the first time: saw men vote—even black men—who had not voted before. They saw contending armies march over Fairfax roads and camp in Fairfax fields. They saw political office pass from the hands of old families to those of newcomers; they saw black slaves emancipated and black children skip off to school. They saw aristocrats disfranchised and well-to-do men impoverished; they saw their farms denuded and their homes ravaged. They saw, in short, the destruction of a way of life that some of them cherished and others deplored. In the pages that follow, the reader will meet some of the people who created the history of Fairfax in these decades, as they struggled to determine the course of their lives and of their future.

I

Yankees Come to Fairfax

Travelers in large parts of Fairfax in the 1840s sometimes spoke of an oppressive "air of desolation" hanging over the county. Where luxuriant fields of tobacco, wheat, and corn had once supported thriving planters, there were now pine forests, abandoned fields, briars, and sedge grass; one might travel for twenty or thirty miles without seeing another human being.[1]

And then, suddenly, to one's surprise, one might come upon a settlement of neat, attractive homes, handsomely cultivated gardens, and sleek cattle housed in well-built barns. The curious traveler soon learned that these were areas of Yankee settlement. For in Fairfax, Reconstruction did not await the Civil War. A full quarter century before the war was over, Yankees, replete with carpetbags, began to move into the county and sought to reorder it in the image of the rural North. These antebellum Northerners, unlike those who came during and after the Civil War, were warmly welcomed in Fairfax. Like other Virginians of the 1840s, Fairfax citizens greatly admired Northern progress, energy, and prosperity, and they saw these Yankee settlers as harbingers of a new prosperity for "old Fairfax."

1. [Samuel M. Janney], *The Yankees in Fairfax County, Virginia* (Baltimore, 1845), pp. 4, 5, 11 (hereinafter cited as Janney, *Yankees in Fairfax*); S[amuel] S. R[andall], "Emigration to Virginia: Fairfax County Lands," Albany, N.Y., *Cultivator* 4(March 1847):77-78 (hereinafter cited as Alb. *Cult.*); "Virginia Lands," *Country Gentleman* 6(6 September 1855):155 (hereinafter cited as Count. Gent.); "Letter from Virginia," 9 November 1850, *American Agriculturist*, 10 (January 1851); 21-22 (hereinafter cited as *Amer. Agr.*); Frederick Law Olmsted, *A Journey in the Seabord Slave States*, 2 vols. (New York: G.P. Putnam's Sons. 1904), 1:238; Sir Charles Lyell, *Travels in North America: With Geological Observations on the United States, Canada, and Nova Scotia*, 2 vols. (London: John Murray, 1845), 1:198 (hereinafter cited as Lyell, *Travels*). The footnotes for this section of the book have been extensively abridged. A copy with full documentation is on deposit at the History Office, Office of Comprehensive Planning, Fairfax, Va., and in the Archives Division, Virginia State Library, Richmond, Va.

Thomas ap Catesby Jones was a naval hero in the War of 1812. He inherited land in Fairfax County near Great Falls and was one of the first Americans to make use of guano, which proved to be an extremely effective fertilizer for Fairfax soil. Virginia State Library.

For several decades, the county, despite its proximity to the national capital, had been in the throes of an agricultural depression. Between 1800 and 1840, the population had fallen by more than 30 percent. Much of the loss resulted from a sharp decline in the number of slaves, but there had also been a significant decrease in the number of white persons. To all appearance, the unproductive lands of Fairfax had become incapable of supporting a growing population.

Observers agreed that much of the land had been worn out by careless farming and absentee ownership. Of those owners who continued to live in the area, many were too fond of the fox and the horse to take time to develop an interest in the pursuits of agriculture. Ignorant of the needs of plants and of the means necessary to redeem the soil, they had allowed their lands to be excessively cropped. When one section of the naturally fertile soil of their estates appeared worn out, they cleared, cropped, and finally abandoned another portion of their land. They then repeated the procedure until, as one contemporary critic wrote, "the wide domains that descended from opulent ancestors become insufficient to supply this system of wasteful extravagance," and the "impoverished proprietor" sells his lands "for a small consideration, and . . . with his family and slaves sets off to . . . the fertile regions of the South West, there to pursue, from incorrigible habit, the same blighting and ruinous system."[2]

2. Janney, *Yankees in Fairfax*, pp. 4-5, 7, 11.

The malaise of the countryside gripped the towns as well. In the late 1830s, writers spoke of the decline of Alexandria, which was then still part of the District of Columbia. By the late 1830s, the Baltimore and Ohio Railroad carried to Maryland ports much of the Shenandoah Valley produce which had once made up a major portion of Alexandria's maritime trade. As the town fell on hard times, houses in the suburbs were vacated, and some fell into ruin. Within the town itself, many houses had no occupants, cattle grazed in grassy side streets, the theater grew "old, dilapidated and crumbling," and the "unbusiness-like" main streets went ill-paved and unlighted. Alexandria, in short, had "nothing of the stir and bustle so characteristic of American towns." It had become a "somnolent village," awake only during the fishing season in late winter and early spring. South of Alexandria, where tourists flocked to see the home and tomb of the revered George Washington, Mount Vernon was in disrepair, and Pohick Church, long since abandoned, had become so dilapidated that the door to George Washington's old pew had come to adorn a free black's chicken house.[3]

Just what led these Northerners to think of buying land in Fairfax is not entirely clear, but several unlikely elements played a role. Who would have supposed that elephants, Peruvian bird droppings, and the agricultural experiments of a Virginia naval hero would combine to lure Yankees to Fairfax? Yet these and more basic factors (the high price of farmland in the Northeast, the growing markets of the District of Columbia, the introduction of commercial fertilizers, and major improvements in transportation) all contributed to the rejuvenation of the county.

The first step toward the new order of things was taken as Fairfax continued to slip into economic stagnation. In the mid-1820s Thomas ap Catesby Jones, a native of Westmoreland County and a career naval officer who had distinguished himself at New Orleans in the War of 1812, inherited Sharon, an "utterly barren and unproductive" estate near the Great Falls of the Potomac.[4] Intrigued by the challenge of the sterile soil and undaunted by a current aphorism which maintained that "the more Fairfax land a man had, the poorer he was," Jones set his slaves to work applying lime and other manures, and he made use of a subsoil plough to turn up fertile soil. In the early 1820s, after a naval expedition to the west coast of South America, he returned with several tons of guano (partially decomposed bird droppings), which he applied to his lands. By such means, Jones soon developed "a pattern farm of the entire region."[5]

3. James S. Buckingham, *The Slave States of America*, 2 vols. (London: Fisher, Son & Co., 1842), 2:564, 570; Janney, *Yankees in Fairfax*, p. 5.

4. Charles Lee Lewis, "Thomas ap Catesby Jones," *Dictionary of American Biography*, Allen Johnson and Dumas Malone, eds. 20 vols. (New York: Charles Scribner's Sons, 1928-36); S.V.; A New-Yorker, "Letters from Virginia—No. 5," *Amer. Agr.* 7 (April 1848):122-23; Alexandria *Gazette*, 2 June 1858 (hereinafter cited as *Gazette*).

5. Samuel S. Randall to John S. Skinner, 15 January 1847, in *Monthly Journal of Agriculture* 2 (April 1847):448 (hereinafter cited as *Mo. Jnl. Agr.*). Ibid., 443-44; *Gazette*, 28 September 1852, 3 November 1868.

Lewis Bailey, the son of Hachaliah Bailey, of circus fame, was one of the first Northerners to begin farming in Fairfax County. By the time of the Civil War the area in which Bailey had settled had become known as Baileys Cross Roads. Virginia State Library.

Northerners somehow learned of his success, and needing land for their expanding population, some began to think of moving to Fairfax to make similar efforts.

Perhaps the first of the Northerners to settle permanently in Fairfax to farm was Lewis Bailey, an upstate New Yorker and the son of Hachaliah Bailey of circus fame. In 1837, the elder Bailey, who needed a place on which to winter his circus animals, bought hundreds of acres of Fairfax land, much of it on the outskirts of present-day Arlington County in the area now known as Baileys Cross Roads. Shortly afterward, Lewis Bailey bought 150 acres of land from his father for ten dollars an acre. Included in the purchase was a "good dwelling-house," but there were "no other buildings of value, and little or no fence." The farm itself, he wrote later, consisted of "cultivated worn-out lands, too poor to produce a crop of grass, or pay for cultivation without manure."[6]

---

6. Lewis Bailey thought he was "the first farmer from the state of New-York, that purchased a farm in this county, with the intention of making it a permanent residence." Bailey to Editors, *Count. Gent.* 6(9 August 1855):90; Janney, *Yankees in Fairfax*, p. 14; Fairfax County Deed Books, D3, p. 395; F3, pp. 134, 137, 225, 254, 258; H3, p. 192 (microfilm copy, Archives Division, Virginia State Library, Richmond, Va.; hereinafter cited as VSL-A); Jane C. Whitt, *Elephants and Quaker Guns: A History of Civil War and Circus Days* (New York: Vantage Press, 1966), p. 17.

Some of Bailey's neighbors considered the farm the poorest in the vicinity. When he built his first small barn, twenty-four by thirty-six feet, they asked him if he "ever expected to fill it." The question was scarcely a jest, for Bailey did not make enough hay the first year "to winter two horses." Nevertheless, the purchase was a wise one. Within a decade Bailey had a fine herd of dairy cattle and had become one of the more prosperous farmers in the area.[7]

A few other New Yorkers were moving into Fairfax in the late 1830s. Among them were Ambrose Cock of Westchester County, Elida Watkins of Ulster County, and Henry Steers of Sing Sing, all of whom became prominent Fairfax citizens. In 1842 Jacob Haight, a dour, industrious Quaker from the Hudson River Valley, made one of the most significant purchases of the decade when he bought the old Richard Bland Lee estate of Sully in the western part of the county. At fifty-nine, Haight was a generation older than most of the farmers who were moving from New York to Virginia. Already prosperous, he and his wife were eager to live in a milder climate. Haight learned of Sully from an advertisement in a New York paper and traveled to Fairfax to inspect the property. Pleased with what he saw, he bought the 750-acre estate at public auction for $12,145, about sixteen dollars an acre, and moved his family to Virginia.[8]

Like other "emigrants," as they were called, Haight worked diligently to improve his land. Using scientific techniques, some of them similar to those employed by Lee a half century earlier, he brought the land to "new life." By crop rotation, applications of sheep manure and guano, and the sowing of timothy and clover, he developed a model farm in western Fairfax, just as Jones had done in the northeastern part of the county.[9]

Over the course of the next three or four years, a number of Northern families migrated to Fairfax. Like the Haights, many of them came from counties in the Hudson River Valley south of Albany, where Quakers had long been known for their prosperous farms and their superior methods of farming. By the 1840s, that region had become overcrowded, land prices were high, agriculture was declining in importance, and competing farms areas had arisen in central and western New York. Many young people moved to the West, but a handful began to see that the upper South offered opportunities to continue the scientific agriculture at which they were expert. With the markets of Washington, Georgetown, and Alexandria nearby, Fairfax and other counties near the

---

7. Bailey to Editors, *Count. Gent.* 6:90.
8. Robert S. Gamble, *Sully: The Biography of a House* (Chantilly, Va.: Sully Foundation, Ltd., 1973), p. 73 (hereinafter cited as Gamble, *Sully*).
9. Ibid., pp. 73-76, 78-81; *Gazette*, 18 February 1860.

District of Columbia appeared quite attractive,[10] especially with land prices running approximately $5 to $15 per acre compared to farms of similar intrinsic value in the North selling from $40 to $70 an acre.

The first newcomers settled in three or four principal areas of the county: along the Little River Turnpike near Sully, in the vicinity of Fairfax Court House, along the Georgetown Turnpike, and on the Leesburg Turnpike around Baileys Cross Roads. By the mid-1840s, many of the newcomers, including Haight and Bailey, had prospered to such an extent that several newspapers began to speak with admiration of the changes they had wrought. One of the earliest accounts to appear in print was carried in an April 1844 issue of the Alexandria *Gazette*. The paper noted that the village of Fairfax Court House "has greatly improved in late years. Several handsome and spacious buildings have recently been built, the lots improved, and other marks of enterprise and industry exhibited."[11] In 1845 Samuel Janney, a prominent Quaker minister, educator, farmer, and writer of Loudoun County, remarked that members of the community had recently erected "a number of commodious and tasteful dwellings," and that "the price of improved land had doubled since 1840."[12]

The farming methods of the newcomers became a matter of curiosity not only to natives of Fairfax and adjoining counties but also to men interested in scientific agriculture all along the Eastern seaboard. Janney was so impressed by the signs of prosperity that he wrote a series of unsigned articles which appeared in both the Alexandria *Gazette* and the Richmond *Whig*. The series was reprinted in pamphlet form and circulated widely in Virginia and states to the north.[13] Janney described at length the agricultural practices of the newcomers and attributed the Yankees' successes to their energy, hard work, superior farming methods, and use of free labor. Within the next few years, one agricultural journal after another carried detailed accounts of emigrants who had redeemed some portion of the "barren lands" of Fairfax.

A letter to the *American Agriculturist*, a New York journal, from an anonymous Fairfax emigrant was typical. This correspondent had bought what was once a "fertile and very profitably productive tobacco plantation" and had later become "a wild and barren-looking waste." The owner had abandoned it, the fences had gone to ruin, the land had "nearly all grown up to old-field pines, persimmon, sassafras, and broom straw. All the buildings [were] in ruin except the dwelling, and that

10. R[andall], "Emigration," Alb. *Cult.* 4:77-78; R[andall], "Fairfax County Lands: Emigration to Virginia, No. II," Alb. *Cult.* 4(March 1847):299-300.

11. *Gazette*, 4 April 1844.

12. Janney, *Yankees in Fairfax*, p. 8.

13. *Gazette*, 12, 20, 25 September, 3, 10, 27, 28 October 1845; the Richmond *Whig* carried the articles on 12, 19, 23 September; 4, 10, 24, 28 October 1845.

nearly so." All thought that the soil was exhausted and "would not produce enough to keep the hands alive who planted it."

Examining the land, the Yankee found that it had never been plowed with a team stronger "than one horse, and of course a very light plow in a very shallow furrow which only stirred the surface." He had decided to purchase this "almost worthless" land. As he set to work to farm it, he found that he could not manure the land for it "would hardly support a single sheep to the acre." He had to find the fertility in the soil itself, and he did just that with "one of your No. 19 plows," which he "set as deep as four good stout Virginia Yankeeised oxen could pull it."

His neighbors ("even the negroes") were sure he was crazy, but he astounded them by producing the "best crop of wheat in all that section of the country," fifteen bushels an acre upon "old broomstraw field," and the next season he had as "luxuriant a crop of clover" as one could wish. Upon this he "sowed a bushel of plaster to the acre, the effect of which, if possible, was still more astonishing" than his wheat crop.

Each year thereafter he added a "new field to my cultivation, and by means of lime, ashes, plaster, clover, and manure" had "rendered a barren waste a fertile spot, supporting herds of cattle and flocks of sheep, and affording sustenance and happiness for many human beings." His "great engine of improvement" had been the plough, and he had sometimes used a subsoil plough "so as to get a mellow tilth from ten to fifteen inches deep."[14]

Like this anonymous correspondent, many of the Yankee emigrants were enthusiastic about their new homes and farms, but there were some who failed or were otherwise discontent with the change. Most observers agreed that the chief reason for failure was the buyer's error in purchasing larger quantities of land than he could afford, leaving himself with insufficient funds to make the needed improvements or to care for the requirements of his family before his land became sufficiently remunerative. Other factors caused some to return home after a year or two: occasional crop failures, overexertion during the long hot summer days, ill health, homesickness, or the purchase of cheap land only to learn later that it was unfavorably or unhealthily situated.[15]

By and large, however, the efforts of the Yankees met with success, and as news of that success spread, more Northerners began to make inquiries about the worn-out lands of the county. Perhaps the most significant group to buy land in Fairfax in the late 1840s was composed of Friends from the vicinity of Philadelphia, who bought the Woodlawn estate after it had become so unprofitable that expenses of cultivation

14. "Letter from Virginia," 9 November 1850, *Amer. Agr.* 10:21-22.

15. Janney, *Yankees in Fairfax*, p. 15; A New-Yorker, "Letters," *Amer. Agr.* 6(December 1847):368; L. Dederick to L. Tucker & Son, *Count. Gent.* 9(8 January 1857):35; R[andall], "Fairfax County Lands," *Alb. Cult.* 4:299-300.

exceeded the selling price of the products. Seven years earlier, the owner, Lorenzo Lewis (the great grandson of Martha Washington and the son of Nelly Custis Lewis) had abandoned the cultivation and offered the land for sale. Years passed and he did not receive an offer; by the time of the Quaker purchase, the Woodlawn fields were overgrown and only a few old slaves remained in some rickety cabins. The Quakers, who were engaged in supplying shipbuilders with timber, bought the two-thousand-acre estate largely for its fine forests. Much of the timber was white oak, especially valuable for shipbuilding.[16]

Jacob and Paul Hillman Troth and Chalkley and Lucas Gillingham, partners of the timber farm, bought the Woodlawn estate and settled there with other members of their families. They decided to sell the land in parcels ranging from one hundred to two hundred acres, on condition that the lumber firm might cut and remove the timber and that the purchaser would not sell intoxicating liquor. Within the next few years, more than forty Quaker families left New Jersey and Pennsylvania to settle on former Woodlawn lands and on adjoining land that had once been the Hollin Hall estate of George Mason's son Thomson.[17]

The Quakers, however, were not interested solely in lumbering and farming. They also were embarking on what they saw as a great moral mission: they hoped to demonstrate to Virginians that slavery was not necessary to the economy of the Old Dominion. The Quakers planned to establish a community of farms worked with free labor and thereby convince Virginians that they could abolish slavery without impairing either their own prosperity or that of the state.[18] The role the blacks were expected to play in the new order of things is not entirely clear, but the Quakers seem to have hoped that eventually the blacks would be freed, that they would have opportunities to gain at least a modicum of formal education, and that someday they would become enterprising wage earners.

The Woodlawn Quakers were not aggressive in pushing their antislavery views. Theirs was to be a peaceable crusade. Rejecting the rhetoric and tactics of abolitionists like William Lloyd Garrison, they hoped to win Virginians to their views by friendly measures, by simply demonstrating what they saw as the superior virtues of their own way of

16. Dorothy Troth Muir, *Potomac Interlude: The Story of Woodlawn Mansion and the Mount Vernon Neighborhood, 1846-1943* (Washington, D.C.: Mount Vernon Print Shop, 1943), pp. 33-37 (hereinafter cited as Muir, *Potomac Interlude*); *Gazette*, 29 April 1846.

17. Muir, *Potomac Interlude*, pp. 40, 50-51, 65; Society of Friends, Alexandria Monthly Meeting Minutes, February-November 1847, July-October 1848, May-July 1849, et passim (microfilm copy, Friends Historical Library, Swarthmore College, Swarthmore, Pa.). I have substituted the names of the months for the numbers that Quakers customarily used.

18. Muir, *Potomac Interlude*, p. 65. Also see Horace D. Buckman, "The Quakers Come to Woodlawn," *Yearbook of the Historical Society of Fairfax, Virginia, Inc.*, 9 (1964-65):65 (hereinafter cited as Historical Society *Yearbook*); Griscom to Janney, 21 April 1846, Samuel McPherson Janney Papers (Friends Historical Library, Swarthmore College) (hereinafter cited as Janney Papers).

life. But there is little evidence that they and other Fairfax Yankees with similar views met with success in converting the natives to their values and their views on slavery. It is also impossible to determine just how much of the new prosperity could be attributed to the enterprise of the newcomers. The Yankees got most of the publicity, particularly in Northern journals, but much of the credit for the agricultural revival of Fairfax must go to native Virginians as well. [19] Participation in Fairfax County agricultural fairs and societies, for example, and the prizes awarded do not seem to have been disproportionately in favor of either Yankee or native. [20]

The extent of influence of newcomer on native—and of native on newcomer—is unclear. What is clear is that Fairfax in 1850 was no monolithic society. Alongside the native aristocratic families, merchants and small farmers, poor whites, free blacks, and slaves were hundreds of enterprising and ambitious Northerners strongly committed to middle-class values and the Protestant ethic.

By 1847, some two hundred Northern families, averaging six members to a family, had moved into the county. They had invested more than two hundred thousand dollars in the purchase of land for farming purposes, paying an average of five to ten dollars per acre. The highest price paid had been for an improved farm of 200 acres, which sold for $26 an acre. Most of the settlers had bought farms of 150 or 200 acres, though several who had purchased as few as 25 to 50 acres found themselves "well to do in the world with these humble allotments, and . . . managed through intensive cultivation of every portion of their lands to compensate for their limited acres." Little land had been purchased for speculation because so much was available that many years would elapse before the supply would be short enough to create a rise in market prices. [21]

By 1850, about one of every three adult white males living in Fairfax had migrated from the North or from outside the United States. They came from all of the states north of the Potomac, as well as from Ohio and the District of Columbia, and from the British Isles, Germany, New Brunswick, and the West Indies. Though about half of the men were engaged in farming and though scores of others undoubtedly worked as farm laborers, many found other economic opportunities. There was a scattering of professional men: lawyers, teachers, physicians, six clergymen (several of whom taught at the Episcopal seminary outside of

19. "The Yankees in Virginia," *DeBow's Review* 22(June 1857):621-23.
20. *Gazette*, 1847-1860, passim.
21. Randall to Skinner, 15 January 1847, in *Mo. Jnl. Agr.* 2:445-46.

Alexandria), an editor, a surveyor, and an engineer. About seventy-five were skilled craftsmen and businessmen including millers, innkeepers, contractors, shoemakers, blacksmiths, brickmakers, wheelwrights, stonemasons, and so on. And there were numerous white laborers, some two hundred from Ireland alone.[22]

That Fairfax in the last antebellum decade was a more cosmopolitan society that has heretofore been suspected seems evident. One might well argue that there was as much diversity in lifestyles in Fairfax in 1850 as in the 1970s—and perhaps more. But what is most significant about the statistics is that they show that the population of the county had surged upward for the first time in the nineteenth century. Somehow the Fairfax economy was becoming capable of attracting and supporting hundreds of newcomers.

22. U.S. Census Office, Virginia Census Schedules, Inhabitants, Fairfax County, 1850 (National Archives, Washington, D.C.; microfilm copy, VSL-A) (hereinafter cited as Fairfax County MS Census).

II

A Comparative Eden

Agriculture and a Diversifying Economy, 1840-1860

The first Northerners who bought land in Fairfax in the late 1830s and early 1840s must have had a sharp eye for its potential, for in those years the Fairfax economy was perhaps more depressed than at any other period in the county's history. The long agricultural depression which followed the Panic of 1837 had worsened the generally poor economic situation of Tidewater Virginia, and in 1842 a severe money shortage squeezed the entire state of Virginia. In Fairfax that year, "likely slaves" brought a hundred fifty dollars or less, and land which ordinarily sold for eight to ten dollars an acre fell under the auctioneer's gavel at little more than two.[1]

In the absence of a major agricultural staple and in the face of apparently exhausted lands, county residents made what money they could from three principal sources: marketing, fishing, and the sale of slaves. Farmers fortunate enough to live along the turnpikes carried wood and a few other agricultural products to Alexandria, Washington, and Georgetown. Their work was time-consuming, and the financial rewards were low. They went to market at least two or three times a week, and in the fall and winter some of them made two or three trips a day into Alexandria carrying loads of wood.[2] Though a few farmers, most notably Thomas ap Catesby Jones near Great Falls, were beginning to prosper, others found it difficult and sometimes impossible to make a profit, or even to remain solvent. Fairfax, complained one citizen, "is a distressed community oppressed by debt."[3]

---

1. Fairfax County Legislative Petitions, 27 December 1842 (VSL-A).
2. Ibid., 11 December 1835, 25 January 1840, 1 January 1841, 3 January 1842; *Gazette*, 1 February 1853.
3. Fairfax County Legislative Petition, 27 December 1842. Also see *Gazette*, 29 January 1853, 27 February 1854, 9 March 1859.

A major staple of the Fairfax economy was the fish caught in the Potomac and its tributaries each year during the fishing season. In good seasons, owners of the fisheries could make a handsome profit, and many poor people who lived close enough to the water found opportunities for temporary employment. Whites, slaves, and free blacks worked as "occupiers of fisheries, haulers of seines, or curers of fish." One legislative petition reflected (and perhaps exaggerated) the role of fisheries in the economy when it maintained that since the "worn-out soil" possessed "but few inducements to bind to it its present owners and occupants . . . the strongest, and almost the only" inducement to remain in the county was "that afforded by the fish . . . [of] the Potomac and its waters."[4]

But the fisheries were scarcely more reliable than the soil. In the 1830s the tremendous seines used on the Delaware and Susquehanna rivers had been introduced on the Potomac. "Extending nearly across the river," the seines, declared one Fairfax petition, measured "one thousand to one thousand two hundred fathoms in length [that is, six thousand to more than seven thousand feet], with an equal or greater length of rope attached to each end," and were "dragged up and down the stream with the tide, so as to sweep away everything within its bed." The use of seines destroyed the spawn, and the costliness of the operation meant the destruction of many small fisheries which had once lined the Potomac and been valuable to their owners and to the communities around them.[5] Though the General Assembly enacted a series of laws designed to protect the fisheries,[6] they played a diminishing role in the Fairfax economy in the midnineteenth century.

Another major source of income for Fairfax residents (and one which they preferred not to talk about) came from selling or hiring out their excess slaves. It is not difficult to imagine what Northern settlers, especially the Quakers, thought of the slave markets run by Joseph Bruin at West End and by Alexander Grigsby at Centreville, or of the frequent slave auctions at the front door of the Fairfax courthouse.[7] Virginians themselves were none too proud of the traffic in slaves and often patronized the traders with reluctance.

But economic and social pressures meant that there was no way by which Fairfax residents could profitably utilize the increasing number of blacks. If the black population of Fairfax had increased as rapidly

---

4. Fairfax County Legislative Petitions, 10 December 1833, 11 December 1835, 20 December 1836, 3 April 1839, 25 January 1840, 4 January 1841, 3 January 1842.

5. Ibid.

6. Acts of the General Assembly of Virginia, 1831-61, passim (hereinafter cited as Acts of Gen. Assem.).

7. Bruin regularly advertised in the Gazette that he offered "cash for Negroes," and that he was "at all times in the market" for "likely young negroes for the South" and would "pay liberal prices for all negroes from 10 to 30 years of age." Gazette, 20 March 1844 ff.

Seine fishing. Among the staples of Fairfax were the shad and herring caught each year in the spring. The introduction of large seines (up to fourteen hundred fathoms or more than seven thousand feet, in length) on the Potomac in the 1830s, however, drove many small fisheries out of business. Virginia State Library.

between 1800 and 1860 as did the black population in the United States as a whole, Fairfax would have had about 25,000 blacks by 1860, or three to every one white. Instead, the number of black people declined from 6,282 in 1800 to 3,788 in 1860; and the number of slaves dropped from 6,078 in 1800 to 3,116 in 1860.[8] There is no doubt that the sale of slaves was the chief reason for their declining population in the county. Just how much money the slave trade brought into Fairfax is impossible to determine, but undoubtedly the depressed slave market of the early 1840s was a major factor in the depressed economy of those years.

Fairfax slave owners could also make money by hiring out unneeded slaves, but just how extensive such practices were in the early 1840s, when money was scarce and the demand for labor relatively low, is not clear. It seems likely, however, that a good many were hired out in neighboring localities. In 1841, Dennis Johnston, for example, a county magistrate and one of the largest slaveholders in Fairfax, advertised that he would have for hire at John Smith's Tavern on Cameron Street "several valuable Servants, Men, Women, Boys, and Girls."[9] And there is evidence that slaves were hired out in other states, some as far as Mississippi.[10] Proceeds from such arrangements must have helped a number of

8. Francis A. Walker, [comp.], *The Statistics of the Population of the United States, Ninth Census, (June 1, 1870)* (Washington, D.C.: Government Printing Office, 1872), 1:69, 70.

9. *Gazette*, 2 January 1841.

10. George W. Hunter to George Richard Lee, 15 July 1840, Stuart Family Papers, Box 2, 1835-1852 (Alderman Library, University of Virginia, Charlottesville).

Fairfax men to feed and clothe their families when little other money was forthcoming.

In the early 1840s these three sources of income—marketing, fishing, and selling or hiring out slaves—were barely enough to keep the Fairfax economy alive. Yet there is evidence in the population statistics of 1840 that the downward trend of the economy had halted. After a steady decline in both the total and white population figures from 1800 to 1830, there was actually an increase between 1830 and 1840. Though the total population rose by less than 2 percent, the white population rose by more than 11 percent.[11]

In the two decades preceding the Civil War, the upward economic and population trends accelerated. Throughout the South the picture brightened with the expansion of the "cotton kingdom"; and in Virginia, agriculture flourished throughout the formerly depressed Tidewater. The change was particularly dramatic in Fairfax.[12] The availability of guano and other commercial fertilizers, the growth of urban markets, revolutionary changes in transportation, the beginnings of economic diversification, a rising white population, and significant changes in the role of slavery all played a part in the rejuvenation of the county.

While considering the developments of the antebellum decades, it is well to recall that Virginians of the 1840s and 1850s were not anticipating the onslaught of war. One has but to read of their optimistic plans for economic expansion to realize that—until after John Brown's raid on Harper's Ferry—Virginians fully expected an indefinite continuation of domestic peace. As they undertook the work that was to make Fairfax County a "garden spot," they had no idea of the destruction that would soon lay waste their fields.

The first step in the agricultural revival of Fairfax was a shift from extensive to intensive cultivation of the soil.[13] Though George Washington and other leading planters of earlier years had experimented with deep ploughing, methodical fertilizing, and the use of grass crops and green dressing in crop rotation, such improvements had not been profitable.[14] Not until the experiments and publicity of Edmund Ruffin did the problem of too much acidity in the soil of Tidewater Virginia become widely known. In Fairfax, Thomas ap Catesby Jones and some of

11. See above, p. 154.

12. Avery O. Craven, *Soil Exhaustion as a Factor in the Agricultural History of Virginia and Maryland, 1606-1860* (1926; reprint ed., Gloucester, Mass.: Peter Smith, 1965), pp. 160-61 (hereinafter cited as Craven, *Soil Exhaustion*); Frederick Law Olmsted, *The Cotton Kingdom: A Traveller's Observations on Cotton and Slavery in the American Slave States* (New York: Mason Brothers, 1861), p. 89; *Gazette*, 29 January 1853.

13. Craven, *Soil Exhaustion*, p. 89.

14. George Washington, "Observations on Mr. Anderson's Accounts," 1798, cited in ibid., p. 110; also see ibid., pp. 86-99; *Gazette*, 31 July 1854, quoting letter from Washington, 1794.

his neighbors apparently made similar discoveries: they stressed the use of lime whereas Ruffin used marl to reduce the acidity. Lime not only reduced acidity but also released other nutrients beneficial to the soil and made them available to plants.[15]

In the mid-1840s, after guano was found to be especially effective on poor pine lands and was being imported in large quantities, farmers who could afford the high price (around forty-five dollars a ton) began to apply it liberally to their lands. John A. Washington, who had inherited Mount Vernon in 1829, declared in 1852 that the use of guano caused wheat yields in the area to rise to ten and fifteen bushels an acre.[16]

With the application of lime, guano, and other commercial fertilizers and the adoption of other modern agricultural practices, Fairfax farmers made great progress in raising both the quantity and the quality of their produce. Proud of their excellent crops, they frequently took specimens by the office of the Alexandria *Gazette*, where editor Edgar Snowden was happy to give both farmer and product a boost. In the 1850s, he commented on potatoes ("the finest . . . ever seen in the county"), on corn (twelve feet high), on oats ("The best we've ever seen"), on apples (the "finest flavored and largest"), on honey (the "purest"), on parsnips ("unsurpassed"), and on many other fruits and vegetables, all grown in Fairfax. Grain production also rose significantly: in 1850 the *Gazette* declared that the "best wheat in the market comes from Fairfax County."[17]

Improvements in animal husbandry as well as in the cultivation of the soil contributed to the revival of Fairfax. Leading the way was Lewis Bailey, whose experience with his father's circus animals undoubtedly stood him in good stead. Bailey repeatedly won prizes for his cattle, not only at county agricultural fairs, but also at regional and state fairs in both Maryland and Virginia.[18]

Such advances were possible in the midnineteenth century largely because of the growth of nearby urban markets. Whereas the total po-

15. Craven, *Soil Exhaustion*, pp. 140-43; Lewis C. Gray, *History of Agriculture in the Southern United States to 1860*, 2 vols. (reprint ed., New York: Peter Smith, 1941), 2:804, 805.

16. John A. Washington, 30 August 1852 in *Prairie Farmer* 12 (October 1852):464-65, cited in Paul W. Gates, *The Farmer's Age: Agriculture, 1815-1860*, Economic History of the United States (New York: Holt, Rinehart and Winston, 1962), p. 108.

17. *Gazette*, e.g., 13 July 1854, 21 April 1859. The statistics of grain production in Fairfax County show that it produced 24,630 bushels of wheat in 1840 and 56,165 in 1850; 158,012 bushels of Indian corn in 1840 and 207,531 in 1850; 1,594 bushels of buckwheat in 1840 and 5,153 in 1850; 66,806 bushels of oats in 1840 and 76,798 in 1850. The flour mills at Alexandria were said to be the second largest in the United States, surpassed only by the Gallego Mills in Richmond. *Compendium of the Inhabitants and Statistics of the United States, . . . Sixth Census* (Washington, D.C.: Thomas Allen, 1861), p. 155-56; J.D.B. DeBow, *The Seventh Census of the United States: 1850*, [Book 1] (Washington, D.C.: Robert Armstrong, Public Printer, 1853), pp. 275, 277: *Gazette*, 11 March 1854.

18. Janney, *Yankees in Fairfax*, pp. 3-4; Fairfax County MS Census, Agriculture, 1850, 1860; *Gazette*, 17 June 1850, 3 November 1851, 20 January 1853, 6 October 1854, 3 November 1855, 6 October 1860. For comments on the excellent livestock of other Fairfax farmers, see *Gazette*, 1 November 1854, 11 October 1860, 5 April 1861.

pulation of the District of Columbia, including Alexandria, was only fourteen thousand in 1800, it was more than three times that by 1840. In 1860, despite the retrocession of Alexandria to Virginia in 1846, the population of the district had reached seventy-five thousand, and that of Alexandria had risen to more than twelve thousand, for a combined population of almost ninety thousand. The presence of these nearby markets enabled many a Fairfax farmer to undertake improvements in his land that would not otherwise have been practical.

Without adequate means of transportation, Fairfax farmers could not have risen to the challenge of growing cities. It was in the field of transportation that Fairfax made its most revolutionary strides—and continued to experience its greatest difficulties. By the midnineteenth century, Fairfax farmers relied primarily on overland transportation to carry their goods to market. The construction of two major rail lines in Northern Virginia in the 1850s, one running from Alexandria to Gordonsville and the other from Alexandria to Leesburg, brought dramatic changes to the county.[19] Though average speed was only about twenty miles an hour, trains were far faster than wagons that lumbered along at two or three miles per hour, when they managed to stay out of mudholes. Because rail transportation sharply reduced the cost of getting goods to market and of getting fertilizer and other items to the farmer, some farmers who had not previously found it profitable to buy commercial fertilizers now found it feasible to do so.[20]

Rail lines also brought an influx of new residents to areas of Fairfax previously "as unknown as the wilds of Kansas." Thriving hamlets sprang up along both the Orange and Alexandria and the Alexandria, Loudoun and Hampshire lines. In 1859 at the new village of Vienna Station, in an area previously known as Ayr Hill, a large country store, "several handsome dwellings," and "an extensive foundry and manufactory of agricultural implements" were under construction. Farther west, the village of Herndon was growing up. By 1859 a locksmith shop and a steam sawmill were in full operation, a post office had been established, and a Methodist Church had been erected. No one, wrote an enthusiastic newspaper correspondent, had "any doubt that the future will witness at this beautiful spot a busy, active population, who may en-

19. For a petition in behalf of the Orange and Alexandria Railroad, see Alexandria (Town) Legislative Petitions, 7 January 1847 (VSL-A). For the acts of incorporation, see *Acts of Gen. Assem.*, 1846-47, p. 101; 1848-49, p. 107. For progress of construction, see, e.g., *Gazette*, 11 February 1850 to 25 October 1860, passim; Virginia Board of Public Works, *Annual Report*, 1851, pp. 546, 549. For progress on the branch line from Manassas Junction to the Valley, which was incorporated as the Manassas Gap Railroad, see *Gazette*, 1 March 1850 to 11 May 1861, passim.

20. In Winchester, Virginia, the opening of the railroad and competition with the C&O Canal caused the price of plaster (gypsum) to fall from $12 to $15 a ton in 1833 to $9 to $10 in 1840 and to $4 in 1845. Virginia Board of Public Works, *Thirtieth Annual Report*, 1845, p. 144. Also see *Gazette*, 24 September, 6 October 1851.

joy all the luxuries of the city without any of the annoyance of brick walls, dusty streets, and the noise and bustle of daily business."[21]

Northern Virginians were as much in love with the locomotive as more recent Americans have been with the automobile. The excitement of workers on one railroad line was said to be "tremendous." The editor of the *Gazette*, an ardent advocate of railroads, commented: "Men worship their idol with a perfect love . . . . In their dreams the ringing of the alarm bell, and the shrill neighing of the iron horse as he prances on his rapid journey, fall upon the ears as the most delightful music."[22]

The condition of Fairfax roads was reason enough for county citizens to prize their railroads. Rarely in satisfactory shape, the roads were a subject of complaint throughout the midnineteenth century, especially during winter rains and spring thaws, when the notorious Virginia mud made many of them virtually impassable. Nevertheless, there were advances in road construction during the 1840s and 1850s. Reflecting both the rising prosperity and the improvements, the number of carriages and other taxable vehicles in the county rose from 89 in 1840 to 610 in 1861.[23] 1860.[23]

Presumably the best roads in the county were the turnpikes chartered by the General Assembly. In the 1850s, several major new roads were constructed in Fairfax. In 1851 the General Assembly authorized the construction of two log roads ("plank roads," as they were called) from Fairfax Court House, one running to some point on the Alexandria and Gordonsville railroad at or near Fairfax Station, and the other to a point on the Potomac River near Georgetown. In 1856, after both natives and newcomers complained of the existing roads leading from Alexandria south into Fairfax County, the Assembly authorized the construction of the Alexandria, Mount Vernon and Accotink Turnpike, designed to serve not only the residents but also the increasing traffic of sightseers to Mount Vernon.[24]

Speed of communication advanced even more rapidly than speed of travel. Samuel F. B. Morse's invention of the telegraph in 1844 meant that man could, for the first time in human history, send written messages faster than he could carry them. In November 1846, the Fairfax County court agreed that the county would provide poles for the telegraph lines from Washington to Richmond that crossed the county.[25]

21. *Gazette*, 9 March. 29 August, 21 November 1859.
22. *Gazette*, 28 January 1851, quoting Warrenton *Flag*, n.d.
23. "A Statement of Taxes . . .," 1840, 1861, in Virginia House of Delegates, *Annual Message of the Governor of the Commonwealth and Accompanying Documents* (title varies), 1840-41, Doc. No. 2, [p. 8]; 1861-62, Doc. No. 5, p. 374 (hereinafter cited as *House Docs.*).
24. Fairfax County Legislative Petitions, 7 January 1856, 22 January 1858; *Acts of Gen. Assem.*, 1855-56, pp. 127-28.
25. Fairfax County Court Minute Books, 16 November 1846.

Everywhere in Fairfax in the 1850s, a spirit of progress was in the air. By 1850 writers rarely spoke of Fairfax "desolation." The "waste" had become a "comparative Eden" of "airy fields, green pastures," "yellow grain," and "fat flocks and herds." Though much Fairfax land remained covered with pine, the traveler along the turnpikes saw at every hand productive dairy cattle, fine orchards and vegetable gardens, and superb fields of corn and wheat. Rising land prices accompanied the rise in productivity. A farm that had sold for $6 an acre in the late 1840s brought $28 in the mid-1850s; one selling for $11 an acre in 1850 brought $25 in 1854; land selling for $10 an acre in 1853 brought $12 to $14 and on one occasion $50 an acre in 1854; land selling in September 1853 for $40 went for $70 an acre eight months later.[26] In 1859 the *Gazette* declared that lands around Alexandria had increased in value by 400 percent in recent years and commented, "There is no part of the State where lands are more valuable or command better prices than in Fairfax."[27]

As Fairfax farmers began to profit from their lands, they searched for new ways of investing their excess capital. Some dreamed of establishing a great manufacturing city at Great Falls; others had hopes of finding rich mineral resources in the rolling hills. Overlooking the irregularities of the water supply of the Potomac, Thomas ap Catesby Jones and several other men organized the Great Falls Manufacturing Company in 1839, and in 1851 petitioned the Assembly for permission to build a rail line from Great Falls to a point on the O&A.[28] Hoping to rival the great new England mill town, the founders named the new community South Lowell. One enthusiast wrote that "the wheat of the Valley and the eastern side of the Blue Ridge country will find its way to this point to be converted into flour. The wool of the west and east can here be manufactured into cloth. The iron, the copper, and other metals can here find a . . . sure means of conversion into the implements of husbandry."[29]

There were other attempts to establish "manufactures" at Great Falls. In 1854 several citizens organized the Potomac Manufacturing Company for "manufacturing paper and other articles." Others organized the Farmers Milling Company "for the purpose of manufacturing flour and other things" at Great Falls. Still others formed the Virginia Company for the "manufacture of iron, machinery, locomotives, and other articles which they may desire to . . . make at the Great Falls."[30]

26. *Gazette*, 27 February 1854. The *Gazette* cites many other instances to substantiate these statistics.

27. Ibid., 27 July, 16 September 1859.

28. Fairfax County Legislative Petitions, 11 January 1839, 12 December 1850, 27 February 1851; John W. Gilmer to [Robert] Craig, Chairman of the Committee on Roads, 5 February 1851, in Alexandria County Legislative Petitions (VSL-A); *Acts of Gen. Assem.*, 1838-39, p. 184. For a history of the Great Falls Manufacturing Company, see *United States v. Great Falls Manufacturing Company*, Deposition of Witnesses (Washington, D.C.: United States Government Printing Office, 1862).

29. Gilmer to Craig, 5 February 1851, Alexandria County Legislative Petitions.

30. *Acts of Gen. Assem.*, 1853-54, pp. 75-77; 1855-56, p. 253; 1859-60, pp. 603, 609, 610; *Gazette*, 18 January, 15 February 1854. For other efforts at manufacturing, see *Gazette*, 11 April 1854, 28 August 1855, 14 June 1856, 21 September 1860.

More down-to-earth residents petitioned the county court for permission to construct water, grist, and saw mills, and in the 1850s even steam mills on the smaller streams in the county.[31] In addition, there was a rash of interest in mining and quarrying in the 1850s.[32]

Increasing economic diversification can be seen in the statistics of occupations for 1860. The manuscript census for that year shows that although more than 650 Fairfax men classified themselves as farmers, there were also about 120 who described themselves as mechanics (blacksmiths, wheelwrights, coopers, and the like), about 100 as professional men (lawyers, doctors, teachers, clergymen, surveyors, and students), 53 as carpenters, 32 as merchants, 11 as millers, and 11 as landlords. A number of others were in a variety of occupations: butchering, wagon-making, boating, and so on.[33]

Despite the varied economic activity, Fairfax in 1860 remained a thoroughly rural county, its principal commercial center still in Alexandria. There were, of course, numerous taverns and general stores, a few hotels, and even a newspaper and one savings bank in the county. Small, localized commercial centers were growing. In 1840 Dranesville secured an act of incorporation, partly to give town officials authority "to prevent and punish by reasonable fines the practice of firing guns and running horses in said town." And in 1842 Fairfax Court House, or Providence, extended its limits and incorporated as a town.[34]

Population statistics best show the highly rural nature of the county (see Table I). Though there were comfortable advances in the population figures, the density per square mile remained low. In 1840 the total population was 9,370; in 1860 it was 11,834, an increase of 26.3 percent. In 1840 the total white population was 5,439; in 1860 it was 8,046, an increase of more than 45 percent.[35] The increase in population density was consequently insignificant, from twenty-one persons per square mile in 1840 to twenty-seven in 1860 (compared with 1,390 persons per square mile in 1976).

31. Fairfax County Court Minute Book, 18 June 1844, p. 148; November 1846; May, June, July, September 1847, pp. 36, 48, 49, 55, 69; June 1848, p. 119, et passim; *Gazette*, 13 April, 12 June, 17 November 1854; 17, 26 February, 10 March, 21 May, 13 June, 18, 19 September 1855; 10 January 1857; 11 October 1859; 29 June, 12, 16 July, 29 December 1860; 26 February 1861.

32. For acts of incorporation of mining companies, see *Acts of Gen. Assem.*, 1852-53, pp. 271, 273, 279; 1855-56, pp. 253, 254. Large deposits of granite of high quality were found on the line of the O&A, and copper and iron ore were discovered on lands of Elder Samuel Trott, pastor of Frying Pan Baptist Church. *Gazette*, 24 May 1850; 9 April 1852.

33. Fairfax County MS Census, Inhabitants, 1860.

34. For accounts of a typical country store, see S.C. Drane, Account Book, 1841-1842 (Virginia Historical Society, Richmond, Va.; hereinafter cited as VHS). For hotels and taverns, *Gazette*, 16 November 1850 through 18 February 1861, passim. The *Gazette* frequently quoted from the Fairfax *News*. For the acts incorporating the Fairfax Savings Bank and the towns of Dranesville and Providence, see *Acts of Gen. Assem.*, 1841-42, pp. 126-27, 1850-51, p. 147.

35. Walker, *Statistics of Population, Ninth Census*, 1:68-69.

Table I
Population of Fairfax County
1840-1860

	White	Black		Total
		Slave	Free	
1840	5,469	3,453	448	9,370
1850	6,835	3,250	597	10,682
1860	8,046	3,116	672	11,834

Source: U.S. Census, 1870. *Compendium*, pp. 68-70.

In the same two decades, the black population (slave and free) declined slowly, falling from 3,901 to 3,788, a loss of 3 percent. Most significant is the fact that all of the loss occurred in the number of slaves: from 3,453 in 1840, it fell to 3,250 in 1850, and to 3,116 in 1860. The proportional decline was even more rapid, especially in the decade from 1840 to 1850. Slaves, who had constituted more than 45 percent of the total population in 1800 and almost 37 percent in 1840, made up less than 31 percent in 1850 and less then 27 percent in 1860. Interestingly enough, while the white population rose dramatically (+45%) and the black slave population declined significantly (-10%), the trend of the free black followed that of the free white rather than that of the black slave. In fact the free black population rose more rapidly than did the white; it rose exactly 50 percent between 1840 and 1860.[36] In other words, several decades before the Civil War, Fairfax County, for one reason or another, was showing that it could utilize increasing numbers of free men (regardless of color) but not increasing numbers of slaves.

It would probably not be fair to describe Fairfax in 1860 as an essentially slaveholding society. The changing population patterns both resulted from and contributed to the changing agricultural patterns: a shift from what may have been little more than subsistence farming to truck and dairy farming and a scattering of other enterprises. Probably the most significant development in the economic history of antebellum Fairfax was the emergence of prosperous farms. Slowly but surely, the county was turning from an aristocratic, structured society dominated by the great planters of the Potomac into an increasingly middle-class society holding middle-class values and middle-class attitudes.

36. Ibid.

III

Social Classes and Shifting Values

In 1840 the social structure of Fairfax County was still unquestionably hierarchical. People had a rather clearly defined place in society, they knew what that place was, and they knew as well what everybody else's place was. Social position in the 1840s was determined far less from what people did or failed to do than from what they were; and what they were resulted primarily from what their recent ancestors had been and had done.

There was without doubt some economic mobility in Fairfax County. We know that land and slave values were going up on the one hand and that some large landholders were losing their property on the other. We also know that some formerly propertyless persons were acquiring land. But economic mobility did not necessarily mean social mobility. It seems unlikely that individuals who became more affluent than their associates began to mix as social equals with persons higher on the social scale.

To say that people had a clearly defined place in the social hierarchy is not to say that the socioeconomic structure of antebellum Fairfax was like a ladder with separate, clearly defined steps. In describing the social gradations of Fairfax society one might better speak of a social ramp, for one social class merged imperceptibly with the next, and knowing one's place on the ramp was actually a very subtle thing.

At the very bottom of that ramp were the slaves, though some were a little further from the bottom than others. They did not necessarily consider themselves at the bottom, however, for some of them identified with their masters and felt themselves superior to the poor whites—and perhaps a good many other people as well.[1] But in the eyes of the law

1. The most thorough investigation of status among slaves is Eugene Genovese, *Roll, Jordan, Roll:*

slaves had fewer rights than any other group. Though they were held responsible for crimes they committed, they were not legal persons. A slave could not sue or be sued,[2] he could not make legally binding contracts, and hence he could not marry. He could be sold or whipped at the whim of his owner,[3] and if he left home without his master's permission, he could be hunted down like an escaped convict. Further, he could not own property. and if he were hired out. the pay for his work went to his master.[4]

The vast majority of male slaves worked as farmhands. Others worked as laborers on railroads and other internal improvements. as waiters, blacksmiths, rough carpenters, boatmen, drivers of oxen, haulers of seines during fishing season, and as servants in inns, hotels, taverns, and private homes.

Barely above the slave on the social ramp was the free black. He had so few legal rights and was bound by so many restrictions and was subject to so much prejudice that his situation, often as not, was little better than that of the slave. Any person with as much as one-eighth Negro blood came under the aegis of Virginia's black code. He was presumed to be a slave; it was his responsibility to carry with him the papers stating his freedom. If he did not, he could be taken up and imprisoned on suspicion of being a runaway slave. If it took him some time to prove his freedom, he had to pay his jail costs; and if he were unable to do that, he could be sold into slavery to pay them.[5]

The World the Slaves Made (New York: Pantheon Books, 1974), pp. 327-98. John H. Russell deals briefly with the subject in his *Free Negro in Virginia, 1819-1865* (Baltimore: Johns Hopkins University Press, 1913), pp. 133-37 (hereinafter cited as Russell, *Free Negro in Virginia*).

2. A slave could sue (*in forma pauperis* only) for his freedom if he had some reason to claim he was illegally enslaved. For such suits on the part of Fairfax slaves, see *Gazette*, 19 August 1854; Petition of George Mason of Hollin Hall, John A. Washington, and Dennis Johnston, 14 January 1851, Fairfax County Legislative Petitions. Also see James C. Ballagh, *A History of Slavery in Virginia* (Baltimore: Johns Hopkins University Press, 1902), pp. 123-26 (hereinafter cited as Ballagh, *Slavery in Virginia*); Samuel Shepherd, comp., *The Statues at Large of Virginia From October Session 1792, to December Session 1806 . . .*, 3 vols. (Richmond: Printed by Samuel Shepherd, 1835), 1:363-65.

3. For sales of Fairfax slaves, see *Gazette*, 2 January 1841, 12 April 1861; G.W. Hunter to Charles C. Stuart, 30 June 1833, George Mason to S.T. Stuart, 9, 22, 23 February, 2 March 1851, Stuart Family Papers. Just how much whipping occurred in Fairfax in this period is uncertain. It may be that masters did *not* ordinarily resort to whipping adult slaves as a means of discipline. Slaveholdings were small, and recalcitrant blacks could always be sold south or disciplined and rewarded in more subtle ways.

4. A good brief abstract of slavery legislation in Virginia is in James Codman Hurd, *The Law of Freedom and Bondage in the United States*, 2 vols. (Boston: Little, Brown, 1858), 2:2-13. For a full-length treatment, see Ballagh, *Slavery in Virginia*. The laws in practice, however, were often mitigated. See the *National Era* (Washington, D.C.), 7 January 1847, for the ruling of a Loudoun County judge who recognized the marriage bonds of a female slave. See Willie Lee Rose, ed., *A Documentary History of Slavery in North America* (New York, London and Toronto: Oxford University Press, 1976), for insight into the complexities of slavery and the difficulties of generalizing. Helen Tunnicliff Catterall, ed., *Judicial Cases Concerning American Slavery and the Negro*, Vol. 1: *Cases From the Courts of England, Virginia, West Virginia and Kentucky* (Washington, D.C.: Carnegie Institution of Washington, 1926), pp. 53-265, gives an indication of the interpretation of the slave code by state courts in Virginia.

5. For a summation of the Virginia black code see Russell, *Free Negro in Virginia*, pp. 88-122. See

In Virginia, a slave manumitted after 1836 had to obtain the permission of the county court to remain legally in the state for more than a year after his manumission.[6] Until the mid-1850s, the Fairfax court routinely permitted reputable, newly emancipated slaves to remain in the county. But in 1855 when Lewis Casey, a "free man of color" who had been recently manumitted by will and was known to be "honest, sober and industrious," petitioned the court for permission to remain, the justices refused. It was, they declared, "impolitic to encourage any larger increase in this class of our population."[7]

Free blacks had long been feared and distrusted in Virginia. They were accused of being unwilling to work, of spreading discontent among the slaves, and of causing a disproportionate amount of crime. Nevertheless, their numbers rose steadily in both the state and county in the nineteenth century. By the 1850s, the Virginia legislature, angered by Northern demands for the immediate abolition of slavery, was prepared to make the black code even harsher. One or two Virginia governors advocated that all free blacks be forcibly expelled from the state.[8] Though the Assembly refused to accede to the governors' requests, it provided for the voluntary enslavement of free blacks, made it illegal for free blacks to purchase slaves, authorized the sale into slavery of free blacks convicted of certain crimes, and enacted legislation which made the escape of slaves more difficult.[9]

Despite this harsh legislation, blacks were not without friends. Individual blacks sometimes knew individual whites to whom they could turn for assistance. Fairfax Quakers evinced some interest in the education of free blacks, and some slaveholders manumitted their slaves or permitted them to earn some money and purchase their own freedom.[10] There were even a few outright abolitionists in the county, one of whom was charged in 1860 with circulating material likely to incite a slave insurrection.[11] Undoubtedly a few free blacks managed to

also Ballagh, *Slavery in Virginia*, pp. 116-47; Luther Porter Jackson, *Free Negro Labor and Property Holding in Virginia, 1830-1860* (New York and London: D. Appleton-Century Company, Inc. [1942]), pp. 3-7 (hereinafter cited as Jackson, *Free Nego Labor*).

6. *Acts of Gen. Assem.*, 1836-37, pp. 47-49. The law does not appear to have been enforced until the 1850s.

7. *Gazette*, 29 September 1855. Observers expected the decision to set a precedent for action on similar cases in the future.

8. See various opening messages of the governors of Virginia to the General Assembly, 1846-1857, *House Docs.*, 1846-1858, Doc. No. 1.).

9. *Acts of Gen. Assem.*, 1855-56, pp. 37-45; 1857-58, p. 46; 1859-60, pp. 140, 163-64.

10. See Society of Friends Fairfax Quarterly Meeting Minutes, 1847-48 (Friends Historical Library, Swarthmore College); Fairfax County Legislative Petition, 26 February 1848, quoted in Willian C. Dunlap, *Quaker Education in Baltimore and Virginia Yearly Meetings* (Philadelphia: The Science Printing Company, 1936), pp. 496-97; *Gazette*, 25 December 1854, 4 February 1861.

11. *Gazette*, 20 January 1853, 21 January 1860; *Acts of Gen. Assem.*, 1859-60, p. 670.

Among the black landowners in Fairfax before the Civil War was West Ford. When Harpers Magazine ran an article on Mount Vernon in 1859 the artist-reporter spent a good deal of time talking with seventy-one-year-old West Ford, who as a child had been a slave in the Washington family. Ford agreed to sit next day for a sketch. When the artist arrived, he found Ford prepared, "having on a black satin vest, a silk cravat, and his curly gray hair arranged in the best manner. 'For,' he said, 'the artists make colored people look bad enough anyhow.'" Virginia State Library.

improve their economic status and acquire some property during the 1840s and 1850s.[12] One of the more outstanding of Fairfax black land-holders was Moses Hepburn, who lived in Alexandria, owned valuable land near the canal, and apparently had an icehouse in Maryland. Another was West Ford, a former Mount Vernon slave, who owned land at Gum Springs.

Free blacks in Fairfax seem to have worked at about the same occupations as slaves, and like many slaves they often hired themselves out on an annual basis. Unlike the slaves, however, the money earned was their own to save or spend. The annual hirings took place on or near New Year's Day at Centreville, Fairfax Court House, and Dranesville. But the largest gathering of hiring hands in the county was at West End on Little River Turnpike just outside Alexandria. The correspondent of a Boston newspaper described the scene in 1861 (in an article which reflects as much about the racist views of the period as about the institution of hiring day):

"On New Year's Day, West End is 'waked up'—it becomes an institution. [There are] congregated all the hiring hands in the adjacent country; men, women and children, mechanics, field hands, dining-room servants, cooks and house servants, of every color from the Octoroon . . . to the real wooly-headed Congo; all decked out in their new suits of full cloths and linsey woolseys—(for in the bond which each

---

12. Black landholding in Virginia almost doubled between 1830 and 1860. Jackson, *Free Negro Labor*, pp. 109-10.

hirer gives the owner, is stipulated, besides good treatment and full fare, two suits of clothes for the slave, one of which is given at the end of the year)—eating, drinking, fiddling and dancing; all their own masters, so far as having the privilege of selecting their homes for the next year goes—and consequently as airy and high-flown as possible when consulted with reference to that—and all as lively and noisy as blackbirds, though the whole party had been on a general and continued spree since Christmas Eve, the commencement of the holidays. . . . Commingled with [the blacks are the hirers, looking for their servants for the upcoming year], the contractor seeking his complement of force, the small farmer [looking for] three or four able bodied fellows [to help cultivate his fields], the citizen of the town hunting his porter or house servants, and the spinster or childless widow looking for a girl "tween ten and twelve to raise.'"[13]

Rates paid for blacks were especially high in the 1850s. The rates for girls ranged from $20 to $60 a year; women, from $50 to $80; and men, from $60 to $150. In 1860, however, the number of servants available for hire dropped, as did the price paid for them.[14]

Though blacks served chiefly as domestic and agricultural workers throughout most of the year, many of them worked on the fish wharves in late winter and early spring. Alexandria was the principal center for the shad and herring trade of the upper Potomac, and every March a teeming but temporary community sprang to life in the town. Located along the river between Princess and Oronoco streets and know to one and all as Fishtown, it was filled with shacks erected each March from rented lumber. These crude shanties housed the blacks who did much of the manual labor, sheltered such activities as salting fish and selling and packing fish spawn, and were used as well for the eating establishments "with drinking accommodations" that appeared each year during the fishing season. [15]

In 1852 a visitor described what it was like

> standing among the fishermen who, at this period of every year, gather their harvest of shad and herrings. It was a kind of fair-day in that usually quiet town . . . . For nearly a quarter of a mile the dock was lined with crowds of colored

13. *Gazette,* 14 January 1860. Also see *Gazette,* 2 January 1861.

14. Prices in 1861 were about the same as in 1860. The reasons for the lower demand are not clear, though the unsettled political situation may have been a factor. At the same time, however, slaves sold for very high prices. For hiring rates and practices in Fairfax County, see, e.g., *Gazette,* 25 December 1850, 1 January 1852, 2 January 1853; Arthur W. Machen, Jr., comp., *Letters of Arthur W. Machen with Biographical Sketches* (Baltimore, 1913), pp. 31-33, 35 (hereinafter cited as Machen, *Letters*); R.E. Lee to William O. Winston, 8, 10 July 1858, William Overton Winston Papers (VHS); Letters and papers concerning *Hunter Trustees* v. *Stuart,* Stuart Family Papers, Box 1. Fairfax slaves on occasion were hired out as far away as Mississippi and Arkansas. See Col George W. Hunter to George Richard Lee, 15 July 1840, Stuart Family Papers, Box 2.

15. *Gazette,* 19 April 1860.

A description of Fishtown in an April 1860 issue of the Alexandria Gazette described the "Fish Wharf, yesterday morning," as "alive with business." A pungy, schooner-rigged "alongside the wharf. Her cargo was quickly cried, and sold; and in less time than it takes us to tell it, a block and tackle was rigged, two men got into the hull of the vessel, among the fish, and filled a couple of large buckets, as fast as they could be hauled ashore and emptied on the wharf. No sooner had the pile of fish on the wharf attained a moderate size than three negro women—two wearing old cloth coats, one of which was blue with 'brass buttons,' and large aprons—took seats beside the fish. One sat on a stool, which she had brought with her; the second took up a bucket and sat on that; whilst the third, for want of better accommodation, squatted upon the wharf . . . . The negro women, with sharp knives, were soon at work." Undated photos from Virginia Historical Society.

men and women, washing and cleaning fish, while in the roads adjacent might be seen numbers of wagons, waiting for their loads of this, the grand staple of Alexandria trade. It was an interesting sight . . . . The women were especially worthy of observation. Covered from head to heels with scales, they stood or sat among the piles of fish that lay heaped around them; and in the midst of songs and laughter they performed their tasks with wonderful alacrity and skill. Knife in hand, they clean and wash shad and herring with singular rapidity. Their costumes defy all descriptions. Some wore men's boots—some men's hats. Over their own rough dresses, they had coarse sacks of overhauls crusted with the scaly armor. They did the packing, and hundreds of barrels were filled ready to be transported to market. Customers were waiting for their loads for Pennsylvania and different parts of Maryland; and the whole aspect of things was business-like and cheerful. In the cabins hard by were the hotels and shanties which the colored tribes occupied. One dilapidated shed rejoiced in the title of "Astor House," and bad liquor was sold to the thirsty blacks for three cents a glass in utter defiance of the . . . Liquor Law. The atmosphere was redolent of fish; fish-scales lined the walks and pavements, fish were being cooked in every form; fish were given away; everything was fishified. [16]

Many poor whites also worked on the boats and wharves during the fishing season, but we have very little direct information of their other social and economic activities. Most were illiterate and left no records; they did not live in such close contact with upper-class whites (whose papers have been preserved) as did the slaves; and they were not considered so colorful by newspaper correspondents. We can surmise, however, that there were white people in Fairfax who were destitute, undernourished, unwashed, unchurched, unable to read or write, and perhaps feebleminded. Unemployed and unemployable, such families may have lived in filthy hovels without the amenities of even a privy. Pitied, despised, avoided, and ignored, they were in a sense further outside of society than the blacks and were looked down upon even by them. They received, no doubt, some attention from the Overseers of the Poor and some must have become inmates of the county poorhouse and farm. [17]

16. *Gazette*, 24 April 1852.

17. See letter from "One of Them," Fairfax County, 29 June 1844, printed in the *Gazette*, 2 July 1844. There were individuals who objected to the "heavy burden of Taxation placed upon the shoulders of the citizens" for the support of "lazy" paupers. In the mid-1840s, county and state taxes for the poor amounted to $1.64 on each tithable.

Undoubtedly there were others who were more intelligent, perhaps owned a bit of land, and had a garden of sorts. They were the "poor honest labourers" who worked with varying degrees of regularity. To earn a little money they may have sold some wood in town or set their wives and children "to gather Shumac in the heat of Summer." They may have made some whisky or helped out during the fishing season or worked as farm hands or as road or railroad construction workers.[18]

Unskilled laborers earned wages of seventy-five cents to a dollar and a quarter a day, depending on whether board was included. Some of them went to one of the hiring places along with the blacks and hired themselves out for the year. As Northerners moved into Fairfax and started new farms and new businesses, as the population rose, and as roads and railroads were constructed, opportunities for employment increased substantially. In fact, between 1840 and 1860 several hundred white laborers, principally from the North and from Ireland, moved into the county to do some of the work needed.[19]

Except for the poorhouse and farm, Fairfax had few facilities to care for people unable to support themselves, but in Alexandria the poor may have fared somewhat better. Alexandrians provided a home for destitute widows, an orphanage and female free school, a long-established free school for boys, and a free night school for poor people who worked during the day. And every winter they opened a soup kitchen for unemployed workers and their families.[20] To what extent such institutions served the needs of the Fairfax poor is unknown, but at least two Fairfax citizens contributed to their success. George Washington founded the free school for boys,[21] and in the midnineteenth century, Fairfax attorney Thomas R. Love gave so much support to the Alexandria orphanage that he became known as the "Orphan's Friend."[22]

A step or two higher on the social ramp than the "ne'er do well" and the unskilled laborer were subsistence farmers, carpenters, blacksmiths, watermen, and certain other skilled tradesmen. Good carpenters, brickmasons, and the like earned as much as $2.50 a day, and some of them no doubt were thrifty men who managed to save a bit, make a good garden, buy a cow, do some truck farming on the side, and perhaps improve their lot in life. Ordinarily not slaveholders, some of them were able to hire the services of a slave or free black on a daily or weekly basis, if not for an entire year.[23]

18. Ibid.

19. Fairfax County MS Census, Inhabitants, 1850, 1860.

20. *Gazette*, 13, 29 January 1852, 14, 21, 22 December 1855, 15, 19 January, 8 February 1859, 6 January, 1 March, 26 April, 31 December 1860, 2 January 1861: *Acts of Gen. Assem.*, 1853-54, pp. 70-71; 1857-58, p. 221.

21. *Gazette*, 1 March 1860.

22. *Gazette*, 1, 18 February 1851.

23. Fairfax County MS Census, Inhabitants, Slave Schedule, 1850, 1860, gives an indication of the

It is difficult to define the middle class in Fairfax. They are generally thought of as the farmers who owned one to three hundred acres of land and a few slaves, or the tavern owners, innkeepers, millers, carriage-makers, storekeepers, postmasters, preachers, teachers, surveyors, and the like. Yet some of the best families in Fairfax also operated stores, taverns, mills, or schools; and some of the most prominent of county citizens with some of the most distinguished names had only moderate land and slave holdings.

Whatever the situation of the middle classes in Fairfax in 1840, there was plainly room for more of them. The vast majority of Northern newcomers and many of those from Europe were thoroughly middle class and they brought with them large doses of what are generally considered middle class values. They believed wholeheartedly in the virtues of hard work, thrift, and neatness; they thought it essential to respect labor, turn a profit, succeed in one's field of endeavor, and get ahead in the world.

Virginians had few objections to the Yankee system of values, but they simply could not commit themselves fully to such values. They were not greatly concerned with "getting ahead in the world," and pleasure was far more important to them than to the Yankee. Thus William Selwyn Ball, son of the Fairfax clerk of the court, could write of the "glorious life, from a worldly point of view" that "old Captain Chichester" led before the Civil War: "Passionately fond of hunting and the chase, [he had] his horse saddled every morning and hitched to the rack near the house, and all he had to do was walk across the yard, mount and ride over the plantation, go hunting or follow the hounds after fox or deer."[24]

And William H. Snowden fondly remembered Charles A. Washington, who lived at Wellington on the Potomac until 1859:

> Charles was a genial, jolly fellow, but not so well up in the arts of practical farming as his illustrious uncle. On one occasion, he went into town to have some ploughshares sharpened which were urgently needed to make ready his grounds for wheat sowing, but falling in with some old cronies he was induced to make a month's visit to the "Springs"; but it was all the same to [his servant] Uncle Toby and the rest of the waiting "hands," for they had a long holiday, though the wheat crop went by default.
>
> In farming he was an experimentalist, though always disastrously. He read in the *Country Gentleman* of the great profits of barley growing, and so resolved to try his hand

variety of occupations and of slave and real property holdings of men in those occupations. *Gazette,* 24 August 1860, reports average wages for several classes of laborers.

24. William S. Ball, "Reminiscences of an Old Rebel," 1929, pp. 6-7 (Xerox copy, VHS).

also. One morning in spring, when the robin and bluebird were piping their jubilant songs, he had his "gang" ploughing a ten-acre field. The barley was sown, and the harvest time came, and the grain was flailed out and loaded on a two-horse team for the Alexandria market. The hopeful proprietor mounted his saddlehorse and rode in, in advance to dispose of his crop. But barley was an unknown quantity, he found, on arriving at the store of his merchants; but later, however, he succeeded in bartering his grains to a brewer for a barrel of beer, which he sent home to his cellar. The tidings of the transaction soon spread among his many jolly town companions, and slipping down the river by boat after night-fall to the Wellington House, they succeeded before morning in drinking up the entire crop of barley.[25]

For the Virginians, work often tended to follow rather than to precede the pleasures of daily living—and sometimes it failed to follow at all.

Northerners often evaluated a man by judging the quality of his crops. But to Virginians the quality of crops had little significance in their estimation of the individual. In the eyes of his fellow natives, the Virginian's status rested not only on the quality of his crops, but also on such matters as how large the landholding, how numerous the slaves, how prominent the ancestors, how big the house, how many the books, how sterling the character, how pleasing the personality (and how delightfully eccentric), how amusing the raconteur, how skillful the hunter, how fine the horses, how expansive the host, how charming the wife, how amiable the guest, how pious the churchman, how eloquent the orator, and how abundant the repast. Any or all of these, and other attributes as well, played a part in determining just what old residents of Fairfax thought of their neighbors.[26]

Perhaps the quality most valued by the old families was that of character. Though Virginians in those days had a good deal of humility—if we are to believe the essayist and lecturer George William Bagby[27]—they were nonetheless convinced that they were the very best people in the whole world. Had they not produced Thomas Jefferson, George Washington, George Mason, Patrick Henry, and a whole host of only slightly lesser lights?

25. W.H. Snowden, *Some Old Historic Landmarks of Virginia and Maryland, Described in a Handbook for Tourists* . . . (Philadelphia: J.B. Lippincott Company, 1894), p. 13.

26. For the values of Virginians, the Alexandria *Gazette* and other contemporary newspapers are an excellent source. And humorist George W. Bagby in *The Old Virginia Gentleman and Other Sketches,* ed. Ellen M. Bagby (Richmond: The Dietz Press, 1938) (hereinafter cited as Bagby, *Old Virginia Gentleman*), offers some fine glimpses into the virtues and foibles of "old Virginians" of the midnineteenth century.

27. Ibid., p. 20.

Abundantly endowed in those prewar days with a happy sense of humor, they sometimes laughed at themselves in delight for being so sure they were the best. They were willing enough to admit that they had faults. They knew they were often careless and lazy and thriftless. And procrastination was said to be "*the* grand characteristic of the native Virginian." Nevertheless, they considered themselves quite outstanding, and after the war one of them explained how they had come to be so. The reason, said humorist Bagby in a lecture in Alexandria in 1866, was that they had grown up on bacon and greens. Not just any old bacon and greens, but the very best bacon and greens in the entire world. "Who ever would have supposed," he asked, "that the savage boars of the German forest and the ugly pot-herbs" of the English sea cliffs "would come together in the same dish to produce the Virginian? So true it is that truth is stranger than fiction. I say the Virginian; for while other prople eat bacon and greens (and thereby become every decent people indeed), the only perfect bacon and the only perfect greens are found in Virginia; and hence it follows, as the night the day, not that the Virginians are the only perfect people, but that they are a peculiar and a very remarkable people."[28] Virginians were sure that Dr. Bagby was telling the plain truth. As the Alexandria *Gazette* put it: "The lecture . . . though it afforded amusement to some, to us . . . contained a sad but truthful history of a noble race of men, doomed alas! we are afraid, to speedy extinction. The character of the Virginian, from his birth to settled manhood, was accurately portrayed—his wildness and recklessness, his indolence, improvidence and negligence; his openhanded generosity and simple minded credulity; his love for politics; his pride, [and] his honor were delineated with an artist's skill."[29]

The life of the "old Virginia" aristocrat, even that of the most impoverished, probably differed somewhat from that of his native middle-class neighbor and the lifestyle of both unquestionably differed from that of the Fairfax Yankee. Contemporaries who were aware of certain differences commented upon them on more than one occasion. We know that the Virginians, certain that nothing occuring on the public road was really worth their attention, tended to live in houses secluded from passers-by. "The mansions of the proprietors [are] thrown back for nearly a mile, and approached by circuitous and wooded lanes," wrote one Northerner, who also noted that the Yankee, on the other hand, uniformly located "within a few rods at farthest, from the highway" in order to keep informed as to what was going on.[30]

Virginians tended to be terribly careless in maintaining their property. Confirmed postponers, they could think of many reasons that

28. Ibid., pp. 180-81, 191.
29. *Gazette,* 14 February 1866.
30. R[andall], "Emigration to Virginia," Alb. *Cult., n.s.,* 4:77-78.

a hole in the lane need not and indeed most advantageously should not be filled. A hole in the road could throw a pretty girl into one's arms or help a young black develop his driving skills. The old Virginia gentleman, declared Bagby in telling exaggeration, "is so incurably conservative that he won't fill up the mudpuddle in front of his gate, won't mend the lock on his back door, or whitewash his worm-fence, or paint his crank-sided carriagehouse." But in the Yankee settlements "neatness and order seemed to prevail in every dwelling." The trim courtyard, the spruce flower bed, the neat garden, and the flower pots set in the windows offered a striking contrast to the less carefully maintained homes of the Virginians and inspired some of them to spruce things up a bit.[31]

Other differences too could be noticed. Virginians went to market in what one Fairfax Yankee ridiculed as a "vast, lumbering, unsightly and cumbrous market wagon with its retinue of five powerful horses, surmounted by 'out-riders,' and filled with supplies adequate to the relief of any ordinary garrison, to say nothing of beds and bedding to the accommodation of men, women and children during the journey of two or three days and nights to the market town." The Yankee's "two-horse lumber-wagon," maintained the writer, "could easily transfer to Washington and Georgetown, in a single day, at least twice the quantity and value stored in these immense formidable machines." (The Yankee observer, perhaps failing to reckon with the Virginian's desire to turn any event into a social occasion for the entire family, felt certain that within a decade the Virginian vehicle would be "ranked among the curiosities of the past.")[32]

If the market wagons of natives and immigrants represented a difference in values, perhaps the barns reflected more than a difference in climate. "Seldom," declared the same observer, did one "find a good, substantial barn on a Virginian farm of ordinary pretensions. Never do you find a Yankee without one, even though the expense may seriously cripple and retard the construction of his dwelling."[33]

The values and life styles of the newcomers contrasted in other ways with those of old Fairfax residents. Jacob Haight made a comparison with which many Virginians agreed. New Yorkers, he said, were accustomed to working for themselves; Virginians were reluctant to stoop to manual labor. It was not uncommon for the son of a prosperous Yankee farmer to hire himself out as a common laborer, whereas many a son of Virginia, he added disapprovingly, spent his time "lounging about taverns or going to races, cock fighting, or other places of amusement; where they fall into habits of vice and dissipation that bring them to

31. Bagby, *Old Virginia Gentleman*, pp. 3, 191; Janney, *Yankees in Virginia*, p. 5.
32. Randall to Skinner, 15 January 1847, printed in *Mo. Jnl. Agr.* 2 :446.
33. Ibid.

ruin." An upstate New Yorker who so spent his hours "would lose his standing in society, no one would trust him, and he could not get ahead in the world."[34]

With the Yankee's greater commitment to achievement, it is not surprising to find also a greater interest in efficiency. There is evidence suggesting that Yankees were quicker to accept the cookstove, which made its debut in Virginia in these decades, than were the natives. And by extension, we may assume that the newcomers, with their emphasis on efficiency and their lack of slave labor, were also somewhat quicker to accept such other technological advances as sewing machines, subsoil plows, and other advances in farm and mill machinery.[35]

Virginians, on the other hand, were more readily outgoing than the Northerners. A Fairfax farmer felt offended when he called on a Yankee newcomer early one morning to lend him some tools. The family was just ready to eat breakfast, and to the caller's amazement and chagrin, they sat down without asking him to join them and ate in silence. The lack of hospitality would have been a studied insult if shown by a native family, and the Virginian visitor, who interpreted it as such, never returned to the house.[36]

Perhaps the most significant difference between the two cultures was the difference in labor force: Virginians relied chiefly on slaves; most Yankees used free labor.[37]

Newcomers were also likely to be more idealistic and high-minded about the blacks than were the natives; it may even be that some of the Quakers came to Virginia chiefly to demonstrate the advantages of free labor to slaveholders.[38] Such men were in a sense soft-spoken abolitionists who preferred to set examples for the wicked rather than merely to

34. Janney, *Yankees in Fairfax*, p. 7. So far as I have seen, midnineteenth century Virginians did not speak of "getting ahead in the world," though they sometimes referred to "bettering one's lot in life." The more dynamic quality of the first expression compared with the more static implications of the second reveals a world of difference in social philosophy and expectations.

35. See Ross D. Netherton, *The Colvin Run Mill* (Fairfax, Va.: Fairfax County Office of Comprehensive Planning, 1976), p. 1.

36. Ralph LeRoy Milliken, "Then We Came to California: A Biography of Sarah Summers Clarke . . .," Historical Society *Yearbook* 8(1962-63):5 (hereinafter cited as Milliken, "Clarke").

37. The Northerner's desire to avoid the use of slave labor created some problems. If a man's family were not large enough to supply the required number of workers, he could sometimes employ one of the laboring men who had made their way to Fairfax from New York and other Northern states. But many Northern laborers, some of them single men finding manual labor not held in respect in Virginia, returned to the North. It was perfectly acceptable, it appears, for a middle-class Northerner's son to do manual work for someone else; a middle-class Virginian might do that kind of work on his own or his father's farm—but he would scarcely have hired out to do manual work. Some of the newcomers hired "the poorest class" of the white population. Though the poor white's work habits were not of the best, his prejudices against such work appeared to at least one observer to be lessening and his habits improving. Some newcomers hired free blacks (though the state's black code had caused many of the more industrious to leave Virginia and go north), some felt they had no choice but to hire slaves and a few purchased slaves themselves. See, e.g., Randall to Skinner, 15 January 1847, printed in *Mo. Jnl. Agr.* 2:446; Janney, *Yankees in Fairfax*, p. 15; Muir, *Potomac Interlude*, pp. 76, 122-23; Gamble, *Sully*, pp. 77-78; Alice M. Coates, ed., "The Civil War Experiences of a Northern Family Settled in Virginia," Historical Society *Yearbook* 8(1962-63): 45-46.

38. Muir, *Potomac Interlude*, pp. 122-23.

castigate them. Most natives, on the other hand, were not at all high-minded about the blacks. Though Virginians in these years evinced some interest in getting rid of slavery, they hoped to get rid of the blacks along with the institution.

A letter from John A. Washington, master of Mount Vernon, just after Woodlawn was sold to New Jersey Quakers, illustrates perfectly the prevailing attitude of many Virginians toward the blacks. If the Woodlawn Quakers, he wrote in a letter to his wife,

> are successful in their undertaking, of which there is little doubt, they will produce quite a revolution in our neighborhood, for others will unquestionably follow them and in no distant date we shall have a population around here very far superior to our present inhabitants. We shall eventually be obliged to send off our slaves and have recourse to white labour for the cultivation of our lands & in our domestic employments, and this change alone, when it can be effected, I firmly believe will benefit us beyond any present calculation.
>
> The introduction of industrious and respectable people in the place of an ignorant slave and in some cases a still more degraded white population will be followed by the division and improvement of farms, the formation of schools and a general diffusion of knowledge, and morality that can never otherwise take place in this region of our State. Added to this, I am fully persuaded, that in less than ten years our lands will double in value.[39]

Though Washington's letter was clearly antislavery, it was also clearly anti-black. He was no abolitionist. As long as there were black slaves about, he and other Fairfax natives intended to keep full control of them.[40]

Though it seems probable that most Northerners who migrated to Virginia were opposed to slavery and secession, they were also interested in maintaining peaceful relations with their Virginia neighbors; they did not expect to spread their antislavery views in such a way as to create undue hostility among the long-time residents. Some were converted to Southern views, but most seem to have retained their Union loyalties and their antipathy to slave labor.

Neither Northerner nor Virginian, it appears, had an edge on kindness of heart. Despite the increasing sectional tensions of the mid-1850s, old and new residents got along together surprisingly well. Some of them went to the same churches, joined the same agricultural societies, read the same local newspapers, sold goods in the same

39. Quoted in Barbara T. Spann, *Carlby* (Fairfax, Va.: Fairfax Office of Comprehensive Planning, 1976), p. 106. For proslavery views in Fairfax, see *Gazette,* 22 February 1851, 25 August 1860.

40. See petition of George Mason et al., 14 January 1851, Fairfax County Legislative Petitions.

markets, harvested their crops under the same sun and rain, fretted over the same drought, complained about the same mudholes, signed the same petitions, worried over the same wolves and crows and the same Hessian flies and joint worms that threatened their livestock and their wheat.

More important they dreamed some of the same dreams: of better schools and roads, improved mail service, trains that ran on time, cheaper fertilizers, easier access to market, lower prices for the goods they bought and higher ones for those they sold, and adequate protection against rowdies and horse thieves. There were, in short, many reasons for them to cooperate.[41]

Despite the haphazard lifestyle of Virginians and the influx of Northerners, the power structure of Fairfax did not change radically before the Civil War. Continuing to wield power were men bearing the old Fairfax names of Mason, Fairfax, Fitzhugh, Huntt, Thomas, Love, Washington, Moss, Dulany, Burke, Ball, Gunnell, and Stuart. Many of these men were related to each other through ties of marriage, kinship, and friendship. They were the men who served in the General Assembly and on the county court. They became Overseers of the Poor, school officials, and commissioners of elections. They got up petitions and led political rallies; they sponsored balls and tournaments and barbecues. They became deacons, elders, and vestrymen in their respective churches. They served as directors of railroads, banks, and canals. They founded companies to look for mineral wealth and tried to establish manufactories at Great Falls.[42] With their fingers in every pie, little went on in the county that they did not know about.

But their days of dominance—though not of prominence—were numbered. Their political power was somewhat reduced by the new state constitution in 1851. Their cultural and economic leadership was significantly diluted by the influx of enterprising Northerners, and a war they did not really anticipate was to bring an end to their control of the county.

41. *Gazette*, 15 April, 23 October, 18 November 1850, et passim; *Southern Planter* 14(January 1854):4, 7; *Act of Gen. Assem.*, 1859-60, p. 501; Machen, *Letters*, pp. 36-39.

42. Fairfax County Court, Minute Books, 1840-1861, passim; *Gazette*, 1840-1861, passim; *Acts of Gen. Assem.*, 1841-42, p. 106; 1846-47, p. 99; 1850-51, pp. 82-83, 137-38, 147; 1852, pp. 131-32, 217, 313-14; 1852-53, pp. 271-73; 1853-54, pp. 75-77; 1855-56, pp. 123, 127-28, 252-54; 1859-60, pp. 501, 603, 609; Fairfax County Legislative Petitions, 1840-1861.

IV

Preachers, Teachers, and Tournaments

Aspects of Antebellum Culture

By the midnineteenth century, technological advances in agriculture, manufacturing, and transportation, and even in the home, meant that fewer man-hours of labor brought higher standards of living. The advances that brought new opportunities to the average man also made new demands on his talents, and consequently meant that such qualities as energy, intelligence, and enterprise were becoming increasingly desirable characteristics. As the common man became more self-reliant and aggressive, several institutions that had once catered principally to the upper classes came to be patronized and even dominated by the middle classes. The rise of the common man was reflected in many aspects of Fairfax culture in the decades before the Civil War: in the churches and schools and in forms of entertainment that brought together people of varying social classes from many parts of the county.

In 1840 there were few active churches in Fairfax: an Episcopal church, a Baptist church, and perhaps five or six Methodist churches.[1] But in the next two decades there was a surge of interest in religion, and the Methodist church more than any other denomination stimulated, encouraged, and profited from the individual's rising concern with the state of his soul. Despite a national schism over slavery in the 1840s,[2]

1. There was no Presbyterian church in the county until the mid-1840s. See Presbyterian Church in the U.S.A., Winchester Presbytery Minutes, 1840-1860 (microfilm copy, Union Theological Seminary Library, Richmond, Va.; hereinafter cited as UTS). The only active Episcopal church in the county was at Fairfax Court House, and Frying Pan Springs was apparently the only Baptist church. Because of imprecise record keeping, the exact number of Methodist congregations is not known. See *Minutes of The Annual Conference of the Methodist Episcopal Church, 1840-1860; 1871 Handbook of the Baltimore Conference: Methodist Episcopal Church, South* (Baltimore: King Brothers, 1871). Church statistics were not reported in the United States census returns until 1850.

2. See Donald G. Mathews, *Slavery and Methodism: A Chapter in American Morality, 1780-1845* (Princeton: Princeton University Press, 1965), pp. 246-82. For some data on the schism in Fairfax, see Melvin Lee Steadman, Jr., *Falls Church: By Fence and Fireside* (Falls Church, Va.: Falls Church Public Library, 1964), pp. 98-99, 105 (hereinafter cited as Steadman, *Falls Church*).

Methodism had grown rapidly in Northern Virginia. Whereas in 1788 there had been only a dozen or so Methodist believers in Fairfax (including Alexandria),[3] by 1860 there were fifteen congregations in the county (excluding Alexandria).[4]

In the 1840s and 1850s itinerant circuit riders preaching at "protracted" camp meetings drew throngs of people to the woods of Fairfax. From miles around, from Alexandria and from neighboring counties, they came on foot, in wagons, on horseback, and by train to one or another of Fairfax farms. They camped out or boarded in nearby villages and sometimes stayed for days. On several occasions there were thirty or more clergymen on the grounds and as many as a hundred tents. With a number of preachers holding services at the same time and hundreds or even thousands of people screaming and shouting, the meetings were always lively and often emotional affairs.[5]

The Methodist doctrine of grace for all was especially appealing to poor people. From the lips of shouting exhorters many a poor white learned that the Lord loved the poorest sinner, that any man could accept Jesus Christ as his Savior, give up his sins, stop drinking and gambling and carousing, work honestly and diligently, and so gain eternal life and joy. Many a man went away afterward with a new sense of his own worth and a determination to labor for the Lord (and himself as well). It would be difficult, in fact, to imagine a more efficient, effective, and systematic purveyor of middle-class values in a nonmass media era than could be found in the itinerant Methodist preachers who urged the people of Fairfax to repent of their sins and be saved.[6]

Growing prosperity, an increasing population, and rising religious interest brought a wave of new church construction in Fairfax in the 1850s. Most of the new buildings were for the Methodists: Ryland Chapel at Fairfax Court House, Andrew Chapel at Vienna, Lewis Chapel at Lorton, and a stone church at Centreville. A nondenominational

---

3. *Gazette*, 12 November 1855.

4. Most of the growth appears to have occurred in the 1850s. In 1850 there were 16 churches reported in Fairfax: 6 Methodist, 3 Baptist, 3 Episcopal, 1 Presbyterian, and 3 "Free." J.D.B. DeBow, *The Seventh Census*, Book 1, pp. 285-93. In 1860, the census reported 1 Catholic, 15 Methodist, and 7 Presbyterian churches in the county for a total of 23. The number of Presbyterian churches reported appears to have been an error: there seem to have been just three Presbyterian churches in the county in 1860. See Winchester Presbytery Minutes, 1840-1860; Presbyterian Church in the U.S.A., Winchester Presbytery ("New School") Minutes, 1856-1860 (microfilm copy, UTS Library, Richmond, Va.).

In addition, although they did not appear in the census, there were a Quaker meeting house, 5 or 6 Episcopal churches, and at least 3 Baptist churches. *Statistics of the United States . . . in 1860; Compiled from the Original Returns of the Eighth Census*, Book 4 (Washington, D.C.: Government Printing Office, 1866), pp. 477-85. For comments on the state of churches at Fairfax Court House, see *Gazette*, 7, 12 November 1859; for "union" prayer meetings at Centreville, see *Gazette*, 2 April 1859.

5. See *Gazette*, 27 June, 9, 27 July, 9, 19 August 1850; 3 September 1851; Gamble, *Sully*, p. 79; Milliken, "Clarke," Historical Society *Yearbook* 8:5.
Clarke . . .," Historical Society *Yearbook* 8:5 (hereinafter cited as Milliken, "Clarke").

6. See *Gazette*, 27 February 1852. Also see *The Southern Methodist Pulpit* 1-5(1848-52); Machen, *Letters*, pp. 82-87.

structure was built in Dranesville and used primarily by Methodists.[7] Other denominations also expanded, though not so dramatically. There were Presbyterian churches at Lewinsville and Falls Church. Roman Catholics, many of them Irish immigrants who had come to Fairfax to work on the railroad, constructed St. Mary's Church at Fairfax Station in 1858[8] and Quakers in the Woodlawn area erected a small frame meeting-house, both of which are still standing today.[9] Episcopalians, spurred on by a plethora of divines and would-be divines at Seminary Hill, built Holcomb Chapel in eastern Fairfax, constructed a Gothic Revival frame church at Centreville, reactivated a congregation at Pohick, and alternated with "Protestant Methodists" to renew usage of the handsome colonial Falls Church. In addition, the Episcopal church at Fairfax Court House continued to hold services, some county citizens frequented Christ Church and St. Paul's in Alexandria, and after 1844 there were Sunday services at the seminary.[10] Near Alexandria, the Episcopal Theological Seminary was flourishing. By the eve of the Civil War it had more than seventy students and a whole group of impressive brick buildings, one of which an enthusiastic *Gazette* reporter described as "the handsomest thing of brick we have ever seen."[11]

The blacks also appear to have had a growing interest in the church, perhaps partly because white clergymen and laymen were paying more attention to their spiritual needs. The Reverend James T. Jackson, rector of St. Paul's Church in Alexandria from 1830 to 1859, baptized over a hundred black people and officiated at "marriages" of a number of slaves.[12] Though blacks in Fairfax had no church building of their own in the county, they did attend local white churches. There were, to cite but one example, twenty-nine black members of Frying Pan Springs Baptist Church in 1840.[13] And it was becoming customary among blacks

7. The *Gazette* carried frequent notices of church activities in Fairfax. Steadman, *Falls Church*, pp. 26-27, 110-22, passim, has much information about churches of several denominations in the Falls Church area.

8. *Gazette*, 25 September 1860.

9. Muir, *Potomac Interlude*, pp. 54-57; Alexandria Monthly Meeting Minutes, January 1850-May 1851, passim. .

10. *Gazette*, 9 May 1850, 2 April, 12 November 1859, 6 March, 12 June, 24 September 1860, 19 March 1861; Margery A. Hall, "History of Saint Paul's Church, Fairfax Parish, Alexandria, Virginia, 1810-1932," 1932, pp. 10, 11, 19 (mimeographed, VHS) (hereinafter cited as Hall, "History of Saint Paul's"). For mention of Protestant Methodists meeting on alternate Sundays at the Falls Church to "cast out devils," see Churchill Jones Gibson to Ann Elizabeth Gibson, 2 November 1839, Chamberlayne Family Papers, 1821-1938 (VHS). For seminary activities, see *Gazette*, 13 July 1850; 14 July 1851; 13 November, 15 December 1855; 7 May, 16, 24 September, 4, 7 October, 10 November 1859; 10 March, 5 October 1860. Also see R.J. Packard to Mrs. Robert E. Peyton, 9 January 1844, Peyton Family Papers, 1770-1913 (VHS).

11. Fairfax County MS Census, Inhabitants, 1850, 1860; *Gazette*, 8 June, 16 September 1859. William Archer Rutherfoord Goodwin, ed., *History of the Theological Seminary in Virginia and Its Historical Background*, 2 vols. (New York: E.S. Gorham, 1923-24), 1:218 (hereinafter cited as Goodwin, *History of Theological Seminary*).

12. Hall, "History of Saint Paul's," p. 7.

13. [Flossie C. McNicol], ed. and comp., "Records of Frying Pan Springs Baptist Church . . .," 1946 (VHS). For black members of Fairfax Methodist and other churches, see Steadman, *Falls Church*, pp. 26, 103-6.

to be baptized in the Potomac River just south of Alexandria. The *Gazette* noted a number of these baptisms before, during, and after the Civil War.[14]

Interest in church activities reinforced a growing preoccupation with questions of moral self-worth. The self-appraisals of Virginians in these years sometimes remind one of the agonizing over sins of Massachusetts Bay Puritans two centuries earlier. One young man of the county in a letter of condolence to a bereaved family wrote modestly that he had few hopes of meeting "the deceased" in heaven as "my *natural* wickedness is *too great* for me to hope for such a total reformation."[15] Wilson Miles Cary Fairfax, a civil engineer, confided in his diary after the birth of a son, "How sweet is youth till tainted by the actual development of the baser passions!" Fairfax agonized frequently and at length over his own sins, writing on one occasion, "I see that there is no good thing left in me but that I am more wicked & less fit for Heavenly peace each day that I exist." And on another, "Oh make us alive to the enormity of sin. Oh what I would not give for 5 minutes sensation of the joy of a regenerate one. But the shades of lust must be torn from the soul ere we can see the nature of such joy. For it springs from the very things which the unregenerate man hates." And he commented repeatedly on an able and friendly fellow worker who had become "the unfortunate victim of various lusts & evils which render him unstable as water."[16]

Robert E. Lee's outlook was far more optimistic. In a letter to his wife written while on duty in Missouri in 1855, he told her that he considered his separation from his family "a just punishment for my sins." It was also, he continued, an opportunity for her and the children to prepare for the time "when I shall have passed that bound from which no traveller returns. . . . For myself I only ask that before that day, I may truly repent of the many sins of my life. That my sins may be forgiven & my pardon sealed in heaven. Then the day of my death will be better for me than the day of my birth."[17]

Of all "sins," the misuses—or simply the use—of alcohol seemed to many the very worst. In antebellum Fairfax the temperance movement had quite vocal advocates (though the frequency with which the Fairfax court granted licenses for taverns and ordinaries inclines one to be a bit skeptical of their effectiveness). They gave much free advice on the evils of ardent spirits and sponsored parades and picnics, the last often at the "grove" in Langley. A "temperance festival" there in the summer of 1852 was "a grand affair" with "seven or eight hundred

---

14. *Gazette*, 3 April 1860, 16 March 1863, 1 February 1864, 17 July 1865, et passim.
15. John S. Blackburn to Margaret C. Peyton, 8 November 1855, Peyton Family Papers.
16. Wilson Miles Cary Fairfax, Diary, 1834-61, 6 June, 29 September, 10, 24 November 1835; 3 May 1836; 16 February 1837, et passim (pages unnumbered) (VHS).
17. Robert E. Lee to Mary Anna Custis Lee, 3 September 1855, Lee Family Papers, 1824-1918 (VHS).

ladies and gentlemen" present. They listened to a "number of very interesting addresses," feasted "free of charge" on a "sumptuous dinner," and climaxed the events of the day by watching "Mrs. Langdon's presentation of a beautiful banner . . . on the part of the ladies."[18]

Participation in temperance activities was just one of several ways in which Fairfax women managed to play a role outside their own homes in the midnineteenth century. They conducted numerous church fairs for a variety of worthy projects, often to aid the Sunday schools which were becoming a popular means of religious education. They sometimes attended political gatherings, even though they could not vote. They participated in the fairs sponsored by local and state agricultural societies, entering a variety of domestic articles.[19] In March 1855, for example, Mariah Bailey, the wife of Lewis Bailey, entered two grass vases at the state agricultural fair in Richmond, "which were among the most interesting features of the department, consisting of sixty-two varieties of grass, tastefully interwoven and arranged."[20] In 1854 the officers of the Fairfax Agricultural Society even decided to permit female membership. Under the presidency of Thomas ap Catesby Jones, they invited the ladies to become members and so unite with the men in the "great cause of Agricultural and Floral production."[21]

From the earliest colonial days a minority of women had not, for one reason or another, been content to be housewives only. They had found employment in several ways, and they continued to do so in the midnineteenth century. A good many women owned and operated farms, usually after inheriting them from deceased husbands. The wealthiest person in Fairfax was Anna Maria Goldsborough Fitzhugh of Ravensworth, the widow of a maternal uncle of Mrs. Robert E. Lee. She owned more land and more slaves than anyone else in the county and personally managed the operations of her farms.[22] Another prominent Fairfax aristocrat, Margaret Love Jackson, the widow of George W. Jackson and the sister of Thomas R. Love, managed Jackson's (now Dranesville) Tavern on Leesburg Turnpike, which the *Gazette* described as "one of the best roadside inns in the state of Virginia."[23]

---

18. *Gazette*, 17 August 1852.

19. For participation in church and agricultural society fairs, see *Gazette*, 11 June 1850, 26 May, 20 September 1851, 9 July 1859, et passim. For attendance at political gatherings see *Gazette*, 13 June 1844, 24 October 1860.

20. *Gazette*, 3 November 1855.

21. *Gazette*, 25 March 1854.

22. See Robert E. Lee to Mary Anna R. Custis Lee, 3 September 1855, Lee Family Papers; George Washington Parke Custis to E. Agnes Lee, 14 October 1853, George Bolling Lee Papers, 1732-1870 (VHS); Fairfax County MS Census, Slave Schedule and Schedule of Inhabitants, 1850, 1860; Fairfax County Land Tax Books, 1840-1860 (VSL-A). For other Fairfax women operating farms, see *Gazette*, 2 November 1855, 19 October 1860; Milliken, "Clarke," Historical Society *Yearbook* 8:8-9.

23. *Gazette*, 17 May 1865.

*Anna Maria Fitzhugh, the widow of an uncle of Mrs.
Robert E. Lee, was the largest property owner in Fairfax
in the mid-nineteenth century. Despite advancing age,
she remained at Ravensworth throughout the Civil War.
She was granted "protection" by Federal troops and unlike that of many of her neighbors, her property suffered
little damage during the war. She died in 1874, leaving
Ravensworth to Mrs. Lee and her heirs. Portrait by
Thomas Sully. Virginia State Library.*

A number of women taught school, a few conducted boarding
schools for "young ladies," and several served as matrons of the
Episcopal seminary.[24] One woman earned a little money for her writing:
in 1859 Sarah Cornelia Jones of Melrose received thirty dollars for a
short story entitled "Two Little Orioles." One Fairfax woman operated a
tollgate, at least two women were appointed postmasters to fill vacancies
created by the deaths of their husbands, another kept store and received
a license to retail "ardent apirits," and still another ran a "boarding and
accommodations tent" during revivals.[25] Lower class women (many of
them black) worked as nurses, maids, seamstresses, laundresses, cooks,
and cleaning women.[26]

Though there were no women ministers living in the county, Fairfax
citizens had the opportunity to hear several who were members of the
Quaker faith. In the 1840s they turned out early at Fairfax Court House

24. *Gazette*, 3 March, 21 August 1852; 21 December 1854; 13 December 1855; 12 September
1860, et passim; Milliken, "Clarke," Historical Society *Yearbook* 8:9-12; Goodwin, *History of
Theological Seminary*, 1:403-9, 2:411-12.

25. Sarah Cornelia Jones to [Nanette L. Peyton], 1 November 1859, Peyton Family Papers;
Fairfax County Court Minute Book, 15 May 1843, p. 61; 21 August 1843, p. 83; May 1844, p. 140;
August 1845, p. 231; 18 May 1847, p. 39; Janney, *Yankees in Fairfax*, p. 17.

26. Fairfax County MS Census, Inhabitants, 1850, 1860, 1870. The *Gazette*, 25 March 1844, praised
the use of steam-driven power looms because "a little girl or any inexperienced person, may tend several
machines at once."

one November Sunday to hear "Friend Rachel Barker" of Poughkeepsie, New York.[27] A year earlier some of them may have heard the sermons of abolitionist Lucretia Mott, a leading Philadelphia Quaker, who met a favorable reception in Loudoun County when she toured the Fairfax Quarterly Meeting.[28] And in the 1850s two of the more prominent female Quaker ministers of the day, Miriam Gover and Louisa Steers, lived next door in neighboring Loudoun County.

Fairfax residents also had an opportunity to see or hear of women in other roles. A drama by a woman playwright was presented in Alexandria and a male lecturer spoke there on female poets.[29] A woman lecturer gave a series of talks on the rights of women (the *Gazette* lifted an eyebrow and commented that the rights of Virginia women were just as illimitable as they chose to make them), and a women medical doctor gave a series of six lectures "to the ladies of Alexandria on the Laws of Life, and the Means of Preserving Health."[30] And in Fairfax in 1858 the most hallowed spot in the county fell into the hands of the gentler sex. Under the leadership of Miss Ann Pamela Cunningham of South Carolina, a group of patriotic and enterprising ladies purchased part of the decaying Mount Vernon estate, including the mansion, from John A. Washington and began their very successful efforts to preserve it.[31]

Despite all their activities—not the least of which was running a household filled with numerous children, several slaves, occasional dependent relatives, and frequent guests—antebellum Southern women sometimes have been portrayed as vapid, idle, empty-headed beauties. But contemporary letters and newspapers do not substantiate the stereotype. Though Southern women were expected to be past masters of the social graces, they were expected to be much more as well. In the eyes of the Alexandria *Gazette*, "A Good Wife" was one who had read

> Her father's well filled library with profit,
> And could talk charmingly; then she could sing
> And play, too, possibly, and dance with spirit;
> Yet she was knowing in needle-work
> And shone in dairy and in kitchen, too,
> As in the parlor.[32]

27. Rebecca Turner to Joseph Turner, 7, 23 November, 4 December 1843, Turner Papers, Record Group 5 (Friends Historical Library, Swarthmore College).

28. Society of Friends, Fairfax Monthly Meeting (Waterford, Va.) Minutes, 16 November 1842 (microfilm copy, Friends Historical Library, Swarthmore College); James and Lucretia Mott, *Life and Letters*, ed. Anna Davis Hallowell (Boston: Houghton, Mifflin and Company, 1884), pp. 236-39; Patricia Hickin, "Gentle Agitator: Samuel Janney and the Antislavery Movement in Virginia, 1842-1851," *Journal of Southern History* 38 (May 1971): 164-65.

29. *Gazette*, 11, 14 January 1859, 3 January 1860.

30. *Gazette*, 27, 31 March, 1 April 1854; 16 April 1855.

31. *Gazette*, 11 July 1859; Elswyth Thayne, *Mount Vernon Is Ours: The Story of the Preservation and Restoration of Washington's Home* (New York: Duell, Sloan and Pearce, 1966), pp. 4-180.

32. *Gazette*, 14 January 1852.

Among the responsibilities of Fairfax women was the matter of the health care of family and servants. Though women and men shared the responsibility, the women undoubtedly carried the burden of the actual nursing. In the 1850s people seemed to worry almost constantly over the state of their own or someone else's health. Illness held no respect for social class, and physicians had so few resources at hand that they could do little to alter the progress of many diseases, regardless of the financial resources of the patient or his family.[33] The ill-heated and unscreened houses; the limited knowledge of medicine, sanitation, nutrition, and anesthetics; and the absence of hospitals and professional nursing care meant that illnesses were frequent and often fatal. Death was no stranger to children and young people, and its hand seemed to fall with undue frequency on some families. One especially stricken was that of Daniel F. Dulany, who was to become a prominent Unionist during the Civil War and who lost five members of his family in nine months in 1852.[34] In the absence of aspirin or other modern painkillers, physical suffering was, of course, commonplace, and use of opium and laudanum became a serious problem in all too many families.[35]

The well-to-do frequented the socially popular Virginia springs, and people of all classes turned in desperation to the patent medicines that promised so much. The Alexandria *Gazette* in 1845 advertised "Sands Sarsparilla" before which "hygean influence Scrofula, Cancer, Leprosy, all Ulcers, . . . and all Diseases of the Skin . . . springing from a diseased circulation, give way." "Dr. Upham's Vegetable Electuary" was "A Certain Cure for the Piles," while "Fever & Ague . . . & all the various forms of Bilious Diseases" could be "SPEEDILY & THOROUGHLY CURED by Dr. Osgood's India Cholagogue."[36]

At times, resort to patent medicines must have been a good deal less dangerous than seeking out the attention of professional physicians, as a letter from wealthy George Mason of Hollin Hall to a physician cousin shows. In 1838 Mason was deeply concerned about his young son, who, in recent years, had frequently suffered a "slight epileptic affection, a petit mal . . . a momentary loss of sensibility attended by a rolling of his eyes." Though the attacks had never lasted more than eighteen seconds, Mason was determined to find a cure, if one existed. The family

33. Physicians' fees were, however, relatively low. Dr. William B. Day of Dranesville, one of the most prominent and respected doctors in the county, charged five dollars for one maternity case involving an all-night visit and a return next day to deliver the placenta. On another case he charged eight dollars to visit the wife of John Reed for two nights "including accouchement." William Benjamin Day, Account Books, 1853-1889, Book I (VHS). For care of the insane, see "Reports of Directors of the Eastern Asylum and of the Western Asylum," *House Docs.*, 1840-1860. For care of the handicapped, see "Report of the Visitors of the Virginia Institute for the Deaf and Dumb and of the Blind" (title varies), *House Docs.*, 1840-1860; Fairfax County Court Minute Books, 18 March 1844, p. 125.

34. *Gazette*, 8 October 1855.
35. *Gazette*, 8 September 1854.
36. *Gazette*, 1-31 October 1845, passim.

physician had been treating the boy, giving him preparations of "Iron & Zinc, Quinine, Strychnine & Valerian," seeing to it that he used the "Salt Bath Electro magnetic machines—relaxed from all Study and irksome occupations, [and] exercised constantly & fully in conformity with the latest approved practice of the French & English Schools."

Mason had tried himself to learn all he could about the problem. He read everything he could lay his hands on "from Hippocrates to the present day." He imported a new work on "Epilepsy," and "observed carefully its prescriptions." But thus far, all the efforts had been in vain, and the family physician was now proposing "the administration of Arsenic." Understandably, Mason "demurred."

"I have such an horror of that accursed mineral," he wrote his cousin, "that altho' I am perfectly aware of its very general use nowadays in many diseases, I cannot consent to his taking it, except as a dernier resort . . . . Still I am willing & anxious to try every safe remedy that has been supposed efficatious, even from the Jewish exorcism to the Druids mistletoe; but I cannot wish any danger to his general health, by a resort to violent & subtile agents of unknown efficacy."[37]

Despite the constant concerns over health, the people of Fairfax, whatever their race or their status in society, found many ways to lighten the burdens of daily living and some of them found ways to broaden their intellectual horizons. Children who grew up on large country estates where there were a number of slaves had a fine opportunity to savor the out-of-doors and also to learn something of and come to appreciate a culture very different from their own.

For a boy in rural Fairfax, the summers when school was out were a delight. William Selwyn Ball described years later the joys of his boy-hood days in northern Fairfax: "If ever there was a Boy's Paradise on earth it was here," he wrote. "It is hard to conceive of a happier environment. The Potomac River within easy walking distance . . . fields and glorious woods, swimming, fishing, hunting and trapping . . . . But to me the crowning joy was the cornshuckings in the fall . . . . The ears had been pulled from the stalks, hauled in and placed in a long pile near the cornhouse. Invitations had been sent to all the neighbors to let their darkies come. About dusk you would hear the various clans in the distance singing as they came. On arriving they were given a drink and lined up along the cornpile, and the singing and shucking went on until the job was finished. Each clan had a leader who would stand on top of the corn pile and lead the singing,—to my ears it was more thrilling than grand opera. If I could only give the music! I will try to give a part of [one] of these peculiar cornshucking songs. One very popular one was:

37. George Mason to Dr. Richard H. Stuart, 1 November 1838, Letters of George Mason of Hollin Hall (UVa).

O Ladybug, Ladybug, fly all around me, ho Nancy ho,
O, Ladybug, Ladybug, fly all around me, ho Nancy ho,
For seven long years I courted Miss Nancy, ho Nancy ho,
And tomorrow's the day that Miss Nancy will marry,
        ho Nancy ho!
    Ladybug, Ladybug fly all around me."[38]

In the fall when schoolbells clanged, white children of almost all social classes trooped off to the one-room country schools. For decades it had been customary for families to get together and hire a teacher for the school year. For those families who could not afford to contribute to the teacher's salary, the state and county paid the teacher a fee of four to six cents a day per child. In 1846 Fairfax made a special effort to set up a "district" school system. Under the authority of a special act of the Assembly, the county was divided into twenty or so districts and a commissioner was appointed to each district. There was, apparently, supposed to be at least one school in each district.[39] But staffing even one-room schools was always a problem. The school commissioners complained repeatedly of "the great want of well qualified teachers." In the mid-1850s they began to require the examination of teachers both as to their academic and moral qualifications. Though there was some satisfaction with this system, the superintendent continued to complain that funds were "entirely insufficient to educate all the children," that many of the districts as laid off were yet without schools, and that there was a lack of organization on the part of the commissioners.

In 1853, the superintendent complained that the fund was insufficient to enable any commissioner to employ a teacher in his district; instead the county paid to send children to teachers "employed by the citizens" and therefore not under the control of the commissioners. Nevertheless, the superintendent declared that some schools were well conducted and that some children advanced rapidly. He thought that if funds were sufficient to keep them at school through the year, "great benefit would result therefrom." Some commissioners were negligent, reported the superintendent; some were diligent. In some districts where schools were convenient children had the "full benefit of the appropriation allotted to their district." In others only "a small portion of the sum allotted had been absorbed for want of convenient schools or inclination of parents to send them."[40]

38. Ball, "Reminiscences of an Old Rebel," p. 7.

39. Milliken, "Clarke," Historical Society *Yearbook* 8:3, 9-10; Steadman, *Falls Church*, pp. 128-30; "Abstract of School Commissioners Reports," 1840-1860, *House Docs.*, 1840-1860; Fairfax County Legislative Petitions, 19 December 1843; *Acts of Gen. Assem.*, 1845-1846, pp. 37-41.

40. "Extracts from Reports of School Commissioners and County Superintendents Relating to the Primary System for Educating Indigent Children of the State in 1854 . . .," Doc. 4-L, p. 45, *House Docs.*, 1853-54; Doc. 8-L, p. 106, ibid., 1855-56; Doc. 7-L, p. 23, ibid., 1857-58.

The sparseness of the population made the support of even this meagre system all but impossible. Nevertheless there was some progress. Boys and girls were taught without regard to sex, the average daily attendance of poor children who did go to school rose from thirty-six to sixty or sixty-five days, and the number of schools rose from twenty-three in 1841 to forty-five in 1855. But there was not a corresponding increase in either the absolute or relative number of poor children in school. Of 500 poor children in the county in 1840, 313 attended school; of 515 in 1855, just 330 were in school.[41]

As a general rule, the higher the social class (and the nearer the school), the better the child's attendance record and the more years he remained in school. Probably most middle-class children, especially the boys, received an elementary education, and some of them went on to high school at one of the day or boarding schools in the area. Among the upper classes, both sons and daughters went to boarding schools, and some of the young men went on to college.

For boys there were a number of good schools in Northern Virginia. Episcopal High School at the Episcopal seminary, located in what was then part of Fairfax County, was one of the best schools in the state, as was Quaker Benjamin Hallowell's fine school in Alexandria. Both attracted students from many states and both provided stern discipline. The course of study with the former was in true Southern style, stressing a classical education; the latter, in good Quaker fashion, placed greater emphasis on a practical English education.[42]

Fairfax County could take pride in the academic abilities of several of its young men. Mottrom Dulany Ball, son of the former clerk of the Fairfax court, was valedictorian at William and Mary in 1854

41. "Abstracts of School Commissioners' Reports," Doc. 4-I, p. 17, *House Docs.*, 1842-43; Doc. 7-K, p. 17, ibid., 1857-58.

42. Robert E. Lee, who had himself studied at Hallowell's, had little desire to see his son Custis go there. Though he admitted that "Benjamin at one time was an excellent teacher, especially for those desirous of learning," he hoped that Custis "will not become like 'Hallowell's boys' as they were termed some years since. I would rather be pierced by a hundred Mexican balls than to see him so." Lee to Mary C. Lee, 24 March 1848, Lee Family Papers. For the life of one of those boys who liked the school, see Letters from William W. Griscom, 1848-1849, Griscom MSS (Friends Historical Library, Swarthmore College). Also see Benjamin Hallowell to William H. Taylor, 1840-1841 (two letters); Certificate of B. Ogle Temple, 15 November 1841, Tayloe Family of Richmond County, Va., Papers, 1650-1970 (VHS); Benjamin Hallowell, *Autobiography of Benjamin Hallowell* (Philadelphia: Friend's Book Association, 1883), pp. 95-130, 154-162. For rules of order at Hallowell's, see *Circular of Alexandria Boarding School*, 19 February 1851 (leaflet, VHS). For comments on the excellence of Alexandria schools, see *Gazette*, 28 August 1851, 26 August 1852, 25 August 1854, 20 September 1855. For the incorporation of Episcopal High School, see *Acts of Gen. Assem.*, 1853-54, p. 65. For further information on the high school, see *Gazette*, 23 July, 13 August, 9 October 1852; 14 July 1853; 31 July 1854; 29 June, 2 July 1859; 14 July 1860; Benjamin Harrison McGuire, Letters 1859-1861, Byrd Family Papers, 1791-1867 (VHS); Robert E. Lee to Martha Custis Williams, 16 September 1853; 31 July 1854; 29 June, 2 July 1859; 14 July 1860; Benjamine Harrison McGuire, Letters 1859-1861, Byrd Family Papers, 1791-1867 (VHS); Robert E. Lee to Martha Custis Williams, 16 September 1853 (photocopy), George Bolling Lee Papers, 1813-1924. For information on other Fairfax boys' schools see E.C. Thom to mother, 25 January 1848, Miscellaneous Papers (VHS); Robert E. Lee to the Rev. George A. Smith, 14 July 1843, 18 September 1845, 26 January 1846, Robert Edward Lee Letterbook, 1838-1860, Lee Family Papers; Petition relating to Fairfax Academy, 13 December 1850, Fairfax County Legislative Petitions; *Gazette*, 9 August 1852, 9 July 1855, 31 January, 23 July 1859; Goodwin, *Theological Seminary in Virginia*, 2:336-412.

and delivered an address, "The Old Dominion," which was described in the Williamsburg *Gazette* as "very far above, both in manner and matter, what we usually hear at College commencements . . . . The production was considered by the Faculty, the Visitors, and the audience one of peculiar merit."[43] And in 1859 Douglas Forrest delivered at the University of Virginia the "Final Oration" to the Washington Society, the first person ever to have been "unanimously selected" to do so by that society.[44]

After receiving much the same elementary training as boys, Fairfax girls found their subsequent education rather different. Aristocratic families tended to believe that a classical training stressing philosophy, science, mathematics, Greek, and Latin was necessary for the education of a gentleman. Girls, on the other hand, were expected to master only the English language, although some hoped to become proficient in French as well. Music and needlework, arithmetic, and some instruction in drawing often completed the training.[45]

Yet some women received an education more commensurate with that of the men. At Clarens, one of the numerous girls' boarding schools in Fairfax County, the Reverend George A. Smith, in addition to "all the subjects usually taught in the best institutions," offered "when desirable . . . instruction in the Latin language, and in Natural, Moral and Mental Philosophy and Belles Lettres." And at Strawberry Vale Seminary, a few miles from Langley, there was a young teacher who had graduated from the Buckingham Female College, "the oldest and perhaps the best female College in the State." She was "well qualified" not only to "teach all the branches usually taught in the English course of studies [but] also Algebra, Geometry, Trigonometry, and Mensuration in Mathematics, French [and] Music."[46]

One's education did not, of course, cease with the completion of one's formal schooling. There were many opportunities to extend one's store of information, especially if one lived near Alexandria or frequented the District of Columbia. The Alexandria *Gazette*, published six days a week, carried a wealth of information: detailed European news, historical and literary articles, as well as thorough coverage of congressional and state legislative debates and proceedings.[47]

Though coverage of contemporary events was sometimes haphazard and analysis was often quite partisan, the literary quality of the *Gazette*

43. Williamsburg *Gazette*, n.d., quoted in *Gazette*, 13 July 1854.

44. *Gazette*, 11 April, 2 June 1859.

45. See *Gazette*, 1, 8 January, 12, 14 August, 11 September, 13 December 1850; 27, 30 January, 20, 26 February, 22 July, 4 October 1851; 7 August 1852; 1 February 1853; 5 August 1854; 27 August 1855; 27 January 1859; for advertisements of girls' schools in Fairfax and adjoining counties.

46. *Gazette*, 11 September 1850; 28 August 1859; 23 January, 18 February, 12 March, 20 August 1860.

47. Microfilm copies of the *Gazette* are readily available at the Virginia State Library, Richmond; the Fairfax County Library, Fairfax, Va.; and the Alexandria Public Library, Alexandria, Va. Original issues are at the Library of Congress, Washington, D.C.

in the antebellum decades was far superior to that of the average metropolitan newspaper today. The amount of information the paper managed to squeeze into its four pages (or just one-and-a-half if ads are excluded) is amazing. Seven columns of tiny print per page and the absence of headlines and features helped to save space and enabled the editor to find room for the usual commercial, religious, political, and agricultural news, and for human interest items.

Stories of arson and suicide, bizarre crime, freakish birth, tragic death, strange coincidence, and dread disease were among the favored items. One could learn that the wife of Henry Nelson, who lived "between Pohick Church and Colchester" had died suddenly of apoplexy, "superinduced by her dissipated habits"; or that a black woman had poisoned a white family in Richmond, then drunk coffee with arsenic in it and died herself; or that a "most foul murder" had been committed at Dranesville on hiring day when Robert Dickey, "a fellow of notorious bad character," had murdered Henry Clay Sinclair, a young man of "excellent character."[48] When there was room, a column on the back page carried historical or literary articles, advice on child rearing, reflections on the beauties of nature or the loveliness of woman, or a description of life in some far-off exotic spot. The Gazette, in short, could be lively, informative reading.

If one desired other reading material, one could visit book stores in Alexandria, Washington, or Georgetown, where one might purchase works on history, religion, medicine, or the latest novels by Charles Dickens, Jane Austen, Walter Scott, or George Eliot. (On the eve of the Civil War, Eliot's Adam Bede was an especial favorite among the ladies with its tale of a pure and lovely female Methodist preacher, a wayward farm girl, and the very upright young man who loved them both.) On occasion, one could hear local lectures on intellectual topics at meetings of the Providence Literary Society, which met sporadically at Fairfax Court House.[49]

Local and traveling lecturers, musical groups, and art exhibits offered numerous opportunities for entertainment and enlightenment. In the mid-1850s in Alexandria one could go to the Lyceum, Sarepta Hall, Alexandria Academy, Washington Hall, or Liberty Hall for lectures on geology, the "steam flying machine," or Professor Johns' travels from London to Alexandria, Egypt, "with color illustrations." One could see a magician or a ventriloquist, view "Stanley's Western Wilds Exhibit—a great Panorama of Indian Life," attend a series of "Philosophical and

---

48. Gazette, 4 January 1855.

49. For the popularity of Adam Bede, see Sarah Cornelia Jones to [Nanette L. Peyton], 1 November 1859, Peyton Family Papers. For the Providence Literary Society, see Gazette, 27 October 1851, 29 October 1859.

Political rallies were a favorite pastime. Woodcut from a book published in 1860 concerning a political rally and barbecue in Northern Virginia. Virginia Historical Society.

Chemical Lectures" two evenings a week at Hallowell's school, or watch "dramatic presentations" of selections from *Hamlet* or *Macbeth* or from "J.A. Keenan's *True Southern Life.*" [50]

Occasionally there were such traveling art exhibits as statuary illustrating the "trials of our savior" and a panorama depicting the "Creation and the Deluge." There was professional musical entertainment by the "American Mocking Bird," the "Orphan Brothers," the "Swiss Bell Ringers," and numerous minstrel and burlesque opera troops.

Fairfax residents did not always have to travel to Alexandria or Washington to view visiting entertainers. In 1851 the "Great Southern Circus" came to Fairfax Court House. White adults paid fifty cents and children and blacks half that to see "unsurpassed and unrivalled lady equestrians" and a chariot in the style of the "ancient War Chariots of Rome" with "carving and gilding of the most massive and beautiful description." Drawn by "Twenty Beautiful Cream Horses," the

50. *Gazette*, 1850-1860, passim.

"Chariot" conveyed into the circus arena the New York Brass Band, led by Mr. Willis, "the Apollo of Sweet Sounds." [51]

The entertainment event of the decade, however, came in 1854. That year "General Tom Thumb" created a sensation in Centreville when he and a "part of Barnum's Exhibition" delighted the village with a visit. Everybody for miles around turned out to see him. The roads, wrote one Centreville man, were "thronged with spring wagons, carriages, persons on horseback, and pedestrians, all hastening to the spectacle." As one inhabitant put it, "That a panther and elephant should be seen in Centreville is not a subject for wonder; but that the special favorite of Parisian and London crowds" should hold forth in the village "is one of those events which must stagger the credulity of the age." [52]

The people of Fairfax found many ways to have fun. They spent holidays in community celebrations. They attended balls on George Washington's "birth night," held parades and excursions on the Fourth of July, exchanged gifts and shot off firecrackers on Christmas Day, and visited neighbors and relatives, or the president of the United States, on New Year's. [53]

Like other Virginians, Fairfax natives mixed socializing with everything they did. They loved river excursions for Sunday School classes, barbecues at political rallies, and festivals for temperance gatherings. Hunting had long been a favorite pastime, and game abounded in many parts of the county. Near Centreville, the *Gazette* reported on the eve of the Civil War, there were "otters, foxes, wild turkeys, robins, partridges, pheasants, and the bald or white-headed eagle (that marauder of poultry and young lambs)." [54]

In the pre-Civil War years, the people participated in few organized competitive sports. Horseracing, a perennial favorite, does not appear to have been especially popular in either Fairfax or Alexandria in the midnineteenth century. In the late 1850s, intrigued by Sir Walter Scott's tales of medieval chivalry, Virginians developed a mania for jousting tournaments. Many a tournament took place in Fairfax and adjoining counties in the years before and after the war. Young men on horseback competed to spear the smallest ring and to win an opportunity to honor a young lady of their acquaintance. [55]

One such "numerously attended" occasion when chivalry flowered at Fairfax Court House was sponsored by the Fairfax Rangers, a volunteer military company. The festivities began at noon on a Tuesday in October 1859, when nine mounted "Knights" formed a line in front of

51. *Gazette*, 15 April, 14 June 1850; 19 May 1851.
52. Machen, *Letters*, p. 87.
53. The best source for descriptions of holiday festivities is the *Gazette*, 1850-1860.
54. *Gazette*, 13 October 1860.
55. For interest in horse racing, see *Gazette*, 1 December 1859. For tournaments at Fairfax Court House, see *Gazette*, 17, 24 September, 1, 25, 29 October, 1 December 1859; 14, 15 June, 17 July, 14, 21, 28 September 1860.

Barbecues at political rallies were among the favorite activities of antebellum Virginians. The woodcut above is from a book describing a barbecue and rally in Northern Virginia. Virginia Historical Society.

the Union Hotel. They were escorted to the field, "preceded by Prof. Walters' splendid Band and followed by a goodly crowd of citizens." There they were called to the judges' stand, where sat Fairfax Sheriff Orlando Huntt and several other local dignitaries. The knights listened attentively while William Smith, former governor of Virginia, made a "pertinent, happily conceived and handsomely delivered" charge replete with appropriate "historical allusions, eloquent thoughts and sound practical advice."

Next came the jousting. It consisted of a series of "spirited contests" in which the mounted "knights," their horses at full gallop, attempted to spear small rings that steadily diminished in size with each contest. Eventually the "knight of Alabama" emerged triumphant, with the knights of "the Village," the "Old Dominion," and the "Silver Rose" coming in second, third, and fourth. Each of the four elated victors thereupon chose an equally elated young lady to receive the honors, the winner naming "the Queen of Love and Beauty" and the runners-up each choosing a maid of honor. The queen was then escorted to her throne and, surrounded by her "sweetly beautiful" maids, prepared to receive her crown.

Chief Marshall William H. Dulany, Fairfax commonwealth's attorney, again introduced Governor Smith, this time to do the crowning. The governor, after delivering a "very pretty and felicitous speech to the Queen and her Maids, in the course of which he paid a deservedly high compliment to the Virginia ladies," proceeded with the coronation. And then the maids and the queen (who "bore her honors with bewitching grace and commanding dignity") led off in the "exhilerating exercises of the Dance," which was "right merrily kept up by those participating." At nine there was "a sumptuous Supper, which had been provided by Mr. J. W. Jackson, and his estimable lady, the host and hostess of the Union Hotel," but not till the early morning hours did the ball close and the guests "wend their way" homeward.[56]

To all appearances this tournament, the second of several held at Fairfax Court House, was a happy occasion. But under the gaiety and merriment there must have run a somber strain, for just one week earlier, less than fifty miles away, John Brown had made his notorious raid on Harper's Ferry.

More than any other event, John Brown's attack prepared the Southern mind for secession and for war. Abraham Lincoln would be elected president in little more than a year; and within two years, Fairfax famers would have contending armies encamped in their woods and on their fields. A number of those at the tournament were to play a prominent role in the conflict. Chief Marshall Dulany served as the Fairfax delegate to the Virginia secession convention; Judge Orlando Huntt served as the Fairfax delegate to the General Assembly throughout the war. Former Governor Smith was reelected governor in 1864 only to give up his office after Lee's surrender to Grant. Union Hotel proprietor James W. Jackson killed the first Union officer to die in the Civil War. And Jackson, in turn, became not only the first Confederate casualty in the war but also the first civilian to lose his life on either side.

---

56. *Gazette*, 29 October 1859.

V

A Peal of Thunder on a Cloudless Day

Politics, John Brown, and Secession, 1840-1861

On the third Monday of each month, three to five of the leading men of Fairfax County assembled at the courthouse to take care of the official business of the county. The function of these "gentlemen justices" was very much what it had been from the time the county first came into existence, for in the midnineteenth century, they still had both administrative and judicial duties. In the 1840s, they heard most civil suits, held preliminary hearings in criminal cases that would be tried in the circuit court, licensed taverns, naturalized new citizens, decided whether a manumitted slave might remain in the county, were responsible for the condition of county roads, and so on.[1]

On court days, the village of Providence sprang into life. Citizens from all over the county flocked to town, often with their families in tow. They traded farm produce for groceries and dry goods; went to meetings of the county agricultural society; attended auctions of slaves, cattle, and real estate at the courthouse door; participated in heated rallies for political candidates; and spent a good deal of time talking, visiting, and having a good time generally. An English traveler who passed through the village on a September court day in the late 1830s described the scene:

> A numerous assemblage of people from the neighboring country were . . . in attendance here. Besides the parties having actual business at these courts, very many of the country residents came into town on those public days, in the hope of meeting their friends, and thus a sort of Social

---

1. For the evolution of the county courts of Virginia, see Albert Ogden Porter, *County Government in Virginia: A Legislative History, 1607-1904* (New York: Columbia University Press, 1947), pp. 109, 163, passim, (hereinafter cited as Porter, *County Government in Virginia*).

Establishment is established, where for two or three days in succession, the principal farmers of the country and their families have a re-union several times a year, which maintains their friendly relations, and keeps up a kind feeling among them all.[2]

Until 1852, the court was in essence a self-perpetuating body comprised of the leading men of the county, just as it had been from the time it was first appointed. It seems impossible today to determine just how much satisfaction Fairfax citizens ordinarily felt with its authority. In the mid-1840s there was clearly a surge of discontent with the court, over which the citizens had relatively little control. Perhaps the dissatisfaction had been there all along and was brought to a head by the economic stagnation that still hung over the county.

At any rate, in the winter of 1844 more than 350 men—a sizable portion of the white adult male population—signed an angry petition to the General Assembly complaining bitterly of the existing court system and the property requirements for the suffrage. They urged the Assembly to plan for a state constitutional convention to reform both.

Your petitioners respectfully call the attention of the Legislature to the County Court system of Virginia: a system derived from the Jurisprudence of the Mother Country, but one which they believe wholly unsuited to a republican form of government, and which in their opinion ought to be entirely abolished. They cannot perceive why the Justices of the Peace should be wholly independent of the people of the Counties in which they reside, why they should have arbitrarily and corruptly, if it should suit their purposes or designs, the appointment of members of their own body whose duty it is, or may be, to decide questions of law and Equity, when many of them have neither the information nor capacity to decide Either. It is indeed a solecism to assert, that men shall decide questions of law for their fellow citizens, who do not know the first principles of the Science which they are called upon to adjudicate. Connected with this subject is the appointment of Sheriffs, deputy sheriffs, and other County offices of the various counties of the State. The situation of the debtor class of the community is at all times *hard*, but it is doubly so when a set of men are let loose to prey upon them, who seem to disregard in many instances all considerations of propriety, who have no sympathy for their situations, and from the manner of their appointment are wholly independent of *the people*. Your petitioners respect-

---

2. Buckingham, *Slave States*, 2:564. Also see Porter, *County Government in Virginia*, pp. 162-63.

fully represent that these officers are elected in every State in the Union (Virginia Excepted) by a direct vote of the People, and they earnestly insist that the welfare of the State would be greatly promoted by a change in the Existing laws in this respect.[3]

There were, apparently, no further such petitions from Fairfax; but in 1850, when there was a statewide referendum on whether to hold a constitutional convention, Fairfax voters heavily approved the measure, as did Virginians in general.[4]

Among the principal changes made in the new constitution, which was drawn up in 1850-1851, was a provision abolishing the property requirements for voting and substituting residential requirements. The right of suffrage was extended to white males over the age of twenty-one who had been residents of the state for two years or more. The new constitution also provided that the governor, heretofore elected by the legislature, the county magistrates, and other local officials were to be elected by the people.[5] Fairfax voted overwhelmingly for the new constitution, as did the entire state, which approved ratification by a ratio of approximately 7 to 1.[6]

In making the local courts elective bodies, the constitution provided that each county was to be divided into a number of districts (six in Fairfax County) with four justices who were residents of their respective districts, to be elected in each.[7] Virginia counties held their first local elections in May 1852, and as a result a number of new men took their seats on the Fairfax court in June of that year. Nevertheless, there were at least a half-dozen men who had served before, and Silas Burke, presiding justice, had also been presiding justice in the preceding and earlier courts.

It is not clear whether the election of the county court had any significant impact on its partisan alignments, though Thomas R. Love, a leading Fairfax Whig, implied in a letter written in 1851 that popular elections and the provision for white manhood suffrage might have an adverse effect on the Whig Party in the county.[8] But as a rule, party affiliations were not emphasized in local elections, and Fairfax voters apparently did not hesitate to cross party lines. Undoubtedly the court became more responsive to the people, but just how that responsiveness was manifested is not clear without further study.

3. Fairfax County Legislative Petitions, 26 January 1844.

4. *Gazette*, 29 April 1850; William J. Van Schreeven, *The Conventions and Constitutions of Virginia, 1776-1966* (Richmond: Virginia State Library, 1967), p. 7 (hereinafter cited as Van Schreeven, *Conventions*].

5. *Virginia Constitution*, 1851, article III, section 1; V, sec. 2; VI, secs. 27, 30. The new suffrage residential requirements meant that residents of other localities with a freehold in Fairfax County could no longer vote in Fairfax.

6. *Gazette*, 30 April 1851; Van Schreeven, *Conventions*, p. 7.

7. *Virginia Constitution*, 1851, article VI, sec. 27.

8. See T.R. Love to S.T. Stuart, 19 February 1851, Stuart Family Papers, Box 2.

Perhaps at no period in American history was there more "participatory democracy" for the male portion of the population (women, of course, did not have the suffrage) than in antebellum America.[9] Virginians, some of whom could not previously vote because of the property requirements, could now cast their ballot for congressmen, governor, lieutenant-governor, state attorney-general, county magistrates, county sheriff, and several other local officials. Previously they had voted only for congressmen and members of the General Assembly.[10]

In addition to taking part in elections, the men of Fairfax had ample opportunities for political participation in the numerous county and neighborhood political rallies. Controversial political matters led to frequent local gatherings, both planned and impromptu, at which time those attending adopted sets of resolutions and sent copies of them off to local newspapers as well as to their state legislators and congressmen. More often than not, such gatherings were partisan in nature, with local political leaders calling them in order to drum up discontent with the opposing party and to build support for their own.

In the two antebellum decades, partisan political divisions in Fairfax were quite close. Though Whigs usually carried the county, they often did so by a narrow margin.[11] The great Whig hero in Fairfax and throughout Virginia was the personable Virginia-born Kentuckian Henry Clay, who had lost none of his popularity in Fairfax with the passing years. In 1844, the last time that the great "Harry of the West" won the Whig presidential nomination, a typical Clay gathering in Fairfax went like this:

In March, the Mount Vernon Clay Club—made up of a portion of the Whigs of Fairfax—met at J. H. Zimmerman's tavern in West End to urge Clay's nomination. It adopted the usual Whig platform favoring a sound national currency, restrictions on the executive power, a single six-year term for presidents, a "judicious tariff," and a nineteenth-century version of revenue-sharing (this distribution among the states of proceeds from the sale of Western lands). Anticipating the Democratic nomination of former President Martin Van Buren, it described that consummate politician's regime as an "incompetent, extravagant, corrupt and disastrous administration."

Fairfax Whigs intended to have none of such evils. Taking a firm stand for Patriotism and for Virtue, they "*Resolved, That armed in the*

9. Women were beginning to attend political gatherings, which apparently had been almost exclusively for males in earlier decades.

10. *Virginia Constitution*, 1830, article III, sec. 14, et passim; cf. *Virginia Constitution*, 1851, article III, sec. 1; V, sec. 2; VI, secs. 27, 30.

11. *Gazette*, 29, 31 May 1852; 28 May 1853; 26 May 1855; 29 May 1860, et passim. In the 1830s, however, Democrats had frequently carried the county. See Henry Harrison Simms, *The Rise of the Whigs in Virginia, 1824-1840* (Richmond, Va.: William Byrd Press, Inc. 1929), pp. 167-92.

panoply of truth, impelled by love of Country, her honor, happiness and glory, we, the sons of Virginia, faithful to the revolutionary ancestry of many of us, and the Whig principle of that period that tried men's souls, will go forth to battle under the flag of Henry Clay."[12]

By and large, Whigs managed to retain a tenuous hold on Fairfax throughout the antebellum period. When the party was torn apart in the 1850s over the question of slavery and related issues, Fairfax and other Virginia Whigs rejected the newly organized Republican Party: in their eyes, it was composed of fanatical abolitionists bent on fomenting "servile insurrections." Instead they supported the nativist-oriented American (better known as the "Know-Nothing") Party.[13] The American candidate for governor, Thomas S. Flournoy, carried Fairfax in 1855 by a vote of 631 to 512, but in the presidential elections of 1856 the majority of Fairfax voters turned to Democrat James Buchanan in preference to American candidate Millard Fillmore, 727 to 650.[14] And Republican John Charles Frémont might as well not have been on the ballot in Virginia, for he received few if any votes. Three years later, in 1859, the Whig gubernatorial candidate, William L. Goggin, barely carried the county, receiving 719 votes to Democrat "Honest John" Letcher's 695.[15]

In the 1840s and 1850s, national agitation of the searing question of slavery and abolition had repeatedly angered Fairfax natives. Partisan controversy and congressional battles over such issues as the return of runaways and the extension of slavery into the territories locked Congress in debate for months on end. But after a decade of bitterness, actions of both Congress and the Supreme Court made it legally possible for masters to carry slaves into all of the territories, and Virginians became reasonably content with national policy on slavery.

By the late 1850s, they were beginning to forget the bitterness of the recent controversies. In the fall of 1859, the people of Fairfax were occupied with their usual concerns, unaware that a small band of Northern abolitionists had gathered at a Maryland farm near Harper's Ferry and were planning to precipitate an uprising of Virginia slaves.[16] In mid-October, Fairfax citizens were excited about the opening of the Orange and Alexandria Railroad to Lynchburg, delighted with the

12. *Gazette*, 20 March 1844.

13. *Gazette*, 21 March, 2 April 1855, et passim.

14. *Gazette*, 1 January 1857, gives the returns for both the 1855 and 1856 elections.

15. *Gazette*, 28 May 1859.

16. John Brown's goals have been a matter of some historical debate. See Oswald Garrison Villard, *John Brown, 1800-1859: A Biography Fifty Years After* (Boston and New York: Houghton Mifflin Company, 1911), p. 314, passim; Stephen B. Oates, *To Purge this Land with Blood: A Biography of John Brown* (New York, Evanston, and London: Harper & Row, 1970), pp. 278-80; J.C. Furnas, *The Road to Harper's Ferry* (New York: William Sloane Associates, 1959), pp. 20-27, passim; Benjamin Quarles, *Allies for Freedom: Blacks and John Brown* (New York: Oxford University Press, 1974), pp. 46-51.

attention the Alexandria *Gazette* was giving the "pretty residences" of Providence, and looking forward to a "grand tournament" at Fairfax Court House on October 25.[17]

In western Fairfax, Centreville residents were feeling especially optimistic. They had had an excellent growing season. There had been fine yields of cabbage, turnips, and salsify, to say nothing of other fruits and vegetables. Land was selling at ten to twenty dollars an acre. Pennsylvanians who had been visiting in the neighborhood were returning with families and friends to locate permanently. Best of all, there were now three rail lines within a few miles of the village. In addition to the O&A and the Manassas Gap lines, the railroad to Leesburg was just coming into operation. Two miles northeast of town, wrote a correspondent of the *Gazette*, residents "already welcome the shrill cry of the locomotive, as it dashes proudly over the track of the Alexandria, Loudoun and Hampshire a few miles distant."[18]

A week before the grand event was to take place, court day, Monday, 17 October, began like any other day. Despite rainy weather most families went about their usual chores, not knowing that less than fifty miles away, at Harper's Ferry, the notorious John ("Ossawattomie") Brown and his followers were in possession of the principal arsenal of the United States government. Those who braved the wet weather and went to Alexandria early in the day to market or shop or visit could have watched the arrival of the new and elegant steamer *Mount Vernon*, which docked at 7:30 a.m. She came in with freight and passengers from New York after a pleasant run of thirty hours, undeterred by the loss of her fore-topmast in a collision with another ship while leaving New York harbor. [19]

A Fairfax visitor in town for fall shopping could stop at H.E. Gregory's stand on King Street to look over the "largest and best assortment of stoves ever offered on this market, . . . cooking stoves, . . . parlor stoves, . . . office and Bar Room Stoves." Or visit William H. Fowle & Son to order one of their various guanos, "Peruvian, Californian, Nevassa, Mexican, and Sombrero." Or take his horse to the Hodgkins' on Pitt Street, who had just "secured the services of . . . one of the best Horse Shoers in this State."[20]

His "lady" may have stopped in at "R. H. Miller, Son & Co., Importers of Queensware," for that establishment had recently received "134 crates and hogsheads" of French porcelain and English china. Or she may have visited Jefferson Tacey, who had been "two years amongst them" as a "paperhanger, upholsterer, gilder, and House Decorator in

17. *Gazette*, 1, 4, 7, 8, 18, 20 October 1859.
18. *Gazette*, 22 October 1859.
19. *Gazette*, 17 October 1859.
20. Ibid.

General." Or she might have taken a shawl to "Monsieur Baudouin" to
to be bleached or dyed in the "French Dyeing and Scouring
Establishment."[21]

A visitor who liked to read might have browsed in James
Entwhistle's and Robert Bell's bookstores. There were volumes on every
topic one could wish. If one had a taste for the exotic, there was a work
by "two late Missionaries" on *Fiji and the Fijians*. If one were a housewife
in search of ideas, *Breakfast, Dinner and Tea, viewed Classically,
Poetically, and Practically, containing numerous dishes of all times and
countries, besides three hundred modern receipts* was at hand. *The Art of
Extempore Speaking, Hints for the Pulpit, the Senate and Bar* might
attract the interest of an ambitious young attorney or clergyman. And
Alvah D. Hovey, D.D., offered reassurance to the devout and a word of
warning to the doubter in *The State of the Impenitent Dead*, while
J. Oswald Jackson spoke to the pure in heart—or those who hoped to be—
in *Jesus Only*.[22]

The visitor who had time for the *Gazette* found it notable only by
the dearth of major news. He had to be content with a story of the "latest
Parisian decree" mandating "thirty flounces per dress, and not one less";
with a report that a Winchester newspaper hoped to see the introduction
of "*steam* carriages on the turnpikes in that neighborhood"; with a
description of eight-year-old "Mad'lle Christians Milly," who possessed
"two fine heads, four arms, and four feet, all concentrated in one perfect
body" and could "dance, walk, or run with as much style and rapidity as
any child of her age"; and with an obituary of nineteen-year-old Lucy
Taylor of Madison County, who, dying of typhoid, had embraced "her
mother round the neck" and asked her "not to mourn for her, but meet
her in Heaven."[23]

The visitor with a few dollars in his pocket may have planned to stay
at the Marshall House, operated by two Fairfax men, James W. Jackson
and Amos Fox. At that hostelry, there was no "fashionable printed bill of
fare," but among the "articles that graced the table" were "boiled ham,
baked ham with champagne sauce, roast beef, corned beef boiled, roast
pig, baked pork, saddle mutton, boiled lamb [with] mint sauce, wild
turkies [sic], pheasants, partridges, rabbits, oppossums, together with
the et ceteras of vegatables of all kinds, the whole concluding with an
afterpiece made up of puddings, tarts, &c, &c." All this plus room for a
dollar and a half a day.[24]

All was quiet. All was business as usual, though perhaps a trifle dull.
All was peace, prosperity, and progress.

21. Ibid.
22. Ibid.
23. Ibid.
24. *Gazette*, 31 October 1859.

Then suddenly that Monday morning at the Alexandria office, the wires of the "magnetic telegraph" crackled with a dispatch from Frederick, Maryland, by way of Baltimore:

October 17th a.m. There is an insurrection at Harper's Ferry. A band of armed Abolitionists have full possession of [the] United States Arsenal. The express train was fired into twice and one of the railroad hands—a negro—killed while trying to get the train through the town. The insurgents arrested two men who came into town with a load of wheat, took the wagon, loaded it with rifles, and sent them into Maryland. The band is composed of a gang of about 250 whites, followed by a band of negroes, who are now fighting.[25]

The Baltimore dispatcher who forwarded the wire warned that it had just been received in that office and "as it seems very improbable, it should be received with great caution until confirmed." The train due that morning from Frederick had not yet arrived, he added. The telegraph wires were cut. "Many wild rumors" were circulating, but there was "nothing authentic yet."[26]

At first, townspeople and visitors alike discounted the news: they thought it was "merely an exaggeration of . . . difficulties among the workmen at the Armory, which would speedily be settled." But the day wore on, and new dispatches reached the city. "Reports of riot, insurrection and murder," declared the *Gazette*, raised public concern "to the highest pitch." Residents and visitors could talk of little else.[27] There had been no warning, no hint of trouble, except perhaps in the news of a "stampede" of slaves who had run off from their master and escaped with several other slaves in the neighborhood.[28] The news of the outbreak at Harper's Ferry, declared the *Gazette* next day, "has come upon us as suddenly and unexpectedly as would a peal of thunder fall on the ear on a clear and cloudless day."[29]

While guerrilla warfare raged between John Brown's men and the people of Harper's Ferry, word of the insurrection spread quickly to Fairfax County. By afternoon it had reached Providence, where the county court was in session. There were fewer visitors in the village than usual, "inclement weather" having "prevented many from paying their regular visit" to town. Only three justices were in attendance. Joshua C. Gunnell was there as presiding justice; Richard Johnston and James Hunter, as associates. There was the usual business to take care of: the recording of deeds, a consideration of disputes about proposed roads and

25. *Gazette*, 18 October 1859.
26. Ibid.
27. *Gazette*, 19 October 1859.
28. Ibid.
29. Ibid.

bridges, the naturalization of an Irishman. The minute books give no hint of how or when the court learned of the insurrection, or of whether the justices learned of it while they were in session. But the minutes of the second day were unusually brief—perhaps gentlemen justices and citizens alike were too excited for routine affairs.[30]

By Thursday, 20 October, the essentials of the insurrection were known to all. The chief leader, reported the *Gazette*, was "undoubtedly Captain John Brown, whose connection with . . . border warfare in Kansas made his name . . . notorious to the whole country." He had first appeared "in the vicinity of Harper's Ferry more than a year ago, accompanied by his two sons." They had left, then returned with several others, and Brown had laid his plans "for an insurrection, which was supposed to be successful in exterminating slavery in Maryland and western Virginia."

The "first active movement in the insurrection" had occurred about ten-thirty on Sunday night, 16 April, while the town slept. On Monday a kind of guerrilla warfare broke out between the insurgents and the people of the town and surrounding countryside. That night United States troops under the command of Colonel Robert E. Lee arrived at Harper's Ferry and on Tuesday after brief but intense fighting, "the work was done" and the uprising had been quelled.[31]

In Fairfax the insurrection became "the principal theme of conversation." A correspondent to the *Gazette* wrote that it had come "too near home" for county citizens not to feel "a lively interest in the matter." Suspicion of the Yankee newcomers arose immediately, and native citizens expected the circuit judge, when he convened the grand jury in November, to "charge that body to look carefully into the present state of things." And, concluded the correspondent with a flourish, "if it finds in our midst" any "who improperly tamper with Southern institutions upon them let the law take its course."

Northerners in Fairfax immediately took steps to reassure their neighbors that they too deplored the outbreak of violence. After talking with a number of his fellow emigrants, Daniel G. Roberts of Centreville wrote the Fairfax *News* "that so far from entertaining the least sympathy with these disturbers of the public peace, they are not a whit behind the native citizens in expressing their indignation at this high-handed outrage against the laws."[32]

The Alexandria *Gazette*, always hostile to the newly formed Republican Party and eager to see both its demise and the return of

---

30. Fairfax County Court Minute Books, 17, 18 October 1859, pp. 234-42.

31. *Gazette*, 20, 21 October 1859; Douglas Southall Freeman, *R.E. Lee: A Biography*, 4 vols. (New York and London: Charles Scribner's Sons, 1945), 1:394-403 (hereinafter cited as Freeman, *R.E. Lee*).

32. *Gazette*, 12 November 1859; Daniel G. Roberts to Fairfax *News*, 10 November 1859, printed in *Gazette*, 19 November 1859.

straying Whigs to the old party, thought there could be a silver lining to the whole affair. The raid, wrote the editor, might thoroughly discredit the Republican leaders who had condoned it. He was pleased with the "tone of the conservative presses of the North" and was "in hopes that . . . this matter . . . may assist in utterly breaking up and destroying what is called the 'Republican' Party."[33]

But Virginia's trial, sentencing, and execution of Brown had an adverse effect on Northern opinion. By the latter part of November it became clear to the people of Northern Virginia that throughout the North there was a great deal of sympathy for Brown's action. A number of Northern abolitionists not only approved the idea of a general slave rebellion, but some had also actually participated in planning the raid, and worse yet a large segment of Northerners condoned their actions.[34] For years, Virginians had thought of abolitionists as people who were deliberately fomenting slave uprisings; now it seemed they had been right. For the first time the depth and breadth of Northern disapproval of slavery was becoming apparent to Virginians.

As Southerners came to realize that John Brown was emerging as a Northern hero, the horror they felt can scarcely be exaggerated. Fears of servile insurrection always lay in the Southern subconscious; remembrance of the chilling Nat Turner rampage in Southside Virginia less than thirty years before was still vivid in the minds of older citizens, and rumors of slave insurrections had precipitated a new wave of racial fears during the 1856 elections. More than any other single event, the John Brown raid aroused in Southerners the old fears of racial uprisings; and more than any other single event, it estranged North and South.[35]

What it all meant was that for most Fairfax natives, love of Union was not so strong as a sense of identification with the South. A Washington *Star* correspondent who traveled through Fairfax and several adjoining counties in November 1859 appraised prevailing rumors of widespread excitement over the John Brown affair: "This excitement," he wrote, "is not a wild one . . . . It is a calm and clear sentiment in favor of a speedy end of the Government of the United States, if it is to continue to be a means through which parties from the North may steal into the South, and their stealing and burning Southern

33. *Gazette*, 26 October, 17 November 1859.
34. See *Gazette*, November-December 1859, passim, especially 22, 23 November.
35. Steven A. Channing, *Crisis of Fear: Secession in South Carolina* (New York: Simon and Schuster, 1970), pp. 20-26, 117, 120, 255-56, et passim, emphasizes the role of the John Brown raid in readying South Carolina for secession and also indicates the reaction to the raid in Virginia; Elbert B. Smith, "The Coming of the Civil War" (paper delivered at the Southern Historical Association Convention, Washington, D.C., 9 November 1975), emphasized the threat to Southern self-esteem in the abolitionist attack and in Lincoln's election. Also see *Gazette*, October-December 1859; Richmond *Whig*, October-December 1859.

property and murdering Southern citizens may be countenanced in such acts by an almost universal expression of Northern sentiment in their favor."[36]

On 29 November, a letter from Fairfax. declared that "military movements" were "the rage at present."[37] On 5 December, the *Gazette* urged the promotion of home manufactures as a good way of making the South economically independent of the North and of supporting "Southern institutions" generally. In January, a Fairfax correspondent noted that "the fair daughters of Fairfax, like their sisters in Alexandria, Richmond, and Norfolk" were glorying "in the independence of patriotic homespun."[38] Meanwhile, in December, William H. Dulany took the lead in organizing the Fairfax Rifle Rangers, and the following summer there was a reorganization of the county militia and a dress parade of the "Gallant Rangers."[39] During. the same period there were public meetings at Falls Church and Fairfax Court House condemning the invasion of Virginia "by that thief and murderer John Brown." Nevertheless, it was apparent that some county citizens were more upset than others. Whereas the Falls Church gathering, chaired by the thoroughly Unionist Daniel F. Dulany, deprecated "all sectional feeling or action," the Fairfax Court House meeting called for state encouragement of "domestic manufactures in all branches" so that "Virginia may be always in a position to act promptly, efficiently and independently."[40]

It is difficult to overestimate the impact of the 1859 raid in readying Fairfax natives and other Southerners for secession in 1861. By the beginning of 1860, talk of a separation of the states abounded as never before in Unionist Virginia as well as in secessionist South Carolina. Though Northern Virginia remained Unionist, its commitment to the Federal government had been significantly weakened, not so much by the raid itself as by the general Northern reaction to it.' In Southern eyes, Northerners who extolled Brown's act and condemned his hanging had loosened the bonds of Union.

In the upcoming presidential year, the Democratic Party followed the Whigs into sectional schism. An overwhelming majority of Fairfax Democrats supported John C. Breckinridge, the candidate of the Southern Democratic Party, clearly preferring him to Stephen A. Douglas, the thoroughly Unionist candidate of the Northern Democrats. Similarly, the vast majority of Fairfax Whigs, feeling nothing but hostility for Republican nominee Abraham Lincoln, supported John 'C.

36. *Gazette*, 23 November 1859.
37. Gazette, 29 November 1859.
38. *Gazette*, 6 December 1859.
39. *Gazette*, 10 January 1860.
40. *Gazette*, 21 January 1860.

Mottrom Dulany Ball. One of the most outstanding men in Fairfax just before the war was this able young school teacher. Ball had graduated from William and Mary, where he delivered an unusually fine valedictory address. Before the war broke out he organized a local cavalry unit. Through a fluke his unit was captured by Union troops in the course of the occupation of Alexandria. He was later released and joined the Confederate Army. After the war Ball went into law practice with his first cousin, William H. Dulany. Ironically, they often defended local blacks charged with crimes by the local government, then under the control of Unionists from the North. Virginia Historical Society.

Bell, the candidate of the Constitutional Union party, a new organization composed primarily of old-line border-state Whigs.

The presidential election in Fairfax was more exciting in 1860 than any other in recent memory. There were rallies for "LIBERTY AND UNION, NOW AND FOREVER, ONE AND INSEPARABLE."[41] There were Breckinridge poles, and Douglas poles, and Bell poles. There was even a Lincoln pole, raised by a Falls Church Yankee, but quickly knocked down.[42] In the election, Fairfax, still loyal, cast a majority of Unionist votes. Though 685 Fairfax men voted for the Southern Democratic nominee, 807 others voted for Unionist candidates, with Bell receiving 692 votes, Douglas 91, and even "Black Republican" Abe Lincoln garnering 24 votes.[43]

Excitement did not abate after the election and the news of Lincoln's victory. Rumors of slave insurrections flooded the county. Meetings were held; resolutions adopted. At Langley, Frying Pan, Sangster's Station, Centreville, and Fairfax Court House, slave patrols were appointed.[44] A few days before Christmas, word came of the secession of South Carolina.

At Lewinsville, several young men organized a cavalry company and elected a talented, witty schoolmaster, Mottrom Dulany Ball, as captain.[45] On hiring day at Fairfax Court House, Dranesville, and Centreville, there was little demand for servants because the people felt conditions were too unsettled.[46] By mid-January, forty-two new members had joined Ball's company. Rumors spread of "incendiary documents" in circulation. And there were more meetings.[47]

On January 15, John Letcher, the new governor of Virginia, reluctantly issued a proclamation authorizing the election of delegates to a convention to discuss Virginia's relations with the Federal Union.[48] In Fairfax, William H. Dulany ran as a candidate for convention delegate on a moderately Unionist platform; Alfred Moss, on a mildly secessionist platform. On 21 January the two men expounded their views at Fairfax Court House before a crowd of citizens who had come to town for court day. Moss was in favor of seceding just as soon as the convention

41. *Gazette*, 6 November 1860. For this election, the Whigs referred to themselves as the Constitutional Union Party.

42. Ibid.; Goodwin, *History of Theological Seminary*, 2:427.

43. *Gazette*, 8 November 1860.

44. *Gazette*, 24 November, 1, 4, 8 December 1860.

45. *Gazette*, 15 December 1860.

46. C.L. Fendall (?) to R.H. Stuart, 22 January 1861, in Stuart Family Papers, Box 2; *Gazette*, 8 January 1861.

47. *Gazette*, 15 December 1860; 3, 15 January, 4 February 1861.

48. In his address to the General Assembly, Letcher had opposed such a convention, but the Assembly nevertheless authorized it. See Francis N. Boney, *John Letcher of Virginia: The Story of Virginia's Civil War Governor* (University, Ala.: University of Alabama Press, 1966), pp. 102-5.

assembled, unless some prospect of compromise with the Federal government was clearly visible. Dulany advocated further efforts at compromise but did not altogether rule out secession.[49]

The vote was heavy, and the county went for Dulany, who defeated Moss 836 to 628. An even heavier majority of voters insisted that any convention decision to secede must be subject to a state-wide referendum; the vote favored reference 856 to 524.[50]

Even Dulany said that "he would never consent to purchase" peace and unity "at the price of the honor and interest of Virginia."[51] When he set out for Richmond, he and most Virginians undoubtedly hoped that some compromise could yet be agreed upon that would keep the Old Dominion in the Union.

Despite repeated efforts (peace conventions and delegations of emissaries), that compromise never materialized. By spring, six more states had left the Union. All efforts at compromise ceased after Confederates bombarded Fort Sumter on April 12. In Virginia, pressures for secession immediately skyrocketed. As the convention entered its last days of debate, excitement mounted in Northern Virginia as well. At Fairfax Court House, the Reverend G. A. Carter made an address favoring immediate secession, and was said to have "created much enthusiasm." On the same day at Fairfax Court House, a meeting of the Union Party gave its "entire and hearty approbation" to the antisecessionist course taken by William H. Dulany at the convention.[52] In Washington, President Lincoln called for volunteer troops to put down the "insurrection." Virginia was asked to furnish over two thousand of the seventy-five thousand men called for.

For most Virginians the call for troops was the final blow. Two days later in Richmond the convention voted 88 to 55 in favor of secession. Fairfax delegate Dulany was among the 55 who voted nay.[53] Undoubtedly he had some vision of the turmoil and heartache that the decision to secede would bring to Fairfax County.

49. *Gazette*, 23 January, 5 February 1861.
50. *Gazette*, 8 February 1861.
51. *Gazette*, 9 February 1861.
52. *Gazette*, 16, 17, 18 April 1861.
53. "Portions of Journal of Secret Session of the Convention . . .," 17 April 1861, p. 10, in *Journals and Papers of the Virginia State Convention of 1861*, 3 vols. (Richmond: Virginia State Library, 1966), 1.

VI

War Comes to Fairfax

From Secession to First Manassas

A group of children are at play in the yard of a one-room country school a short distance from Fairfax Court House. Nearby sits Sarah Summers, just sixteen years old and already a veteran teacher, chatting with several girls. A few of the boys have wandered down to a stream which flows over a narrow dirt road passing the school. It is a bright spring afternoon, Friday, 24 May 1861.

Suddenly Sarah catches sight of a surrey coming at full speed from the direction of Alexandria. It stops at the water to let the horses drink, and she sees that the driver is her uncle Amox Fox, an owner of the Marshall House in Alexandria. With him are two ladies. As the surrey heads toward her grandmother's house nearby, Fox calls out to her: "You better dismiss your school at once and go right home to your mother. The Union Army is advancing!"

The boys from the stream run up to Sarah. Full of excitement, they report that the ladies' clothes are covered with blood! Hurriedly Sarah sends the children home, then runs to her grandmother's house. There she finds her uncle with the wife and daughter of James W. Jackson—the co-proprietor of the Marshall House—and hears the story of their day in Alexandria.[1]

In this and in hundreds of different ways, Fairfax citizens learned that May morning and afternoon of the Federal invasion of Virginia. For weeks, for months, even for years—ever since John Brown's raid—they had been talking of war, but only in recent weeks had it seemed ominously close. Then suddenly in mid-April the firing on Fort Sumter,

---

1. Milliken, "Clarke," Historical Society *Yearbook* 8:12. The school was located near the intersection of Fox Mill and Waples Mill roads.

Lincoln's call for troops, and the Virginia convention's approval of secession (subject to a May 23 referendum) made the outbreak of war seem all too imminent.

Everywhere there were signs of war in the offing. In Washington, citizens fretted over the city's vulnerability to potential secessionist mobs, then sighed with relief in late April as the Seventh New York Regiment ("the pride of Gotham") detrained in the city.[2] In Richmond, Governor John Letcher called for volunteers and placed them under the command of Robert E. Lee, late United States Army colonel and a frequent visitor in Fairfax.[3] In Fairfax, three volunteer companies, two cavalry and one infantry, were mustered into state service.[4] By election day, May 23, when men all over Virginia turned out to vote on the secession ordinance, the state had taken control of the two rail lines that ran through Fairfax, a handful of Virginia troops had gathered on the Potomac heights overlooking Washington, and thousands of Federal troops were stationed in the capital city.[5]

There was no question that day that Virginians would approve secession. Many who had opposed secession until after the convention had made its decision announced in favor of the ordinance. In Fairfax at a public meeting in mid-May, William H. Dulany declared that despite his nay vote at the convention, he thought "there should be no division" among Virginians: "The [uncompromising] course of the [Lincoln] administration made it the imperative duty of every loyal son of Virginia to strike for her independence." At the same meeting, State Senator Henry W. Thomas also spoke in support of ratification.[6] In many areas where antisecessionists were expected to appear at the polls, hotheads had threatened violence to anyone who dared vote against the ordinance. In Fairfax, too, the adamant "Secesh" warned many a Unionist not to vote, and undoubtedly succeeded in intimidating a good many.[7]

2. Benjamin Franklin Cooling, *Symbol, Sword, and Shield: Defending Washington During the Civil War* (Hamden, Conn.: Archon Books, 1975), pp. 35, 37 (hereinafter cited as Cooling, *Symbol, Sword, and Shield*); Emmons Clark, *History of the Seventh Regiment of New York*, 2 vols. (New York: Published by the Seventh Regiment, 1890), 1:498; 2:1, 3-4.

3. Freeman, *R.E. Lee*, 1:439-42; Douglas Southall Freeman, *Lee's Lieutenants: A Study in Command*, 3 vols. (New York, London: Charles Scribner's Sons, 1942-44), 1:5 (hereinafter cited as Freeman, *Lee's Lieutenants*); "Ravensworth," Historical Society *Yearbook* 3(1954):29.

4. William B. Hurd, *Alexandria, Virginia, 1861-1865* (Alexandria: City of Alexandria, 1970), pp. 9, 62 (hereinafter cited as Hurd, *Alexandria*). The muster roll of Ball's company, Co. I of the Northern Virginia Cavalry, 11th Regiment, 1861 (VHS) shows four officers, nine noncommissioned officers, and thirty-one privates, all of whom enlisted in Charlottesville or Fairfax, and gives age, height, complexion, eye and hair color, place of birth, and occupation of each of the men and officers.

5. Hurd, *Alexandria*, p. 31; Cooling, *Symbol, Sword, and Shield*, pp. 40, 44.

6. *Gazette*, 22 May 1861.

7. Henry T. Shanks, *The Secession Movement in Virginia, 1847-1861* (Richmond, Va.: Garrett and Massie, Publishers, 1934), pp. 212-13. Also see despositions in Southern Claims Commission Papers, Fairfax County, 1871-90, Records of the Third Auditor of the Treasury, Records of the United States General Accounting Office, Record Group 217 (National Archives, Washington, D.C.) (hereinafter cited as Southern Claims Commission Papers, Fairfax County).

Voter intimidation. This cartoon ridiculing the lack of freedom in voting or secession was carried in Harpers Weekly. *A number of Fairfax residents who would probably have voted against secession stayed away from the polls because of intimidation and threats of violence by secessionists. Fairfax voted overwhelmingly in favor of seceding. Virginia State Library.*

The story of one who remained unintimidated is an example of the kind of coercion which Unionists encountered. When William D. Smith, a farmer and gardener, went to Accotink to vote, he found the "rebel cavalry" there. "When I presented myself to the poll," he later recounted, "I was told by a rebel that if I voted against the ordinance I would lose my property and perhaps get greased before I got home. I saw Mr. Devers [the illiterate owner of a thirty-acre farm near Accotink] there and two sons, I told him [and his two sons] my greavances [*sic*] . . . . I think both of them [the sons] pulled their coats off and told me I should vote if I wanted to, that they intended to vote against the ordinance of secession. They went in and beckoned me to follow. When they came out they said they had voted. The old man said, 'I have voted against the damned sons of bitches.' . . . I heard the rebels at Accotink at the election call him a damned villain. They appeared to hate him very much then and don't like him now."[8]

8. Deposition of William D. Smith, Claim of John W. Devers, Southern Claims Commission Papers, Fairfax County.

There is no way of knowing the actual uncoerced opinion of Fairfax citizens. The total number of votes cast was 1,520, about the same number as in preceding elections.[9] Nevertheless, there is good reason to believe that as many as several hundred who would have voted against secession simply did not cast a vote. In view of the deep interest that every Fairfax citizen must have felt in the election, it might be expected that the vote would have been unusually high, and after the war many maintained that they had been afraid to go to the polls.[10] Undoubtedly the turnout of prosecessionists was heavy. Of the 1,520 votes, 1,231 were in favor of secession to just 289 against. In three precincts, the vote for secession was unanimous: at Bailiss, Ross's, and Centreville. At West End, only one vote was cast against secession.[11] Of the 289 votes against the ordinance, 240 were cast in three precincts where Northern immigration was heavy: Accotink, Lewinsville, and Lydecker's, in each of which a majority opposed secession.[12]

Once the formality of referendum was over, the Union acted quickly. In the early hours of 24 May, on orders from President Lincoln and General Winfield Scott, eleven regiments of Union troops moved out of the District of Columbia. They crossed the Potomac, its waters lighted by a full moon, over the Aqueduct and the Long Bridge, and by boat from Anacostia. Soon after two in the morning, Federal troops, most of them raw young volunteers, stepped onto Virginia's renowned "sacred soil" and took possession of the Virginia end of the bridge without encountering Rebel resistance.[13]

Meanwhile, the handful of ill-provisioned Virginia troops in Alexandria, including the three volunteer companies from Fairfax, received orders to withdraw to Manassas.[14] There, at the critical junction of the Manassas Gap and the Orange and Alexandria railroads south of Bull Run in neighboring Prince William County, Confederate troops

---

9. *Gazette,* 8 November 1860.

10. See various depositions in Southern Claims Commission Papers, Fairfax County.

11. *Gazette,* 24 May 1861. Also see testimony in claim of Joseph W. Sewell, Southern Claims Commission Papers, Fairfax County.

12. In Alexandria, only 48 votes were cast against secession to 958 for. Hurd, *Alexandria,* p. 11. For the returns of the referendum in Fairfax, see an undocumented article by Thomas P. Chapman, Jr., "The Secession Election in Fairfax County, May 23, 1861," Historical Society *Yearbook* 4(1955):51; and cf. Fairfax County Precinct Returns, 23 May 1861, Referendum, Records of 1861 Virginia Convention (VSL-A). There are minor differences between the precinct returns published in Chapman's article and those sent to state officials by the election commissioners. One resident of Falls Church, Lewis A. Crump, said that of the two hundred inhabitants there at the beginning of the war, only two families (Buck and Williams) were Rebels. Claim of Reuben Ives, Southern Claims Commission Papers, Fairfax County.

13. See United States Department of War, *War of the Rebellion: A Compilation of the Official Records of the Union and Confederate Armies,* 1st ser. (Washington, D.C.: Government Printing Office, 1880-1901), 2:40-41 (hereinafter cited as *OR*).

14. Report of Col. A.S. Taylor, quoted in Hurd, *Alexandria,* p. 10.

were just beginning to mass.[15] There was to be no attempt to hold Alexandria, which Virginia and Confederate officials considered undefendable.

One of the Fairfax units, the cavalry company commanded by Mottrom Dulany Ball, did not make the train to Manassas—the last to leave Alexandria under Southern control for the duration of the war—and quickly found itself a prisoner of the Union troops. No blood was shed in that episode; in fact, only two lives were lost in the occupation of Alexandria.[16]

As the New York Zouaves marched into Alexandria, Colonel Elmer Ellsworth and his men saw a Rebel flag flying proudly over the Marshall House. Hoisted by the fiery "Secesh" proprietor James William Jackson, of Fairfax, the flag seemed to Ellsworth a deliberate insult to the power of the United States government. Intent on cutting it down, he dashed into the hotel, ran up the steps, climbed a ladder to the roof, and hauled down the flag. As Ellsworth started back down the stairs, Jackson—intent on protecting his property and incensed by Ellsworth's attack on the Confederate flag—shot down the Union officer. A Union corporal accompanying Ellsworth then fired at Jackson, mortally wounding him. Jackson's remains were interred at the Jackson house on Swinks Mill Road. His wife and daughter escaped with his partner Amos Fox to Fairfax.[17]

Within a matter of days, Union troops began to build a ring of forts along the Alexandria-Fairfax line for the inner defenses of Washington. Army camps covered Seminary Hill and Cameron Valley. From a distance, the countryside—covered with white tents and red clay fortifications—seemed a study in contrasts.

In the weeks that followed the Union occupation, changes in Fairfax occurred so rapidly, events became so confused and lacking in focus, that attempting to impose some intelligible pattern seems almost to do violence to history. One can envision the fear, the excitement, and the uncertainty of Fairfax citizens as they sought to decide whether it would be safe to remain at home, as people in eastern Fairfax fled to the homes of relatives and friends in western parts of the county, as men went off to war (and sometimes to prison for purely political reasons), as they attempted to deal with slaves eager to escape to freedom, and as they tried to make up their minds about what they should do regarding their gardens and their fowl and livestock. One can imagine some of the questions they asked of the future: How much actual fighting would take place? How long would it last? Where would it occur? What dangers

15. For the withdrawal to Manassas, see *OR*, 1st ser., 2:42-43. For the strategic strengths and weaknesses of this area, see Freeman, *Lee's Lieutenants*, 1:688. That the Occoquan and Bull Run and the topography of the land immediately north of those streams constituted a natural barrier is evident even today.

16. Hurd, *Alexandria*, pp. 14, 31; Cooling, *Symbol, Sword, and Shield*, p. 45.

17. See Hurd, *Alexandria*, p. 15; *Gazette*, 24 May 1861; *OR*, 1st ser., 2:41.

would they meet if they stayed at home? What would happen to their property if they left? One can imagine their despair as they watched troops camp on their lawns, chop down their timber, and slaughter their livestock. One can imagine the new hostility between neighbors, friends, relatives, even members of the same family when one opted to support the Confederacy, the other to support the Union, and as "rebels" threatened Unionists with lynching, arrest, and even hanging.[18]

The problems would have been desperate enough if there had been a local government to help keep order, but the Fairfax court did not meet after Virginia joined the Confederacy. Despite strong Unionist sentiment, Fairfax had remained loyal to the Old Dominion: all the "Magistrates except three" had turned "secessionist."[19] By mid-June, when the court was scheduled to meet, the presence of Union troops and the possibility of arrest made it unsafe to assemble.

To make matters worse for Fairfax farmers, military needs disrupted their markets. Railroads became virtually inaccessible for shipping produce. In the eastern and northern parts of the county, Federal troops had taken possession of the Alexandria, Loudoun and Hamphire line as well as of several miles of Orange and Alexandria tracks. In western Fairfax, Confederates controlled the Orange and Alexandria, which they used as their main line of supply to troops at Centreville and Manassas Junction.[20]

The movement of the military was a subject of paramount interest to Fairfax citizens. Between the Union forts on the outskirts of Alexandria and the Confederate forces that were just beginning to mass at Manassas Junction, the county was rapidly becoming a no-man's-land. News was limited, largely because the Federal government suspended publication of the Alexandria *Gazette*, and much of what was heard was based on hearsay. Both sides sent scouting and reconnaissance parties into the county, and clashes between Yankees and Rebels became inevitable. On 1 June there was a Union cavalry raid on Fairfax Court House in which both sides claimed victory, and on 17 June, there was bloody fighting at Vienna.[21]

In the meantime, a handful of Unionists in Fairfax and Alexandria began to lay plans to take control of the local governments and to cooperate with the "loyal" Virginia government being organized in Wheeling. In late May and in June, as most state legislators gathered in Richmond, conventions of loyal delegates (all or most of them from northwestern Virginia) met in the panhandle city. There they agreed that

18. Cooling, *Symbol, Sword, and Shield*, p. 47; Southern Claims Commission Papers, Fairfax County.

19. Stephen S. Shinn to Francis H. Pierpont, 8 October 1861, in Miscellaneous Papers of Francis H. Pierpoint [sic] and the "Restored" Government of Virginia (VSL-A). Hereinafter cited as Pierpont Executive Papers.

20. Hurd, *Alexandria*, pp. 31-32.

21. For descriptions of the cavalry raid on Fairfax, see, e.g., *OR*, 1st ser., 2:59-64; for an account of the fighting at Vienna, see *OR*, 1st ser., 2:124-30.

"Brilliant charge of United States Cavalry through the village of Fairfax Court House," 1 June 1861. Virginia State Library.

a "Restored" Virginia General Assembly composed of the loyal delegates and senators elected on 23 May would meet in Wheeling on 1 July. The convention also chose Francis Harrison Pierpont, an old-line Whig and a native of Monongalia County, as acting governor.[22]

Word of the upcoming session of the loyal General Assembly had reached the Alexandria area by 2 July. On that date Union men in Northern Virginia "after some considerable vexation" but without aid from Federal troops or "wavering Union men," managed to hold an election for delegates and senator to the Restored legislature.[23] To represent them in the Assembly, Fairfax men chose as their delegate John Hawxhurst, a Quaker miller living on Difficult Run who had come to the county from New York in the late 1840s.[24] James T. Close was selected as senator, a man better known for his energy than his intelligence. A

22. For the action of the conventions, see Charles H. Ambler, *Francis H. Pierpont, Union War Governor of Virginia and Father of West Virginia* (Chapel Hill: University of North Carolina Press, 1937), pp. 85-90, 96-98, 108-9 (hereinafter cited as Ambler, *Pierpont*); Hamilton James Eckenrode, *The Political History of Virginia During the Reconstruction* (Baltimore: Johns Hopkins University Press, 1904), pp. 10-11; George Ellis Moore, *A Banner in the Hills: West Virginia's Statehood* (New York: Appleton-Century Crofts, Division of Meredith Publishing Company, 1963), pp. 57-62, 79-84; "Restored" Virginia Convention, "An Ordinance for the Reorganization of the State Government," n.d., in Ordinances of the Convention of West Virginia, 1861 (manuscript journal in Pierpont Executive Papers). For the varied spellings of Pierpont's name, see Ambler, *Pierpont*, pp. 3-4.

23. Charles H. Upton to Francis H. Pierpont, 3 July 1861, Pierpont Executive Papers. How the election was conducted is not clear. Richard H. Follin, a middle-aged, illiterate farmer of Prospect Hill, once testified that he had voted for Hawxhurst as a delegate to the Wheeling convention (but probably meant to the Wheeling Assembly). Claim of Richard H. Follin, Southern Claims Commission Papers, Fairfax County.

24. *Journal of the House of Delegates of the* ["Restored"] *State of Virginia for the Extra Session, 1861* (Wheeling, 1861), p. 27 (hereinafter cited as JHD[R]). For biographical material concerning John Hawxhurst and his brother Job, see Alexandria Preparative Monthly Meeting, Minutes, 16 November 1854, 12 April 1855; Edward Stabler to Samuel M. Janney, 4 August 1846, Janney Papers.

"newcomer" like Hawxhurst, Close had come to Alexandria more than a decade earlier as an agent for the Southern Protection Insurance Company. The two men and a third novice legislator representing Alexandria managed to arrive in Wheeling within a few days after the Assembly began to meet. Though none of them, apparently, took an especially active part in the remainder of the proceedings, their very presence reflected the spirit and energy of Fairfax and Alexandria Unionists. No other area outside a distance of 150 miles sent representatives to the July Assembly.[25]

While Hawxhurst and his companions politicked in Wheeling, Union troops went on the offensive in Virginia. For weeks Northern newspapers and political leaders had demanded that Federal troops move "forward to Richmond." It would be a simple matter, they said, to capture the Confederate capital, prevent the Confederate Congress from meeting, and bring the war to a quick and glorious end.[26] Lincoln too thought an early move had merit. Military action was needed to sustain morale; Federal troops were no greener than Confederate; and by capturing Manassas Junction and destroying the Rebels there, Union forces would gain a chance to move south, take Richmond, and end the war.

On 16 July, Union troops marched out of Alexandria and Washington into the Virginia countryside. Commanding them was Brigadier General Irvin McDowell, a brusque and censorious but capable career officer from Ohio. McDowell, who had deep doubts as to the wisdom of so early a move, had apparently been won over by the time he undertook the attack on Manassas.[27] Few others had any qualms at all; but the naive confidence of Union troops as they set out for Manassas, accompanied by political leaders, journalists, and sightseers, was to be short-lived. The march was slow, and there were frequent interruptions as the officers repeatedly ordered their men to fall out to search out any masked batteries. Bored and exasperated by the slow pace, the undisciplined Union troops loitered, picked berries, and inflicted destruction on homes and property that appalled Fairfax Unionists.[28]

As the Federal troops marched through the county, one family after

25. *Journal of the Senate of the [*"Restored"*] Commonwealth of Virginia (Extra Session) Begun and Held in the City of Wheeling, July 1861* (Wheeling: "Daily Press" Book and Job Office, 1861), pp. 38-39. The manuscript of the "Restored" Virginia Senate Journal, 1 July 1861-15 May 1862 is in the Pierpont Executive Papers.

26. Allan Nevins, *War for the Union*, 4 vols. (New York: Charles Scribner's Sons, 1959-71), 1:214 (hereinafter cited as Nevins, *War for the Union*). Proud Virginians had insisted that if the state seceded, Richmond must be the capital of the Confederacy, a bit of vainglory for which the state paid heavily in the four years of war. On 21 May, two days before the referendum, the Confederate government officially decided to make the move. Cooling, *Symbol, Sword, and Shield*, p. 44.

27. T. Harry Williams, *Lincoln and His Generals* (New York: Alfred A. Knopf, 1952), pp. 19-21.

28. Kenneth P. Williams, *Lincoln Finds a General: A Military Study of the Civil War*, 5 vols. (New York: Macmillan Company, 1949-1959) 1: 77-80 (hereinafter cited as K. Williams, *Lincoln Finds a General*). For the destruction, see claims of Lyman Broughton, Wait Broughton, Robert Carter, Southern Claims Commission Papers, Fairfax County.

another fled to relatives and friends living safely within Confederate lines. But many natives refused to leave home and many Northern immigrants felt safe enough with Union troops approaching.

On 18 July, Federal troops met their first organized opposition in a minor engagement at Blackburn's and Mitchell's fords on the Bull Run, the first where the main road from Centreville to Manassas crossed the stream and the other a half-mile upstream.[29] The skirmishing, which left about 83 Federal and 68 Confederate casualties, gave young Yankees and Rebels alike their first confrontation with violent death. One young Confederate later recalled the sight: "Up on the bluff we saw the first dead Yankee—he lay stark and cold . . . among the trees in . . . the gathering twilight; the pale face turned towards us . . . we looked [upon it] with feelings . . . [of] awe and dread."[30] Three days later, on a hot and humid Sunday, the two armies met in full battle.

At the beginning, matters went well for McDowell. But for the first time in history, the use of railroads affected the outcome of fighting. Just hours before the battle, Confederate General P.G.T. Beauregard began to receive reinforcements from General Joseph E. Johnston's army at Winchester.[31] By Sunday morning, when heavy fighting began, four of Johnston's five brigades had reached Manassas. Later, on that hot July afternoon, one of those brigades took a stand "like a stone wall against the enemy," as Thomas Jonathan Jackson's men turned the tide of battle. The Union advance halted, became first an orderly retreat, and then a rout. Panic-stricken, Federal soldiers turned on their heels and ran blindly, like wild beasts from a fire.

Sarah Summers, whose home was in the path of the retreating soldiers, remembered the Northern soldiers "running like mad to get back to Washington . . . so scared they hardly knew which way they were running." Some fled pell-mell through her house. Next morning the Summers found bales of blankets and uniforms in their yard, barrels of fish and flour and beef tongues, and even a crate of champagne, all left behind in the haste of the flight.[32]

Overnight, the sultry summer weather had given way to heavy rains. Along the muddy roads (and there was no mud like Virginia mud, commented one Yankee after another), Union soldiers, tired, footsore, and rainsoaked, struggled to make their way back to Washington. Fleeing with them were Fairfax Yankees, some not to return for the duration of the war, a few never again to set foot in the county, all eager to reach the safety of Union lines before the Confederates advanced.

29. Virgil C. Jones, *First Manassas: The Story of the Bull Run Campaign* (Gettysburg, Pa.: Historical Times, Inc., 1973), p. 2.

30. William H. Morgan, *Personal Reminiscences of the War, 1861-5* (Lynchburg, Va.: J.P. Bell Company, Inc., 1911), p. 51.

31. Nevins, *War for the Union*, 1:217; K. Williams, *Lincoln Finds a General*, 1:85-88.

32. Milliken, "Clarke," Historical Society *Yearbook* 8:17, 18-19.

VII

Turmoil, Occupation and a New Government

July 1861-May 1862

After their victory at Manassas, Confederates, for a variety of reasons, did not pursue the Union forces. By Monday morning heavy rains made any kind of movement impossible. For a few days, they remained along the Bull Run, occupying only Centreville, Fairfax Court House, and several other spots in the county. Then in early August, Beauregard moved his men forward. His advance posts even reached the heights of the Potomac, across the river from Washington (a position President Lincoln found more than disquieting). But when Beauregard suggested initiating a full-scale offensive against Union troops, the cautious Johnston, who had remained at Manassas and who outranked him, demurred. Beauregard countered with a proposal to move into Maryland, and in October, Jefferson Davis came to Fairfax Court House to discuss, and reject, the proposal.[1]

A few weeks later Johnston withdrew the entire army to a triangular-shaped line with its apex on the high grounds of Centreville, its sides running back to the Bull Run at Union Mills (near present-day Clifton) and at the Stone Bridge. It was along this line that the army, by then known officially as the Department of Northern Virginia, went into winter quarters.[2] Through the winter months, stories of the great strength of the Confederate fortifications circulated freely among Union troops, until eventually they came to believe that the Rebel defenses at Centreville were virtually impregnable.

---

1. T. Henry Williams, *P.G.T. Beauregard: Napoleon in Gray* (Baton Rouge: Louisiana State University Press, 1954), pp. 89-90, 99-101, 104 (hereinafter cited as Williams, *Beauregard*); K. Williams, *Lincoln Finds a General*, 1:122-24; *OR*, 1st ser., 2:98. For an account of Confederate action in an eastern portion of Fairfax, see John W. McDonald, "Skirmishes near Bailey's Cross Roads, Fairfax County, Virginia, August 25 to September 1, 1861," Historical Society *Yearbook* 2(1852-53):23-27.

2. Williams, *Beauregard*, pp. 101, 104.

Julia Ward Howe was visiting in Washington in the fall of 1861 when, after watching a review of Union troops at Upton's Hill (not to be confused with the Grand Review held on Munson's Hill, Baileys Crossroads, a few days later), she was inspired to write new words to the music of "John Brown's Body." The result was "The Battle Hymn of the Republic." Virginia State Library.

While the Confederates tried to decide what to do with their victorious troops, Union officers set about building an efficient fighting force from their beaten, demoralized men. As commander, there could have been no better choice than Major General George Brinton McClellan. Fresh from victories in western Virginia, the magnetic thirty-four-year-old West Pointer and Ohio railroad executive was a master organizer. He approved plans for a series of forty-eight forts to defend Washington against Confederate attack,[3] and, working systematically and efficiently, he created from his dispirited troops an army that believed in itself and passionately loved its commander.[4]

By mid-autumn, McClellan was eager to show off his army. On 20 November at Munson's Hill near Baileys Cross Roads, he staged a full-scale review of tens of thousands of Federal troops. The artist of *Harper's Weekly* sketched the scene and briefly described it. Moving "in most perfect order," troops, including seven divisions—seven regiments

3. Cooling, *Symbol, Sword, and Shield*, p. 66.
4. Charles Winslow Elliott, *Winfield Scott: The Soldier and the Man* (New York: Macmillan Company, 1937), p. 733. After the war when Robert E. Lee was asked to name the best Union general he had faced, he was said to have declared emphatically, "McClellan by all odds!" Warren W. Hassler, Jr., *General George B. McClellan: Shield of the Union* (Baton Rouge: Louisiana State University Press, 1957), p. 326.

Union General George Brinton McClellan who took command of demoralized Union troops after their defeat at the First Battle of Bull Run, was a superb organizer. In November 1861 he staged the largest review of troops yet to have taken place in the western hemisphere, at Baileys Cross Roads. Virginia State Library.

of cavalry, ninety regiments of infantry, and twenty batteries of artillery—came onto the field. The president and his cabinet arrived for the review. Philippe, Comte de Paris, aide-de-camp to General McClellan, later wrote that "No such spectacle had ever been seen in the United States; the novelty of the display caused the liveliest interest among the inhabitants of Washington. But to a European, not the least curious part of the pageant was the President, with his entire Cabinet, in citizens' dress, boldly caracoling at the head of a brilliant military *cortege*, and riding down the long lines of troops to the rattle of drums, the flourist of trumpets, and the loud huzzas of the whole army." The largest review of troops yet held on the North American continent, the display—wrote one of the men who was in it—"was grand and imposing in the extreme. The troops occupied nearly 200 acres of land."[5]

The presence of so large a fighting force meant that the need for supplies was immense, especially for rails, lumber, and timber. Forts, barracks, campfires, and railroads all required wood. In Fairfax and Alexandria counties, Federal troops felled whole hillsides of timber at a single cutting. A New York soldier described the process: "The choppers would begin at the foot of the hill, the line extending for perhaps a mile, and cut only part way through the tree, and in this way, work up to the crest, leaving the top row so that a single blow would bring down the trees; then, when all was ready, the bugle would sound as a signal, and the last stroke of the axe be given, which brought down the top row;

5. Philippe, Comte de Paris, "McClellan Organizing the Grand Army," in *Battles and Leaders of the Civil War*, ed. Robert Underwood Johnson and Clarence Clough Beel, 5 vols. (New York: Century Co., 1887), 2:118; *Harper's Weekly* 5(7 December 1861): 775-76, 779.

these falling on those below would bring them down, and like the billow on the surface of ocean, the forest would fall with a crash like mighty thunder."[6]

Foraging expeditions were the order of the day. Fairfax families watched helplessly as soldiers, sometimes acting on orders, sometimes simply plundering, carried off potatoes and cabbages, hogs and cattle, grain and hay, and even furniture and bedding. Sometimes they saw their barns and outbuildings dismantled and removed to become part of a barracks, a barricade, or a floor for a tent. Some were the subject of outright vandalism. One noncommissioned Union officer, for example, described in disgust the destruction of property belonging to the heirs of Thomas ap Catesby Jones: "The soldiers are playing shameful havoc with the property. The members of the family are rebels and have deserted the premises . . . . The house presents a complete scene of plunder and vandalism. Everything movable, even down to family portraits, has been carried away and what could not be taken away was destroyed."[7]

By late fall, all of McClellan's supplies were brought to him by train and wagon, for Confederate forces had succeeded in gaining control of the Potomac River, cutting off water travel to and from Washington. In actuality, the capital of the United States was the only city in either the North or the South that was then effectively blockaded, though Lincoln had issued a "paper" blockade of Southern ports on 21 April. None of the Confederate river batteries was located along the Potomac in Fairfax, however, as Confederate hold of the land north of the Occoquan was not sufficiently secure to permit the erection and protection of batteries.[8]

In other ways too, the presence of contending armies disrupted the lives of Fairfax citizens, large numbers of whom spent the remaining war years away from the county. By the summer of 1863, the *Gazette* reported that the "old residents of Alexandria" had mostly departed. "Not one-third of the original inhabitants now remain . . . . Many of the old mansions . . . have been deserted by their owners, and are now used as barracks or offices for the military authorities."[9] Undoubtedly the number of Fairfax residents also decreased. The wisdom of leaving the county became especially apparent when men suspected of Confederate sympathies were arrested and committed to prison. Of those who remained, most stayed at home as much as possible. As Frank Wooster, a Virginian "bred and born," put it: "It was troublesome times and men

6. Quoted in Cooling, *Symbol, Sword, and Shield*, p. 67. For a description of the loss of timber to Union forces, see testimonies in the various claims for damanges, Southern Claims Commission Papers, Fairfax County.

7. Jacob Heffelfinger, Diary, 10-11 October 1861, *Civil War Times Illustrated* Collection, United States Military History Research Collection, Carlisle Baracks, Pa. (hereinafter cited as *CWTI* Collection).

8. Mary Alice Wills, *The Confederate Blockade of Washington, D.C., 1861-1862* (Parsons, W. Va.:

9. *Gazette*, 10 August 1863. See also "Sunday in Camp," *New York Times*, 12 February 1862, p. 7.

Foraging parties were the order of the day in Fairfax during many phases of the war. A decade after the war was over, loyal Fairfax citizens whose personal property had been seized by Union troops acting on orders of Union officers were able to receive some compensation from the Federal government for the losses they had suffered. Their accounts of those losses are in the National Archives in Washington. Virginia State Library.

did not go about but very little . . . . Men who work for their living, earn their money, and get it and don't ask any questions, and that was my style of work."[10]

Numbers of Union sympathizers deserted the county. Some left because of Rebel threats at the time of secession; others remained until the Union defeat at Manassas, then fled to Alexandria and Washington, and often found work outside the county for the remainder of the war. After Bull Run, Lyman Broughton, for example, went to Washington and worked in the arsenal yard, then took charge of government stables, and was finally appointed watchman of the government lumberyard. A brother, who became a sutler in the Union army and was captured in 1862, was sent to Libby Prison in Richmond, almost died, and had not fully recovered by the early 1870s. Henry D. Biggs, a farmer and storekeeper who lived four miles from Vienna, voted against secession, and was threatened with arrest by Confederate sympathizers, left Fairfax and entered the huckstering business in Washington. Thomas T. Johnson, a neighbor of Biggs, left at the same time and served the Union army as a detective and scout. Josiah Bowman, the owner of Ayr Hill in Vienna, had a hundred acres in woodland when the war began, and only five when it ended. When the Rebels advanced, Bowman went to Washington and was on the role of Baker's detectives, later acted as a guide and scout for the Federal army, and when at home, stayed quiet, going out only to Hawxhurst's mill on Difficult Run for breadstuffs.[11]

Some of the more politically minded Fairfax Unionists joined the Unconditional Union Association of Alexandria, which met weekly. In September 1861 it numbered 150 men and was "constantly increasing," thanks partly to Unionists moving into the area. By October, it numbered over 300 men, and by November, over 400. On 24 October, it somehow managed to hold a highly irregular congressional election in Alexandria and perhaps in parts of Fairfax and Prince William counties. At that time, S. Ferguson Beach, a long-time resident of Alexandria and a leading attorney who practiced frequently in Fairfax and was to become a mainstay of the Pierpont government, was elected to the United States House of Representatives, though he was never granted his seat. In late fall, association members also began to think of holding local elections in Alexandria and perhaps in Fairfax.[12]

In the fall of 1861, Unionists also talked of getting up some kind of local military organization. Several who were receptive to the Restored

10. Claim of Wait Broughton, Southern Claims Commission Papers, Fairfax County. Also see Claim of William Ferris, ibid.

11. Claims of Lyman Broughton, Henry D. Biggs, Josiah B. Bowman, ibid.

12. See, e.g., James T. Close to Pierpont, 7 September 1861; J.C. Clayton to Pierpont, 25 September 1861, Pierpont Executive Papers; U.S. House of Representatives Committee of Elections, "S. Ferguson Beach: Report," No. 42, *Reports of Committees of the House of Representatives*, 37th Cong., 2nd sess. 1862.

government in Wheeling wrote to Pierpont, hoping to secure his assistance in establishing some form of protection against Confederate marauders. John Hawxhurst, his Quaker pacifism notwithstanding, was eager to see the formation of a home guard and wanted to be sure Pierpont would commission it.[13] There were others communicating with Pierpont as they attempted to form loyal military units. In Alexandria, Restored State Senator James T. Close was among several talking of organizing a home guard, a militia company, and an army brigade. For a time, however, all the efforts came to naught. Close antagonized too many people; there were petty jealousies among several of the others; and in one way or another, all the attempts went astray.[14] When the war was a year old, Fairfax had companies in several Confederate regiments, but not so much as a single company in the Federal army.[15] Union men in Fairfax, many of them Quaker pacifists, apparently had little desire to take up arms against their former neighbors.

While local Unionist leaders attempted to recruit men for the Federal army, Confederate troops shivered on the hills at Centreville and Federal soldiers struck up an all too intimate acquaintance with Virginia mud. "Such mud you have never seen," commented a Union soldier at Fairfax Station, while another writing in the winter of 1863 described the land as "one great quagmire." "Pilgrim's 'Slough of Despond,' " he wrote, "ain't a circumstance to the great slough which extends from Fairfax" to Stafford. The road along the way had been "strewn with mules and horses dead and dying, choking in the mud."[16]

For the troops on both sides in the winter of 1861-1862, the war was new and the sights were new. Though Federal troops expected an attack momentarily, there was little fighting—the principal event in Fairfax was a skirmish at Dranesville in December between Federal forces commanded by General Edward O. C. Ord and Southern forces led by a flamboyant young Virginia cavalryman, James Ewell Brown Stuart.[17]

Time hung heavy on the hands of the men in winter camp, and diary keeping became a major activity. A Confederate private, Randolph Harrison McKim, described camp life at Centreville that winter: His "mess" was composed of "a rare group of men to be serving as *private soldiers*." There were "a country gentleman of large means," "a lawyer

13. John Hawxhurst to Pierpont, 29 August 1861, Pierpont Executive Papers.
14. See letters from B.F. Wall, Stephen S. Shinn, James T. Close, J.C. Clayton, John C. Underwood, Henry C. Cooper, and James A. Hardie written in the fall of 1861, the winter of 1861-1862, and the fall of 1862 in the Pierpont Executive Papers.
15. Lee A. Wallace, Jr., comp., *A Guide to Virginia Military Organizations, 1861-1865* (Richmond: Virginia Civil War Commission, 1964), pp. 308, 312, 343, et passim.
16. Alexander Caldwell to his brother, 11 January 1863, Caldwell Family Letters, Xerox copy, *CWTI* Collection; Heffelfinger, Diary, 15 March 1862, *CWTI* Collection; Capt. James Gillette to mother, 29 January 1863, James Gillette Letters, Xerox copy, *CWTI* Collection.
17. John W. Thomason, *Jeb Stuart* (New York: Charles Scribner's Sons, 1930), pp. 124-28.

who left a good practice in Baltimore," "a highly educated Irish gentleman," "a graduate of Harvard," "a second-honor man at Princeton," "a master of several modern languages educated in a European university," and a "candidate for Holy Orders in the Episcopal Church." McKim, who had devoted himself "at the age of sixteen to the ministry of the Gospel," thought the conversation in their log hut "was of a very high order." Among other topics, they discussed international law, the work and travels of Humboldt, and "the influence of climate on . . . human features." They also passed the time in less exalting ways: in discussion of the latest rumors, in quarreling and fisticuffs, in reading (often aloud to each other), in visiting friends or relatives who lived nearby, in improving and cleaning their huts. Sometimes there were feminine visitors. One day, two "famous beauties" came to visit McKim, riding out to Fairfax Station on the cowcatcher of an engine. Religious services were commonplace and generally well attended. At the beginning of December, McKim instituted nightly "prayer meetings." Held at first in private tents, they were soon moved to a larger tent especially provided for the services. As winter approached, men on both sides did what they could to make their quarters warm. McKim remembered how they "suffered with the cold on that bleak hilltop . . . . Some of the men excavated the entire space under their tents to the depth of three or four feet, and so slept snug and warm, while the less energetic of the company were exposed to the keen, cold winds."[18]

While the armies shivered, their commanders laid plans for spring. Johnston decided that he would fall back behind the Rappahannock to keep Union troops from landing at Aquia Creek, from which point they could have reached Richmond before him. He waited until early March to withdraw, and Federal forces were not aware that he was contemplating the move until he had virtually completed it.[19]

The Union troops that marched out to occupy Manassas were shocked at the appearance of the countryside between Alexandria and Centreville. Jacob Heffelfinger, a Union officer, wrote that "nothing along our whole route appears to have been held sacred from the devastation of the war. At one place I saw traces of a camp in a graveyard, some of the tents having been pitched immediately over the graves. The blackened ruins of dwellings line the road. At one place I saw a dead horse in one of the rooms of a deserted dwelling house." As they passed through Centreville, Union troops were chagrined to find that much of the rumored impregnability of that Confederate stronghold was

18. Randolph Harrison McKim, *A Soldier's Recollections: Leaves from the Diary of a Young Confederate* (New York: Longmans, Green, and Co., 1910), pp. 49-61. For a description of similar activities in a Union camp, see letters and diaries in *CWTI* Collection, especially the diary of Jacob Heffelfinger.

19. Freeman, *Lee's Lieutenants*, 1:135-41.

Quaker guns. In the winter of 1861-1862 the principal Confederate fortifications in Northern Virginia were located on the heights of Centreville. Rumors of their impregnability were widespread among Union troops who were later chagrined to find that many of the guns they feared were mere logs. Virginia State Library.

a sham. In some of the forts were "Quaker guns," maple logs that the Rebels had painted to resemble cannon. One correspondent noted that "There were no platforms on which to work guns, nor any appearance of there having been any." Heffelfinger, however, was impressed with the winter huts of departed Rebels, all undisturbed, and thought them "much better than our winter quarters." When they reached Manassas, there was a gruesome rage to get mementoes of the battle of Bull Run. "The curiosity of some men," he wrote, "makes them forget they belong to the human species. Some have even brought teeth into camp which they extracted from the heads of bodies at Bull Run, not content to allow the dead bodies of friend or foe to rest in peace in their sad and shallow graves."[20]

McClellan, meanwhile, had been urging a roundabout attack on Richmond. Instead of a direct frontal assault on the Confederate lines still at Manassas, as Lincoln favored, he wanted to move his troops by water down the Potomac, landing at Urbanna near the mouth of the Rappahannock and thereby forcing the Confederates to move their forces away from Manassas. The issue was unresolved when McClellan fell ill in December, but finally, on 13 March 1862, a meeting of corps commanders at Fairfax Court House agreed on a water route to Richmond. They insisted, however, that the movement be made by way

20. K. Williams, *Lincoln Finds a General*, 1:153; Heffelfinger, Diary, 13 April 1862, *CWTI* Collection.

of the peninsula between the York and James rivers rather than by way of Urbanna. To quiet Lincoln's fears for the protection of Washington, McClellan agreed to leave behind a force large enough to give the citizens a feeling of complete security, some 33,000 to 40,000 men. But just at that point, "Stonewall" Jackson became so active in the Valley that Lincoln, frightened for the safety of the capital, detained McDowell's corps as well in front of Washington.[21]

In late March and early April, tens of thousands of McClellan's troops began to embark from Alexandria for the peninsula. Transports, steamers, and vessels loaded and left "hourly," and Unionists grew optimistic that the war, or at least Virginia's part in it, would soon be over. Lewis McKenzie, organizer and president of the Alexandria, Loudoun and Hampshire Railroad, and the most competent Unionist in Alexandria, wrote Pierpont that if McClellan were to succeed in taking Richmond, Virginians would perhaps decide they had "had enough of it" and be willing to let the Union exercise its authority. At the same time would-be Congressman Ferguson Beach thought there were waiverers in Fairfax who, as they began to see the "futility" of the Confederate cause, would cooperate with Unionists in organizing a local government "upon a respectable and sound basis."[22]

Meantime, Fairfax Union men, undoubtedly encouraged by their Alexandria compatriots, were becoming increasingly eager to reestablish civil law in the county. Daniel F. Dulany of Falls Church, a leading native Unionist, complained to Pierpont that "We are totally without civil law, and maurauders [sic] are daily destroying the country." On 22 March 1862, shortly after Johnston's withdrawal, a number of these men gathered at Fairfax Court House to see what could be done. At the meeting, they appointed a committee of three, including John Hawxhurst, to draw up a formal request that Pierpont reestablish civil government in the county.[23] Their appeal was successful. On 7 May, Pierpont, after a visit to Washington, where he apparently met with a number of local Unionists, issued a proclamation declaring Fairfax County offices vacant. The holders, he said, had failed to take a loyalty oath prescribed the previous June by the Wheeling Convention. On the

21. Cooling, *Symbol, Sword, and Shield*, pp. 112, 117.

22. Hurd, *Alexandria*, p. 19; S. Ferguson Beach to Pierpont, 27 March 1862; Lewis McKenzie to Pierpont, 29 March 1862, Pierpont Executive Papers. McKenzie wrote that about 65,000 infantry, cavalry, and artillery had left Alexandria for Old Point Comfort and that he expected another 35,000 would be got off in the next week. Despite his optimistic predictions concerning the establishment of a Union government, he admitted that he had never known Virginians to be so bitter, "the women and preachers especially."

23. Close to Pierpont, 19 March 1862; Dulany to Pierpont, 24 April 1862, Pierpont Executive Papers. Charles H. Upton, John Hawxhurst, H.W. Throckmorton to Pierpont, 29 March 1862, Pierpont Executive Papers.

Professor Lowe's balloon. Among the many technological advances in the Civil War was the use of balloons in order to map the countryside and determine the location of opposing troops. Professor Lowe makes a balloon ascension on a reconnoitering expedition to Vienna. Virginia State Library.

same day, he issued a writ of election for 22 May 1862, the regular election day. Job Hawxhurst, the brother of John, and Jonathan Roberts, both leading Fairfax Quakers who had migrated from the North in the 1840s, were named as election commissioners.[24]

Although the writ did not reach Alexandria until 14 May the election was held on schedule.[25] Only 260 men voted, most of them Yankee emigrants, but they managed to elect a full slate of officers.[26] For the first time in a year, Fairfax had a functioning government.

24. Francis H. Pierpoint [sic], Executive Journal, 22 June 1861-20 February 1865, p. 62, manuscript journal in Pierpont Executive Papers (hereinafter cited as Pierpont Executive Journal).

25. Roberts to Pierpont, 14 May 1862, Pierpont Executive Papers.

26. *Gazette*, 26 May 1862.

VIII

Difficult Days for Loyal Fairfax

May to December 1862

Just how much popular support the new government had is impossible to determine. It seems likely that it had the approval of most of the "emigrants" (as Fairfax Yankees called themselves) and of some native Unionists. Certainly many of the emigrants tried diligently to cooperate with native Unionists. Yet bitter feelings soon sprang up between Daniel F. Dulany, whom Pierpont named in June 1862 as his aide and as colonel of a nonexistent cavalry, and Jonathan Roberts, a transplanted Northern Quaker who was elected sheriff of the county at the May elections. Roberts was convinced that Dulany was no true Union man, a charge Dulany hotly denied and Pierpont eventually decided to ignore.[1]

As Fairfax held its election, McClellan, after two months on the peninsula, was finally drawing near to Richmond, convinced as usual that his force was "undoubtedly inferior to that of the rebels." In actuality, he probably had twice the effective strength of Johnston. As the two armies made ready to join battle, Union hopes were running so high that recruiting had been discontinued. Federal troops had recently blunted a Confederate advance at Shiloh in Tennessee and had captured New Orleans, the most important city in the Confederacy. Now they stood on the outskirts of the Confederate capital with the largest, the best equipped, and the best trained army the New World had ever seen.[2]

1. Jonathan Roberts to Pierpont, 24 June 1862; Daniel F. Dulany to Pierpont, 24 April, 19 July, 12 September 1862. Pierpont Executive Papers. For McKenzie's confidence in Dulany see McKenzie to Pierpont, 19 July, 16 September 1862, ibid.; *Gazette*, 26 May 1862. Dulany, a resident of Falls Church, was the brother of William H. Dulany, Fairfax delegate to the 1861 Virginia convention. Testimony of Daniel F. Dulany, Claim of Edwin C. Fitzhugh, Southern Claims Commission Papers, Fairfax County. For a breif description of Dulany, see Ball, "Reminiscences of an Old Rebel," p. 68. For Roberts's affiliations with the Quakers, see Alexandria Monthly Meeting Minutes, 1847 ff., passim.

2. Nevins, *War for the Union*, 2:62, 105-6; K. Williams, *Lincoln Finds a General*, 1:154-65.

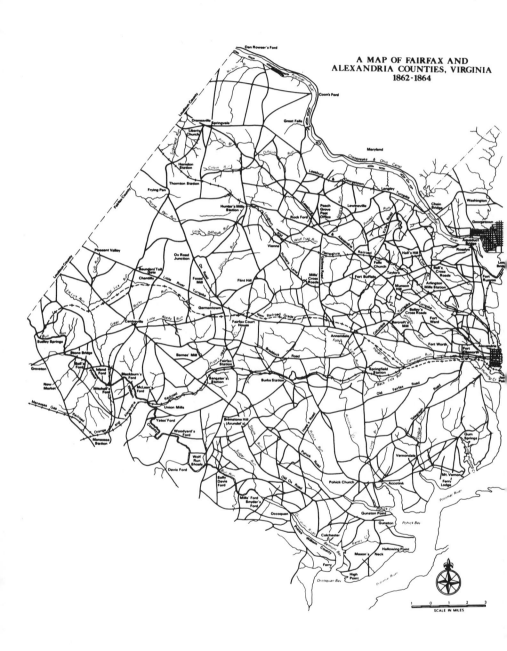

Map of Fairfax and Alexandria, 1862. From Gen. Irvin McDowell's map of northeastern Virginia at the Library of Congress. Redrawn by Sue Beatty, Fairfax County Division of Mapping.

Six weeks later that army stood defeated, its commander dis-
credited, its long and costly campaign a failure. Somehow McClellan had
gotten his forces divided astride the erratic Chickahominy just before
torrential rains brought it to flood stage, and the battle of Fair Oaks on
31 May, though indecisive, had brought Robert E. Lee to the command
of the Confederate army, a general far different in temperament from the
cautious Johnston and the slow-moving McClellan.[3] Lee was the epitome
of the Christian warrior. He loved the battlefield; he was daring and
aggresive; he attacked when less aggressive commanders would have
waited or withdrawn. In late June, several weeks after assuming
command, he called Jackson from the Valley and in the vicious Seven
Days' Battles which followed, he ended McClellan's peninsular
threat—but failed in his attempt to annihilate the Union army.

Meanwhile, life in Fairfax began to take on a semblance of normal
activity. In May 1862, postal service was resumed in parts of the county.
Two or three Fairfax fisheries carried on limited operations. Some
fugitive slaves, unable to find work, were said to be returning to their
masters; a number of citizens began to put in gardens (though very little
wheat was raised); a few farmers visited Alexandria to buy food and
clothing, "but only to a limited extent." The Alexandria market was
reported "well supplied" and prices were said to be reasonable. And
numerous citizens complained of the heat.

But signs of war were everywhere. Soldiers and strangers roamed
the streets of Alexandria; Negro "contrabands" flocked into Alexandria
and Washington; Unionist courts issued warrants for selling goods
without a license; and several Fairfax men suspected of entertaining
Confederate sympathies were arrested and confined in prison. Cattle
owners complained that their cows yielded little milk. In June, area
hospitals overflowed with men wounded in the battles around
Richmond, the Episcopal seminary became a hospital for about a
thousand Union convalescents, and Fairfax citizens received news of
friends and relatives killed and wounded in battle. The *Gazette* reported
that men could think and talk of nothing but war.[4]

As summer wore on, Lincoln, in dire need of Eastern victories,
brought Henry Halleck and John Pope in from the West, the first as
commander in chief of the Union armies, the latter as commander of the
newly created Army of Virginia. Pope promptly made himself both a
laughing stock and an ogre. He bragged to his troops about having seen
only the backs of his enemies in the West; and he won derisive jeers for

3. Lee became commander of the Army of Northern Virginia after Johnston was wounded at the
Battle of Seven Pines, just east of Richmond. Freeman, *R.E. Lee*, 2:72-74.

4. *Gazette*, 26, 29, 30 May, 2, 13, 16-18 June 18⨍⨼. Those arrested and confined to prison in June
included Joshua C. Gunnell, a former county magistrate; Joseph Bruin, the West End slave dealer; and
Dr. J.B. Day, considered by some the most ardent secessionist in the county. Ibid., 18 June 1861.

stating that his headquarters would be "in the saddle" (where, Confederates jocularly noted, they kept their hindquarters). Pope also issued a set of orders which sent his army to live on the countryside, cracked down harshly on Southern sympathizers, and held the citizens of the Shenandoah Valley and Northern Virginia responsible for Confederate guerrilla activities in those areas. Wisdom, it appeared, was not one of Pope's principal attributes.

During the summer of 1862, efforts were once again afoot in Alexandria and Fairfax to raise a regiment of loyal eastern Virginians. The attempt began inauspiciously and ended in disgrace. It got under way in June when Pierpont asked Dulany, McKenzie, and apparently Close, to see what they could do to raise a company or two each in Fairfax and Alexandria. The responses were not encouraging. Dulany wrote that "Unfortunately we have very few fighting men [left]—most of our population having [already] taken up arms," and Close declared that "after several days investigation in regard to obtaining volunteers," he had concluded "there is but very little Patriotism in the counties of Alexandria and Fairfax."[5]

Close broached the subject of a home guard. After all, he argued, in a strange burst of enthusiasm for state rights, "Virginia forts should be guarded by Virginia men." Pierpont suggested that he carry the idea to Lincoln's Secretary of War, "stating to him that it would be a source of much pleasure to our loyal men to know that Virginia cities and Virginia forts could be guarded and defended by Virginia men." Close called on the Secretary and either obtained his approval or thought he had obtained it. And somehow he obtained from somebody, apparently Pierpont, an appointment as colonel of the regiment.[6]

The appointment outraged most Unionists, at least those of the native variety. In a hot letter to Pierpont, McKenzie declared that it was "a most unfortunately Injudicious selection . . . . This Man Close is perhaps the most unpopular man in Alexandria and acts in such a Manner as disgusts our People with the Union cause. Neither by Education or Manners is he fit to command a Company let alone a Regiment. And yet he has Industry and a large share of assurance." McKenzie urged Pierpont to give Dulany—whose course he thought was "generally approved in Fairfax"—authority to raise a company in the county.[7]

As Close began to make some progress in enlistments, military activities in Northern Virginia picked up. Federal authorities suddenly realized that Lee and Jackson had turned north from Richmond and were

5. Dulany to Pierpont, 10 August 1862; Close to Pierpont, 14 July 1862, Pierpont Executive Papers.

6. Close to Pierpont, 8 August 1862; McKenzie to Pierpont, 16 August 1862, Pierpont Executive Papers.

7. McKenzie to Pierpont, 16 August 1862, ibid.

Clara Barton, founder of the American Red Cross, was a maiden government clerk when, after the Second Battle of Bull Run, she cared for wounded Union soldiers at Fairfax Station. Virginia State Library.

threatening to cross the Rappahannock. They must make an all-out attempt to reinforce Pope. Most of McClellan's forces, enroute from the peninsula, began landing at Aquia Creek, though one corps disembarked at Alexandria and was sent by rail to the Rappahannock.[8]

But Union forces moved too slowly. By 27 August, Jackson had flanked Pope's army, crossed the Rappahannock, gotten in behind him at Manassas, and put his troops across the Orange and Alexandria Railroad to the north of the town. The Confederates were just thirty miles from Washington.

In the Union capital, no one knew what had happened. They knew only that the telegraph had gone dead, and that there was no word from Pope. McClellan left Aquia and went to Alexandria to give advice to Halleck, who sent McClellan's army to Pope. Just who was in command of what was not clear to anyone.[9] And so it was that on the last days of August 1862, a year and a month after First Manassas, Confederate troops won another resounding victory on the banks of Bull Run.[10]

8. Ibid.

9. Williams, *Lincoln and His Generals*, p. 156.

10. Freeman, *Lee's Lieutenants*, 2:120-30, 135-43.

The only major battle to occur on Fairfax soil in the war took place at Ox Hill, or Chantilly, on the heels of the Second Battle of Bull Run. Though Union General John Pope managed to deflect Lee's advance on Washington, Union control of Fairfax was in disarray for months after the fall 1862 campaign. Union Generals Isaac I. Stephens and Philip Kearny were killed during the battle. The above illustration is titled, "The Death of General Stephens." Virginia Historical Society.

Union casualties ran into the thousands. Hundreds upon hundreds of the wounded men were taken to Fairfax Station, where they lay on a hillside under the trees awaiting transportation to hospitals in Fairfax, Alexandria, and Washington. Among those who nursed them was a forty-year-old maiden government clerk. Although Clara Barton had no official connection with the army, she ministered as best she could to the thousands of sick and wounded men lying on beds of scattered hay while "hundreds of wagons" continued to bring the wounded in "from the field still held by the enemy."[11]

Despite their heavy losses, Federal troops made an orderly retreat. The next day, 1 September, when Confederates sought to cut off Pope's forces near Chantilly and move closer to Washington, the result was a stalemate. Though two Union generals, Philip Kearny and Isaac Stevens, were left dead on the field, Pope was able to save his army from destruction and was also able to prevent a Confederate movement toward Washington. It was the only major battle of the war fought on Fairfax soil.[12]

As the exhausted Union forces retreated slowly toward Alexandria, rain began to fall "in torrents," just as it had after First Bull Run. One

11. Percy H. Epler, The Life of Clara Barton (New York: Macmillan Company, 1915), p. 42, quoting Clara Barton, n.d. Also see pp. 36-47.
12. See Freeman, Lee's Lieutenants, 2:130-35 for an excellent account of the battle.

soldier described the "tiresome and tedious" retreat: "Sometimes we marched about ten or fifteen steps . . . . When the word came 'Halt!' we dropped down, and when we were hardly down came the words, 'Forward, March!' the dropping down and getting up, two hundred times or . . . oftener, was tiresome beyond description."[13]

As Federal troops withdrew to the fortifications in front of Alexandria, nearly all of Fairfax County was left outside Federal lines, and Union men who lived in western and northern Fairfax were compelled "to escape for their lives." Many went to Washington; some were caught by the Rebels and imprisoned in Richmond. In most cases, however, their families remained at home and found themselves behind Confederate lines. One Fairfax Unionist declared that Northern families had "been robbed of nearly everything on earth, so that they are all in absolute want and as things now are, no relief can be sent to them, and they have no means of coming away."[14] To make matters worse, there were rumors that Rebels in Fairfax and Prince William had begun to organize guerrilla bands.

Meanwhile, halted at Ox Hill near Chantilly, Lee had moved north across the Potomac and into Maryland. While the two armies met at Antietam in mid-September in the bloodiest battle of the war, Fairfax Unionists intensified their efforts to establish a home guard. Eventually, several local units were established, all of them, apparently, in areas where the Northern population was heaviest. Reuben Ives, a farmer at Falls Church who had voted against secession, was captain of the guard at that village. Robert Pettit commanded the Home Guard at Accotink, composed primarily of black men (according to the Alexandria *Gazette*). Alexander Haight was captain of a company in western Fairfax.[15]

But attempts to raise a regular army unit of eastern Virginians continued to flounder. Close was accused of "imbecility" and corruption, and one of his second lieutenants—who was said to reside at "a most infamous House of Prostitution kept by a colored prostitute on Henry

13. Henry Gerrish, Memoirs, 1909, n.p., Xerox copy, *CWTI* Collection.
14. Joseph Stiles to Pierpont, 16 September 1862; Andrew Wylie to Pierpont, 16 September 1862, Pierpont Executive Papers. The Union army encamped a half-mile east of Falls Church "and from there all the way to Arlington." Claim of Reuben Ives, 2 May 1871, Southern Claims Commission Papers, Fairfax County. For one description of Union forces commandeering civilian supplies, see testimony of General O.O. Howard, who commanded a portion of Pope's rear guard, part of which fell back through Fairfax to the Washington side of the Episcopal seminary. "There was much disorder in the army," said Howard. "The necessities of the army frequently required the pressing of wagons . . . . We had to pick up vehicles of all kind to carry the sick & wounded." Claim of James O.C. Haskins, Southern Claims Commission Papers, Fairfax County. Also see Claims of Reuben Ives and Betsy Johnson, ibid., for a graphic description of Union troops carrying off civilians' food, clothing, bedding, blankets, and furniture at the time of the retreat. For an excellent account of the experiences of a Northern family in western Fairfax during the war, see Gamble, *Sully*, pp. 91-114.
15. Wylie to Pierpont, 16 September 1862, Pierpont Executive Papers; Claim of Reuben Ives, 2 May 1871, Southern Claims Commission Papers, Fairfax County. For interest in establishing a home guard, see James T. Close to Pierpont, 31 March 1862; McKenzie to Pierpont, 12 May, 19 July 1862, Pierpont Executive Papers.

Street" in Alexandria—"was dragged through the streets by the Provost guard between two negro prostitutes, with his knuckles bleeding, and his pantaloons down, to the Provost Marshall's Office." Yet somehow he remained in the regiment.[16]

The Sixteenth Virginia Volunteers was preeminently a regiment of "Skedadlers," declared one of Pierpont's correspondents; then added, "No that ain't the right name either, they were deserters, and I honestly believe and know that three fourths of the men and one third of the officers were of that class . . . instead of the regiment being made of eastern Virginians they were eastern deserters & scoundrels . . . . And as you know it is hard to make an Eagle out of an oyster." The army apparently agreed that making eagles of the Sixteenth Virginia Volunteers was a hopeless task. In June 1863, the unit was mustered out of service, to the relief to everyone.[17]

It was little wonder that efforts to enlist Northern Virginia Unionists in the fall of 1862 had met with so little success, for Union armies after their losses before Richmond and at Second Manassas and the stalemate at Antietam were so thoroughly demoralized that many were ready to desert. J. H. Atkinson, a western Virginian who had gone to Washington after Second Manassas at Pierpont's request, reported on 10 September that the First Virginia Infantry was "nearly used up and could not send into a fight much over 100 men and these tired, worn out, and dispirited." Though Atkinson "had but little experience in military affairs," he had "enough to know that our armies were very much demoralized by the manner in which our Generals headed them for the last month. The city is full of stragglers from the army who have lost their regiments and it seems as though no one knows where they can find them. The Provost Marshall says a regiment is one place, at Head Quarters they tell you it is at another and in half the cases the enquirer finds that neither knew anything about it."[18]

Another visitor from northwestern Virginia, whose son was in the Fourth Brigade, First Virginia Infantry, had spent "10 days eating & sleeping with the men." On 14 September he wrote:

> The 4th Brigade now numbers about 1000 worn, haggard men, without energy, and most wofully demoralized. Since the departure of Maj Duval they have no respect for any officer left. Genl carrol never comes into camp sober, & then only to give peremptory marching orders to some point within our lines opposite the city, every order evidently aimless and foolish. Last Saturday week they were hurriedly

16. H.B. Davis to Pierpont, 7 October 1862, Pierpont Executive Papers.
17. [Anon.] to Pierpont, 12 June 1863 (fragment), Pierpont Executive Papers.
18. J.H. Atkinson to Pierpont, 10 September 1862, Pierpont Executive Papers.

ordered to a point above Georgetown by way of Uptons Hill, and were scarcely encamped until they were ordered back to Alexandria within ½ mile of where they were before, they encamped about a half a day and were again ordered to march to the heights near Georgetown where they now are. By this process our men are wore down until all energy & hope are gone. I have heard men say they will never fight again until they have had time to rest. I have seen men throw away their guns on march. I have heard them bitterly curse the officers in loud tones, I have heard them swear that in the next fight they will not stand fire, that they will run, or throw down their guns . . . . Sir, they are no longer a regiment to be relied upon. a Spirit of recklessness, and almost hopelessness has seized them, and woe to the man who leads them to battle in their present condition, discomfiture & lasting disgrace awaits him and them . . . . During the first march from alexandria to georgetown there was scarcely a line officer in the brigade. Corporals commanded companies, sargents led regiments, The general & his staff were absent, and all went recklessly along within one mile of the rebels at Uptons Hill, outside of our own lines.[19]

Conditions in the Union hospitals were also deplorable. The heavy casualties of the summer campaigns had strained the medical facilities on both sides. From Camp Convalescent at the Episcopal seminary, one northwestern Virginia soldier wrote Pierpont in December that he and several other Virginia boys had been "Put in tents with out fire or Blankets and we have to pack our Wood a mile and two Boys frose to Death and three more Died By Being Chiled."[20]

The demoralization of the Federal military made it impossible for Fairfax Unionists to retain control of the county. Despite the draws at Chantilly and Antietam, the disaster at Bull Run and Pope's subsequent retreat had thoroughly disrupted civil government in Fairfax. In March 1863, Fairfax clerk of the court Henry T. Brooks wrote that on the day prescribed by law, 31 December 1862, four months after the retreat, it had been "impossible . . . to make a certified return of the number of acting Justices in our County—Pope's defeat having so deranged everything with us that no Court had been held since the August Term."[21] Pope's retreat also disrupted commerce for the remainder of 1862. William Bushby, the flour inspector in Alexandria, wrote to Pierpont on 24 December that since the August retreat he had "not inspected but 14

19. John J. Johnson to Pierpont, 14 September 1862, Pierpont Executive Papers.

20. William H. Blankenship to Pierpont, 7 December 1862, Pierpont Executive Papers.

21. In the six magisterial districts of the county, there were, reported Brooks, a total of fourteen acting justices (one of whom was a prisoner in Richmond) and ten vacancies. Brooks to Pierpont, 17 March 1862, Pierpont Executive Papers.

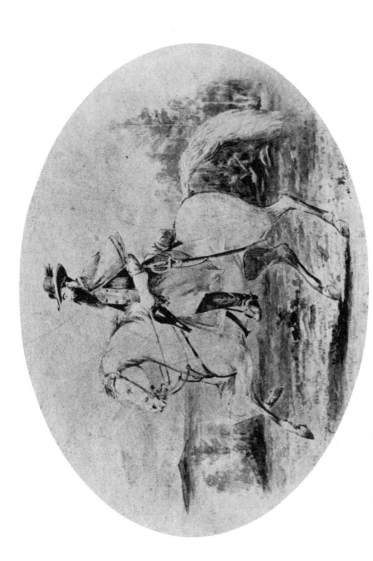

Confederate Major General James Ewell Stuart was just twenty-nine years old when he made his famous raid into Fairfax County in December 1862. With a handful of Confederate cavalry, he captured supply wagons, cut telegraph lines, tore up rail tracks, and took two hundred prisoners. At Burke the intrepid Stuart sent off a wire to Union Quartermaster General Meigs complaining of the quality of his newly acquired Union mules. Virginia State Library.

Bbs" of flour. On Christmas Day 1862, it seemed that matters for Fairfax Unionists were just about as bad as they could get. They did not know that J.E.B. Stuart and John Singleton Mosby were still to come on stage.

More than ever Fairfax at the end of 1862 was a no-man's-land in which Union and Confederate troops and sympathizers struggled sporadically and violently for control. Though the Army of the Potomac was in full operation, though Federal troops operated beyond Fairfax throughout the fall (primarily in Maryland and along the Rappahannock), and though Federal cavalry outposts held a line from the town of Occoquan through Manassas Junction, Centreville, Chantilly, and Frying Pan Church to Dranesville, Confederates made one of their more daring penetrations into Fairfax in the last days of 1862.[22]

On 26 December, twenty-nine-year-old Major General James Ewell Brown Stuart crossed the Rappahannock and headed toward the Occoquan with 1,800 men and four guns. Two days later he was in Fairfax County. He got as close to Washington as Burke Station on the Orange and Alexandria Railroad, capturing supply wagons, cutting telegraph wires, tearing up railroads, and capturing 200 prisoners. He himself suffered only 28 casualties, including one death. At Burke he sent off an impertinent telegram to the United States quartermaster general that was to become famous. The Union mules he had captured, complained Stuart, were of such poor quality that they could scarcely pull his newly acquired Union wagons.[23]

Stuart spent three days inside Union lines before moving out of the county by way of Vienna and Frying Pan Church to rejoin the Army of Northern Virginia at Fredericksburg.[24] His effrontery and his wit delighted Fairfax Rebels. Northern abolitionists might insist that Southern slaveholders were wicked sinners, but Stuart had shown that those virtuous Yankees were surely incompetent fools.[25]

22. John W. McDonald, "Stuart's Burke Station Raid: 26-31 December 1862," Historical Society Yearbook 4(1955):67.

23. Ibid., p. 70; Freeman, Lee's Lieutenants, 2:399-407; Freeman, R.E. Lee, 2:475-78.

24. Freeman, Lee's Lieutenants, 2:405 and note.

25. The Gazette, 27 December 1862, for example, has a delightful story of a Stuart squad's capture of a Union train "by diplomacy rather than the exercise of force" because of the presence of 1,500 Union troops.

IX

Yankee Reformers and Mosby Rangers

1863

By December 1862 it appeared to Fairfax Unionists that matters had settled down enough to hold court. On 1 December presiding justice Thomas P. Brown asked Pierpont to order the court to meet near the Episcopal seminary or at West End. The justices had not held court in recent months, he said, because of the advance of Confederate troops, the occupation of the courthouse by Federal forces, and the "delapidated condition" of the building. At the same time, Brown told Pierpont that the court was moving county records to Alexandria for safekeeping because it appeared likely that Federal forces would evacuate Fairfax Court House.[1]

Three days later on 4 December, Pierpont authorized the Fairfax justices to meet in the village of West End, as it was hazardous to hold court in the courthouse "on account of the proximity of the public enemy."[2] In other words, by the end of 1862, Union control of Fairfax was so tenuous and "Secesh" guerilla activities were so threatening that the Unionist court felt safe only if it met in the shadow of Alexandria and under the protection of Federal troops.[3]

On 1 January 1863, before the court was able to gather, Lincoln's Emancipation Proclamation became effective. Although it applied only to states and areas still in rebellion and although West Virginia, the

1. Brown to Pierpont, 1 December 1862, Pierpont Executive Papers.
2. Francis H. Pierpont, Proclamation of 4 December 1862, Pierpont Executive Journal; Francis H. Pierpoint [sic], Record Book of Proclamations and Messages, 1861-1863, p. 108, Pierpont Executive Papers; Fairfax County Court Minute Book, 19 January 1863, p. 108.
3. Eckenrode, Virginia During Reconstruction, p. 14. Eckenrode maintained that the "Pierpont administration at Alexandria existed only·in the shadow of the Federal armies and would have been summarily expelled by the people but for them. It . . . must not be thought that the Alexandria government was based upon the consent and approval of the governed." A reading of the Pierpont Executive Papers shows that Eckenrode's assessment was only too accurate.

Eastern Shore, and counties in the Hampton Roads area were excluded from its provisions, Fairfax and Alexandria were not exempted.[4] Among fugitive slaves in the Washington area, the proclamation brought a wave of rejoicing. Though some of the runaway slaves in the crowded contraband camps in Washington and Alexandria were suffering a smallpox epidemic, many of them, reported the *Gazette*, "are holding meetings, and having a fine time generally, over the Proclamation. Singing, praying, shouting, speeches &c., are the 'order of the day.' "[5]

On 19 January 1863, less than three weeks after presidential emancipation, the Fairfax court convened for the first time in almost five months. It met at West End in a house known as Bruin's Building, a site that must have been especially pleasing to the antislavery court, for Bruin had for years been one of the largest slave traders in Fairfax County, and it was here that he had bought and sold hundreds of slaves.[6]

A week later, there was a special election for the United States House of Representatives in the Seventh Congressional District. Originally ordered for 31 December it had been postponed, perhaps because of Stuart's raid.[7] Though there were ten counties in the district, precincts apparently were open only in Alexandria and Fairfax. Voting seems to have been by ballot rather than *viva voce*. All told, 554 votes were cast (327 in Alexandria, 227 in Fairfax) for five candidates and Lewis McKenzie emerged triumphant with a plurality of just twelve votes. The election was in vain, however, for Congress refused to seat the Virginia Republican, maintaining that the election procedures had been irregular, that only two of the nine counties in the congressional district had held elections, and that in view of the few votes cast, no valid election had taken place.[8]

In 1863 with the courts again in operation, some individuals were engaging in business more or less as usual. A petition to the Unionist court was, of course, a recognition of its authority; it was made by some willingly and gladly, by some with great reluctance, and by some not at all.[9] Elizabeth Catts, "sober" and "responsible," received a license to operate an ordinary. Joseph T. Janney was authorized to establish a ferry at Occoquan. George Tucker, a newcomer from Vermont who was to become a major figure in the reconstruction government, secured the

4. The text of the proclamation was carried in the *Gazette*, 3 January 1863.
5. *Gazette*, 3, 14, 17 January 1863.
6. Fairfax County Court Minute Book, 19 January 1863.
7. Pierpont Executive Journal, 4 December 1862.
8. Jefferson Tacey, clerk, "A Statement of the result of the Special Election," 28 January 1863 (Pierpont Executive Papers), gave the official report of the election. For the official vote and the rationale for refusing to seat McKenzie, see U.S. House of Representatives, Committee of Elections, "Lewis McKenzie: Report," Report No. 33, *Reports of Committees of the House of Representatives*, 37th Con., 3rd sess., 1863, p. 1.
9. For the feelings of individuals who, despite their opposition to secession, considered the Pierpont government illegal, see John Muir to Pierpont, 8 March 1863, Pierpont Executive Papers.

court's permission to practice law, and was named commonwealth's attorney.[10]

There were numerous indictments for doing business without a license, a move that was essentially antisecessionist and pro-Pierpont.[11] To secure a license, the applicant was required to take an oath of loyalty to the Pierpont government, an act that was anathema to citizens still loyal to Confederate Virginia.[12] As Fairfax Union men sought to wrest political control of the county from the Rebels, indictments for doing business without a license were a handy means of cracking down on the "Secesh."[13]

An even harsher means of intimidating Rebels and bringing them to financial ruin was by confiscating their property. So far as is known, there has been no adequate study of attempts to confiscate Confederate property during and after the war, and until such a study is made, it is impossible to know just what occurred in this respect. Nevertheless, it is clear from the minute books that the Fairfax court did confiscate a great deal of property. Undoubtedly the magistrates were encouraged to do so by John C. Underwood, perhaps the most important Republican in eastern Virginia, who as fifth auditor of the United States Treasury was doing his utmost to make the Civil War a thorough-going social and economic revolution.[14]

Though Underwood's support of confiscation won him the deep and bitter hatred of Virginia Confederates, his motives were high-minded enough. In December 1862, he wrote Pierpont: "I am doing all I can in this Treasury Department to bring the old plantations of the rebel & emigrant refugees in the East to sale for taxes hoping that they will thereby soon pass into the hands of loyal liberty loving & labor honoring men & that in this way the east may be prepared to enter on a race of competition with the West for the blessings of education, moral mental & physical, resulting in an improved condition of arts manufactures agriculture & all the comforts & refinements of the highest civilization."[15] In other words, Virginia was to be remade in the image of the antebellum North.

With Fairfax again in Union hands, its position as part of a state comprised chiefly of counties in northwestern Virginia was drawing to a

---

10. Fairfax County Court Minute Book, May-July 1863.

11. Ibid., January 1863 ff.

12. For the text of the oath, see box of oaths in Pierpont Executive Papers.

13. Jonathan Roberts to Pierpont, 1 June 1862; Oath of E.H. Delahay, 6 June 1862, Pierpont Executive Papers. For opposition to some of the arrests, see McKenzie to Pierpont, 19 July 1862, ibid.

14. See Patricia Hickin, "John Curtis Underwood and the Antislavery Crusade, 1809-1860," *Virginia Magazine of History and Biography* 63(April 1865):156-68, for information concerning Underwood's egalitarian ideals.

15. Underwood to Pierpont, 19 December 1862, Pierpont Executive Papers.

close. Sentiment for the permanent division of Virginia into two separate states had become vociferous enough to win consent of the Lincoln government and of Congress. Though the inconsistency of refusing to permit the secession of Southern states from the Union and of allowing the secession of northwestern counties from the Old Dominion was troubling to many, Congress finally agreed to make a separate state of West Virginia.[16] It was to enter the Union on 20 June 1863. The question of whether Pierpont would remain in West Virginia and attempt to win office in the new state or whether he would move his small government to eastern Virginia now had to be resolved, and in Alexandria and Fairfax, Unionists for a time did not know what was to happen to their state government.[17]

Pierpont, a fair, kind, conscientious man with a deep concern for the welfare of the people he governed, was at that time deservedly popular with Unionists in eastern Virginia. By early May, he had decided to remain with the Restored Virginia government, and on 12 May 1863, a Unionist convention in Alexandria unanimously endorsed him for governor. Presided over by Job Hawxhurst, the convention reflected the egalitarian ideals and the radical tendencies of the delegates. It adopted four resolutions as a "basis of principles": the first approved the Emancipation Proclamation and the abolition of slavery as an efficient aid in suppressing rebellion; the second called for arming the blacks for service to the United States as a "proper, wise, and just measure"; the third approved the Conscription Act; and the fourth directed the Unionist congressional candidate to use his influence, if elected, to support the first three measures in Congress.[18]

Elections were held on 28 May 1863. Pierpont was elected to a four-year term as governor, James T. Close was chosen as state senator in the district composed of Alexandria and Fairfax, and there was a referendum on whether the two counties should become part of West Virginia. In Fairfax, the proposal carried by a vote of 155 to 30,[19] but the

16. James G. Randall, *Lincoln the President*, vol. 2: *Springfield to Gettysburg* (New York: Dodd, Mead & Company, 1945), p. 13 and note; Close to Pierpont, 20 August 1861, Pierpont Executive Papers. See *Debates and Proceedings of the First Constitutional Convention of West Virginia (1861-1863)*, ed. Charles H. Ambler et al., 3 vols. (Huntington, W. Va.: Gentry Brothers, Printers, n.d.), 1:547-57; 3:409-15.

17. W. J. Cowing to Pierpont, 12 March 1863, Pierpont Executive Papers. On 10 December 1862, State Senator Close had introduced into the Assembly at Wheeling a resolution to move the capital of "Restored" Virginia to Alexandria after West Virginia's statehood became effective. The Senate had adopted the resolution on 17 January 1863. *Journal of the Senate of the ["Restored"] Commonwealth of Virginia, Extra Session, 1862-1863* (Wheeling, W. Va.: A.S. Trowbridge, State Printer, 1862), pp. 27, 29, 58, 62, 66, 70.

18. Ambler, *Pierpont*, p. 13; *Gazette*, 12-14 May 1863.

19. Pierpont Executive Journal, 1 January 1864; Jefferson Tacey, clerk, Statement of election results, 14 July 1863, Pierpont Executive Papers; *Gazette*, 29, 30 May 1863. Hawxhurst was apparently reelected to the House of Delegates. See *JHD*(R), 1863-64, p. 32; [Certificate of election], 1 June 1863, signed by Daniel W. Lewis, Henry Studds, and Robert F. Roberts, commissioners, Pierpont Executive Papers. The West Virginia constitutional convention had already rejected the admission of Fairfax and several other

small turnout reflected no consensus on the question, and the matter was eventually allowed to drop.

Magisterial elections also were held on 28 May to fill ten vacancies on the Fairfax County court. Clerk of the court Henry T. Brooks was quite encouraged by the results of the election. He wrote Pierpont, "We are doing our best to unite & consolidate the elements of loyalty of every character & I think we are making great progress. Our vote in this county has increased at this election 100% beyond our best heretofore & I think in a year from now we can increase it by 200% more." Brooks, an emigrant, was also happy to report the seating of George F. M. Walters, a "native unionist." Like many other Unionists, Brooks saw the war as a great moral mission: "We have a fearful struggle before us. Our Horeb hath prizes worthy the ambition of the giants of any age—worthy the efforts of the best of men—shall we reach the Goal? Let pertinacity, faith and duty answer." [20]

Though an influx of Yankee "carpetbaggers" following on the heels of Union troops was a constant vexation to many areas of the conquered South, the problem seems to have been somewhat less severe in Fairfax.[21] Northerners had been residents of the county for a decade or more, and most had been careful to build up a large reservoir of good will. Virtually all of the acting justices in 1863 were "emigrants" who had been in the county for a number of years, were familiar with local problems, and had been and often still were on at least fairly friendly terms with the natives, despite the hostilities that had emerged over the secession crisis.

Nevertheless, there were problems in the county, especially concerning Pierpont's military aide, Colonel Daniel F. Dulany, who was not considered loyal by some of the more radical Unionists. In early May, in fact, several of them had threatened to dump Pierpont as their gubernatorial candidate if he did not dismiss Dulany.[22] But Pierpont apparently managed to smooth over the disagreement for Dulany remained his aide throughout the remainder of the war.[23]

In August, after visiting several cities in eastern Virginia, Pierpont announced that the capital of what was left of Restored Virginia would be at Alexandria.[24] Though the area he was to govern was much diminished

counties in eastern Virginia to the new state, once on 13 December 1861, and again on 11 February 1862. *Debates and Proceedings,* 1:557; 2:415.

20. Henry T. Brooks to Pierpont, [1863], Pierpont Executive Papers.

21. See McKenzie to Pierpont, 23 August 1862, 29 June 1863, Pierpont Executive Papers.

22. D. Spaulding to Pierpont, 13 May 1863, Pierpont Executive Papers.

23. Though Dulany's loyalty to the Union seems to have been sincere, he had close ties to Fairfax natives who were secessionists. His own son, in fact, became an enthusiastic Mosby man and was killed while serving under Mosby. *Gazette,* 30 January 1864. On one occasion, the younger Dulany captured his father.

24. *Gazette,* 7, 8, 22, 29 August 1863.

after West Virginia won her statehood, Pierpont's problems did not abate with the move to Alexandria. As the months passed, Pierpont, in fact, barely managed to hold on to his office. At times it seemed that his jurisdiction encompassed no more than Alexandria city and county. On the Eastern Shore and in the Hampton Roads area, the Union army wielded the real power. And in neighboring Fairfax, though the Unionist court met regularly for the remainder of the war years, it did not again hold sessions at Fairfax Court House.[25]

The reason was simple enough. It could be summarized in one word: Mosby.

The very name was enough to strike terror into the hearts of Union soldiers. Mosby was everywhere. Mosby destroyed railroad tracks. Mosby robbed sutlers and paymasters. Mosby captured pickets and shot down stragglers. Mosby, with a price on his head, crossed Long Bridge to Washington in the full light of day, hobnobbed with Union officers at the bar of a crowded hotel, slept in bed next to one of them, and returned unharmed to Virginia. Mosby stopped ladies on their way to Washington and sent a lock of his hair to President Lincoln. Mosby captured Union generals in their beds at two in the morning. Mosby was everywhere.[26]

Everywhere and nowhere. Certainly nowhere that Union search parties could find him. He was not to be found in Loudoun County when Sheridan sent a search party of almost five thousand men with torches and—license to destroy—over the Blue Ridge in November 1864. Mosby turned and disappeared into the mountains when a party sent by Meade during the Gettysburg campaign ambushed him in the eastern foothills of the Blue Ridge. And on one occasion late in the war, after Union soldiers had wounded him, Mosby tricked a liquor-befuddled Union major into thinking him a dying Rebel lieutenant and so was left, "presumably to rest in peace," at a Loudoun County farmhouse.[27]

Fact mingled with fiction, but there was too much fact in the legends to suit the Union. Mosby, who had grown up in the shadow of the central Blue Ridge, attended the University of Virginia, and practiced law in Southwest Virginia, had signed up for Confederate service shortly after the firing on Fort Sumter. By summer 1861, he was part of Jeb Stuart's

25. Fairfax County Court, Minute Books, 1863-1865.

26. For these and other rumors that circulated among Union troops, see Joseph Schubert, "How I was Captured and My life in different Rebel Prisons [and] Penns," unpublished MS, n.d., CWTI Collection. Schubert wrote that Mosby had told him that he had recently been in Washington in disguise as a Union officer and had had a drink with a Union officer at a Washington hotel. Later Schubert heard of Mosby's sleeping in a bed with a Union officer and, next morning, leaving a note telling the officer that he had had "the pleasure of sleeping with Col. John S. Mosby." See also Mosby, The Memoirs of Colonel John S. Mosby, ed. Charles Wells Russell (Boston: Little, Brown, and Company, 1917), pp. ix-xiii. For contemporary items in relation to Mosby's activities, especially in Fairfax, see Gazette, 9-18 March, 7 August-3 September 1863, 3 November 1863-30 January 1864, 5-30 August 1864, 28 January-22 March 1865. passim.

27. Virgil Carrington Jones, Ranger Mosby (Chapel Hill: University of North Carolina Press, 1944), pp. 141-42, 233-41, 247-50 (hereinafter cited as Jones, Ranger Mosby).

John Singleton Mosby, an obscure lawyer in Southwest Virginia at the outbreak of the war, became one of the most lasting of the war-time heroes. A number of his more celebrated exploits took place in Fairfax County. Mathew Brady photo. Virginia State Library.

cavalry; by the following spring he had been promoted to first
lieutenant; and in June 1862, during the peninsular campaign, he had
suggested to Stuart the ride around McClellan's army which has been
celebrated in Civil War annals. He served as Stuart's scout throughout
much of 1862 and accompanied him on his Fairfax raid in December of
that year. When Stuart rode out of Fairfax County three days later,
Mosby. with nine men. had permission to remain behind.[28]

And so it was that Mosby began his career as a partisan ranger.
operating extensively in Fairfax and other counties in Northern Virginia
and the lower Shenandoah Valley. By late January 1863, his men, many
of whom were from Fairfax County, were making news in the Alexandria
Gazette, harassing the forces of Colonel Percy Wyndham at Fairfax
Court House, capturing twenty-eight Yankee cavalrymen, and
furnishing Stuart with information of Union movements.

One of Mosby's more celebrated exploits occurred on 9 March 1863 in
the very center of Fairfax Court House. There the twenty-five-year-old
Union Brigadier General Edwin H. Stoughton had made his headquarters
at the comfortable brick home of Dr. William Presley Gunnell. On this
chilly Sunday night shortly after falling asleep, Stoughton suddenly
awakened to a sharp slap on his bare rear. Stoughton, a lover of wine
and of women, had spent the evening enjoying both and was none too
alert. "General," asked a slim figure above him, "did you ever hear of
Mosby?" "Yes, have you caught him?" "No, but he has caught you."
Minutes later, Stoughton with two Union captains, thirty privates, and
fifty-eight horses found himself unhappily accompanying Mosby and his
men.

Four days later, pretty Antonia Ford, nineteen-year-old daughter of
a prosperous local merchant whose sympathies were warmly
Confederate, found herself in a Washington prison, arrested for her role
in obtaining information from Stoughton and other Northern officers
and men and passing it on to Confederates. She even had a "commission"
from fun-loving Jeb Stuart as his honorary aide-de-camp with a rank of
major.[29]

A rash of other arrests of Fairfax Court House residents suspected of
entertaining Confederate sympathies followed Mosby's raid. Thomas R.
Love. Joshua C. Gunnell. Amos Fox. and Antonia's father. F.R. Ford.
were all seized and imprisoned for a time at Old Capitol Prison in
Washington. The Washington *Star* commented that the government had
"determined to remove from the vicinity of the Federal lines in Fairfax all
residents not known to be reliably loyal."[30]

28. Jones, *Ranger Mosby*, pp. 16-35, 45, 55, 59-60, 68.

29. Jones, *Ranger Mosby*, pp. 90-97; V.C. Jones, *Gray Ghosts and Rebel Raiders* (New York: Henry
Holt and Company, 1956), pp. 150-59 (hereinafter cited as Jones, *Gray Ghosts*); Jones, "General
Stoughton's Capture," Historical Society *Yearbook* 4(1955):52-57.

30. *Gazette*, 10, 17, 18 March 1863.

Like many Virginia women, pretty nineteen-year-old Antonia
Ford of Fairfax Court House was an enthusiastic supporter of
the Confederate cause. She was so assiduous in supplying
General JEB Stuart with information about Union movements
in the neighborhood that he gave her a "commission" as
major and named her his honorary aide-de-camp. Above is a
Harper's Weekly cartoon ridiculing the whole affair.
Antonia was imprisoned for a time in Washington but
eventually married Joseph Willard, a Union officer. Virginia
State Library.

Tales of this and other of Mosby's escapades have been told too
often and too well (especially by Virgil Carrington Jones) to need
repeating here. But the account of a Union soldier captured by Mosby
near Baileys Cross Roads shows how legendary a character he became.

Joseph Schubert, a private Union soldier, knew little about spelling
and punctuation, but in his handwritten reminiscences of later years, he
captured vividly his experiences as a prisoner of Mosby and his men.

Schubert, on a date still not ascertained, was sent to a "dismounted"
camp on the outskirts of Washington. After receiving a new horse, he
rode into Fairfax County with several other men. He had gotten about a
mile beyond Baileys Cross Roads when his horse went lame. Schubert
dismounted and had started leading his horse back to camp when two
men in blue overcoats emerged from the woods and forced him to go
with them back into the trees. It was there that he met Mosby:

> I saw a man mounted on a fine looking bay Horse . . . .
> he says to me young man do you no who I am. I told him I did
> not. well he says I am the man they call Mosby, I suppose I
> have got a very heard name in your lines Havent I. well yes sir
> you have got a pretty heard name. then I commenced to feel
> pretty shakey for he had the name all through our lines shoot-
> ing or Hanging one Half of the Prisenars he Captured. well he

said I dont Harm any of you men nor I dont alow any of my men to Harm you although I dare say when I am not about and my men Captures your men they take most any thing they can get. the only men I Rob is your Soldiers Robbers. pointing down in the woods where he had 4 large Suttler Wagons loaded down with suttler goods . . . . these men comes out Here to rob you Soldiers and when I capture them I take every thing away from them. he had Captured about 25 or 30 of our men . . . .

he asked me if I would like to join his command. I told him I could never do that . . . so then he told me to go and Join the rest of the prisenors. this was in the afternoon between 2 and 4 o'clock In sight of Washington and alexandria . . . so about Sun down he . . . Orded his men to get ready and move on . . . so we road along through the woods untill it got dark . . . that night we layed clost along the Orange and Alexandrew Rail Road we could see the sparks from the Smoak stack. I though to myself is this posible, a prisenor In the Hands of the Enemy and looking at our own cars passing by us . . . about day Brake we all got up and rooled up our Blankets and started of through the Woods . . . .

it was not long until we came to a House. 2 weoman came out and had a short talk with Mosby. I heard him ask the weoman if any of the yanks had bin along. she told him there had bin a large party of Cavalry along the day before . . . it was not long untill Mosby marched us in the house to get our Breakfast. it was a very good meal . . . . after we were all done he counted all of us prisenars and his men and paid the weoman 25 cents for each man . . . I think he had regular places to stop they all knew who he was and they would give him All the information about our men . . . .

of we started again through the woods and through Swamps. we often thought he was lost and did not no where he was a going but we found different from that. this is the way he travled for 5 or 6 days but at Meal time he would always manage to Strike a house and feed us and the Horses. he always paid them in our money for this was in our lines. with all our marching them 5 or 6 days we never saw one of our men . . . .

Mosby was a man about 5 feet 6 or 7 in High Sandy Complexion rather slinder not a noble looking man but a very nicespoaken man. he was very dairing . . . he was a terra to our army. he has distroyed millians as Burning Bridges tearing up railroads Capturen supply trains goverment Wagons . . . Capturen Suttler wageons . . . he has Captured men and officers . . . . Mosby lived In our lines all the time all of this kind of work was going on in the rear of our army. his head quarters the most of his time was in his Saddle always ready

Mosby troops in ambush waiting to capture a bearer of dispatches. Virginia State Library.

for duty . . . when we arrived on the Blue Reidge Mountains Mosby gave us some Rations and told us he was going to send us to Richmond va so he started us prisenors off with some of his men.[31]

Though rumors were widespread of ill-treatment and even death at the hands of Confederate rangers, Schubert and a number of others captured by the "Grey Ghost" said they were "well-treated by Mosby's men." But by late 1863 Lee, who initially had favored such guerrilla activities and been quite favorably impressed with Mosby's work, had grown disillusioned. The ranger, Lee thought, was spending too much time capturing and selling sutlers' wagons and goods and not enough of his energies on disrupting the enemy's transportation and communications networks. Nevertheless, in 1864, when the law authorizing such organizations was repealed, Lee recommended that Mosby and his men be exempted; and in February of that year, at the urging of both Stuart and Lee, Mosby was promoted to lieutenant colonel and allowed to continue his guerrilla activities.[32]

31. Schubert, "How I Was Captured," *CWTI* Collection (periods and paragraphing, but no other punctuation, have been added).

32. Jones, *Gray Ghosts*, pp. 155, 192-93, 214; Jones, *Ranger Mosby*, pp. 171-75.

Union forces made repeated efforts to end the "depredations committed by rebel banditti." Pierpont urged Provost Marshal Colonel Henry Horatio Wells to see if something could not be done for the "suppression of the evil." Though the governor was deeply anxious for the most stringent measures to protect the loyal citizens, his urging resulted in no effective action. Confederates even managed to seize within Federal lines a number of prominent citizens who had publicly adhered to the Union and carry them to Richmond. Pierpont feared if such conduct were not halted, "Union sentiment within our lines will be demoralized," and he urged that Rebels within Union lines be held as hostages until the Confederate government released such political prisoners.[33]

If, in the view of Unionists, Mosby's band was no better than a pack of thieves and robbers, in Confederate eyes he was a hero: the Gray Ghost who outfoxed, embarrassed, and chagrined powerful Union forces. Superior numbers and superior supplies might finally vanquish a prostrate Confederacy, but through Mosby, Southerners everywhere, and especially those in Northern Virginia, could laugh at their Northern victors and soothe their own trodden pride with tales of a pesky Virginian who gleefully tantalized and frustrated the self-righteous Yankees. Other Confederate heroes lost their lives or eventually were forced to lay down their swords, but John Singleton Mosby continued to baffle his Union opponents until well after Lee's surrender at Appomattox.[34]

Mosby was a true folk hero. He was David against Goliath, the little guy against the big boys, the individual against the mammoth organization, the human being against a war machine. Mosby, clearly something of a ham actor playing to the audience, had a feel for the spotlight, a flair for the dramatic, a knack for action that would create a superb story. Because the scene of Mosby's operations was the outskirts of the national capital; because it was the president of the United States and the highest-ranking of Union generals that he annoyed, frustrated, and humiliated, Mosby's exploits came to seem larger than life, a fit subject for legend and myth-making.

33. Pierpont to Wells, 30 September, 20 October 1863, Pierpont Executive Papers. Also see *Gazette*, 10 December 1863.

34. On 21 April 1865, after disappearing from the view of the Federals, Mosby disbanded his command "in preference to surrendering to our enemies." Mosby to soldiers, 21 April 1865, quoted in Jones, *Ranger Mosby*, p. 271. Also see *Gazette*, 5 May 1865, which commented that "the visions they cherished for an independent country have vanished."

X

A Preview of Reconstruction

August 1863-April 1865

So long as the capital of the Pierpont government was in Wheeling and so long as western Virginia was part of Restored Virginia, Fairfax and Alexandria were at the periphery of Pierpont's concern. But with the admission of West Virginia as a new state and the removal of the Restored Virginia capital to Alexandria, Northern Virginia became the most important area governed by Pierpont, especially after he lost all control of the Eastern Shore and Norfolk areas to Federal military authorities in the summer of 1864.[1]

In the last two years of the war, many of Pierpont's chief associates and advisors were Fairfax and Alexandria men. After the war, when President Andrew Johnson recognized Pierpont as governor of the entire state and when Pierpont moved to Richmond to displace Governor William Smith, a number of these men continued to play a leading role in his administration.[2] Though there were undoubtedly among them some self-interested adventurers, and though it is not possible to determine where altruism began and self-interest ended, it seems safe to say that there was a good deal of sincere egalitarian sentiment in the Pierpont administration.

In a sense, the reconstruction of Fairfax and Alexandria began in 1863 with the removal of the Pierpont government from Wheeling to Alexandria, though it did not begin officially throughout the South until congressional passage of the Reconstruction Acts in 1867. Technically, reconstruction had to do with the way in which seceded states were brought back into the Union, that is, with who would restore them and who would govern them. In actuality, the chief question had to do with the

1. Eckenrode, *Virginia During Reconstruction,* pp. 21-23.
2. Ibid., p. 25.

Souvenir cards published in 1863 to celebrate Lincoln's Emancipation Proclamation depict the evils of the slave trade, the traditional black balls and other festivities of Christmas week, the noble Union soldier freeing the humble slave and a black man rejoicing in his new-found freedom. Virginia Historical Society.

status of blacks and with what rights they were to be accorded.[3] The racial issue involved the motives of both idealism and self-interest. Soon after the war ended, it became clear that if the blacks were not only freed but also given the franchise they could help to offset the votes of ex-Confederates and thus help to perpetuate in office men who otherwise could not win reelection.[4]

The period from the summer of 1863 until 1865 was a kind of holding operation for Pierpont. So long as he was recognized as "governor of Virginia," no matter how little territory he actually controlled, he maintained a claim to the governorship of the entire state

3. Hans L. Trefousse, *The Radical Republicans: Lincoln's Vanguard for Racial Justice* (New York: Alfred A. Knopf, 1969), pp. 266-304 (hereinafter cited as Trefousse, *Radical Republicans*), is one of the best accounts of "wartime reconstruction" in the border states.

4. See S. Ferguson Beach to Pierpont, 26 May 1865; Yardley Taylor to Pierpont, 17 June 1865, Pierpont Executive Papers.

(minus West Virginia) when it could be loosened from the clasp of the Confederacy and returned to the Union. The Pierpont government that moved to Alexandria was of necessity thoroughly dependent on the good will of Federal authorities for its continued existence.[5] Both that government and its approval of West Virginia statehood had been sustained and recognized by some of the more radical elements in Congress, by men who were intent on emancipation.[6] It seems likely that these men encouraged and perhaps pressured the Pierpont government to provide for emancipation of the blacks, though there appears to have been a good deal of local support as well.[7]

When Pierpont arrived in Alexandria, the Emancipation Proclamation had been in effect about seven months, but its legality and constitutionality were dubious and it had specifically exempted slaves on the Eastern Shore and in the Norfolk area. For one reason or another Pierpont decided in the fall of 1863 to ask the Restored legislature to provide for emancipation of all slaves in Virginia.

From the very beginning of the war, blacks had considered the conflict a struggle over slavery, had viewed Union troops as their liberators, and had flocked to them in large numbers. They had created a whole host of problems for the Union authorities. Border state slaveholders insisted that runaway slaves must be returned to their owners, abolitionists cried out for immediate emancipation, and Union generals issued conflicting orders concerning blacks within their jurisdictions.[8] In the early days of the war, however, Union General Benjamin F. Butler excused their presence within his lines on grounds that as Confederate property they were "contraband" and need not be returned.[9] (The name stuck and even after Lincoln issued the Emancipation Proclamation the freedmen were commonly referred to as "contrabands.") Though the Federal government equivocated for a time about their official status, by the spring of 1862 Congress had forbidden the return of slaves to their owners, and by summer of the same year had declared that all Rebel-owned slaves escaping to Union lines were free.[10]

Federal authorities were ill-prepared to cope with the problems of work, food, and shelter for the tens of thousands of slaves who looked to them for protection. When Pierpont moved to Alexandria he found the

5. Eckenrode, *Virginia During Reconstruction*, p. 23.

6. Trefousse, *Radical Republicans*, pp. 270-71.

7. See Pierpont to [Edwin M. Stanton], 27 January 1864 (draft), Pierpont Executive Papers.

8. See Dudley Taylor Cornish, *The Sable Arm: Negro Troops in The Union Army, 1861-1865* (1956; reprint ed., New York: W.W. Norton & Company, Inc., 1966), pp. 11-15; James M. McPherson, *The Struggle for Equality: Abolitionists and the Negro in the Civil War and Reconstruction* (Princeton: Princeton University Press, 1964), pp. 63-133 (hereinafter cited as McPherson, *Struggle for Equality*); Trefousse, *Radical Republicans*, pp. 203-230.

9. McPherson, *Struggle for Equality*, pp. 69-70.

10. Benjamin Quarles, *The Negro in the Making of America* (New York: Collier Books, 1964), p. 112.

Fairfax slaves fled the county early in the war to take refuge behind Union lines. All too often they found their new living conditions more deplorable than those they left behind. Virginia State Library.

city full of the blacks' shanties, a number of them no doubt occupied by Fairfax slaves. Wherever there was space, in the outskirts at the north and south ends of town and in vacant lots, there were, according to the Alexandria *Gazette*, rude houses "huddled together, with no convenience for drainage." The freedmen's villages swarmed "with a mass of men, women, and children, generally orderly." The men sometimes found work as laborers for private individuals or for the United States government; the women found employment as servants in taverns and private houses. By the beginning of 1865 there were reportedly forty thousand blacks in Washington, eight thousand more in Alexandria, and hundreds of others in freedmen's villages at Falls Church and Arlington. The greatest destitution was said to prevail among them.[11]

The blacks met a mixed reception at the hands of their liberators. Some, like a Union officer stationed at Fairfax Court House, were ardent champions of emancipation. In January 1863 the captain of a Pennsylvania company wrote his brother that the war was a contest "not between North & South; but a contest between human rights and human liberty upon the one side and eternal bondage upon the other . . . . The downtrodden and oppressed of earth," he declared, "are watching us with fearful anxiety."[12] But a New Hampshire man stationed in Alexan-

11. *Gazette*, 2, 5 February 1864; 10, 20 January 1865.
12. Alexander Caldwell to brother, 11 January 1863, Caldwell Family Letters, *CWTI* Collection.

Freedmen's Village. Throughout the war many Fairfax blacks sought freedom by escaping to the protection of Union lines. In Alexandria there were several new "Negro villages," where shanties were "huddled together, with no convenience for drainage." In Washington "the greatest destitution" was said to prevail among the escaped slaves. There were also freedmen's villages at Arlington and Falls Church. Virginia Historical Society.

dria, writing in his diary about the same time, thought that "No one can come out here and believe his senses and remain an abolitionist. I have seen a good many that have been converted." Though he was for "putting away any institution if . . . it will help put down the rebellion," he thought that "if the war lasts a year longer, a nigger can't live in the Army of the Potomac, for now they are in danger of their lives all the time. Our division," he added complacently, "killed a lot of them in Alexandria last fall."[13]

Pierpont, fortunately for Northern Virginia blacks, held a fairly idealistic view.[14] In December 1863, when the new legislature assembled for the first time, he had already decided to ask it to authorize a state constitutional convention that could abolish slavery.[15] The legislators, consisting of just six senators and eleven delegates representing only Northern Virginia, the Eastern Shore, and the Norfolk area, was so tiny that it was easily accommodated in the chambers of the Alexandria city council. In the Senate, Thomas P. Brown, presiding justice of the Fairfax court, represented the district composed of Fairfax and Alexandria;[16] in the House, Job Hawxhurst replaced his brother John as the delegate from Fairfax.[17]

13. John Henry Burrill to parents, 1 January, 6 February 1863, John H. Burrill Letters, Xerox.

14. See Benjamin F. Butler to Pierpont, 3 December 1863; Pierpont to Gov. Andrews,—186[4] (draft), Pierpont Executive Papers. He was opposed, however, to using "colored troops to act as a provo guard" on the Eastern Shore on grounds that they were insolent to white citizens and that their use was "a terrible shake to the Union cause in that section." Pierpont to Secretary of War [Stanton], 27 January 1864 (draft), ibid.

15. *JHD*(R), 1863-64, p. 39; Eckenrode, *Virginia During Reconstruction*, p. 17. The 1851 constitution prohibited the General Assembly from abolishing slavery. *Virginia Constitution*, 1851, article IV, sec. 21.

16. James T. Close had resigned. A special election was held on 28 May 1863 with Thomas P. Brown opposing James Purdy. Purdy contested the election but Brown kept his seat. *Gazette*, 15, 16 December 1863.

17. *Gazette*, 14 December 1863; *JHD*(R), 1863-64, p. 32.

Most legislators, including those from Fairfax, were just as eager as Pierpont to provide for emancipation,[18] and both Hawxhurst and Brown were named to committees to consider the portion of the governor's message dealing with slavery.[19] Ironically, as the legislature set to work to carry out its democratic ideals, it found it necessary to resort to some undemocratic tactics to achieve them. It rushed the bill for a convention through the House in just four days,[20] and disfranchised a good portion, probably a majority of the electorate; only persons loyal to the United States since 1 September 1861, were to be permitted to vote for convention delegates. And it refused to permit a referendum on the adoption of the constitution to even this limited electorate.[21]

The tiny legislature became the butt of a good deal of ridicule. Many observers, both in and out of the state, took its pretensions to authority lightly. Massachusetts Senator Charles Sumner referred to it as "little more than the Common Council of Alexandria." The Springfield, Illinois, Republican called it "that funny little body"; the Alexandria Gazette, refusing to dignify it with the name of General Assembly, dubbed it simply "the legislature in session at this place."[22]

Nevertheless, the governor and the Assembly continued to attempt to exercise the powers of government. The most radical measures the legislature considered had to do with the status of blacks. It passed a resolution encouraging the formation of black Virginia regiments as a means of "suppressing the rebellion"; it considered (but refused to enact) a bill introduced by Hawxhurst to permit the education of blacks;[23] and it passed, on 19 December 1863, the bill for the constitutional convention over the objections of two or three delegates[24] who argued that because the new constitution would be the work of only a handful of men and would not be submitted to the voters for ratification, it would consequently not be legal.[25]

The election of convention delegates was scheduled for Thursday, 21 January 1864. On 31 December Fairfax Unionists had held a meeting at West End and nominated Job Hawxhurst as their candidate.[26] Also running was Felix Richards. Though Fairfax County was still subject to

---

18. JHD(R), 1863-64, pp. 14-16.

19. Ibid., p. 31; Gazette, 15, 16 December 1863.

20. Gazette, 18, 19 December 1864; JHD(R) 1863-64, pp. 31-38.

21. Gazette, 8, 21 December 1863.

22. Gazette, 30 December 1863, 8 February 1865, et passim.

23. JHD(R), 1863-64, p. 43.

24. Ibid., pp. 46, 51; Gazette, 12 January 1864.

25. JHD(R), 1863-64, p. 38; Gazette, 23 December 1863. Delegates Reuben Johnston of Alexandria and Thomas H. Kellam of Accomack County made such protests. Gazette, 5 January 1864.

26. Gazette, 29 December 1863, 1 January 1864. The Gazette said that the meeting was "not a large one." At a similar meeting in Alexandria, there was a lengthy argument as to whether it was wiser to treat secessionists harshly or with leniency. Gazette, 6 January 1864. Whether there were similar disagreements at the Fairfax meeting, which seems likely, is not known.

guerilla raids and influenced by the anti-Pierpont sentiments of many of its leading citizens and though it was so deranged that Sheriff Jonathan Roberts complained he could not "ride it with safety,"[27] polls were open in seven of the fourteen precincts. More than two hundred votes were cast, about one-seventh the usual prewar number, and Hawxhurst easily defeated Richards, 195 to 16. Former Alexandria delegate S. Ferguson Beach was elected to represent the Fairfax-Alexandria senatorial districts.[28] Altogether, a total of seventeen men representing fifteen counties in eastern Virginia were elected as convention delegates.

At the convention, which met in Alexandria from 13 February through 11 April 1864, Hawxhurst and Beach were among the leaders in advocating advances for Virginia blacks.[29] They favored immediate, uncompensated emancipation and urged that testimony in court cases be permitted without regard to color.[30] They were not, however, among the members who advocated harsh treatment of the native white population, for they supported in vain a move that would have submitted the constitution to the voters for ratification.[31] In other words, their stance was conciliatory as well as liberal. Neither man, it seems, could then be classified as a thorough-going radical or conservative.

Though Hawxhurst, Beach, and one other delegate cast the only votes in favor of permitting Negro testimony in court cases without restriction, they were not in a minority in their support of emancipation.[32] There was only one dissenting vote when the convention on 10 March passed an ordinance providing for immediate, uncompensated emancipation.[33] The vote was a moment of triumph for Unionists. To announce the great event, the convention ordered that cannon be fired and town and firebells be rung. The *Gazette*, which had little respect for the Restored government, spoofed the little celebration. It reported that around noon Alexandrians had been startled to hear "the rapid discharge of Artillery and the violent ringing of the Town and Fire Engine bells." Someone had raised a cry of fire and "citizens and soldiers went running about in every direction, in quest of the supposed conflagration." The cannon "soon ceased firing, but the bells kept up a furious gingle," and as no fire was to be found, "a thousand and one reports were set afloat," until word

27. Statement of Jonathan Roberts, quoted in the *Gazette*, 7 January 1864.

28. The *Gazette*, 23, 26 January 1864, gives the total number of votes cast at 208. The report of the election commissioners in Fairfax, 21 January 1864, gave the total as 211. Pierpont Executive Papers.

29. *Gazette*, 12 January 1864; *Journal of the ["Restored" Virginia] Convention which Convened at Alexandria on the 13th Day of February, 1864* (Alexandria: D. Turner, Printer to the State, 1864), pp. 2, 14, 23, 26 (hereinafter cited as *Journal of Convention*).

30. *Journal of Convention*, 1864, p. 2.

31. Ibid., pp. 18, 30.

32. Ibid., pp. 47, 49.

33. Ibid., p. 18.

finally spread that the firing and ringing had been ordered to announce the passage of the emancipation ordinance.[34]

Whether Fairfax and Alexandria slaves were now legally free depended on the legality and constitutionality of the president's Emancipation Proclamation and the Virginia convention ordinance. Either, if enforced and not overturned in the courts, was enough to free the slaves. In the meantime, however, Congress had under consideration a constitutional amendment providing for emancipation in all the states. It passed the Senate in April 1864, but not until 31 January 1865 did it win approval in the House of Representatives, and not until December 1865 was it ratified by the requisite number of states.[35] The Virginia delegates no doubt took great pride in providing for emancipation in Virginia a year before the United States Congress was able to ensure emancipation in the South.

In other respects, the constitution that emerged from the convention was almost identical to the 1851 constitution. In addition to prohibiting slavery in the state "forever," the more important changes provided for voting in elections by ballot rather than by oral vote, for a reduction in the residence requirement for voters, for disfranchising certain office-holders under the Confederate government, and for requiring of voters and officeholders a long loyalty oath to the United States and Pierpont governments. In addition, the convention passed an ordinance outlining the method by which additional Virginia counties were to come under the aegis of the Restored government.[36]

In 1864, the battlefields of war were becoming more and more remote from Fairfax. Mosby's raids into the county declined sharply (though as late as March 1865 the *Gazette* reported that Mosby's men had seized horses a few miles from Alexandria).[37] Grant came east in March 1864 to assume command of all the Union armies and, in effect, of the Army of the Potomac. Though there was a Confederate raid into Maryland in July, which appeared to threaten the Federal capital, the Southerners returned to Virginia without mounting a major attack.[38]

But the growing certainty of ultimate Union success did little to stabilize the Pierpont government. Having lost control of the Eastern Shore and Norfolk areas to Federal military authorities during the summer,[39] Pierpont found his hold on Northern Virginia tenuous. By the

34. Ibid.; *Gazette*, 10 March 1864.

35. Trefousse, *Radical Republicans*, pp. 298-300; McPherson, *Struggle for Equality*, pp. 126-27.

36. Eckenrode, *Virginia During Reconstruction*, p. 21; "Restored" Virginia Constitutional Convention, 1864, "Ordinance for the establishment of the Restored Government, adopted 14 April 1864," Pierpont Executive Papers.

37. *Gazette*, 8, 9 February, 22 March 1865.

38. Cooling, *Symbol, Sword, and Shield*, pp. 207-12.

39. Eckenrode, *Virginia During Reconstruction*, p. 23.

Francis Harrison Pierpont, an old-line Whig from northwestern Virginia, became governor of loyal Virginia in 1861. In August 1863, shortly after West Virginia was admitted to the Union as a separate state, Pierpont moved his government to Alexandria and came in close contact with a number of Fairfax Unionists. Several of them came to play a leading role in the reconstruction of Virginia. In the winter of 1864-65 the tiny Alexandria legislature authorized a state constitutional convention which provided for the immediate emancipation of Virginia slaves. Virginia State Library.

end of 1864 a number of Northern Virginia Unionists had grown thoroughly disillusioned with his regime, and some of them were eager to see the military supplant him in their part of the state as well. Petitions began to appear requesting suspension of the civil government on grounds that its jurisdiction was limited to only a few counties and that even there it was ineffective.[40]

Other groups, however, came to Pierpont's rescue. A public meeting in Alexandria chaired by Lewis McKenzie went on record as recognizing "the restored government . . . as the only legitimate government of Virginia," and Pierpont, with Lincoln's support, managed to hold on to the reins of power.[41]

40. For such a petition to Congress from Woodlawn-area Unionists, see *Gazette*, 7, 12 January 1865.
41. *Gazette*, 20 January 1865.

In the meantime, on 5 December 1864, the Restored Assembly met for its second session. Its most significant action was the adoption of the Thirteenth Amendment on 9 February 1865 which provided for immediate, uncompensated emancipation of all American slaves. The Restored Senate unanimously approved it; only two votes in the House (both from Accomack County delegates) were cast against it. The Assembly refused to go beyond this measure. Though Pierpont urged new, liberal legislation concerning the blacks, and though bills were introduced establishing free public schools and permitting the testimony of blacks in legal proceedings, they were not enacted.[42]

Soon after the Assembly adjourned, several Northern immigrants with a genuine concern for blacks manifested their interest in private attempts to assist them in the transition from slavery to freedom. In March 1865 a number of these men met in Alexandria to establish the Freedmen's Relief Association, an auxiliary of the National Freedmen's Association. Several Fairfax men, including the Sully Quakers Alexander Haight and his brother-in-law James P. Barlow, were members. They planned to send teachers and goods to ex-slaves, to establish schools, and to relieve the "destitute."[43]

As the winter of 1864-1865 progressed, it became increasingly evident that the Confederate armies would soon capitulate. On 1 April, when word came of the fall of Richmond, there was celebrating and rejoicing among Unionists but no great surprise. On 9 April, when news arrived of Lee's surrender earlier that day, it too was expected.[44] Though to Confederates it seemed that "the world had fallen," there was widespread agreement—even among some of the more ardent—that it was best the Union had won and that slavery had been abolished.[45] To Unionists, already rejoicing over news of the capture of Richmond, it was the occasion for further celebration. They gathered in large numbers in Alexandria on Sunday, 10 April, at the theater and at Liberty Hall to listen to the orators for the occasion. Pierpont, Underwood, and a number of Fairfax men including George Tucker, Reuben Ives, Gilbert S. Miner, and former Restored State Senator Thomas P. Brown "delivered animated speeches," the *Gazette* reported, "which were received with great applause by the audiences . . . . Much enthusiasm prevailed and music and song enlivened the occasion."[46]

The celebrating continued until Saturday. On Friday, 14 April, a fine spring day with the trees in full blossom, Alexandria streets were thronged for a "Military and Civic Procession" to honor the rehoisting of

42. *Gazette*, 9 February 1865; JHD(R), 1864-65, pp. 8, 26, 70; Eckenrode, *Virginia During Reconstruction*, p. 19. Hawxhurst was one of three delegates favoring additional rights for Negroes. JHD(R), 1864-65, p. 70.

43. *Gazette*, 21 March 1865.

44. *Gazette*, 2-10 April 1865, passim.

45. See Milliken, "Clarke," Historical Society *Yearbook* 8:37.

46. *Gazette*, 11 April 1865.

the American flag over Fort Sumter. It was said to be "one of the largest displays of the kind ever held" in Alexandria, and it came off in fine order. "The military were out in full force, accompanied by . . . bands of music," and followed by representatives of various associations. The fire department, the Sons of Temperance, and a "Lodge of Colored Free masons dressed in their regalia" were among the paraders. The fourteen-block-long procession passed stores and houses decorated with flags and banners. Crowds cheered and church bells rang in celebration of peace and victory.[47]

But the next morning brought news that ended the rejoicing. Stores had not been open long when word arrived that the president had been killed. At first Alexandrians refused to give credence to the rumors. No American had ever been assassinated, wrote the editor of the *Gazette* in disbelief. No one thought that "such an awful tragedy did or could happen . . . assassination is foreign to the habits and disposition of our race." It was an "Appalling Tragedy," an "atrocity." "All men—all brave men—all honorable men," he continued, "abhor murder and assassination—cowardly and atrocious as they are."[48]

As the news spread, Alexandria church bells began to toll. The mayor issued a proclamation suspending all business. Stores closed, black crepe was draped on public buildings, "and before night every house occupied within the limits of the city displayed the emblems of mourning . . . . The aspect of the city was that of deep grief at the awful catastrophe that had occurred."[49] For four days, until after the funeral on Wednesday, the columns of the *Gazette* were bordered in black.[50] On the day of the funeral, Alexandria was "clothed in mourning," church bells tolled at intervals, guns were fired throughout the day, and large numbers of loyal Fairfax and Alexandria citizens went to Washington for the services. "Everything," declared the *Gazette*, "wore an air of deep sorrow."[51]

47. Ibid., 14, 15 April 1865.
48. Ibid., 15 April 1865.
49. Ibid.
50. Ibid., 15-18 April 1865.
51. Ibid., 21 April 1865.

XI

Old Virginia Done With

Reconstruction, 1865-1870

As the funeral train bearing the remains of Abraham Lincoln made its slow journey from Washington to Illinois,[1] the people of Fairfax turned to face the problems of peacetime living. For both Rebels and Yankees who had refugeed or gone off to fight, coming home could be heart-wrenching. Too many familiar faces were gone forever; too much property had been carried off or damaged beyond repair.

Though some parts of the county were "relatively untouched" by the war, other areas had been denuded of everything familiar. Southward from Alexandria along the railroad lines, the land was like a "prairie." For miles there was not a fence. Dwellings were rare. In the area of Bull Run there were only plains, stockades, and entrenchments, "nought but bushes, weeds, and grass. Dwellings, fences, wood"—all were gone.[2]

Many of those returning home were as stricken as the land. Depressed by their defeat, ex-Confederates were especially stunned. Saddened by the loss of loved ones and the destruction of homes and property, many found it difficult to resume a normal life. Some were never able to accept the change.[3] After learning of Lee's surrender and being mustered out of service, nineteen-year-old William Selwyn Ball rode home from the Shenandoah Valley to the Potomac estate in

---

1. The train left Washington on 21 April and did not arrive in Springfield until 4 May after numerous stops along a roundabout way. Carl Sandburg, *Abraham Lincoln: The War Years*, 4 vols. (New York: Harcourt, Brace & Company, 1939), 4:387, 393-413. The funeral car had been built in Alexandria as a private car for the president. Hurd, *Alexandria*, p. 33.

2. *Gazette*, 20 June, 2, 7 October 1865. For other accounts of wartime destruction and of families returning to Fairfax after the war, see Milliken, "Clarke," Historical Society *Yearbook* 8:38-39; Joan Gibbs Lyon, "The Home Place," Historical Society *Yearbook* 9 (1964-65):76; Gamble, *Sully*, p. 115; and depositions in Southern Claims Commission Papers, Fairfax County. For an account of the war-time "plundering" and post-war condition of the Episcopal Theological Seminary, see *Gazette*, 19 February 1866. Also see Goodwin, *History of Theological Seminary*, 2:223-32.

3. Milliken, "Clarke," Historical Society *Yearbook*, 8:42.

northern Fairfax where he had grown up. There he found his brother Mottrom and several cousins, just returned from Appomattox, "sprawled out on the lawn . . . dazed and unable to realize that actually all was lost." Elmwood, their "dear old home" (he wrote many years later), "had been pulled down and its fine timbers used for other purposes. Nothing left save the foundations of the buildings to show that it ever had been a home. The splendid trees all gone."

Though Mottrom, older than Selwyn and one of the most capable young men in the county, soon developed a thriving law practice, Selwyn felt utterly lost. For him, "the world seemed to . . . come to an end with the losing of the war." Nothing appeared worthwhile; he had "no ambition left." He went to work for a time on the family farm, but spent much of his time "getting into every kind of devilment." "Penniless, with no education, bashful as a girl," he thought the future was hopeless and "gave way to drink." Though he got "gloriously drunk" on one occasion, he was usually more circumspect; he "rarely . . . took too much, just enough to feel lively and full of fun." "Why not go to the Devil?" he felt. "We were only ten miles from Washington and Alexandria, an easy walk, every dance and tournament within that radius saw us."[4]

The feelings of rootlessness and lost purpose afflicted many. What better way to lift the shades of despair, if ever so briefly, than by a frolic? For generations Americans had found solace in getting themselves thoroughly soused; but "Demon Rum" never beckoned with more allure— or to more people—in Virginia than after the war.

Houses of entertainment sprang up quickly in Fairfax in 1865,[5] and Alexandria was infested with saloon keepers. The Rev. Mr. S.S. Roszell, on an autumnal visit to preach to a flock of Southern Methodists in Alexandria, "was surprised and saddened to see [written] over almost every other door, the word "S-a-l-o-o-n."' Those "degrading dens of destruction" made men who were strictly temperate, "prominent church members, honored esteemed and loved" four years earlier into "dancing theatre-going, rum-guzzling mutilated images of manhood." He prayed that "'the sword of the Lord and of Gideon' [would] speedily descend upon every 'Saloon' in this community and country, and not one 'wet nurse' be left therein to 'suckle the grown-up babies of the bottle!' "[6]

But the sword of Gideon did not descend that winter. The Richmond *Sentinel* complained that "thousands of our most gifted and promising young men are fast becoming confirmed sots," and the editor of the Alexandria *Gazette* was certain that "the vice of intemperance is

---

4. Ball, "Reminiscences of an Old Rebel," pp. 57-64.
5. See Fairfax County Court Minute Book, 1865, passim.
6. *Gazette*, 12 October 1865.

Intemperance, always a problem in midnineteenth century America, became especially widespread—at least in Virginia—after the war. The Reverend Mr. S.S. Roszell, a leading Methodist clergyman, visited Alexandria in the fall of 1865 and was appalled at the number of saloons. In a sermon preached during his visit, he deplored those "degrading dens of destruction" that had turned "prominent church members" into "rum-guzzling mutilated images of manhood." Virginia State Library.

alarmingly on the increase—it attacks indiscriminately in this city young and old, rich and poor, men and women." And at Fairfax Court House on a January court day, there was a "free fight" caused by "bad whiskey and too much of it."[7]

But for Fairfax citizens intent on picking up the pieces of broken lives, the summer of 1865 meant neither frivolity nor inebriation, but just plain hard work. As the spring sun warmed the Virginia soil and as thousands of Union troops marched through the county on their way to a final "Grand Review" in Washington, Fairfax farmers began to cultivate parcels of land, hoping to make "at least small crops this year." Women used all their housewifely talents to make whatever living quarters they had into homes, and ladies once accustomed to leisurely living prepared meals over open fires and scrubbed family laundry. Schoolmasters and schoolmarms began to fit up cabins or a room or two in their homes in order to open schools for neighborhood children, all too many of whom had not been in a classroom for four long years. Clergymen and lay

---

7. *Gazette*, 12, 17 January, 28 February 1866. A year later, the problem must still have been serious. The *Gazette* on 15 April 1867 carried an article entitled "What Makes Young Men Drunkards."

people reclaimed the churches that had served as hospitals or storehouses in the war. Laborers, white and black, worked to rebuild roads and bridges and rail lines. County officials searched for missing record books, lawyers hung out shingles, millers replaced damaged equipment, and merchants restocked their stores. And almost everyone went in search of loans and credit, for Confederate money was worthless and other kinds seemed impossible to come by.[8]

As citizens began to resume business "as well as they [were] able," events in that first postwar summer and fall seemed at times to conspire to prevent recovery. High prices, a severe drought in late summer, a crime wave (from the Long Bridge to Baileys Cross Roads the road was said to be so "infested with footpads" that it was "extremely dangerous" to travel at night), a rash of horse stealing, the difficulties of getting steady work from the freedmen, and an epidemic of "hog dipthcria" that ravaged the already short supply of swine: all made the plight of Fairfax farmers just that much more difficult.[9]

Yet efforts at rebuilding somehow continued. Despite the lack of money, there were compensating factors. Northern merchants were more than willing to extend credit to old customers. Farmers who were able to buy horses at government sales often obtained good bargains. At army warehouses there were huge auctions of supplies no longer needed, many of which could be put to good use on Fairfax farms.[10] By the end of June, most of the military hospitals in Northern Virginia had closed, Union troops garrisoning the forts in Alexandria and Fairfax had been sharply reduced, and plans were afoot to return railroads to civilian control.[11] In August, the Fairfax court, still dominated by Northerners, assembled at Fairfax Court House for the first time in three years.[12] By October, the village was showing signs of rebuilding: "Stores are being reopened," wrote a *Gazette* correspondent, "houses repaired, [and] fencing replaced . . . . The day may come when desolated Fairfax [will] again . . . rise from the ruins and call upon her friends to settle within her borders."[13]

Meanwhile political leaders had taken steps to restore Virginia and other Southern states to more normal, peacetime relations with the Federal government. A few weeks after taking office, President Andrew Johnson removed wartime commercial restrictions, granted full amnesty

8. For evidence of Fairfax citizens resuming their work and undertaking unaccustomed chores, see the *Gazette*, 1, 13, 24, 25 May, 5, 13, 16, 20 June, 19, 22, 26 July, 16, 23, 30 August, 6, 12, 16, 28 September, 2 October, 22 November 1865.

9. For the problems brought by the summer and fall of 1865, see ibid., 14, 29 May, 14 June, 5, 20, 27 July, 8, 30 August, 8, 18 September, 9, 10, 11, 24, 30 October, 11, 16, 21, 22 November, 18, 29, 30 December 1865.

10. *Gazette*, 1, 9, 11, 13 May, 1, 16 August, 2 September, 10, 29 November 1865.

11. Hurd, *Alexandria*, pp. 21-22.

12. *Gazette*, 19 July, 21, 24 August 1865.

13. *Gazette*, 20 October 1865. For the simultaneous revival of the Herndon area, see ibid., 2 October 1865.

and pardon to most of those who had participated in the rebellion (except for the more prominent) and recognized Pierpont as governor of all Virginia.[14] Pierpont himself had moved to Richmond to begin the arduous, as well as impossible, task of keeping his old Unionist supporters happy while he set about winning the favor of former Confederates.[15] Throughout the spring and summer, returning Rebels began to take the amnesty oath as prescribed by the president, swearing they would "faithfully support, protect and defend the Constitution of the United States, and the Union of the States" and "abide by and faithfully support" all existing acts and proclamations "having reference to slaves."[16]

The people of Fairfax shed few tears over the end of slavery. As one Confederate sympathizer put it years later, they thought the war ended "just right." Most had never really wanted to leave the Union; many had long had qualms about slavery, and almost all soon found "that it was much better for them that the Negroes were free."[17]

Though most Fairfax natives were willing enough to relegate the peculiar institution to the past and though they felt, to varying degrees, some interest in wiping out the old evils of poverty and illiteracy among white people, they had little desire to make basic changes in their society. They hoped and expected to regain control of local government, and despite Pierpont's efforts at conciliation, they were eager to see his administration replaced by the old leadership. They also expected to meet (moderate) Northern demands for readmission and they were ready to resume their place in the Union without great ado or undue delay. They had suffered through so much change during the war that they were more inclined to feel a deep nostalgia for the familiar ways of "old Virginia" and to attempt to preserve the old customs and ways of life as best they could.[18]

Not everyone in Fairfax, however, felt those deep yearnings for the Virginian past. The blacks were eager to hold on to their new-found

14. *Gazette*, 1, 10 May 1865. See Eric McKitrick, *Andrew Johnson and Reconstruction* (Chicago: University of Chicago Press, 1960), pp. 48-49, for the pardon. It excepted fourteen classes of former Confederates including those owning $20,000 worth of taxable property. Those excepted could, of course, apply directly to the president for an individual pardon.

15. Ambler, *Pierpont*, pp. 269-301; Eckenrode, *Virginia During Reconstruction*, pp. 29-34; *Gazette*, 15, 25 May 1865. For Pierpont's rising favor with former Confederates and declining favor with many Unionists, see *Gazette*, June-July 1865. Also see Lewis McKenzie to Pierpont, 23 June 1865, and Daniel F. Dulany to Pierpont, 28 June 1865, Pierpont Executive Papers.

16. For the full text of the amnesty oath, see *Gazette*, 3 May 1865. Orlando Huntt, former sheriff of Fairfax and "delegate" to the Virginia General Assembly throughout the war, was one of the first in Northern Virginia to take the oath. Ibid. Also see ibid., 8 May 1865.

17. See Milliken, "Clarke," Historical Society *Yearbook* 8:39; and the synopsis of a speech by Daniel F. Dulany at Fairfax Court House, 18 September 1865, in *Gazette*, 19 September 1865.

18. See *Gazette*, 15 April-31 December 1865, passim. The nostalgia is especially evident in the Alexandria *Gazette*, 1865-1870, passim, as it repeatedly comments on celebrations or other events that were reminiscent of "old Virginia": the dedication of a church, the celebration of a holiday, or some special evidence of hospitality reminiscent of antebellum years.

freedom and to expand upon it.[19] Many Northerners who had come into Fairfax before or during the war had found Virginia ways strange and inefficient, and Virginia government much too undemocratic. Most of them had no longing to preserve the old ways, and some were eager to see them destroyed. Antislavery men tended to be firm advocates of an egalitarian society and as such had little patience with the social structure of eastern Virginia and no desire whatsoever to see old leaders restored to office.

A handful of these egalitarians were determined that the war must eventuate not just in emancipation but also in the widespread acceptance of a whole gamut of egalitarian values which they were convinced constituted the only moral basis of organizing society. In their eyes, equal civil rights for all men, a system of public education, a more equitable distribution of land, equal opportunity to climb the social and economic ladder, a more efficient exploitation of natural resources, the fuller development of commerce, manufacturing, and transportation, and hence more material prosperity for everyone were all absolute goals. Further, they were convinced that the fulfillment of their goals would make the nation a virtual utopia. The Yankee emigrant abolitionist John C. Underwood put it quite well in 1856 (while campaigning for emancipation, public education, and the Republican presidential ticket) when he rhapsodized,

> I believe we are at the commencement of a Revolution destined to be more magnificent in its progress, more glorious in its results than the Revolution of 1776 . . . . A revolution more beneficent in its effects upon the south than upon the north—filling our valleys with arts and manufactures and doubling the value of our lands—causing the music of the spindle to drown the noise of the hitherto undisturbed waterfalls—making our hillsides smile with plentious beauty and our deserts blossom like the rose. Converting our grog shops into school houses and temples for the worship of Almighty God. Where anthems of liberty shall rise like incense to the great Father and bring down blessings immeasurable upon our redeemed and regenerated land.[20]

Though Underwood, the most prominent Yankee settler in Northern Virginia, apparently failed to convince many of his white compatriots

19. A few days after Lee's surrender, Negroes in Alexandria secured the suspension of the Virginia black code. *Gazette*, 4 May 1865. The blacks, with the active support of the egalitarians, held a major meeting in Alexandria in August 1865, the proceedings of which were published. *Gazette*, 30 June, 28 July, 1, 5, 15 August, 14 November 1865.

20. Underwood to Samuel M. Janney, 9 August 1865, Janney Papers. For a discussion of the ideals, values, and goals of leading antislavery men in Virginia, see Hickin, "Underwood," *VMHB*, 72:156-57, 162; Hickin, "Gentle Agitator," *JSH*, 37:166, 182; Hickin, "John Curtis Underwood and the Antislavery Crusade, 1809-1860" (master's thesis, University of Virginia, 1961), pp. 93-95 passim; Hickin, "Antislavery in Virginia, 1831-1861" (Ph.D. dissertation, University of Virginia, 1968), pp. 570-73, 578, et passim. Also see *National Era*, 1847-1860.

that the key to utopia was at hand, there appear to have been some enthusiastic egalitarians in the area. One or two hundred men in Alexandria and fifty or so others in Fairfax, including several of the more prominent Unionist leaders—Underwood, John and Job Hawxhurst, Jonathan Roberts, and George Tucker—seem to have been undeviating advocates of such policies. If they were to effect the social, political, and economic revolution which they deemed not only desirable but essential and moral, they had, of course, to see that they and men who held similar views also held the reins of power.

At first they seemed fairly confident of their ability to do just that. They assumed that both the president and Governor Pierpont were in sympathy with them and that the working people of Virginia would turn their backs on old leaders and support the new ones.[21] They had every expectation that the old Rebel leadership would be stripped of its political power and they hoped to see slaveholders stripped as well of their economic power.[22] Some of them believed that suffrage should be granted to blacks, at least to those who could meet certain requirements of literacy. As the weeks and months passed, however, they began to see that some of their bases of power did not materialize and that they were hard-pressed to find the support they needed if they were to remain in office. Governor Pierpont and President Johnson seemed more interested in conciliating former Confederates than in remodeling the South, and the working men showed no inclination to turn their backs on the traditional leadership.

When legislative elections were held in May 1865 in Fairfax and several other reorganized counties with only white men participating, egalitarians were appalled at the results.[23] In Fairfax, despite a close vote, native Unionists, who tended to be conservative in their social and political philosophy, defeated the Northern and more radical incumbents.[24] In other counties, the outcome was much the same. If such results were to be had when few but Unionists were voting, egalitarians could envision nothing but disaster as more ex-Rebels gained the suffrage. The echoes of cannon had scarcely died away, and already their own power and their dreams of a real revolution in Virginia were threatened.

21. See Job Hawxhurst to Pierpont, 22 June 1865, Pierpont Executive Papers.

22. See below, p. 380.

23. See S. Ferguson Beach to Pierpont, 26 May 1865, Pierpont Executive Papers.

24. Pierpont's former aide, Daniel F. Dulany, a native Unionist, easily defeated Thomas P. Brown, an "emigrant," for the office of state senator from the Alexandria-Fairfax senatorial district, though Brown carried Fairfax 178 to 175. In a five-way race for a seat in the House of Delegates, Daniel W. Lewis, a native Unionist, won over the incumbent Job Hawxhurst, a native of New York, by a vote of 212 to 137, with each of the three other candidates winning about 50 votes. For the campaign and the election results, see Gazette, 13, 23, 26, 27, 29 May, 3 June 1865. For a statement by Lewis indicating that the status of the freedmen was a chief issue in the campaign, see ibid., 5 January 1867. Votes were cast in only eight Fairfax precincts. Ibid., 26 May 1865. The low turnout seems to have been due in large part to voter apathy, a chronic problem in Virginia in the reconstruction period. See Gazette, 19 September 1865, et passim.

"Ultra men" began to realize rather quickly that suffrage qualifications must be radically changed: only truly "loyal" men should have the franchise and they should have it regardless of race.[25]

Actions of the General Assembly later in the year and of provisional legislatures in other Southern states (all of them set up under the none-too-demanding eye of President Andrew Johnson) did little to reassure the egalitarians.[26] In Virginia, the legislature set aside the disfranchising and test-oath clauses of the 1864 constitution, ex-Confederates were elected to a variety of offices in preference to Pierpont men, and there was no attempt to extend suffrage to even a limited number of blacks.[27] Though the Assembly did remove certain racial distinctions from the law books, it also enacted a stiff vagrancy law which, in the eyes of many Northerners, would have been "slavery in all but its name."[28]

In 1866, after Congress assembled for the first time in Johnson's administration, the Republican leadership secured the passage of a civil rights bill over Johnson's veto and incorporated its provisions in the Fourteenth Amendment to the Constitution.[29] But the Virginia

25. For early interest in extending the suffrage to black men, see S. Ferguson Beach to Pierpont, 26 May 1865, Pierpont Executive Papers.

26. For an excellent account of Johnson's influence (and lack of influence) on the actions of Southern legislatures, see McKitrick, *Johnson and Reconstruction*, pp. 186-213.

27. On 20 June 1865, Pierpont urged the Assembly to remove the restricting clause of the 1864 constitution (as it had power to do under that constitution). *Gazette*, 23 June 1865; ["Restored"] *Virginia Constitution*, 1864, Article III. In a statewide referendum in October 1865, a small turnout of Fairfax voters, most of them no doubt Unionists, overwhelmingly (244 to 33) approved repeal of both clauses and gave the Conservative candidate for Congress a lopsided majority. *Gazette*, 12, 20 October 1865. A lame duck session of the old Alexandria legislature, which met in Richmond 19-23 June 1865, and consisted of a dozen delegates and five senators, showed little interest in black suffrage. At the end of the session, Speaker J. Madison Downey of Loudoun County congratulated the legislature because he thought abolitionists "cannot now saddle negro suffrage upon us." Quoted in *Gazette*, 27 June 1865. Also see *Gazette*, 19, 26 June 1865; Eckenrode, *Virginia During Reconstruction*, pp. 29-30; Ambler, *Pierpont*, pp. 272-75; JHD(R), 1865; *Journal of the Senate of the* ["Restored"] *Commonwealth of Virginia: Begun on Monday, the Nineteenth Day of June, . . . in the Year One Thousand Eight Hundred and Sixty-Five* (Richmond: James E. Goode, Senate Printer, 1866). Fairfax Delegate Job Hawxhurst was unable to attend the session because of illness in the family. Hawxhurst to Pierpont, 23 June 1865, Pierpont Executive Papers.

28. Eckenrode, *Virginia During Reconstruction*, pp. 41-45; *Gazette*, 5, 12, 14, 18, 20, 23 December 1865; *Journal of the House of Delegates of the State of Virginia for the Session of 1865-66* (Richmond: Allegre & Goode, Printers, 1865), pp. 168, 231-32, passim; *Journal of the Senate*, 1865-66 p. 116, et passim. Gen. Alfred H. Terry suspended the Virginia vagrancy law on 25 January 1866 because its "ultimate effect" would be to "reduce the freedmen to a condition of servitude worse than that from which they have been emancipated." Eckenrode, *Virginia During Reconstruction*, p. 43; *Gazette*, 25 January 1866.

29. Northern Virginia Radicals played a major role in encouraging Congress to involve itself in the reconstruction process. See *Gazette* 23 June, 5 July, 16 September, 11 October, 29 December 1865; 30, 31 January, 6, 13, 17, 20, 24, 26, 27 February 1866 for their meetings urging that Virginia be stripped of its statehood and returned to territorial status. Also see *Report of the Joint Committee on Reconstruction at the First Session Thirty-Ninth Congress; Part II: Virginia, North Carolina, South Carolina* (Washington, D.C.: Government Printing Office, 1866), pp. 20-25, 33-35, for the testimony of Fairfax Yankees to the effect that freedmen, Northerners, and other Union men would be in danger if the military were withdrawn. The testimony was given in secret and little evidence was offered to substantiate the charges and complaints. The *Gazette*, 17, 21 February 1866, et passim), hotly denied the thrust of other, similar complaints being made publicly. Also see Eckenrode, *Virginia During Reconstruction*, pp. 45-48.

legislature—ignoring the advice of Governor Pierpont—flatly and unwisely refused to ratify the amendment. Only Fairfax delegate Daniel W. Lewis, a native Unionist, was wise enough and courageous enough to vote for it.[30] Only one Southern state, Tennessee, ratified the amendment and was readmitted to the Union. Virginia and the other Southern states remained recalcitrant, refusing to take the measures that congressional Republicans, urged on by Southern Unionists, deemed essential for readmission.

Finally, in March 1867, almost two years after Lee's surrender, radicals in Congress, again urged on by radical Southern Unionists, found a new way to secure the satisfactory "reconstruction" of the South. In the Reconstruction Acts of that year, it turned the Southern states into military districts and charged the military authorities with making a new registration of voters, one that would include the blacks and exclude large numbers of former Confederates. The electorate in each state would then choose delegates to a state constitutional convention that would draw up a constitution acceptable to Congress and to the voters in the state, as listed in the military registration.[31]

When elections for convention delegates were held in Virginia in October, seventy-two Radical and only thirty-three Conservative members were elected.[32] Fairfax was one of those counties in which Radicals won election. Among the more prominent Radicals of the convention, in fact, were those from Northern Virginia. Representing Fairfax was Orrin E. Hine, who had come to the county after the war as the local agent of the Freedmen's Bureau;[33] representing Alexandria was former Fairfax resident John Hawxhurst; representing the Alexandria-Fairfax senatorial district was Linus M. Nickerson, a "recent settler" living in Falls Church; and presiding over the convention was John C. Underwood. Both Hine and Hawxhurst took prominent roles in the debate and were among the most radical of the white delegates in the convention. Hine, in fact, was the leading force in securing the incorporation of a

30. Eckenrode, *Virginia During Reconstruction*, p. 51; *Gazette*, 9, 10 January 1867. The *Gazette*, 5 March 1867, carried a speech by the elderly Lewis (known popularly as the "old man"), commenting on his sole vote against rejection of the amendment.

31. Among the better accounts of congressional reconstruction are McKitrick, *Johnson and Reconstruction*, pp. 253-363, 448-85; Martin E. Mantell, *Johnson, Grant, and the Politics of Reconstruction* (New York: Columbia University Press, 1973), pp. 23-25; Joseph B. James, *The Framing of the Fourteenth Amendment* (Urbana: University of Illinois Press, 1965); Trefousse, *Radical Republicans*, pp. 266-370; McPherson, *Struggle for Equality,* pp. 341-432; William C. Gillette, *Right to Vote: The Fifteenth Amendment* (Baltimore: Johns Hopkins University Press, 1965).

32. Of the Radicals, 25 were Negro. Eckenrode, *Virginia During Reconstruction*, pp. 84, 87.

33. For the nomination of candidates, see *Gazette*, 24, 27, 30 September, 7, 8 October 1867. Hine was opposed by Mottrom Dulany Ball, but in Fairfax and throughout Virginia, many Conservatives were so disaffected by congressional reconstruction that they stayed away from the polls, refusing to cooperate in any way. See *Gazette*, 8 October 1867, which urged Virginians to vote and to vote for Conservative candidates. Almost all of Hine's support came from black voters. See Fairfax County, Certificate of Election, 22 October 1867, Pierpont Executive Papers.

stringent disfranchising clause though it was not so severe as he and other Northern Virginia Radicals would have liked.[34]

At the time, native Virginians were horrified at the newcomers and blacks who constituted the majority of delegates at the "black and tan" convention; Virginia newspapers ridiculed them mercilessly. Yet many Virginians came to admit that the convention drew up a constitution which provided for several desirable changes. Provisions for a system of public education and for a new form of local government were the chief innovations of the convention. Counties were to be subdivided into townships in good Yankee fashion, and the administrative functions of the old county courts were given to a board of supervisors which was to be elected, one member from each township. The constitution wiped out racial distinctions in civil rights and suffrage requirements and contained test-oath and disfranchising clauses that would have effectively disbarred many former Confederates from voting and officeholding. Except for the suffrage and test-oath clauses, the Underwood constitution contained no really radical provisions.[35]

Even so, the Radicals had outreached their grasp. Largely because of the provision for black manhood suffrage and the inclusion of the test-oath and disqualification clauses, the constitution was not submitted to the voters for more than a year after it was drawn up. Native white Virginians opposed it adamantly and Federal officials, including many congressional Republicans, had serious reservations about its punitive features.[36]

Among the principal reasons for Virginians' antipathy to black suffrage was the illiteracy of blacks. But the most important reason was, undoubtedly, the natives' realization they they could not control the black vote and their fear that the blacks might support social and economic programs they opposed. At the end of the war many blacks had hoped that they would receive small farms from confiscated lands that had belonged to the Rebels. That dream had not materialized. The Bureau of Refugees, Freedmen, and Abandoned Lands returned most of the lands to antebellum owners, though it also worked to help the blacks adapt to emancipation.[37]

34. For Hine's role in the convention, see Eckenrode, *Virginia During Reconstruction*, pp. 89, 98-101; *The Debates and Proceedings of the Constitutional Convention of the State of Virginia, Assembled at Richmond, . . . December 3, 1867* (Richmond: Printed at the Office of the New Nation, 1867), passim. Nickerson, though less vocal than either Hine or Hawxhurst, ordinarily voted with them.

35. Eckenrode, *Virginia During Reconstruction*. pp. 101-3. For an annotated edition of the constitution, see Armistead R. Long, *The Constitution of Virginia: An Annotated Edition* (Lynchburg, Va.: J.P. Bell Company, 1901), pp. 1-106. Despite their defeat and their poverty, Virginians in the post-Civil War era had not entirely lost their sense of humor—at least when Radical politicians on either state or local level could be made the butt of their ridicule. For a denigrating, spoofing account of a session of the Fairfax Court, dominated by "emigrants" throughout the reconstruction period, see "Pequod, Letter from Fairfax County, Va.," 11 November 1867, printed in *Gazette*, 14 November 1867.

36. Eckenrode, *Virginia During Reconstruction*, p. 103.

37. See *Gazette*, 9, 27 October, 3, 23 November 1865, for information concerning the return of

The Freedmen's Bureau opened offices in Fairfax County in August 1865. The agent, George Armes, had been directed to protect the former slaves "from oppression and imposition and encouraged them to industry and economy." He was to make certain that they secured "a fair remuneration for faithful labor" and that families were not separated "merely for the convenience of employers." In addition, his office was to care for any destitute freedmen, to see that no black was still held as a slave, to settle matters of contention between whites and blacks, to help blacks secure homes and land either by purchase or rent, and to provide schools for black children.[38]

One of the agents' first duties was to take a census of the black population in each county. Of the 2,941 blacks reported to be living in Fairfax County in the fall of 1865, none were living in freedmen's villages. There were, however, at least three communities in which a number of blacks had gathered. There was a group of about thirty at Lewinsville, a similar number at Fairfax Station, and an additional 130 at Fairfax Court House. The others were scattered about, many of them living where they had always lived, on the lands of former masters.[39]

The freedmen, according to a succession of bureau agents, had few problems finding work. By November 1865, not one Fairfax black was "dependent on the charity of the Bureau for his or her support." The prevailing wages were five dollars a month for women and ten dollars a month for men, about what they had been before the war, even though prices had risen dramatically. Though some freedmen complained of destitution, the agent declared that it was by "their own want of frugality and industry" that they experienced such difficulties.[40]

By 1867, blacks were reported to be showing "increasing intelligence" in drawing up contracts with whites, making stipulations they would not have thought of a year or two earlier.[41] Sharecropping had become more widespread, and those who had been "industrious" the past year found "little difficulty in obtaining land again." That spring the demand for labor was greater than the supply. Wages advanced from ten dollars to twelve dollars and even fifteen dollars for men for a month's work, and

property to antebellum owners. It was thought that the blacks expected to be given the land on New Year's Day 1866 and there were rather extensive but unfounded fears of an insurrection when they discovered the land was not forthcoming. *Gazette,* 26 December 1865.

38. James I. Ferree to George Armes, 3 August 1865, Letter Book (Letters Received), Record Group 105, Bureau of Refugees, Freedmen, and Abandoned Lands, Fairfax County, Virginia, 1865-1868 (National Archives, Washington, D.C.) (hereinafter cited as Freedmen's Bureau Papers).

39. Freedmen's Bureau, Census 1865, Fairfax County, Va., printed in *Gazette,* 21 November 1865; Lt. Sidney B. Smith to Ferree, 1 October 1865; Smith to Col. John Eaton, Jr., 1 November 1865, Letter Book (Letters Sent), Freedmen's Bureau Papers.

40. Smith to Eaton, 1 November, 31 December 1865 (Letters Sent), Freedmen's Bureau Papers. Also see *Gazette,* 1 December 1865.

41. Orrin E. Hine to Col. S.P. Lee, 1 January 1867, Letter Book (Letters Sent), Freedmen's Bureau Papers.

went up from five dollars to six dollars a month for women.[42] The agent who took office in April found the freedmen "generally in a contented and prosperous condition" with none in "extreme want . . . or suffering for want of employment." Though some had taken up trades, most were renting "little spaces of ground and . . . cultivating corn, oats, &c." Some were working the land for half the crops, others were paying a small yearly rent. Agent William Shields wrote, "They display great energy and perseverance, seeming to feel a pride in thier success, and very great ambition to own their farms, both men and women working on the crops." All in all, their general condition was advancing "with astonishing rapidity."[43]

By the end of the decade, a number of blacks had managed to purchase some land. By 1870 approximately 120 blacks and mulattoes, at least nine of whom were female, owned some land in the county. If their families averaged just six members per household, then approximately 17 percent of the freedmen (or about one out of six) were living on their own land. Though most of the holdings were valued at five or six hundred dollars or less, some were worth a good deal more. Several owned land valued at more than $2,000, and one eighty-year-old black farmer in the Centreville area was reported to have land worth $6,000. The most prosperous black in the county, however, was Jackson Hampton, a forty-year-old black farmer in Lee Township whose lands were valued at $24,000. Hampton's holding was more than respectable. Though the wealthiest person in Fairfax was Anna Maria Fitzhugh of Ravensworth, with real property valued at $160,000, such prominent Fairfax citizens as attorney and farmer Thomas R. Love and dairy farmer Lewis Bailey owned less than Hampton, $20,000 and $13,400 worth of real property, respectively. Nor were Hampton's personal property holdings valued at $1,000 insignificant. Although Love reported personal property worth $10,000, Mrs. Fitzhugh reported only $3,000, and Bailey, despite his fine herd of dairy cattle, just $2,000.[44]

Black people struggling to make a success of their new lives were determined to see that their children attended the new schools being operated under bureau auspices.[45] By December 1866, there were eight black schools in Fairfax County, most of them supported and staffed by the Friends' Aid Society of Philadelphia. Though the "malicious burning"

42. Hine to Lee, 2 March 1867, ibid.

43. William Shields to Lee, 30 April, 31 May 1867, ibid.

44. Fairfax County MS Census, Inhabitants, 1870. One of the principal Negro landholders was Frederick Foote, a fifty-six-year-old mulatto of Falls Church who took an active role in Radical politics in the county. Ibid.; *Gazette*, 30 September 1867. For additional information concerning black landholding in Fairfax County after the Civil War, see Andrew M.D. Wolfe, "Black Settlement in Fairfax County, Virginia, During Reconstruction (independent history project, St. Albans School for Boys, Washington, D.C., 1975).

45. See Lt. Sidney B. Smith to Ferree, 1 October 1865, Letter Book (Letters Sent), Freedmen's Bureau Papers.

Black children on their way to school. After the war and before public schools were set up in Virginia, the Friends' Aid Society of Philadelphia supported and staffed a number of schools for blacks in Fairfax. The children were described as progressing "with rapidity, showing invariably an eager desire to learn." Virginia State Library.

of a school in the vicinity of Frying Pan and the "breaking up of the one near Lewinsville somewhat discouraged" the blacks, the number of children in school was "constantly increasing."[46] By March 1867, 440 black adults and children were attending school. The bureau agent declared that the "scholars" progressed "with rapidity, showing invariably an eager desire to learn." Discipline was "admirable"; the children were "docile and intelligent." One of them was especially bright, he reported. "Only six years old, and very black, she reads so fluently that the family in which she lives, white (unable to read) take a weekly newspaper, which she reads to them in the morning. Her correctness and expression in reading would be wonderful in a much older child."[47]

But physical facilities left much to be desired. "The schoolhouses," wrote agent Shields in April 1867, "are totally inadequate; . . . most of them are very low, built of logs and mud, poorly ventilated, miserably furnished, and so small that half the scholars must remain outside while the other half recites. Some of them, when I came, had neither locks nor hinges on the doors."[48]

---

46. Hine to Lee, 10 December 1866, ibid.
47. Hine to Lee, 6 February, 6 March 1867; Shields to Lee, 30 April 1867, ibid.
48. Shields to Lee, 30 April 1867, ibid.

384   Fairfax County, Virginia—1840-1870

The poverty of the freedmen caused other problems. In January 1868, though there was "work for all," teachers reported that some children could not attend school for want of shoes and proper clothing. [49] In general, the bureau agents thought that the "better class whites" were disposed to assist the freedmen in improving their condition. [50] The agent initially thought the extension of suffrage to the blacks would bring them better treatment. Before the October 1867 elections for delegates to the state constitutional convention—the first Virginia election in which blacks participated—the bureau agent wrote that the blacks "seem to have risen suddenly to a much higher standard of civilization in the estimation of the native whites, and are treated with much more consideration." [51]

But when the whites found that the blacks refused to follow the advice of their old masters and voted instead with the Radicals, there was a severe backlash. Several black laborers were discharged for voting the Radical ticket, for the whites were determined to make the blacks vote as the whites wished. Within a few months, the Ku Klux Klan had been organized in Fairfax and was beginning to cause problems for both blacks and loyal whites. [52]

The decisions handed down by Judge Henry W. Thomas at the November 1867 term of the Fairfax Circuit Court may well have constituted part of the backlash. Of the ten persons found guilty and convicted at that session of the court, nine were black. Thomas apparently handed out harsh sentences. An Alexandria *Gazette* reporter commented with obvious approval that "a severe lesson was given to criminals in the verdicts found in the different cases" (including four years each for two convicted of grand larceny and eighteen years for one convicted of horse stealing). One of those convicted was a black boy, James Stewart, accused of stealing a watch. Though he had as his defense counsel Mottrom Ball, one of the ablest attorneys in the area, the jury found the boy guilty, and Judge Thomas sentenced him to five years of imprisonment. Ball moved for a new trial on grounds of the boy's youth and the cruelty of sentencing a boy so young to a long prison term where he would be thrown in with hardened criminals and learn "vicious habits." [53]

The judge agreed that the case called for sympathy for the boy "and all his class," but he refused the plea for a new trial, and in his reply he undoubtedly reflected the rationalizations in which Fairfax natives liked to indulge. The *Gazette* summarized his remarks:

49. W.S. Chase to John Burrill, 31 January 1868, ibid.
50. Shields to Lee, 30 April, 31 May, 30 June, 31 July 1867, ibid.
51. Shields to Lee, 30 June 1867, ibid.
52. Chase to O[——] Brown, 31 October, 31 December 1867, 30 April 1868, ibid.
53. *Gazette*, 6 November 1867.

It was [said Thomas] a fair illustration of the benefits conferred on the negroes by elevating them to the rights of the whites, and giving them the same mode of trial for offenses, that before the changes we have been forced lately to make in our criminal laws, this little boy would have been turned over to his master, and after proper correction by him, would have gone gaily to his work and soon have been free of the pain of it, . . . "but," said the Judge, "we must administer the laws as we find them, and the qualms of conscience, if there should be any, for the terrible visitation of his fault on this poor little boy, must be with those, who, having the power to do so, forced us to make these changes, by the fiat of a mistaken fanaticism."[54]

The difficulty most Fairfax natives faced in accepting black suffrage can scarcely be overestimated, especially after it became clear that the blacks were thoroughly radical in their politics and had not the slightest intention of voting as their former masters wished. Probably nothing that happened in the course of the war was more traumatic to the whites after the war than sharing the ballot with former slaves whom they could not, at least in this respect, dominate. Whites were even sometimes denied the ballot while illiterate black farmhands determined who would govern them. To vote as equals with former chattels, and in fact to lose to them at the polls, as they did in 1867, probably brought home to them most sharply the defeat they had suffered in the war.

Despite the hostility, the vast majority of Fairfax citizens, whatever their color or political persuasion or place of birth, probably spent more of their energies in cooperating with each other than in fighting. A few months after Lee's surrender, Radical James T. Close and Freedmen's Bureau agent George Armes could join with such ex-Rebels as Amos Fox and William H. Dulany to sponsor a tournament at Fairfax Court House—surely an effort to promote good will within the county.[55] In subsequent years, men forgot political differences enough to join the same agricultural society (at least until one of the Radical members urged the admission of a black postmaster and farmer).[56] Freedmen's Bureau agent and Radical delegate to the convention Orrin E. Hine later became not only mayor of Vienna (a community dominated by Northerners) but also one of the most widely respected residents of the county.[57] By 1870 in Alexandria, to the astonishment of the spectators, Radical Judge John C. Underwood and the old fire-eating governor of Virginia, Henry A. Wise, were even to be heard in the courtroom exchanging pleasantries of

54. Ibid.
55. Ibid., 1 September 1865.
56. Ibid., 10 November 1868.
57. See below, p. 432.

a most complimentary nature.[58] Old bitternesses by no means disappeared, but good will existed too.

By 1870, the Fairfax economy had substantially recovered from the effects of the war. Though many Northerners and other citizens had left and had not returned, the population had risen to 12,952, a respectable (9 percent) increase over that of 1860 (almost as high a rate as had occurred in the preceding decade when it had risen by almost 11 percent).[59] Schools were in session, more churches than ever were holding services, and canals were back in operation. Railroads were again in private hands, ruined bridges had been rebuilt, and new lines of track laid. A third railroad from Alexandria, which was to bring direct connection with Richmond, was under construciton. New telegraph lines had gone up; old post offices had reopened, and new ones had been established. Old turnpikes and county roads were undergoing improvements and new roads were under construction. One new town had been founded (Clifton in 1868), and several other towns were attracting Northern emigrants, especially Thornton, in the area of present-day Reston.[60]

Even before the war ended, some of the mills were back in operation; and after the war was over, others were built or rebuilt. In 1870 the county had a total of ninety-four milling and manufacturing establishments using ten steam engines and nineteen waterwheels; they employed a total of 224 hands (6 "youths" and 218 males over sixteen years of age). The manufactured products were typical of rural counties in eastern Virginia. Twelve carriage and wagonmakers employed a total of 25 hands; two brickyards had 33 hands; four "flouring mills," 22 hands; and six lumber mills, 36 hands. The four grist mills produced "flouring-mill products" worth more than $150,000 annually, the six lumber mills produced lumber products worth a total of almost $40,000, and the other enterprises combined produced slightly over $10,000 worth of goods each.[61]

Yet Fairfax remained a primarily agricultural county. The number of farms had increased significantly, with the highest percentage of increase coming in farms of fewer than fifty acres, many of the new ones undoubtedly among those owned by blacks. Productivity also had

58. *Gazette*, 29 January 1870.

59. Walker, *Statistics of Population, Ninth Census*, p. 68.

60. *Gazette*, 29 June, 5, 30 October 1869, 2, 13, 25 January 1870, et passim; Richard Randolph Buckley, "A History of Clifton," Historical Society *Yearbook* 4 (1955):58-59; Virginia Board of Public Works, Journal N, 18 February 1861-1 December 1883, Minutes, pp. 138-305 (VSL-A). Also see Pierpont Executive Papers, 1865; Fairfax County Court Minute Books, 1865-1870, passim.

61. Fairfax County MS Census, Industry, 1870; Francis A. Walker, *The Statistics of the Wealth and Industry of the United States . . . Compiled from the Original Returns of the Ninth Census (June 1, 1870)* (Washington, D.C.: Government Printing Office, 1872), p. 739.

recovered.[62] The county, though it ranked twenty-ninth in the state in total population and twenty-sixth in the number of acres in improved farmland, was at or near the top in the production of several agricultural commodities. It was the largest milk producer in the state and the eighth largest butter producer. Only one Virginia county (Accomack) produced more Irish potatoes; only three (Augusta, Loudoun, and Rockingham) grew more hay; only four raised more market products; and none outdid Fairfax in the value of its forest products. It was among the larger corn producers in the state (ranking thirteenth), and one of the largest fruit growers (ranking fifth). Not surprisingly, the total cash value of its farms was near the top: sixth highest in the commonwealth.[63]

By the time of the 1870 census, Fairfax residents were once more full-fledged American citizens. In January of that year, Virginia finally gained readmission to the Union. In 1868, several months after the constitutional convention adjourned, a number of moderately conservative Virginians, eager to bring an end to military rule, had taken steps to secure the adoption of the constitution. They urged their fellow Virginians to accept the constitution with its provisions for black suffrage if the federal government would permit them to vote separately on (and likely reject) the disfranchisement and test-oath clauses. The arrangements were eventually worked out with Congress and the president, who was then Ulysses S. Grant, and elections were slated for 6 July 1869.[64]

The referendum on the constitution and the the two clauses and elections for governor, legislators, and congressmen all took place at the same time. In Fairfax, voters showed themselves to be more conservative than in the 1867 elections. Like the rest of the state, they approved the constitution almost unanimously: 2,223 to 13. Few but blacks voted in favor of retaining the disfranchising clause (983 for; 1,247 against). The Republicans, always quarrelsome in Virginia in the postwar years, had suffered a major schism. In a close race, the moderate candidate for governor, New York native Gilbert C. Walker, carried Fairfax by a vote of 1,177 to 1,036 (and the state by a ratio of six to five) to defeat the Radical candidate Henry Horatio Wells, another New York native and a long-time resident of Michigan. Radicals fared less well in the Fairfax legislative elections. Orrin E. Hine lost, 983 to 1,259, to the somewhat more moderate Job Hawxhurst. And in the congressional race, the

62. Also see Fairfax County, MS Census, Agriculture 1870; Walker, *Statistics of Wealth and Industry*, pp. 268-69, 364. For an excellent description of the revival of agriculture along the Columbia and Little River turnpikes, see *Gazette*, 6 May 1867. Also see ibid., 26 October 1869.

63. Walker, *Statistics of Wealth and Industry*, pp. 268-71.

64. Eckenrode, *Virginia During Reconstruction*, pp. 104-25; Alex[ander] H.H. Stuart, *A Narrative of the Leading Incidents of the Organization of the First Popular Movement in Virginia in 1865 . . . and of the Subsequent Efforts . . . to Secure the Restoration of Virginia to the Union* (Richmond: Wm. Ellis Jones, 1888), pp. 17-72.

Lewis McKenzie, president of the Alexandria, Loudoun
and Hampshire Railroad, was the most prominent
Unionist native of Northern Virginia. Despite repeated
conflicts with Yankee Unionists, he won election as the
first congressman from the district after Virginia was
readmitted to the Union. Virginia State Library.

Radical Charles Whittlesey lost to the more moderate Lewis McKenzie,
1,002 to 1,243.[65]

Virginia's ratification of the constitution meant that the way was
clear for the Old Dominion's readmission to the Union just as soon as
Congress could agree that the commonwealth had been sufficiently
reconstructed. The legislature on 8 October had already ratified not only
the Fourteenth Amendment but also the Fifteenth, providing for equal
suffrage rights for blacks.[66] Though a few congressional diehards still
attempted to postpone Virginia's readmission, Congress finally agreed in
January 1870 to restore Virginia to statehood and to permit Virginia
representatives to take their seats in Congress.[67]

65. Jonathan Roberts, president, Board of Canvassers, Fairfax County, "Canvass Return Showing
the Result of an Election Held on the Sixth Day of June, 1869," Pierpont Executive Papers. Though
Roberts ignored the racial subtotals on the form, it seems likely that as many blacks voted in the
October 1868 elections as in those held in July 1867 when some nine hundred blacks went to the polls.
See Fairfax County, Certificate of Election, 22 October 1867, ibid. It is also likely that most blacks
voted a straight Radical ticket. Also see Eckenrode, *Virginia During Reconstruction*, p. 125.

66. *Gazette*, 9 October 1869; Eckenrode, *Virginia During Reconstruction*, p. 126-27.

67. *Gazette*, 25, 26 January 1870; Echenrode, *Virginia During Reconstruction*, p. 127.

Native Virginians felt a kind of quiet, resigned relief to be once more in the Union, but there was little inclination to celebrate. They had detested being treated like a conquered people, and they felt that they had been badly abused during reconstruction. The war itself had left relatively little bitterness; reconstruction had left a great deal. In addition, people felt that the new commonwealth would be quite unlike the old one, and they were none too sure the change was to be for the better.

Most Fairfax citizens probably felt much as did the editor of the *Gazette*, who despite his long years of advocating "real, honest, material 'progress,' and advancement," loved many of the ways of old Virginia. A few days after Congress had agreed to the commonwealth's readmission, he wrote,

> We are regaled now, in some quarters by the cry of "Good bye *Old* Virginia—Hurra for new Virginia," "The New Era has come—All hail to the New Era,"—"Old Virginia done with," &&. These cries are uttered sometimes for taunt or derision—sometimes in jest—sometimes in unconsidered desire for novelty and change.—We say, too, in sadness and sorrow of heart, "Good bye, *Old* Virginia"—the greatest, truest, noblest, best Commonwealth that ever existed on the earth—with all its faults and failings. Farewell to it! We ne'er shall see its like again, we fear; in this country.[68]

Glad (but not overjoyed) to be back in the Union, hoping (but not quite sure) that better days lay ahead, the people of Northern Virginia reluctantly made their farewells to a past they would be slow to forget. There was, somehow, a feeling that they might be losing more than they would gain, that the progress they valued might not offer so good a life as the careless but gracious ways they had known in bygone years. Fairfax natives were in no mood to march boldly forward. They walked instead backward into the future, their gaze still fixed on the past they left behind.

68. *Gazette*, 28 January 1870.

1870 — 1925
Patrick Reed

Section One, 1870-1900

Fairfax: Phoenix or Failure

Previous monographs have not done justice to Fairfax County's experience in the last third of the nineteenth century. The explanation rests simply in the fact that when compared to the Revolutionary era when such historic giants as George Washington and George Mason called Fairfax home, or to the Civil War period when the legendary John S. Mosby made his most daring raids behind northern lines in the county, the late nineteenth century must seem uneventful. The conclusions of the sparse studies of this period have fallen consistently into two categories. Several accounts depict the defeated yet determined citizens stoically scratching out an existence from the war-torn countryside as the region reeled in the recesses of Reconstruction-bred turmoil. One life-long resident of the county, whose "family had lived through this," recalled an invasion of "carpet baggers" and "scalawags," while a 1924 University of Virginia-sponsored economic survey of the county concluded that "the scars of war were left deep upon the breast of Fairfax County. Probably no other county in the state suffered to an equal extent. Only [after 1900] did the anemia of war give place to returning vitality."[1] An alternate but equally unsubstantiated treatment of the period found that the county "was not scarred by . . . great and decisive military events."[2] Like the mythical phoenix, the populace threw off its postwar problems and oppressors and arose from the ashes of wartime and Reconstruction destruction.

Neither of these conclusions will stand serious scrutiny. On the contrary, Fairfax County's story between 1870 and 1900 is neither one of unrelieved suffering and stagnation, nor of unparalleled progress. It is one of a quiet agricultural area, drifting through times of both moderate difficulties and moderate advance. Yet, lest one conclude that earlier students were correct in largely ignoring this period in favor of more colorful and heroic times, the era's established rural and emerging village patterns of life reveal not only a charming serenity, but also some subtle hints of new directions the county would take after the turn of the century.

1. John C. Mackall, "McLean, Fairfax County, Virginia," *Yearbook of the Historical Society of Fairfax County, Virginia*, 4 (1955):5 (hereinafter cited as Historical Society *Yearbook*); Lehman Patton Nickell and Cary J. Randolph, *An Economic and Social Survey of Fairfax County*, University of Virginia Record Extension Series, vol. 8, no. 12 (Charlottesville, Va.: Michie, 1924), p. 16 (hereinafter cited as Nickell and Randolph, *Economic and Social Survey*).

2. Frederick Gutheim, *A History Program for Fairfax County, Virginia* (Fairfax County Park Authority, 1973), p. 33.

I

Postwar Conditions

Even though earlier evaluations of events were undeniably exaggerated, previous historians were quite accurate in their estimates of obstacles to be overcome as the people of Fairfax faced the post-Civil War era. Because of the county's strategic location between and behind the lines of both armies during the war, physical damage had been substantial. John F. Trowbridge, a northerner who visited Virginia shortly after Lee's surrender at Appomattox, described the area between Alexandria and Manassas as showing "no sign of human industry, save here and there a sickly, half-cultivated corn field. The country for the most part consisted of fenceless fields abandoned to weeds, stump lots and undergrowth."[3] A United States Department of Agriculture survey of farm conditions in Virginia in 1870 prefaced its findings with the comment "that only five years have elapsed since the agriculture of the state was utterly prostrated. The people waked up as out of a dream, to see their labor system overthrown, and their lands lying idle. Nearly all kinds of farm stock had been swept off by the hurricane which passed over the country, and but few agricultural implements remained."[4] And even exceeding the physical decimation of the county were the remaining emotional burdens, the still divided loyalties, the loss of loved ones, and the utter lack of hope that must have accompanied such conditions.

Despite these adversities, there appeared signs of awakening almost immediately after Appomattox. Oddly enough, or perhaps

---

3. John F. Trowbridge, *The South: A Tour of its Battlefields and Ruined Cities* (Hartford, Conn.: L. Stebbins, 1866), p. 82.

4. "Status of Virginia Agriculture in 1870," *Report of the Commissioner of Agriculture, 1870* (Washington, D.C.: Government Printing Office, 1871), p. 291 (hereinafter cited as "Status of Agriculture in 1870").

Great Falls (Forestville). From G.M. Hopkins, Atlas of Fifteen Miles Around Washington, 1879.

appropriately, the source of new hope was the North which sent out many of its sons in search of at least potentially greener pastures after the war. Cheap land prices, the proximity of Washington, D.C., and the milder climate made Fairfax County an attractive area to northerners, many of whom had probably passed through the region during the war and now returned with their families to become permanent settlers. Small colonies of these northerners settled in and around the communities of Accotink, Chantilly, Clifton, Herndon, Vienna, Merrifield, and Falls Church, and the settlers quickly became leading and widely respected citizens. The United States Department of Agriculture team even noticed the change in Virginians' attitude "toward the outside world. Formerly they were indisposed to encourage immigration from other states . . . . Now . . . strangers from every state . . . are cordially welcomed whenever they show any disposition to become permanent settlers and industrious citizens . . . . In many counties a strong tide of immigration is setting in, bearing with it improved stock and better implements, which cannot fail to import a healthy impulse to improvement."[5] The following decades demonstrated that the department's report did not exaggerate the significance of these newcomers to Fairfax County.

Reconstructed Institutions

In the meantime, residents of Fairfax went about the business of restructuring their institutions to meet the realities of the postwar situation. The Underwood Constitution, ratified by Virginia voters in 1869 while still under a Reconstruction regime, required that each county establish a board of supervisors as its chief administrative agency, preempting many of the duties of the old county court system. In December 1870, the Fairfax County Board of Supervisors, members of which were elected from each of six townships, officially took charge of county property from the court.[6]

Most of the board's energies were expended in raising revenue and paying the county's bills. Taxes in late nineteenth-century America were extremely low: federal and state income and sales taxes were nonexistent, and county taxpayers had only to fund a budget of $9,904 in fiscal 1880. In that representative year, a tax rate of only fifty cents per $100 in real and personal property, plus a fifty cent "tithe" for each adult male and each dog owner produced a surplus of $973.[7] However, at a time when

5. Ibid.

6. Fairfax County's first Board of Supervisors, representing the Centreville, Lee, Mount Vernon, Falls Church, Providence, and Dranesville Townships, included H.D. Rice, Dr. William H. Day, Courtland Lukens, J.Y. Worthington, Judge Jonathan Gray, and Richard Hirst. Board of Supervisors Minute Book, 1:15 (hereinafter cited as BOSMB).

7. Ibid., 1:209. The entire budget for 1874 amounted to only $3,548.10. That year, the salary of county Judge James Sangster was $259.50, while Superintendent of the Poor, Thomas T. Burke, received $250 for his services. Fairfax News, 28 February 1875 (hereinafter referred to as News).

county newspapers were continually referring to "hard times" and "a stringency in the money market," even these tax rates must have seemed steep to many. The long lists of delinquent taxpayers published annually in the local newspaper attest to this fact, and in 1874, the Board of Supervisors found itself with no money in its treasury and $1,500 in outstanding bills. At this point some county residents seemed uncertain about the board's activities; the Fairfax *News* called on county officials "to make all expenditures public to help the people understand this new system of local administration."[8]

During this period of adjustment and despite its seemingly miniscule budgets, the Board of Supervisors performed a number of essential services for county residents. Unquestionably, the board saw as its first duty the protection and promotion of its constituents' leading economic pursuit: agriculture. A cause with which both the Board of Supervisors and the Fairfax *News* seemed preoccupied in the 1870s and 1880s was the protection of farmers' sheep and other livestock from stray dogs and wild predators. During the campaign for the General Assembly in 1873, the *News* felt that a firm stand on the "dog issue" was the chief qualification a candidate must possess. "Our next representative should be a man of nerve," it declared. He must help secure a dog law "which will have the effect to exterminate the whole useless canine breed . . . that literally infest[s] every square mile of territory in the County." When the new legislature failed to act promptly on the issue, the editor declared that the solution lay not simply in "taxing ·dogs to pay for the sheep destroyed . . . . That is dodging the question, and will not protect the sheep . . . . Kill first and tax afterwards, and allow none but farmers to keep dogs."[9] Tired of waiting for the General Assembly to act, the Board of Supervisors took the more moderate course of requiring owners to register their dogs and contribute fifty cents per dog to a "dog fund." Farmers whose animals were killed were reimbursed from the fund. Along with the bounties paid for fox scalps, hawk and owl heads, and dogs not wearing collars, these claims continued to demand a substantial portion of the county's budget. In 1881 alone, the board paid farmers almost $1,000 for their losses, some $80 more than had been collected for the dog fund.[10]

Another issue which accounted for much of the Board of Supervisors' agenda was the county road network. Again, the central concern was agriculture, as the roads, in the words of the board's minutes, "accomodate . . . a large population of the county in reaching the markets of Alexandria and Washington." In 1871, the board took

8. *News,* 28 February 1874; 26 June 1874.
9. Ibid., 6 June 1873; 13 February 1874.
10. BOSMB, 2:1.

over operation of the Little River Turnpike (Route 236) and the Falls Bridge Turnpike (Route 193) from the state, and in 1872, it paid $300 to the Middle Turnpike (Route 7) Company to make it a free road owned and maintained by the county. In 1876, the supervisors appointed eighteen road commissioners, three from each district, and adopted "the mixed system of contract and laborer [sic] for making the roads," meaning that, in addition to a small tax levy for road maintenance, county citizens could be compelled to contribute up to three days of labor each year on the roads. By the early 1880s, road maintenance and bridge construction had become a major county expense, with more than $5,500 spent between 1881 and 1884 to bridge Pohick, Scotts, Difficult, and Accotink runs, and Hunting Creek.[11]

In addition to its activities on behalf of the area's agrarians, the Board of Supervisors was concerned with the care of the county's convicts and paupers. In several annual reports these items represented the largest single outlay in the county budget. For example, in the 1880 budget of $9,904, appropriations for indigents accounted for $4,345. Although most of these bills were incurred in the operation of the county jail and poorhouse, miscellaneous expenses were regularly required. In 1879 the county appropriated $94 for coffins for paupers, and the following year the supervisors agreed to assume a $5 obstetrical fee for paupers and an additional fifty cents for medicine, an amount that might lead a modern-day obstetrician to wonder if his predecessor were not a resident of the poorhouse himself. In 1882, the board directed Overseers of the Poor in each district to spend $10 "for vaccinating people who cannot pay for it." The board authorized the sheriff to purchase "3 pair of hand cuffs and 1 pair of ankle chains for the jail" in 1875, and a year later a major expenditure of $8,000 was needed to replace the jail when it was destroyed by fire. This emergency necessitated a request to the General Assembly for permission to borrow $5,000 to pay for the jail and a new Hunting Creek Bridge which had recently collapsed.[12]

With the county's welfare obligations continuing to mount, the Board of Supervisors attempted in 1875 to offset some of these expenses by authorizing the use of "Chain Gangs" on county projects. By late 1877, "since the Poor House [was] filled to its utmost capacity," the supervisors directed the Overseers of the Poor to arrange for "a suitable person or persons" to support paupers "on as reasonable terms as they can obtain." Sealed bids were used to auction off responsibility for the poor to county residents. Though the supervisors required that "the board . . . furnished shall be of a good, plain and substantial character," the care of an "outside pauper" had cost the county a mere $15 to $20

11. Ibid., 1:1, 47, 91, 95, 193, 225, 235, 263; 2:2.
12. Ibid., 1:79, 175, 208-9, 261, 270-71; 2:1.

per year in 1873. By 1880, however, the board allowed one Rebecca Marders $60 a year "for the support of a colored girl named Hannie Garrett." The growing welfare costs were accompanied by fears that this activity would contribute to an erosion of economic individualism and the work ethic. In 1875, the board resolved to "suppress as far as possible, the disposition on the part of a certain class of individuals in our community, to expect assistance outside the Poor's House, believing that the custom is abused [and] that imposition has been, and will be practiced if the greatest vigilance is not used."[13]

Reconstructed Politicians

A final important responsibility of the County Board of Supervisors was the establishment and support of a new system of public schools called for by the Underwood Constitution of 1870. Before looking at the politics of public education in the county, however, one must consider this and other issues on state and national levels, where the foundations for so many Fairfax programs and attitudes were laid.

As might be expected following the bitter hostilities and bloodshed of the 1860s, many old wounds were slow to heal. While more moderate and realistic Fairfax voices argued that "the time has [come] for a united sentiment," even the appeals of the Fairfax *News* for "the American people . . . to stand forth shoulder to shoulder . . . and restore the ancient *regime*" obscured a number of still unsettled disputes. Despite the fact that Reconstruction had ended in Virginia by 1870 and the Conservative or Democratic Party had been restored to power in the state in 1869, S. Simpson, editor of the *News*, still saw "tangible proof of the existence of *Imperialism* in our midst" in 1874. President U.S. Grant was criticized for his refusal to grant a general amnesty to Confederates and for his continued "intermeddling" in southern affairs. Centreville Conservatives called the Republican-sponsored pay raises for Congress and the President in 1873 "an outrage," and the *News* felt the Civil Rights Bill of 1875 was "full of evil" and evidence of "an ingrained, malicious feeling on the part of Northern members against Southern people." The act was seen as a means of assuring Grant a third term on the strength of black votes from the southern states. The editor argued that to allow the county to fall into Republican hands would be to "acknowledge ourselves to be inferior to our late slaves" and warned that should "the *knot* of *imperial* consolidation be drawn tighter . . . a culminating point shall have been reached, when its *anaconda* folds will again be severed by the sword."[14]

---

13. Ibid., 1:83, 88, 122, 182, 254.

14. *News*, 17 June 1874; 14 December 1872; 18 July 1873; 5 March 1875; 31 October 1873.

The views of the staunchly conservative Fairfax *News* were not unanimously held throughout Fairfax County. On the contrary, the large number of northern immigrants in the area and the newly granted political rights of the county's blacks assured local Republicans of a significant voice in county affairs. The six members of the Board of Supervisors elected in 1874 were evenly split between Conservatives and Republicans, and the *News* wondered "why are Republicans winning in Providence [Fairfax] Township when Conservatives have a majority there?"[15] Several years later the editor of the Fairfax *Herald* offered an explanation for continuing Republican strength. Even though the Conservatives had "a good majority" estimated at 12,500 of the 21,000 eligible voters in the Eighth Congressional District, of which Fairfax was a part, he felt that "the Republicans can throw a full vote without much trouble, owing to the fact that the negro would rather vote than anything else." Whether relative white apathy was really the reason or not, as late as 1888 general elections in Fairfax County continued to be hotly contested. That year, Grover Cleveland, the Democratic presidential candidate, outpolled Republican Benjamin Harrison in the county by a vote of 2,010 to 1,824, and Democrat Fitzhugh Lee defeated his Republican challenger Park Agnew in the Congressional race by the nearly identical margin of 2,004 votes to 1,836.[16]

A still better indication of the lack of politican unanimity in the county can be seen by focusing on a pair of statewide issues, on which there even appeared serious disagreements within the Conservative ranks. The most divisive issue among Virginians in the fifteen years following Reconstruction was the state debt controversy, a question closely linked to the second serious dispute, over the future of public education in Virginia. Would Virginians honor their pre-Civil War obligations, which by 1870 had risen to $45,000,000, or could the state justifiably declare bankruptcy and cancel at least a portion of its debt? Advocates of full payment, the "Funders," included many older, aristocratic, and politically powerful planters and businessmen, or "Bourbons," while less conservative middle-class whites and newly enfranchised blacks argued that if saddled with such an obligation in already depressed conditions, the state could not meet the ordinary expenses of government, much less fulfill its recent commitment to build a statewide system of free public schools. These "Readjusters" chose as their standard bearer a controversial ex-Confederate and soon-to-be-dominant Virginia politico, General William Mahone, who "weighed about 100 pounds, had a squeaky voice, and was so fastidious as to his clothes that his tailor said he would rather make dresses for eight women

15. Ibid., 5 June 1874; 3 October 1873; 9 October 1874.
16. *Fairfax Herald*, 5 October 1888; 9 November 1888 (hereinafter cited as *Herald*).

than one suit for the general." When Funders, including Governors James L. Kemper and Frederick W.M. Holliday, continued to impound constitutionally appropriated school funds in the 1870s, support grew for the Readjusters, and in the elections of 1879, they swept into the majority in both houses of the General Assembly. Mahone himself was elected to the United States Senate. In 1881, Readjuster William E. Cameron, handpicked by Mahone, captured the gubernatorial contest by defeating John W. Daniel, who had recently declared that he would "rather see a bonfire made of every schoolhouse in the state" than see the debt reduced. Following Cameron's victory, the debt was legislatively lowered to about $21,000,000 and funds desperately needed were freed for the state's struggling schools.[17]

The dispute over the debt and public education in Fairfax County mirrored and, on occasion, contributed to the statewide disagreements during the 1870s and 1880s. Despite the highly controversial tactics of General Mahone (his means of achieving power had been ruthless; he used his position to reap large personal profits and reward his followers; and he openly appealed to the state's black voters, even becoming a Republican after he was safely entrenched as a Conservative in the U.S. Senate), both he and his policies enjoyed substantial support among county residents. His Readjuster stance had at least the unequivocal support of the editor of the Fairfax *News* who proclaimed in 1875 that "we have ever had but one opinion about the State debt, and that is, despoiled, subjugated, and dismembered as the State has been, we have no State debt that we are bound either in honor or in law to pay one cent of." The editor then revealed what seems a glaring contradiction between his opinion on the fate of the debt and his earlier denunciations of federal "intermeddling" and "imperialism." "The whole responsibility of payment of what was once the debt of Virginia," he argued, "now rests upon the government of the United States . . . . Funding bills and Court of Appeals decisions are all swept out of sight by the avalanche of Federal responsibility."[18]

With no tradition of free public education to build on, many local citizens were skeptical of the need for and feasibility of the Underwood Constitution's "Act to Establish and Maintain a Uniform System of Public Free Schools." The already overburdened economy and the rural character of the county were other obstacles to an early implementation and efficient operation of the new educational system. In spite of opposition from "some narrowminded and contrary people" in the county, and largely because of the energy of the state's first

17. Virginius Dabney, *Virginia: The New Dominion* (Garden City, N.Y.: Doubleday, 1971), opposite p. 367, pp. 381, 386-87 (hereinafter cited as Dabney, *Virginia*).

18. *News*, 8 January 1875.

Superintendent of Public Instruction, William H. Ruffner, Fairfax County had forty-one schoolhouses in operation by the fall of 1870. Although the report of Thomas M. Moore, the county's first Superintendent of Schools, admitted that all but one of these primitive schools consisted of a single room, only sixteen were equipped with outhouses, and the school term averaged less than five months, their very existence reveals a strong determination on the part of many county residents to provide their children with educational opportunities.[19] But hurdles remained. In 1873, the Fairfax *News* criticized the new brick school under construction "at the eastern end of the village," costing between $2,500 and $3,000, as being too expensive. The editor called the building "better than what [the children] live in," and pointed out that since the county had "to sustain two separate school establishments . . . the negro people . . . will demand one for their use equally expensive."[20] The following year, a group of local citizens circulated a petition calling for the removal of County Superintendent of Schools Daniel McCarty Chichester. The County School Board refused to dismiss the superintendent, and praised "his efficiency, indefatigability, and unbounded feeling toward free schools." Chichester, however, was convinced by the incident that "there are still many enemies of the system."[21]

Destined to be an even more serious enemy of the system was the economic situation and the desire by the state's Funders to deprive the schools in order to honor Virginia's mounting debt. Annual school taxes of ten to twenty cents per $100 probably played a large part in the protests of local property owners, and when the dominant Bourbon element in the General Assembly voted the Funding Act of 1877, schools in all parts of the state felt the impact. With the state's supplements severely slashed, there were seven fewer Fairfax schools in the fall of 1878 than in the previous year, and the length of the average school term was cut from almost five and a half months in 1876-77 to barely three months in 1878-79. Enrollment in Fairfax schools fell from 2,839 in 1877-78 to 2,190 the following school year, and teachers' salaries fell from an average of $33 per month in 1876-77 to only $22 in 1879-80. The assault on the young school system reached a climax when the State School Board considered a motion that public schools be closed altogether for the ensuing year. Although the motion was defeated, inadequate funds ultimately forced a number of schools to close their doors. At the end of

19. Virginia Andrus, "Selected Phases of Early Public Elementary Schools in Fairfax County, Virginia" (M.A. thesis, George Washington University, 1947), pp. 27, 29, 92-93 (hereinafter cited as Andrus, "Selected Phases").

20. *News,* 5 September 1873.

21. John K. Gott and Katherine S. Hogan, "Fairfax County Public Schools: A Brief History," *Legato School: A Centennial Souvenir* (Fairfax, Va.: Office of Comprehensive Planning, 1976), p. 25 (hereinafter cited as Gott and Hogan," Fairfax Public Schools").

the first decade of Fairfax County's experiment in public education, only 50 percent of its school-age population had been enrolled, and a mere 30 percent were actually attending its schools.

The fall elections of 1879 witnessed the statewide triumph of Mahone and the Readjusters, with their promises to free impounded state funds for education, so that progressive local citizens could confidently look forward to a more certain future for Fairfax schools. Despite the problems encountered in the late 1870s, F.D. Ficklin, who had replaced Chichester as County Superintendent in 1878, attested to the continuing determination of county residents when he "reported in 1879 having trouble with the clamor of people compelling the trustees to open more schools than the funds on hand justified."[23] These brighter prospects were deceiving, for not long after the Readjusters had succeeded in reducing the debt in early 1882, the Mahone machine began a wholesale housecleaning, dismissing Funders from state offices and replacing them with loyal Readjusters. "Worst of all," according to Virginius Dabney, "was the discharge of William H. Ruffner, the able and devoted head of the public school system, and his replacement with Richard R. Farr," former County Treasurer, Surveyor, and three-term delegate to the State Assembly from Fairfax.[24]

Though they had never been known as friends of the schools, Funder reaction to the appointment of Farr was hysterical. Delegate Charles E. Stuart of Alexandria told the General Assembly that he had lived near Farr for many years and had "never known that he was fit to be superintendent of the public schools in any county, let alone . . . Superintendent of Public Instruction of Virginia." He concluded that Farr was "thoroughly incompetent."[25] The Alexandria *Gazette* published "a few of Mr. Farr's far-away and funny fights against ordinary spelling," and the Richmond *State* continued the attack in verse:

> Haste thee, teacher, haste away,
> Farr too long has been thy stay;
> Farr too bad thy words are spelt
> Much too strong thyself hath smelt . . . .[26]

Since their concern was obviously not the fate of the system, Funder opposition to Farr may have been based on a fear that he favored "Mixed Schools." Not to his credit, Farr unequivocally denied this charge,

22. Andrus, "Selected Phases," pp. 29, 38.

23. Ibid., p. 31.

24. Dabney, *Virginia*, p. 389.

25. Clayton Beverly Phillips, "Education in Virginia Under Superintendent Richard Radcliffe Farr, 1882-1886" (M.A. thesis, University of Virginia, 1932), p. 26 (hereinafter cited as Phillips, "Education Under Farr").

26. Alexandria *Gazette*, 9 January 1882 (hereinafter cited as *Gazette*); *Richmond State*, 31 January 1882, and 2 February 1882.

stating that "nobody wants mixed schools . . . . So repugnant is this matter to our people that our Governor [Readjuster Cameron] made special mention of it in terms of condemnation." Yet while the criticism would continue, Farr received high marks for his four-year tenure in office from two former political opponents. Dr. J.L.M. Curry, the southern representative of a northern philanthropist of public education and "a national figure," wrote in 1885 that "in my work as Peabody Agent I found no superintendent more devoted to the cause of public schools, more energetic, more faithful, more efficient than Mr. Farr."[27] Even the replaced Dr. Ruffner saw "a vigor and a laudable progressive spirit" in Farr's administration.[28]

The effects of political upheaval on education continued to be felt in Fairfax. In 1883, the regrouped Conservative Party, having accepted the downward adjustment of the state debt, recaptured control of the General Assembly from Mahone, and the General's supporters braced themselves for the backlash. When Eugene F. Crocker was appointed by the State School Board to replace F.D. Ficklin as Fairfax Superintendent of Schools, surely on Farr's recommendation, the new State Senate refused to confirm the nominee. After Crocker was again appointed and again rejected, the State Board nominated M.E.J. Northrup, who was approved by the Senate only to be dismissed when he failed to meet the literacy requirement for the position. Jacob M. Troth of the Woodlawn Quaker community was the next nominee, but as the Senate failed to take action on his appointment, the twice-rejected Crocker continued to serve as Acting Superintendent until Milton Dulany Hall finally received all the necessary endorsements in 1886 and began his forty-two-year tenure as Superintendent of Fairfax Schools.[29] Remarkably, through all the instability in local leadership, the county's schools recovered rapidly from the hardships of the late 1870s. By 1886, when Hall's administration began, there were seventy-eight schools operating in the county, an increase of fourteen since 1880. Seventy-three were equipped with outhouses, all had "suitable grounds," fifty-two of the buildings were actually owned by the county, and the school term had been stretched to almost six months. Still, only six of the schools had more than a single room, less than thirty-five percent of the county's youth attended, and teachers' salaries averaged around $27 a month. By this time, however, open opposition to the principle of public education had evaporated, and the people of Fairfax had "demonstrated an admirable determination to continue to improve the system."[30]

27. Phillips, "Education Under Farr," p. 160.
28. Gott and Hogan, "Fairfax Public Schools," p. 26.
29. Ibid., p. 27.
30. Andrus, "Selected Phases," pp. 51, 53, 59.

Reconciliation and Assimilation

The decade following Reconstruction did not witness an end to either internal disputes or the sectional conflicts of the previous twenty years. In addition to the continuing criticism of "Black Republicanism" and "Federal Imperialism," Fairfax voices regularly invoked the memories of the "Lost Cause" and its heroes. The front page of local newspapers was given over to circulation-boosting romances and recycled histories, more often than not detailing clashes from the late war from a decidedly Confederate perspective. If the Fairfax *News* and Fairfax *Herald* accurately reflected the interests of local residents, the people of Fairfax spent much of their time reliving the raids of Colonel Mosby, reasserting their respect for Robert E. Lee, and reassessing the reasons for the southern defeat. The county's Confederate veterans received unending recognition from the newspapers, from the podium at practically all public gatherings, and from every serious political hopeful who stumped the area, urging the voters to "honor the dead! Save the Living!"[31] The greatest political advantage one could possess was the ability to add "C.S.A." after signing one's name, particularly if the name was preceded by "Col." or "Gen." Only if the name itself were "Lee" could one's chances be further enhanced. General William Henry Fitzhugh Lee, Robert E. Lee's son who settled at "Ravensworth" in Fairfax County after the war, used these advantages to secure a seat in the State Senate, and then to win election to the United States Congress three times. His cousin Fitzhugh Lee, originally of Fairfax and former Commander of Cavalry in the Army of Northern Virginia, was elected governor of the state in 1885. The climax of county salutes to the Confederacy came in the fall of 1890, when the $1,200 Confederate monument was dedicated at the Fairfax Town Cemetery. Former Governor Lee, U.S. Senator John W. Daniel, and a generous supply of Confederate officers and enlisted veterans joined the crowd of two thousand, who "in their enthusiasm to view everything, delayed the parade for one and a half hour."[32]

Perhaps an even better indication of the strength of county ties to the Confederacy can be seen in the gradual assimilation of former Northerners into the culture of the "Lost Cause." Robert S. Gamble, in his exemplary study of Sully Plantation and its inhabitants, revealed that the offspring of New York-born Quaker Alexander Haight "were growing up to speak and think not like New Yorkers, but like Virginians; later, with their playmates who were sons and grandsons of Confederate veterans, his grandchildren would yell as loudly as their companions when an aged Southern officer spoke to a cheering crowd in front of the

31. *News*, 24 October 1873.

32. Jeanne Johnson Rust, *A History of the Town of Fairfax* (Washington, D.C.: Moore & Moore, 1960), pp. 64-65 (hereinafter cited as Rust, *Town of Fairfax*).

William Henry Fitzhugh Lee, was a Confederate General of
Cavalry, state senator, and congressman. He died at
"Ravensworth." Fairfax County Courthouse portrait.

courthouse about 'whipping the Yankees' up and down the county, or
when the band struck up 'Dixie' at a local political rally . . . . Possibly
nothing expressed so well this assimilation as when, in October 1874,
Margaret Haight—returned from a proper boarding school education in
New York—was married at Little Sully by the Episcopal minister to
Thomas W. Lee. The bridegroom, a son of William F. Lee, was a direct
descendant of Richard Lee III, London merchant and the eldest brother of
the first Henry Lee who had patented the lands encompassing Sully."[33]

Amid the reminiscences and rebel yells, there were occasional
indications of reluctant realism, if not sincere reconciliation. Even the
recalcitrant Fairfax News seemed to see the wisdom in moderation during
the congressional campaign of 1874, warning its readers that they must

---

33. Robert S. Gamble, Sully: The Biography of a House (Chantilly, Virginia: Sully Foundation,
1973), pp. 118-19 (hereinafter cited as Gamble, Sully).

"stop opposing the federal government if the South wants relief." After arguing in July that incumbent General Eppa Hunton's "secession proclivities before the war" and "his chivalry in the field throughout the bloody contest" should be no political handicap, the editor began to have second thoughts by late September and used the occasion of a debate in the courthouse between Hunton and his opponent, James Barbour of Culpeper, to reveal his misgivings: "If Barbour is elected a full share of the public patronage will be equally distributed over this Congressional district; and *per contra*, we may infer that if Hunton shall be the man, it will be hereafter as it has been heretofore, *nil*; not because of any present fault of General Hunton, but because he has neither the ear of Congress nor of the Executive of the United States, being an original secessionist . . . . We regard these two gentlemen as Conservative men, with this difference, Mr. Barbour brings us one step nearer peace and prosperity than Gen. Hunton . . . . That difference is an important one to us in our present needy condition."[34]

While county conservatives were willing to make only backhanded concessions to cooperation, and then only with the other hand out, the weakening of radical Republican reformism and northern concessions to southern intransigence closed the sectional gap considerably. When a relative of the Alexander Haight family at Sully visited the county in early 1877, she wrote to her own family in Kansas "that 'most all' of the people of the area were 'bitterly disappointed' at the election of Republican Rutherford B. Hayes over the Democratic nominee, Samuel Tilden. [But] after her nephew, Henry Haight, attended inaugural ceremonies in Washington, she reported how his attitude toward the new President changed upon hearing Hayes' avowal to win the goodwill of the South."[35] Symbolic of the reconciliation of Fairfax to postwar realities was the visit of President and Mrs. Hayes to the county in 1878. After sightseeing at Mount Vernon and Woodlawn, the first family accepted an invitation to meet neighborhood residents at "Grand View," the home of Jacob M. and Ann Troth. The occasion was by all accounts pleasant. In fact, the Troth's daughter Sallie recalled that "Chalkley Gillingham, in Quaker fashion, addressed the charming wife of the President as 'Lucy.'" In his diary, President Hayes described the day in Fairfax as "delightful."[36]

---

34. *News*, 9 October 1874; 24 July 1874; 25 September 1874.

35. Gamble, *Sully*, pp. 117-18.

36. Dorothy Troth Muir, *Potomac Interlude: The Story of Woodlawn Mansion and the Mount Vernon Neighborhood, 1846-1943* (Washington, D.C.: Mount Vernon Print Shop, 1943), p. 137 (hereinafter cited as Muir, *Potomac Interlude*).

II

Agricultural Aggravation

Only the most optimistic of Virginians could look to the future with confidence as they exchanged swords for plowshares after 1865. The United States Department of Agriculture survey of the state in 1870 found that "the conditions on which agricultural prosperity rests have been so unsettled by intervening events, and the tenure of lands to a great extent rendered uncertain, that few farmers have been influenced by a spirit of improvement. The great object has been to make a livelihood. The efforts both of farmers and planters have been vigorous . . . but rather with a view to speedy returns than ultimate improvement. No systematic rotation has been practiced . . . . They are still wedded to old habits, from which no change of circumstances has sufficed to divorce them."[37]

Yet despite the survey's conclusion that "in but few sections of the State has agriculture made any progress within the last ten years," its findings for Fairfax were extremely favorable. For example, it was found that "probably two-thirds of the land seeded to wheat and one-quarter of the corn have commercial fertilizers applied to them," and "barnyard manure is husbanded with some care." While "the attention given to alternation of crops is probably not increasing, the rotation before and since 1860 being usually corn, oats, and wheat, then clover and timothy for two or three years, . . . under this system, with the judicious application of fertilizers and farmyard manures, lands in the western part of the County have risen in value from $20 to $40 per acre, and their productive capacity increased from fifteen or twenty bushels to forty bushels of corn per acre; oats from ten bushels to twenty-five or thirty

37. "Status of Agriculture in 1870," pp. 269-70.

bushels; hay, threefold." The survey also reported that the "surface of the county is well adapted to labor saving implements, and they are generally in use for cutting grain and grass."[38] The explanation for this relatively positive evaluation lies not only in the determination of native Fairfax farmers, but also in the influx of a group of highly industrious immigrants from the north.

As the Fairfax *News* pointed out in 1874, one of the most serious problems facing Fairfax farmers after the war was "the want of an adequate and regular supply of trained labor."[39] Despite the Department of Agriculture's confidence that "with kind treatment and payment according to contract, the negro" would be "as tractable as ever," many blacks were still unwilling to voluntarily return to dependent status by whatever name.[40] A Union veteran who had served as tutor to the Fitzhugh family at "Oak Hill" before the war returned to Fairfax County after Appomattox to find the mansion abandoned. After acquiring the property, he described in letters the hardships encountered in rebuilding the estate "when servants and field workers were gone" and with "no one to till the fields."[41] A second obstacle to improvement was a shortage of capital. Even those who were well established reported difficulties, as did George Mason of "Spring Bank," the grandson of the author of the Fairfax Resolves and the Virginia Bill of Rights, in a letter dated 1868 to Edward Curtis Gibbs, a Quaker who had bought "Hollin Hall" from Mason in 1852: "My son is so delighted with your success in raising Wheat, that he has persuaded me to try a Field this Fall in that Grain; but to do so effectually, will require a heavy expence in Seed and Fertilizers, and Money is now so scarce with me, that I am getting nothing of the Interest on all my Investments for nearly Thirty Years in Virginia Stocks." Mason also told of his inability to find an insurer for his house and property, as "they ceased to insure during the war."[42]

Northern Immigration

If Edward Curtis Gibbs's "success in raising Wheat" contradicted the Department of Agriculture's report for Fairfax County that "wheat has been an uncertain crop for several years," his accomplishment was to be typical of the experience of other former Northerners who were finding their way to Fairfax.[43] For while many long-time residents were saddled with debts and deprived of their accustomed labor, newcomers were able to take advantage of deflated land prices and the local demand for cash.

38. Ibid., pp. 269-70, 274, 279, 282-83.
39. *News*, 17 July 1874.
40. "Status of Agriculture in 1870," p. 291.
41. Jean Geddes, *Fairfax County: Historical Highlights from 1607* (Middleburg, Va.: Denlinger's, 1967), p. 78 (hereinafter cited as Geddes, *Historical Highlights*).
42. Mrs. Winfield Scott Macgill, "Hollin Hall," Historical Society *Yearbook,* 9 (1964-65):41.
43. "Status of Agriculture in 1870," p. 274.

These conditions must at least partially explain the decision of seven
Union veterans from New York, who had seen the area during the war,
to settle with their families near Merrifield on land made available to
them at $25 per acre.[44] This may explain as well the arrival of Harrison
G. Otis whose family "was among several that migrated to Clifton from
the North just after the Civil War," and the actions of Ancel St. Johns of
New Jersey, who "with a number of friends," bought up much of the land
surrounding Herndon.[45] Perhaps this also accounts for the affliction of
Jonathan Magarity, an Irishman described as "land crazy" by one of his
granddaughters. In 1869, Magarity bought "Windy Hill Farm" and soon
added "Storm Farm," both near Lewinsville, and several other tracts to
his holdings.[46] That same year, the Gibbs family relocated in the Mount
Vernon neighborhood, selling three hundred acres of "Hollin Hall" to a
New York Quaker, Theron Thompson, whose family would soon pioneer
the rise of the dairy industry in Fairfax County.[47] By 1879, the Virginia
Commissioner of Agriculture estimated that "six hundred families . . .
from the northern and western States have settled in this county since the
war."[48]

Among the most successful Fairfax farmers in the immediate
postwar period were a pair of earlier immigrants from the north, James
Barlow of Sully Plantation and his neighbor Alexander Haight of Little
Sully. Soon after the war, Barlow built a general store and a
steam-powered grist mill on the Little River Turnpike, and after several
other businesses were added, including Haight's sawmill and a post
office, the community casually acquired the name "Chantilly."
According to the census of 1870, Haight and Barlow had recovered from
setbacks suffered during the war and both were worth more than
$50,000. James Barlow's decision to sell Sully to Stephen Shear of New
York and Shear's son Conrad of Michigan in 1870 for $20,000 was
certainly not prompted by a need for quick capital. The elder Shear, "a
Bible-carrying Quaker," soon returned to New York, but Conrad Shear
stayed at Sully for thirty-seven years and prospered by preserving "the
pattern of farming established years before, raising hay, wheat, corn and
some livestock," including a small dairy herd. The availability of
dependable farm hands, many of them former slaves in the area, also
contributed to the success enjoyed by Haight and Shear.[49]

44. Pearl Dunn, transcribed interview with Stephen L. Matthews, Fairfax, Virginia, 20 August
1971, pp. 1-2 (hereinafter cited as Dunn-Matthews interview).

45. Richard R. Buckley, "A History of Clifton," Historical Society Yearbook; 4 (1955):60; Nickell
and Randolph, Economic and Social Survey, p. 26.

46. Susan Collet Butler, "Windy Hill Farm," Historical Society Yearbook, 11 (1970-71):64.

47. Charles Kirk Wilkinson, "Sherwood Farm and Surrounding Area," Historical Society
Yearbook, 9 (1964-65):80-81.

48. Commissioner of Agriculture, A Handbook of Virginia (Richmond, Va.: Superintendent of
Public Printing, 1879), p. 96.

49. Gamble, Sully, pp. 116, 117, 122-24.

The advantages of those with adequate capital are easily recognized in the experience of Edward Daniels. By his own account, Daniels "came to this State in 1870 from Chicago and purchased 'Gunston Hall,' with a thousand acres of neglected and run down land. The old mansion was a ruin and the whole region was grown up to old field pine, briars and foul weeds. We put in a large force of men, with two sawmills, cleared two hundred acres, restored the old Hall at a cost of five thousand dollars, built barns and tenant houses, and began at once to plant [fruit] trees in all the open land."[50]

Another successful northern immigrant was William E. Clark who bought "Hayfield," originally a part of Mount Vernon, in 1874 and soon enlarged the estate from 360 acres to 814 acres. Even more impressive was the double-octagon, or sixteen-sided barn which Clark constructed, obviously enlarging on the plans of a barn built in the vicinity by George Washington in 1793, but which had since been destroyed. Clark's barn reportedly cost $30,000, its first story constructed of brick and containing thirty-seven horse stalls. Four hundred tons of hay could be stored above and fed efficiently to the livestock by means of a 250-ton silo in the center. The side walls of the horse stalls were decorated with cast iron ornaments which featured Clark's initials.[51]

Still another section of the original Mount Vernon estate passed into the hands of recent northern arrivals soon after the war. Stacy H. Snowden, a Quaker who had bought 652 acres on the Potomac from Charles A. Washington, the General's great nephew, in 1859, sold 820 acres known as "Wellington" to a three-man northern syndicate in 1866. Snowden, who called his home "Collingwood" after his birthplace in New Jersey, and his brother Isaac, who moved from "Wellington" next door to "Riverview" in 1866, were joined in 1869 by a third brother, William, who bought a small tract back from the syndicate and built his home there. The Snowden family became tied to another group of recent arrivals when Isaac's daughter Elizabeth married Daniel Dickinson Thompson of "Hollin Hall," whose sister Theresa Thompson later acquired "Wellington" from the defunct syndicate. Although the Thompson family continued to spread through the neighborhood as their dairy interests grew, the dominant character in the community remained the colorful "Captain" William H. Snowden, who was a poet and historian as well as a farmer on this twenty-four acres. Because the post office in Alexandria would entrust the Captain with his neighbors' mail, his pantry window became a popular gathering place. After providing this service informally for several years, he was allowed to establish an official post office in his home in 1893. This office, which he romantically

50. *Herald*, 4 January 1907.
51. Marguerite Marigold, "Hayfield," Historical Society *Yearbook*, 9, (1964-65):52, 54.

called "Arcturus" after a star, operated until 1902 and was not the extent of the Captain's development schemes for the neighborhood. [52]

Although these recent northern arrivals were by no means the only Fairfax farmers to prosper in the postwar years, their accomplishments were exceptional. Easily outnumbering these success stories were ones of those who struggled or even failed altogether, usually without either the education or the economic means to leave either records of their efforts or descendants able to do so for them. For prosperous and poor alike, the work was hard and the diversions few, and it is little wonder that county farmers soon turned to cooperative action. It should be added, however, that while there is no evidence of open hostility, neither are there indications of close economic, social, or political alliance between the northern newcomers and native southerners. A candid assessment of "regional relations" in the county appears in the Syracuse (New York) *Journal* in July 1875. The correspondent, identified only as "A.F.B.," filed his article from "Huntley," the Fairfax County estate of Albert W. Harrison who had arrived from Montclair, New Jersey, in 1868 to buy the property near Mount Vernon. "A.F.B." wrote that "The Southern people are not considered by these northern farmers [in the Woodlawn community] especially unfriendly. There is little social intercourse, however, because the women got so thoroughly mad [during the war] that they will never get over it in this world . . . . Nevertheless, there is such a sprinkling of Yankees in these parts that life here has its social attractions." [53] Economic envy on the part of county natives, differences in social and political outlook, and plain xenophobia are certainly more reasonable explanations than the correspondent's simplistic one of female intransigence, but his basic premise, that relations were neither unfriendly nor completely comfortable, remained essentially accurate for some time.

Agrarian Organization

Undoubtedly the forerunner of formal agricultural organization was the spontaneous gathering at the country store. At Barlow's Mill, built between 1865 and 1870, farmers from the Chantilly area "gathered to swap news and transact business with one another as they waited for their corn to be ground, or for a load of the powdered sumac which was used in tanning." [54] Years later, Hummer's Store remained the community center for Langley farmers, its airtight stove making it a comfortable place to pass a cold winter evening. Mr. Hummer, a

52. Mayme Parker, "Along the River Front," Historical Society *Yearbook*, 9 (1964-65):82-85.

53. Tony P. Wrenn, *Huntley: A Mason Family Country House* Fairfax, Va., 1971;, pp. 15-17 (hereinafter cited as Wrenn, *Huntley*).

54. Gamble, *Sully*, p. 116.

Confederate veteran who kept his mustache "fairly well darkened with stove polish," kept his patrons fairly well entertained with stories of the "Damn Yankees" he had killed in the war and with his unorthodox business practices. Hummer was hard of hearing and often misunderstood orders, but customers learned to take whatever they were given rather than cause a ruckus; his method of weighing flour or sugar was to balance the scale with varied quantities of nails. John C. Mackall remembered only one occasion when Hummer's method and integrity were questioned, then by a "smart alec" young man to whom Hummer replied, "dod-zackit get your flour elsewhere!" as he poured the flour back. In addition to these anecdotes, Mackall recalled that "the subject of conversation was usually farm questions," with national and local politics "gone into fully."[55]

The farmers who first recognized the economic and social benefits of organization in the postwar period were the Quakers of the Woodlawn community who were already closely linked by family, regional, and religious ties. In October 1865, twenty-one men, including the most prominent members of the community, signed the Constitution of the Woodlawn Horse Company, which they deemed "necessary for our mutual protection against horsethieves." Charles Kirk Wilkinson, descendant of a charter member, wrote that the organization consisted of "horse owners, regardless of race, who immediately formed vigilante-type groups to seek out and recover a member's lost, strayed or stolen horse. The members met once a year, always on the last Monday in December. It was obligatory for a member to attend regardless of his own illness, illness in his family or because of the meeting . . . falling on Christmas Day. If a member did not attend he was fined $2.00 . . . quite a large sum in those days."

No doubt more enjoyable were the monthly meetings of the Woodlawn Farmer's Club organized in 1866. Meetings always fell on the Saturday nearest the full moon, for after a full day of business meetings, "old-fashioned conversation," and dinner, furnished by the host family, there would be more light for finding the way home.[56] The minutes for the May 1870 meeting provide a summary of the club's activities:

> The regular monthly meeting of the Woodlawn Farmers' Club was held on Saturday . . . at Huntley, the residence of A.W. Harrison. The President being absent, Courtland Lukens was appointed Chairman pro tem. Twenty four members were present. Theron Thompson was admitted as a member. The report of the committee on vegetables . . . was . . . discussed at some length. The committee on cereals pre-

55. Mackall, "McLean, Fairfax County Virginia," Historical Society Yearbook, 4 (1955):3-4.
56. Wilkinson, "Sherwood Farm and Surrounding Area," Historical Society Yearbook, 9 (1964-65):78-79.

sented their report on the condition of things about the farm
and premises of Huntley, which was a good one and rather
commendatory of Mr. Harrison, as a practical farmer, and
elicited several pertinent questions and answers. Some discussion ensued as to the best method of ridding farms of garlic.
E.E. Mason produced several "Pips" taken dexteriously with
the thumb nail from under the tongue of young chickens. The
"Pip" is a little boney substance similar to a fish scale, a negative of the tongue, and prevents the chick from eating unless it
is removed. A conversational style of discussion ensured [sic]
on the subject of poultry. An invitation to supper, as usual,
was unanimously accepted without debate. The club then
adjourned to meet one month hence at Edward Daniels'.[57]

Members of both the Woodlawn Horse Company and Farmers' Club
undoubtedly participated in the three-day Farmers' Fair held at
Woodlawn in September 1877, called "the largest, best conducted one
ever held in that section of Fairfax County," and both groups continued
to meet well into the twentieth century.[58]

The largest organization to involve Fairfax farmers in the late
nineteenth century was the Potomac Fruit Grower's Association.
According to Edward Daniels, "its membership extended on both sides of
the river including the whole section tributary to Washington. The exhibits of this society were magnificent; they were made monthly . . .
often in the summer on steamboats chartered for the occasion."[59] In 1876,
400 members and guests of the group were entertained aboard the *Mary
Washington*, a steamboat operated from 1874 to 1882 between
Washington, Alexandria, and Mount Vernon by Paul Hillman
Troth, a prominent resident of the Woodlawn community.[60] The
Virginia Commissioner of Agriculture, Thomas Whitehead, testified to
the success of the organization in 1880 when he found Fairfax "at the
head of the list of counties in the value of orchard products."[61] Even
though the Fruit Growers' Association disbanded during the 1880s
because of "the stagnation of trade" and inadequate transportation
facilities, its example was cited by subsequent leaders of organizational
efforts among county farmers.[62]

57. Wrenn, *Huntley*, p. 16.
58. Muir, *Potomac Interlude*, p. 135. A Board of Supervisors' publication reported that the
Woodlawn Farmers' Club was "forty-one years old, and has never missed a monthly meeting." Fairfax
County Board of Supervisors, *Industrial and Historical Sketch of Fairfax County, Virginia* (Falls
Church, Va.: Newell, 1907), pp. 29-30 (hereinafter cited as Supervisors, *Industrial and Historical
Sketch*).
59. *Herald*, 4 January 1907.
60. Muir, *Potomac Interlude*, p. 148.
61. Thomas Whitehead, *Virginia: A Hand-book* (Richmond: Everett Waddey Co., 1893), p. 243;
U.S. Bureau of Census, *Compendium of the Tenth Census of the United States, 1880*, part I
(Washington, D.C.: Government Printing Office, 1883), p. 822 (hereinafter cited as Bureau of Census,
Compendium of Census, 1880).
62. *Herald*, 4 January 1907.

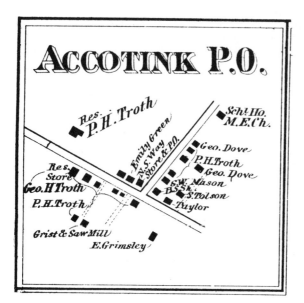

Accotink. From G.M. Hopkins, Atlas of Fifteen Miles Around Washington, 1879.

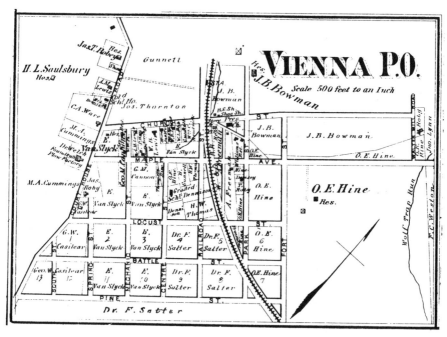

Vienna. From G.M. Hopkins, Atlas of Fifteen Miles Around Washington, 1879.

By the 1870s a number of other farmers' clubs had been organized. In 1873, the Fairfax *News* published a letter from the Farmers' Club of Accotink urging legislation to compel people to take care of their own animals and pay for the use of neighbors' fences. The following year the paper reported the formation of the Central Farmers' Club which met at Fairfax Court House and became an outspoken voice for more effective dog laws and more and better railroad service to Washington's markets. At other meetings in 1874, the fourteen to seventeen members in attendance discussed the relative merits of grazing and cropping, the best methods for preparing the ground for corn crops, and the techniques for improving land and cutting hay. Equally active was the Vienna Farmers' Club which included women participants in its business as well as its social gatherings and which discussed such issues as "cultivation of the potatoe" and the relative profits of dairy farming and fruit growing. The Fairfax *News* not only regularly reported the activities of these organizations, but also encouraged them to increase their cooperative efforts. In early 1874, for example, the editor urged county farmers to patronize the new Guanahani Guano Company of Alexandria, insisting that if the fertilizer distributor had been in operation the previous year, over half a million dollars "would have been kept at home."[63]

Destined to play a more influential role in the future of county agriculture was the Piedmont Milk and Produce Association, which held its first annual meeting in February 1873. This organizational gathering was devoted to preaching the benefits of dairying, such as the improvement of worn-out lands by dairy stock manure and the promise of a steady cash income rather than the uncertainty of fluctuating market prices once or twice a year. One Fairfax dairy farmer was reported to have netted $450 from eight cows in only eight months. The spokesman also called for a daily milk train with a refrigerator car from Fairfax County to Washington, a suggestion that the *News* seconded, calling it the key to realizing the full potential of the Washington market. At the association's second annual meeting in 1874, both progress and problems were reported, but prospects for the future seemed bright. Although there was still no night train to Washington and wagons had to be sent over the twenty-four-mile distance daily, the association reported that members had realized $13,092 in gross sales of milk, and $1,335 for other produce, while paying $2,987 in railroad and wagon freight charges. The report added that the price received for milk had averaged fourteen cents per gallon. Finally, the members decided that in the following year, farmers using their facilities would be charged a fifty-cent membership fee whether they wanted to belong to the organization or not. At its 1875

63. *News*, 31 January 1873; 27 February 1874; 13 March 1874; 1 January 1875; 10 April 1874; 8 May 1874; 26 June 1874; 10 July 1874; 15 May 1874; 11 September 1874; 6 March 1874.

meeting, the Piedmont Milk and Produce Association reported 67,582 gallons of milk shipped, with gross receipts increasing to $15,538 and shipping costs falling to $2,598. The average profit per cow for the year was $57.33.[64]

The names of individual members of the Piedmont Milk and Produce Association are no longer available, but neither its membership nor its potential was any secret to the Fairfax *News*. An editorial appeared in the paper in February 1874 concerning the association's second annual meeting, pointing out that "all but one or two members are Northerners . . . . There is money in it and our northern friends are first to find it out and profit by it."[65] It can safely be assumed that even if they were not active participants in the association (and they probably were), the experience of this early cooperative effort was not lost on the Theron Thompson family of "Hollin Hall." In 1881, Thompson's son John rented a building in Washington to receive and process milk produced by his father and brothers. The milk was shipped by wagon to Alexandria, then by ferry to the Washington distribution center. After processing, John Thompson would peddle it door-to-door to capital residents from a horse-drawn wagon.[66] In 1886, the Fairfax *Herald* reported that James Duncan of Vienna had also started a milk route to Washington, and that "besides milk that is being shipped by the railroad, there is now milk being shipped by three daily [wagon] routes from that vicinity."[67] By the mid-1890s, John Storm had developed a large dairy farm near Lewinsville, also transporting the milk daily by wagon to his own processing plant called the Storm and Sherwood Dairy located on Q Street in Georgetown.[68] With markets, herds, skilled farmers, and entrepreneurs on hand, only the highly inefficient transportation system still stood between these modest successes and state leadership for Fairfax in the dairy industry, a development which awaited the arrival of electric trolley lines around the turn of the century.

Although there is no evidence that directly links these local cooperative efforts to national agricultural organizations, any or all of them may have been at least loosely associated with the Patrons of Husbandry, better known as the Grange. The appointment of Richard R. Farr as Local Deputy of the State Grange in 1876 attests to the existence of the organization in Fairfax, though another reference to the group does not appear for a decade when a post office was established at

64. Ibid., 14 February 1873; 6 February 1874; 19 February 1875.
65. Ibid., 6 February 1874.
66. Wilkinson, "Sherwood Farm and Surrounding Area," Historical Society *Yearbook, 9* (1964-65):80; Parker, "Along the River Front," Historical Society *Yearbook, 9* (1964-65):88.
67. *Herald,* 2 July 1886.
68. *The McLean Scene,* (McLean, Va. magazine-advertiser), August 1965.

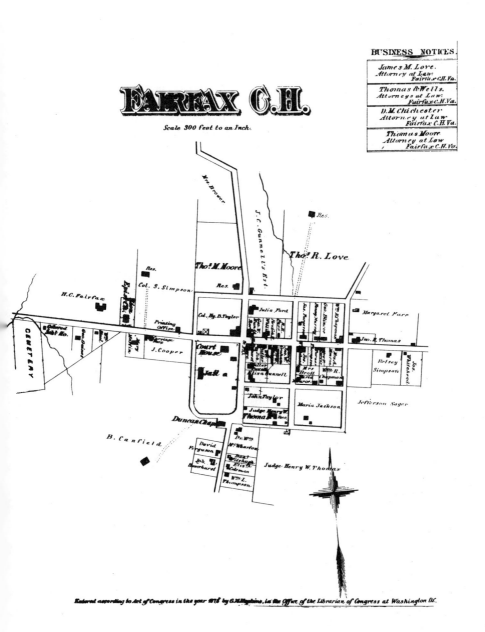

Fairfax Court House. From G. M. Hopkins Atlas of Fifteen Miles Around Washington, 1879.

"Grange Camp" just west of Vienna.[69] Nationally, the Grange was founded to provide a social outlet for farmers, but it soon turned to economic and political action as well. Local Grangers may have fit into this pattern, for in 1886 the County Board of Supervisors gave "grangers and others interested" permission to erect a flagpole on the courthouse lot for weather signals and flags, although the board specified that no political flags would be permitted.[70] Grangers may also have been responsible for the "First Annual Farmers' Institute and Exhibition" which met at Fairfax Courthouse for three days in 1891. The meeting, held "for the interest of agriculture, to promote the welfare of our county, and to aid in its development," attracted "large crowds" and was described as "very successful."[71]

There is also no direct evidence that the Populist Party made significant inroads in the county in the 1890s, despite the fact that Fairfax farmers surely felt the pinch of falling farm prices in the nationwide depression of those years. In the 1893 state elections, Fairfax voters gave only 162 of their 1,580 votes to Edmund R. Cocke, the Populist candidate for governor. However, William Jennings Bryan, the Populist as well as the Democratic presidential candidate in 1896, outpolled Republican William McKinley in the county 2,109 to 1,877, and Bryan increased his margin to 2,136 to 1,507 in a 1900 rematch.[72] The best evidence that the Populists' frustrated and confused cry for help did not go completely unheeded in Fairfax County may have been the political metamorphosis at Sully Plantation. Robert S. Gamble wrote that Conrad Shear, who lost one son fighting for the Union and whose parlor prominently featured an engraving of Abraham Lincoln, "did not waver in his Republicanism— though he found himself in the midst of a staunchly Democratic countryside—until 1896. Then, swayed by the fiery populist appeal of William Jennings Bryan and the spectre of the "Cross of Gold" upon which the American farmer was being crucified by monied Eastern interests, he forsook the GOP for the first time and voted the Democratic Ticket."[73]

69. Phillips, "Education Under Farr," p. 44; Mayo S. Stuntz, "Development of Postal Services in Fairfax County, Virginia, 1750-1890" (history seminar project, George Mason University, 1975), p. 21.

70. BOSMB, 2:42.

71. *Herald*, 10 January 1891; 4 August 1891.

72. Ibid., 10 November 1893; 16 November 1900.

73. Gamble, *Sully*, p. 125.

III

Community Cooperation:
Religion and Education

While most Fairfax residents lived and labored on the land in the late nineteenth century, community life was coming to play an increasingly important role in the county. The center of most communities had always been the church, so it is natural to find that many citizens' earliest efforts after the war were to rebuild their places of worship. During the war, many county church buildings had been occupied by troops from both armies and used as everything from hospitals to stables. The Lewinsville Presbyterian Church manse, stable, and school were occupied by federal troops for about two years, and it was not until forty years later that the federal government repaid the church for the severe damages its buildings had suffered.[74] The historic Pohick Church suffered extensively, though by 1872, $1,250 had been raised and the church was restored to usable condition.[75] The Reverend W.A. Aldrich, who was sent soon after the war to reorganize the Fairfax Zion Episcopal Church which had been completely destroyed by Union troops, found only eighteen participants at services held in the courthouse, yet reported "a deep interest manifested in religious matters, and a willingness to make every sacrifice for the sake of the Master and His cause. The people, in their impoverished condition, are making an earnest effort to rebuild." In 1869, Washington's Bishop Whittle, who conducted a service for fourteen participants in their roofed but still unfinished new building, wrote that he knew of "no congregation in the Diosese more deserving of help than this, where the people have shown such a determination to help themselves." Whether assistance was forthcoming or not, the building

---

74. Butler, "Windy Hill Farm," Historical Society *Yearbook*, 11 (1970-71):64.
75. Supervisors, *Industrial and Historical Sketch*, p. 82.

was completed in 1872, and by 1876 it was furnished and out of debt.[76] Despite these hopeful signs, disputes and hardships were not at an end. The war had split many churches into northern and southern branches, and congregations giving allegiance to the different governing bodies continued to overlap geographically and to compete, so that long after sectional squabbles had subsided, county churches remained centers of both cooperation and occasional conflict.

Second sources of community spirit and community pride after the Civil War were the new schoolhouses which spread over the county after the passage of the state school law in 1870. Actually, because of the depressed economy and the political conflicts surrounding the education issue, the guidelines established by the state guaranteed neither the implementation nor the success of the new system. A State Board of Education appointed a county school superintendent and three local trustees; their duties included examination and certification of teachers, management of school properties, administration of an annual school census, and arranging votes on school taxes. The burden for making the principle of public education a reality, however, remained in each individual community. As John K. Gott and Katherine S. Hogan pointed out in their brief history of county schools, it was the parents who "petitioned the district to start a school, and had a great deal of influence on the location, often providing the land, the school room or house, and making contributions of time, money and labor. Teachers, [although] appointed by the district trustees, were often located by the parents and boarded in a patron's home . . . . While the state provided books for indigent children other students had to supply their own."[77] Perhaps a most appropriate means of beginning an estimation and an evaluation of the growth of both new and existing communities would be to account for the establishment and growth of these two centers of community spirit—the churches and the schools.

Friendly Persuasion

Quakers had been the predominant religious group in the Woodlawn community since the large-scale migration of Friends into the area had begun in 1846. Although their pacifism had temporarily brought mistrust from both sides during the Civil War, rapid recovery in the neighborhood was stimulated by the wave of new arrivals after the war. In fact, about 1866, the size of the meeting house was doubled, and the meeting flourished through the remainder of the century, reflecting the prosperity the area farmers enjoyed.[78] Education had always been a chief

76. Rust, *Town of Fairfax*, pp. 61-62.

77. Gott and Hogan, "Fairfax Public Schools," pp. 21, 24. Among the first textbooks prescribed by the State Board of Education were Holmes's Speller, Reader and History of the United States, McGuffy's Reader, Venable's Arithmetic, and Maury's Geography.

78. Horace D. Buckman, "The Quakers Come to Woodlawn," Historical Society *Yearbook*, 9 (1964-65):69.

concern for these thrifty Quakers, and their postwar efforts in this area were exemplary. By 1868, they had organized the Woodlawn School Association, to which Courtland Lukens deeded a half acre of land for a proposed school. Though not used at the time, the present Woodlawn Elementary School was erected on this site in 1937.[79] Meanwhile, the Snowden School was organized about 1870, at first meeting in the home of Valentine Baker, a member of the syndicate which had bought "Wellington" from Stacy Snowden four years earlier. Soon a one-room school building was erected by Baker, Snowden (who donated the land), William Hunter, and Theron Thompson. Kate Snowden, Stacy's daughter-in-law, later recalled that "the benches were crude and the only desks were boards around the sides of the room. Children worked facing the wall." For many years the school seems to have functioned independently of the new state system, serving neighborhood children whose parents were willing and able to operate the school on their own. Mrs. Snowden wrote that "school was held off and on for many years in the one room," with classes conducted in turn by Josephine Baker, Alice Dove, Nellie Nevitt, who would remain in the county system for over fifty years, and Mrs. Emmet Finks, whose son contended that she "taught there two years, without pay, before the County School Board knew Snowden School existed!" Even after the county had acquired the school and property and had taken over its administration, the minimum required attendance could not always be maintained, and for two years Daniel Dickinson Thompson, who had married Isaac Snowden's daughter, operated the school in his father-in-law's home, "Riverview," with Miss Dove the teacher. The building burned around 1900, was replaced in 1903, and burned again in 1941.[80]

While their neighbors were struggling to keep the Snowden School in operation, the founders of the Woodlawn Quaker colony were attempting to follow the guidelines established by the state. Chalkley Gillingham, who had been an original member of the settlement in 1846, wrote in his diary in January 1871 that "I have been busy the past two weeks attending to help the inaugurating [sic] public free schools, according to a recent act of the state legislature." Gillingham expected "to start a white school on the 2nd day next in our meeting house," but was evidently encountering problems collecting authorized school taxes in the community. He wrote that despite "having a fund of our own, of which we can have the use of $100 per annum . . . we have had considerable difficulty in getting it up, there always being some narrow minded and contrary people to contend with. If this were not true," he concluded,

79. Katherine S. Hogan, "Fairfax County Public Schools: A Centennial Chronicle, 1870-1970" (Fairfax, Va.).

80. Kate Snowden, "The Passing of a Landmark," Historical Society *Yearbook* 9 (1964-65):92, 93.

"the world would move on more rapidly in reformation from the oldness of the letter, into the newness of the spirit." By April, however, the problems had been overcome, for Gillingham's diary reported, "we have started the white free school in our meeting house. Sallie, the wife of John Parrish, as teacher, with upwards of 30 scholars . . . remained two months, after which Maria Troth, the daughter of P.H. Troth of Accotink, took it and continues the teaching successfully." The school was supported by "15 dollars per month from the state and 15 per month from the Philadelphia Friends Fair Hill school fund."[81] As in agriculture, the Woodlawn Quaker community set an admirable example for their fellow residents of Fairfax, both in their moral outlook and conduct and in their educational achievements.

Yet if the Friends of Woodlawn were thriving economically and academically, there were occasional signs that their religious influence might be waning. In an isolated example from the Woodlawn community, a disagreement arose when Edward Curtis Gibbs failed to request the permission of the congregation to marry. When called on for an apology, Gibbs reportedly answered, "I'll be damned if I'll apologize to anyone for marrying my wife," and the family subsequently became Presbyterian.[82] Nor was this the only case of diminishing devotion to the meeting. As Robert S. Gamble reported in his history of Sully Plantation, James Barlow, in one of his last acts before leaving Virginia for Kansas in 1873, gave $40, and along with fellow Quaker Alexander Haight, was one of the largest contributors toward the construction of Christ Episcopal Church at Chantilly. "The younger Haights affiliated in the 1870s with the small Episcopal flock . . . , worshipping of a Sunday morning with the Lees, the Turbervilles, and the proud, ruined Stuarts, in the diminutive Gothic-style chapel they had helped to build."[83]

Shear Determination

At the same time establishment Episcopalians were converting their northern neighbors at Chantilly, educational opportunities in the area were expanding. By 1873, a school had been opened at Chantilly, and its teacher, Miss Frances Sherman, boarded with the Conrad Shear family at Sully.[84] The Legato School, originally four miles southeast of Chantilly on Lee Highway but restored and relocated on the courthouse grounds during school centennial celebrations in 1970, was built in 1877.[85] The Rotchford School on Ox Road must have been built about the same time

81. Andrus, "Selected Phases," pp. 92-93.

82. Joan Gibbs Lyon, "The Home Place," Historical Society *Yearbook, 9* [1964-65]:76.

83. Gamble, *Sully*, p. 119.

84. Ibid., *p. 121.*

85. Virginia B. Peters, "History of the Legato School," *Legato School: A Centennial Souvenir* [Fairfax, Va.: *Office of Comprehensive Planning* [hereinafter cited as Peters, "Legato School"].

Legato School, built about 1877, is shown after it was moved to the county government complex in Fairfax. Photo by Wm. Edmund Barrett, 1977.

Miss Lillian Millan was a teacher at Legato School for many years. Fairfax County Office of Public Affairs.

and was described by Edna Force Davis, who attended the school in the 1880s, as a "small log school house with hand made board benches and desks, running to the wall from a narrow aisle in the middle. From four to six pupils sat in each seat." By 1890, Davis was the teacher at the one-room Ashford School near Burke. Usually about twenty of the forty students enrolled attended, and for her efforts, she received about $25 per month, $10 of which went to pay her board. Lillian W. Millan, who taught for forty-four years in Fairfax County schools, rode five miles on horseback every day to her first job at "Navy," two miles east of Chantilly. Her fifty students (of all ages) were crowded into a single room. These working conditions, her transportation hardships, and her $22.50 monthly salary were not her only difficulties. "One session," Millan remembered, "I had twenty pupils with the same surname, all related." She subsequently taught in one-room school houses at Chantilly, Pender, Legato, and Jermantown.[86]

A former student's remembrances of Miss Millan were affectionate if not entirely happy ones. Mary Elizabeth Balderson vividly recalled the day she absentmindedly tapped her pencil on her desk while studying. Not only did Miss Millan scold her before her classmates, but also accompanied Mary Elizabeth home, where she told the girl's mother that the child had been "flippin' her garters." But Balderson also remembered that while "discipline was stern, enterprising students did manage a few pranks. One teacher kept a clock on her desk, but during the winter months she would often go down into the room in order to sit by the stove as much as possible . . . . While she was working with a class, some big boy would sidle up to her desk and set the clock ahead. Then all the children could go home early."[87] The contributions of such a dedicated teacher as Miss Millan to all these Fairfax communities certainly outlived the long years of her service.

Immigration and Accusation

A new station was located on the Orange and Alexandria Railroad in southern Fairfax County in 1869 to provide an outlet for the area's farm products, pulp wood, and the soapstone mined nearby. Harrison G. Otis, whose family had immigrated to the area along with others from the north after the war, became the first postmaster of Clifton Station, probably naming the new community for a town near his home in New York. Otis also built the Clifton Hotel, which became a "popular vacation resort for families from Alexandria, Washington and Baltimore," and promoted the development of the town through his real estate business.[88] An 1868 article in the Alexandria *Gazette* advertised

86. Andrus, "Selected Phases," pp. 89-92.

87. Peters, "Legato School," pp. 47-48.

88. Buckley, "History of Clifton," Historical Society *Yearbook,* 4 (1955):59-60; Geddes, *Historical Highlights,* p. 117.

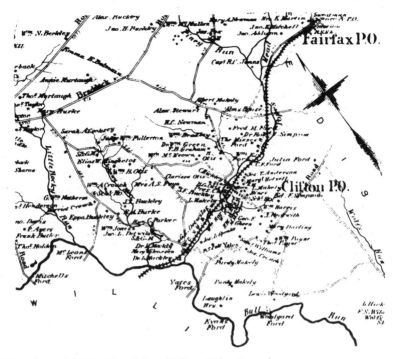

Clifton. From G.M. Hopkins, Atlas of Fifteen Miles Around
Washington, 1879.

that "immense tracts of open and waste land adjoin that now owned by
Mr. Otis, which can be bought for comparatively a mere song, and
which, with but a slight overlay could be made to 'blossom the rose.'"[89]
Even before the train began to stop, the newcomers had organized a
Presbyterian Sunday school, and two years later, in 1870, they laid the
cornerstone of their new church building. In 1872, the Clifton Baptist
Church was organized, a one-room schoolhouse was in operation,
replaced in the late 1870s by a two-story frame building, and the town's
Masonic Lodge was chartered in 1877. [90]

Despite the evidence of religious, educational, and fraternal
cooperation, all was not peaceful in Clifton. When Mary A. Otis, wife of
the postmaster and proprietress of the hotel, accused Margaret Hetzel,
widow of a U.S. Army veteran killed in the Mexican War in 1847, of
being a southern sympathizer during the late "War of the Rebellion,"
Hetzel was ostracized by her neighbors and reportedly investigated by
the U.S. Pension Office. She responded with a $10,000 libel suit against
Mrs. Otis. Though the outcome of the case is not known, here is a clear

89. John Hebert and Celeste Hebert, "The History of the Town of Clifton, Virginia" (Fairfax, Va.:
Office of Comprehensive Planning, 1975), p. 5 (hereinafter cited as Hebert and Hebert, "Clifton").
90. Buckley, "History of Clifton." Historical Society Yearbook, 4 (1955):61.

indication that bitter sectional and social tensions could arise even amid the rural tranquility of late nineteenth century Fairfax County. [91]

Relative Diversification

Despite its distance from Washington, a total of twenty-one miles, the town of Herndon from its beginning was a relatively cosmopolitan community. This is due in part to the route of the Washington and Ohio Railroad, the link completed to Herndon in 1856-57, and in part a result of the arrival of a number of northern newcomers following the Civil War. In 1858 the town received a post office named for Captain William Lewis Herndon, a Virginia-born sea captain who had heroically gone down with his ship after directing his passengers and crew into lifeboats. A survivor supposedly told this story at a meeting held to choose a name for the new post office and persuaded the village fathers to honor the dead hero. [92] Ancel St. John, originally from New Jersey, seems to have been a leader of the new arrivals after the war, a group which also included families from New York and Pennsylvania. These families were probably instrumental in the construction of the Methodist Episcopal Church in Herndon in 1872, which affiliated with the northern governing body of that denomination. Lottie Dyer Schneider, in her own *Memories of Herndon*, wrote that "about this time, a number of New England people had come to town who were Congregationalists. The Methodists graciously offered the use of their church to these people for worship."[93] By 1873 the Congregationalists had completed their own building, and by 1876 local Episcopalians, including the Castelmans, Thorntons, Cockerills, Fitzhughs, and other families with southern roots, had done likewise. [94]

Herndon citizens were early and enthusiastic in their support for public education, completing their first school building the year before the state school system began operation in 1870. Rita Schug, in a study on the community, attributed this interest to the fact that so many townspeople came from the north and were accustomed to the principle of public support for schools. When the original building burned down in the early 1870s, residents were quick to rebuild, using their own cash subscriptions and contributions of labor. [95] By the early eighties, this school was one of only five "graded schools" in the county, boasting of two teachers for its seventy-nine first- and second-grade students. [96] The

91. Hebert and Hebert, "Clifton," p. 13.

92. Herndon's daughter, Ellen Lewis Herndon,married Chester A. Arthur in 1859 and thus became First Lady twenty-two years later. Lottie Dyer Schneider, *Memories of Herndon, Virginia* (Marion, Va., 1962), p. 6 (hereinafter cited as Schneider, *Memories*).

93. Nickell and Randolph, *Economic and Social Survey*, p. 26; Schneider, *Memories*, pp. 6-7, 23.

94. Rita F. Schug, "The Town of Herndon" (research paper, George Mason University, 1973), p. 24 (hereinafter cited as Schug, "Herndon"); Schneider, *Memories*, p. 7:

95. Schug, "Herndon," p. 19.

96. Andrus, "Selected Phases," p. 68.

public schoolhouse was not the only educational facility in the town, for by 1876, Mrs. Robert Allen Castleman, a widowed first cousin of Robert E. Lee, along with her son and four daughters had established the Herndon Episcopal Seminary for Girls. Mrs. Castleman's son later became the Episcopal minister at Falls Church, but all four daughters remained at home and continued to hold classes and board students until the mid-1920s. The sisters taught the Episcopal catechism, but excused students from this instruction at their parents' request. The school also featured individualized instruction beyond the primary grades, promoted one sport, girls' basketball, and in all things stressed "discipline, deportment and poise." Tuition was $10 per month.[97]

The detailed study of town records by Rita Schug and the personal remembrances of Lottie Dyer Schneider, born the year Herndon was incorporated, provide a unique view of the vision and experience of a growing Fairfax community in the late nineteenth century. Following reception of the town charter in January 1879, officials were elected, including Mayor Isaiah Bready, originally of New York, Town Clerk Howard Blanchard of Maine, and Town Councilmen Ancel St. John of New Jersey, Stephen Killam of Nova Scotia, William D. Sweetzer of New England, William Urick, Lawrence Hindle, and C.H. Hathaway.[98] "To preserve order and property," the Council soon passed a series of ordinances, making it a crime to injure a tree on public or private property, to loiter, to insult passersby, to disturb a religious congregation, to deface property, to throw missiles, or to allow stock to wander into the "built-up" area of the town. Ball playing on Sundays was also prohibited, as were profanity or indecency in dress, manner or speech, carrying a concealed weapon, and trespassing.[99] Although the population was only 442, the incorporated area included 4 1/3 square miles of land, supposedly so that "saloons could not be established within easy walking distance of the railroad station and so create a 'town nuisance.'"[100] Schneider, whose father Elisha Dyer was Mayor, President of the School Board, or Town Sergeant for many years, remembered that "when Father was active in town affairs he had many problems with men of both races drinking and with petty thefts. I recall at one time that he had the jail full and had to house a few in the cellar. Mother was loud in denouncing this, and I think it only occurred once." On another occasion "a note was fastened to the gate threatening Father if he put any more animals in the pound. People would let their animals roam the streets and would get angry when they had to redeem

97. Schug, "Herndon," p. 21.
98. Schneider, Memories, p. 5.
99. Schug, "Herndon," p. 5.
100. Bureau of Census, Compendium of Census, 1880, p. 315; Geddes, Historical Highlights, p. 119.

Funeral procession in Herndon about 1900. Print courtesy of J. Berkeley Green. Copy by Bernie Boston.

them . . . . It worried me as a child when Father buckled on his pistol and went out to do his duty, giving little heed to threats. Gradually the town became a saner and safer place to live."[101]

    With its access to Washington markets, Herndon was destined to become another center of the dairy industry in Fairfax County, but already the train had brought a new type of citizen to the community: the commuter. Schneider recalled that "many of the Men from the North commuted to Washington daily where they held government offices." These northern newcomers were credited with adding "much to the cultural atmosphere of the community." They and their families certainly contributed to the formation and success of the Fortnightly Club, a literary group, in 1889, the Herndon Citizens Association and School

---

101. Schneider, *Memories*, p. 28.

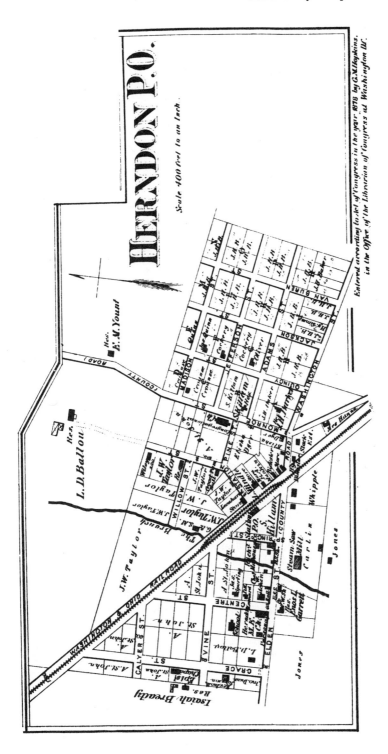

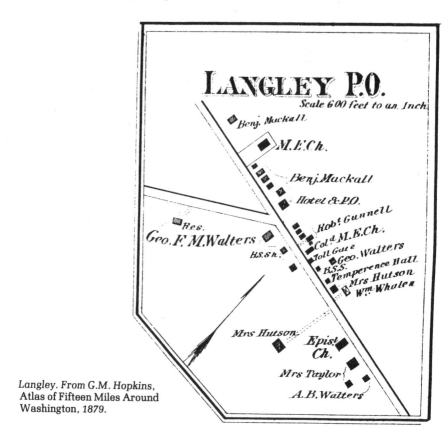

Langley. From G.M. Hopkins,
Atlas of Fifteen Miles Around
Washington, 1879.

League in 1897, the occasional singing clubs, oyster suppers, strawberry and ice cream festivals, and other church and civic activities. The train was also responsible for bringing in a number of summer residents and vacationers from the city, as well as a group not considered so desirable by the permanent populace. Especially unwelcome were the beggars and bands of gypsies who often came to town. Schneider vividly remembered the visits of the medicine man selling bottles of a dark liquid guaranteed to cure rheumatic aches and pains, the man with the dancing bear, the organ grinder and his monkey, and the gypsies who would push "their way into houses and business places, eager to tell fortunes and get money. Their clothes were gay but dirty, and they had the reputation of stealing things. When they became angry they would spit upon people. Everyone seemed relieved when they moved on to other destinations."[102] While the early arrival of the train had brought Herndon relatively great diversity, the coming of the electric trolley in the early 1900s would bring changes still unimagined in the late nineteenth century.

102. Ibid., pp. 7, 26, 27.

Languid Isolation

A log schoolhouse was in use early in the 1870s at Langley, with Miss Cordelia Slade the teacher. Several young Episcopalians, including Martha Reid, Fannie Mackall, and Kate and Helen Smoot, also used the building to give religious instruction on Sundays. By the midseventies, students from the Alexandria Theological Seminary had accepted the invitation of local Episcopalians to conduct weekly services "in the public school which had by then been established in the Methodist Church building" on the Georgetown Pike. But the trip was a difficult one for the students over undependable roads, and the congregation soon determined to erect its own building and secure a permanent minister. Both Arthur Taylor and General Benjamin F. Mackall, an honored Confederate veteran, generously offered tracts of land for the church, both sites near the intersection of the Georgetown Turnpike and Chain Bridge Road. A controversy arose, however, when it was realized that the Mackall site was directly across the road from the local tavern, which also served as a relay station for the stage line from Washington to Leesburg. Bertram G. Foster wrote in *St. John's First Fifty Years* that some parishioners contended "proximity to a barroom, or as one designated it, the 'very gates of Hell,' was no place for a church, whereas others as vigorously held that such was an ideal place for it. Whether the . . . danger to the weaker brethren" played any part in the decision is unknown, but Mr. Taylor's offer was finally accepted.[103]

St. John's Episcopal Church was consecrated in 1877. Within a few years neighbors had added by stock subscription a town hall, the scene of dances, drama productions, and civic meetings. Despite these diversions, however, and the entertainment always available at Hummer's Store, the community was struggling by the turn of the century, primarily because of its isolation, even though the nation's capital lay within five miles. As John C. Mackall, one of the General's five children who attended school in Georgetown, remembered, "due to the terrible condition of the roads and the fact that my father also had his law office in Washington, my family had been compelled to take up quarters in Georgetown for the winter months."[104] For the Mackalls' less affluent neighbors, trying to reach markets, schools, and churches must have been a real hardship. Even St. John's, only two decades after its completion, "fell on evil days. It was actually closed for a year or so for lack of a minister, and some referred to it as 'St. John's in the Wilderness.'"[105] But the Langley community, like several others in the county, would be transformed within a few years by the arrival of the electric trolley.

103. Louise L. Smith, "St. John's Episcopal Church in McLean," Historical Society *Yearbook*, 5 (1956-57):33-34.

104. Mackall, "McLean, Fairfax County, Virginia," Historical Society *Yearbook*, 4 (1955):13.

105. Smith, "St. John's Church," Historical Society *Yearbook*, 5 (1956-57):34.

Restoration and Fraternization

At least some county residents were desperate for new neighbors in the 1850s, for when Dr. William Hendricks offered to settle at "Ayr Hill" if the citizens would change the community's name to "Vienna," Hendrick's hometown in New York, they agreed.[106] Another New Yorker, Orrin E. Hine, arrived in 1866 and had an even greater impact on the community. William West, born in Vienna in 1873, explained 102 years later that during the Civil War northern "men were soldiering through here [and] could see what the prospects were for peacetime . . . . Major Hine was one of those who after the war came back and bought quite a tract of land." Tax records back up this assertion, for by 1885 Hine owned 6,440 acres in the vicinity, with property and buildings appraised at more than $45,000.[107] In addition to running his extensive farm and a real estate office, Hine has been credited with straightening and widening the town's streets and then lining them with six miles of maple trees. When the town was incorporated in 1890, "in order to improve its public schools and . . . streets," he became its first mayor, a position he held until 1900.[108] If these activities and honors are not tribute enough, in 1897, the Hamilton (Loudoun County) *Telephone* evaluated his contributions to Vienna over three decades: "to the credit of Major Hine . . . after the late war was over he came back to the very section where, per force of the necessities of cruel war, his men had contributed to the desolation of the country, and has devoted all of the succeeding years in 'making glad the waste places' and surely, it can be truthfully said of him that he has restored to this section more than he destroyed."[109]

Major Hine was also deeply interested in the principle of public education, for in 1868 he went to Richmond where he testified before the General Assembly on the operation of public schools in the North, and two years after the state's system had been established, Vienna had a two-story frame school house.[110] By 1882, it was another of Fairfax County's five "graded schools," with two teachers and two grades for its sixty-seven students.[111]

Vienna Presbyterians completed their church in 1874, while Methodist and Episcopalian congregations were organized in the 1890s.[112] Perhaps equally important to many residents were the

106. Supervisors, *Industrial and Historical Sketch*, p. 12.
107. Andrew M.D. Wolf, "Black settlement in Fairfax County, Virginia during reconstruction" (Fairfax, Va., unpublished study, 1975), p. 32 (hereinafter cited as Wolf, Black settlement).
108. Elizabeth C. Burke, "History of Fairfax County," Historical Society *Yearbook,* 5 (1956-57):11.
109. Wolf, Black settlement, p. 33.
110. Burke, "History of Fairfax County," Historical Society *Yearbook* 5 (1956-57):11.
111. Andrus, "Selected Phases," p. 68.
112. Burke, "History of Fairfax County," Historical Society *Yearbook* 5 (1956-57):11.

Vienna School. From Industrial and Historical Sketch of Fairfax County, Virginia, 1907.

numerous clubs and secret societies around which "the principle warfare of the town is centered" and "for which the town is famed," according to the *Industrial and Historical Sketch* of the county published by the Board of Supervisors in 1907. Among the organizations listed were the Woman's Club, the Business Men's Club, the Daughters of the American Revolution, the Masons, the Odd Fellows, the United Woodmen, the Good Templars, the Village Improvement Society and the Junior Order United American Mechanics.[113]

Enthusiasts for Education

Other nearby communities were showing a similar interest in education if not for civic and fraternal affiliation. In fact, there is at least one claim that the one-room school at Flint Hill, later Oakton, was the first "public" school in the county, that is, the first supported by the tithes of local residents. It held its first session in 1849. This school burned soon after the war, but was replaced by another one-room

113. Supervisors, *Industrial and Historical Sketch*, p. 12.

building at the intersection of Hunter's Mill and Chain Bridge Roads in 1874.[114] The seven northern families who had settled at Merrifield after the war also refused to wait for state and county assistance, instead taking "matters into their own hands to provide an education for their children." Pearl Dunn recalled that "first, they organized the Mill's Crossroads Literacy Society . . . . Some gave money, [up to] $10 per family . . . . Others gave materials; some gave labor . . . . Results . . .a one room log school" completed in 1874.[115] Parents were not alone in their desire to help. Mrs. Arthur Wynkoop proudly remembered the efforts of older students a few years later to obtain a new school to replace the old store building on the corner of Hunters Mill and Lawyers Roads which had been leased by the school board. The students, "so anxious for a school house, had strawberry and ice cream festivals and oyster suppers and raised $100 which they gave to the School Board . . . for the new building."[116]

Isolated Stagnation

Although it was the county seat and famed for the sweetness of the water from the well on its public square, Fairfax Court House could hardly be described as a thriving community in the late years of the nineteenth century. The opposition to the town's new brick school under construction in 1873 has been mentioned, as have the hardships of the Zion Episcopalians in trying to rebuild their church after the war. When the town abandoned its former name "Providence" in favor of "Fairfax" in 1874, Providence seems to have abandoned Fairfax in return.[117] In 1875 the locally published Fairfax *News* folded. The town of 376 received a booster in 1881 when Captain Stephen R. Donohoe arrived from Alexandria to establish and edit the Fairfax *Herald*, and more capable leadership was provided through the 1880s by Frank Page, Rector of Zion Church from 1878 to 1889 and brother of Thomas Nelson Page whose romantic novels about the Old South made even Northerners shed nostalgic tears.[118] But the "scattered rural membership" of the Duncan Chapel Methodist Church (South), which replace an earlier church in 1882, "was hampered by severe winters, bad roads, and diphtheria epidemics," and in 1888 its minister, Rev. O.C. Beak, wrote of a "general business depression in this area" which caused the church and no doubt

114. Helen Rector Jones, "A History of the Oakton School," Historical Society *Yearbook*, 7 (1960-61):27, 28. When Squire E. Smith applied for a post office at Flint Hill in 1883, he learned that another Virginia community had already claimed the name, so he chose "Oakton" for the huge oak tree then at the intersection of routes 674 and 123. The tree was cut, as were most of Major Hine's maples, when the roads were widened to accommodate automobile traffic in the twentieth century.

115. Dunn-Matthews interview, p. 2.

116. Peters, "Legato School," p. 37.

117. The county seat of Culpeper County had formerly claimed the name Fairfax, but freed the name for the Fairfax County seat and changed its name to Culpeper.

118. Candace Jo Sheris, "Truro Rectory," Historical Society *Yearbook*, 11 (1971):96-97.

FAIRFAX C. H., VA.

—o—

THOSE in want of Riding Vehicles, such as

Daytons, Spring Wagons,

SURRYS,

BUGGIES,

with and without Tops, New and Second-hand, I would say give me a call, I think I can suit you, both in price and quality,   If I have not what you want, leave your order and it will be filled at short notice REPAIRING and PAINTING DONE, AND SATISFACTION GUARANTEED. New BUGGY TOPS fitted to old Jobs, as usual.   Prices to suit the times.

JOSEPH COOPER.

Old Fairfax Herald Print Shop, Friday, 13 July 1888.

the entire community to suffer "from removals."[119] Even the town's most treasured possession, the will of George Washington, was threatened with removal to the State Library in Richmond by action of the General Assembly in 1876.[120] The standard explanation for the town's troubles, appearing regularly in the *Herald* until the arrival of the trolley line in 1904, was the lack of a rail link and the unreliable roads, isolating the courthouse from most of the county in bad weather. Whatever the reason, when Fairfax Court House received its charter of incorporation in 1892, its population had fallen, by one estimate, to two hundred; it had three white and two black churches, a school for each race, three or four stores, a newspaper office, an old-fashioned tavern, a coach and wagon maker, and seemingly busiest of all, an undertaker's establishment. [121]

Pachyderm's Predilection

Two families played leading roles in the growth of the settlement surrounding Baileys Cross Roads in the thirty years after the war: the Munsons and the Baileys. Timothy Munson, a New York Presbyterian, had brought his family to the area in 1851, and in 1869, Daniel Munson inherited his father's 260-acre nursery known as Munson Hill Farm. A

119. Rust, *Town of Fairfax*, p. 62.

120. *News*, 11 December 1874. County protests against the move were ultimately successful, and the historic document remained in the historic old courthouse. BOSMB, 1:90, 96.

121. Rust, *Town of Fairfax*, p. 66. As early as 1873, in sharp contrast to realities two decades later, the Fairfax *News* had proudly boasted of the town's amenities and limitless future: "We have four stores, two merchant tailors, one grocery, one bakery, one wheelwright and carriage shop, two hotels, one hostelry, a travelling butcher, two bar rooms, three schools, two doctors, six lawyers, three churches, with a fourth in expectancy, a brick kiln, a full share of fourteenth amendments and a lot of free dogs. . . . But what especially gives interest and a name to the place is . . . the old Court House, with an unrivalled *well* outside, and Washington's *will* inside. Enough said. Quantum sufficit. Glory, honor, ancient Romans. Spartans nowhere." At least the well had not gone dry twenty years later. *News*, 28 March 1873.

Northern sympathizer during the war, the younger Munson had the distinction of being kidnapped by the legendary Colonel Mosby in 1863, and his good fortune in escaping earned him his own claim to the title "Colonel." Daniel Munson's biographer called him "a mighty successful horticulturist, having business relations from Maine to Texas," and from Munson's correspondence comes a more revealing assessment of the scope of his business. In 1883 he wrote, "I am very busy, having from 20 to 30 men to attend in my nursery and also 40 agents to look after." More lasting but unfortunately not permanent testimonials were the hundreds of Munson maples which lined the streets of Falls Church, making that village a "riot of color" every fall until they fell to the wider streets which the automobile demanded in the twentieth century.[122]

The source of the settlement's name was Hachaliah Bailey, "Father of the American Circus," in the words of the greatest showman of them all, P.T. Barnum. The crossroads had been the winter home of the famed Barnum & Bailey Circus for many years, but as Jane Chapman Whitt wrote in her lively account of *Elephants and Quaker Guns*, "the upkeep of circus menageries had become a luxury that Hachaliah Bailey descendants, divided by the war, found difficult to maintain." Remaining animals returned to the circus circuit, but Mariah Bailey, Hachaliah's daughter-in-law, who had inherited the Baileys Cross Roads property in 1843, stayed on. In the 1870s, Mariah deeded land to Fairfax County for the settlement's first public school, and in 1886 she not only donated the two-acre site, but also volunteered her carpenter son Theodore's labor for the construction of St. Paul's Episcopal Chapel. In addition, she always entertained the students, who came from the Alexandria Episcopal Seminary to conduct weekly services, at the boarding house she had fashioned by moving the old Cross Roads Inn to adjoin the family mansion "Maury." According to Whitt, Maury" became a popular resort for Washingtonians "who would come to the countryside to spend a weekend or the summer. Guests who enjoyed riding to hounds could find Virginia hunters in the stable [or] would head for the old circular riding ring." Ironically, an injury forced the energetic matriarch to spend her last years bedridden, but she was no doubt provided constant company by her eight children and their offspring, her two greyhounds, and her South American parrot, a gift from sympathetic circus friends. The bird's vocabulary was described as "a shocking jargon of Espanol and circusese." Mariah Bailey died in 1896, but as if to commemorate the colorful past her family had contributed to the community, soon after the turn of the century, an electrical storm caused a stampede of terrified elephants from a nearby amusement park.

122. Jane Chapman Whitt, *Elephants and Quaker Guns: A History of Civil War and Circus Days* (New York: Vantage, 1966), pp. 62-63, 75-76.

"Trumpeting wildly . . . one of the animals crashed his way up the slopes from Four Mile Run to Bailey's where he was lassoed in a cornfield," still another symbol of the county's past that was, by then, vanishing rapidly.[123]

The Barroom's Rejection

Vestiges of the past were vanishing even more rapidly down the road at Falls Church, speeded by the postwar arrival of a large number of Northerners to what had been a "mere hamlet of perhaps a dozen houses." One of the first was Isaac Cross, a Pennsylvanian attracted to the village by the farmland available so close to Washington at $40 per acre.[124] Far more representative of Falls Church's future, however, were Charles H. Buxton and W.W. Kinsley, both government clerks in Washington who decided to make their homes in the village in 1871. Despite the fact that "at that time the railroad facilities to Washington were most unpromising," others soon followed these "pioneers" of the town's "department colony," including G.A.L. Merrifield and M.S. Roberts, employees of the Pension Bureau, Albert P. Eastman of the War Department, and George F. Rollins of the Treasury Department.[125] In 1873, Joseph S. Riley, also of Washington, took up residence at Cherry Hill Farm, one block northeast of Route 7, where he would hold court sessions after he became Town Magistrate and Justice of the Peace.

According to Melvin Lee Steadman, Jr., "Judge Riley was almost solely responsible for the incorporation of the town in 1875, and at his own expense went to Richmond to lobby the charter through the General Assembly." Charles E. Gage was told by Riley "that one of the impelling reasons behind [the incorporation] was the deplorable conditions in the village due to the unregulated sale of drink. Apparently, there was so much loafing and drinking that ladies could not walk about without embarrassment."[126] Besides banishing the barrooms, the charter gave residents the power "to lay off new streets, alleys and sidewalks; to regulate or prohibit the running at large of animals; to provide for order and quiet, and the observance of the Sabbath . . . ; to provide and protect shade trees; to establish a fire department . . . , [and] to regulate in reference to contagious diseases."[127] Still another newcomer,

123. Ibid., pp. 82-83, 85-88.

124. Charles Alexander Stewart, *A Virginia Village: Historical Sketch of Falls Church and the Old Colonial Church* (Falls Church, Va.: J.H. Newell, 1904), pp. 2, 22 (hereinafter cited as Stewart, *Virginia Village*).

125. Nickell and Randolph, *Economic and Social Survey*, p. 21; Stewart, *Virginia Village*, pp. 7-8.

126. Melvin Lee Steadman, Jr., *Falls Church: By Fence and Fireside* (Falls Church, Va.: Falls Church Public Library, 1964), pp. 76, 407 (hereinafter cited as Steadman, *Fence and Fireside*).

127. Tony P. Wrenn, *Falls Church: History of a Virginia Village* (Falls Church, Va., 1972), p. 27 (hereinafter cited as Wrenn, *Falls Church*).

Merton E. Church, who arrived in Virginia from Vermont in 1879 and settled in Falls Church in 1886, would seek even more far-reaching changes in his efforts to develop the community into a suburb of Washington.

In the meantime, residents of Falls Church were devoting abundant attention to their schools, but occasionally inappropriate attention to their churches. Another M.E. (Methodist Episcopal) Church came to town when newly arrived northern Methodists, apparently feeling unwelcome in the Dulin Chapel Methodist Church (South), established

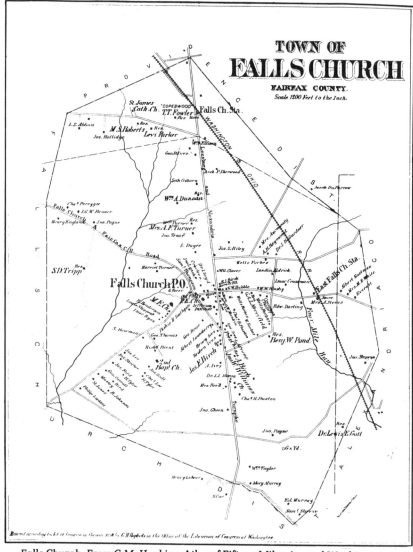

Falls Church. From G.M. Hopkins, Atlas of Fifteen Miles Around Washington, 1879.

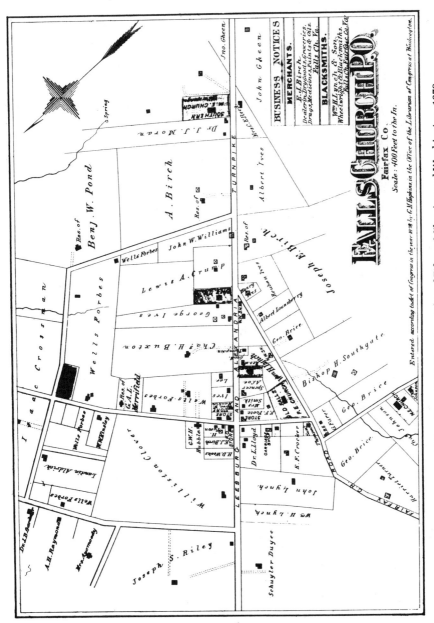

Falls Church Post Office. From G.M. Hopkins, Atlas of Fifteen Miles Around Washington, 1879.

their own in 1875. Antagonism over religious matters was heightened the following year when recent emigrants from New England organized a Congregational Church. Even a purely promotional pamphlet, printed by a local developer a number of years later, admitted "that some residents had thought" that another church in such a small town would result in dissension among the Christian people." At its first meeting, the new church felt called upon to issue a resolution expressing its "good wishes toward every church of Christ in this place," and its "desire to co-operate with them in every good work."[128] With evidently more unanimity, inhabitants initiated a drive for a local educational institution. Many signed a petition in 1875 pledging themselves to the principle of public education and binding themselves "for the purpose of aiding and sustaining a public graded school in the Village of Falls Church."[129] Already in 1871, a school had been established, probably meeting in the Columbia Baptist Church, and by the early 1880s, the two-story brick Jefferson School had been completed, built largely with the contributions of local citizens.[130] County school records reveal that the town's school, even in the seventies, was graded and consistently had the highest enrollment and attendance of any in the county. For several years after moving into the new building in the 1880s, the school had an unprecedented three teachers, and it divided as many as 193 students into as many as seven grades. These were accomplishments which would not be approached anywhere in the county through the remainder of the century.[131]

Ada Walker's *Memories of Old Jefferson Institute* provides a former student's intimate look into this exceptional school and into the Falls Church community in the early 1890s. In a tribute to James Isaac Brown, a Quaker from Loudoun County and the school's principal from 1890 until his death in 1893, Walker cited the kindness and flexibility with which he administered his considerable authority. To illustrate, she told of a request made by the school's older girls that they be permitted to include a "college song" in each day's opening exercises, along with the usual hymn and Bible reading. Brown gave his permission, leaving the girls with the responsibility of preparing the other students, and on the following morning, Walker recalled, they most inappropriately led the class in "There is a Tavern in This Town." "Principal Brown sat quietly with his arms folded until the song was concluded. With no apparent feeling, he broke the strange silence . . . by saying, 'if that is a good example of college songs, I think we'll sing no more of them.'" Yet when the girls apologized for their mistake, Brown granted them a second

---

128. Nickell and Randolph, *Economic and Social Survey*, p. 22; Stewart, *Virginia Village*, p. 81.

129. Steadman, *Fence and Fireside*, p. 407.

130. Burke, "Fairfax County," p. 9; Ada Walker, *Memories of Old Jefferson Institute* (Falls Church, Va., 1964), p. 3 (hereinafter cited as Walker, *Old Jefferson Institute*].

131. Andrus, "Selected Phases," pp. 49, 68, 85-86.

chance, and "the next day when the singing of 'The Spanish Cavalier' was concluded, Mr. Brown said pleasantly, 'that is more like it, and you will do even better than that,' and they did." Another of Brown's students, William H. Emerson, remembered that occasionally the principal would allow schedule changes so that male students could accept the standing challenge of unenrolled working boys in the village to a noontime baseball game. Word would rapidly spread, and no doubt many of the more than eight hundred residents of Falls Church would assemble to witness the big event.[132] Although these innocent pleasures persisted, Falls Church was becoming even more impatient than other Fairfax communities in awaiting the arrival of the electric trolley, an event which would cause the developments of the coming decade to quickly overshadow the progress of the previous three.

Deserved Diversion

Church services and socials, school activities, and fund raisers for churches and schools provided the residents of every Fairfax County community with enjoyable and meaningful diversions from their labors. Although it was hardly an abundant commodity in the late nineteenth century, what the people did with their leisure time can tell much about their interests, values, and goals. A turn-of-the-century county directory revealed that several communities other than Vienna featured professional societies, fraternal lodges, and patriotic organizations. Listed were five Masonic lodges, three chapters of the Independent Order of Odd Fellows, five of the Junior Order United American Mechanics, two of the International Order of Good Templars, many Sunday school associations, a businessman's club, a medical society, Daughters of America and Daughters of the American Revolution chapters, a fruit growers' association, and a Confederate veterans' camp.[133] County newspapers regularly reported that the carnivals, expositions, jousting tournaments (the target being a small metal ring on a rope), picnics, and even balloon ascensions sponsored by these groups were open to the public and were well attended. Baseball was the leading athletic pastime, but tennis was also popular, as the organization of a lawn tennis club in Fairfax in 1887 indicates. Shopping or sightseeing excursions into Washington, except for farmers going to market, were infrequent for most, but competition from large Washington, D.C., stores may have been responsible for the Fairfax merchant's offer in 1886 of a $75 bedroom set to the couple who would agree to be married in the store's show window. The Fairfax *Herald* reported that there were five applicants, and a large crowd was no doubt entertained by the ceremony for the lucky pair. An even more

132. Walker, *Old Jefferson Institute*, pp. 2, 3.
133. William G. Collins, ed., *Fairfax County, Va., Directory, 1906* (Falls Church, Va., 1906), pp. 15, 17, 19, 21.

The Fairfax Baseball Team, about 1910. Photo courtesy of Wilmer Holbrook. Copy by Lee Hubbard.

amusing spectacle may have been the occasional "masked ball" at which the guests appeared disguised as anyone from "Alonzo the Fair" to "Black Eyed Susan."[134]

Edification and Organization

A more serious activity was the lyceum held regularly in several Fairfax County communities including Fairfax, Flint Hill (Oakton), and Herndon during the fall and winter months. Among the questions discussed or formally debated were "Does temptation lessen the baseness of crime?" (no); "Which is most useful to mankind, gold or iron?" (iron); "Which exercises the greatest influence on the minds of the people, the press or the pulpit?" (pulpit); "Does civilization tend to abolish military ambition?" (yes); and "Lady Jane Gray justly beheaded?" (no). "Another interesting feature of the Lyceum" at Flint Hill, the Fairfax *News* reported, "is, that to each member is assigned a question to be answered at the next meeting. These questions are of almost every describable kind, relating to history, geography, botany, &c, and form no small part of the profit of the meeting."[135] Equally constructive and providing a

---

134. *Herald*, 27 May 1887; 3 December 1886; 29 December 1893.
135. *News*, 13 November 1873; 18 December 1874; 29 January 1875.

much needed social outlet for the county's rural residents were the meetings of the various farmers' clubs. The monthly meeting of the Woodlawn Farmers' Club, for example, was an anxiously anticipated event. Charles Kirk Wilkinson, who grew up at Sherwood Farm in the vicinity, remembered one meeting hosted by his parents at which "we served dinner for over one hundred members and guests." Wilkinson also remembered that the men and the women held separate business meetings, adding that "the men were mainly interested in their agricultural and business pursuits," while "the ladies were responsible for the religious and charitable organizations in the community." One such organization was the Mount Vernon Circle of the King's Daughters, a nonsectarian group chartered in 1872 which contributed time, labor, and money to the Alexandria Infirmary Association, the Chautauqua Fund, war orphan support, and other causes.[136]

Sexual Limitation

Despite their involvement in these worthy causes, it is interesting to note that women never actively participated in the debates of county lyceums. Instead, women served as secretaries for the groups and were occasionally allowed to read "a select piece," recite a temperance poem, or on one occasion, to render "a humorous dialogue, entitled 'Mrs. Tweezle and Sir Peter.'"[137] Meanwhile, women teachers in county schools received salaries averaging ten percent less than men doing the same job.[138] Since there is no evidence of dissent, the Fairfax *News* may have accurately reflected a county consensus on the role and position of women when it responded in 1874 to a recent incident in Ohio where "women banded together in a crusade against barrooms, converting them, for the moment, into places of prayer. The design may have been good, and the effect may have been felt, still we do not think 'the end justifies the means,' as it cannot be the duty of women to foresake their homes and household affairs and wander about in that manner. It is not their province, nor have they the power to suppress the liquor traffic, or the drinking of liquor. It must come chiefly (if at all) through other instrumentalities, such as legislation and the united action of men."[139]

---

136. Wilkinson, "Sherwood Farm and Surrounding Area," Historical Society *Yearbook*, 9 (1964-65):78-80.

137. *News*, 29 January 1875.

138. Andrus, "Selected Phases," pp. 29, 53.

139. *News*, 22 May 1874. In this same year the *News* argued that the General Assembly was "wasting time in discussing the rights of married women." *News*, 27 March 1874.

IV

Legacy of Emancipation

To imply that the few farms and the dozen communities touched upon to this point embodied life in Fairfax County in the late nineteenth century would be to perpetuate a deplorable injustice. For until the recent completion of Andrew M.D. Wolf's path-breaking study of "Black Settlements in Fairfax County" in the postwar period, little had been recorded and nothing of substance had been published on this subject. It has been argued that a minority group should not be afforded separate treatment in a historical survey; rather its members should be given proportional attention among the community at large. Although there was much interaction between the races, in this case it seems appropriate to deal with the black experience in Fairfax independently, first of all because, whether by circumstance or design, blacks remained essentially a group apart from the white majority. Furthermore, in addition to the basic problems shared by all Fairfax residents in the aftermath of the war, blacks faced a set of social, economic, and emotional difficulties unparalleled in our history. While they were freed from the burden of slavery, most blacks suddenly found they had neither the capital nor the experience necessary to establish a foothold and to enjoy the American dream of equal opportunity that the verdict of war and constitutional amendments had promised them. Their efforts to overcome these handicaps, however successful, deserve express attention. Finally, this focus is justified by the unique opportunity it provides: the examples of intolerance, as well as the sincere efforts to provide assistance, will add to the material measure a meaningful evaluation of the quality of county life during the final third of the nineteenth century.

Racial Intimidation

If the editorial voices of the Fairfax *News* and Fairfax *Herald* were representative of the racial views of the county's Conservative (Democratic) majority, for whom both claimed to speak, many whites had neither confidence in blacks' ability to overcome their handicaps nor great concern over the prospect of their failure. The response of the *News* to a speech delivered by Governor James L. Kemper to the black members of the Virginia Assembly in 1874 was typical. The Governor insisted that "we must all enjoy a common prosperity, or we must all go down in a common ruin," and that "each race [must] stand up for the interests and rights of the other and of both," to which the *News* replied, "we do not believe one word of it. . . . We do believe . . . that the negro is wholly dependent upon the white race for his prosperity as he now enjoys it, [but] the white race is in no degree, or sense, dependent upon the colored race for a like condition. In short, we think the two races would be infinitely better off if they were separated by an impassable gulf. The Anglo-Saxon's career is onward and upward, regardless of what the colored race may do. The only question to be considered is, will the negro follow our example, and keep up in the great contest for the acquirement of property and general intelligence? We have the gravest doubts that he will, and the more pertinent question is, how much is he likely to clog and retard the advancement of the white race by his inactivity and uncongenial presence?"[140] While few blacks would have read this reply, it was hardly calculated to heighten blacks' self-esteem or to harmonize relations between the races. On the contrary, the more likely purpose of such diatribes was the aggravation of tensions, both out of sheer bigotry and in an effort to enhance a political advantage.

Several other items from the newspapers seem studied attempts to stimulate fear of the black man among white readers. At the end of its two-column report on a rape-murder in West Virginia in 1873, the *News* warned "that there have been more negroes hung for rape and murder during the last eight years of freedom, than altogether during the two hundred and forty years of their bondage in the United States. This is civilization with a vengeance! and how much longer will the high-toned Anglo-Saxon blood submit to see these brutal outrages perpetuated upon their wives and daughters, by tamely waiting the slow, and sometimes uncertain process of the law [?]"[141] The Fairfax *Herald* regularly reported the percentage of black prisoners in the local jail, while ominously detailing the crimes they had committed. The editors of both papers also appealed to their readers' pocketbooks, lamenting the terrible cost of

140. Ibid., 15 May 1874.
141. Ibid., 10 October 1873.

crime in the state, especially in operating "that public negro boarding house called the State Penitentiary." *Herald* editor S.R. Donohoe then found the crime rate among blacks difficult to understand in light of "the millions of dollars spent to educate and enlighten the negro since the war," and "the further fact that the Southern people in their personal intercourse with the negroes are universally kind to them."[142] After saddling blacks with practically complete responsibility for crimes committed in the county and state, the *News* continued vigorously to condemn every civil rights bill brought before Congress on the grounds that "we do not believe in any sort of class legislation."[143] The real object of these scare stories, it seems, came out at the end of an article in the *Herald* in 1889. After reporting that all four county jail inmates were black the paper stated that "still, there are white people who think that the republican party, a majority of which are negroes, should have control of the state."[144]

The decision by county Republicans to nominate a black for constable in the Providence District in 1889 gave the Fairfax *Herald* an opportunity to get maximum political mileage out of its appeal to its readers' fears. The paper admitted that it knew nothing about the candidate, but explained that "it is the suicidal and pernicious policy of electing negroes to office to the injury and detriment of our county, to which we wish to call the attention of the people. . . . A negro constable *now*, means a negro overseer of the poor, negro justices, and negroes for all the other offices after a while. It is useless to deny the fact, for we can name counties in this State where Republicans have had control. . . . In one case . . . under the old whipping post law, a white girl sixteen or seventeen years of age, charged with petty larceny, was sentenced to be whipped, and the lashes were actually administered by a negro sheriff! . . . If you are opposed to negro rule, you should not only vote against the negro candidate, but against *all the Republican nominees*, . . . and thus administer a rebuke to that party that it will not soon forget."[145] The black candidate was not elected.

Despite the vehemence of their convictions, the views of the Fairfax *News* and Fairfax *Herald* were not universally held in the county. Indeed, there seems to have been a general recognition of the value of black labor in the postwar period and, therefore, of the need to maintain at least stable race relations. Even the *Herald* admitted that "with all his faults, the black man is the best laborer the South could have, and his place, were he to leave, would be hard to fill."[146] Furthermore, it seems that

---

142. Ibid., 17 January 1873; *Herald*, 28 December 1888; 29 March 1889; 11 December 1891; 19 April 1889; 9 March 1889.

143. Ibid., 5 December 1873; 29 May 1874.

144. *Herald*, 19 April 1889.

145. Ibid., 17 May 1889.

146. Ibid., 7 December 1888.

while many county whites may have responded to the newspapers' general attacks on the black race, they were much less temperamental in their personal contacts with county blacks. Their fears were directed at some unknown and distant threat rather than toward their black neighbors whom they had known (or until recently owned) and depended upon all their lives. Finally, it must be remembered that after the war, the county experienced a large-scale influx of newcomers from the North who, while not wholly altruistic, tended to have fewer ingrained prejudices against blacks. The demand for black labor, the proximity to Washington, D.C., low land prices, and the presence of liberal Northerners must have made Fairfax a relatively attractive area for blacks, because even immediately after the war, when many former slaves were migrating to the North or to the developing Southwest, both black population and property ownership increased steadily in the county. Between 1860 and 1870, the number of blacks increased thirteen percent; between 1870 and 1880, it increased another twenty-three percent to 5,264. Despite the occasional outbursts of bigotry, in several communities there was evidence of genuine cooperation and friendship between the races.[147]

A Fordable Privation: Affordable Habitation

The black settlement at Gum Springs could trace its origin back to 1829 when West Ford, a former slave, was willed a tract of land by Bushrod Washington, the General's nephew. Ford eventually divided his 211 acres among his children who, in turn, subdivided, and by 1880, this settlement of freedmen included twelve families, among them Ford's grandson West who was the florist at nearby Mount Vernon. The availability of steady employment at Washington's home, by then open to the public with a large maintenance staff, must partially explain these blacks' ability to acquire their own land so quickly, for census records reveal that several other members of the community were also employed there. A second explanation was the cheapness of the marshy Gum Springs property, which certainly deserved its name. One of the men, whose name was King, attempted to improved his plot by promoting it as one of the county s first land fills, and the new home he built there was a testament to his success.[148]

The community s center was the Gum Springs School, established for area blacks in 1871 by the Woodlawn Friends. Ever since their arrival in the 1840s, the Quakers had been generous toward their black neighbors, and Chalkley Gillingham's diary reported in early 1871 that

---

147. Bureau of Census, *Compendium of Census, 1880*, p. 376.
148. Wolf, Black settlement, pp. 23-24.

they had "started two colored schools, one on each side of my place at Woodlawn and Gum Springs." In addition to $15 per month from the state, the schools received "the assistance of Friends in Philadelphia with their fund—giving 10 dollars per month to each school—we have a colored teacher in the Woodlawn and a white one in the Gum Spring School and about 40 scholars in each on the list, 37 being present yesterday at Gum Spring and 34 at Woodlawn." In April 1871, Gillingham wrote that "we had to change the teacher in the Woodlawn school from colored to white and one of our daughters, Hannah W. Cox, is teacher there [but both] schools are now in successful operation."[149] At a time when fewer than 50 percent of the enrolled students countywide were actually attending schools, the extremely high percentage of blacks in attendance at Gum Springs and Woodlawn is noteworthy. It must have been with great pride and self-confidence that West Ford told the census taker in 1880 that six of the nine members of his family, excepting only his wife and two small children, could read and write.[150]

The Accustomed Occupation

Contrary to the case in most parts of the south, there was little sharecropping in Fairfax County, so the vicious cycle of diminishing crops and rising debts was avoided. But unless a freedman possessed some skill or trade, he had few employment alternatives to farm labor, which often too closely resembled his former condition in slavery, with the exception that he received wages of fifty to seventy-five cents per day. Blacks in the Chantilly vicinity seemed satisfied to remain on the land they had worked as slaves. Jacob Barlow of Sully Plantation recorded a payment of $45.98 to Caleb Ray, a freedman, his wife, and his son on 1 January 1868, and over the coming years, George Currie, Oscar Mason, and other workers, "most of whom had once been slaves in the area, . . . performed the myriad tasks that kept Sully going: baling hay, repairing fences, plowing, sowing, and reaping." Currie and his wife Ellen, "also . . . born in slavery but now . . . a paid domestic," would continue to work at Sully and neighboring farms into the twentieth century.[151]

A similar pattern, though on a larger scale, was taking shape at Herndon. As Rita Schug concluded, "since Herndon was off the beaten track and settled primarily by northerners, it offered a snug haven for the freedman, not far enough north to be inhospitable climatically and offering sufficient employment on small local farms."[152] A late nine-

149. Andrus, "Selected Phases," pp. 92-93.
150. Wolf, Black settlement, p. 26.
151. Gamble, *Sully*, pp. 116, 122, 124.
152. Schug, "Herndon," p. 36.

teenth-century white resident gave a serene, if stereotyped, picture of Herndon blacks, remembering that "in the evening some of our colored citizens would . . . assemble on [the railroad] platform and to the accompaniment of their banjoes sing songs and while away the twilight hours."[153] In neither Chantilly nor Herndon, however, does it seem that many blacks were able to acquire land. The 1880 census reported thirty-four black families in the Herndon area; with the exception of a blacksmith, several railroad workers, and two independent farmers, all the men were listed as farm laborers. William West, the centenary citizen of Vienna, could remember only one black, Arch Shirley, who owned a farm near Herndon.[154] Still, area blacks were taking advantage of educational opportunities. As early as 1866, a school for blacks had been organized at nearby Frying Pan, although the building was the target of an arsonist in November of that year.[155] An 1878 map reveals that a "Colored Schl. Ho." could be found at Chantilly, and of the three schools designated in Herndon, one must have been for blacks, for Harrison Moulton, remembered as an "outstanding . . . colored citizen," went on to graduate from the Hampton Institute at Hampton, Virginia.[156]

Emancipated Congregation

Late in 1863, Cyrus Carter, the freeborn son of Lancaster County, Virginia slaves, brought his family by boat up to the Potomac to Washington, D.C. It was probably during his wartime service in the ambulance corps, carrying the sick and wounded across Chain Bridge to the capital, that Carter first noticed the nine acres of heavily wooded and apparently uninhabited Fairfax County property which he bought soon after the war from John S. Crocker, a Union general who invested in several parcels of depreciated county land. While Crocker seems to have planned to make his property available to freedmen, charity was clearly not his only motivation. In 1876, he sold an additional four acres to Carter for $450, to be paid over five years "under legal interest." In the meantime, the Carters had been joined by several other Lancaster County families who christened their community "Lincolnville" after their recently killed commander-in-chief. Soon other black migrants arrived, including Hiram James Kinner, a former slave in New Orleans. The 1870 census listed Kinner as a farmhand living with the Sliptoe Darby family of Lincolnville, though by 1877 Kinner was able to buy a five-acre farm from Pierce Shoemaker who was subdividing a piece of land he too had acquired from General Crocker. The easy access to

153. Schneider, *Memories*, p. 11.
154. Wolf, *Black settlement*, p. 65.
155. Gamble, *Sully*, pp. 115-16.
156. G.M. Hopkins, *Atlas of Fifteen Miles Around Washington Including the Counties of Fairfax and Alexandria, Virginia* (Philadelphia, 1879), p. 69 (hereinafter cited as Hopkins, *Atlas*); Schneider, *Memories*, p. 28.

Aqueduct Bridge and Long Bridge over the Potomac as viewed from Georgetown, 1875. From Keims, Washington and Its Environs, *1880, United States Commission of Fine Arts.*

Washington markets allowed the community to thrive. Cyrus Carter made an agreement to supply the Washington, D.C., jail with cabbage, string beans, corn, and other vegetables, while Christopher Columbus Hall, who came to Lincolnville from Loudoun County before 1870, anticipated the rise of the dairy industry in Fairfax County when he established a twenty-six-acre dairy farm in 1872. Before long he also owned a store in Washington, operated by one of his sons, where he marketed his milk products.[157]

The Christian religion had always been important to black Americans: a comfort, a diversion, and a promise that unrelieved suffering was redemptive. Probably no county resident realized more clearly the continuing importance of the church to blacks after emancipation than did Cyrus Carter. Soon after their arrival, Lincolnville residents organized a Baptist Church and held services in members' homes. Then in December 1866, barely a year after the community had been established, a small wooden church building was dedicated, built on Carter's land. Carter also donated a one-acre cemetery plot and served as pastor of the church until his death in 1891. For fourteen years Carter also served as minister to the Baptist congregaton at Odricks Corner, and he may have been instrumental in the establishment of other freedmen's churches in Vienna and Falls Church.[158]

157. Wolf, Black settlement, pp. 45-48.
158. Ibid., pp. 70-71.

Conspicuous Cooperation

Freedmen in the Vienna vicinity probably had the widest range of economic opportunities in the county, although those able to acquire land remained a distinct minority. William West recalled in a recent interview that his maternal grandparents, Simon and Lucinda Alexander, were among the earliest local black landowners. The Alexanders had been slaves at "Woodacre," the plantation of Frank Williams, a captain in the company of Colonel Mosby. Although the property had been devastated during the war, the former slaves remained, and for their loyalty through the difficult times, the captain's mother, Frances Williams, deeded them a parcel of land for $1.00 in 1869. William West's paternal grandfather Thomas and his father Daniel West were among the many laborers on the extensive farm of Major Orrin E. Hine. By 1870, the Wests had acquired their own small plot, valued by the census taker at $100. Equally important to the black community was the arrival of another Northerner, Captain Harmon L. Salsbury, who, according to William West, had commanded a division of blacks during the war and had developed "a great and civil regard for his men." His Vienna property must have amounted to several hundred acres, for in the 1870 census it was valued at $10,000. And as Andrew Wolf observed, "since the names in the census were . . . listed in the order of the families along the roads, it could be seen that there was a cluster of black families in the immediate area of Salsbury's home. This certainly stands to reason, for . . . not only did he make the property available, he also facilitated the obtainment of his lots by extending easy credit to the Vienna blacks, few of whom had . . . capital. West [recalled] that when he bought his first acre from Salsbury in the early 1890's, he was charged $100, but was given ten years to pay the money. During the first five years, no interest was demanded; after that there was only a minimal rate." In addition to the work available on the large farms, blacks in the area could find employment at several local industries. The Moses Commins Plow Factory, which operated until the late 1870s, paid its workers $1.00 per day, considerably higher than current farm wages. A fertilizer plant and a tomato canning factory also provided blacks with opportunities to acquire capital and eventually, perhaps, a piece of property. William West described relations between the races in Vienna as "very good; a black could go into any white store, and none were prevented from buying land."[159]

Soon after his arrival in Vienna, Major Hine heard his field hands discussing their desire to organize a church. At his suggestion they applied to the government and were given permission to use the lumber

159. Ibid., pp. 30, 34-37.

in the numerous abandoned ammunition shelters left in the area. On a plot donated by Hine, they erected a Baptist Church in 1867.[160] An 1887 county map labeled this building "Cold. Schl Ho.," so it clearly served a dual purpose.[161] While not debunking Hine's generosity, one life-long county resident suggested that there may have been an ulterior motive behind the major's gift. Captain Harmon L. Salsbury, 'Hine's rival in real estate," owned the property adjacent to the church site, she explained, so Hine may have hoped to depreciate the value of Salsbury's land, "since he believed that whites were often wary of living near freedmen." However, considering Salsbury's open-mindedness and Hine's record as an employer and civic leader, such an explanation seems unlikely. Both of these men were probably deserving of the praise given Hine in 1897 by an area newspaper, which saluted "the applied energy of the new men and new money that he had been instrumental in locating here," and "the forceful effect of the . . . progressive ideas that he has helped introduce."[162] Certainly the blacks of Vienna had benefited by their presence in the community.

Constructive Occupations

Two other successful and very self-sufficient black settlements were located near Vienna at Odricks Corner and on what is now Belleview Road. Alfred Odrick, who gained his freedom from the Coleman family of Dranesville on Proclamation Day, 1863, was a skilled carpenter, and by 1872 he had saved $450 with which he bought thirty acres of land. He evidently succeeded at farming, for he soon replaced his log hut with a large, comfortable house for his family. The 1880 census reported that eight or nine more black families settled nearby, including Cyrus Carter's son Andrew, a skilled craftsman in his own right from the Lincolnville settlement, who had married Odrick's sister-in-law. Interestingly, Carter bought his seventeen acres at Odricks Corner from General John S. Crocker who had sold the original Lincolnville property to his father shortly after the war. Even before Alfred Odrick built his own home, he constructed a community schoolhouse on his property, and beginning in 1873, Cyrus Carter came to conduct weekly Baptist services in the building. In 1887, the elder Carter laid the cornerstone for the Shiloh Baptist Church, also built on property donated by Odrick. Meanwhile, less than a mile away, another community was crystallizing around the homestead of Samuel Sharper whose grandfather had earned his freedom and acquired the thirty-four-acre farm in 1825. The 1870 census valued Sharper's real property at $1,000, an amount to which he added $500 in

160. Ibid., p. 71.
161. Hopkins, *Atlas*, p. 69.
162. Wolf, Black settlement, pp. 23, 34.

1874. That the community was growing is obvious from the successive marriages of three of Sharper's daughters to three sons of Albert Henderson, a neighbor. John Jackson, another neighbor, was probably not alone in seeing that his children got an education, but he was surely a proud father when his son Lewis became the teacher at Odricks School, indicating that the two communities worshipped and studied together.[163]

A Fairfax Conflagration

Just as it lagged behind the rest of the county economically after the war, Fairfax Court House needed to improve relations between its two racial groups. Perhaps the rhetoric of the locally published Fairfax *News* and Fairfax *Herald* contributed to the ill feelings, for in November 1873, the *News* reported that a recent political rally and barbecue "came near to ending in a general row. Some colored blood was made to flow, rocks were in demand, and some powder was burnt. Fortunately, . . . the propelled lead flew wide of its mark. Some were seen down in the streets hunting for specimens of quartz rocks, while others went down because they could not help it . . . . Several sore heads were felt the next morning. All this was the result of an attempt to harmonize the races."[164] Fortunately also, such an occurrence was not representative of all contact between blacks and whites in the vicinity. Francis Honesty, a life-long resident of Fairfax, recalled that Dr. Clarke Brooke, a large landowner and the local tax collector, employed many freedmen on his farm, and later sold land to a number of them. Honesty's wife's grandfather operated a general store in this black community about a mile south of town on Braddock Road. Honesty also remembered that many blacks "found employment in the saw mills which were busily producing ties for the expanding [railroads, and] blacksmithing evolved as a popular trade among the freedmen below Fairfax, for the saw millers often needed worn equipment and broken bolts . . . replaced."[165]

Within the village of Fairfax itself, almost one-third of the inhabitants were black. Easily the most successful was James Ferguson, known locally as Jim Fogg. Before the census of 1870, Fogg purchased at public auction the "Allison Stable Lot" and began his own livery stable. According to William West, "Fogg could always count on his best business every third Monday . . . when officials came from various parts of the county to attend meetings at the courthouse." In 1874, Fogg bought another lot at auction, this one located "in front of the door of the Courthouse," where he must have erected the "eating house" that the 1880 census reported he owned. The census, however, failed to mention

163. Ibid., pp. 51, 53-55.
164. *News*, 7 November 1873.
165. Wolf, Black settlement, p. 63.

the small rooming house Fogg and his wife operated, probably above the restaurant.[166] In addition to Jim Fogg's enterprises, local blacks had organized a school for their children and two churches by the time of the town's incorporation in 1892.[167] Even in the face of verbal and physical animosity, blacks like Jim Fogg were able to become successful and respected members of the Fairfax community.

Genealogical Amalgamation and Admirable Ambition

Although the William Boston family was not a part of a black community, its struggle for a foothold affords a revealing view of the black experience in the postwar years. Boston was the son of a racially mixed couple, and his wife, Henrietta, had a genealogy which included General James Jackson of Civil War fame, an eighteenth-century Algonquin Indian, and assorted other ancestors, both black and white. It may have been the family's "white roots," Andrew Wolf suggested, that caused the Bostons to feel "no need to seek the security of a black community." For many years after their marriage in the 1870s, William and Henrietta Boston rented their home from the Ball family, "apparently one of those countless southern families devastated by the Civil War." In 1889, Boston was able to take advantage of the Ball's continuing financial difficulties by selling his horse and cow, then paying all back taxes in addition to the purchase price on fifteen acres of Ball property located on the Georgetown Pike near Great Falls. The income from their small farm and from Henrietta's job as a cook for two neighboring white families was still inadequate, so William took a job at a stone quarry on the Chesapeake and Ohio Canal in Washington, for which he was paid fifty cents per day. And as Florence Smith, Boston's granddaughter, recalled, "that wasn't for eight hours. That was from the time he could see until the time he couldn't see."[168]

Cross Roads Integration

The John Bell family joined the Daniel Munson and the Mariah Bailey families as leaders in the Baileys Cross Roads community after the Civil War. Bell, who had received an education from his former master or employer, left North Carolina in the 1860s for Washington, D.C., where he took a job in the U.S. Patent Office. After several years in the city, Bell decided that he wanted his children to grow up in a rural environment, so, like the thousands who would follow him, he came to northern Virginia in search of a home within commuting distance to his government office. In the early 1870s, Miles Munson, Daniel's younger brother, heartbroken over the recent loss of his new home and young

166. Ibid., pp. 63-64.
167. Rust, *Town of Fairfax*, p. 66.
168. Wolf, Black settlement, pp. 67-69.

daughter in a tragic fire, decided to leave Virginia and sold his fifty-acre tract near the Columbia Pike to John Bell. By 1880 Bell had hired a live-in farm attendant, a freedman named Jefferson Davis. There were many other employment opportunities for blacks on several large white-owned farms in the area (Munson Hill Nursery was probably the biggest employer), and Bell's granddaughter Mrs. Julia Bell Sheppard recalled that several white families subdivided and sold parcels of their land to local blacks. The 1880 census found that fifty of Baileys Cross Roads' eighty-nine inhabitants were black, so this must have been one of the more densely and peacefully settled black communities in the county. John Bell was clearly a leader in maintaining this happy condition, for his granddaughter remembered stories of how "he used to set up long wooden tables on his lawn where officials and citizens of both races who were concerned for the development of the area would spend many an afternoon discussing various local problems."[169]

Pleasant Consolidation

In the midst of the Civil War, a group of newly freed blacks from southern Virginia found their way to Alexandria, where, homeless and jobless, their plight came to the attention of Charles H. Brown, a resident of New York who owned sixty acres of Fairfax County land a short distance south of Baileys Cross Roads. The freedmen eagerly accepted Brown's offer to subdivide the property, evidently on terms within their means. Andrew Gaines and Andrew Jackson, who bought and built homes on their plots in the late 1860s, did not have their deeds recorded until 1873 and 1875, respectively, indicating that they were given several years to complete payment. The new arrivals, numbering about a dozen families, called their settlement Mount Pleasant, and by 1867 they had erected a Baptist church on land set aside for that purpose by Brown.[170] John Bell, from Baileys Cross Roads and a devout Baptist, was surely among many from that community to attend the church. And though black children from Baileys attended the small frame school built on land donated by Bell for several years, they later walked the short distance to a "consolidated" school which met in the Mount Pleasant Church.[171]

Economic Diversification and Foote-dragging Segregation

The largest and most diversified group of blacks in the postwar period settled in the vicinity of Falls Church. Frederick Forrest Foote, a slave of the Minor family until 1863, was the first to acquire land. To accomplish this, Foote enlisted in the Union Army while continuing to

169. Ibid., pp. 57-61.
170. Ibid., pp. 49-50, 72.
171. Whitt, *Elephants and Quaker Guns*, pp. 78-79.

Frederick Forrest Foote was a merchant and member of the Falls Church Town Council, 1881-1889. From Melvin L. Steadman, Falls Church By Fence and Fireside.

work nights on the Chesapeake and Ohio canal, and by 1864, he was able to make a down payment to his former owner on a twenty-eight-acre tract where he built his home. Although Foote did not complete payment on the property until 1882, he acquired several other plots of land before 1878, including three lots in Falls Church valued at $2,100. It may have been on these lots that Foote's son, Frederick, Jr., established his shoemaker's shop and his large grocery and provisions store. In 1881, the voters of the village elected Frederick Foote, Jr., to the Falls Church Town Council, evidently the first black to hold such a position in the county. Foote remained on the council until his death in 1889. Six years later, when Frederick, Sr., died at the age of ninety-five, a member of the Minor family paid tribute in a deposition, writing that "old Frederick Foote was thought a great deal of by the white people and children used to very frequently go to their house and stay all night."[172]

Despite the high regard of the white community for the Frederick Foote family, census records indicate that Falls Church blacks lived in three very distinct and segregated neighborhoods. The first, called simply "the hill," was settled by the freed slaves of the Dulany family

172. Wolf, Black settlement, pp. 37, 39-40.

Mrs. Louisa Marrs Henderson was a leader in the black community in Falls Church. She is shown about 1886 with her children, Edwin B. (standing) and William A. Henderson. From Melvin L. Steadman, Falls Church By Fence and Fireside.

whose land was subdivided for them after the war. Immediately after this was done, a man was reported trying to take "advantage of the naivete of these blacks as landholders by imposing upon them monthly rents . . . . This corrupt activity was discovered, however, and the scoundrel was apprehended."[173] A second settlement was the "Southgate Subdivision," one of many developments conceived and promoted by entrepreneur extraordinaire Merton E. Church who arrived in the town in 1886. By the early 1900s, this settlement was reported to include "probably a hundred cottages with a population of between 400 and 500 . . . . Many of the little cottages and surroundings indicate industry and thrift in the occupants."[174] The third black settlement was in West Falls Church and was known as "Gravel Banks." As Andrew Wolf observed, the census taker in 1880 must have begun "his trek through the village in one of [these] communities, because the list . . . commences with 29 black families, or 149 individuals. The striking feature of this group [was] the degree of occupational variation among the working men." On the list Wolf found "a carpenter, a Baptist minister, a blacksmith, a wheelwright, several schoolteachers, and even an enterprising banker."[175]

173. Ibid., p. 40.
174. Stewart, *Virginia Village*, p. 22.
175. Wolf, Black settlement, pp. 40-41.

Although blacks in Falls Church were finding opportunities not available elsewhere in the county and though race relations were described as "very good" by E.B. Henderson, a descendant of Frederick Foote, even here there was a lingering fear among whites of the black population.[176] By 1873, 232 of the town's 632 registered voters were black, a percentage which prompted the white majority to seek to limit black political influence in 1879.[177] As Henderson explained, "there existed in those days a real two-party system. Many of the settlers from the North were Republicans and all the Negroes were Republicans. All the Southerners were Democrats, and they were the dominant party in Falls Church. To improve the political situation, the colored section was cut off from the town to remain in Fairfax County. It was not an unusual practice. It was just a case of simple gerrymandering."[178]

The Falls Church community featured examples of the best and near worst in late nineteenth century race relations. The recognition of ability regardless of race, symbolized by the election of Frederick Foote, Jr., to the Town Council in 1881, demonstrated how far county residents had come in fifteen years. Probably only the viciously racist attacks by county newspapers and the physical violence they may have inspired were more detrimental than the denial of political rights to Falls Church blacks by the racially motivated boundary change. The postwar period witnessed significant progress for many individual blacks: physical freedom for all, political rights for most, education for many, economic sufficiency for some, land ownership and independence for a small minority, and social acceptance for a fortunate few. But seen as a group, blacks had few of the comforts and fewer of the freedoms that twentieth-century Americans have come to expect as their birthright as citizens of this country. Furthermore, with the exception of their self-segregation into separate communities, where they were often forced to make their homes and spend their lives, blacks had not yet begun to realize that only through unity, and in some cases only by demonstrating their discontent and inviting suffering, could they win recognition of the common humanity they share with all men. In the midst of their late nineteenth-century difficulties, it is doubtful that county blacks would have found comfort in the knowledge that the worst was yet to come.

176. Wrenn, *Falls Church*, p. 30.
177. *News*, 31 October 1873.
178. Wrenn, *Falls Church*, p. 30.

V

Conclusions and Projections

As in the particular case of relations between the races, so, in general, was Fairfax neither phoenix nor failure in the late nineteenth century. Population growth was steady, reflecting a mood of moderate optimism. Not quite 13,000 people inhabited the county in 1870; by 1900 the figure had reached 18,580, an increase of 43.5 percent.[179] Meanwhile, land values, the county's key economic gauge, had not kept pace. Just two years after the war, the county's 265,153 acres had an average assessed value of approximately $17. By the mid-1870s, this figure had fallen to $15, then to less than $14 in 1883. By 1896, county properties at $15.38 per acre, were still well below their value of thirty years before.[180] Statistics can never stand alone, but the glimpses of farm and community life, the accounts of religious and educational institutions, and the sketches of individual endeavor have confirmed this conclusion, disclosing both successes and serious remaining obstacles to progress. Since one of man's unique characteristics is his imagination, perhaps the plans and the dreams of a people are as important as contemporary realities in an evaluation. An effort to determine how the people of Fairfax viewed their personal and their county's future is in order.

The Railroad's Invitation

In 1874, the Fairfax *News* felt its readers had every reason to look with confidence to the future: "the county of Fairfax is destined, at no

179. U.S. Bureau of Census, Ninth Census, *The Statistics of the Population of the United States* (Washington, D.C.: Government Printing Office, 1872), 1:68; U.S. Bureau of Census, *Twelfth Census of the United States*, 1900, (Washington, D.C.: Government Printing Office, 1902), 1:lvi.

180. *Chataigne's Virginia Gazetteer and Classified Business Directory*(Richmond: J.H. Chataigne, 1877-1878), p. 463; *Chataigne's Virginia Gazetteer and Classified Business Direcotry* (Richmond: J.H.

distant day, to become one of the wealthiest agricultural counties in the State . . . . Nothing is more probable than that within a period of ten or twelve years from this time, all the lands, especially east of the Court House [sic] and around it, will be taken up and cultivated as market farms, . . . by which time lands will range from $50 to $100 per acre because of their proximity to Washington City, Georgetown and Alexandria, affording . . . the finest markets in the world for every thing our soil will produce." The only obstacles the *News* perceived to this Arcadian vision were "the want of an adequate and regular supply of trained labor" and the want of an adequate and regular supply of trains. The newspaper's assurances that the former shortage "in a few years will be overcome . . . by tha [sic] farmers doing their own work on the small farm system" were largely accurate.[181] In addition, the several thousand landless freedmen provided a most reliable labor force, whether or not the *News* cared to admit the county's economic dependence on this group. The second shortage proved more stubborn, but so did the *News* and other county voices in their advocacy of the railroad as the key to both present and future prosperity.

By the early 1870s, there were three rail lines traversing the county: The Washington & Ohio Railroad, soon the Washington, Ohio & Western which passed through Falls Church, Vienna, and Herndon to Leesburg; the Orange, Alexandria & Manassas, soon the Virginia Midland Railway, passing through Fairfax Station and Clifton; and the Alexandria & Fredericksburg Railroad which linked those cities by way of Woodbridge, through the Woodlawn neighborhood. As important as the railroads were to these communities, and as large as they loomed in the county's anticipated agricultural development, other means of transportation still figured more prominently, and caused more headaches, in the day-to-day lives of most county residents.

Wagons continued to carry the bulk of Fairfax farm goods to Washington markets, and most farms and communities were connected only by usually uncomfortable and often impassable roads. Notwithstanding the avalanche of editorials and the plethora of public meetings on the necessity of good roads, there appears to have been little permanent improvement in county roadways during the late 1800s. Stage service was discontinued from Alexandria to Middleburg through Fairfax County in early 1873, and the *News* could not convince anyone to invest the estimated $150,000 needed to extend the King Street horse car service from Alexandria to Fairfax Court House.[182] As late as the turn of the

---

Chataigne, 1884-1885), p. 232; *Chataigne's Virginia Gazetteer and Classified Business Directory* (Richmond: J.H. Chataigne, 1897), p. 408.

181. *News,* 17 July 1874.

182. Ibid., 11 April 1873; 1 August 1873.

century, much of the wagon and buggy traffic still favored the "shun-pikes," as the ersatz parallel roadways formed by those who shunned the rough and rutty turnpikes were called. As John C. Mackall recalled, even "the shun pikes were narrow and in wet weather full of mud holes . . . . When two vehicles met going in opposite directions, . . . it was sometimes necessary for one to back out."[183] Still more frustrating must have been the frequent inaccessibility of existing railroad facilities. In January 1873, the Fairfax *News* happily reported the completion of the depot on the Orange, Alexandria & Manassas line at nearby Fairfax Station, but by June, the paper was again demanding direct rail access from Fairfax Court House to Alexandria and Washington. The following year, the editor wrote bitterly of the "terrible condition of the road from the Court House to Fairfax Station" and concluded that "if we cannot get a railroad let us, by all means, have a passable dirt road to our place."[184] Eighteen years later, the editor of the Fairfax *Herald* was still complaining about the poor and inconvenient railway service available to Fairfax Court House residents.[185]

Even when they were able to reach the railroads, county customers often found their expectations unfulfilled. Service was neither certain nor always safe, largely a result of the continuous financial problems suffered by all three roads. The experience of the Washington & Ohio was typical. Restored to service in 1867 after suffering severe damage during the war, the W&O was bankrupt and in receivership by 1878. The line was sold twice in 1882, the second time to New York investors who renamed it the Washington, Ohio & Western. But each year brought new deficits, and in 1894, the new Southern Railway Company acquired the line through foreclosure proceedings.[186] Such difficulties made it impossible for the line to respond to the appeals of the Fairfax *News* that it fence its right-of-ways, notwithstanding the 1873 accident in which a cow derailed and destroyed an engine, which, in turn, tore up fifty feet of track.[187] Nor could railroad officials be certain of the intentions of county authorities who seemed torn between their desires to encourage improved and expanded service and to collect much needed revenues by more heavily taxing railroad real estate and equipment in the county. The Board of Supervisors equalized tax rates on railroad and other county properties in 1880, and two years later, the assessment of railroad property was increased from $5,000 to $15,000 per mile of track.

183. Mackall, "McLean, Fairfax County, Virginia," Historical Society *Yearbook*, 4(1955):6.

184. *News*, 17 January 1873; 27 June 1873; 1 May 1874.

185. *Herald*, 19 February 1892.

186. Louise C. Curran and William J. Curran, *McLean Remembers* (McLean Scene, Inc., 1967), p. 28 (hereinafter cited as Curran and Curran, *McLean Remembers*); Ames W. Williams, *The Washington and Old Dominion Railroad* (Springfield, Va.: Capital Traction Quarterly, 1970), pp. 27-28, 41-42.

187. *News*, 26 September 1873.

Second thoughts about the impact such a tax hike might have on a rail service, along with an injunction obtained by the W&O Railroad against the County Treasurer to restrain him from collecting the taxes, convinced the board to reduce the assessment back to $5,000 per mile. Further railroad investment in Fairfax was certainly not encouraged by the board's action, and poor service continued.[188] A Falls Church developer's handbook in 1906 described the rail service to Washington of thirty years earlier as "unpromising. The coaches were little better than the present freight car caboose, and the schedule was unreliable, the trains slow, and a change of cars had to be made at the Alexandria junction."[189] A more recent monograph described "the road's operation . . . as attuned to its surroundings, being slow moving, casual and carrying a halcyon air."[190] Despite the railroad's nineteenth-century shortcomings, probably most county residents continued to agree with the Fairfax News that the railroad was the "greatest invention in history."[191] While some would argue a qualitative meaning for "greatest" in this claim inaccurate, the quantitative impact on the county could hardly be exaggerated after existing railroads were converted to and supplemented by electric trolley lines in the 1890s and early 1900s.

Suburbanization

The Washington, Ohio & Western's route through Fairfax was responsible in 1887 for the evolution of a new conception of the county's future. That year the newly-formed Loring Land Improvement Company announced that it had "secured a tract of land in Fairfax County on the Washington, Ohio & Western Railroad, about fourteen miles from Washington, and midway between Falls Church and Vienna." Although a number of county residents, from Falls Church to Herndon, were already commuting daily over the line to jobs in Washington, the Loring Company's proposed new commmunity of "Dunn-Loring" was the first organized effort to present the county as a suburb rather than as an agricultural supplier to the District of Columbia. "The nearness of the town of Washington," the company's promotional pamphlet explained, "being only forty-five minutes from the Baltimore and Potomac Station, renders it most desirable to persons employed in that city and wishing for a healthful country home. Good railroad accomodations are provided . . . and telephone and postal arrangements have been made . . . . The lots range in size from 80 x 160 feet to five acres . . . . The price and terms of sale will be reasonable and easy; and every inducement will be

188. BOSMB, 1:173, 207-8, 212.
189. Stewart, Virginia Village, p. 3.
190. Curran and Curran, McLean Remembers, pp. 28-29.
191. News, 14 December 1872.

The East End railroad station at Falls Church, about 1898. During the Spanish-American War, visitors came by train to see soldiers at Camp Alger near Merrifield. From Melvin L. Steadman, Falls Church By Fence and Fireside.

afforded to those who desire an attractive residence."[192] Unfortunately for its promoters, before the first two houses could be completed, General William McKee Dunn, "a wealthy man living near Lewinsville [and] the driving force behind the development," died, and his chief partners, George B. Loring, a Washington, D.C., occulist, and George H. LaFetra, the proprietor of a temperance hotel in Washington, were unable to keep the project alive. Not until the company was reorganized in 1913 did the community again awaken, and not until after the second World War did rapid growth begin.[193] Despite the original failure of "the Dunn-Loring Subdivision," had the county been paying attention in 1887, it could have caught an accurate glimpse of its future.

Military Invasion

If the W, O & W and the Dunn-Loring development had struggled since their respective inceptions, both enjoyed a brief period of

192. Loring Land and Improvement Company, *Town of Dunn Loring* (Judd & Detwiler, 1887), pp. 3-4.

193. Prentiss A. Shreve, "A Short History and Some Anecdotes of Dunn Loring, Virginia, and Neighboring Towns," *History of Dunn Loring and Vicinity* (Dunn Loring Volunteer Fire Department and the Ladies Auxiliary, Souvenir Program, 1954), p. 7; Edgar Shreve, "Reminiscences of Mr. Edgar Shreve," *History of Dunn Loring and Vicinity* (Dunn Loring Volunteer Fire Department and the Ladies Auxiliary, Souvenir Program, 1954), pp. 11, 15.

prosperity during the Spanish-American War, when the United States Army took advantage of existing transportation and communications facilities in choosing a site between Falls Church and Dunn-Loring for Camp Russell A. Alger. By August 1898, more than 35,000 troops were stationed at the camp, and though the fighting would be over before many of these soldiers would see action, "troop trains arriving or departing, drills at camp and practice marches . . ., martial music from army bands, reveille and taps, all contributed to impress [county] folk with the fact that the country was at war."[194]

President Willam McKinley came often to review the troops, among them the future biographer of another president. In his renowned study of Abraham Lincoln, Carl Sandburg included a brief description of the soldier's life at Camp Alger:

> I did in 1898 wear the same light-blue trousers and dark-blue jacket with brass buttons as the troops of the Army of the Potomac, and near Falls Church, Virginia, only a few miles from the Capitol dome, I lived in a tent, answered roll call six and eight times a day, cut saplings and built myself a bunk, more than once made a practice march in hot weather carrying in the first weeks a Springfield rifle, later a Krag-Jörgensen rifle, cartridge belt, canteen, and blanket roll.[195]

Occasionally, the monotony of camp life was broken by a trip to see the sights of Washington on one of the hourly trains of the temporarily solvent W, O & W Railway, or by an outing into surrounding Fairfax County. A company of midwesterners reported tasting their first corn pone at a farm house near camp, and rated it a "fair addition to the [usual] ration of bacon and hard tack."[196] Another source reported that "the homes of the citizens were thrown open to soldiers . . . , and the ladies . . . vied with each other in contributing to the comfort of sick soldiers at the camp."[197] While appreciative, the soldiers no doubt felt entitled to this attention since they blamed local water supplies, rated "anything but good," and "the imitation pastry sold as pies" by local peddlers, rated a "disgrace [to] a 10 cent restaurant," for their sickness. But the worst complaints were reserved for "the roads of Virginia," which the newspaper correspondent for an Indiana regiment camped near Clifton reported "were experienced in all their glory of mud."[198]

194. Stewart, *Virginia Village*, pp. 27, 29.

195. Carl Sandburg, *Abraham Lincoln: The War Years*, 4 vols., (New York: Harcourt, Brace & Co., 1939), 1:ix.

196. Terre Haute, Indiana newspaper, [1898, Terre Haute *Express*], from a personal scrapbook of articles on Camp Alger in Fairfax County.

197. Stewart, *Virginia Village*, p. 28.

198. Terre Haute *Express*, [1898].

The Search for Perfection

Beyond Dunn-Loring, the Washington, Ohio & Western passed through Vienna, Hunter's Mill, and Thornton Station, where yet another nineteenth-century vision of Fairfax County's future received a brief trial. In 1886, General William McKee F. Dunn of the Loring Company and Dr. Carl Adolf Max Wiehle, a German-born, recently retired physician from Philadelphia, jointly bought, then divided 6,449 acres in the vicinity, with most of Wiehle's 3,500 acres north of the railroad line. According to a subsequent owner of the property, Dr. Wiehle was a "perfectionist," who "dreamed of a Utopia carved out of this virgin forest of white oak." To give his dreams credibility, he convinced the government to establish a post office at "Wiehle" in 1887, and to prove his personal commitment, he built for his family a gingerbread-covered summer home there the following year. Then to shape his vision, he imported a professional city planner from Germany, who by 1892 had produced a detailed map of the proposed community. To convey order, streets were systematically and symmetrically laid out, and given such names as Paris, London, Berlin and Vienna avenues to add a cosmopolitan flavor to the town. Washington, New York, and Philadelphia avenues provided a proper patriotic balance, while Oak, Maple and Hickory avenues conveyed the tranquility that every small American town should offer. For sentiment's sake, Wiehle's seven children were also honored with street names. Lakeside Avenue, bordering three hand-dug lakes, separated the residential section from the railroad and an industrial area, indicating that Wiehle hoped the town would be self-sustaining rather than a bedroom community, and would attract an economically heterogeneous population. Finally, in 1893, to give substance to his plans, Wiehle deeded the property to the Virginia Lumber and Manufacturing Company, "a closely-held family company," and the construction of the new town began.[199]

A brick kiln and a sawmill were first erected to produce building materials for the town, and soon the Maryland and Virginia Serpentine and Talc Company located a mill at Wiehle to take advantage of locally available soapstone deposits. A four-room schoolhouse was erected on a lot donated by Dr. Wiehle to the county, and a brick-steepled town hall was added, serving for many years not only as a civic center, but also as a sanctuary for the Wiehle Methodist Church.[200] With an industrial base and its religious and educational facilities, the town's future seemed

199. A. Smith Bowman, Jr., "A History of Sunset Hills Farm," Historical Society *Yearbook*, 6(1958-59):39-41.
200. Ibid., p. 41.

Fairfax Herald building with the Town Hall in the background.
Photo by Wm. Edmund Barrett, 1968.

promising. In 1892 the Fairfax *Herald* reported the town "steadily growing," after earlier warning residents of Herndon and Vienna that they "must bestir themselves or, ere they know it, the new town of Wiehle will become a dangerous rival."[201] Through the 1890s many visitors from Washington were attracted to the town's Aesculapian Hotel, "a rambling 35-room building with towers, gables and many porches. It sported a bowling alley and tennis courts, the lakes afforded swimming, fishing and boating and the surrounding woods offered cool bridle paths and good hunting. [It] was filled to capacity each summer at monthly rates of $30.00 including board. Its chef had once worked for J.P. Morgan and its cuisine and the excellent quality of its spring water [were] known for miles around. There was a continual waiting list." But despite Wiehle's popularity as a resort, its founder's vision was evidently ahead of its time. Between 1895 and 1898, only five town lots were sold, and by the turn of the century, the population had leveled off at about fifty.[202] Disillusioned and in debt, Dr. Wiehle died in 1901. Yet on this site three-quarters of a century later, his dream of a self-contained, socially integrated, model community would be revived, constructed, and inhabited by over 25,000 northern Virginians, who would call Reston home.

201. *Herald*, 11 March 1892; 5 April 1889.
202. Bowman, "A History of Sunset Hills Farm," Historical Society *Yearbook*, 6(1958-59):41-42; U.S. Bureau of Census, *Twelfth Census of the United States, 1900*, (Washington, D.C.: Government Printing Office, 1902) 1:lvi.

Section Two, 1900-1925

The Electric Connection

The tracks of the electric trolley traced a distinct line between nineteenth- and twentieth-century Fairfax County. More than any other development, this new form of transportation caused the changes of the first quarter of the new century to come at a rate and with an impact unimagined in the final third of the last. Just as the steam train, described as "attuned to its surroundings, . . . slow moving, casual and carrying a halcyon air," accurately reflected the less ambitious aspirations and accomplishments of the earlier period, so the trolley embodied both the county's confidence in and its anxieties about the future.[1] Although the trolley itself would be replaced by the automobile as the leading force shaping the county's development in the mid-1920s, its tracks left a path that the people of Fairfax would follow for the next half century.

1. Curran and Curran, *McLean Remembers*, pp. 28-29.

VI

Political Reaction

"Progress" was the most important proposed product of the electric age that was dawning on Fairfax as the new century began. Yet amid the plans for growth and economic development, the county's conservative contingent was rapidly becoming the political consensus. Even though the Democratic party had been the dominant political party since the end of Reconstruction, the county Republicans, including most of the many postwar northern emigrants, had offered the majority worthy opposition, rarely failing to receive less than forty percent of the vote in federal and state elections and holding on to a number of local offices by dominating several magisterial districts. But by the turn of the century, Fairfax County was well on its way toward joining the solid Democratic South. Between the presidential elections of 1896 and 1900, Democrat William Jennings Bryan increased his margin over the incumbent Republican William McKinley by 6 percent to win almost 59 percent of the Fairfax County vote; in 1904, the Democratic candidate Alton Parker outpolled Republican Theodore Roosevelt with 65 percent of the county's votes; in 1908, Bryan was endorsed on 74 percent of the Fairfax ballots against Republican William Howard Taft; and in 1912, Democrat Woodrow Wilson defeated both Taft and Roosevelt, this time the candidate of the Progressive Party, with the approval of 75 percent of Fairfax voters. State and local elections were becoming equally embarrassing for local Republicans, with Democratic gubernatorial and legislative candidates carrying the county by better than three-to-one margins in 1906 and 1909; and Democrat Charles C. Carlin of Alexandria, who represented the county in Congress from 1907 to 1919, was consistently reelected with the votes of approximately 80 percent of his Fairfax County constituents. Only in the Mount Vernon and the adjacent Lee districts, where post-Civil War northern settlement had been most dense, did county Republicans maintain a respectable but minority representation.[2]

Constitutional Corruption

The most obvious explanation for the mounting Democratic majorities was the fact that on Virginia soil, appeals to the "Lost Cause" simply outlasted those of Republicans to the "Bloody Shirt." Even those northern newcomers who kept the faith no doubt found it difficult to pass on to their children the idealism that had characterized Republicanism at its best. The growing association of the party with the nation's big business interests, and the concurrent identification of the Democrats with the farmer-dominated Populists through their common candidate, William Jennings Bryan, helped secure the Democratic hold on the county. Yet there was another more sinister cause for the evolution of the countywide conservative consensus: the deliberate disfranchisement of Virginia's blacks by means of a new state constitution. In his study of the Virginia Constitutional Convention of 1901-1902, Ralph Clipman McDaniel wrote that through the late nineteenth century, "the conservative whites had a majority statewide and retained power in areas in which they were a minority through control of the government machinery or outright fraud . . . . Rising concern over the legality of depriving the Negro of his vote was unquestionably the leading motivating force for the Constitutional Convention."[3] In other words, the concern of many Virginia conservatives was not to eliminate the corruption, but to legalize it.

In an 1888 referendum, Virginians had been apathetic about the need for a new constitution, with fewer than 6 percent of the voters approving of a convention; but by 1897, 32 percent supported the idea. Finally in 1900, the state's voters accepted the call for a convention with 56 percent of the vote. In none of the referenda had Fairfax voters endorsed the constitutional convention. Fewer than 20 percent had approved in 1888 and 1897, and only 43 percent agreed with the statewide majority in 1900.[4] Even after the final vote, opposition from the county continued. In August 1900, the Fairfax Herald reported that "the colored people of this vicinity recently held a meeting to express their opposition to the proposed constitutional convention" and elected John H.H. Bush to represent them at a conference on the issue in Charlottesville. But Fairfax conservatives were clearly coming to recog-

---

2. Herald, 16 November 1900; 18 November 1904; 13 November 1908; 15 November 1912; 17 November 1905; 12 November 1909.

3. Robert A. Alden, "Fairfax County and Constitutional Conventions: 1774-1956," Historical Society Yearbook), 7(1960-61):17.

4. Ibid.

John Quincy Marr Monument dedication on the courthouse lawn, 1904. Copy by Lee Hubbard

nize the convention as an opportunity to strengthen their political grip on the county. Although the staunchly Democratic *Herald* had previously opposed the movement, the paper decided to make the most of the situation once Virginia voters had given their consent. As the delegates began their deliberations at Richmond in 1901, the *Herald* admitted that "the openly avowed object of this convention is to deprive the most ignorant and indolent members of the colored race of the right to vote," a goal which it wholeheartedly endorsed.[5]

Equally enlightening was the role played by R. Walton Moore, Fairfax County's delegate to the convention. Moore was named Chairman of the important Legislative Committee, although the work of the Committee on the Elective Franchise overshadowed Moore's and every other committee's activities. After meeting for more than a year, the convention accepted the Franchise Committee's recommendations that after 1903, a prospective voter would be required to give, "in his own handwriting, without assistance," his name, age, and address, and to "answer on oath any and all questions affecting his qualifications as an elector, submitted to him by the officers of registration." Since this provision could be applied at the local registrar's discretion, it hardly eliminated the irregularities, although it would eliminate thousands of blacks from the state's electoral processes. Registrants would also be obliged to pay a poll tax of $1.50, with the tax due a full six months before the next election or primary. Thus, the state's well-organized Democratic machine would gain an added advantage over the less informed and less prosperous blacks upon whom Virginia Republicans depended.[6]

With these provisions agreed upon, the convention next had to determine the process by which the new constitution would take effect. Disregarding the instructions of the General Assembly that they submit their work to the state's voters for approval, the delegates decided to simply proclaim the document law, fearing that the targets of the new franchise provisions would block ratification. Robert A. Alden, R. Walton Moore's biographer, found that although the Fairfax delegate had personal misgivings about the legal and ethical propriety of this decision, "he favored the constitution and did not want to see it overthrown." Therefore, immediately after the vote for proclamation, Moore offered a resolution "that as it has been determined to proclaim the Constitution, provision should be made for its recognition . . . by the political departments of the Government, and to that end the General Assembly shall be convened at an early date."[7] Within a few days of the

---

5. *Herald*, 24 August 1900; 19 April 1901.

6. Dabney, *Virginia*, p. 437.

7. Alden, "Fairfax County and Constitutional Conventions: 1774-1956," *Historical Society Yearbook*, 7(1960-61): 19-20.

adoption of this resolution, the Assembly convened in special session and its members were sworn in under the new constitution. A lone Republican holdout saw his seat declared vacant, and all judicial challenges brought by Virginia Republicans failed, with the United States Supreme Court weakly concluding that the convention's actions "cannot be undone by any order of the court."[8] Although Fairfax had not been in the forefront of the movement for a new constitution, the county's role in its implementation was significant, and the impact of the constitution was no less profound in Fairfax than in other parts of the state. Between the elections of 1900 and 1904, the number of voters statewide fell by more than 50 percent, while in Fairfax County fewer than one-third as many votes were cast. In elections since the Civil War, the 15 to 25 percent of the population of Fairfax which had voted had given the county a degree of truly representative government. But after the Constitution of 1902 took effect, the 6 to 10 percent of the population still eligible and casting ballots allowed conservative Democrats complete political control of the county.

Educational Exceptions

After taking from blacks their political rights, conservative whites used their political advantage to crush a movement to improve blacks' educational opportunities. When the 1905 Republican gubernatorial candidate John F. Lewis advocated free textbooks for the state's school children, the Fairfax *Herald* charged that "if the Republican plan is carried out, it will cost the people of Virginia $500,000 the first year, and after that . . . at least $300,000 a year . . . . How would this Republican plan of free books affect Fairfax County? The negroes of this county constitute 26 percent of the school enrollment, they own 4 per cent of the property in the county. This means that out of every $26 worth of books furnished to negroes, the white people would pay $22 of it; and the negroes would pay $4." Nor was the projected cost of the program the only objection, as the *Herald* ridiculed the "ambition to make classical scholars . . . of the negro race," while wondering who would remain to do "the hewing of wood, the drawing of water, and the hoeing of corn . . . since they have to be done by somebody."[9] Over and above the *Herald's* poor arithmetic, the most striking feature of these arguments is the absolute illogic of penalizing an already politically impotent people for their economic disability by denying them the basic educational tools

---

8. Dabney, *Virginia*, p. 440.

9. *Herald*, 10 November 1905; 13 October 1905. The paper further revealed its priorities by noting that "the Confederate soldier is not mentioned in the Republican platform. The Democratic Party gives to the old soldiers $300,000 per year. Do the Republicans propose to take this money to provide free books for the negroes?" See also *Herald*, 13 October 1905; 20 October 1905.

they needed to overcome their handicaps.[10] By 1920, the annual cost of instruction for each white pupil in the county was $13.29, while $6.44 was spent for each black student. White teachers received an average annual salary of $408, while blacks got but $239.[11] Despite the emphasis on "progress" in the early years of the twentieth century, the county's conservative white establishment continued to deny county blacks the basic rights and opportunities of American citizenship. And as rapid economic development caused disruptions in established patterns of life over the coming twenty-five years, some whites sought scapegoats for their personal frustrations. Disadvantaged blacks furnished them a convenient target.

A Politician's Projections

Easily the most influential political figure in Fairfax County at the turn of the century was Joseph E. Willard. A brief look at his career will provide an introduction to several other issues that would concern residents of the county over the following two and a half decades. Although he was not even born at the time, Willard's background in politics can be traced to the legendary exploits of Colonel John S. Mosby and his beautiful Fairfax County "informant" Antonia Ford. After one of Mosby's raids behind enemy lines, Union officers became convinced that the popular Miss Ford was serving as a spy for the "Gray Ghost." She was arrested and imprisoned in Washington, D.C. where she met a young Union officer, Major Joseph C. Willard, who secured her release, then married her. The story was given pathos when, "weakened by her imprisonment," Antonia died seven years later. The child of this wartime romance, young Joseph E. Willard, was sent to Fairfax County to live with his grandfather Ford, while his father and uncle Henry Willard became fabulously wealthy as the proprietors of Washington's famous Willard Hotel.[12] In a letter dated August 1900, Colonel Mosby discounted all connection between himself and Antonia Ford. "There is not a particle of truth in the statement that she ever acted as a spy," he

10. Actually many black leaders of the period, including Booker T. Washington, urged blacks temporarily to accept white political and social domination and to strive instead for economic equality through technical and vocational education. Hollis B. Frissell, head of the Hampton Institute which pioneered the movement for vocational training for blacks, said in 1901 that "the study of books in the case of the blacks was of secondary importance. That the question of decent living and intelligent industry was the [main] goal." *Virginia*, p. 450.

11. Virginia Education Commission and Virginia Survey Staff, *Virginia Public Schools*, part I, Educational Survey Series, VII (New York: World Book Co., 1920), pp. 393, 397.

12. Geddes, *Historical Highlights*, p. 113.

wrote. "She was innocent as Abraham Lincoln." Then referring to the fable that Antonia Ford had gotten her revenge against him by marrying a Union officer, Mosby joking added, "if it hadn't been for me there never wd have been a Joe Willard . . . . Now don't you see the obligation that Joe Willard is under to me? . . . Don't you think he ought to pay me an annuity? Ask him."[13] If Willard ever answered, he probably agreed, for he certainly could have afforded it, and whether fact of fiction, he surely realized that the stories connecting his mother to Colonel Mosby were partially responsible for the political popularity he enjoyed.[14]

Willard's political career actually began soon after his graduation from the University of Virginia Law School, when in 1893, he was elected to the State House of Delegates from Fairfax County. When the Spanish-American War erupted in 1898, he organized, equipped, and commanded a company of men from Fairfax, and in 1901, still only thirty-five years old, he was elected Virginia's Lieutenant Governor. Willard also remained active in local affairs. In 1900, he joined with R. Walton Moore in organizing the Fairfax Democratic Club, and on one occasion in 1904, he presided over the Fairfax Town Council in the absence of Mayor Walter T. Oliver. His estate, located just north of the courthouse, was a county showplace, "where every stalk of corn contains two or three splendidly developed ears." When Lieutenant Governor Willard announced his candidacy for the governorship in 1905, the Fairfax *Herald* declared that he would be "strongly supported here" and became his unswerving ally in the campaign. In fact, in the eyes of the *Herald*, Willard could do no wrong. Typical was the paper's report of a recent rabbit hunt, at which Willard declined to shoot the lone rabbit sighted. "'I'll give it a chance for its life,' he said, throwing down his gun. 'If it beats me running it can go free.' The chase that followed across an open field was an exciting one. Colonel Willard won and brought the rabbit back in his game bag." On weightier issues, the *Herald* was equally full of praise, if conveniently vague, citing the candidate's enthusiasm for education, roads, and business. Willard himself displayed political adeptness when asked his opinion on the proposed Mann Bill which would regulate the sale of liquor in Virginia. Willard neatly side-stepped the loaded question by responding, "I approve the Mann bill when construed as controlling and regulating the sale of whiskey, but I do not approve of it when construed as prohibition."[15] Despite the support from his home county and the $18,000 he spent during the

---

13. John S. Mosby, "Letter to Mr. Thomas Keith, August 20, 1900," Historical Society *Yearbook*, 1 (1951): 26.

14. According to the Fairfax *Herald*, Willard was "said to be the richest man in Virginia." *Herald*, 22 January 1904.

15. Ibid., 18 March 1904; 28 September 1900; 19 August 1904; 2 September 1904; 22 January 1904; 27 January 1905; 21 April 1905.

campaign, almost twice as much as spent by each of his opponents, Willard ran a distant third behind Claude Swanson and Judge William Hodges Mann in the Democratic primary and called an abrupt halt to his career in politics.[16]

Yet Willard's prominence in Fairfax County was far from finished. The marriage of his daughter Belle to Kermit Roosevelt, the son of the former president, in 1913 focused nationwide attention on the county, and the Fairfax *Herald* reported that "Layton Hall, the elegant home of Mr. Joseph E. Willard," was often "the scene of a very handsome entertainment." Willard was appointed to the State Corporation Commission in 1905, and two years later, he anticipated a concern of county residents for highway safety when he was arrested by a bicycle policemen in New York for driving his automobile at a reckless thirty miles per hour. His philanthropy regularly won him more complimentary headlines, especially when his wealth was used to stimulate the "progress" that county leaders so anxiously awaited in the early 1900s. When the Fairfax Central Road League reported its financial condition "very good" in 1904 it especially acknowledged the "very substantial assistance" of J.E. Willard. One week earlier, the *Herald* reported Willard's offer of $25,000 to the Washington, Alexandria & Falls Church Railway if it could complete the electric trolley line then under construction to Fairfax within four months. With this stimulus, the county seat acquired the long-anticipated direct rail link with Washington well before the deadline. Willard's contemporaneous campaign for governor may have helped to stimulate these acts of generosity, but even after he had left the county to become Woodrow Wilson's Minister to Spain from 1913 to 1921, he continued to remember his friends in Fairfax. In 1916, the organizers of the Fairfax County Fair gratefully acknowledged the "liberal contribution" of $150 from Fairfax County's fair-haired favorite son, Joseph E. Willard.[17]

16. *Richmond Times Dispatch*, 9 September 1905; *Herald*, 29 September 1905.

17. Ben Miller, "Antonia Ford," reprinted from an unknown Washington, D.C., newspaper, *Historical Society Yearbook*, 1 (1951): 30; *Herald*, 29 December 1893; 6 October 1905; 19 July 1907; 8 July 1904; 20 October 1916.

VII

Transportation Transformation

The introduction of steam-powered trains in the midnineteenth century marked the first significant improvement in communications and transportation in Fairfax County since the construction of rolling roads in the colonial period. The trains created new towns, reinvigorated old ones, and became a symbol of hope for a more prosperous future. But plagued by financial difficulties, poor management, frequent accidents, and inadequate service, the steam trains failed to approach the impact predicted by postwar prophets of progress. Another advance arrived in 1887, when a telephone line connected Centreville, Fairfax Court House, Annandale, and Alexandria. From the Willcoxon Tavern at Fairfax, a caller could reach Alexandria for fifteen cents or other county exchanges for ten cents.[18] Until the twentieth century, however, telephones were generally found only in public buildings, and certainly only a small percentage of the population was affected by the accessibility of instantaneous information by phone. Electric power and lights would not be available to most households and communities until the 1920s. Therefore, by comparison or by itself, the first technological innovation to deserve the description "revolutionary" in its impact on the county was the electric trolley. The University of Virginia's *Economic and Social Survey* of the county supplied an accurate, if unintentional, forecast in

18. Rust, *Town of Fairfax*, p. 64.

Fairfax Station, 1919. Print courtesy of Southern Railway. Copy by Wm. Edmund Barrett.

citing "the development taking place in the County as a result of the trolley lines" to back up its belief that "the day is not far distant when war stricken Fairfax will be a veritable land of Goshen, flowing with milk and honey."[19] For even if beekeeping would never again approach housekeeping as a major activity in the county, the trolley allowed Fairfax dairy farmers to keep enough milk flowing to quench the demand of the expanding Washington and suburban Virginia market.

Stimulus to Suburbanization

Just four years after the inauguration of the first successful trolley line in the world at Richmond in 1888, the Fairfax *Herald* announced with enthusiasm that "a syndicate of Western capitalists . . . has secured the right of way over the streets of Alexandria for an electric railway, . . . embracing the principal streets of the city and running from the steamboat and railroad depots to Mt. Vernon, the whole scheme involving the expenditure of not less than a half million dollars." The New Alexandria Land and River Improvement Company also bought "1,600 acres of land in [Fairfax] county, across Hunting creek, south of Alexandria, between that city and Mt. Vernon."[20] Within four months

19. Nickell and Randolph, *Economic and Social Survey*, p. 18.
20. *Herald*, 8 January 1892.

Mount Vernon trolley station, about 1930. The Tea Room was next to the visitors' entrance to the estate. Photo courtesy of Joan Gibbs Lyon.

of the project's inception, the Washington, Alexandria, & Mt. Vernon Electric Railway was "practically completed," and residents of the Mount Vernon-Woodlawn neighborhood began to prepare for an immediate "advance of progress."[21] Although a nationwide depression had since set in, a promotional pamphlet reported in 1894 that the syndicate's development "already numbers two factories, a spacious hotel, and a number of neat cottages—a nucleus which will no doubt be, ere long, rapidly augmented with the revival of financial confidence."[22] Equally ambitious were the schemes of Captain William H. Snowden who had recently established a post office in his home "Arcturus" on the Potomac, and now envisioned the arrival of a host of new postal patrons. To encourage this development, he surveyed a portion of his own property into seven lots with seven streets, one of which, Mount Vernon Avenue, would service the station he built on the new electric line. He even prepared a guidebook which included historical sketches of local landmarks to be sold to passengers on the trolley.[23] In his book, Snowden

21. Mayme Parker, "Along the River Front," Historical Society *Yearbook*, 9 (1964-65): 86.

22. William H. Snowden, *Some Old Historic Landmarks of Virginia and Maryland, Described in a Handbook for the Tourist Over the Washington, Alexandria and Mt. Vernon Electric Railway* (Alexandria, Va.: G.H. Ramsay & Son, 1901), p. 12 (hereinafter cited as Snowden, *Some Old Landmarks*).

23. Parker, "Along the River Front," Historical Society *Yearbook*, 9(1964-65):86.

confidently predicted "large accessions of new settlers from localities far
less favored, to occupy the divisions and subdivisions of the many large
farms of the [original Mount Vernon] estate," his own among them.[24]

Despite these displays of confidence, the plans of both the New
Alexandria Company and Captain Snowden proved unrealistic. Nothing
more was heard from the former, while only "a few" of the latter's lots
were sold in the 1890s.[25] More successful were the plans of the heirs of
David Frost, a member of a three-man syndicate which had bought the
Wellington estate from Snowden's brothers, Stacy and Isaac, back in
1866. In 1912, several buildings from a defunct amusement park were
moved on flat cars to Wellington Station on the trolley line; there they
were unloaded and placed on half-acre lots to serve as summer cottages
for vacationers from the city. One resident attributed the success of
"Wellington Villa" as a summer colony to the fact that "it was just far
enough from town to be quiet and rustic, and easily accessible by the car
line, and the river afforded excellent swimming, boating, and fishing
facilities."[26]

Access to Education

Although the county's earliest electric line did not immediately have
the effect desired by developers, its impact was nonetheless substantial.
For if city dwellers still found Fairfax only a nice place to visit, county
residents quickly took advantage of their new access to Washington. By
1906, there were thirty daily trains between Washington and Mount
Vernon and a total of 1,743,734 passengers for the year.[27] The
destinations of many Fairfax County customers were District of
Columbia schools, for despite the progress made by Fairfax public
schools over their first quarter century, the State Board of Education
required that "the teaching to extra branches [high school subjects] shall
always be secondary and subsidiary to the interests of elementary
education." Although there were already seventy-five high schools in
Virginia, Fairfax County had none as late as 1906 when a new state
school law provided especially for their establishment. As the Board of
Supervisor's promotional *Industrial and Historical Sketch* explained in
1907, "the ease with which students were able to attend High School in
Washington probably accounts, in no small degree, for the late establishment of high schools in Fairfax County."[28]

24. Snowden, *Some Old Landmarks*, p. 67.
25. Parker, "Along the River Front," Historical Society *Yearbook*, 9 (1964-65): 86-87.
26. Harry B. Lyon, "Wellington Villa and Vicinity," Historical Society *Yearbook*, 9 (1964-65):91.
27. Ibid., pp. 90-91. pp. 90-91.
28. Lonnie J. Hinkle, "A History of Public Secondary Education in Fairfax County, Virginia" (Ed.D. diss. George Washington University, 1971), pp. 46, 50, 69 (hereinafter cited as Hinkle, "Public Secondary Education").

The particular ease with which students in the Mount Vernon neighborhood could reach District schools by the Washington, Alexandria & Mount Vernon Electric Railway must account for the even later establishment of a high school there. Charles Kirk Wilkinson, born in 1894 and raised on the Sherwood Farm near Woodlawn, received two years of schooling at home, then took his lessons for four years at the nearby one-room Snowden School. By the age of twelve, Wilkinson had been exposed to all which local schools could offer, and so, along with many young neighbors, he began to make the daily trolley trip to the Sidwell Friends School in Washington.[29] Though the new $7,500 four-room school built in 1917 at Potter's Hill in the Mount Vernon District probably offered some high school work, county school records still show no students attending high school in either the Mount Vernon or the adjacent Lee districts as late as the mid-1920s. In an effort to alleviate this obvious deficiency, the Fairfax County School Board gave the Mount Vernon and Lee School districts $500 each in 1918 to help pay tuition and transportation costs for their students at Alexandria public high schools. Two years later, a committee was formed to help Fairfax County School Superintendent Milton Dulany Hall decide which students should receive assistance, with the board matching each $25 payment made by eligible students' parents. In 1925, Hall stated his continued opposition to opening a high school at West End, actually at the northeastern edge of the county, since it would cost twice as much to operate the school as to continue paying tuition for Fairfax students going to schools in other jurisdictions.[30] Although the trolley may have provided county officials an excuse for delaying the badly needed expansion of the local school system, it at least provided access to an adequate education elsewhere for those students who were able and willing to make the extra effort.

Pathway to Pasteurization

While young people determined to complete their education would continue to be steady customers of the Washington, Alexandria & Mount Vernon Electric Railway, bringing the line even more business was the area's second most important, but much more easily spoiled resource: milk. Fairfax dairy farmers had always enjoyed an advantage over other Virginians because of their proximity to the Washington Market; but now freed from dependence on the weather, the condition of the roads, and the unreliable steam trains, county dairymen could enlarge their herds and expand their facilities, confident that their milk would

29. Charles Kirk Wilkinson, "Sherwood Farm and Surrounding Area," Historical Society *Yearbook,* 9 (1964-65): 77-78.

30. Hinkle, "Public Secondary Education," pp. 141-42.

arrive fresh and find a ready market. The family of Theron Thompson, who immigrated to the Mount Vernon neighborhood from New York in 1869, played a central role in the rise of the county's dairy industry. Thompson's son John had established a Washington distribution center for the family's dairy products in 1881, and when the trolley line was completed in 1892, he acquired a parcel of land from his neighbor, Stacy Snowden, on the line at Herbert Springs, where milk was collected for shipment to the Washington plant. John's brother Egbert soon took over the Herbert Springs facility, while brothers Daniel, of nearby Riverview Farm, and Arthur, who developed a dairy farm in Maryland, also shipped milk to the Washington center.[31] Eventually the business of farmers from all over the county would help make Thompson's Dairy one of the Washington area's most successful enterprises and the Fairfax County dairy industry supreme in the state of Virginia.

Clifton Station's Stagnation

The railroad had created the community of Clifton in the late 1860s, and the town had grown steadily through the early years of the twentieth century. In 1902, the approximately 150 residents received a charter of incorporation and elected R.R. Buckley their first mayor.[32] Following the passage of the new state school law in 1906, the Fairfax County School Board appropriated $250 for the establishment of a high school at Clifton, and the fifteen students who met in a room hastily added to the town's grade school in the fall of 1907 had the privilege of attending the county's first high school. By 1912, Clifton could boast of a new school building with six classrooms, a library, and an assembly hall.[33]

Proud town officials soon came to feel that the kerosene lamps on the streets of their progressive community were old-fashioned, and when the Bull Run Power Company brought electricity to the town in the 1920s, the lanterns were ceremoniously replaced with electric street lights. Despite Clifton's confidence, these symbols of progress during the next thirty years would light the way for no more than two hundred inhabitants the town had counted in 1910. Clifton's economy had suffered an irreversible setback when the pulpwood supplies which had furnished the railroad the bulk of its local business were exhausted shortly after the turn of the century, and the automation of railroad switching and loading devices eliminated a number of residents' jobs on the line, by then a part of the Southern Railway system.[34] Several citizens of Clifton rode the train to jobs in Washington daily, but because

31. Wilkinson, "Sherwood Farm and Surrounding Area," Historical Society Yearbook, 9 (1964-65): 80-81.

32. Hebert and Hebert, "Clifton," pp. 10-11.

33. Hinkle, "Public Secondary Education," pp. 70-71, 85.

34. Richard R. Buckley, "A History of Clifton," Historical Society Yearbook, 4 (1955): 61-62.

the steam service was not geared to handle commuter traffic, prospective suburbanites sought homes in Fairfax County communities more accessible to the capital. By the time the private automobile replaced the electric trolley in other communities as the more convenient, although more expensive, means of commutation, Clifton had been bypassed by the developmental schemes and patterns which accompanied the trolley to the county over the first quarter of the century. As a result, the town remains uniquely unchanged from its turn-of-the-century appearance.

A Sully and a Sullen Reorientation

Just as it had done through the late 1800s, the community of Chantilly surrounding Sully Plantation reflected the changes that were coming to Fairfax County as a whole in the early years of the twentieth century. Conrad Shear, who had lived at Sully longer than any previous resident, retired to Herndon at the age of eighty-seven in 1910, conveying the farm he had worked for almost forty years to William Eads Miller, a Herndon realtor. After briefly advertising the property in a list of "some nice Northern Virginia homes," Miller sold himself on its potential and converted Sully into a dairy farm "to take advantage of the milk and cheese industry flourishing around Washington in the wake of improved rail transit and rapid advances in refrigeration techniques." As Robert S. Gamble found in his study of Sully, "even [the] quickly-spoiling [skim] milk was made profitable shortly before World War I, when George Haight of Little Sully initiated a regular milk pickup service for area farmers, transporting the milk to Herndon, whence it was shipped on the [recently electrified] Washington and Old Dominion Railroad to Chestnut Farm Dairies in the District of Columbia." Although Miller and his wife lived at Sully for only five years, the imprint of their occupancy clearly revealed the growing importance of Fairfax communities that lay along the lines of the electric railroads. With his real estate business in Herndon and the Presbyterian Church he had helped found at Floris— "the name that a more self-consciously sophisticated generation had given to the old settlement of Frying Pan—the Millers proceeded to reorient Sully toward the north rather than the south, to the lane connecting the house to the Centreville [Herndon] Road. Accordingly, a long wooden porch was added to the north side of the house. The backyard—filled during the Shears' time with growing things in a pleasantly-informal, country way—became the front, the two-seater privy there was removed to a less-conspicuous spot."[35]

From its location on the railroad line to the west from Washington, Herndon had served rural northwest Fairfax County as a market

35. Gamble, *Sully,* pp. 126-27, 129.

community and social center since the 1850s. While Herndon's population had always been diverse, with many post-Civil War northern emigrants and a number of daily commuters to government jobs in Washington, the conversion of the steam-powered Washington, Ohio & Western Railroad to the electric Washington & Old Dominion Railway in 1912 coincided with the beginning of a fundamental change in the town's character. Initially, the trolley enhanced Herndon's role as a market town, expecially for the milk produced on dairy farms from Chantilly to Dranesville. The continuing importance of agriculture in the area was emphasized in 1920 by the designation of the four-room brick school at nearby Floris as the county's agricultural and vocational high school.[36] During the 1920s, according to Rita Schug, "the majority of the leading milk producers in Fairfax County were located around Herndon."[37]

While Herndon farmers were expanding their dairy operations, however, they were gradually losing their influence in town political affairs. The University of Virginia's 1924 survey noted that "after the installation of the electric road, interest in the town quickened. Employees of Washington saw in it a quiet place for a home, and one easily accessible to their place of business."[38] The year before the trolley's arrival, the Herndon Town Council had been deadlocked over the choice of a mayor from among its own members, half of whom were farmers, the other half businessmen. They finally compromised by choosing Dr. Ernest Robey, a farmer and a pharmacist. By the midteens, the changing character of the town was evident by the majority of shopkeepers and town-based professional men whom Herndon citizens had begun to elect to the council.[39] The emphasis of Herndon's new $10,000 high school, erected in part through the sale of bonds issued by the town council in 1911, was not on agriculture, but on athletics and commerce. In 1924, the school had the county's first athletic director, and its grounds included two basketball and two tennis courts, a baseball diamond, and a 220-yard track. In 1925 a business course, part of the county's first commercial department, was added to the school's curriculum.[40] While William Eads Miller could hardly have complained about the business the trolley was bringing his Herndon real estate office, many less affluent fellow farmers were beginning to feel frustrated in the face of the rapid changes coming to their county and community.

---

36. Nickell and Randolph, *Economic and Social Survey*, pp. 70-71.
37. Schug, "Herndon," p. 10.
38. Nickell and Randolph, *Economic and Social Survey*, p. 26.
39. Schug, "Herndon," pp. 7, 14.
40. Hinkle, "Public Secondary Education," pp. 128-29.

Wagon load of hay. A two-horse team was necessary to pull 1,000 pounds of hay over muddy roads near Langley in 1911. Virginia Department of Highways and Transportation.

Three-Cornered Evacuation

Until 1906, Lewinsville and Langley were languishing agricultural communities, isolated three miles apart in northeast Fairfax County. John C. Mackall, who grew up in Langley, remembered that only "the arrival of the steam threshing machine that moved from farm to farm at harvest time" disturbed "the peace and quiet of these two 'little communities." The threshing machine also added to the area's transportation problems, since "many horses would shy or run away when they were approached by the terrific engine and its appendages . . . . When it left Lewinsville and headed for Langley a daily check as to its whereabouts was kept, in order to avoid meeting it on the road." But the stir caused by the annual visit of the threshing machine could not have compared to the impact of the news in 1905 that Davis Elkins, son of Senator Stephen B. Elkins of West Virginia, and John R. McLean, "owner and publisher of the *Washington Post,* were planning to run an electric car line from Rosslyn . . . to Great Falls [which] would pass . . . somewhere between Lewinsville and Langley. The entire countryside . . . was a bustle. Where would the line come? How long would it take? What effect would it have?" Simply, but accurately, Mackall answered his own question: "the advent of the railroad changed everything."[41]

41. John C. Mackall, "McLean, Fairfax County, Virginia," Historical Society *Yearbook,* **4** (1955): 11-12.

The first cars of the Great Falls & Old Dominion Railway rolled into Great Falls Park on 3 July 1906, and "by 1907, 1,600,000 passengers were being carried annually . . . past . . . crossroads which were soon to bear the names of the developers."[42] The station erected where the line bisected the road connecting Lewinsville and Langley was christened McLean and soon became a collecting point for area farmers' milk and produce, which was then shipped to Washington markets. Far more noticeable were the changes in community life. Again in John C. Mackall's words, "the two communities became one." A new central post office replaced those formerly in each town. The old Langley hotel and Hummer's store, which had housed Langley's post office, were razed since their locations off the trolley line made them obsolete. Prior to 1906, "due to the terrible condition of the roads," the Mackall family had been forced to take up winter quarters in Washington, where John, his three brothers, and sister attended school and their father practiced law. But "the railroad solved the problem of getting from McLean to Georgetown."[43] Another resident remembered that though "the rest of the county was impossible to get to, . . . Georgetown was very accessible. . . . That's where we did our banking and got our groceries. . . . And really going in on that electric train was . . . a social event, because you just knew everybody on it."[44] As Mackall observed, however, "the problem of getting over that road from Langley to McLean had not been solved. . . . My father rented houses on the car line for two winters and finally solved the problem by building a house at McLean where we lived during the bad winter months, and then back a mile and one-half to Langley for the rest of the year."[45]

Also indicative of the trolley's effect was the fate of Langley's St. John's Episcopal Church which had suffered since the late 1890s for lack of members and a minister. After heated discussion, a majority of the remaining members decided that "however much sentiment might urge the contrary, the church's usefulness depended upon its being moved to McLean. . . . Accordingly, . . . the church was mounted on casters and made a 'dignified and stately progress' through the fields to . . . a piece of land . . . within a few hundred feet of the trolley line." Furthermore, from Bertram G. Foster's history of *St. John's First Fifty Years*, "the move proved a wise one. The minister's duties became so heavy it was no longer possible to share him with the old Falls Church. In 1913 a rectory was completed, and St. John's had its first full-time minister."[46]

42. Curran and Curran, *McLean Remembers*, p. 29.

43. Mackall, "McLean, Fairfax County, Virginia," Historical Society *Yearbook*, 4(1955):13.

44. Charlotte Corner, transcribed interview with Stephen L. Matthews, McLean, Virginia, August 12, 1971, pp. 26-27, 42 (hereinafter cited as Corner-Matthews interview).

45. Mackall, "McLean," Fairfax County, Virginia," Historical Society *Yearbook*, 4(1955):13.

46. Louise L. Smith, "St. John's Episcopal Church in McLean," Historical Society *Yearbook*, 5 (1956-57): 34.

Few residents of Langley and Lewinsville could have afforded to rent or build a second home at McLean, and their homes and farms could hardly have physically followed St. John's to the proximity of the trolley. Yet whether or not they approved, the trolley transferred still another center of community life to McLean. Charlotte Corner, who came from an "old rundown one room school in Giles County" to the new Franklin Sherman School at McLean in 1914, remembered that "the few people that lived [at Langley and Lewinsville] didn't want to give up their one room schools because they were afraid they might never have another school. . . . The idea of the consolidated school was new. . . . And then . . . there was a tremendous opposition to having a school [at McLean] because there weren't [many] children. . . . But you see, all this had to be built up. . . . It was the electric railroad that dictated what we would do, and . . . the children . . . came down here to McLean."[47]

In addition to emphasizing the trolley's impact, Corner's recollections provide a frank look at the disappointments and rewards a dedicated young teacher found in Fairfax County public schools in the 1910s. "The first day we opened," she recalled, "we raised the flag and tried to sing the Star-Spangled Banner but we broke down before we finished it. . . . We only had 29 pupils . . . and there was quite a bit of opposition to that great big [six-room] building, and only using two rooms. . . . The only equipment [we] had was a broom and a box of chalk. . . . The sun would glare in there in the afternoon . . . and we had no electricity, no running water. . . . The teachers . . . certainly couldn't have taught for money, because I don't think I got but fifty dollars a month for eight months, and the others got maybe forty-five or six." Another problem may have been a lack of leadership from county school authorities, for Corner complained that Superintendent Hall "was of the old school . . . and I don't think I saw him but several times, the whole time I taught."[48]

To combat these hardships, Corner had only her enthusiasm. She maintained that "if you wanted anything . . . you had to get out and get it. . . . I was just bursting with [the] idea that the school should be a community center, [so] one of the first things we [did] was to organize the School and Civic League. . . . We had a play every month . . . and [had] suppers to get money." The Masonic Order and local Baptists, both of whom met in the school building for many years, were a "tremendous help," but Corner had special words of praise for her pupils: "The boys used to bring shovels and rakes . . . and they leveled off the ground and planted trees. . . . The four years I was there, I never had one problem in

47. Corner-Matthews interview, pp. 13-14, 17.
48. Ibid., pp. 15-39.

discipline, I never had one act of vandalism. . . . When you work hard to get those things, you're not going to destroy them."[49]

Also important to the school, and to the entire community, was the annual observance of McLean Day, beginning in 1915. John C. Mackall remembered a "carnival atmosphere" and that the "entire neighborhood worked for days in preparation." Since the event was held on the Saturday in August before the Democratic primary, "politicians were always on hand to make their final appeal to the voters." From nine in the morning until eleven at night, there were games of skill, baseball, a baby contest, dancing, and a jousting tournament, usually won by Henry Hirst who rode as the "Knight of Langley." By running his lance through more metal rings than anyone else, Hirst won the honor of crowning his sweetheart and future bride, Mafie Carper, "the Queen of Love and Beauty." Proceeds from the occasion went to the Franklin Sherman School and other community projects.[50] More than fifty years after the first McLean Day, Charlotte Corner complained that developers had "cut down every tree and put up townhouses" in her formerly wooded neighborhood, but she continued to insist that "McLean was a wonderful place to live."[51]

Hine-sighted Progression

Like his father before him, Colonel Charles A. Hine had his ear to the ground and his eye on the horizon. Major Orrin E. Hine, a Union veteran, had come to Vienna in 1867, had acquired a great deal of the former and had lined the latter with six miles of maple trees.[52] His son evidently heard the rumble and saw the lines of the electric trolley, because after his graduation from West Point and law school, he went to work for the railroad, in turn as a brakeman, switchman, yardmaster, conductor, chief clerk, trainmaster, assistant superintendent, right-of-way agent, and general superintendent. He also took over his father's 6,440-acre farm and real estate office. Early in 1904, his influence and investment secured an extension of the Washington & Falls Church Electric Railway to Vienna.[53] Then, "largely through the untiring efforts of Hon. R. Walton Moore . . . and the generous aid of Lt. Gov. Jos. E. Willard," the line was again extended so that by December 1904, the Fairfax *Herald* could joyfully announce that "after many years of weary waiting, Fairfax has at last realized her fondest dream. We now have direct railroad connection with the National Capital. . . . Three or four

49. Ibid., pp. 14-15, 17-18, 20-22.
50. Mackall, "McLean, Fairfax County, Virginia," Historical Society *Yearbook*, 4(1955):14; Curran and Curran, *McLean Remembers*, pp. 18-21.
51. Corner-Matthews interview, p. 34.
52. Elizabeth C. Burke, "History of Fairfax County," Historical Society *Yearbook*, 5 (1956-57): p. 11.
53. *Herald*, 25 June 1909; Nickell and Randolph, *Economic and Social Survey*, p. 25.

years will show marvelous growth and development, not only here, but along the entire line of the road."[54] Three years later, the County Board of Supervisors' *Industrial and Historical Sketch* confirmed the prediction, reporting "great activity in suburban home-building . . . especially . . . along the lines of the electric railway." Though its estimate that "over fifty of the five hundred inhabitants of [Vienna] are employed in Washington" probably exaggerated both figures, the promotional brochure hardly overstated the trolley's impact on either community.[55] Even before the completion of the line to Fairfax, R. Walton Moore and Walter T. Oliver, who had recently resigned as the town's mayor, purchased forty acres of land adjacent to the railroad route, which they and the Fairfax *Herald* hoped would "make a very desirable sub-division. Already a number of lots have been sold at reasonable prices."[56] And in 1911, fresh from the success of their Great Falls & Old Dominion line, John R. McLean and Senator Stephen B. Elkins bought and electrified the Washington, Ohio & Western Railroad, renaming it the Washington & Old Dominion, whose tracks also passed through Vienna. "With two electric lines," the 1924 University of Virginia survey accurately concluded, "the numerous Government clerks and other employees of Washington who largely compose the 800 or more of Vienna's population, find convenient transportation to their places of business." The town had become "primarily a residential community."[57]

Once again the availability of trolley service delayed the expansion of the Fairfax County school system. The 1907 *Sketch* noted that Vienna's "advanced pupils take advantage of the educational opportunities afforded in nearby Washington, and many go there daily."[58] Soon these students had to ride with their commuting fathers only as far as Falls Church where the county's second high school was organized in late 1907.[59] Despite the convenience, the Fairfax *Herald* found citizens of Vienna "bending their energies towards establishing a high school" in 1909, though local school officials Franklin Sherman and Franklin Williams cited a number of obstacles, including "the lack of funds . . . the limited number of pupils mature enough for the curriculum," and the need to make "the present primary school as perfect as possible." To these problems, the paper added that it was "impossible to get a mongrel population to act together unitedly in any given direction." In the meantime, citizens of Fairfax Court House were involved in a similar debate. Letters and editorials in the Fairfax *Herald* continually stressed

54. *Herald,* 2 December 1904.
55. Supervisors, *Industrial and Historical Sketch,* p. 13.
56. *Herald,* 23 September 1904.
57. Nickell and Randolph, *Economic and Social Survey,* pp. 25-26.
58. Supervisors, *Industrial and Historical Sketch,* p. 13.
59. Hinkle, "Public Secondary Education," p. 89.

the "advantages of a good high school in reach of our children where they can be under the care of their parents," but in 1909, the editor lamented the fact that "people here in Fairfax have been so indifferent to this all important subject." Later that year, the paper reported the results of a recent poll "in which every person approached pledged hearty support" to a high school scheduled to open that fall.[60] The plans did not materialize, however, and the frame high school built on the trolley line between Fairfax and Vienna at Oakton in 1910 continued to serve the needs of all three communities for several years.[61]

A Church Profession

"In the summer of 1901 when my father had a job in Washington," wrote one of Falls Church's most famous residents, "my mother couldn't stand the heat of the city and so we rented [a] house on Maple Avenue. . . . It was there that, one Sunday, I was struck in the left eye by an arrow fired by my older brother. He was seven, and I was six, and [another brother] Robert was four, and I'm sure we all threw up together." But James Thurber also recalled that "a lot of good things as well as bad happened in that house. . . . We had a big back yard and an apple orchard, and there were some seckel pear trees. . . . We had the colored maid who served dinner in her bare feet and burned her finger in the steam of the kettle so that she could try out the salve she had bought at a traveling medicine show, complete with banjos and ballyhoo, that visited the town. Our garbage was collected by an ancient white-haired negro not more than five feet tall, whose two-wheeled oxcart was pulled by a brace of oxen. His appearance never failed to enchant us boys, for he was not only out of the South, but out of the past." Almost sixty years later, Thurber remembered the Falls Church of his childhood as "a quiet little village," and added, "I often wonder what it has become."[62] Had his memory been less selective, he could have easily imagined many of the changes that had come to the village, for by the turn of the century, Falls Church was well on its way to becoming a streetcar suburb for the nation's capital.

In 1897, Fairfax County's second electric railway, the Washington & Falls Church, connected those cities and was celebrated by local citizens in both poetry and prose. Frank L. Ball remembered that "these roads were great friends. . . . We used to go up and down . . . everybody on the car—the whole community out—the car packed and jammed—to Falls Church and back [to Clarendon] three or four times, singing hymns and

60. *Herald*, 2 July 1909; 7 May 1909; 14 May 1909; 3 September 1909.

61. Hinkle, "Public Secondary Education," pp. 103-4, 137.

62. James Thurber, letters to Mrs. Frank Acosta, 26 December 1958, 29 November 1959, quoted in Wrenn, *Falls Church*, p. 35.

*Uncle "Pete" Gillam was the first garbage collector in Falls Church, about 1890.
From Melvin L. Steadman, Falls Church By Fence and Fireside.*

songs . . . great doings all evening." Another contemporary of the trolley
wrote in verse:

> You've heard them singing of the grapevine swing
>   I sing of the grapevine road.
> It goes with many a jog and a lurch
>   From Aqueduct Bridge to the town of Falls Church
>   Past many a rural abode.[63]

But amusement was not the only result of the trolley's arrival, nor would
the countryside along its route long be rural, for the trolley was
responsible for the development of Falls Church as a suburb. As a 1904
developer's brochure predicted, with "the improved facilities for reaching
Washington by means of steam roads and trolley lines, the tide of
suburban home seekers from the capital city must turn this way,
whereby this Virginia village is destined to become a Virginia city."
Already, the pamphlet boasted, Falls Church was "thoroughly
cosmopolitan" and "the largest town in the county. . . . According to a
recent census only about fifty per cent of its inhabitants are natives of
Virginia, the rest coming from the various States of the Union or from
foreign countries. Falls Church might properly be called a national

---

63. Frank L. Ball, "Electric Railways of Arlington," *Arlington Historical Magazine,* 3 (1966): 35, 40
(hereinafter cited as ball, "Electric Railways").

village, since its citizens are chiefly employees of the government, and the interests of its 1,100 people naturally center at the National Capital."[64]

The man responsible for this pamphlet was also largely responsible for the way Falls Church developed following the arrival of the trolley in the 1890s. Merton E. Church had left his native Vermont in 1879 and settled in Falls Church in 1886, where, according to the brochure, he immediately became the "most prominent" of local "pioneer business-men." For twelve years he operated a drug store and was unanimously elected President of the State Pharmaceutical Association in 1889, before training and selling out to his successors. In 1888, he "established telephonic communications between Falls Church and Washington [and] built up an extensive telephone system extending over Fairfax and Alexandria counties and reaching to Bluemont in the Blue Ridge Mountains." For many years he remained chief stock holder, president, and general manager of the local telephone company, positions he also held in the Falls Church Improvement Company, which "successfully developed the 'Sherwood Sub-Division,'" a black settlement south of Falls Church, and "one of the first sub-divisions put on the market in Fairfax County." Through his loan business, Church brought together "those who wish to borrow money with which to buy or build a home, and those who wish to invest funds, thereby enabling the worthy home-seeker to own his own home, making him not only a prominent but more interested and desirable citizen." The brochure concluded that "in the development of Falls Church, Mr. Church has been indefatigable, and has been personally identified with every progressive movement. In addition to his drugstore, real estate and telephone business, he has been largely interested in procuring better transportation facilities in the way of electric railroads; he has built many houses in the town and . . . is at present engaged in organizing an electric light company . . .; he has got faith in the future of the town and is not afraid to invest his money in home enterprises . . . to him more than any other one man, is due the growth and development of our beautiful little village." It should be added that Church edited the weekly Falls Church *Monitor,* whose press undoubtedly printed this praise and promotion of his schemes to capitalize on the suburban development made inevitable by the advent of the electric trolley.[65]

---

64. Stewart, *Virginia Village*, pp. 1-2.

65. Ibid., pp. 22, 91-92. Jeanne Rust, in a privately published study of Falls Church, implied that the desire for development of Falls Church was not unanimous: "there were always the two factions in Falls Church; the Southerners who worked six days and worshipped on the seventh, taking life as it came; and, the Yankees who worked seven days and looked for more. The Southerners were reluctant to accept the migratory government workers, and they, in turn, were impatient and frustrated with their 'Southern gentlemen.' " Jeanne Johnson Rust, *All-American Crossroads* (Fairfax, Va., 1970), p. 26.

Merton E. Church, about 1900. From Melvin L. Steadman, Falls Church By Fence and Fireside.

Merton E. Church's most characteristic appeal issued a welcome to "the jaded fathers and mothers from the city to the place where children may enjoy life with nature, where the climate, conducive to refreshing sleep, soothes tired nerves and makes life to such again buoyant with youthful hopes and joys."[66] But perhaps more indicative of the changing character of Fairfax County was the fate of a wildcat sighted near the courthouse on Braddock Road shortly after the arrival of the trolley in 1905. "What it was doing in this part of the country is a mystery," reported the Fairfax *Herald*, but "after an exciting chase of about two hours, the animal was caught and killed."[67] Despite Church's invitation to "enjoy life with nature," the tracks of such creatures would be permanently lost beneath those of the electric trolley as rapid suburbanization of the county continued.

66. Stewart, *Virginia Village*, p. 32.
67. *Herald*, 27 October 1905. By 1918, County Game Warden E.B. Donaldson reported that "game of all kinds is scarce." *Herald*, 6 December 1918.

VIII

Wartime Mobilization

Since the turn of the century, the focus of Fairfax residents had been fixed firmly on local affairs. Although a growing number of them commuted daily to jobs in the nation's capital, the central concerns of most continued to be their families, homes, shops, and farms, their churches, schools, community social affairs, and civic responsibilities. Only during national elections did local newspapers seriously address wider issues, and even then with emphasis on local implications. Charlotte Corner, who arrived in the area in 1914 to teach at McLean's new Franklin Sherman School, recalled that her first stop had been the White House in Washington. A cousin who was "very high in the government at that time" had given her a ticket for a special White House tour, which included an audience with President Woodrow Wilson. "There were just about ten people there," Corner remembered, "but one was a great big Indian Chief. . . . He'd come to see his Great White Father. And I was so interested in this chief that I really wasn't too much interested in Wilson. . . . He didn't impress so much at that time, he seemed rather cold. . . . Of course the [First World] war [in Europe] had just broken out but wars were something I didn't know much about then. . . . Washington was more or less a country town. I didn't think too much of meeting all those people. It was just natural, we just took it for granted."[68]

68. Corner-Matthews interview, pp. 10-11.

Corner also vividly recalled election night two years later, when Democrat Wilson sought reelection against Republican Charles Evans Hughes: "We thought it would be so nice to have a meeting in the school house, and have a special phone put in. . . . Every half hour or so . . . the returns would come in. . . . By the time that we couldn't stay there any longer, I guess about midnight, it was decided that Hughes was elected. . . . Well, that pleased the Republicans very much [but] Mr. [Benjamin F.] Mackall was a very staunch Democrat. . . . Several of the men went down and draped the entrance to his home in black crepe to console him. And then of course, the next morning the report came in that Wilson was reelected so the tables turned."[69] Five months later, county residents acquired a new and deeper awareness of the wider world when Woodrow Wilson, so recently reelected on the platform "he kept us out of the war," requested and received a declaration of war against Germany, and Fairfax prepared to fight the First World War.

Social Evaluation

The war years may seem a most inappropriate period in which to attempt an evaluation of social attitudes among county residents, and yet the emergency caused them to look more deeply at themselves as well as at national and international issues. As Woodrow Wilson promoted the war as an effort to "make the world safe for democracy," the people of Fairfax were stimulated critically to examine their own ideas and institutions. Like other Americans, they wondered whether their society would meet the challenge or would find itself wanting in the showdown for leadership of the Western World. Furthermore, their experiences during the war shaped and sometimes altered their outlook toward such issues as the limits of legal dissent; the proper extent of federal and state interference in their schools, the criminal justice procedures, and the maintenance of public health; and the appropriate role and position of women, blacks, and other minority groups in their society. The wartime self-evaluations provide a candid look at the social concerns of Fairfax County citizens during the early years of the twentieth century.

Cause for Contribution

A few days after American entry into the war, the people of Fairfax County held a public meeting to pledge their support to the war effort, and within a few weeks, they found a variety of ways of expressing their loyalty and contributing to the cause. Most honored were those who enlisted in the armed forces, and of those, almost 100 made the supreme sacrifice. By early June, 1917, fifteen hundred Fairfax men between

69. Ibid., pp. 27-28.

twenty-one and thirty-one years of age had registered for the selective military draft, and of the seven hundred assigned draft numbers, 314 were called in late July. "Ovie Mitchell Beach, of Woodbridge, had the honor of being the first man drawn for war service in the national army," while Colonel Charles A. Hine of Vienna, a graduate of West Point and a veteran of the Spanish-American War, was given command of the Sixty-ninth New York Infantry which sailed for the French front in early fall. Those left at home were constantly reminded of the reality of war by the establishment of federal forts in Fairfax. Although the small garrison at Fort Hunt, just across Hunting Creek from the Mount Vernon estate, was declared superfluous for the defense of Washington by the War Department and had its guns dismantled, the fifteen hundred acres of nearby Belvoir Manor, purchased by the War Department in 1910 and designated Camp A.A. Humphreys in 1917, later renamed Fort Belvoir, became a major training center for the Army Corps of Engineers. A seven-mile-long railroad spur, called the "first military railroad the United States has ever built," connected Camp Humphreys to the Richmond and Fredericksburg steam railway line at Accotink. In 1918, the Fairfax *Herald* reported that "flying machines in the air above Fairfax are becoming a familiar sight," adding that a Captain Jack Davis flew to Fairfax to see his mother. "While he did not land he did all sorts of stunts in the air . . . and several residents of Fairfax nearly had heart failure."[70]

Civilians also responded to appeals for their time, money, and moral support. R. Walton Moore, prominent lawyer and politician from Fairfax, was named by Governor Henry C. Stuart to the Virginia Defense Council, whose role it was "to co-ordinate the work of all organizations and patriotic agencies working for the general good." Foremost among those agencies in Fairfax County were the "Home Guards," groups which could not "be ordered out of the State for any purpose, but [were to be] used for the preservation of order within [Virginia's] border." At a patriotic rally held at Potter's Hill School near Accotink, attended by over five hundred citizens, more than seventy-five men joined the Franconia, Potter's Hill, and Accotink "Guards," and "a full-fledged company of . . . 70 members" was organized for Fairfax and Falls Church. More constructive were the activities of the twenty-two branches of the American Red Cross in Fairfax County. At the close of the war in late 1918, the combined county chapters reported that over the previous eight months, 2,216 garments, eighteen thousand surgical dressings, a large number of sheets, towels, napkins, and handkerchiefs, and $14,000 had been made or raised and donated to the national

70. *Herald*, 13 April 1917; 8 June 1917; 27 July 1917; 24 August 1917; 26 July 1819; 11 October 1918.

organization for shipment to the European theatre. In addition, a fully equipped ambulance, bearing brass plates advertising "Fairfax County, Va., U.S.A.," was sent abroad, while county school children who had enrolled in the Junior Red Cross worked to raise the $700 needed to send a "kitchen trailer" supplied with food and coffee to the front.[71]

However admirable these activities, county residents were occasionally overzealous in their efforts to aid the cause. For example, in the early months of the war, the Fairfax *Herald* reported a short-lived movement "in the town of Vienna to bring about a change in its name. . . Many residents of the town contend that it is not proper for their home place to be named in honor of one of the nations supporting Germany in its ruthless warfare." More serious were the threats to civil liberties, whether actually carried out or not. A presidential proclamation required that "alien enemies," or German-born males over fourteen years of age, register at their local post office, and Franklin Williams, Jr., of Vienna indicated that local harassment of German-Americans might go farther when he felt it necessary to remind participants at a patriotic rally that the county's citizens of German birth "were in nowise responsible for the war." The county's leading supporters of the war effort were quick to condemn any sign of disloyalty, or any measure of enthusiasm unequal to their own. The Fairfax *Herald* wholeheartedly agreed with the "Go to Work or Go to Jail" policy of the State Commissioner of Labor, warning that "there is no room for idlers in Virginia at this . . . critical time in the history of our State and nation." The *Herald* was even harsher with Wisconsin's Senator Robert LaFollette, an outspoken opponent of American participation in the war: "when you hear a man condemning the war and opposing necessary war measures, you may know that he is in the pay of the German government as a pacifist, or hasn't enough intelligence to comprehend the vital interests involved in the war." La Follette and "the rest of the disloyal gang . . . are morally . . . guilty of treason. . . . They should be expelled from the Senate and if they continue their disloyal acts they should be imprisoned or shot." Finally, at one of the many rallies to boost the sale of the war bonds, F.S. McCandlish of Fairfax, Chairman of the County United War Work Campaign, threatened to make public the names of men who refused to contribute to the war fund.[72]

Cause for Disillusion

Despite their nearly unanimous support of Woodrow Wilson's conduct of the war, disillusionment among county residents with the

71. *Herald,* 4 May 1917; 7 September 1917; 25 May 1917; 5 April 1918; 26 November 1918; 6 July 1917; 23 November 1917.

72. *Herald,* 27 April 1917; 1 February 1918; 13 April 1917; 24 May 1918; 26 October 1917; 31 August 1917; 8 November 1918.

president's idealism may have anticipated that of most of the nationwide majority which eventually came to regard American participation in the war as a tragic mistake. Wartime sacrifices undoubtedly disenchanted some. The *Herald* reported "a bad shortage of coal oil [kerosene] within most of Fairfax County" during the severe winter of 1917-1918, and at least one of the county's railroads, the Southern, was forced to curtail its passenger service in order to meet the expanded demands on its freight service.[73] Charlotte Corner graphically revealed a more serious sacrifice, as well as her own growing doubts about Wilson's goal of creating a new world order, when she recalled that "during [1917] everybody was very enthusiastic, we were going over there and beat up the Germans and that was going to end wars forever. . . . And then that next year, . . . the bodies of the soldiers were . . . coming back to Arlington. . . . I used to go over there, they were just piled up one on top of another. Oh, it was just pathetic."[74] Within weeks of the armistice, the *Herald* criticized Wilson's decision to attend the peace conference at Versailles. The paper feared that the president would be "influenced by a beautiful conception of what should be rather than by a realization of the stern requirements of the occasion. . . . The celebrated [but ill-fated] fourteen principles as enumerated by Mr. Wilson . . . were never really officially endorsed by this country [and are] vague." Like most Americans during the "Red Scare" of 1919 and the early 1920s, the county's disillusionment was not reserved for Wilson alone, but was also directed at his erstwhile Russian allies and his socialist adversaries. In 1921, the editor of the *Herald* came out strongly against a pardon for Eugene Debs, the perennial presidential candidate of the Socialist Party of America, whose crime had been his pacifism, and recommended that "all radicals in this country" be sent "back to Russia as rapidly as possible and let them get a view close by of what their doctrines really are. The country will be rid of bad rubbish."[75]

Contagion and Immunization

Along with the veterans and corpses returning from the war in Europe came yet another tribulation. Charlotte Corner well remembered that "on top of [the war deaths] we had that awful outbreak of flu. . . . You couldn't bury people 'cause they didn't have enough coffins. . . . And there were not enough doctors, there were not enough nurses. . . . My husband had the flu . . . my sister had the flu . . . the little boy had the flu. That . . . was just awful."[76]

Although the County Board of Supervisors had adopted a "Code of Ordinances for the Protection of Public Health" in 1913, creating a Board

73. *Herald*, 1 February 1918; 15 June 1917.
74. Corner-Matthews interview, pp. 32-33.
75. *Herald*, 6 December 1918; 1 April 1921; 15 April 1921.
76. Corner-Matthews interview, pp. 33-34.

Dr. Louis E. Gott and daughter Alys, about 1910, on the front porch of their Falls Church home. Note the horse and buggy in the yard. Virginia State Library.

of Health, appointing a Sanitary Inspector, and regulating the disposal of garbage and the running and slaughtering of animals, not until the First World War and the infamous influenza epidemic of 1918-1919 did public health become a major local concern. A week after the declaration of war, the Fairfax *Herald* announced the inauguration of a Health Inspection Campaign to include an examination of all county school children and a sanitary survey and medical census of county households. Dr. E.L. Flanagan, the county's first public health officer, "found the largest percentage of defects in the teeth," but also urged "every mother . ...to have her children examined for intestinal parasites," and recommended that "all grown people. . .should be examined for hookworm disease." Early in 1918, the County School Board hired a public health nurse, Lena G. Townshend, who organized hygiene leagues and health campaigns at schools all over the county. Later that year, after Flanagan left the county for service in the army, the *Herald* reported that Fairfax County had no cases of typhoid "due largely to the excellent work done by. . .health officials in. . .educating the people to disease prevention."[77]

Even had he been available, Flanagan could have done little to alleviate the influenza epidemic that fall, for as the *Herald* lamented, "the medical profession has discovered no means of checking the disease," but could only, as did the paper, "urge the people . . . to stay away from . . .Washington and Alexandria" where the flu was raging.[78] One of the few remaining doctors in Fairfax County paid a high price for his diligence, as Mrs. Frances Van Patten, a lifelong resident of the Great Falls area, called the death from influenza of Dr. Alfred Lewis Leigh, "our old country doctor, the greatest blow for the whole neighborhood."[79] Schools and churches were closed, the county fair and other community gatherings were cancelled, masks were worn by many in public, and by the time the disease subsided in the spring of 1919, more than eleven thousand Virginians were dead. Fairfax County's toll of 531 was higher than that of any other Virginia county with the exception of Prince George.[80]

Undoubtedly, the influenza experience was responsible for the intensified interest in public health following the war. R. Walton Moore, wartime Chairman of Red Cross activities, was instrumental in

77. *Herald*, 13 April 1917; 27 April 1917; 4 May 1917; 22 June 1917; 18 January 1918; 22 March 1918; 12 April 1918; 31 May 1918; 12 July 1918.

78. *Herald*, 27 December 1918; 18 October 1918.

79. Frances Van Patten, transcribed interview with Stephen L. Matthews, Great Falls, Virginia, 19 August 1971, p. 24.

80. *Herald*, 4 October 1918; 11 October 1918; 13 December 1918; Virginia State Health Department, *Report of the Bureau of Vital Statistics for the Year 1918* (Richmond, Va., 1919), pp. 24, 26; Virginia State Health Department, *Report of the Bureau of Vital Statistics for the Year 1919* (Richmond, Va., 1920), pp. 204, 205.

Dr. Alfred Leigh, about 1916. Photo courtesy of Hassell Leigh. Copy by Bernie Boston.

establishing a new public health program in 1919. The program's field director reported that "public talks were given in schools and halls and frequently lantern slides were employed." On his first inspection tour, he found that "only 5 per cent of the 2,007 houses examined had sanitary toilets; afterwards the number was increased to 47.6 per cent. . . . During the summer of 1919, a dental dispensary was inaugurated," and 269 young people were treated. The same year, 2,128 examinations were conducted for intestinal parasites, and treatment was given to all 574 who were found infected. Notwithstanding this progress, a 1924 evaluation admitted that "the work has had its ups and downs, due mainly to the bad condition of the roads and insufficient finances. From the spring of 1922 to that of 1924 there was no inspector."[81] The County Health Agent's Report for 1924 listed sixty-six cases of scarlet fever with one fatality, twenty cases of diphtheria also with one death, one hundred cases of tuberculosis, twelve incidences of smallpox, and four each of typhoid and polio.[82] But, continued the 1924 evaluation, "the people are realizing the importance" of public health activities. "Several ladies organizations are interested, and there is a possibility of obtaining

81. Nickell and Randolph, *Economic and Social Survey,* pp. 108-9.

82. *Herald,* 20 July 1923; 27 February 1925. A 1922 survey found the county's death rate relatively low, but the birth rate was extremely low. Fairfax whites ranked ninety-fifth and blacks ranked ninety-third out of one hundred Virginia counties. Perhaps in increasingly suburbanized Fairfax, parents were finding children an economic burden rather than a convenient source of labor, as children had often been in rural America. Nickell and Ranolph, *Economic and Social Survey,* p. 46.

a nurse by private subscription." More vital still was the growing commitment of the county's public officials: the Board of Supervisors' budget for 1924-1925 included $5,300 for the maintenance and promotion of public health.[83]

Noble Experimentation and Excessive Expectation

Another public health concern and a nationwide social crusade which reached fruition as a result of World War I was prohibition. After all, beer was "German," and as the Fairfax *Herald* argued in an article entitled "John Barleycorn a Poor Soldier," "prohibition is needed in the ranks as well as in the file," and "war is a sober business."[84] Actually, although the struggle had been long and hard, Fairfax County and Virginia proponents of prohibition had achieved their goal several years before the ratification of the Eighteenth Amendment to the United States Constitution in 1919. Since its beginning in the midnineteenth century, the temperance movement had been characterized by a strongly evangelical appeal. Perhaps the fact that the movement in the county and state had also gained the support of influential political figures and secular groups by the turn of the century explains its early realization in Virginia.

The Sunshine Lodge of the International Order of Good Templers, probably centered at Fairfax Court House, claimed fifty-six members in 1904, twenty of them women, and invited their fellow citizens to "help us . . .close up all the speakeasies in the community."[85] The Pioneer Lodge of Falls Church had been organized in 1887, and by 1906 its membership had grown to eighty-five. In fact, Falls Church, which had been "dry" since its incorporation in 1873 under Virginia's local option law, was the headquarters of the Grand Lodge of the State, and local Postmaster George W. Hawxhurst served as Grand Secretary for Virginia's Good Templars for more than three decades. [86] The Anti-Saloon League and the Women's Christian Temperance Union were active in several other Fairfax communities, and together these organizations spearheaded the movement in Fairfax for statewide prohibition over the following decade.

An indication of the growing popularity of prohibition followed a statement before the General Assembly in 1910 by Delegate Walter T. Oliver, former Mayor of Fairfax, that "there are more drunkards in the dry towns than in the wet." The Fairfax *Herald* feared the statement would "create an erroneous impression" about Fairfax, which was a

83. Nickell and Randolph, *Economic and Social Survey*, p. 108.
84. *Herald*, 25 May 1918.
85. *Herald*, 5 August 1904.
86. Stewart, *Virginia Village*, pp. 85-86.

"dry" town, and argued that "there is nothing like as much liquor sold here now as would be sold if we had licensed bar rooms." The present mayor and members of the town council followed with their own indignant statement that Fairfax had no "confirmed drunkards." In 1908, the *Herald* announced that E.B. Sisson, who operated a distillery at Legato, could legally distribute his product to only a single licensed tavern keeper in the county, M.R. O'Sullivan, whose busy establishment was located in a part of Alexandria City which, at that time, was still in Fairfax County. Already, prohibition had become the predominant issue in state and local elections, and a 1914 petition signed by 69,936 Virginians, 571 of them from Fairfax County, finally convinced Governor Henry C. Stuart to call a referendum on the question of state-wide prohibition. With almost unanimous support, or embarrassed silence, from the county's press and political and moral leadership, Fairfax voters joined the statewide majority by endorsing prohibition on fifty-seven percent of their ballots, a decision which took effect throughout Virginia in 1916.[87]

The enthusiasm of prohibitionists was exceeded only by their expectations of what their success would mean. Many seriously believed that jails, asylums, and poorhouses would soon be empty, disease would be eliminated, and the sanctity of the home, womanhood, and the family would be restored.[88] The Fairfax *Herald* happily heralded progress toward these goals by listing the net reductions in inmates at the state penitentiary during the first year of prohibition; but by 1918, second thoughts were creeping into its pages. Reports of raids and confiscations of illegal liquor began to appear more frequently, including a 1924 estimate that over a thousand dollars worth of stills, one holding two hundred gallons of whiskey, had been captured and destroyed by the sheriff during the preceeding eighteen months. During 1924, sixty-five of the county jail's 109 inmates had been convicted of a prohibition law violation, and in 1925, the exasperated editor of the *Herald* reported "an orgie of law breaking . . . . The Fairfax Circuit Court is again . . . clogged with trials of violators of the prohibition law and conditions seem to improve but little, in spite of all efforts to enforce the law."[89] Disillusionment with the noble experiment was rapidly replacing the unrealistic hopes of Fairfax County prohibitionists.

87. *Herald*, 17 August 1906; 4 October 1907; 26 November 1909; 28 August 1908; 28 December 1906; 12 November 1909; 28 January 1910; 27 March 1908; 10 July 1914; 17 July 1914; 14 August 1914; 25 September 1914.

88. R.E. Lee, Jr., attorney and delegate to the State Assembly from Burke, supported the movement for the "happiness of the home; the protection of women and children; the stopping of crime . . . ; the peace and pleasure of public gatherings; and the removing of temptation from young men." *Herald*, 14 August 1914.

89. *Herald*, 28 December 1917; 25 January 1918; 15 August 1924; 9 January 1925; 20 March 1925.

Strained Relations

Of greater concern to the county's law-abiding citizens than their own criminals were those incarcerated in the District of Columbia's Fairfax County workhouse. When Congress gave its approval for the reformatory and acquired fifteen hundred acres of land on Belvoir neck adjacent to the Woodlawn estate and three and one-half miles from Mount Vernon in 1910, the reaction from county residents, especially in the vicinity of the proposed facility, was hysterical. The Mount Vernon Ladies Association filed a formal protest against the plan, charging that "it would be sacrilege to establish a reformatory for criminals on land which has been so closely identified with the history of the Country," and appealed to Governor William Hodges Mann and President William Howard Taft to intercede against the project. The Fairfax *Herald* further stirred the controversy by reporting a false rumor that a Congressional subcommittee had recommended including Mount Vernon within the reformatory grounds. The protests only succeeded in having the facility moved a few miles to the west, between Lorton and Occoquan, and it was in operation by January 1911. Shortly thereafter, Howe Totten, a Washington lawyer whose Fairfax County home adjoined the new site, filed a $20,000 suit, alleging that inefficiency and a lack of discipline in the conduct of the workhouse had made the neighborhood dangerous and had forced him to abandon his home. Neighborhood nerves were certainly not soothed by the workhouse riot in February 1911, in which a guard was beaten and six prisoners escaped. Two months later, Joseph M. Springman, who operated a general store near Lorton, filed an affidavit in support of Totten's suit, claiming that his business had declined and that his store was no longer safe. In 1912, the *Herald* acknowledged that "the D.C. work house has made great improvements, and has certainly been helpful to this part of Fairfax County." The paper credited Lorton Superintendent W.H. Whittaker for the fine condition of Telegraph Road between Lorton and the facility and for providing employment for many Fairfax County residents. In 1915, the *Herald* even agreed with Whittaker that "the only punishment necessary to teach 'a normal' man to behave is to deprive him of his liberty," and seemingly approved of his exaggerated boast that "at Occoquan we have no guards and no walls." But the overwhelming sentiment in the county remained negative, especially in the wake of continued escapes. When an escapee attempted to assault two Fairfax County women within twenty-four hours of leaving Lorton in 1917, the county asked that federal authorities furnish more guards and tighten security at the facility, a request that would be renewed regularly over the following sixty years.[90]

90. *Herald*, 14 October 1910; 13 January 1911; 20 January 1911; 27 January 1911; 10 February 1911; 28 April 1911; 17 May 1912; 26 February 1915; 28 September 1917.

Religion's Attrition

Several other issues of public morality surfaced in the years surrounding World War I. Strengthening the Sunday blue laws was a leading concern of many citizens, including the members of the Sunshine Lodge of Good Templars, who in 1904 asked for support in their efforts to "stop the gatherings on Sunday for the purpose of drinking and playing cards." In 1916, the Fairfax *Herald* criticized the "peculiar language" of the present blue law, which provided that "ice cream made on any [day other] than Sunday, can be delivered on Sunday on the ground of necessity."[91] But a 1916 United States Census of Religious Bodies revealed that many county residents may have preferred ice cream and social gatherings to churchgoing on Sundays. The survey found that more than two-thirds of the county's church members were either Baptists or Methodists; 12 percent were Roman Catholics; 9 percent were Episcopalians; 5 percent were Presbyterians; 3 percent were Brethren; and one percent were Disciples of Christ. However, the 6,872 church members accounted for only 44 percent of the county's population over ten years of age, a statistic termed "not creditable" and "most lamentable" by the 1924 University of Virginia survey. By comparison, 61 percent of Virginia's population claimed church membership, with Fairfax ranking eighty-sixth out of one hundred counties in this category.[92]

Even more distressing to many was the county's embarrassingly high divorce rate. In 1907, Lewis H. Machen of Alexandria, who represented Fairfax County in the State Senate, suggested fixing the marriageable age at twenty-one for both sexes: "such a law . . . would probably prevent many of the matrimonial mistakes resulting from the heedlessness of youth and might thus obviate the necessity for many divorces."[93] But by 1922, even though the county's marriage rate was less than half that for the state as a whole, the divorce rate continued to climb, with Fairfax fifth among Virginia counties in per capita divorces.[94] The Fairfax *Herald* noted that four years earlier, the county had ranked seventeenth in the state, and blamed the county's proximity to a growing Washington for the increase. In 1925, the paper called Virginia's divorce laws "too easy," and asked that they be tightened, failing to realize that stricter laws could hardly solve conjugal differences and that the days of rural stability, and domestic tranquility, were rapidly drawing to a close in Fairfax.[95]

In addition to marital misunderstandings, the period witnessed a protracted misunderstanding involving a newly arrived religious group

91. *Herald*, 5 August 1904; 23 June 1916; 11 February 1921.
92. Nickell and Randolph, *Economic and Social Survey*, pp. 46-47.
93. *Herald*, 9 August 1907.
94. Nickell and Ranolph, *Economic and Social Survey*, p. 46.
95. *Herald*, 12 January 1923; 21 August 1925.

(the Dunkards), and the near extinction of another sect of long standing in the county (the Quakers). A small group of Dunkards had organized a German Baptist Brethren Church at Oakton in 1903, and counted 113 members when they dedicated "their commodious new church-house" in 1905. Then in 1912, the Fairfax *Herald* announced that "a large colony of Dunkards is to be established on Hayfield Farm, consisting of 804 acres of land . . . on the telegraph road."[96] Soon thereafter, another group of Dunkards requested permission to use the Legato School building between Centreville and Fairfax for a Sunday school, but then refused to accept local school trustees' negative response. Virginia Peters, in a history of the Legato School, wrote that "one B.F.A. Meyers was forbidden to enter the school and the trustee[s]. . .appointed a committee of one to 'fix secure fasterners on the windows and the door.' These measures apparently did not deter the Dunkards because the school board minutes for one meeting in 1913 reveal that the group had been informed once more that since there was a church for such purposes, the Legato School was not available." In 1915, the Dunkards requested permission again, but "after due consideration and a great deal of controversy, it was decided not to grant the request."[97]

Meanwhile, next door to the new colony at Hayfield, the Quaker community which had been centered at Woodlawn since the 1840s. continued to thrive, as it had since recovering from substantial Civil War setbacks. But in 1917, as Horace D. Buckman wrote in his brief study of the Woodlawn Quakers, there came "a second invasion by the armed forces. Fort Belvoir [then Camp Humphreys] was established in the area, and some of the members had their homes taken over by the military reservation. When the war ended and the Meeting could catch its breath and take stock it found most of its members had moved away. It struggled on for a few years, then regular Meetings were discontinued, though the Meeting was never 'laid down.' "[98] Two hundred and fifty years earlier, William Penn had counseled his pacifist followers that "truth often suffers more by the heat of its defenders, than from the arguments of its opposers." Even as much of the community made a quiet exodus from the Fairfax County farms they had made flourish for seventy years, the Friends continued to set an admirable example for their neighbors.

Enfranchisement's Fruition

The turn of the twentieth century brought many American women an opportunity to question the roles and restrictions that had been

96. *Herald*, 29 September 1905; 22 November 1912.

97. Peters, "Legato School," pp. 39-40.

98. Horace D. Buckman, "The Quakers Come to Woodlawn," *Historical Society Yearbook*, 9 (1964-65): 69. During World War II, Fort Belvoir was expanded further, and "the Meeting House is now completely surrounded by the bustling army post."

maintained for them since colonization. Only upper class women had earlier escaped the drudgery of making clothes and soap, preserving and preparing food, working beside husbands or fathers in fields or factories, and at the same time bearing and rearing children. But as commercial ice, packaged and canned foods, electric ranges, and sewing and washing machines became available, females from less prosperous families were discovering the unfamiliar commodity of leisure time.

Many Fairfax women found alternatives to traditional domestic duties in Washington, especially as the first World War caused a rapid expansion of the federal bureaucracy. Jobs were available not only in government offices, but also at telephone company switchboards and department store sales counters; women from surrounding farms and suburbs flocked to fill them. The University of Virginia cited these employment opportunities in explaining the significant drop in the female percentage of population in Fairfax, from 49 percent in 1910 to only 46.2 percent in 1920.[99] Other county women found outlets for excess energy in volunteer war work and other social causes. For example, in 1874, the Fairfax News had editorially condemned a group of women who had tried to close down a bar room in Ohio, but forty years later, the Fairfax Herald called the statewide passage of prohibition "a Great Victory" and admitted that the "voters of Virginia were encouraged and inspired by the women of the State." Furthermore, in the war's early months, the Herald reported that "women have gone to work to give aid to our country." At a "Colored Preparedness Meeting" at Fairfax, the wives of prominent town officials "made speeches along patriotic lines," and the extensive Red Cross activities of Fairfax women have been cited.[100]

Impressed by the admirable response of women to the wartime emergency, establishment voices called on women to accept an even more active role in the crusade, and in social and political circles as well. In 1918, the Herald reprinted an article from Physical Culture entitled "Silly Corseted Girl a Slacker." While the writer acknowledged that "women are gradually encroaching upon the occupations once followed by men," he decried "the simpering, corseted product of modern methods in the training of girls . . . . While the boys are making men of themselves, it should be considered the duty of the girls to [make] themselves fit mates for those who come back from the terrible conflict that is now upon us."[101] Undoubtedly, the author would have applauded

99. U.S. Bureau of Census, Thirteenth Census of the United States Taken in the Year 1910, III, Population 1910 (Washington, D.C.: Government Printing Office, 1913), p. 943; U.S. Bureau of Census, Fourteenth Census of the United States Taken in the Year 1920, III, Population 1920 (Washington, D.C.: Government Printing Office, 1922), p. 1064; Nickell and Randolph, Economic and Social Survey, p. 44.

100. Fairfax News, 22 May 1874; Herald, 2 October 1914; 11 May 1917; 27 April 1917.

101. Herald, 8 March 1918.

the wartime activities of Ivakota, the county's home for unwed mothers. According to the University of Virginia survey, "no more interesting chapter of war work was ever written . . . . Here many a girl was given a chance to do her 'bit' for the country, which without the guiding and restraining hand of Ivakota, would have been an unconscious enemy of the cause she longed to serve! Many an unthinking boy in *khaki* was led to understand the unworthiness of leaving his own flesh and blood on some doorstep while he went to war to avenge the wrongs of Belgian and French girls at the hands of an alien foe! Many today are happy and prosperous possessing that greatest of all boons, self-respect."[102] While the values embodied by "Ivakota" have not always persisted, the new respect given women, and the self-respect they gained as a result of their contributions to the cause, were real, and undoubtedly played a vital role in the culmination of the movement for women's suffrage. In March 1917, the recently organized Shakespearean Literary Society of Fairfax High School debated the following question: "Resolved, That Women Should Vote in Virginia on the Same Basis as Men." Although it is impossible to know whether the views of the participants were sincerely held, Judges J.W. Ballard, John W. Rust, and T.R. Keith, mayor and town councilmen of Fairfax, respectively, decided unanimously in favor of the affirmative.[103]

Even after women had acquired the vote with the ratification of the Nineteenth Amendment to the U.S. Constitution in 1920, serious obstacles to true equality remained. The Fairfax *Herald's* condemnation of Mrs. Nicholas Longworth of Fairfax for "embrac[ing] the cigarette habit" is an example of the separate standards maintained for the sexes. The paper found it "hardly believable" that a woman who was "looked upon as a leader [would] sacrifice the confidence of her sex by setting an example so demoralizing and pernicious." Meanwhile, many men, whether from personal insecurity or sheer selfishness, continued to confine women to a separate and consistently inferior role in their male-dominated political structure. When Mattie Gundry, who had operated the Gundry Home and Training School for Feeble-Minded near Falls Church for many years, was nominated to be a school trustee by the Falls Church District School Board in 1908, County Superintendent of Schools M.D. Hall declared her ineligible because of her sex, a decision sustained on appeal by Circuit Court Judge J.B.T. Thornton. Equally detrimental to the movement for equal rights were the women who preferred the pedestal and continued liberation from the responsibilities of equality. Furthermore, once they had acquired the ballot, suffragettes

102. Nickell and Randolph, *Economic and Social Survey*, p. 106.
103. *Herald*, 23 February 1917; 30 March 1917.

discovered that they were divided along political, economic, and philosophical lines just as were men. The unity forged by the prohibition and suffrage movements had been dissipated by their successes. Evidence of progress toward equal rights would occasionally appear. In the early 1920s, the Fairfax *Herald* expressed its support for the "efforts. . .being made to have the women of the town take an interest in local affairs and to become candidates for the town council. Mattie Gundry who three times was elected to the Falls Church Town Council certainly kept the faith.[104] But it would be half a century before men and women again organized to secure the basic human rights promised all Americans, regardless of their sex.[104]

The Paternalistic Tradition

The war years were a critical time for black residents of Fairfax County as well as for women. In the half century since the Civil War, race relations in the county had remained stable as long as blacks remained satisfied at the bottom of the social, economic, and political ladder. Evidence of interracial cooperation was overshadowed by the more numerous and effective efforts to limit opportunities for black advancement. The successful crusade to disfranchise black voters through the Constitution of 1902 is a prime example. Whites treated blacks like children, and many blacks behaved accordingly, gratefully accepting whites' occasional benevolence and patience with their mistakes. Blacks regularly had to be scolded for "loafing" and "skylarking," but little more was expected or given. "Ungrateful" blacks continued to receive most of the blame for crime in the county, but occasionally a black would earn the patronizing praise of county whites. P.H. Hughes, "the teacher at the Fairfax colored school," professed to "have tried in every conceivable way to make my humble race better citizens," and for his efforts was labeled "a Benefactor to His Race" by the Fairfax *Herald*. When World War I began, blacks were told to display their patriotism by planting gardens, and when county conscription quotas were still unfilled in early 1918, blacks were called to the colors. According the the *Herald* they displayed "fine spirit" and "much willingness to take up military life."[105] This is not surprising since, even though army battalions, barracks and blood banks remained strictly segregated, blacks in the service experienced a degree of equality they had never known. This was especially true for those who served in Europe where segregated public facilities were not maintained. Even more blacks found new economic and

---

104. *Herald*, 12 August 1910; 11 December 1908; 24 June 1921; 24 March 1922; 22 June 1923; Steadman, *Fence and Fireside*, p. 144.

105. *Herald*, 18 August 1916; 25 August 1916; 2 April 1915; 5 April 1912; 27 April 1917; 28 June 1918.

social opportunities in northern factories and neighborhoods, both opened to large numbers of blacks for the first time because of the emergency of the war. The 6.5 percent decrease in the county's black population between 1910 and 1920 is evidence that many Fairfax County blacks participated in the "Great Migration" from the rural south to the urban north, and most probably had their expectations raised considerably by the experience.[106] But an indication of how little the attitudes of county whites had changed came when the Fairfax *Herald* glibly noted that race riots had broken out in many parts of the north following the migration, and suggested that "the negroes should learn from this that their truest and best friends are the Southern people, who understand their weaknesses and limitations."[107]

Education's Condition

The education offered the county's young people was another object of evaluation during World War I. School children contributed to the war effort through the Junior Red Cross, health, hygiene, and canning clubs, and the Junior Farm Bureau and the U.S. Boys Working Reserve, both of which sought to supplement the seriously depleted farm labor supply. At the same time, despite the increased demands on students' energies, state and local school and political leadership sought to insure and improve their educational opportunities. The state's first compulsory attendance law took effect in the fall of 1918 and required that all children between the ages of eight and twelve attend school at least sixteen weeks during each academic year. School funding continued to increase, as it had since the turn of the century, so that by 1917, the county school budget of $87,000 accounted for more than all other county expenditures combined.[108]

"In the last few years," the University of Virginia's 1924 survey reported, "the amount of consolidation that has occurred has materially helped the school situation in the county . . . . Trucks have been used to transport children to school, thus assuring a larger attendance than would otherwise be the case."[109] According to Virginia Peters, William Halley, who built a school at Lorton at his own expense when the old school building there burned in 1918, "may have introduced the first public transportation of school children in Fairfax County. For a year, he drove eight children to and from school . . . so that they would not have to walk through the grounds of the Lorton Correctional Institution."[110]

106. U.S. Bureau of Census, Thirteenth Census, III, *Population 1910*, p. 942; U.S. Bureau of Census, Fourteenth Census, III, *Population 1920*, p. 1064.

107. *Herald*, 6 July 1917.

108. *Herald*, 22 February 1918; 3 May 1918; 23 August 1918; 28 November 1917.

109. Nickell and Randolph, *Economic and Social Survey*, p. 100.

110. Peters, "Legato School," p. 37.

Superintendent Hall's 1924 report counted "fourteen bus, or wagon routes," and in 1925, four new buses were purchased "to help solve the problems of consolidation."[111] Although parents in Lewinsville and Langley spoke nostalgically of their neighborhood schools when the more central Franklin Sherman School at McLean superseded them in 1914, genuine complaints about consolidation and the transporting of students to achieve it seem to have been nonexistent. In fact, by the early 1920s, Langley parents had acquired a Model T Ford to take their children to the McLean school. Charlotte Corner remembered that "the children just climbed on that Ford, just like bees around a hive. If they could [not] get in . . . they'd just hang on the outside."[112] Despite the addition of seven fully accredited four-year high schools, at least three junior high schools, and an almost three-fold increase in the county's school attendance between 1907 and 1928, the number of school buildings in Fairfax County fell from ninety-four to sixty-five.[113] The quality of education available in these enlarged and better-equipped institutions had improved markedly.

The best indication of the job Fairfax schools were doing and of the changing character of the county since the arrival of the electric trolley was the revelation that in 1920 the county ranked first in the state in literacy. The census of 1900 had found almost 16 percent of the population illiterate, and in 1910, almost 11 percent. But ten years later, only 4.3 percent could not read or write.[114] The 1924 University of Virginia-sponsored survey gave county schools high marks in several other areas. The Fairfax system ranked eighteenth out of one hundred Virginia counties in the average annual salary paid its teachers ($684.40); it ranked nineteenth in the value of property per school room ($1,383.75); sixth in per capita cost of instruction ($23.15); twentieth in length of the school term (161 days); and seventeenth in its "relative educational efficiency," an overall evaluation of the system's financial resources and operations.[115]

Despite this positive rating, several serious shortcomings remained. Most surprising was Fairfax County's ninety-eighth position in the state in the percentage of its school-age population attending its schools. Of 8,968 children between six and eighteen years of age, only 4,989 were enrolled, and only an average of 3,556 actually attended Fairfax public schools. The fact that many older students, particularly from the Mount

111. Hinkle, "Public Secondary Education," pp. 19-20.

112. Corner-Matthews interview, p. 24.

113. Gott and Hogan, "Fairfax Public Schools," p. 30.

114. U.S. Bureau of Census, Thirteenth Census, III, *Population 1910*, p. 943; U.S. Bureau of Census, Fourteenth Census, III, *Population 1920*, p. 1,064.

115. Nickell and Randolph, *Economic and Social Survey*, pp. 73-74.

Accotink School interior. From Industrial and Historical Sketch of Fairfax County, Virginia, 1907.

Vernon and Lee districts, had to travel to Washington or Alexandria to
attend high school was partially responsible for this unfavorable
ranking, but the 1924 survey correctly found this "a startling condition to
exist in a county that ranks first in the state in literacy," and warned that
"if the compulsory school law is not enforced more rigidly, we will not be
able to hold our rank in the. . .future."[116]

Not so surprising but equally serious was the lack of adequate
funding for, and apparently interest in, the black students of the county's
strictly segregated school system. A Virginia Education Commission
study in 1920 found that the cost of instruction per pupil in Fairfax
County varied from an average of $13.29 for each white child to $6.44
for each black. The school term lasted twenty days longer in the county's
white schools, and although black teachers had an average of
thirty-seven pupils in their classrooms compared to thirty-one for white
teachers, blacks received an average annual salary of only $239
compared to the $408 per year received by whites.[117]

Along with the prejudices that these statistics suggest, leadership, or
lack of it, may have been a major problem. During M.D. Hall's
forty-two years as County Superintendent of Schools, from 1886 to
1928, great progress was made. In the value of school property alone, the
system saw an increase of over two thousand percent, from $32,500 to
$707,000.[118] But several subtle and some not so subtle criticisms of Hall's
administration were surfacing by the early 1920s. It was Hall's
opposition which stopped the much-needed expansion of the system in
several school districts, and Charlotte Corner confessed that she finally
went to Richmond to ask state school authorities to "please . . . get us a
new superintendent."[119] When Hall was finally convinced to retire at the
age of eighty, school officials, teachers, parents, and students displayed
their deep affection and appreciation, not only for this final decision, but
for his devoted efforts to guide the system through its formative years.
Under the more energetic leadership of Wilbert T. Woodson and his
successors, Fairfax County public schools continued to improve and to
set an example for the systems of other counties and other states to
follow.

116. Ibid., p. 123.
117. Virginia Education Commission and Virginia Survey Staff, *Virginia Public Schools*, pp. 393, 397.
118. Gott and Hogan, "Fairfax Public Schools," p. 30.
119. Corner-Matthews interview, p. 39.

IX

The Agrarian Situation

Another activity of county residents which received added attention and assistance during the war was agriculture. In fact, it is in this area that the impact of the technological changes coming to the county can be seen most vividly. Along with the Fairfax County Board of Supervisors' efforts on behalf of area farmers, the state had begun to provide aid by the early years of the twentieth century. The Virginia Agricultural and Mechanical College, for example, offered free, three-week demonstration courses during the winter of 1907 on subjects which included horticulture, animal husbandry, and dairying. The Virginia Polytechnical Institute also offered winter courses for farmers, while the Virginia Agricultural Experiment Station regularly held public meetings in Fairfax communities to present its latest findings. In 1910, the "Farmers' Institute Train," a traveling exhibit of farm implements, products, and literature, stopped at Burke and Fairfax Station for large meetings. [120] Then in 1914, the outbreak of the war and its demands on the nation's goods and manpower brought a new appreciation for America's farmers, their labors, and their products.

The War's Stimulation

With the war in Europe threatening to directly involve Americans at any time, county farmers called a meeting to discuss the new United States Farm Loan System, and in January 1917, they became "the first on record to make application for membership." [121] The Fairfax *Herald* announced that the Fairfax Farm Loan Association was "ready to do

---

120. *Herald*, 22 November 1907; 23 December 1910; 15 December 1905; 6 May 1910.
121. C.L. Fowler, Fairfax County Agricultural Agent, *Annual Reports*, 1916, p. Y-2.

business as soon as the national government completes its plans for the loaning of money to farmers at a moderate rate of interest." In June 1917, the Fairfax County Agricultural Defense League bought and distributed more than $1,200 worth of seeds to county farmers. The following January, the *Herald* disclosed that the U.S. Department of Agriculture would sell at cost a supply of nitrate of soda, purchased through the War Industries Board to stimulate agricultural production.[122] And of greater significance to the farmers of Fairfax County was the appointment in 1917 of Harry B. Derr to the recently created post of County Agricultural Agent.

For twenty-one years, Harry B. Derr was the Fairfax farmer's friend, advisor, and liaison for federal, state, and local agricultural programs. Further, his annual reports became a fascinating chronicle of the fruits and frustrations of farming in an area undergoing the fundamental transition from rurality to suburbia. Although his initial annual report was incomplete, the Fairfax *Herald* provided a synopsis of Derr's work during the war's and his own first year. Undoubtedly, the period's most pressing problem was the perennial shortage of farm labor, aggravated now by the draft and the better-paying jobs available in Washington and in war industries elsewhere. Derr sought to alleviate this shortage by organizing and promoting the Junior Farm Bureau and the U.S. Boys Working Reserve, and awarding "junior buttons" to the young volunteers. The agent also urged county farmers to file affidavits on behalf of their employees to prevent their being drafted for military service. Despite these efforts, Derr warned in late 1918 that "farm labor conditions are getting worse" and that there had been an outbreak of hemorrhagic septicemia, or "blackleg," among unvaccinated calves. He also complained that he had found "considerable sappy corn being put in the cribs," that wheat and potatoes had done poorly due to unfavorable weather and blight, and that much of the county's winter oat crop was badly infested with cheat, "a pernicious weed."[123]

If farmers were limited by bad luck and a lack of farm labor, Derr tried to make the most of the situation by encouraging cooperative enterprises, from boys' and girls' corn and canning clubs, to a large-scale milk producers' association. He may have instigated the mass meeting of farmers from Fairfax and Loudoun Counties that met in June 1917 to discuss "Rural Organization and Co-operation," and he surely called the meeting in February 1918 "to form a County Farmers' Bureau [to] assist the County Demonstrator in his efforts towards the betterment of the agricultural conditions in the county." Three months later, a "Threshing Association" was organized for "the standardization of prices for

122. *Herald,* 19 January 1917; 15 June 1917; 25 January 1918.

123. *Herald,* 22 February 1918; 3 May 1918; 5 April 1918; 2 August 1918; 11 October 1918; 22 November 1918.

threshing and bailing, the putting in repair of machines to make them 100 percent efficient, and the formation of plans whereby all farmers in a neighborhood will have grain ready at the same time so that the machines will have to pay but one visit to a section." The benefits of group action would not become apparent until after the war in most cases, but the agent's efforts to teach individual farmers better book-keeping and business practices enabled them better to cope with the abnormal wartime conditions.[124]

A Fair Indication

The postwar period produced prosperity for some, but problems for most county farmers. First, the positive accomplishments. Cooperative wartime experiments along with the experience gained at the annual county fair convinced many to continue both of these efforts. The county's earliest successful cooperative organizations, the Piedmont Milk and Produce Association and the Potomac Fruit Growers' Association, had been organized in the 1870s, but their example was evidently not followed until the early 1900s when the Milk Producers' Association of Maryland, Virginia, and the District of Columbia and the Fairfax County Fruit Growers' Association made short-lived efforts to encourage joint action. A number of neighborhood farmers' clubs had been organized and met irregularly, but their activities were often more social than economic, and in 1909, the Fairfax *Herald* regretted that "there being no farmers' club in the vicinity, it is hard to get the farmers to act with any degree of unanimity." A recent farmers' meeting at the courthouse was "not largely attended." Later that year, the paper expressed its opinion that in this "one respect, at least, Fairfax lags behind her sister counties," and suggested that an annual agricultural fair would create "bonds of friendship and good fellowship among our people."[125]

In the fall of 1912, when the county's first fair was held, not only was the *Herald's* prediction fulfilled, but Fairfax farmers found an opportunity to exhibit the fruits and vegetables of their labors. The fair also provided an opportunity for discussing the merits of union, for farmers' clubs were formed at Fairfax and Annandale during the following year, and at organizational meetings in 1914, members of the Andrew Chapel and Vale Farmers' clubs stressed the need for cooperation and laid plans for group participation in the next fall's fair. Meanwhile, young people organized corn, tomato, poultry, and canning clubs, and a 4-H club, all undoubtedly anticipating the annual fair with great excitement. By the fair's fifth edition, even though it fell in the midst of the World War I, it had become Fairfax County's favorite

124. *Herald*, 15 June 1917; 15 February 1918; 24 May 1918; 18 January 1918.
125. *Herald*, 20 October 1905; 4 January 1907; 2 April 1909; 27 August 1909.

attraction, featuring in three very full days a brass band, balloon ascensions, comic knife throwing, high-wire walking, health demonstrations, an automobile parade, precision drills, parachute drops, moving pictures, Punch and Judy shows, a school parade, and the prize-winning produce and livestock of the county's farmers and future farmers.[126] Over and above its significance as a social occasion, the fair provided Fairfax farmers a forum from which to build more enduring and economically important cooperative organizations.

The Benefits of Cooperation

First to take the cow by the horns, along with other extremities, were the "milk producers of this and other nearby counties . . . who supply the City of Washington." They organized in 1916, and according to the Fairfax *Herald*, were "enthusiastic over the plan for a centralized distribution of the milk supply."[127] By the early 1920s, the Maryland and Virginia Milk Producers' Association, Inc., claimed 121 members in Fairfax County, and when reorganized in 1923, it represented the owners of over fifteen thousand dairy cows.[128] In his 1925 report, County Agent Derr credited the group with handling "the greater portion of the milk produced in the county."[129] The success of this organization may have been the responsibility of the several Dairy Herd Improvement Associations organized by Derr to test herds and to cull from them cows whose milk production did not reach a profitable level. In 1923, the *Herald* reported that three Fairfax dairy farmers "led the list for the ten best cows in all the cow testing associations of the State," while other county dairymen consistently received top recognition in the Sealtest Milk Company's monthly awards for milk purity.[130] In 1924, the agent's annual report reproduced a study revealing that the average milk cow in Virginia produced 2,511 pounds of milk the previous year, the national average was 3,527 pounds, and the average for cows in testing associations nationwide was 6,077 pounds. But the cows from Fairfax County's leading testing association produced an average of 8,066 pounds of milk, and the association's leading herd gave a remarkable 11,764 pounds per cow.[131] The University of Virginia's 1924 survey found that Fairfax County "has twenty percent of the cow testing associations operating in Virginia," and concluded that "these and other considerations," certainly including the easy access via trolley to the

---

126. *Herald*, 20 December 1912; 26 June 1914; 14 August 1914; 5 July 1912; 1 November 1912; 28 September 1917.

127. *Herald*, 3 November 1916.

128. Nickell and Randolph, *Economic and Social Survey*, p. 112; *Herald*, 2 March 1923.

129. Harry B. Derr, Fairfax County Agricultural Agent, *Annual Reports*, 1925, p. 13 (hereinafter cited as Derr, *Reports*).

130. *Herald*, 27 July 1923; Schug, "Herndon," p. 10.

131. Derr, *Reports*, 1924, p. 12.

excellent Washington market, "have combined to give Fairfax first place in the State in the value of its dairy products."[132] In 1923 county dairymen received "a return of nearly one million dollars from milk and its by products."[133]

Agricultural agent Derr found a number of other positive achievements to report in the early twenties. In 1922 he announced the formation of the Northern Virginia Bee Keepers' Association, and he annually praised the work of the County Farm Bureau, the two county granges, the three Fairfax communities which held yearly agricultural fairs, and the four farmers' clubs, each composed of twelve families which met once a year at each home. Derr described the meetings of these clubs in his 1925 report: "After dinner the ladies visit while the men go over the farm and discuss current farm problems. Then they return to the house and listen to some speaker who has been invited for an informal talk. . . . It was at one of these meetings," Derr continued, "that the agent first broached the subject of an Agricultural Vocational High School, and the plans . . . terminated . . . with . . . the Floris School, one of the best in the state." The members, many of whom were dairy farmers, also "built three miles of rock road upon which they all had to travel to get their farm products to town and rail road."[134] Derr had kind words as well for the county's Home Demonstration Agent, Lucy Steptoe, whose work was supported by school leagues, local railroad companies, the Fairfax County Chamber of Commerce, 4-H clubs, the Daughters of the American Revolution, and other interested individuals. Activities included clothing, canning, cooking, bread baking, poultry, and gardening clubs, kitchen improvement contests, and short courses in first aid and other subjects. Four hundred and twenty-five girls and forty-one women participated in these activities in 1925.[135]

Corn production, valued at $569,590 in 1922 and second in importance only to the county's dairy goods, received a boost in 1925 with the introduction of a locally produced hybrid called "Fairfax County White." Several experimental fields produced yields of eighty to ninety bushels per acre, better than three times the average yield for the state. Although "horse drawn machinery [was] still in the majority" in 1925, the agent hoped his advocacy of "labor saving machinery [could] remove some of the drudgery our farm labor complains of" and convince them to stay on the farm. His annual report always optimistically noted the number of new tractors and trucks in the county. In 1919, there

132. Nickell and Randolph, *Economic and Social Survey*, p. 99; U.S. Bureau of Census, Fourteenth Census of the United States Taken in the Year 1920, VI, part 2, *Agriculture* (Washington, D.C.: Government Printing Office, 1922), p. 166.

133. Derr, *Reports*, 1923, p. 13.

134. Ibid., 1922, p. 14; 1925, p. 14.

135. Lucy Steptoe, Fairfax County Home Demonstration Agent, *Annual Reports*, 1924, p. 1; 1925 (n.p.), p. 4.

were five new tractors and two motor trucks; in 1924, he happily announced that "Mr. H.C. Clapp of this county has invented a four row picker with which 20 acres of beans per day were harvested."[136] These factors no doubt contributed to the University of Virginia's 1924 findings that, in addition to its number one position in milk production, Fairfax ranked sixth out of one hundred Virginia counties in wheat yield per acre, eleventh in total production of Irish potatoes, sixteenth in sweet potatoes, eighteenth in per capita egg production, within the top third in corn, butter, hogs, hay and forage, and orchard fruit production, and sixteenth in the total value of farm property, assessed at almost $20,000,000.[137]

Postwar Prostration

And now the problems. Life had never been easy down on the farm, but in the wake of World War I, it was growing decidedly more difficult, especially relative to the comforts and conveniences that were becoming available to Americans living in cities and towns. Fairfax farmers were not alone in feeling the effects of the nationwide economic slump immediately following the war, but even after the advent of "Coolidge Prosperity" in the early 1920s, the Fairfax *Herald* reported county farmers in "serious straits" and unable to buy fertilizer because of the low prices their goods were bringing.[138] County agent Derr emphasized this difficulty in his 1920 and 1921 reports, adding that the scarcity of money had prevented construction of planned lime warehouses. The money squeeze was surely responsible for the "positive antipathy towards buying medicine or paying for veterinarian work" that Derr recognized in 1922, and the following year he "regretted that some of our farmers refuse to pay the increased price for certified seed and continue to purchase cheaper but inferior seed with its resultant loss." In his 1924 report, Derr blamed the preference for the cheaper seed on the county's "disastrous" corn year, with yields falling from thirty to fifteen bushels per acre.[139]

The University of Virginia's 1924 survey revealed a more ominous statistic when it found 492 of the county's 2,253 farms (22 percent) mortgaged, a higher percentage than in all but three other Virginia

136. U.S. Bureau of Census, Fourteenth Census, vol. VI, part 2, *Agriculture*, p. 166; Derr, *Reports*, 1925, p. 2; 1922, p. 21; 1919, p. Y-2; 1924, (n.p.). Traditionalists no doubt regretted Derr's conclusion in 1924 that "modern machinery on the farm by means of which farmers grind their own feed, in addition to buying ready mixed feeds from the large manufacturers is causing the closing down of many of the grist mills formerly operated. Exit the old-fashioned corn pone enter bakers bread . . . which is delivered to the stores by the leading Washington bakeries." Derr, *Reports*, 1924 (n.p.).

137. Nickell and Randolph, *Economic and Social Survey*, p. 122.

138. *Herald*, 15 April 1921.

139. Derr, *Reports*, 1920, p. X; 1921, p. 1; 1922, p. 12; 1923, p. 2; 1924, p. 3. In contrast, Derr claimed that his demonstrators, using only certified seed, reaped an average of fifty-two bushels per acre from their corn fields. Derr, *Reports*, 1924, p. 3.

counties.[140] In 1922, Derr described the difficulty Fairfax farmers were having "in obtaining money to pay off loans," and added that "a number of homes have been lost from this cause."[141] The University's report blamed "poor management" and the efforts of farmers "to purchase luxuries that they cannot afford," along with the economic situation, for the rise of mortgages, while Derr hoped that as a director of the Federal Farm Loan Bank, he could induce county farmers "to become members of the bank, rather than run chances of being picked up by loan sharks." In 1925, he told of convincing an eighty-seven-year-old farmer to sell a portion of his farm rather than extend his loan by mortgaging his farm for thirty years! Tight money was also responsible for the growing "hesitancy about cooperating in buying and selling farm supplies" that Derr recognized in 1921. He blamed the tendency from solidarity to solitariness on "what appears to be a fear of being beat, or jealousy that one man may succeed better than his neighbor," and on the fact that co-oping "meant cash transactions and that their credit at the stores would be denied them."[142] The 1924 survey added its criticism of the "lack of cooperation and organization between our producers and consumers."[143] A 1925 United States Bureau of Census Report on Cooperative Marketing found that only thirty-two of the county's 2,367 farms had made joint sales, and only nine had made joint purchases during the preceding year.[144] Even the dairyman, whom Derr recognized as "the only farmer to come out ahead" in 1923, was not immune to these hardships. In 1924, the agent advised able farmers to purchase "a high quality pure bred bull [rather] than to buy pure bred cows. The latter represents an enormous outlay of cash and several dairymen have gone under trying to carry such a load." Derr also realized that not all farmers wanted to be dairymen; one farmer told him that "he did not want to be tied to a cow's tail 365 days in the year."[145]

Politicians' Protestations

Other economic hardships for area agrarians could be traced to a gradually growing insensitivity among local political leadership to farm problems. The County Board of Supervisors had continued to devote a large share of its energies in the early 1900s to the interests of its mostly agricultural constituents, building and maintaining roads to markets, and protecting livestock by taxing dog owners to pay bounties for

140. Nickell and Randolph, *Economic and Social Survey*, p. 122.

141. Derr, *Reports*, 1922, p. 13.

142. Nickell and Randolph, *Economic and Social Survey*, p. 122; Derr, *Reports*, 1925, p. 12; 1921, p. 7.

143. Ibid., p. 89.

144. U.S. Bureau of Census, United States Census of Agriculture, 1925, part II, *The Southern States* (Washington, D.C.: Government Printing Office, 1927), p. 206.

145. Derr, *Reports*, 1923, p. 22; 1924, p. 11; 1923, pp. 22-23.

predators and to reimburse farmers for killed animals.[146] In 1907 the Board of Supervisors made an extraordinary appropriation of $1,000 to assist the Fairfax County Fruit Growers' Association in its crusade against a blight called "Peach Yellows," and in 1910 the board matched a $400 state appropriation for agricultural experimentation in the county. Local political rivals competed in their protestations of concern for farm problems, and the acid test of an incumbent's performance was the length of his list of contributions to farmers. Supporters of C.C. Carlin of Alexandria, Fairfax County's congressman from 1907 until his resignation in 1919, cited his advocacy of rural free delivery, postal savings banks, good roads, and marketing legislation during his successful 1918 reelection bid, and the Fairfax *Herald* endorsed Carlin in part because he was a farmer and owned more land and grew bigger crops than his opponent, E.B. White of Loudoun County.[147] R. Walton Moore, Fairfax lawyer who won Carlin's vacated seat in a special election in 1919 and remained in Congress until 1931, distributed 800 packages of seeds in 1921 to affirm his own concern for the farmer. The Board of Supervisors' annual reappointment of Harry B. Derr as County Agricultural Agent and its support for the work of the home demonstration agent were the most significant contributions of all. Although the board's 1922 appropriation of $3,000 to assist Derr in his cow-testing activities and its creation of an agricultural and vocational high school at Floris in 1920 seemed to indicate a still-growing commitment to agriculture, several other issues reveal that by the early 1920s, the concerns of local politicians, and the character of the county, were changing.[148]

The Agent's Fulminations

One "glaring inequality" recognized by the University of Virginia's 1924 study was the favoritism shown the county's "gentlemen farmers." Since tax assessors were "left to set their own standards," the survey

146. As Fairfax County became less rural in character and as dairy cows replaced more vulnerable sheep on many Fairfax County farms, withdrawals from the "dog fund" to pay for destroyed livestock became smaller. In 1909, claims amounted to only $55.50, and the large balance left was channeled into the school fund. *Herald*, 9 July 1909.

While most other county expenses had increased over the final decades of the nineteenth century, economic assistance to the poor was a second exception to this trend, decreasing in both a relative and absolute sense. In 1910, the 150-acre poor farm located in southwestern Fairfax County was sold, and a new but smaller poorhouse was built near Jermantown. One explanation for the county's diminishing welfare commitment may have been a gradually improving economy which enabled some to escape poverty. But the popularity of "Social Darwinism," the belief that charity improperly interfered with operation of the law of survival of the fittest in the social order, may also have convinced county authorities to be less generous with the poor. Social Darwinism had won wide acceptance in America with the rise of big business and colonialism in the expansionist 1890s, and it would take the tragedy of the Great Depression of the 1930s to convince most Americans that poverty was not necessarily a result of moral weakenss, but often the responsibility of an increasingly impersonal economic system. *Herald*, 19 August 1910.

147. *Herald*, 11 January 1907; 4 November 1910; 12 April 1918; 28 June 1918.

148. Derr, *Reports*, 1921, p. 6.

found that "the average county estate of $10,000 and upward is assessed at a little more than a fourth of its true value," while the owner of a small farm "pays in taxes . . . nearly twice as much in proportion to its worth."[149] Representative Carlin, who owned more than forty-one thousand acres of land in Fairfax and four other Virginia counties, may have profited from these underassessments, even though, as the Loudoun *Mirror* pointed out, both Carlin and his opponent in 1918, E.B. White, "farm by having someone else do the work for them."[150] And at least one county resident doubted R. Walton Moore's claims that he cared about the common farmer. Pearl Dunn, a teacher in Fairfax schools for many years, remembered seeing Moore driven to the Capitol in his chauffeured limousine: "He never spoke, never looked at anybody or anything."[151]

County agent Derr also bitterly criticized county officials' unwillingness to offend the wealthy. In 1923 and 1924, he reported "considerable losses of poultry . . . from fox raids," and added that "as fox hunting is a popular sport among . . . a few of our citizens regualaratory [sic] measures are . . . left to other parties. . . . It is to be regretted that one of our most profitable industries should suffer in order to furnish sport for our . . . idle rich." Even more exasperating to Derr was his conviction that except for

> the splendid opportunities for [an] education in our county agricultural high school at Floris . . . our schools give absolutely no assistance in agricultural education. . . . A very small percentage of our farm boys go to college and agriculture should be the elective course where the student does not expect to go farther. . . . Of what use will be the Latin or French learned by a farm boy except to cuss something in a language unknown to his companion. . . . The present curriculum is absolutely unfair to the 90% of our farm children who do not get beyond the grades.

"In an effort to assist boys to work their way through school," Derr "made arrangements with farmers and dairymen in the vicinity of [Floris High] school who will give room and board to boys for what work they can do out of school." The agent's other attempts to supplement the opportunities for agricultural training, however, met opposition in high places. When the plans for a young people's center for club and extension work fell through in 1924, Derr suspiciously "hope[d] politics had nothing to do with it." The following year, he joined the chorus of criticism against M.D. Hall, citing the "almost hostile attitude of the

149. Nickell and Randolph, *Economic and Social Survey*, p. 126.
150. *Herald*, 19 July 1918.
151. Dunn-Matthews interview, p. 20.

County Superintendent of Schools towards any form of Club Work."
Gradually, and with some reason, Derr reached the conclusion that
county schools were "deliberately educating the farm children from the
farm."[152]

152. *Herald,* 10 August 1923; Derr, *Reports,* 1924, p. 11, (n.p.); 1923, p. 19; 1922, p. 3; 1925, p. 8.

Harry B. Derr, County Agricultural Agent, about 1928.

X

Transportation Aggravations

The most serious problems facing Fairfax farmers, and affecting the remainder of the population as well, could be traced to the transportation system connecting the county to the capital. For nonfarmers, the problem was the system's relative inefficiency; for the farmer, the central problem stemmed from its relative efficiency, as rails and roads to Washington provided alluring occupational alternatives to declining farm income. Before we return to the farm, as did few who left it in the 1920s, a look at the difficulties that plagued the transportation system is in order.

The Trolley's Transgressions

Although its proponents had seen many of their expectations fulfilled, the electric trolley brought aggravation as well as accommodation for many of the suburban commuters it had enticed to the county. Complaints of poor service, exorbitant fares, and unsafe conditions on the trolley lines appeared with regularity in the Fairfax *Herald*, including an early 1907 report that the State Corporation Commission was investigating a number of charges against the Washington, Alexandria & Falls Church Electric Railroad. Customers criticized the line for its failure to properly heat its cars, maintain published schedules, prevent accidents, and provide adequate lighting, and for its inequitable rates, especially the recent fare increase from seven to eight cents for the Falls Church-Aqueduct Bridge run. In May, the *Herald* was "appalled at the increasing number of railroad accidents," and accused the trolley's management of having "little regard for [the] lives and safety of passengers." One month later, and shortly after the State Corporation Commission's verdict against the line, a crowded trolley on the WA&FC

Railroad crashed into a freight car on a steep grade near Alexandria Courthouse, completely demolishing the trolley and killing one passenger. Several of the many injured had to have limbs amputated. The repercussions of the accident, including suits, further investigations, and mortgages, led to receivership and sale of the line before the end of the year. But the problems of the WA&FC were not over. By 1908, just four years after celebrating the completion of the line's extension to Fairfax, the *Herald* called the existing station "disgusting," and townspeople petitioned for the construction of a new station nearer to the business district, a demand renewed when the old depot burned, or was burned, the following year. The State Corporation Commission threatened the line with formal proceedings if a suitable station were not soon erected, but it was almost a year before the WA&FC acquired the lobby of an abandoned hotel near the courthouse for its new terminal.[153]

Other lines were not immune from such problems. In 1908, the United States Secretary of War, whose department oversaw rail and road connections with the nation's capital, warned the Washington, Alexandria & Mount Vernon Electric Railway that its tracks approaching the Highway Bridge would be removed if they were not relocated in compliance with the law. Following reports in 1914 that cars from McLean were arriving in downtown Washington with as many as thirty-seven standing passengers, the U.S. Public Utilities Commission demanded that John R. McLean's Washington and Old Dominion Railroad furnish improvement proposals within ten days. Two years later, passengers organized the Old Dominion Protective Association for "the mutual protection of patrons, commuters, and shippers living along . . . the Great Falls and Bluemont branches of the Washington and Old Dominion Railroad Company."[154] Louise and William Curran's *McLean Remembers* confirms customers' complaints, finding "rolling stock difficulties, lack of proper terminal facilities, an unbelievably casual organizational structure and a shortage of investment funds" among the line's faults. "Collisions were common occurrences, scheduling was haphazard at best and passengers were often left standing by the tracks waiting for the arrival of a train which had been cancelled or diverted elsewhere." McLean's death in 1916 came of natural causes, but businessmen with fewer problems have occasionally been less patient. According to the Currans, ungrateful heirs were left with huge debts, and so instituted strict economy measures: they refused "to pay debts, deferred maintenance," and spent next to nothing "for equipment replacement. The line was even known to build its own locomotives out

153. *Herald*, 22 February 1907; 1 May 1907; 31 May 1907; 5 July 1907; 12 July 1907; 9 August 1907; 4 October 1907; 11 October 1907; 18 December 1908; 7 May 1909; 14 May 1909; 10 September 1909; 28 January 1910; 4 February 1910.
154. *Herald*, 11 December 1914; 17 November 1916.

Stalled auto on a muddy road near Fairfax, in 1911. Virginia Department of Highways and Transportation.

of boxcars and parts from wrecked, obsolete or otherwise unusable locomotives."[155] The Fairfax *Herald* had to remind itself "that railroads are indispensible to the development of a community" to temper its criticism that "the railroads, in their eagerness to make 'big money,' forget that the people have rights."[156] Even its most earnest advocates were coming to regard the electric trolley as less than the ultimate answer to the needs of the suburban commuter.

The Auto's Limitations

Despite the growing doubts about the trolley, the automobile was hardly an alternative in the early 1900s, because of both the condition of the roads and the vehicle's performance over them. In 1904, Governor Andrew J. Montague stated that good roads were the "mark of the highest civilization."[157] If true, his was a sorry state, for that is what Virginia's roads were in. With allowable exaggeration, Charlotte Corner contended that after the arrival of the trolley in 1906, she "could go [from McLean] to Chicago quicker than . . . to Fairfax." Corner referred to Georgetown as "our hometown," explaining that "we looked towards

155. Curran and Curran, *McLean Remembers,* p. 29.
156. *Herald,* 26 July 1907; 2 August 1907.
157. *Herald,* 16 December 1904.

Washington because the rest of the county was impossible to get to."
During much of the year, she remembered, county roads were "just
rivers of mud."[158]

When he began his work as county agent in 1917, Harry B. Derr
complained that "there were very few miles of hard roads in the county
and much of the work had to be done with horse and buggy." In response
to the State Department of Agriculture inquiry two years later as to
whether Derr had "so thoroughly organized your county that . . . you
can reach every farm family," Derr replied with obvious irritation, "the
perfect man 1900 years [ago] failed to do this. How can ordinary man do
it [?]" he wondered, even though by then, he had obtained a Ford
automobile.[159] The Fairfax *Herald* echoed criticism from all over the
county, much of it concerning roads which had already been
"improved." In 1915, the Fairfax County Improvement League suggested
that "sign boards should be erected all along" the recently paved Chain
Bridge Road between Fairfax and Vienna, designating it the "Fairfax
Folly" because of its poor condition. Several years later, the *Herald* noted
that some parts of the main street through Fairfax were several feet above
the sidewalks while other parts were several feet below.[160] In addition to
the inconvenience, the cost of car and road maintenance and use was
often prohibitive. Although protestations of concern and commitment
were regularly forthcoming from civic leaders and political hopefuls,
Derr reasonably maintained in 1921 that "if anyone should be interested
in the improvement of roads it is the agent as it cost him over fifty dollars
per month to operative his car during the past year."[161]

Even though Derr was just one of many who had become dependent
upon his car by 1920, few residents of Fairfax had foreseen such a
development fifteen years earlier when a single automobile tire could cost
fifty dollars. Furthermore, to most the automobile had seemed more a
public nuisance than a potential necessity. In 1907, the Fairfax *Herald*
observed that the automobile was "getting in disfavor with the general
public because of the recklessness and disregard of public safety which so
often attend its use . . . If only the fools who indulge in such useless sport
could be thus exterminated, the accidents would not be without good
results." The same year, a correspondent to the paper expressed his own
and his horse's fear of automobiles and actually argued that cars "should
. . . not . . . be allowed in the public roads." Editorials continually
condemned the disregard for speed limits and the "'joy riders,' who race
over public highways and streets, with no object in view beyond their

158. Corner-Matthews interview, p. 13.
159. Derr, *Reports*, 1925 (n.p.); 1919, p. A-2.
160. *Herald*, 19 February 1915; 15 June 1923.
161. Derr, *Reports*, 1921, p. 5.

own pleasure." The *Herald* felt "the nuisance . . . even greater" in the country, because "the powdered stuff, with which the new roads are coated, is whirled . . . up by passing automobiles."[162]

Even after the paper had finally acknowledged in 1916 that "the automobile is here to stay" and that "the automobile has become indispensible to modern business life," it continued to find as many liabilities as benefits in the car's increasing conveyance across county roadways. Although the *Herald* recognized that "accidents are not so much the fault of the machines as of those who run them," the abuses of operators remained abundant. Recommendations that traffic policemen be placed at busy intersections on holidays and weekends were regularly offered, but even after speed limit signs of fifteen miles per hour were posted on all five roads leading into Fairfax, a "large number of automobiles . . . with District of Columbia tags" continued to speed into town "in excess of forty miles an hour" and turn corners "on two wheels." Equally upsetting was the fear that the county's dogwood trees would be damaged by the "many thousand city residents [who] motor over our roads" and "who break them to get the blossoms."[163]

The Car's Compensations

Since the 1870s, a large share of state and county tax revenues had been earmarked for roads, but the advent and eventual acceptance of the automobile, despite its cost in money and quietude, forced an inflated fiscal commitment to road construction and maintenance. Although the county had built its first macadamized, or hard-surfaced road between Clifton and Centreville in the early 1900s, individuals were often forced to maintain roads to their own homes and farms, and many of the county's major roadways continued to depend on tolls for their upkeep. The Little River Turnpike required fees from its users until 1896 when the road became a public highway maintained by state and local tax revenues. In 1910, the Washington and Leesburg Turnpike Company sought the permission of the General Assembly to take over several abandoned turnpikes in Fairfax and Loudoun counties and to convert them into "modern high-class turnpikes," with tolls to pay for maintenance. By the late 1910s, however, tolls had become inadequate to meet the growing demand for paved roads by the increasingly car-conscious public, and in 1919, most of the county's tollhouses were closed.[164]

Even the larger share of general revenues devoted to roads soon proved insufficient, and the leading state and local issue became the

162. *Herald,* 27 September 1907; 14 May 1909; 14 June 1912.
163. *Herald,* 6 October 1916; 21 June 1918; 7 September 1923; 29 August 1924; 10 July 1925; 25 April 1924.
164. Geddes, *Historical Highlights,* p. 22; *Herald,* 21 January 1910; 6 December 1918.

desirability of bonded indebtedness for roads and highways. In 1915, a year before the Fairfax *Herald* estimated that there were "more than 200 automobiles in Fairfax County," voters in the Providence District narrowly endorsed a $50,000 road bond issue. By 1920, soon after the Board of Supervisors had ordered "All Road Work Stopped, . . . owing to lack of money," county voters approved by a large majority a $500,000 bond issue for the improvement of the Little River Turnpike from Alexandria to Loudoun County. In 1923, by which time mass production techniques had reduced the purchase price of Henry Ford's Model-T to $300, the state auditor reported 2,775 motor vehicles of all kinds in the county. Another indication of the increasing dependence of county residents on the internal combustion engine was the arrival of autobus service. The Arlington-Barcroft Bus Company established a "New Jitney Line from Aqueduct Bridge to Langley" in 1915, and the Virginia Transit Company and the Suburban Motor Vehicle Company began operating a number of bus lines between Washington, Alexandria, and various Fairfax communities in the early 1920s. In 1924, the Ford Motor Company came to Fairfax County to make a promotional film entitled "The Road to Happiness," featuring a number of local residents in cameo appearances.[165] Evidently, most were convinced, because for better or worse, the heyday of the electric trolley was drawing to a close as northern Virginians expressed their preference for the costly convenience of the private automobile.

The Road to Rejuvenation or Relocation?

Fairfax farmers had always been in the forefront of the movement for good roads. Without exaggeration, roads from farms to markets were their lifelines. When the U.S. Department of Agriculture sponsored an "Economic Study of Small Farms" in the Washington area in 1916, it found that while "the men on the larger farms are beginning to use motor trucks . . . to deliver the vegetables and fruits . . . to the open market in Washington, . . . the common practice for the farmer [of ten to forty acres] is to do the hauling himself with his farm horses and wagons." The farmers in the survey, about half of them in Fairfax County, made an average of seventy-five trips per year. Most arrived at the market by three o'clock in the morning, and were "usually home on the farm by

165. *Herald*, 15 January 1915; 29 September 1916; 24 September 1920; 5 November 1920; 1 June 1923; 26 October 1923; 14 May 1915; 29 June 1923; 3 October 1924; 23 January 1925; 12 June 1925; 21 March 1924. In 1922, Fairfax County ranked tenth in Virginia with the value of its autos, trucks, motorcycles, and bicycles at $376,970. Nickell and Randolph, *Economic and Social Survey*, p. 98. In the Democratic gubernatorial primary of 1925, Fairfax County voters gave a slim majority to State Senator G. Walter Mapp, even though a young State Assemblyman named Harry Flood Byrd, who opposed road bonds with the slogan "Pay As You Go," won the nomination by more than forty thousand votes. But after his election as governor and during his long career in public service to Virginians, Fairfax County automobile enthusiasts would benefit from Byrd's active advocacy of better roads and highways. *Herald*, 14 August 1925.

noon."[166] Whether they drove trucks or wagons, many of these farmers were undoubtedly in attendance at one or more of the seven meetings called by county agent Derr in 1921 to discuss improvement of county roads.[167]

The special need for the county's agricultural goods during the war must explain the special attention to road maintenance noticed by the Fairfax *Herald*, "despite the scarcity of labor and war conditions." Through the war's final fall, the federal government's Rural Motor Truck Bureau operated three truck routes across the county, picking up farm products for the Washington market each morning and delivering supplies to county farmers on its return trip every afternoon.[168] By 1922, "a considerable portion of the milk produced" in the county had been transferred from the trolley and was "being transported into the city by motor truck."[169] In addition to facilitating access to markets, county agent Derr recognized in his 1925 report "a correlation between the improvement of the roads and the painting and fixing up [of] things around the [farm] house. During the past three years over 100 miles of hard surfaced roads have been built and the result is that tourist travel and city joy riders have brought enormous traffic to the county." Far from being annoyed at this invasion, Derr found that "this lends to home improvement along the highway." In contrast, Derr found "in the back sections with its bad roads . . . a corresponding depressing effect, and as a result one rarely sees an improved homestead. . . . Farmers who have an inherent desire for congenial surroundings generally move from such locations." Derr professed to know "of a number of such who are trying to sell their homes for less than what the buildings cost them in order to get away." To counter this tendency, he planned to offer prizes for improvement of homes and grounds.[170]

Despite Derr's outward confidence and the continued improvement of county roads, he, better than anyone, realized that no prize he could offer could convince some county farmers to remain down on the farm. For along with opening up Washington markets, the electric trolley and the improved roads had opened farmers' and their families' eyes to the comforts and conveniences of town and city life. Although telephones had already arrived in most farmhouses, only seventy-five of the county's more than two thousand farms had running water in 1920, and only about 145 had electricity.[171] As Derr frankly acknowledged, even

166. Funk, "Economic History of Small Farms near Washington, D.C.," *U.S. Department of Agriculture Bulletin 848* (Washington, D.C.: Government Printing Office, 1920), p. 17 (hereinafter cited as Funk, "Economic History of Small Farms").

167. Derr, *Reports*, 1921, p. 5.

168. *Herald*, 3 March 1918.

169. Derr, *Reports*, 1922, p. 9.

170. Ibid., 1925, pp. 7-8.

171. Ibid., 1920, p. Y; 1921, p. Y; Fairfax County Chamber of Commerce, *Historic, Progressive Fairfax County in Old Virginia* (alexandria, Va.: Newell-Cole Co., 1928), p. 37.

had such utilities been available, only a minority could have afforded to invest in their installation with farm products bringing such unremunerative prices. As the electric trolley and the automobile made alternatives available, many opted for the inbound trip—one way. In 1909, the Fairfax *Herald* disclosed that "farm laborers are not to be had . . . for either love or money. The electric road offers employment at good wages to an increased force, and men as well as boys avail themselves to it." The following year, the *Herald* noted that "nearly every available colored man is at work upon the improvements along the electric railway, which causes great difficulty to farmers and townspeople in procuring needed laborers."[172] The war aggravated the existing labor shortage, but its end brought no relief. In 1922, Derr received "numerous calls for help with farm labor," but lamented that "little assistance could be given. Several large road contracts in the county, and the high wage paid in the adjoining cities of Washington and Alexandria have induced much of our available farm labor to migrate from our rural communities." In December of the next year, Derr wrote that "much of the corn is still in the field unshucked, owing to the scarcity of labor to do the work." Rather resentfully, he told of "two farm hands that were handy with trowels and tools, that were earning $2.58 per day doing farm work." The men "are now traveling to Washington daily and getting, I will not say earning $12.00 per day at plastering."[173] It seems likely that the 1923 want ad in the Fairfax *Herald* for a farm hand at $30 per month went unanswered, as did the advertisement two years later for a "Man to Work on Dairy Farm," although by then the prospective employer was willing to "furnish house, wood, milk and garden [and] pay $50.00 a month, to start."[174]

Unable to compete with city wages, farmers had to find alternatives. By 1923, Derr knew of "at least 100 . . . who while not all leaving their farms have ceased farming operations, sold their live stock, bought themselves Ford Cars, and are working either in Alexandria or Washington."[175] The 1916 U.S. Department of Agriculture study found that only five of the forty-five farms of fewer than ten acres surveyed realized profits of more than $400 during the year, and that such farms were "worth $234 a year merely as a home for the family of a man working in the city."[176] Many left their farms altogether, tempted by the escalating value of their properties as potential suburban home sites. In 1925, Derr reported that "with the rapidly increasing miles of hard

172. *Herald*, 1 October 1909; 4 February 1910.
173. Derr, *Reports*, 1922, p. 13; 1923, p. 9; 1923, p. 22.
174. *Herald*, 5 January 1923; 6 March 1925.
175. Derr, *Reports*, 1923, p. 22.
176. Funk, "Economic History of Small Farms," p. 9.

A boy and his dog. Thomas Gantt and Hobson, about 1910. The Gantt family lived on the "Walney" estate near Centreville.

surface roads in this county many business men of the city are purchasing farms, either from a speculative or home point of view." After receiving "a number of calls to help make these farms self-supporting at least," Derr again found that "the greatest difficulty is the securing of competent managers" and farm laborers.[177]

For those whose roots went deeper into the Fairfax County soil they farmed, an even more distressing development than the loss of farm labor was the inability to keep wives and children satisfied with life on the farm. Charles Edward Gibbs, whose Quaker father had arrived in the Woodlawn community in 1852, surely suffered to see his loved ones leave the family farm. His wife became a telegraph operator for the Washington, Alexandria & Mount Vernon Electric Railroad, and soon after being given the responsibility for running the farm at the age of twenty-one, his son Edward C. Gibbs sold all but the house and twelve acres, "swore he would never milk another cow," and became manager, freight agent, and restauranteur at the Mount Vernon terminus for the trolley line.[178] Derr's annual reports were full of such stories. For

177. Derr, *Reports*, 1925, p. 12.

178. Joan Gibbs Lyon, "The Home Place," Historical Society *Yearbook,* 9 (1964-65): 75; Harry B. Lyon, "Wellington Villa and Vicinity," Historical Society *Yearbook,* 9 (1964-65): 90-91.

example, in 1921 and every year thereafter, he expressed "great disappointment" with the club work, blaming his inability to interest more young people on the county's "proximity to the city of Washington, and the ease with which the city can be reached. . . . Telephone girls receiving $17 dollars per week as a beginning salary, looks very tempting to many country girls." One farmer told Derr that "one of my daughters is making 22 dollars a week, and my wife is talking of getting a job too. My wife can earn more in the city than I am getting so I guess I will take care of the house and let them go to work."[179]

Derr's disappointment with the county school system and its leadership has been cited, but not his fear that if farm children "get their training in Washington they are lost to the farm." In 1921, he told of "one of my most successful corn club boys [who] used the money he made on his land, and took a business course, and is now assistant to the cashier in one of our county banks. His younger brother . . . also a successful corn grower is dissatisfied with the hard work and no doubt as soon as old enough will hunt an easier job." Derr found some comfort in his belief that "farm boys who are competent get the preference over city grown boys in obtaining positions" in the city, but he again admitted his inability "to make much headway with [club] work, or offer better inducements on the farm . . . . I can hardly blame the young people, as [never] in all my experience have I seen as little return to the farmer from his labor as at the present time."[180]

Countryside Confusion

The belief that farmers possessed special virtues was as old as the American Republic. Not just farmers, but almost all Americans liked to think that honest, hard-working, God-fearing farmers were our best citizens. Even today, when fewer than one American in twenty live on farms, there remains a persistent sentiment that life in the country would in some ways be better. Perhaps this is true, but by the 1920s, farmers were becoming dissatisfied with merely the respect of their fellow Americans. Farmers wondered why they should not share in the prosperity that other Americans were enjoying. They too wanted the Model-Ts, the entertainment, and the electrical appliances that American technology was making available. Yet at the same time, farmers wondered whether they might lose something by joining the materialistic scramble of the 1920s. The new urban mass culture that they associated with bootleg whiskey, organized crime, the Charleston, and short skirts seemed to threaten their traditional values of thrift, hard work, and

---

179. Derr, *Reports*, 1921, p. 1.
180. Ibid., 1923, p. 19; 1921, pp. 1-2; 1925, p. 8.

stability. They especially resented the sight of their own children returning from school or from the motion pictures wearing city clothes and using city talk, and when old enough, rejecting life on the farm for better paying jobs in the city. In short, farmers were confused. They were torn between their desire to share in the material prosperity of twentieth-century America, and their resentment at the erosion of their agrarian values. Most farmers eventually accepted the new urban culture with little complaint; others with quiet resignation. But some remained intransigent in their efforts not only to moderate the changes, but to turn back the clock to simpler and supposedly superior times.

The earliest to openly question the "progress" predicted to follow the trolley and the automobile to Fairfax County was James W. Head, a Vienna farmer, whose 1904 letter to the editor of the *Herald* was entitled, "Poor Old Fairfax . . . a Lament on Introduction into Fairfax Court House of Electric Transportation Facilities." In part, his protest read,

> Dear, quaint old Fairfax! . . . hast harkened to the insistent voice of Progress . . . yielded to the inroads of an implacable civilization! Where now is thy boasted individuality? . . . Thy . . . perfect peace of Arcadian summers? 'Alas! they are all in their graves'; progress hast sounded their deathknell; worldliness hast thrown wide thy portals, and lust will soon stalk boldly across thy threshold . . . . Gain will rob men of their reason, will madden their brains . . . . Poor old Fairfax![181]

Although their own desperate desire for better transportation facilities would allow few to challenge so directly the trolley or the movement for good roads, many farmers over the following two decades did entertain serious doubts about the direction in which the county's transportation revolution was taking them. While few could so eloquently express their feelings, they had an able spokesman in Harry B. Derr.

In 1923, Derr acknowledged that again, "the year has not been a prosperous one," and added that "we are living in hopes that the pendulum will soon begin to swing country wards." But Derr must have known that such a developement was unlikely, that the future of Fairfax would not belong to the farmer. He realized that "owing to the proximity of Fairfax County to the large cities of Washington and Alexandria . . . our small farmers . . . have sold their farms or abandoned their leases and moved into the cities and are earning more money per day, than they made per week in the country." He realized also that "many of them are actually training their children along more lucrative lines, and occupations other than farming."[182] Finally, Derr surely was aware that

181. *Herald,* 30 December 1904.
182. Derr, *Reports,* 1923, p. 22; 1925, p. 8.

the new urban culture of the 1920s had every advantage. The moving pictures shown every Friday evening at the Fairfax Town Hall were as popular among farmers as townspeople, even though they emphasized urban themes and tastes. And soon radio, truly a mass medium, would send its message into every household and help make Americans more alike than different in what they thought and wanted for themselves and their families. In 1925, as if to verify the county's suburbanized future, the U.S. Census Bureau found that for the first time, the farm population of Fairfax County had passed into the minority. Of a total of 21,943 inhabitants, only 10,680, or 49.7 percent, still lived on farms.[183] With the prospects for Fairfax farmers growing dimmer, Derr continued to express his own frustrations and those of many county farmers in his annual reports. But by the early 1920s, a vocal minority were voicing their feelings more forcefully, as members of the Ku Klux Klan.

Agrarian Desperation

The Ku Klux Klan had been reorganized in 1915, ostensibly as a revival of the post-Civil War organization that had helped reimpose white supremacy on the South through terrorism. But bigotry was just one expression of the Klan's desire to reimpose the values of an earlier day on a society changing too fast to suit its members. In 1923, the Fairfax *Herald* reported that "while Rev. J.C. Trasher, of the M.E. Church, South [of Fairfax] was delivering his farewell sermon, ten robed and hooded members of the Ku Klux Klan entered the church and presented the pastor with a purse containing $50.00 in gold. Mr. Trasher," the paper explained, was "much beloved by the people of the community." Two months later, the Klan "staged a spectacular initiation of 103 persons in a field at Five Oaks, not far from the Fairfax-Vienna pike. The ceremonies were attended by several hundred white robed and masked . . . klansmen, and a large throng of spectators witnessed the initiation from a distance. . . . A large fiery cross and torches . . . gave light for the proceedings."[184] Derr acknowledged that klansmen were often "the drawing cards" at agricultural fairs and at gatherings for "community betterment."[185]

Another center of Klan activity was Herndon, where several years earlier a resolution of the town council thanking former Mayor and Town Sergeant Elisha Dyer for his efforts to develop the town had alluded to "the petty cavilling and clamor of those who resent the onward march of civilization." By the midteens, town merchants and commuters to the District of Columbia had wrested local political control

---

183. U.S. Bureau of Census, Agriculture, 1925, part II, *The Southern States*, p. 181.
184. *Herald*, 30 March 1923; 11 May 1923.
185. Derr, *Reports*, 1925 (n.p.).

Ku Klux Klan funeral at the Fairfax Cemetery, about 1929.

from the formerly dominant farmers, and it was undoubtedly this latter element that sought to reassert its influence, or at least vent its frustrations, through the Ku Klux Klan. As Rita Schug pointed out, membership was a closely guarded secret, but the organization was "visibly growing" by the early 1920s. One local resident recalled "being visited by these hooded Americans who sought to initiate him as a member. . . . Although he did not join the Klan, claiming the pressing needs of his family and business, he did enjoy a free showing of 'Birth of a Nation,'" the technically acclaimed but viciously racist documentary film on the origin of the KKK. Schug also found that many of the Herndon Klan's activities were "directed toward the maintenance of morals. . . . One white man was tarred and feathered for deserting his wife and 'running around.' A burning cross warned others of his ilk." "One hundred percent Americanism" was still another of the Klan's prescriptions for the nation's and for their personal problems. Annually during the twenties, flag-waving klansmen "made a parade entrance and culminated [Herndon Day] festivities by fireworks and a cross-burning."[186]

186. Schug, "Herndon," pp. 8, 33; *Herndon Observer*, 10 September 1925; 23 August 1926; 5 July 1928.

In addition to their efforts to monitor public morality and promote a blind patriotism, the Klan sought someone it could safely blame for the disruption of their society. Racial and religious minorities, even more deprived than were farmers, provided convenient targets. The threat of international Judaism was a favorite issue of the Klan nationally, but the lack of Jews in influential positions in Fairfax County probably prevented anti-Semitism from becoming a focus for county klansmen. Anti-Catholicism may have been a local issue during the unsuccessful 1928 presidential campaign of Democrat Al Smith, the Catholic Governor of New York. A Herndon resident recalled that women claiming to be former nuns visited the town and alleged maltreatment at the hands of priests, and a Falls Church resident wrote that on one occasion, the local KKK "turned over the tombstones in the Catholic burying ground."[187] The worst, however, was reserved for county blacks.

White supremacy was a key element in the social order that the Klan was struggling to restore. Fairfax County had never been a haven of racial harmony, and with the anxieties of local whites and the ambitions of local blacks coinciding in the early 1900s, conflict was inevitable. Although there is only one account of physical violence, verbal and visual threats were common. Edwin B. Henderson, a renowned black Washington educator and a resident of Falls Church, recalled in a recent interview that the "headquarters for the Virginia Klan seemed to be in Ballston, in Fairfax County," now a part of Arlington County. "During this period my family and I received . . . many threats by telephone. Before the dial phone, the telephone company would refuse calls to our house after 12:00 o'clock at night. In time it became necessary to have an unlisted phone, which we maintain to this day." One of "over a hundred vile and threatening letters" to Henderson warned that

> some night when you are peacefully dreaming . . . of the charming BABOONS you have been instructing, and sniffing in the delightful odor exuding from their bodies, you will be rudely awakened by GHOSTS . . . and after you have been gagged, you will be born to a tree nearby, tied, stripped and given thirty lashes on your ETHIOPIAN back, and left to be found by some passer-by. We are for law and order just so long as you aforesaid ETHIOPIANS behave, but when you thrust yourselves on your superiors, the white people, your doom is sealed. . . . A word to the wise is sufficient.
>
> [Signed] K.K.K.[188]

---

187. Schug, "Herndon," p. 33; E.B. Henderson, as told to Edith Hussey, *History of the Fairfax County Branch of the NAACP* (Fairfax, Va., 1961), p. 5 (hereinafter referred to as Henderson, NAACP).

188. Henderson, *NAACP*, pp. 5-6.

More effective were the Klan's somber if adolescent ceremonies, always with the featured cross burning. When "members of the Ku Klux Klan from Fairfax and Herndon" joined other klansmen from the capital area for another "spectacular initiation on a hill above Rosslyn" in 1924, "the light from the cross and from the candles carried by the klansmen were [sic] plainly visible from Washington and the surrounding country."[189] Blacks and whites who witnessed this haughty demonstration of hatred surely thought twice before openly advocating such ideas as racial cooperation and the equality of all men.

Trolley Trepidation

Farmers were not alone in suffering psychologically from the speed of the changes brought by the trolley and the automobile. Even the foremost advocates of technological progress and suburban growth regretted some of the side effects of the county's development, for improved rail and road connections to the capital brought not only new settlers, but a number of old problems to the attention of county residents. While the solutions proposed by proponents of "progress" were usually more subtle, they were often no less insidious than those advanced by the Ku Klux Klan.

Even though the 1924 University of Virginia survey found Fairfax County's foreign-born population "so negligible as scarcely to be worth mentioning," the "107 qualified electors" of the Vienna Council, Junior Order United American Mechanics felt sufficiently threatened in 1905 to condemn America's open-door immigration policy as "a menace to our free institutions." The Vienna chapter of the nationwide nativist organization, composed primarily of local merchants, tradesmen, and postal and railroad employees, had been founded in 1896, but it was not until the arrival of the trolley that the local group spoke out against "the tide of immigration"—significantly "not the sturdy people who came before . . . to build up their homes . . . and if necessary, to die in defense of the stars and stripes, Old Glory, our flag—but [those] from the pauper districts of southern Europe and the Oriental Countries, the incubators of nihilism, anarchy, disease and crime."[190] Over the following twenty years, town leaders would continue their efforts to attract "desirable residents who would contribute towards [Vienna's] wealth and progress," but the booster pamphlet circulated in Washington by the Vienna Citizens Association in 1925 was careful to add that "the majority of the people . . . with but few exceptions are of American stock," a condition the town clearly intended to maintain.[191]

---

189. *Herald*, 9 May 1924.
190. Nickell and Randolph, *Economic and Social Survey*, p. 44. *Herald*, 20 October 1905.
191. Nickell and Randolph, *Economic and Social Survey*, p. 26.

A more immediate threat to the county's white establishment was the area's black population, both upwardly mobile local blacks and outwardly mobile Washington ones. As early as 1904, the Fairfax *Herald* argued that the trolley had "brought a large number of lawless characters to the county" as well as the expected and welcomed suburbanites. The paper especially singled out "some of the negroes employed on the new electric railroad" to Fairfax for causing trouble, and in this case, none too subtly suggested that "when again attempted . . . we would advise our people to pump lead into the rowdies until they become fit subjects for a junk shop." The trolley brought another unwelcome arrival to the county in 1907. According to the *Herald*, "Barbara Pope, a colored woman of Washington, . . . declined . . . to take one of the cars assigned to colored passengers." When the train reached Falls Church, she was arrested, fined for breaking the "Jim Crow" law, and "detained for nearly twenty-four hours." Pope brought a $10,000 suit for being "violently ejected from the train," but insult was added to injury when she was awarded one cent for damages.[192]

The following year, an incident on the trolley almost cost two black residents of Falls Church their lives. After being ejected from the trolley for drunkenness, Sandy James, described by a local white as "the hardest man I ever saw," and Lee Gaskins, "a bad one too," were accused of derailing a trolley car near Ballston by piling "a whole lot of stones and things on the line." When word of the incident spread, whites organized a lynch mob, which had "real evil intent in their minds, because they were going to kill 'em. . . . They had shotguns, and pistols and rifles and axes . . . and they searched every colored house there at East Falls Church . . . but they couldn't find them." Gaskins was eventually captured, tried, found guilty, and served a ten-year sentence. Although James's fate is not known, a local white testified that he once heard Sheriff Howard Fields say "that he hit Sandy James with a blackjack with lead in it about 25 times just as hard as he could hit him in the head and it never fazed him."[193]

Evidently, local authorities feared that the trolley would bring still more blacks as permanent settlers, and so in 1915, following passage of a state law permitting residential segregation, the Falls Church Town Council "proposed an ordinance which would have confined Negro residents to a small section of the town, and would have prevented them from living in the area designated for whites even though their homes were already in the restricted districts."[194] In the midst of this controversy, some county blacks began to realize that only through unity could such efforts to deny their rights be defeated, and the movement for racial justice in Fairfax County was born.

192. *Herald*, 25 November 1904; 18 January 1907; 7 June 1907.
193. Ball, "Electric Railways," pp. 38-39.
194. Henderson, *NAACP*, p. 1.

Challenge to Segregation

The Colored Citizens Protective League (CCPL), organized in early 1915 by Edwin B. Henderson, Joseph B. Tinner, and other black leaders in Falls Church, wrote letters of protest to the mayor and town councilmen, then hired a Washington lawyer and brought suit to prevent enforcement of the residential segregation plan. When the town council announced that a referendum would be held on the issue, the CCPL applied for chapter status in the National Association for the Advancement of Colored People, a nationwide, biracial organization founded in 1909 under the leadership of W.E.B. DuBois. In contrast to Booker T. Washington, who called on blacks to temporarily accept white prejudice and patiently work for economic equality through vocational education, DuBois urged blacks to defend their dignity and demand their civil and political rights. With these goals, the Falls Church and Vicinity Branch of the NAACP, called the first rural chapter of the organization, hired two more Washington lawyers who argued the unconstitutionality of the Falls Church segregation plan and finally convinced the town council to abandon the proposal.[195]

As E.B. Henderson explained, however, the organization's role in Fairfax County was just beginning:

> The most consistent work of the NAACP was our effort to improve education and educational facilities for our youth. We learned how bad the school conditions were when my wife, who had been a model teacher in the District schools, was drafted to teach in the colored school in Falls Church during the first World War, when teachers were scarce. Negro teachers received far lower salaries than white teachers of the same qualifications. Teachers of colored children were responsible for janitorial work, whereas such service was . . . provided in schools for white children. The schools for Negro children were in the most dilapidated condition. All were frame buildings and old, with outbuildings to serve toilet needs. At the Falls Church school there was no source of drinking water on the grounds. . . . All the schools for white children, in contrast, were brick construction and equipped with plumbing. There was no high school for colored children in Fairfax County. Those who wanted more than a seventh grade education had to travel to Washington at their own expense or be transported to the Industrial School at Manassas. . . . When bond issues were voted to meet the educational needs, only trifling amounts were allotted to the Negro schools. Once when I approached a superintendent with a request for a larger appropriation for Negro schools, he replied, "We have to look after our own children first."

195. Ibid., p. 2.

Despite this dismal picture, Henderson credited the efforts of the NAACP, and its black and white members and supporters, for the eventual success of the movement for a high school for Fairfax blacks, and for the gradual improvement of educational opportunities for the county's black youth.[196]

Obstacles to Integration

In spite of some hard-earned successes, E.B. Henderson and other leaders of the movement for racial justice fully realized that not just laws, but minds must be changed if true progress toward an equal society were to come. Henderson recalled that during the war, "when Negroes were obliged to enter and leave by the rear door of the street railway cars and sit from the rear, my father on his way to work one morning was rudely pulled from the steps of the car to let a white person enter . . . I entered suit against the offender. Col. Jacob DePutron formerly of the Union army, who had witnessed the incident, consented to represent my father as counsel. When the case was tried in the Falls Church court house, Captain Bethune of the Home Guards, the defendant's attorney, brought into court with him enough of the uniformed Home Guards to fill half the room. Colored citizens occupied the balance of the space. After the conductor and others had refused to testify, Colonel DePutron had himself sworn in as a witness. His account substantiated our case, and the defendent was fined $20 and costs. On the following morning De-Putron, in effigy, was seen hanging from an electric light pole at East Falls Church car stop." A few years later, when cars and buses had supplemented the trolley service to the county, Henderson himself was forcibly put off a bus when he refused to move to the rear before crossing from the District into Virginia. Despite the best efforts of the NAACP, Jim Crow seating on buses involved in interstate travel would not end until after 1946.[197]

Nor were these the only examples of discrimination in the county. In the midteens, the Herndon Town Council passed a resolution denying a Washington *Post* report that "coloreds" must be off town streets by 9:00 P.M., but then in 1923, the council approved an ordinance, later changed to a resolution, "prohibiting the sale of property within the corporate limits to non-whites without council permission." A long-time resident recently denied that there was much of a "to-do," arguing that "Herndon never had a 'colored' problem since Vernon Cockerille, a former blacksmith and town sergeant for many years, would give them the eye and generally keep things in order."[198] Twenty-five years of

196. Ibid., p. 7.
197. Ibid., p. 4.
198. Schug, "Herndon," p. 35.

Sadie, the champion Holstein, after her return from the Virginia State Fair in 1924. Photo courtesy of John Middleton, Herndon.

technological progress, of rapid development of the county, had witnessed little progress toward the ideal that all men are created equal.

In 1900, the majority of Fairfax County's 18,580 residents lived on farms; in 1925, most of the twenty-two thousand inhabitants lived in town. The technological innovation of the electric trolley made possible, though the proximity of Washington made inevitable, this significant change in the county's character. Yet in 1925, Fairfax County was still the leading producer of dairy products in the state of Virginia.[199] Symbolic of this fact was the recognition in 1925 of Ben Middleton's prize dairy cow Sadie as "the best known Holstein in the world." Middleton, a Herndon dairyman, regularly had to give Sadie three milkings per day, and over the previous three years, she had produced more than thirty tons of milk and a ton of butterfat. But Sadie and what she represented were of the past. As if to emphasize that the changes of the previous twenty-five years would seem small in relation to those of the following fifty, on 15 September 1925, a bolt of lightning struck and killed "the best known Holstein in the world."[200] It seems fitting that the force which, harnessed, had connected formerly rural Fairfax with Washington should now so dramatically declare the dawn of a new day.

199. U.S. Bureau of Census, Agriculture, 1925, part II, *The Southern States*, p. 155.
200. Schug, "Herndon," p. 10.

1925 — 1976

Nan Netherton

I

Growing Pains: Population

Hardly any aspect of life in Fairfax County escaped dramatic changes during the years 1925 to 1976. Agricultural growth and, later, urban development characterized the period. Each of these activities drew new population into the county, more than offsetting the movement of black residents who sought greater opportunities in the north and west. The new residents, most of whom were employed in Washington and Arlington, sought homes in the open space within 20 miles of the metropolitan core. Fairfax County offered space for this suburban fringe.[1]

Virginia's strong attachment to tradition and the past were still well represented in Fairfax County and indeed constituted a strong attraction to many outsiders seeking homes near their jobs in the numerous emergency federal agencies created by the Roosevelt administration during the economic depression of the 1930s and the further proliferation of jobs as a result of government expansion during World War II and the Korean War. For Fairfax County, the growing "industry" was the federal government, and the service industries attracted to the government; the failure to develop a broad industrial base was symbolized by the fact that one of the area's chief industrial exports was baled waste paper.[2]

Each year, the burgeoning center of federal bureaucracy continued to stimulate growth; this required the use of more space for more people

1. Thomas Jefferson Center for Political Economy, University of Virginia, *Statistical Abstract of Virginia: 1966* 2 vols., (Charlottesville, Va.), vol. I; Virginius Dabney, *Virginia: The New Dominion* (Garden City, N.Y.: Doubleday & Co., 1971), p. 467 (hereinafter cited as Dabney, *Virginia*); Jean Gottmann, *Virginia In Our Century*, (Charlottesville: University Press of Virginia, 1969), pp. 463-68 (hereinafter cited as Gottmann, *Virginia*).

2. Dabney, *Virginia*, p. 491; Gottmann, *Virginia*, p. 467.

who insisted on more and better services from all levels of government. In 1950, approximately one-half of the civilian work force was composed of government employees; in 1960, approximately one-fifth, and in 1970, almost one-third. During this twenty-year period, the proportion of employed persons providing services and engaged in wholesale and retail business grew from approximately one-sixth of the Fairfax County work force of 21,407 in 1950 to more than one-third of the total 97,206 employed in 1970.[3]

In the 140 years from 1790 to 1930, the county's population doubled; between 1930 and 1950, a mere twenty years, the number of inhabitants had almost quadrupled mainly due to federal government program expansion and the influx of many veterans and their families to the Washington area following World War II. The new residents came from near and far—New England, the Midwest, the Southwest, the West Coast, and from many foreign countries. The 1950 census figures revealed that of the total county population of 98,557, 21,450 (or 21.8 percent) had lived in a different county or abroad in 1949.[4]

The county during the 1950-1960 decade experienced a population growth of 179 percent, from 98,557 to 275,002. This growth was a tremendous burden on the strongly agricultural, rural nonindustrial county which had been furnishing the federal city with dairy and poultry products, meat, fruits, and vegetables, and an ever-increasing number of daily commuters.[5]

Between 1960 and 1970, the county's population rose to 454,275, a total greater than the population of Vermont or Wyoming or Alaska. Natural increase accounted for 26 percent of this number, and 73 percent was from immigration. The county's rate of natural increase was greater than the national average of 23.8 percent that year; and the county death rate of 4.2 percent in 1960 was well below the national average of 9.5 percent. Interestingly, the birthrate in Fairfax County in 1970 dropped to 17.2 percent, a number below the national average of 18.2 percent. The death rate in the county in 1970 dropped to 4.0 percent, even further below the national average of 9.4 percent. The total increase in Fairfax County's population between 1900 and 1970, the largest percentage increase, although smaller numerically than either Prince Georges or Montgomery counties on the Maryland side of the Potomac River, was an astounding 2,349 percent. In that same period of time, including the figures resulting from the acquisition of the five new states of Oklahoma,

3. *Fairfax County Profile* (Fairfax, Virginia: Office of Research and Statistics, February 1977), table 70, p. 106.

4. *Statistical Abstract of Virginia*, vol. I; U.S. Department of Commerce, Bureau of the Census, *County and City Data Book, 1952* (Washington, D.C.: U.S. Government Printing Office, 1953).

5. U.S. Bureau of the Census, *County and City Data Book, 1962* (Washington, D.C.: U.S. Government Printing Office, 1962), p. 392.

New Mexico, Arizona, Alaska, and Hawaii, the population of the United States grew from 75,994,575 in 1900 to 203,235,298 in 1970, an increase of 167.4 percent.[6]

Such growth increased the demand for government and other services and created a voracious appetite for increasingly valuable land and for other resources needed for residential subdivision uses. It had a dramatic impact on life-style and tax base, on forest, field, and stream, in an area where fewer than 400 years before, Indian tribes from both the north and the south had lived, hunted, fished, farmed, and fought.

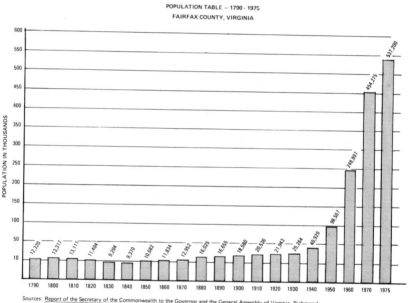

POPULATION TABLE — 1790 - 1975
FAIRFAX COUNTY, VIRGINIA

Sources: Report of the Secretary of the Commonwealth to the Governor and the General Assembly of Virginia, Richmond: Division of Purchase and Printing 1963.
Fairfax County Office of Research and Statistics, Fairfax County Profile, 1977.

6. Bureau of the Census, The Statistical Abstract-of the U.S., The American Almanac (New York: Grosset & Dunlap, 1973), p. 23; Fairfax County Profile, pp. 14-15, 11.

II

The End of the Agricultural Era

An advertisement placed by the National Bank of Fairfax in William F. Carne's *Fairfax Herald* on 2 January 1925 read like a miniature "Who's Who" of Fairfax County of the times and showed the great diversity of occupations and interests represented on the bank's board. There were many professions represented, yet farming was still a major occupation. Officers and directors were listed for the thriving institution, which declared capital and surplus at $100,000 and offered 3 percent earnings on savings accounts. F.M. Brooks, M.D., who lived between Fairfax and Fairfax Station on the present Ox Road, Route 123, was president of the board of directors; Thomas R. Keith, a Fairfax attorney was first vice president; R.E. Thornton, senior judge of the circuit court, was second vice president, and Edgar Littleton, originally from Leesburg, was cashier. The directors were Wilson Farr, commonwealth's attorney, lawyer, and dairy farmer who lived at "Five Chimneys" on Route 236; F. W. Huddleson, county treasurer and farmer who ran a dairy farm west of Fairfax on Route 50, near Chantilly; Dallas Berry, who operated a farm on Route 7 west of Tysons Corner; Ford Swetnam, M.D.; M.D. Hall, superintendent of the county schools; F.D. "Tudie" Richardson, county court clerk; Douglas S. Mackall, an attorney from Langley; Richard Farr, farmer and brother of Wilson; and M.E. Church, a real estate agent and entrepreneur from Falls Church. This was the major bank in Fairfax County at the time, although the First National Bank of Alexandria, Virginia, had an advertisement on the same page stating surplus and profits of $550,000, operating as the "oldest National Bank in Northern Virginia."[1]

1. *Fairfax Herald* (Fairfax, Va, 2 January 1925), p. 1; Interview, Joseph Beard, 23 November 1975.

A brisk business in the sale of cars was indicated in an advertisement placed in the *Fairfax Herald* on the same date; it was placed by the Fairfax Garage for used Ford cars and trucks and tractors of all types. The generally poor condition of the roads was suggested in J.M. McAtee's advertisement for the Oakton Garage: "All makes of autos repaired, welding a specialty."

Some other advertisers were F.D. Richardson and John W. Rust offering farm loans; stores selling feed and fertilizer, insurance agencies; and furniture stores. The Ideal Shoe Repairing Company on King Street in Alexandria advertised work received and returned by parcel post, and N.P. Young, civil engineer and surveyor of Fairfax offered "Surveys and Estimates, Subdivisions a specialty."

The *Fairfax Herald* was the weekly paper many county farmers subscribed to in the first half of the twentieth century,[2] and publisher-editor William F. Carne offered his readers news and editorial commentary on a variety of local, state, national, and even international issues. During 1925, Carne wrote no less than five editorials favoring the establishment of the Shenandoah National Park in the Blue Ridge mountains of Virginia and urging county residents and state officials to support the effort. He discussed the merits of forming a county chamber of commerce on several occasions, stating that even farmers could benefit from more businesslike operations which could be assisted by such an organization. He expressed concern in a February editorial that the recent establishment of a bus line between Alexandria and Washington would have an adverse effect upon the electric railway line between Fairfax and Washington. On the other hand, he predicted that the construction of Memorial Bridge would contribute much to the growth and prosperity of the county. In March, Carne applauded efforts of Dr. J.P. McConnell, president of the Co-operative Education Association, and R. Walton Moore, chairman of the State Council of Rural Agencies, to establish county councils, especially Moore's sponsorship of an essay contest to encourage public interest in the concept. He praised Moore in a March editorial as the original author of the House of Representatives bill favoring United States participation in the World Court. Passage of the $10,000 school bond proposed for completing the "new Fairfax school building" was urged in a May editorial, and two weeks later, Carne was writing in support of Judge S.G. Brent's acquittal of members of the board of supervisors of any wrong-doing relative to road funds. In August, the editor noted that U.S. radio audiences might soon receive goodwill radio broadcasts from England, and in December's final editorial of the year, he urged the passage of a bill to harness power at Great Falls.[3]

2. Interview, Joseph Beard, 9 August 1975.
3. *Fairfax Herald*, 6 March, 20 March, 1 May, 15 May, 25 December 1925.

County Agricultural Agent Harry B. Derr listed dairy cattle and the poultry industry as two major projects in his December 1925 annual report. In addition, Derr noted that an improved and distinct strain of Boone County white corn had been developed and named Fairfax County white corn. High yield was 90 bushels per acres; average, 40. In a year during which roads often were in shockingly bad condition, Derr had traveled 7,000 miles by auto, 32 by horse and buggy, and 626 by train, assisting and training county farmers who were producing a great variety of stock and crops for home consumption and the markets of Washington and Baltimore. Although horse-drawn machinery was still in most prominent use, the cutting of wheat with a mechanical tractor had already been found to be the most economical method because it saved time and labor. The influence of the automobile was given a nod of approval by Derr who observed a definite "correlation between the improvement of the roads and the painting and fixing up things around the house." There were decided disadvantages from a county agent's standpoint to life in proximity to the cities of Washington and Alexandria. The opportunities nearby for shorter work hours and good wages were influencing many county farmers to sell their farms and train their children along more lucrative lines of endeavor.

To whom were they selling their farms? "With the rapidly increasing miles of hard surface roads in this county many business men of the city are purchasing farms, either from a speculative or home point of view. A study of these men reveals the fact that many of them were farm boys who had gone to the city many years ago, and have become well-to-do, and the lure of the land is becoming stronger than the city attractions can obliterate."[4]

Derr was a dedicated public servant who obviously loved his work. He waxed poetic in his comments on a photograph of one type of livestock included with the 1925 report: "If beautiful scenery and fresh water have anything to do with good hog breeding then Collingwood Hampshires lead the world. This is a view of one of many hog pens that lead down to the beautiful Potomac river where they can take their cool bath any time."

In April 1925 a delegation of citizens had appeared before the board of supervisors requesting an appropriation for partial salary for a home demonstration agent "to secure and promote the health, safety and general welfare of the inhabitants of Fairfax County," to begin in the budget year 1926-27; this was approved by the board. The advisory council of rural agencies for several years had raised the necessary funds

4. H.B. Derr, Annual Report of the Fairfax County Agricultural Extension Agent, December 1925 (hereinafter cited as *Report*); Annual reports from the extension office are filed in the Virginiana Collection, Fairfax County Central Library.

through the cooperation of school leagues, citizens associations, the Fairfax County Chamber of Commerce, a Daughters of the American Revolution chapter, local railroad companies, 4-H clubs, and individuals. [5]

The national Agricultural Extension Service had been formally established in 1914 by the passage by Congress of the Smith-Lever Act, placing the responsibility for implementing a countrywide program for demonstration and educational purposes under the U.S. Department of Agriculture. The program had been an outgrowth of work conducted by Dr. Seaman A. Knapp, a field agent for the Federal Department of Agriculture, who had been successful in organizing corn and tomato clubs for farm boys and girls. The program was then expanded to include the whole spectrum of farm activities and scientific methods for adults and children alike. Virginia Polytechnic Institute in Blacksburg had the prime responsibility in Virginia for the training of extension agents and maintaining a steady flow of information and assistance through the local county agents to the county farm population. [6]

Derr stated in his 1927 annual report that Fairfax County was furnishing Washington with a large amount of pulp and cord wood; therefore, the county needed a program of forestry management, not only to rehabilitate abandoned farmland, but also to plant locust trees to furnish fence posts. Chestnut trees which had been used for centuries as fence posts had become virtually extinct because of a blight which had spread across the country in the early years of the twentieth century. He also indicated that wood was being replaced in many cases by concrete, especially to build farm septic tanks to accommodate indoor plumbing.

Leadership training was stressed at a 4-H club camp held at Manassas by placing members on self-governing committees during the meetings. Two 4-H member participants, Omer Hirst and John Webb, later used this training in Virginia's General Assembly; each attested to improvement in his leadership abilities and basketmaking, and Hirst particularly stressed an improvement in his table manners. [7]

Home demonstration clubs engaged in a variety of activities in home and community. Agent Mary Lippard was pleased to announce that no only had a total of seventeen women "quit drying dishes" due to the use of new dish drainers, but also that Annandale was equipping a community kitchen, Burke had secured playground equipment for the school, and the Clifton Home Demonstration Club was building an all-weather road to their schoolhouse. An increased interest in

---

5. Fairfax County Board of Supervisors Minute Book No. 5, p. 86 (hereinafter cited as BOSMB).

6. BOSMB No. 5, p. 86; December 1925 Fairfax County Home Demonstration Agent's Annual Report (hereinafter cited as HD *Report*); Interview, Joseph Beard, 29 November 1975.

7. Derr, *Report* 1927.

Representative members of the Fairfax County Chamber of Commerce in about 1934.
Left to right, front row: C.C. Carr, Town of Fairfax, farmer; unidentified; H. Earl
Hanes, Herndon lawyer; George Harrison, Herndon farmer, member Board of
Supervisors; unidentified; Edmund H. Allen, Newington, insurance agent; George K.
Pickett, Groveton, farmer, real estate, and insurance agent; Norville Larkin, county
civil engineer, roads and highways. Second row: Edward Gibbs, Mount Vernon,
electric railroad; John W. Rust, Fairfax, lawyer; Carroll V. Shreve, Falls Church,
fuel supplier. Third row: W. Cameron Roberts, Woodlawn, feed dealer; W.F.P. Reid,
Groveton, farmer, chairman of the Board of Supervisors; Arthur Buell, Herndon,
realtor; John T. DeBell, Centreville, farmer, chairman of School Board; unidentified;
John W. Brookfield, Springfield, farmer, postmaster; unidentified. Photo courtesy of
Fairfax County Chamber of Commerce.

beautification of home and school grounds was recorded in the 1928
report. Painting, whitewashing buildings and fences, and planting trees
and shrubs were among the activities. The club members also pruned
shade trees and performed tree surgery in the courthouse park. The
Better Food Club introduced a hot lunch program at the Navy
Community School on Ox Road.[8]

Agricultural efforts were tremendously stimulated by the Washington marketplace. "The main factor in placing Fairfax County first in
Dairying in the state is due to the splendid influence of the two Herd
Improvement Associations upon the breeding operations of the county.
Pure bred bulls were used . . . . " The interest and cooperation of the
Fairfax Chamber of Commerce and the county grange were cited in the
1930 report as vital factors in the success of county extension work and
improvement of the county's agricultural and industrial museum which
occupied half of the second floor of the old clerk's office at the courthouse.

8. Lippard, HD *Report*, 1927, 1928, 1929.

An innovation in communications this same year resulted from an invitation by James Vance of Washington, D.C., owner of radio station WJSV at Mount Vernon Hills. He offered free air time to Derr for regular programs of a public service nature. Community clubs and school leagues were asked to participate, and many specialists from Virginia Polytechnic Institute and from the U.S. Department of Agriculture in Washington gave talks on various agricultural subjects. Musical selections for violin and piano added variety to the programs.[9] "Air time" began to pay dividends. The very next year the first annual Piedmont Dairy Festival, with eight counties including Fairfax participating, was held in Manassas in October. Derr gave large credit for its success (8,000 to 10,000 people in attendance) to WJSV's extensive publicity of the effort to increase average milk consumption in the area. Patterned after the famous Winchester apple blossom festival which did so much to assist the orchard industry, the event drew attendance from West Virginia, Pennsylvania, Delaware, Maryland, and New Jersey. "All hail the potent influence of the radio," saluted Derr. The farm and home hour was increased from one-half hour twice a month to forty-five minutes every Thursday, and "five ladies were added who could take part."[10]

Several problems were troubling Derr. "Failure to keep records is the outstanding weakness of the majority of our farmers." Derr was referring not only to vaccination and revaccination records by also to keeping cost accounts of various crops and charging the farmer's free labor against it. It was in the 1930 report that Derr first mentioned what eventually became a major problem in the county. As many as 2,000 hogs were being fed on Washington city garbage by one farmer alone, at no cost, and the farmers feeding their hogs on grain could not profitably compete in the marketplace. He added, "the stench from these places is almost unbearable during the hot weather."

Wells and springs were going dry as a result of an extended drought period, and 727 railroad cars of feed were brought in as drought relief for Fairfax and adjoining drought-stricken counties. The *Fairfax Herald* reported that the water shortage was critical and that Salisbury Spring on Windover Heights in Vienna was being tested for use. Carne urged a water system for the town of Fairfax. The *Herald* commented that although the drought had killed many harmful insects, it had also caused a shortage of berries and seeds—food supply for wildlife during the coming winter. Drought conditions were depressing the area's production of crops. Derr's 1931 annual report urged that every acre which could be spared be planted in alfalfa hay. The soil also needed treatment

9. Derr, *Report*, 1930.
10. Derr, *Report*, 1931.

with tons of lime, and financial conditions were poor. Yet, the county agent consistently counseled farmers against taking out government loans to tide them over because of the uncertain future economic conditions. To support his position, he sent for copies of an article by Dr. Gus W. Dyer from the *Southern Agriculturist* entitled "The Devouring Mortgage" and credited it with persuading many farmers against accepting the loans for which there were no immediate prospects of repayment.[11]

A temporary crisis in the county's dairying industry was brought on by a new requirement for milk sold in Washington to contain 4 percent butterfat, a standard which the champion holsteins of Fairfax could not meet. This resulted in a switch by the dairy farmers to crossbreeding with guernsey and jersey animals for richer milk.

Poultry raising was becoming a big business, and vaccination for fowl chicken pox was in the experimental stage beginning in 1930. John Murphy told Derr in 1932, "By gosh, I learned my lesson last year. I vaccinated my birds and they are just rolling out the eggs, me for vaccinating after this."[12]

The county agent was always alert to new developments of all kinds, particularly media. For educational purposes, with the cooperation of the health department and home agent, the county purchased two movie projectors. Derr cooperated with the Tuberculosis Association, the Red Cross, home demonstration clubs, and dental clinics in presenting movie and slide programs on health, and gardening. "On January 25, at Floris, our farmers were shown the first Dairy talking movie, 'When the Cows Come Home' and several other talking pictures. Judging from the expressions of the audience it must have been the first talking movie given in the County." In a comparison of two communication media, Derr commented, "The radio furnishes an excellent medium to bring subject matter before the people. It is remarkable that so many people will maintain a radio that will not subscribe to a local paper." Three years later, he reported, "We find that we can reach twice the number of farmers in our county with the radio than we can with the county paper."[13]

The pay-as-you-go policy of Virginia, in general, was reinforced locally by agent Sarah Thomas' home demonstration clubs and their thrift campaign of 1933 to grow, can, bake, and sew at home, and to improve grounds and keep accurate family accounts. Their goal was to try to "keep their yearning within their earning."[14]

11. Derr, *Report*, 1930, 1931; *Fairfax Herald*, 22 August, 5 September, 26 September 1930.
12. Derr, *Report*, 1930, 1931, 1932.
13. Derr, *Report*, 1932, 1933, 1936.
14. Thomas, HD *Report*, 1933.

The impact of federal emergency agricultural programs was beginning to be felt. It was time-consuming for the county agent, who made 534 farm visits related to Agricultural Adjustment Administration (AAA) work alone, one-third of the total for the year. The AAA was created by congress in 1933, although opposed by Senator Harry F. Byrd because he disliked the power it gave the federal government. However, the Virginia Farm Bureau Federation, the Virginia Grange, and most farmers of Virginia favored and supported the new agency. They wanted production controls established for some of their crops, particularly tobacco and wheat. The previous year had seen the lowest wheat price in 132 years: fifty cents a bushel. Fairfax County received assistance from the broad-based depression relief program in another way. Thirty to forty men from the local Civilian Conservation Corps (CCC) camp in Prince William County near Manassas came to cut and burn the bark and brush from pinebark beetle-infested trees. They also assembled the 100 tons of framework steel delivered to F.E. Stowe's farm at Pender for a fire tower, which was provided with a telephone and a watchman during dry or dangerous periods.[15]

October of 1933 was the month of Virginia's referendum on repeal of prohibition, which had initially taken effect in Virginia on 31 October 1916, several years before the Eighteenth Amendment to the U.S. Constitution was passed in 1920. The Virginia voters were caught up in the stampede which was sweeping the entire country. They cast approximately 100,000 ballots for repeal of both federal and state prohibition laws, and only 58,000 against. Thus ended "the era of the amphibious statesman—that notorious species which voted 'dry' and drank 'wet.'" It was the beginning of a new era for the A. Smith Bowman family of Fairfax County who had come from Kentucky in 1928 and purchased 4,000 acres of the old 7,000-acre Wiehle tract near Herndon for a beef and dairy farm, renaming the post office "Sunset Hills." When repeal came, the old soapstone mill was converted into a distillery building, and other old buildings were converted to warehouse and other uses. The distilling of Virginia Gentleman and Fairfax County bottled-in-bond bourbons began, produced from grain grown on the farm. The mash by-product was fed to approximately 1,000 beef and dairy cattle. By 1947, the remainder of the old Wiehle acreage was purchased, and Sunset Hills, then totaling 7,200 acres, became the largest farm in Fairfax County.[16]

Because of the relatively small farms (the average size farm in Virginia for 1930 was 98.1 acres, for 1935, 89.3 acres; for Fairfax it was

---

15. Dabney, *Virginia*, pp. 460, 496; Derr, *Report*, 1933, 1934.

16. Dabney, *Virginia*, pp. 461-62; A. Smith Bowman, Jr., "A History of Sunset Hills Farm," *Yearbook of the Historical Society of Fairfax County, 1958-1959,* (Vienna, Va.), 6: 43 (hereinafter cited as Historical Society *Yearbook*).

99.3 acres in 1930 and 70.7 acres in 1935), most farmers found it necessary to rotate crops and were unable to spare land for permanent pasture. One of the most successful dairymen in the county, C.T. Rice, gave a talk on temporary pastures over WJSV radio which Derr mimeographed and mailed to dairymen, small farmers, and every farm paper in the east and central west. Favorable comments resulted. "This plan of temporary pastures has been more widely used and has had more lasting effect than any demonstration we have put on with the exception of dairy herd improvement work."[17]

Derr reported in 1935 that the two industries in the county for the year were dairying and poultry, gross farm profits amounting to over one million dollars. Chicken stealing was becoming so prevalent that a stenciling program was inaugurated for tattooing numbers on birds' wings to facilitate prosecution of the thieves.

The improvement of poultry flocks was a continuously important goal for the county agent, and he even gave specific advice on selecting the best roosters. "The first thing is to look for vigor . . . watch each bird closely, they show their pep and vitality by their carriage in foraging, scratching and fighting. Peppy birds mate often, crow frequently and act gallant while with the hens. The most vigorous males always have a number of females with them as they are attracted by his calls when he finds dainties while scratching in the litter or soil. As the most vigorous females are apparently selected by the male as his companions, no mistake can be made in selecting these birds for your breeding pen if they qualify in other characteristics. Avoid selecting breeding birds from those who loiter on the roosts during the day, no matter how many other qualities they may have . . . ." Charles Darwin himself could not have presented the facts more clearly.

The year 1936 provided some troublesome moments for Derr who was deeply concerned with environmental and conservation matters. Evergreen trees were defoliated by the bag worm, codling moths were attacking orchard trees, and the seventeen-year locust infestation was memorable. Derr philosophized: "The cry, 'FEED THE WORLD' in wartime hastened the clearing of many acres of young forests and today thousands of these acres are unused, growing up to brush. This land should all be reforested and growing in value."[18]

Another area of activity which had received little attention proved beneficial. A 4-H club had been organized at the Vienna Colored School, and Derr stated that he had not expected much from it. When the individual projects were completed, however, almost every child

17. *Statistical Abstract of Virginia*, 2:372; *Fairfax County Farm Statistics, 1910-1966* (Richmond: Virginia Cooperative Crop Reporting Service, August 1967).
18. Derr, *Report*, 1936.

between the ages of nine and eighteen had participated, most of them residents of Vienna where garden space was scarce. The agent was sincere in his praise: "it is a creditable showing for a colored school that has not received its full share of assistance in club work . . . . Efforts are being made to get a competent negro worker for the schools and adult women . . . . The principal, Louise Archer is entitled to considerable credit for creating the interest she did among her pupils."[19]

Work with organizations and federal agencies was increasing. The Izaak Walton League of Arlington held several meetings with the agent on conservation of both flora and fauna. For the first time, aerial photographs were made of Fairfax County by the contractor Fairchild Aerial Surveys, Inc., of New York City. Thirteen flights were taken to complete the record, and the agent and his assistant had to locate each farm on the map and mark it so that the Department of Agriculture supervisor could locate and interview the farmer to ascertain his soil practices. The amount each farmer could earn in 1938 would be gauged by his field performance, cooperating with the Soil Conservation Service. To assist with the growing volume of soil conservation work, Miss Marion Earle joined the office staff.

Twenty years of dedicated service were completed by H.B. Derr at the end of 1937. The statistics for Derr's final year as agent were imposing: 960 farm and home visits; 2,755 office calls; 2,088 telephone calls (many of these were relative to the AAA program and soil conservation work); 2,588 Virginia and United States government bulletins distributed; auto mileage, 12,381; train mileage, 1,000. It was fitting that eight and one-half year old Willowmere Martha 234094, owned by B.F. Salsbury of Fairfax, set a new official national record announced by the American Guernsey Cattle Club. She had during the year produced 14,255.6 pounds of milk and 621.5 pounds of butterfat in Class A.[20] Again, Fairfax County had raised a champion, this time a new breed—Guernsey.

Derr's successor was Agricultural Extension Agent Joseph Beard, whose grandparents and parents had migrated together to Fairfax County from the Shenandoah Valley of Virginia in the first decade of the twentieth century because Fairfax was closer to major markets for farm products. They settled near the Washington and Old Dominion Railroad line where they could ship a live calf, a crate of eggs, poultry, or butter to Washington, Baltimore, or Philadelphia. There commission merchants sold the products and mailed a check for the proceeds to the farmer. This kind of farm-to-market convenience was not available to farmers in the Valley at the turn of the century. Beard's father was a dairy farmer and

19. Ibid.
20. Derr, *Report*, 1937.

*An Award for a successful Fairfax County program of livestock disease control
was given by the Virginia Commissioner of Agriculture, 1958. Left to right:
Maurice T. Rowe, then Assistant Commissioner of Agriculture; Wilson D.
McNair, Herndon dairy farmer; Joseph E. Beard, Agricultural Extension Agent
for Fairfax County; and Richard Lee, Chantilly dairy farmer.*

when his sons reached high school age, he bought a 162-acre dairy farm
near the coeducational Floris Vocational Agricultural High School at
Frying Pan near Herndon so that they could walk to school. When Beard
graduated from Floris in 1927, he went into the dairy business with his
father and brother, but by 1929 the combination of depression and
drought made a four-year college course in dairy husbandry seem
attractive. As he was finishing the fourth year of college at Virginia
Polytechnic Institute at Blacksburg in the Shenandoah Valley, Beard
joined the U.S. Army Reserve because jobs were scarce, although he
finally got a job offer as a milk tester just before graduation. The county
agent in Prince William held the job open while Beard finished his basic
army training. After the milk-testing job came positions as assistant
county agent and county agent elsewhere in Virginia. Then, at the
request of the Fairfax County Grange, whose representatives appeared
before the board of supervisors on his behalf, Beard was hired as
agricultural agent in his own county, an exception to the usual rules.[21]

Twelve farm unit demonstrations were established in 1939 with the
cooperation of the Tennessee Valley Authority and the local soil

21. Interview, Joseph Beard, 9 August 1975; BOSMB No. 7, p. 532.

*Edith Rogers, Herndon dairy
farmer and teacher, was the
first woman member of the
County Board of Supervisors.
Photo in 1940 by Arthur
Rothstein for the Farm Security
Administration. Library of
Congress.*

conservation committee for the purpose of teaching improved farm practices in all local phases of agriculture. Farmers cooperating in these demonstrations kept accurate farm account records in return for phosphate fertilizers distributed by the TVA for pasture improvement. Beard's stated goals for the long-range extension program were adjusting production to market demands, increasing efficiency in all phases of agriculture and country life activities, improving marketing methods, and improving standards of living.[22]

Country life activities were soon to be augmented, and eventually superseded by suburban and urban activities in Fairfax County. In 1939, for the first time, the annual report indicated the growing impact of accelerating in-migration as the federal bureaucracy expanded. Four topics suggested for discussion at a meeting of the Agricultural Committee, an organization of farmers with county-wide representation were: (1) development and sale of sod; (2) room and board of members of families who are employed elsewhere; (3) group marketing of local products by roadside stands; and (4) subdivisions on land considered too

22. Beard, *Report,* 1939.

Mark Turner, *Great Falls dairy
farmer, was Master of the
Virginia State Grange for three
terms, and long-time chairman
of the Virginia Milk Commission.
Photo in 1940 by Arthur
Rothstein. Library of Congress.*

valuable for farming. W. Alvord Sherman stated his belief that the 1940
reassessment for tax purposes would be more accurate and fair, based on
aerial photographing and indexing of land parcels, so "that it will put on
the suburban area their fair share of the tax burden." Those making their
living by farming were eager to have taxes reduced on agricultural lands
and increased on residential holdings for which a higher level of public
services was generally being demanded. According to the 1939 report,
dairying was bringing in $1,300,000 annual income to Fairfax farmers.
Fairfax County poultry enterprises were evaluated as a $1,020,000
industry, with more than half a million birds in flocks.[23]

Conditions which were to develop markedly in the next three
decades were already becoming serious problems: the increasing need for
cash on the home farm (due in great part to mechanization), increasing
taxes, land values, labor costs, a transient, highly mobile population,
and the "back-to-the-country movement."

Special notice was taken in the 1940 annual report of the many local,
state, and federal organizations and agencies which had cooperated with

23. Ibid.

the farm and rural people in the county: the school board, board of supervisors, Farm Security Administration, Rural Electrification Administration, Tennessee Valley Authority, National Youth Administration, Federal Housing Administration, local community chest, welfare department, U.S. Census Bureau, AAA program, and a new agency—the local Selective Service Draft Board. Clouds of war had begun to appear on the horizon. [24]

The influx of government workers employed in the war effort accelerated, and in 1941 a county planning and zoning ordinance was put into effect. The county was divided into districts of agricultural rural residential, suburban residential, general business, and industrial business. Two members on the zoning board represented the farms, one of whom was also chairman of the planning commission. Concern was mounting that real estate agents and others were purchasing land in anticipation of post-war development, and farmers were urged to consider requesting some type of restrictive zoning to prohibit subdivision development in the middle of farmlands. [25]

The county agent's annual reports during the war years provided an important record of life and work on the homefront. Joseph Beard, who had been an army reservist since graduation from VPI, was called to service in World War II. R.B. Davis, Jr., Lawrence Green, and Oscar Turner replaced him for the duration. Scrap aluminum drives, the agricultural defense production campaign, including home "victory gardens," scrap iron campaigns, farm machine rationing, and farm building rationing were some of the war-time projects participated in by the county's extension service. Shortage of farm labor became a problem because so many people were called to arms or were working in government jobs. Some convict help was obtained, but most help was recruited from the District of Columbia. No farm crops went unharvested in 1943. [26]

Although some crops were lost as a result of the shortage of labor in 1944, it was still a problem to obtain an agricultural deferment from military service. Members of the WAC (Womans Army Corps), soldiers, and convicts all helped harvest crops during the week and on Sundays. Throughout the state that year "convict labor was used for approximately 85,000 hours in harvesting farm crops, for which reimbursement was received." [27]

By 1945 land was increasingly being appraised on residential value rather than on farm use. Population in the county had doubled in the previous four years, and as was reported succinctly and prophetically,

24. Beard, Report, 1940.

25. BOSMB No. 9, pp. 447-64; Davis, Report, 1943, 1944.

26. R.B. Davis, Jr., Report, 1941-1943.

27. Davis, Report, 1944; 37th Report of the State Highway Commission to the Governor of Virginia, (Richmond, Va.: Division of Purchasing and Printing, 1944).

"The outlook for agriculture in Fairfax is dismal . . . the people that own homes demand many services and under the taxing system, agriculture carries the burden." Economic realities were producing conflicts between the farmers and the new wave of suburbanites. Agricultural problems shifted from commercial orchards and truck gardening to vegetable gardens, ornamental plants, shrubs, and lawns. Col. Joseph E. Beard returned from his military assignment to his previous job as agricultural agent. Beard found that the conditions of 1946 differed vastly from those existing before the war.[28]

One method of coping with new problems was the regional approach, exemplified by the organization in April 1946 of the Northern Virginia Tri-County Soil Conservation District, consisting of Fairfax, Loudoun, and Prince William counties. One of the major reasons for the formation of this group was a growing awareness of the need for more responsible utilization of natural resources.[29]

Other signs of the times included a demonstration meeting held on C.T. Rice's farm on Hunter Mill Road in Oakton to explain better farming methods, a doubling of the membership in the 4-H youth program within the year, an extensive Japanese beetle control program of poisonous milky spore applications, and an increase of thirty days in the county's grazing season due to soil conservation and enrichment programs. However, "inefficiency and delays occur when the details of the various projects are worked out in a countywide organization of 118 members representing 110,000 people with diversified interests. Garden club members are not interested in the artificial breeding work of dairy cattle anymore than dairy farmers are interested in controlling moles in a peony bed." It was evident that the county citizens knew how to reach the county agent's office: the staff had to be increased several years in a row to handle the more than 500 calls per month asking for information and assistance. The lifestyle of many of the county's young people was changing: "There is little community spirit developed by riding in automobiles and going to the movies. There are 15,000 boys and girls of 4-H club age in Fairfax County and we have less than 1,000 enrolled in club work." The "heads, hearts, hands and health" concerns were, at the very least, finding outlets in other than Fairfax County's traditional rural ways.[30]

The family farm was disappearing, rapidly being replaced by two diametrically opposed land uses: commerical farms were becoming larger and more highly mechanized, and part-time farmers with other occupations were on the increase. The extension service staff had to

28. Davis, *Report*, 1945; Beard, *Report*, 1946.
29. Beard, *Report*, 1946.
30. Beard, *Report*, 1947, 1949.

change its operational procedures in order to accommodate the new trends and greater demand for information. More newsletters, leadership training, and large group meetings were added to the program in order to assist the new or part-time farmers. Orchards had almost completely disappeared. The need for conservation of soils, water, forests, and wildlife was becoming more apparent to everyone. In one area alone, half of the 600 subdivisions in existence in the county in 1952 needed help with erosion problems. This problem was a unifying one. The Fairfax County Federation of Citizens Associations assisted with a detailed two-year survey of soil types. The soils study proved of greater value than initially anticipated for both farmers and the effect on selection of good homesites, septic fields, and wells. Communication methods improved. Just as H.B. Derr had found radio a valuable medium for his extension work in the early 1930s, Beard found television a new and powerful means of disseminating information in the mid-1950s.[31]

By 1956, thirty-five types of soil and soil conditions had been identified within Fairfax County, and information gleaned from the survey was being shared with neighboring Prince William and Loudoun counties. An article published in *Soil Conservation* explained the importance of the survey. Less than one-fifth of the calls made to the County's soil scientist, C.S. Coleman, during one year were from farmers. The remainder, more than four-fifths, were from homeowners or County government officials. The taxpayers' savings effected by the soil survey information were estimated at an average of $2,000 a week. Construction of heavy buildings on shifting soils can be very expensive.[32]

Space age developments had a marked effect on the county agent's work load as relocation of farmers began after the federal government took over 12,500 acres of land in the northwestern portion of Fairfax County and in Loudoun County for the construction of the Chantilly jet airport. Laurence Mitchell, chairman of the Northern Virginia soil conservation district, foresaw future problems of siltation of downstream watersheds during construction of the airport facility and brought his concern and recommendations for impoundment and siltation ponds before the board of supervisors. These recommendations were adopted.[33]

Beard made a plea for more staff and more funds from the county government to handle his department's exceptional work load. One agent per 35,000 residents was very much out of line with the standard recommended ratio of one to 6,000. Urbanization had come about rapidly through the unprecedented population explosion in Fairfax

31. Beard, *Report*, 1951-1955.

32. *Soil Conservation* (Washington, D.C.: Soil Conservation Service, U.S. Department of Agriculture, October 1957), pp. 51-56; Beard, *Report*, 1957.

33. Beard, *Report*, 1958; *Fairfax Newsletter*, ed. Betsy Hinkle (Springfield, Va.: 4 April 1958), p. 3.

County due in large part to immigration of persons connected with the expansion of the federal government bureaucracy and the many support services required by the new residents. [34]

The abrasion and frustration accompanying the proximity of the diverse lifestyles, perspectives, and goals between agricultural and suburban sectors of Fairfax County was well depicted in Beard's 1960 annual report, a classic expression of two distinctly separate interest groups in conflict over land utilization and lifestyles.

> Our farmland is being riddled with government installations, telephone cables, and 350 to 400 foot-wide limited access highways. How does a farmer cross one of these roads to get to either crops or livestock on the other side? Who cares if the silt from one of these giant excavations fills his farm pond or muddies the little streams so that his livestock cannot obtain drinking water? . . . What happened to all of this expended labor, energy, and soil fertility? It certainly hasn't arrived on the lawns of our housing developments, nor is it found with the grass on the 900 acres of Fairfax County school grounds, or athletic fields. . . .

> Why is it exasperated housewives from the urban developments call the County Agent's Office trying to find a quick and simple means of eliminating snakes, field mice, other rodents, skunks, ground hogs? Could it be that when large areas nearby are being bulldozed for an airport, a highway or a housing development that these animals are looking for a new home too?

> What would you do with a dead cow, or a dead pony on a hot day in July if your husband worked for the government and was away on a long trip and you only owned an acre of land and the neighbors were getting nasty about the whole matter? Would you call your County Agent too?

> What would you do if the forty-foot well under the concrete basement of your house went dry just as you were washing the diapers and you didn't expect your husband to come back from his government trip for seven days?

> How will you tell your wife that you can't get a building permit to build the country estate home that you have both planned and dreamed of for years because the soil on the 15 acres you spent $20,000 for will not percolate for a septic tank

---

34. U.S. Department of Commerce, Bureau of the Census, *Statistical Abstract* (Washington, D.C.: U.S. Government Printing Office, 1960).

and it doesn't look like running water and sewage will be available in the community for 10 or 15 years?

Would you call the County Agent's Office if you lived in this urban area with a seventeen-year old son who was getting into trouble and the Welfare Office or the Juvenile Court Officer had advised you to get him out on a farm?

A farmer rarely calls for information on how to destroy ants or poison ivy on his 150 acre farm. But if this 150 acres contains 300 homes, nearly 100 calls will be received during the year from this group and probably twenty-five or thirty of them will be for the control of ants or poison ivy.

Japanese beetles have shown no preference for either farm crops or ornamental plants or shrubs, nor have the soils, sewage and water problems confined themselves to either farm or urban populations.

These are some of the examples of situations which affect both farmers and urban groups when the two are integrated as they are in Fairfax County.[35]

Beard was not defeated by such problems. His report followed the above essay with formal listings of objectives, program suggestions designed to disseminate information, and foster understanding and cooperation between diverse interest groups. He recommended the incorporation of proper conservation measures, and provision for further studies to improve utilization and amenities on the land for its people.

Comparison of land values is informative. In 1920, Fairfax County farmland was valued at $95.40 per acre; the population was 21,943. In 1960, farmland was valued at $753.53 per acre and the population had climbed to 248,897. Forty years of growth had brought about other major changes in county life. Floris Vocational Agricultural High School, which Derr helped to establish, and from which Beard had graduated, was closed in 1929 when Herndon and Floris high schools were consolidated. The building and site were made available to the 4-H clubs in the county for their annual fair and other activities after acquisition from the school board around 1958 by the Fairfax County Park Authority. Frying Pan Park was gradually developed as a living museum to preserve an almost-forgotten way of life in the 1920s when family subsistence farms were numerous in the county, and mechanization had not yet become an integral part of the agricultural system.[36]

35. Beard, *Report*, 1960.
36. Interview, Joseph Beard, 9 August 1975.

A program directed toward providing information on floods, erosion, and siltation control was initiated to make the public aware of the problems, needs, and high anticipated future cost of present neglect. Storm sewers, flood plains, lakes, rivers, and streams had become filled with silt and debris. The raw ground exposed by bulldozing for construction programs reacted to weather conditions in the same way the abandoned tobacco fields of Fairfax County had in the eighteenth century: siltation occurred during heavy rainfall, a frequent problem in northern Virginia with its average annual rainfall of 47.58 inches.[37] The power of the printed word was invoked through the publication of a brochure "for builders and developers outlining simple, inexpensive agronomy practices and engineering procedures" which they could carry out. Steps were taken to establish an experimental development project in the Pohick Creek watershed, approved by the county board of supervisors in November 1967. It was estimated that every dollar spent in preventing and controlling erosion and siltation would mean a saving of $15-$18 in the future.[38]

A valuable profile of agriculture in Fairfax County in 1964 and 1969 is available in an agricultural census published in 1972. The number of and acres in farms actually increased between 1964 and 1969 from 218 farms with 32,369 acres to 278 farms with 36,211 acres. The average size of farms in Fairfax County decreased from 146.5 acres to 130.2 acres. The average value of farmland and buildings per acre in the five years changed from $1,388.95 to $2,049.87, a 47.58 percent increase. The market value of all agricultural products sold in 1969 exceeded 2.5 million dollars, whereas the 1964 figure was only slightly over 2 million. The inventory of cattle had gone up in 1969, but hogs and chickens had each decreased by more than 50 percent. The 59,120 bushels of field corn harvested in 1969 was almost 181.27 percent greater than the 1964 figure; wheat had dropped about 20.14 percent; but soy beans had increased from 288 bushels to 2,825, an increase of 880.90 percent. Productivity per acre had been markedly increased by technological advances.[39]

The population of Fairfax County and city was estimated at 473,700 in 1969. Much of the population was transient or highly mobile, so that every year it was necessary for the extension service to provide many new residents with educational materials and instructions relative to ornamental horticulture, agronomy, erosion, siltation, and conserva-

37. Fairfax County Department of County Development, *Rainfall in Fairfax County*, (Fairfax, Va.: Division of Design Review, 1972).

38. BOSMB No. 47, pp. 33-39; the plan was implemented under PL 566 to provide flood control and silt reduction facilities in the Pohick stream valley in order to prevent eroded soil from being deposited in the Pohick Creek channel and the Potomac River; Beard, *Report*, 1968.

39. U.S. Department of Commerce, *1969 Census of Agriculture, County Data Book*, (Bureau of the Census, U.S. Government Printing Office, 1972), pp. 225-32. The study includes twenty-five analytical tables describing farm size, livestock and produce, land use, income, operators, chemicals and fertilizers used, and forest products.

tion. A plant diagnostic and soil sampling laboratory was established in the extension office, and a new speakers' bureau enabled the staff to work through some of the more than 600 clubs and organizations in urban Fairfax County.[40]

Beard retired from his position as county agricultural extension agent in April 1970. Because of the overwhelming public demand for information, the Tip-a-Phone program had been established by the extension office with different recorded messages every day. Initially, 25,000 to 30,000 calls were anticipated annually. The volume of phone calls was such that in 1969 alone 37,786 conventional phone calls were received in the office, and 79,608 by Tip-a-Phone. The office visits for the same year amounted to 12,016, a total of 128,410 contacts. This was quite a contrast to Derr's office, business, and phone calls totaling 2,310 in 1926. Charles Hall and then Wayne Smith succeeded Beard as directors.

In 1973, a land use tax for farmers was discussed at a countywide meeting with political representatives "with almost perfect attendance by the remaining large farmers in the County." Little more than a year later, Hugh A. Johnson, a nationally recognized agricultural economist wrote in a report for the Office of Comprehensive Planning, "Commercial agriculture in Fairfax County is the remnant of an earlier economy. . . . . County policy since 1965 to assess all land in the County based on probable sales value for non-farm use has resulted in appraised values and real estate taxes unrelated to the land's productivity for agriculture." He further stated that only 37 operating units still existed which could annually produce at least $2,500 in sales of farm products. "Milk handling from the remaining Fairfax County dairy farms happens to be less of a problem than it might otherwise be because the bulk trucks can collect their milk on their way from adjoining counties to the processing plants."[41]

A wide range of subjects interest young and adult citizens of the county, and the extension service has kept abreast of the times, particularly in a multimedia approach to disseminating information. Nutrition and health programs aired over WNVT television (channel 53) were seen by more than 11,000 fourth, fifth, and sixth graders in the county's public schools by 1974 and teachers were supplied with materials to teach good nutrition. A bulletin on the use and care of indoor plants was developed in response to public interest and inquiry, reflecting a national trend. Almost 1,000 garden plots were allocated to citizens who were interested in growing and preserving their own food in 1975. Portable computer terminals were used at four regional libraries to

40. Beard, *Report*, 1969.

41. Charles L. Hall letter to Benjamin H. Weddle, V.P.I., 6 June 1973; Hugh A. Johnson, "The Role of Commercial Agriculture in Land Use Planning for Fairfax County," *PLUS Working Paper No. 6* (Fairfax, Va.: Office of Comprehensive Planning, November 1974).

Rural Scene. A view at harvest time, on Route 7, the Leesburg Pike, near Colvin Run Mill. Photo in 1975 by James K. W. Atherton. The Washington Post. Used with permission.

assist with collecting and analyzing daily nutritional information from cooperating patrons. The Senior Citizens Nutritional Program participants at Groveton agreed to have an analysis run on their dietary habits. Requests for educational programs and information grew from 73,828 in April 1974 to 146,590 in April 1975, indicating an increasing awareness on the part of citizens in the county of the "need to know." Radio also continues to be useful; recorded tapes on timely topics are played every hour on local radio stations.

Many of the youth of today are demonstrating concern for and interest in conservation, environmental quality, and quality of life. In June 1975, the 4-H Congress was held at V.P.I. in Blacksburg, and the thirty-one member delegation from Fairfax was the largest which had ever attended from the county. Jeff Stewart of Fairfax Station won the Virginia 4-H achievement award which is the highest such award in the state and a particularly high honor for a resident of such an urbanized county.[42]

Statistically, the county agent's public service contacts have grown in number. In 1976 there were 8,135 office calls, 58,550 telephone calls, and 42,662 Tip-a-Phone calls, totaling 109,347. Total contacts of all

42. Smith, *Report*, 1974, 1975.

kinds, including publications, tallied 686,853. The role of the county agricultural agent has naturally changed in Fairfax County along with the change to urban use of most of the farmland. Whereas in the first decades of service Derr and Beard and their few assistants made thousands of farm visits, their numerous successors (the extension office staff now numbers 21) have had to change their primary duties to scientific testing of soils and plants in an office laboratory because there is not time to get out in the field to attend to the botanical and home agricultural needs of a population estimated at 554,500. An early accolade to county extension workers as well expressed in 1933 by C.W. Warburton, Director of Extension Work, U.S. Department of Agriculture, when he said: "They have dedicated their efforts to improving the social and economic welfare of farm people. They are always ready to take the lead in any movement for the betterment of agriculture. These are men and women of tremendous influence upon the rural life of the nation." In the case of Fairfax County, the new name of the agency tells the story: The Department of Extension and Continuing Education. The modernized department serves the new needs of both agricultural and urban lifestyles. [43]

In 1925, almost every subsistence farm in Fairfax County had its own woodlot—a stand of trees selectively thinned and periodically reforested to provide a continuous supply of fuel for home use. On a 100-acre farm, possibly 30 to 40 acres would be in woodland. In fifty years' time, the residential lifestyle had changed so much that door-to-door wood salesmen often "short changed" consumers, and periodicals like Fairfax County government's Weekly Agenda found it desirable to explain that "a cord is defined as 'the amount of wood that is contained in a space of 128 cubic feet when the wood is ranked and well-stowed,'" a fact that must once have been common knowledge in every Fairfax County home. [44]

43. Derr, Report, 1935.

44. Interview, Joseph Beard, 9 August 1975; "How to Buy Firewood," Weekly Agenda (Fairfax, Va.: Fairfax County Government, September 1975), 12(36).

III

The Schools
Reading, Writing, and Reorganization

In a survey prepared for the University of Virginia in 1924, Cary J. Randolph stated that the purpose of the chapter on schools was to place before the citizens of Fairfax County the facts concerning education and school standings in the state, in order to interest them in providing the county with the best educational opportunities available. A general index rating, measured by certain financial and academic factors, had been set up by the superintendent of public instruction in the State of Virginia and published as a bulletin of the state board of education. During the 1922-23 session, Fairfax County had the highest state index figure of 80.08, the total average of all counties being 74.86. It stood eighteenth among the counties in Virginia with its higher-than-average annual salary per teacher of $684.40, due in part to its proximity to Alexandria and the District of Columbia, both of which were by 1924 largely urban and paying their teachers well compared to most Virginia counties. However, the Fairfax ranking on school attendance of the population between six and nineteen years was ninety-eighth in the state, although only 39.16 percent attended school regularly. Obviously, the compulsory attendance law enacted by the General Assembly in 1922 was not being enforced in the county.[1]

In Falls Church, the largest town in Fairfax County, the population recorded in the 1920 census was 1,700. The Jefferson Institute, which had been established in 1873, two years before the town had been incorporated by an act of the General Assembly, was still in use but under the new

---

1. Acts of Assembly, 24 March 1922; Lehman P. Nickell and Cary J. Randolph, *An Economic and Social Survey of Fairfax County* (Charlottesville, Va.: University of Virginia, 1924), pp. 60, 64 (hereinafter cited as Nickell and Randolph, *Social Survey*).

name of Falls Church High School. In 1925, only half the students in the town could be housed in the old building. A two-room temporary structure and an old church were being used. Madison school, located on a large lot on Lee Highway (near the State Theatre), opened in 1926. Built of native stone, it had 14 rooms and modern heating, lighting and plumbing.[2]

Herndon had a population of 953 in the 1920 census. In 1925, it had a public high school and a seminary for girls. Vienna, with a 1920 population of 773, had schools for both white and black students in 1925. In 1920, the town of Fairfax had a population of 516; in 1925, it had "a splendid graded school."[3]

A longer school term in cities was thought to have a direct bearing on the cities' leadership over rural counties in literacy standing. Until there was equalization of educational opportunities, enterprising and farseeing parents, who were solicitous for the future welfare of their children, would continue their migration from county to city districts.[4]

One means of obtaining public support for community programs had been envisioned during the first decade of the twentieth century when the Co-operative Education Association of the State sponsored the formation of community leagues to establish Virginia public schools as community centers. The leagues' purposes were to improve the civic, physical, moral, educational, social, and economic interests of the citizens by virtue of cooperative efforts. By 1922, there were twenty-seven such leagues in Fairfax County with a total membership of 843. Some of the activities related to schools cited in the 1923 annual report included the raising of money by the Andrew Chapel League to extend the school term of the seventh and eighth grades from eight to nine months, and add an extra teacher. Franconia worked for road and school improvement. Centreville secured 300 books and cooperated with the county agent and health director. Belle Aire installed a medicine cabinet and first aid remedies. McLean was in the process of raising $25,000 for a new high school building. The Vienna Junior League purchased athletic equipment, and the Floris Junior League spent over $250 raised by a bazaar to purchase dishes, chairs, and rest room furnishings.[5]

2. Sadie C. Detwiler, Hollie Nickell, and Katherine Harrison, *The County of Fairfax* (Charlottesville, Va.: University of Virginia; Fairfax County School Board, 1925), p. 15 (hereinafter cited as Detwiler, *Fairfax*); Melvin Lee Steadman, *Falls Church By Fence and Fireside* (Falls Church: Falls Church Public Library, 1964)(hereinafter cited as Steadman, *Falls Church*). pp. 140-42

3. Detwiler, *Fairfax*, p. 16.

4. Nickell and Randolph, *Social Survey*, p. 61.

5. Nickell and Randolph, *Social Survey*, pp. 64-65.

Public School Consolidation

The *Fairfax County Geography Supplement of 1925* presented a comprehensive picture of the county as it was in that year. The four authors, teachers at Clifton and Floris High Schools, reported that although Fairfax County ranked first in the state in literacy and close to the top in general efficiency, lack of funds had been a major hindrance to improvement in the schools, due in part to the state's low legal ceiling on district and state taxes and also to limitation of the assessment of real property at far below its true market value. In some sections of the county, smaller schools had been closed or consolidated. The school year also had been lengthened to nine months. Five of the high schools, Clifton, Floris, Herndon, Oakton and McLean, were accredited. The Herndon Female Seminary, which had been established in 1876 by Mrs. Mary Lee Castleman, was still furnishing a respected cultural education. The Episcopal Theological Seminary, established in 1827 west of Alexandria, and the Episcopal High School of Alexandria, established in 1839 by the church, were both described as active educational institutions. The seminary had already sent out over 1,500 men to teach and preach the gospel, many on missions to foreign countries.[6]

Milton Dulaney Hall completed forty-three years of administration as superintendent of Fairfax County Schools in 1929. During that period, the county's first public high schools were established, teachers' salaries were raised, and the value of school property had increased by 2,075.4 percent, having risen from a value of $32,500 in 1886 to $707,000 in 1929. Many of the one-room schools had been closed. Transporting of students by county-funded vehicles had begun. When Mr. Hall was appointed in 1886, there were 86 teachers and 3,868 students. The superintendent's salary was $420 per year and teachers were paid $27 per month for approximately six months of teaching. There were, in 1929, 171 teachers in all, 143 of whom were white and 28 black; the average white teacher's salary was $834.85, the average black teacher's salary, $420.00; the superintendent's salary had increased to $1,155.00. There were 44 white schools with 4,130 students and 21 black schools with 856 students, a total of 4,986 in 65 schools. Twenty-nine were still one-room buildings, 18 were two-room, four were three-room. The eleven "trucks or wagons" paid for by the school board transported 509 students, ten vehicles for white, one for blacks. All schools were equipped with "patent desks," 49 with "sanitary outhouses," 56 with "sanitary heat and ventilation." Fifty-two flew the American flag, and six the Virginia flag.[7]

6. Detwiler, *Fairfax*, p. 21; Nickell and Randolph, *Social Survey*, pp. 66-67.

7. John Gott and Kathryn S. Hogan, "Fairfax County Public Schools, A Brief History"(hereinafter cited as Gott and Hogan, "Public Schools."; *The Legato School: A Centennial Souvenir* (Fairfax: Fairfax County History Commission, 1976); Annual School Report to State Department of Education, 1928-1929.

Milton D. Hall was Fairfax County's School Superintendent, from 1886 to 1929. Fairfax County School Board.

Wilbert T. Woodson was Fairfax County's School Superintendent, from 1929 to 1961. Fairfax County School Board.

Hall reluctantly retired in July 1929 and was succeeded by Wilbert Tucker Woodson who had come to Fairfax County in September 1925 as supervisor of schools and clerk of the school board. Woodson served as superintendent of schools for thirty-two years, until 1961. In May 1929, Madison School, in the town of Falls Church, was the scene of one of numerous testimonial occasions honoring Hall's many years of public service. Among many honoring him were Congressman R. Walton Moore, C.J. Heatwole, Secretary of the Virginia Education Association, and Lillian Millan, a teacher with many years' experience at Legato School. The black teachers of the county held a reception at Baileys Crossroads presided over by the principal of Baileys School, Lillian Carey. Mrs. M.E. Henderson of Falls Church and W.D. Gresham, State Supervisor of Negro Education, spoke.[8]

Woodson was born in Crozet, Virginia. He graduated from the College of William and Mary. While in military service during World War I, he received the French Medal of Honor. When he took over his administrative responsibilities, the county was rural with the exception of Falls Church, Fairfax, Herndon, Vienna, and Clifton. Many of the county citizens were employed in the federal or district government in

8. Gott and Hogan, "Public Schools," p. 32.

Washington, although agriculture and dairying were the principal occupations. There was little interest in public schools among the older and more influential citizens who through long Virginia tradition preferred private schools and academies. This group included the local politicians and large land owners, many of whom bitterly opposed repeated requests for increases in taxes for schools and used many means to deny them. The government workers, many being relatively new residents of the county, were interested in public schools and did not think the small rural schools offered the opportunities they felt their children should have. Because children of government workers at the district or federal level were admitted free in the urban schools of Washington, and since public transportation on the steam and electric railways and by bus was economical and convenient for most county children, many parents sent their children to Washington schools. Thus, this group which would naturally have exerted a strong influence for improvement of the local school system in the county was solving the problem of educating their children in another way.

Woodson realized that if he were to build a better school system in the county, he would have to receive support from citizens willing to speak up convincingly and that a majority of voters would have to elect sympathetic members of the board of supervisors, the tax-levying body. Other key local government officials—the treasurer, the commissioner of revenue, the commonwealth's attorney, and the sheriff—would all have to be favorably inclined toward tax increases to support an improved school system.[9]

First, a well-defined, forward-looking program had to be planned. Consolidation of the one-, two- and three-room frame school buildings was desirable in order to provide better facilities and pay higher teachers' salaries. There was a deep loyalty in many rural communities to the local school which "was good enough for me and my father and grandfather." However, Woodson strongly advocated modernization which would replace the pot-bellied stoves, water buckets, outhouses, pumps, and open wells, with modern heating systems, running water, and indoor plumbing, along with better teaching and learning facilities.

The next step was to recommend different sources of funding to the school board which was composed of members appointed by the circuit court-appointed school trustee electoral board to represent the six magisterial districts and towns. Although most members realized that

9. *Who's Who in the South and Southwest* (Chicago: Marquis Who's Who, 1954); *Who's Who in American Education* (Nashville, Tenn.: Who's Who in American Education, Inc., 1955-1956); *Virginia Lives: The Old Dominion Who's Who* (Hopkinsville, Ky.: Historical Record Association, 1964); W.T. Woodson, *Three Decades of Growth and Progress in Public Education* (Fairfax: Fairfax County Public Schools, Superintendent's Report, 1960-1961), pp. 2-3(hereinafter cited as Woodson, *Three Decades*).

consolidation and modernization would require the raising of taxes and issuance of bonds, the school board did favor the plan. During the 1930s, some construction money became available through borrowing from the Literary Fund of Virginia, and some federal grants came through the Public Works Administration. Taxes were allocated in succeeding years to repay the Literary Fund loans.

When the success of the first phase of school improvement seemed assured, Woodson began an intensive campaign to get community leagues and parent teacher associations organized in every consolidated school community, and these in turn organized into a countywide association. These associations became the hard-working cooperative support and encouragement for the school administration. They were united in the stated purpose of education "to provide for the continual development and improvement of every individual to the extent of his abilities" including training in basic skills, citizenship, thinking, knowledge, human relations, health, constructive use of leisure time, Americanism, good behavior, and recognition of the worth of each individual.[10]

By 1940, many of the one-, two-, and three-room schools had been replaced by two new high schools and nine new consolidated elementary schools. The first unit of Fairfax High School was built in 1934, of Mount Vernon High in 1939. The new elementary schools were built as follows: Franconia, 1931; Groveton, 1933; Centerville and Lorton, 1934; Woodlawn, 1937; Fairview, 1938; and Burke, Dunn Loring, and the Vienna Colored School (renamed Louise Archer in 1948) 1939. The total number of schools in 1940 after this consolidation was 39 elementary and 4 high schools serving 6,899 pupils over the four hundred-plus square mile area of Fairfax County. The teaching force had increased to 246 and the average teacher's salary had risen to $972.10. Total cost of education per pupil was $52.87, excluding debt service (repayment of principal and interest on previous bond issues and Literary Fund notes) and capital outlay.[11]

The decade 1941-1951, because of World War II and its aftermath, markedly affected the county's educational program. Some teachers were called to the armed forces; others took higher paying war-related jobs. The federal works programs which had coped with the previous decade's widespread unemployment came to an end. The average teacher's salary in 1941 was $1,117.75, and the competitive job market resulted in resignation of many career teachers and thus the intensive recruiting of retired teachers and married women who had left teaching to devote full time to home and family.

10. Woodson, *Three Decades*, p. 5.
11. Ibid., pp. 6, 7.

In 1946, the eighth grade was added to the state's curriculum, increasing the period of public school education from eleven to twelve years. Other changes were introduced: special education, visiting teacher service, and in-service workshops were added to the program.

Because of building material shortages during and immediately following the war, only six new schools were constructed: Lincolnia, 1942; Falls Church High School, 1945; Oakton, 1945; James Lee, 1947; and Willston and Graham Road, 1951. The school population more than doubled in the ten years; it was 7,755 in 1941 and 16,163 in 1951.[12]

J.H. Rice, principal of Herndon High and Elementary schools, was instrumental in establishing the first cafeteria program in the county. Unable to get official funds appropriated by his local school board, he appealed to the Rotary Club in Herndon and to the PTA. About 1943 the cafeteria program began at Herndon. Kitchen and cafeteria equipment and dining hall furniture were purchased from proceeds of a Rotary carnival and from other activities. Each child brought eating utensils from home each day, and parents often sent in a bushel of potatoes or tomatoes for stew or soup. The cannery at Herndon High was used to put up federal surplus foods, and canned goods were shipped to every school in the county as the program grew. The first meals at Herndon High cost five cents each.[13]

The black community began to voice its opinion regarding black education. Edwin B. Henderson of Falls Church composed a flyer which was issued by the Fairfax County Branch of the National Association for the Advancement of Colored People and the countywide Colored Citizen's Association. The flyer called attention to school conditions and was distributed throughout the county and to the press.[14]

John V. Horner wrote in *The Sunday Star* of 28 May 1950 that the shortage of classrooms in rapidly-growing post-war Fairfax County was estimated at 90 and the projected needs for the estimated school population as of September 1951 would be 600. At the time of writing, Fairfax had little more than half that number, and more than 10 percent of those were substandard: classes were being held in leaky quonset huts, church rooms, lodge halls, and even furnace rooms. The proposed bond issue referendum set for 31 May 1950 not only had the opposition of the pay-as-you-go advocates, but also faced threats of loss of population if the pending annexation suits of Alexandria and Falls Church proved

12. Ibid., pp. 8, 9.

13. Adelaide Neiley in *Fairfax Schools Bulletin*, (Fairfax, Va.: Fairfax County Public Schools, 1975), 12(3):3; Annual Report to the State Department of Education, 1945.

14. Dr. E. B. Henderson, *The History of the Fairfax County Branch of the NAACP*, (Fairfax County Branch, National Assoication for the Advancement of Colored People, 1965) (hereinafter cited as Henderson, *NAACP*).

Our Disgrace and Shame
School Facilities for Negro Children in
Fairfax County

WHITE SCHOOLS	NEGRO SCHOOLS

WHITE SCHOOLS

1. All brick or stone, except 4 wooden buildings
2. Have running water, janitorial service, inside toilets, central heating
3. Children ride in heated busses.

NEGRO SCHOOLS

1. One to three room wooden buildings
2. All have outside "pit" toilets for teachers and children, no running water; all stoves in the rooms
3. No janitorial service—Teachers do all cleaning, haul water, make fires
4. Three schools have no water on premises
5. Some children walk from 4 to 6 miles to school
6. Buses are old and rickety and are not heated.

HOW SCHOOL FUNDS ARE SHARED

In 1935 the School Board sought a grant of $153,022.50 from PWA and a bond issue (which was defeated) to raise $187,027.50. Of this total of $340,050.00 it was proposed to spend for:

White Schools ....$330,750—97.4 per cent
Colored Schools .... 9,000— 2.6 percent

In 1935 this county owed the State Literary Fund $188,739.32 (all of which had been spent on white schools). In that year the colored population of the country was 19 percent.

The 1945-46 PROPOSED budget provided among other items:

FOR WHITE SCHOOLS	FOR COLORED SCHOOLS
Administration $18,380	0
Operation of School Plant 80,350	?
(Salary of janitor, light, telephone and fuel)	
Capital Outlay $745,000	$45,000

The following proposed expenditures of a proposed loan from the State Literary Fund were approved:

WHITE SCHOOLS	COLORED SCHOOLS
$50,000 for Herndon High School	0
$40,000 for 2 classrooms, wash room and cafeteria at Vienna	0
$20,000 for 2 classrooms at Lincolnia	0
$10,000 to complete 2 classrooms at Groveton	0
$40,000 additional was secured to add elementary rooms to Madison School	

(Excerpt from E.B. Henderson, NAACP)

successful. Falls Church became a city of the second class in 1948 and thus a separate political entity and taxation unit responsible for its own school system. The two cities were nibbling away at the more urban and heavily populated portions of the county to add to their own tax revenues. However, the $10,500,000 school bond issue was approved by a more than two to one vote.[15]

Improvement of schools for the black children of Fairfax County was one of the goals of the Fairfax County Branch of the National Association for the Advancement of Colored People. This goal was shared by the Fairfax County Citizens Association, the Countywide Citizens Association, the League of Women Voters, and other organizations and individuals. An interracial committee was formed to work with citizens and the school administration for a black high school within the county. At this time black children of high school age were either being bussed to a regional industrial high school at Manassas or attending District of Columbia high schools. Luther P. Jackson High School was completed in Merrifield in 1954, named after a native of Kentucky who was an admired member of the Virginia State College faculty for nearly three decades and had made "valuable contributions to the history of Virginia blacks." The successful interracial committee was composed of the following members: Mrs. Hannah Keith Rowe, Barrett Pozer, the Rev. Mr. Horace Lukens, Lawrence Kiefer, Mrs. Eleanor K. Morrow, Mark O'Sullivan, Dr. Nelson Podolnick, Stuart DeBell, John A.K. Donovan, the Rev. Mr. Wallace E. Costner, the Rev. Mr. Milton Sheppard, Clayton Frye, J. Sidney Holland, Ollie Tinner, Allen Saunders, Mrs. Sadie Harris, Eugene Rogers, William A. West and E.B. Henderson.[16]

The School Population Explosion

The decade of 1951-1961 was one of more children, classroom shortages, bond referendums, school construction, and expanded school curriculum in the pursuit of excellence in public school education. The pupil membership in the 1951-52 academic year had been 17,680; in 1960-61, 59,870, an increase of 238 percent. The number of school buildings had increased from 42 to 93. In addition to the 31 May 1950 bond issue, three others were passed in February 1953, November 1955, and May 1960 for a grand total of $69,500,000 bonded indebtedness for schools. The willingness of county voters to assess themselves to this extent attracted widespread attention. The National Broadcasting Company, NBC, chose the county to serve as an example of county-

15. Woodson, *Three Decades,* pp. 8-11.
16. Henderson, *NAACP,* p. 7; Dabney, *Virginia,* p. 504.

financed school expansion in a series of ten broadcasts on matters regarding the nation's public schools in November 1955. Stuart Finley of Lake Barcroft interviewed Warren Quenstedt, chairman of the county's "Save Our Schools" committee, for this television program.[17]

One of the increasing expenses in the annual school budget was the fleet of school buses. In the 1952-53 school year, over 90 school buses were in operation, hauling more than 13,000 pupils approximately 600,000 miles per year. Enrichment programs for educational trips and excursions were also being aided by the use of buses. "An official of the State Department of Education recently announced that the Fairfax County School Board is operating the largest school bus fleet of any school district east of the Mississippi River."[18]

The United States Supreme Court Decision and "Massive Resistance"

This 1951-1961 period was an especially difficult one because of racial integration ordered by the United States Supreme Court decision of 17 May 1954 which outlawed segregation in the public schools. The effect was felt far beyond the classroom walls, for it caused a mass migration of whites to the suburbs from cities such as Washington, D.C., which had large black populations.

Virginia's newly installed Governor Thomas B. Stanley at first received the news of the Supreme Court decision calmly and invited the views of both races in order to solve problems created by the court decision. But within the week, Stanley had invited black leaders to his office to urge them to continue to observe segregation and ignore the ruling. This was unacceptable to the black leaders. Stanley said publicly, "I shall use every legal means at my command to continue segregated schools in Virginia."[19]

In contrast to Fairfax County's conciliatory atmosphere, some other Virginia counties encouraged the governor in his resistance to desegregation. A new organization of white segregationists was formed in Prince Edward County, Virginia, whose school board was one of the five defendants in the Supreme Court's segregation cases. The new organization was named "Defenders of State Sovereignty and Individual Liberties" and within two years there were 60 local chapters throughout the state with a total membership of approximately 12,000.[20] As Robert

---

17. *Bulletin of the Federation of Citizens Associations,* 17 November 1955 (hereinafter cited as FCA *Bulletin*); Woodson, *Three Decades*, p. 10.

18. Fairfax County School Board, *Growing Up in Schools* (Fairfax: The Virginia Press, 1953), p. 43.

19. Dabney, *Virginia*, p. 531; U.S. Supreme Court Decision, 17 May 1954; Brown v. Board of Education, of Topeka 349 U.S. 294, 75 S.Ct. 753 (1955).

20. Robbins L. Gates, *The Making of Massive Resistance* (Chapel Hill: University of North Carolina Press, 1964), p. 36 (hereinafter cited as Gates, *Massive Resistance*); Dabney, *Virginia*, p. 532.

Whitehead, a lawyer and member of the House of Delegates from Nelson and Amherst counties observed "the progeny of the southern white man's illegitimate sons and daughters were now giving the southern white man fits in the courts."[21]

The governor appointed a commission to explore legal means of circumventing the Supreme Court ruling, and Garland Gray, a staunch segregationist from Sussex County and an influential state senator, was named chairman. Although Democrat Armistead Boothe of Alexandria, Republican Ted Dalton of Radford, and the Virginia Council of Churches urged the selection of a biracial commission, it was actually composed exclusively of white state legislators. After one public hearing and a year of deliberation, the Gray commission revealed its plan on 11 November 1955. The proposal included local option for integration of races in schools, a state-administered pupil assignment plan, and tuition grants from public funds for attendance at private schools or at public schools in other jurisdictions. The Gray commission requested the calling of a special session of the Virginia General Assembly to consider the holding of a special referendum on a constitutional convention. This session convened on 30 November 1955 and delegate John C. Webb from Fairfax County and Falls Church emerged as the unofficial spokesman for a group of Northern Virginia legislators who had reservations on the bill or on tuition grants as a whole.

A referendum was held on 9 January 1956 at which voters approved the holding of a limited constitutional convention to amend Section 141 for the legalization of tuition grants. The blacks of the state had voted almost solidly against the referendum. 'Dr. E.B. Henderson of Falls Church, vice-president of the Virginia State Conference of the NAACP, reported that 2,071 Negroes in nine northern Virginia counties readily signed a statement opposing all forms of segregation in public life. He said that less than one percent of those asked refused to sign." A Society for the Preservation of the Public Schools had been formed, headed by State Senator Armistead Boothe of Alexandria; many clergymen and labor leaders also opposed the proposed constitutional amendment. The only widely circulated Virginia newspaper which espoused the liberal cause was the Norfolk *Virginian-Pilot*, Lenoir Chambers, editor.[22]

The constitutional convention met on 5 March 1956 and voted unanimously to legalize tuition grants. It was from Senator Harry F. Byrd's statement that "massive resistance is the best course for us to take" that the movement took its name. Governor Stanley summoned the Virginia General Assembly into special session on 27 August 1956 and presented the "Stanley Plan" which included a requirement for the

---

21. Gates, *Massive Resistance*, p. 150.
22. Gates, *Massive Resistance*, p. 71; Dabney, *Virginia*, pp. 532-33.

580   Fairfax County, Virginia—1925-1976

governor to close any school under court order to integrate, and to cut off state funds from any school which tried to open in compliance with the court order. Without state funds, a locality could either try to operate integrated schools with its own funds or close the schools and provide tuition grants where private schools were available. No black student entered a white school in Virginia during the 1956-57 session. Stanley stepped down as governor in January 1957; J. Lindsay Almond took office.[23]

On 30 July 1956, delegate Kathryn H. Stone of Arlington had been interviewed by academician Dr. Robbins L. Gates and had stated that since "academic arguments did not seem to change anyone's mind, she placed great reliance in the ability of church leaders to effect a slow but sure change in attitudes."[24]

The Fairfax County Council on Human Relations was the first group in northern Virginia to affiliate with the Virginia Human Relations Council and their organizational meeting, moderated by C. Douglas Adams, Jr., of Annandale, was held on 4 March 1957. The Rev. Dr. John H. Marion, executive director of the Virginia council, was speaker. The biracial executive board included laymen and laywomen, as well as ministers: Carl Auvil, Sleepy Hollow; the Rev. Mr. Hubert Beckwith, Annandale; Harry Gertwagen, Weyanoke; Leland Hayden, Woodburn; Edith Hussey, Tauxemont; Edwin Lynch and Louise Palmer, Burke; Helen Platt, Chesterbrook; David H. Scull and Father Thomas P. Scannell, Annandale; and the Rev. Mr. Milton Shepherd, Mount Pleasant. At a meeting on 2 May, officers were elected: Rev. Hubert Beckwith, president; Rev. W. E. Costner, Edwin Lynch and David Scull, vice-presidents; Mrs. Albert Hussey, secretary; and Harry Gertwagen, treasurer. A set of purposes and principles had been adopted in January 1957 by the organizing committee:

> The Fairfax County Council on Human Relations is a democratic association of people who share the concern that those of different races, colors and creeds and other conditions of life should come to a better understanding of one another, based on a respect for the inherent worth and dignity of every individual. We believe, unequivocally, that every individual possesses the inalienable right as confirmed by the Bill of Rights in our Constitution, to equal opportunity for the fullest development and use of his capacities. We recognize that legislation to safeguard this right can be fully effective only in an atmosphere of mutual understanding, trust and respect. . . .[25]

23. Dabney, *Virginia*, p. 536.
24. Gates, *Massive Resistance*, pp. 145-47.
25. *Fairfax County Sun-Echo* (Falls Church, Va.: 7 March 1957), *Congregational Christian Church of Fairfax County Newsletter* (Annandale, Va., 13 February 1957).

In this declaration, the Bill of Rights, patterned after the Virginia Bill of Rights by George Mason of Gunston Hall, a large slaveowner, was cited as a guarantee of human rights for all, including blacks.

In August of 1958, a statement by and names of forty-nine ministers of Fairfax County and Falls Church appeared in several newspapers expressing opposition to enforced segregation in the schools on the basis of race, as well as all efforts to provide substitutes for the public school system.[26]

All efforts to circumvent the United States Supreme Court ruling of 1954 were nullified by the decision of the Virginia Supreme Court of Appeals on 19 January 1959 which outlawed school closing and ordered that the state must support public free schools, including those which were integrated. The Massive Resistance movement ended. The Defenders of State Sovereignty and Individual Liberties eventually became the organization called "Let Freedom Ring" (still listed in the Arlington, Virginia, telephone directory). As Mrs. Robert (Minerva) Andrews, 1958-59 president of the League of Women Voters of Fairfax County stated, "that whole period was so completely dominated by the fight to save the school system that everything else pales in comparison."[27]

Educational Expansion

Many new services were offered during the decade 1951-61 by the Fairfax County school system. Homebound teachers, helping teachers in art, music, reading, speech, science, foreign languages, and psychological services provided expansion in the overall program. The Belle Willard School constructed in 1957 served the orthopedically handicapped children in grades 1-8, and opened up new opportunities for exceptional children. A study of the school organizational structure was conducted by representatives of many county organizations in cooperation with the school board and staff. The decision to reorganize the grade division from 7-5 to 6-2-4 was implemented in 1960-61 with the opening of nine new 1,000-student-capacity intermediate schools for grades 7 and 8. The ungraded organization for the elementary level was introduced in several schools to try a system of learning without traditional grade level identifications.

What had the decade's phenomenal growth in school population meant to pupils and their families? As new schools were built closer to the students' residences, redistricting took place, so that during the

26. *Northern Virginia Sun* (Arlington, Va.), 22 August 1958; *Washington Post and Times Herald* (Washington, D.C.), 23 August 1958; *Evening Star* (Washington, D.C.), 23 August 1958; *Fairfax County Sun-Echo*, 28 August 1958.

27. Dabney, *Virginia*, p. 542; League of Women Voters, *20 Years!*, pp. 2, 10; Harrison v. Day, 200 Va. 439 (19 January 1959).

elementary school period, even if a family remained in the same home, (and this was often *not* the case) the children might attend three to five different elementary schools between their first and seventh grade years. In order to build the necessary classrooms, construction and equipment expenses were cut to the bone and new buildings were often left in seas of mud which needed sodding, paving, and landscaping; empty library shelves needed books, and sun-drenched windows needed curtains. Many of these improvements were provided by the parent-teacher associations which sponsored bake sales, carnivals, and other fund-raisers. In the same time period, new churches were being planned and built; citizens associations, the League of Women Voters, and many other organizations were holding regular and special meetings and it soon became a rare experience for active community participants to be at home in the evening. One PTA, Braddock Elementary, took advantage of the situation and in 1960 printed up tickets to "A Night of Peace." Families purchasing the tickets were entitled to spend one evening at home: no meetings. The tickets sold well enough to raise the necessary funds for the year's PTA budget.[28]

W. T. Woodson retired in 1961 after thirty-six years of service in the Fairfax County school system, thirty-two of them as top administrator. He had shown himself to be a man who could change with the times, who could work productively with a multiplicity of situations and people. He looked back on a period of tremendous growth and change in the county's school system, and his own participation, at the state level, in commissions on vocational guidance programs, standards for school buses, and visiting teachers programs. During his tenure the value of school property had risen from $707,000 to $72,116,602; the number of school buildings from 65 to 92, most of them greatly increased in size; the number of students had grown from 4,782 to 59,870, a 1,100 percent increase. The average annual salary of all teachers had increased from $834.85 to $5,416; the superintendent's salary had become $11,160; the figure had been $1,555 in 1929. Instead of the 11 school vehicles ("trucks or wagons" of 1929), the county was operating 253 buses in 1961.[29]

The taxpayers of the county had been heavily involved with the school system, not only in the approval of several bond issues, but in the large proportion of annual expenditures on schools. The tax dilemma of Fairfax County was well illustrated by the county's 1957 fiscal summary pie charts: all real estate and personal property taxes collected by the county represented 62.9 percent of total revenues; the school system represented 63 percent of total expenditures.[30]

28. Woodson, *Three Decades*, pp. 10-14; Interview, Jane Willey Hustvedt, Annandale, Va., 12 December 1975.

29. Woodson, *Three Decades*, pp. 10-14.

30. Hinkle, *Fairfax Newsletter*, 26 October 1957.

School Crossing Guards. Most of the members of the group which was active in 1969, the year the county successfully defended itself against Alexandria's annexation suit. Fairfax County Police Department.

E.C. Funderburk succeeded Woodson in 1961. He was a graduate of the University of North Carolina and had been school superintendent in three different systems in that state before coming to Fairfax. When Funderburk stepped down at the end of the 1968-69 school year, after eight years of service, there were 102,000 students in the Fairfax County public schools. The average teacher's salary had risen from $5,600 to $9,000 per year, and the average per-pupil cost had risen from $384 to $689. The operating budget rose from $24.6 million to $79.5 million. The taxpayers had approved three bond issues: May 1963, $29.9 million; November 1965, $58.5 million; and May 1968, $67 million—a total of $155.4 million of bonded indebtedness for financing schools. Four major programs had been implemented: Head Start, as soon as it had been authorized by Congress in 1965; the first formal agreement between the school administration and the teachers' professional organization, the Fairfax Education Association; the institution of public school kindergarten in 1968-69, adding 8,076 pupils in the first year; and in 1968-69, decentralization of the school administration into four areas. In addition, in 1965, important policy decisions had been made to implement full racial integration of the students and school staffs throughout the system.

The population growth by both natural increase and immigration
was such during the 1960s that a report for 1962-63 stated that one and
one-fourth classrooms were being built each day, and the annual report
for 1967-68 revealed that 413 *new* teaching stations had been established
that school year.[31]

Dr. Lawrence M. Watts succeeded Funderburk in 1969. A native of
Dodge City, Kansas, he had earned degrees at the University of Denver,
the University of Colorado, and at Harvard University. He came to
Fairfax from an upstate New York school district superintendency. The
administration was brief due to his death in June 1970, but he did initiate
a massive staff reevaluation which resulted not only in transfers but also
in new programs for teacher training and development. He organized a
"charette" so that citizens of the Groveton area could meet, discuss, and
assist with the design of the new Groveton High School, which opened in
September 1976. He was influential in the designs of Chantilly and Lake
Braddock secondary schools, both of which opened in September 1973.[32]

A nationwide search for a replacement for Dr. Watts resulted in the
promotion of a man who had been on Fairfax County's school staff since
1963: Dr. S. John Davis, born in Backlick, Pennsylvania, earned degrees
from Indiana University of Pennsylvania, and George Washington and
American universities of Washington, D.C. He was a science teacher and
for five years had directed Flint Hill Preparatory School in Oakton.
When he assumed his new and complex duties as superintendent, the
student population was 133,362, 28.9 percent over the 1965 figure of
94,802.[33]

The 100th anniversary of the state's public free education program
in Fairfax County was being observed as Dr. Davis assumed his new
responsibilities. The school board had established a centennial committee
in 1969 to plan for the observance and had appointed former superintendent Woodson and former school board member Mrs. John E.
Onesty cochairmen. Their first priority was "to establish a school
museum in a restored and refurbished building centrally located and
under constant surveillance to prevent vandalism." Legato, a little one-
room school which had been built in 1877 and closed in 1930 because
of consolidation, was selected, purchased, and moved from its original
location across from Legato Road on Route 29-211 to the east parking lot

31. Fairfax County School-Community Relations Office: Earl C. Funderburk biography; Department
of Instruction, *A Guide to Intergroup Education* (Fairfax: Fairfax County School Board, 1965); *Fairfax
County Sun-Echo*, 30 November 1964; *Alexandria Gazette*, 10 January 1969.

32. Fairfax County School-Community Relations Office: Dr. Lawrence Watts biography; *Reston
Times*, 18 June 1970.

33. Fairfax County School-Community Relations Office: Dr. S. John Davis biography; *Washington
Post*, 26 March 1975; *Fairfax Journal*, 10 July 1975; *Northern Virginia Sun*, 12 May 1975.

Terraset Elementary School, Reston, opened in 1977. The architects of this innovative underground educational building received a national design award for their concept integrating educational, conservation, and ecological goals. The solar energy collectors were funded by Saudi Arabia. Fairfax County School Board.

of the county office building complex on Route 123. There it is to be restored as a museum, with landscaping to approximate its original appearance.[34]

In the fall of 1975, student population climbed to 136,944, only a 2.6 percent increase over the 1970 figure. While two bond issues passed, one in May 1972 and the other in June 1973 for a total of $79,150,000, two others, one in November 1974 and the other in June 1975, were rejected by the voters. Not only was the growth of population slowing down, but its composition was changing. The eastern part of the county, that closest to Washington, D.C., was now densely settled with a combination of older families whose children had completed their years in the public school system, and young "singles" or couples who had no children. Whereas in the 1930s, the rural element in the western part of the county was feeling the impact of the new suburbanites' demand for services, particularly schools, resulting in increased taxation, now, the older, more settled population in the eastern portion was going to the polls and voting down bond issues which would benefit the expanding

34. Tony P. Wrenn, Virginia B. Peters and Edith Moore Sprouse eds., *Legato School: A Centennial Souvenir* (Fairfax, Va.: Fairfax County History Commission, January 1976), pp. 3, 67-73.

western part of the county, particularly the "new town" of Reston with its large school-age population. The two bond issues, one for $60,000,000 in November 1974, and the other for $46,320,000 in June 1975, were rejected at the polls. "I suppose we failed to pass the June bond issue for the same reasons the November referendum failed. We failed to change enough minds, the size of the referendum was too much for some people, and the economic uncertainty continues."[35] A scaled-down school referendum passed in 1976.

The school board, under the chairmanship of Mary Ann Lecos, faced new problems in its primary function of developing policies in written statements of intent which could guide operation of the school program. Appointed by the elected Board of County Supervisors, the school board shared with its chief executive officer, Superintendent Davis, the concern that the very size of the system (by 1976 the nation's twelfth largest) tended to dehumanize the individual student and teacher.[36]

". . . within a day's ride . . ." .

World War II and the Korean conflict drew thousands of new residents to Fairfax County, as they came first for employment connected with war efforts, and then to settle permanently. The speed and size of this growth overwhelmed many of the county's public facilities and services. In the case of higher education, however, these newcomers created almost overnight a demand which might otherwise have been postponed at least another decade. Seeking advanced education for increased competence in their current or prospective employment, or college-level training without leaving their home areas, these people provided one of the county's most important resources, namely: a highly trained and competent citizen population with an interest in community affairs.

In 1950 Northern Virginians who sought college or professional education had to go to Washington, where five major universities and numerous professional schools were located. With facilities which had not been renewed or expanded because of wartime shortages, these schools stretched to accommodate the increased enrollment. It was clear, however, that in the total scheme of regional development, Northern

---

35. David W. Sheatsley, comp. *Fairfax County Profile* (Fairfax, Va.: Office of Research and Statistics, 1976), p. 23; Fairfax County School Board Referendum, 12 June 1973; quotation from Mary Ann Lecos, Chairman, Fairfax County School Board, Dick Hogan, *Northern Virginia Sun*, 11 June 1975.

36. Fairfax County, Virginia, Public Schools, 1975-1976, *Information for Parents*; S. John Davis, "Humanizing the system pays dividends," *Fairfax Schools Bulletin* (Fairfax, Va.: Department of School-Community Relations, June 1975), 2(10):1.

Virginia needed its own facilities for higher education. In the 1960s this resulted in the establishment of two new institutions in Fairfax County: George Mason University and Northern Virginia Community College, a two-year college which in a short time grew to offer a wide range of courses in five branches throughout Northern Virginia.

George Mason University

George Mason University began in 1950 as an extension division of the University of Virginia in Charlottesville. Profesor J.N.G. Finley was selected as the first director of the Northern Virginia Center, to provide higher educational opportunities for a region in which one-eighth of the state's population lived. Finley graduated from Johns Hopkins University in 1926, and did graduate work at the University of Virginia and at Cambridge in England. He received a law degree from Drexel Institute.

Recruiting a faculty was one of the easier tasks confronting Finley. Some faculty members from other universities in the Washington area taught at the extension; many were former professors who had entered government service at the federal or local level, and private industry as well.

Six extension courses were offered in February 1950, and 63 men and women were enrolled. Because high school classrooms were being used, there were no daytime classes at first. In only two years, registration had reached 500. By 1955, more than 1,900 students were registered for 90 different classes.

Planning for expansion entered a new phase after the Virginia Advisory Legislative Council announced in September 1955 that it would recommend authorization of a community college under the direction of the University of Virginia, in the Northern Virginia area. Endorsement of the facility was given by many of the area's community organizations, including the Northern Virginia Regional Planning and Economic Development Commission, the Fairfax County Federation of Citizens Associations, the Council of PTAs and individual PTA groups, Chambers of Commerce, the Board of Supervisors and others. In Thomas Jefferson's 1817 plan for nine area colleges, he had proposed that one should be located in the northern part of the state, "within a day's ride" of the homes of the people it was to serve. Northern Virginia was finally implementing his plan.[37]

The University of Virginia's Board of Visitors authorized the establishment of a coeducational two-year branch college to supplement the extension program. It opened in the renovated 44-year-old Baileys Crossroads Elementary School in 1957 with an enrollment of 17 students.

---

37. William H. Wranek, Jr., "The University Extension Center," *The Commonwealth Magazine* (Richmond, Va.: Virginia State Chamber of Commerce, November 1955).

Professor Finley was the director and ran both George Mason College and the extension.[38]

The search for a permanent site was conducted, and one after another, the Chiles tract (Merrifield), Ravensworth (Springfield), Maplewood (Tysons Corner), and Sunset Hills (Herndon) were rejected. Finally, the offer by Mayor John C. Wood and the Town of Fairfax of 150 acres on Route 123 south of the town limits was accepted. It was named after the Virginia statesman and Fairfax countian, George Mason, in 1959, and was designated a community college of the university.[39]

The institution developed rapidly after the first four buildings opened in 1964. It was elevated to a four-year, degree-granting institution by the Virginia General Assembly in 1966, and given a long-range mandate to expand into a major university. Graduate programs began in 1970, the same year the College Board of Control in northern Virginia acquired an additional 422 acres of land, making a total of 572 acres available for future development. The former Fairfax High School property, now North Campus, was purchased in January 1972. The branch became an independent institution, George Mason University, by an Act of the General Assembly effective 1 March 1972. Dr. Lorin A. Thompson, who had served as chancellor and then president following Professor Finley's administration, retired in June 1973 and was succeeded by Dr. Vergil H. Dykstra. In the 1974 fall semester, 6,134 students were registered, 65 percent of whom were residents of Fairfax County and City, and Falls Church. The largest age group (42.6 percent) was twenty-five years of age and over. The enrollment by fall 1975 was 8,000. Many of the students are teachers earning graduate degrees or complying with their teaching certification requirements.[40]

Northern Virginia Community College

When legislative studies revealed that Virginia had the lowest percentage of college age population in all the states with the exception of South Carolina, the General Assembly created a study commission in 1962 to determine the reasons. The expansion which the commission recommended resulted in the passage by the Virginia General Assembly in 1964 of an Act establishing the Department of Technical Education and a State Board for Technical Education.

The Northern Virginia Technical College was opened in a hastily converted rented warehouse at Baileys Crossroads in September 1965. In just 100 days, its president, Robert L. McKee, had interviewed and hired

38. "History of George Mason University," *George Mason University Catalog, 1973; Globe Newspapers,* 25 September 1975.

39. Hinkle, *Fairfax Newsletter,* 25 January 1958; George Mason University Catalog, 1973.

40. *George Mason University Catalog, 1973; George Mason University Institutional Analysis Report,* 1975.

qualified faculty and staff, established a curriculum, scheduled classes, obtained books, notified prospective students, and enrolled them in scheduled classes. The first board chairman of the college, Dr. Bernard Joy, predicted that within ten years the students would number ten times the initial enrollment of approximately 700. Actually, the enrollment grew 30 times the initial enrollment to a total of 20,854 in spring 1975, and to 27,198 in fall 1975.

A multicampus master plan was developed for five separate campuses in Northern Virginia. Local jurisdictions served by the college provided funds for the purchase of the five sites and partial funding for construction of some of the buildings, the first of which was completed in 1967 on the Annandale campus.

Dr. Richard J. Ernst was appointed president of the college by the Board of Northern Virginia Community College in September 1968. Northern Virginia was the first member of the community college system in the commonwealth to receive full accreditation by the Southern Association. It was granted in December 1968.

The Northern Virginia Education Television Association occupied the specially equipped fifth building which was completed on the Annandale Campus in 1970, and in addition to offering a new broadcast engineering technology program for NVCC, they began beaming color programming to the secondary schools in Northern Virginia and operating a new public television station, channel 53. During the 1969-70 academic year, 10,913 students registered for credit courses, and approximately 4,000 persons took advantage of adult education and community service programs. The very next year, 1970-71, 14,564 students registered for noncredit courses, making NVCC the fourth largest institution of higher learning in Virginia. In that year, plans were finalized for the five different Northern Virginia campuses: Annandale, Alexandria, Loudoun, Manassas, and Woodbridge.

During 1971-72, the Consortium for Continuing Higher Education in Northern Virginia was established with George Mason University, the Northern Virginia Community College, the University of Virginia Extension, and the Virginia Polytechnic Institute and State University, and later, Marymount College, as members. This plan was designed to give new mobility for students, and to coordinate quality programs with maximum transferability of credits.

The growth in college enrollment increased in a manner similar to the public school enrollment patterns in Fairfax County during the 1950s and 1960s. The students, many of whom had for a time left the formal academic scene, were swelling the institution enrollment to a standing of third largest in the state in 1972-73. The Mitre Corporation of McLean selected NVCC as a site for testing new computer-assisted instructional systems, symbolic of rapidly advancing technology.

The fall semester in 1975 saw an enrollment of 27,198 students, the largest number of students ever recorded in the history of higher education in Virginia in either two- or four-year institutions, a ranking which was maintained through spring, 1976. The mean age of the students was 27.7 years in fall 1975.

The wide range of programs offered is exemplified by such courses as animal science technology, automotive body reconditioning, banking and financial management, environmental technology, history, principles of real estate, sociology, waste water treatment, and welding.[41]

Luther Rice College

Founded in 1966, Luther Rice College was established in the educational wing of the Franconia Baptist Church with 87 students. The college was named after a Baptist missionary who was born in 1783. Members of the Board of Directors are Baptists, and the institution's motto is "Learning with a Christian purpose." It had an enrollment of 162 students in the 1975-76 academic year.[42]

---

41. Northern Virginia Community College, *A Decade of Service 1974-1975*, (Annandale, Va.: NVCC Office of Planning Research and Management Services, 19 July 1976), pp. 2-9.

42. Interview, Dr. K. Bruce Miller, President, Luther Rice College, 19 July 1976.

IV

Transportation: Rails, Roads, and Wings

The facility which has of late years been afforded by the improvements of roads and competition of stage coaches, for the personal intercourse of individuals residing at different parts of the kingdom, has contributed much to lessen, if not utterly to abolish, those distinctions and provincial peculiarities which might, under less favorable circumstances, be well-supposed to exist in this remote part of the country. By frequent peregrinations of the natives and the continual ingress of strangers, on commercial or scientific pursuits, those local habits which might once have been deemed unconquerable, have almost completely disappeared.[1]

Automobile, Bus, and Truck

During and immediately following World War I, railroads had fallen into disrepair because of labor and materials problems. In the aftermath of war, the popularity of the auto grew by leaps and bounds and with it, the pressure on all levels of government to improve the roads. Far-reaching changes were to come about in rural life as a result of widespread production and purchase of motor vehicles and improvement and hard-surfacing of roads for their use. Buses were to make it possible for rural schools to consolidate, and other vehicles were to be designed as traveling libraries and mobile highway post offices. The high degree of mobility which this new development represented, accompanied by the gradual acceptance of conveniences such as the telephone, radio, electric power, and television were to make obsolete such common traditions as the old-fashioned country doctor (like Alfred Leigh of Colvin Run) who hastily performed operations on farmhouse kitchen tables.[2]

The problem of financing the building of highways in Virginia was solved to a great extent by county bond issues until 1919 when the state highway system was laid out and a large share of road building was assumed by the state, funded by state and federal appropriations. Under

1. *The Gazetteer of the County of Cornwall* (Truro, England: John Heard, 1817), A copy is located in the British Museum, London.
2. John B. Rae, *The American Automobile*, (Chicago: University of Chicago Press, 1965), pp. 196-97; interview with Hassell Leigh.

the act which established the system, the legislature had attempted to link together the most important towns in the state and to utilize the best roads which had been constructed by the counties. The legislature and highway commission selected trunk roads which made long-distance motor travel possible to the far corners of the state and linked up with other states to form an integral part of the national highway system. Counties wishing to assist with building of roads were allowed to place funds with the highway commission for advance building, the funds to be repaid by the state at a future date.[3]

A widespread demand for better highways rose steadily, an outgrowth of the "Good Roads Movement" and a coalition of farm groups, the League of American Wheelmen, engineers, and road builders. No matter what mode of transportation was in use, the cry in Virginia was "Get the farmer out of the mud!" The problem became that of raising additional revenues to finance statewide improvements. Early in 1923, Governor E. Lee Trinkle called a special session of the Virginia Assembly to consider various solutions. He advocated a pay-as-you-go policy by a direct three-cents-a-gallon tax on gasoline until the question of the issuance of state road bonds could be decided by referendum. The legislature had divided the state into eight highway districts the year before, and available funds were to be distributed to the districts in equal shares.[4]

Harry F. Byrd of Winchester, chairman of the roads committee in the Virginia Senate, among others, opposed the bond issue on the grounds that it would encumber the children, grandchildren, and great-grandchildren of the present generation. A heavy rain fell on the day before the referendum in November 1923, but despite its effects which demonstrated the urgent need for road improvement, the voters rejected the bonds and endorsed the pay-as-you-go plan for highway building. The public demanded improved roadways and accepted the increased taxation necessary to accomplish the objective. It was a victory for rural counties like Fairfax because Virginia's cities would have to contribute the lion's share of any gasoline tax levied. Also, many counties, like Fairfax, already had a certain amount of bonded indebtedness of their own.[5]

Henry G. Shirley, who had been Maryland's highway administrator, was appointed head of the State Highway Commission, which was reorganized in 1927 as the Virginia Department of Highways. He served as highway commissioner until his death in 1941.

3. Susie Chilton Palmer, "The Development of Virginia Highways" (master's thesis, University of Virginia, Charlottesville, 1930), p. 39 (hereinafter cited as Palmer, "Virginia Highways"); Acts of Assembly, 1918, ch. 10, p.9.

4. Albert W. Coates, Jr., . . . the most convenient wayes . . . (Richmond: The Virginia Department of Highways, 1972), p. 17 (hereinafter cited as Coates, wayes).

5. Palmer, "Virginia Highways," p. 45.

On the national level, at the request of the American Association of State Highway Officials, the Secretary of Agriculture appointed a committee in 1925 to select and designate a comprehensive system of through routes and uniform signing throughout the country. Virginia was also moving toward the establishment of a new major transportation system: "The year 1925 was marked by great strides in highway construction and Virginia's highway system was emerging from the mud. . . . The voice of the people of Virginia, however, was still raising the cry for more roads and better roads. . . ."[6]

The first gasoline tax had been levied by Oregon in 1919 and was quickly adopted by other states. It was considered the fairest tax devised for road purposes because the amount of gasoline consumed is relative to distance traveled and traveling conditions, placing the burden directly and proportionately on those who use the roads. At the national level, a gasoline tax approved by Congress was later to become the principal revenue source for the federally-aided highway program as well.[7]

The Fairfax County Board of Supervisors was giving a large portion of its attention at monthly meetings to road matters. Most of the business involved paying warrants to people who had done road work in the highway districts. In February 1926, a request was made to the state for the incorporation into the highway system of a section of road from Gum Springs to Mount Vernon "as this road is heavily traveled by a tremendous number of high class tourists each year and the necessity for its proper maintenance is great."[8]

In a 1928 chamber of commerce publication, the network of transportation lines through Fairfax County was described in glowing detail. Eleven transportation companies with thirteen separate lines were serving the county with steam and electric rail facilities and bus service. "Of the 34 communities and points shown on county maps, 25 are connected by improved, hard-surfaced roads with Washington and Alexandria; 7 are junction points for two hard-surfaced roads, and 3 are junction points for three or more hard-surfaced roads. Railroads serve 22 of the 34 points; 3 have two railroads, 8 have both railroads and hard-surfaced highways. Busses run through 18 of the 34 points, on regular schedules, and in most cases affording frequent service." The booklet's forty-three advertisers with Alexandria addresses far exceeded in both number of ads and space purchased the eighteen advertisers from Falls Church, the seventeen from Fairfax and the eleven from Washington, D.C. Although the transportation systems were drawing shoppers and

6. Coates, wayes, p. 17; The Virginia Road Builder, (Richmond: Virginia Department of Highways, Sept.-Oct. 1955), 11(3).

7. Palmer, "Virginia Highways," pp. 39-45; Coates, wayes, p. 17.

8. BOSMB, No. 5, p. 148.

commuters into Washington, D.C., in increasing numbers, Alexandria was still making a strong bid for county business.[9]

The chamber of commerce publication concluded with a prediction: "to a large extent, the future of Fairfax County is written in the future of the United States and its National Capital. . . . There can be no question that the Nation's Capital will grow in population and size as the United States increases in wealth, population and world-importance. As the southwestern arc of Greater Washington, Fairfax County is destined to develop into one of Washington's most charming environs."[10]

Getting the Farmer Out of the Mud: The Byrd Road Act

By 1930, 386,664 motor vehicles were registered in Virginia alone; they produced license tax revenues of $6,564,000. Gasoline tax in that year produced $7,251,000 throughout the state. The motor vehicle registration had more than doubled the 1920 figure of 145,340. In 1931, Fairfax County registered 2,656 motor vehicles. In addition to the license and gasoline taxes, Virginia used direct appropriation from the legislature, convict labor, and federal aid for the financing of the state road program. This was fine for the major state trunk roads, but the counties were still experiencing problems of improving and maintaining the local roads for which they were responsible. Two-thirds of the state's employed population earned their living from the land, and farm-to-market roads were vital to producing income. This was especially true since by this time, the railroads were providing less frequent and often irregular service, distinct detriments when perishables like milk are involved. The Byrd Road Act passed in 1932 offered counties the option of transferring their road building and maintenance responsibilities to the highway commission, incorporating the mileage into the newly established state secondary road system. Although this meant relinquishing a one-cent county gasoline tax, it also would effect a reduction in the local tax burden and increased efficiency in use of the highway appropriation. Fairfax County voters elected to avail themselves of the opportunity, paving the way for accelerated county road building over the next few years.[11]

In August 1939, roads commissioner Shirley reported, "Practically all horse-drawn equipment has vanished from the highways, and motor equipment has taken its place, requiring a road that can be travelled the

9. Fairfax County Chamber of Commerce, *Historic, Progressive Fairfax County in Old Virginia* (Alexandria: Newell-Cole Co., Inc., 1928) pp. 34-35.

10. Ibid., pp. 44-45.

11. Coates, *wayes*, p. 18; *in Proceedings of the Fourth Annual Virginia Highway Conference* (Lexington, Va.), Address by U.S. Senator Harry F. Byrd; BOSMB No. 6, pp. 260-261; Acts of Assembly, 1932, ch.415, pp. 872-80

Shirley Highway paving proceeds on the main artery in 1948. Virginia Department of Highways and Transportation.

year-round." The number of motor vehicles registered in Virginia had now swelled to 525,877.[12]

Brig. Gen. James A. Anderson began a sixteen-year career as highway commissioner when appointed in 1941. Anderson had taught civil engineering and been dean of the faculty at Virginia Military Institute in Lexington. He had lived in Northern Virginia as a boy and later described the early twentieth-century roads in Northern Virginia as having been "6 feet wide and 9 feet deep," and typical of rural roads throughout the United States of that time. Shortly after his appointment, Anderson had even more serious problems than those of coping with muddy roads, controlling highway speeds, and educating drivers "to the courtesy of the road." The United States became a nation at war with the necessity to move a modern mechanized army, to build new access roads to defense areas, and to keep farm-to-market and industrial thoroughfares open for the defense effort. The rapidly urbanizing Northern Virginia suburbs of Washington, D.C., stimulated active planning for Virginia's first super highway. In 1944, the Federal Aid Highway Act designated a national system of interstate highways "so located as to connect by routes, as direct as practicable, the principal metropolitan areas, cities and industrial centers, to serve the national defense, and to connect at suitable border points with routes of continental importance."[13]

The first two-and-one-half mile section of the Shirley Memorial Highway, from the Pentagon road system to Leesburg Pike (Route 7), was opened to traffic in 1944. It was constructed by the Public Roads

12. Coates, *wayes*, p. 19.

13. *FCFCA Bulletin*, May 1959; Coates, *wayes*, p. 20.

Administration "as a war measure to relieve the extremely heavy transportation of thousands of government employees who work in Washington and live in Arlington and Fairfax Counties." The divided Highway was access controlled and designed for 70-mile-per-hour speed. It was built for $1,268,691. Divided by turfed median strips, with intersecting roads overpassed or underpassed, and landscaped roadsides, the thoroughfare was a fitting memorial to Henry Garnett Shirley, State Highway Commissioner from 1922 to 1941.[14]

The State of Virginia extended Shirley Highway southward to join U.S. 1 at Woodbridge, Prince William County, Virginia, and opened it in 1951. In a short time traffic on Shirley Highway more than doubled from 16,000 vehicles per day to 35,000 per day, the increase attended by serious congestion during peak hours.[15]

French geographer Jean Gottmann described an aspect of the county's and Northern Virginia's plight in his appraisal of the east coast corridor. He coined the word "megalopolis" to describe the "main street" which stretched from New Hampshire to Fairfax County, and made a striking comparison between New York City and the Washington metropolitan area. Although the population of the latter was one-tenth the size of the former, he found that the daily average crossings over the Hudson River from New Jersey to Manhattan during July 1953 were 216,160; this was smaller in volume than the average number of 218,199 crossing over the Potomac from Virginia to Washington in the same period.

It was not until Congress passed the Highway Trust Fund legislation in 1956 that sufficient funding was provided for development of the interstate system, a need sensed by Fairfax Countians for many frustrating years while commuting on choked, inadequate highways to jobs at the Pentagon and in the District of Columbia. The bus systems were inadequate and the routings unresponsive to needs, partly because the population was scattered in many different residential areas. There was a multiplicity of destinations and working schedules.[16]

The Capital Beltway and Interstate 95

Construction of the capital beltway, designated Interstate 495, began in 1958. It was designed to serve as a bypass around Washington,

14. FCFCA *Bulletin*, May 1956; Coates, *wayes*, pp. 20, 22; Federal-Aid Highway Act, 20 December 1944, PL 521, 78th Congress, Second Session; At the time, this modern section of highway represented the most advanced design for combining efficiency with amenities, and controlled access. Ross D. Netherton, *Control of Highway Access*, (Madison, Wis: University of Wisconsin Press, 1963), p. 83.

15. F.W. Cron, *Pentagon Area Transportation Study*, Appendix A (Washington: Bureau of Public Roads, 1960); *Thirty-Seventh Report of the State Highway Commissioner to the Governor of Virginia* (Richmond: Division of Purchase and Printing, 1944), p. 1.

16. Gottmann, *Virginia*, pp. 475, 482; Title II, Federal-Aid Highway Act of 1956, 70 Stat. 374, 29 June 1956.

*Interchange. Just east of Springfield, Interstate 95 meets Interstate 495.
Photo about 1963. Virginia Department of Highways and Transportation.*

D.C., for travelers and as a link between the growing Virginia and Maryland suburbs. In Fairfax County, it served both as a bypass for through traffic and as a distributor for local traffic. The 22-mile Virginia section of the 66-mile circumference stretches from the Cabin John Bridge over the Potomac on the north side to the Woodrow Wilson Bridge at Alexandria on the south side. There are twelve interchanges on the Virginia section. The major ones are located at the George Washington Memorial Parkway, Interstate Route 66, Route 50, Interstate Route 95, and Route 1. Except for uncompleted Interstate Route 66, these are major commuting routes into the central city.

Robert C. Burton of the University of Richmond and Frederick D. Knapp of the University of Virginia began a study in 1958 to determine, over a period of time, the economic and social factors in the vicinity of the Virginia section of the Beltway; that is, the changes in land and real property values, land use, traffic patterns, travel habits, and business activity. The before and after data were collected, prepared, studied, interpreted, and published by the University of Virginia, the Virginia Department of Highways, and the Bureau of Public Roads. The conclusions for the first time show major interaction, other than for through traffic, between the two states. The beltway gave the region a measure of cohesion. Service and distribution centers could now serve the entire metropolitan area. There was some interchange of workers and shoppers. The amount of acreage in industrial uses more than quadrupled between 1958 and 1966. There was a marked increase in the building of multifamily dwelling units in close proximity to the beltway. Because of maximum accessibility, multipurpose areas emerged at places like Tysons Corner (the interchanges of Interstate Route 495, Route 7, and Route 123) where a research park, regional shopping center, and apartment complexes are constantly expanding. The demand for interchange property is indicated by the high land prices paid in interchange areas. In 1966, a daily average of 44,000 vehicles traveled north and south across the county between Cabin John Bridge and the I-95 interchange on the beltway. Most of these trips would not have been made on routes available before the beltway opened. Fairfax County was well on its way to becoming urbanized before the beltway was begun. Nevertheless, the size of an average parcel of land in the vicinity of the beltway fell from 1.5 acres in 1951 to .5 acres in 1964, and during the same period, the average price of improved residential land close to the beltway increased from $1,900 to $16,700 an acre.[17]

An interesting paradox pointed out by Burton and Knapp's study is the number of Maryland commuters (in common parlance, "double-crossers") who cross the Potomac River into Virginia on the beltway and commute to the District of Columbia on Virginia's George Washington Memorial Parkway. They, therefore, cross the river twice in an effort to improve their commuting trip time, adding to the severe peak-hour congestion on the bridges. Another problem, considered dangerous and expensive to solve, is the conflict between the desirability for intensive commercial and residential development of the interchange areas and the ideal engineering function to distribute traffic on and off the beltway efficiently and safely.[18]

Virginia State Highway Commissioner Douglas Fugate wrote of changing highway concepts in 1970 that "it is no longer sufficient to examine highway proposals solely from such standpoints as traffic service, economics, and engineering feasibility. An entirely new range of considerations has developed, and must be accepted by those responsible for the highway program . . . social impact, environmental enhancement . . . pollution . . . mass transportation . . . fresh concepts concerned more with moving people than with moving vehicles. . . . We must

17. Robert C. Burton and Frederick D. Knapp. "Socio-Economic Change in the Vicinity of the Capital Beltway in Virginia," *Highway Research Record Number 75* (Washington, D.C.: Highway Research Board, 1965), p. 32.

18. Bureau of Population and Economic Research, *The Socio-Economic Impact of the Capital Beltway on Northern Virginia*, (Charlottesville, Va.: University of Virginia, 1968), pp. 1, 115-17, 119.

greatly broaden our concepts of the highway's role in an increasingly urban society. . . ." Fairfax County residents had reason to be interested in roads concepts. In 1970 the number of vehicle tags sold was 208,805; by 1975 it had climbed to 322,303.[19]

In the heavily populated northern Virginia suburbs, a special lane of Interstate 95, the old Shirley Highway, was reserved for express buses. Fairfax County, Arlington, and Alexandria commuters were encouraged to leave their cars at home or in fringe parking lots and use the bus to reduce traffic congestion. This idea represented the nation's first experience with setting aside a lane of interstate highway for buses, and the results were impressive. In barely more than three years, more commuters were riding the buses than were driving their personal cars during the morning peak traffic period. The success of the Shirley "busway" led to similar projects in other urban areas.[20] Reston commuters, for example, successfully obtained limited express bus service using the restricted Dulles International Airport access road.

Death of the Railroads

The Washington & Virginia Railway Company, which connected Arlington and Fairfax County with downtown Washington, was the most important suburban railroad operation in the Washington area. One of its lines originated at 12th Street and Pennsylvania Avenue, crossed the Potomac at the Long Bridge, and extended through Alexandria to Mount Vernon. The other extended from Rosslyn through Clarendon and Vienna, to Fairfax, a distance of twenty-one miles, paralleling the Washington & Old Dominion for part of the distance. The company went bankrupt in 1924 due to several years of losses caused by increased use of autos and decrease in passenger business. It was reorganized in 1927, the southern portion becoming the Washington, Alexandria & Mount Vernon, the northern, the Arlington & Fairfax Electric Railway Company. The Washington, Alexandria & Mount Vernon was phased out by the federal government which forced abandonment in 1932 in order to obtain the Washington terminal properties for new buildings. The Arlington and Fairfax operated until 1939, experimenting with rail buses for the last three years of operation. The increasing use of autos and difficulty with regulations eventually caused abandonment of this line. Both lines had been almost entirely passenger carriers, generally operating single cars. Following the Civil War, Virginia roads were in more deplorable condition than most roads in the

19. Douglas B. Fugate, "Changing Highway Concepts," *Traffic Quarterly* (Westport, Conn.: Eno Foundation, April 1970), pp. 165-73; Vehicle Tag Report to Assistant Director of Finance, Fairfax County, Virginia, 1976.

20. Coates, *wayes*, p. 28.

United States at that time. When the Office of Public Roads Inquiries was opened in 1893, its goal was to overcome public apathy and objection to taxation for road purposes by educating the public to the value of good roads. It also was to furnish expertise and sometimes machinery to localities wishing to use scientific and modern methods in their road construction projects. The railroads were anxious to see short-haul roads built to their lines and encouraged the Good Roads Movement. They donated special trains with cars for machinery, and dining and sleeping cars of officials, road experts, and press representatives. They sometimes even provisioned the train and furnished part of the skilled and common labor. Thus, the railroads had an active part in promoting a mode of transportation which later offered them serious competition and, in many cases, caused their demise.[21]

A. Smith Bowman had come to Fairfax County from Kentucky in 1927 and settled his family beside the Washington & Old Dominion Railroad in the neo-Georgian mansion near Herndon which Dr. Max Wiehle, the nineteenth-century new-town dreamer, had built in 1887. Mr. Bowman renamed the Wiehle station Sunset Hills, bought nearly 4,000 acres of the old Wiehle property and began dairy and beef cattle farming on what became the largest farm in Fairfax County. By 1947 Mr. Bowman's holdings in the northwestern end of the county included approximately 7,200 acres. The property lay on either side of the railroad track, facilitating delivery of supplies and shipment of products on the line which once did business under the name of Alexandria, Loudoun & Hampshire.[22]

The very next year after the Bowman family arrived, statements in the chamber of commerce publication concerning the transportation picture and particularly the slant of the ads for the railroads previewed what was to come:"Ten years ago there was not a single mile of modern, improved, hard-surfaced road in Fairfax County. Today, the hard-surfaced road mileage is approximately 160 miles, more than one mile of modern improved road for every three square miles of county area." Advertisements of the two electric railways demonstrated the problems being created by loss of passenger revenue on their lines (although they did not so state) due in large part to the increase of automobile and bus usage. The Mt. Vernon, Alexandria & Washington Railway Company told county residents "to get good service, *support* the Railway," and the Arlington & Fairfax Railway Company (M.E. Church, president) promised that his road could continue to increase land values in Arlington and Fairfax counties "If you are a patron of *Your Railway.*"[23]

21. Mildred L. Barret, "Federal Aid in the Beginning," *Virginia Highway Bulletin* (Richmond, Va.: Virginia Highway Department, January 1948), 14 (3): 4-5; H.H. Harwood, *Rails to the Blue Ridge,* (Falls Church, Va.: Pioneer America Society Inc., 1969) pp. 88-91 (hereinafter cited as Harwood, *Rails*).
22. A. Smith Bowman, Jr., "A History of Sunset Hills Farm," Historical Society *Yearbook,* 6: 36-43.
23. Chamber of Commerce, *Historic, Progressive Fairfax County,* 1928, pp. 35, 38.

The Washington & Old Dominion was one of the few interurbans in the country ever to operate passenger service after the removal of electric facilities and conversion to diesel power. It was built as a steam road in 1858 and was electrified in 1912 while under the joint control of Washington millionaire John R. McLean and Senators Stephen and Davis Elkins, father and son, of West Virginia. Daily commuters from communities including Herndon, Vienna, Dunn Loring, and Falls Church regularly rode back and forth to Rosslyn and Washington. The line was merged with the Great Falls & Old Dominion Railway Company, which had been completed in 1906 as an electric line from Georgetown via the Aqueduct Bridge through Rosslyn to Great Falls, a distance of fourteen miles. The main freight route on the Washington & Old Dominion was from Alexandria to Bluemont, in Loudoun County, a distance of fifty-two miles. As the Virginia suburban area grew, freight and some resort business developed, but eventually the popularity of the automobile and truck brought a decline in rail traffic and the depression of the 1930s forced bankruptcy and reorganization. The Great Falls branch line was abandoned in 1935, and in 1939, the main line was cut back from Bluemont to Purcellville, also in Loudoun County. All passenger service was first discontinued in 1941, at which time the remaining freight service was converted to diesel power. Passenger service was resumed for a time, but then discontinued permanently.[24]

Old Tracks and New Trails

Although limited passenger service was provided during and after World War II, by 31 May 1951 it finally ended, coinciding with the U.S. Post Office Department's decision to award all short-haul mail contracts to truckers. The mail contract, which amounted to $17,000 per year for the W&OD, had raised almost three times the revenue of passenger service in 1950. Davis Elkins, advanced in age, sold the freight line in 1956 to the Chesapeake & Ohio Railroad which acquired it because of Virginia Electric and Power Company's plan to build a coal-fired electric power plant near Leesburg. Coal was a commodity the C&O could supply to the operation. Other projects materialized instead, one of the largest being the supplying of heavy building materials to the Chantilly (Dulles) airport construction effort. The Interstate Route 66 right-of-way acquisition condemnation in 1962 took 2.9 miles of the railroad right-of-way on the north end between Rosslyn and Washington Boulevard in Arlington.

---

24. G.W. Hilton and John F. Due, *The Electric Interurban Railways in America* (Stanford, Ca.: Stanford University Press, 1964), pp. 328-29.

Eventually the railroad's management filed for abandonment of the entire right-of-way. There was an opportunity to go out of business at a profit by selling the right-of-way to the Virginia Department of Highways for additional I-66 mileage. Public hearings began in May 1965. In the next three years the abandonment case became the most controversial and voluminous ever handled by the Interstate Commerce Commission. Finally, the proceedings ended up in federal court in Alexandria which ruled that the railroad was to be abandoned after 8 July 1968. The last two box cars were pulled from the Murphy and Ames Lumber Company siding in Falls Church to the Potomac yards in Alexandria on 27 August.[25]

Throughout this chain of events, one of the country's fastest growing metropolitan areas lost an invaluable potential rapid transit right-of-way at a time when plans were being formulated to build such a system. The Washington & Old Dominion had become a victim of the development it had helped to create. Had it been located almost anywhere else, it might have survived. But in an area of superhighways, highrise office and apartment buildings, and land worth up to $332,000 per acre, a single-track short line with grade-level road crossings was at the time an economic absurdity, and sufficient funds were not immediately available to purchase the right-of-way for rapid transit purposes.[26]

A portion of the W&OD through Falls Church City is now in use as a biking-jogging-hiking trail with Virginia Electric Power Company's permission and cooperation of the city and the Northern Virginia Regional Park Authority. The power company's price for an easement for a permanent trail system, which could run from Purcellville to Rosslyn, is so high that it has prevented the Northern Virginia Regional Park Authority from entering into such an agreement.[27]

Dulles International Airport

First called "Chantilly" after a nearby nineteenth-century plantation and community, this air transport facility was built in 1962 on 12,500 acres, one-third in northwestern Fairfax County and two-thirds (including the terminal building) in Loudoun County. Over 750 parcels of land were involved in the total acquisition This was a new site for the airport, chosen after years of citizen opposition to the establishment of a similar airport on land purchased by the federal government for just that purpose near Burke, Virginia.

The control tower, terminal, and service buildings were designed by architect Eero Saarinen; he also designed the mobile lounges which move

25. Harwood, *Rails*, p., 91.

26. Harwood, *Rails*, pp. 83-91; Fairfax County, Virginia, Deed Book 3095, 14 October 1968, p. 389.

27. Interview, John Davis, Northern Virginia Regional Park Authority, 17 December 1975.

Dulles International Airport, on the Fairfax-Loudoun county line. Architect Eero Saarinen designed the terminal which was completed in 1962. British Airways and Air France began regular Concorde service there on 24 May 1976. Photo by Bernie Boston.

passengers to and from planes and allow for an efficient utilization of the terminal building. Landscaping was designed by Dan Kiley. Before his death in 1961, Saarinen visited the airport then under construction and expressed the opinion that it was the best thing he had done. His plan was to convey the purpose of the jet airport for the nation's capital through architectural design. The excitement of travel and significance of belonging to the federal city were expressed in the entire composition of the terminal, runways, road system, parking lot, and landscaping.

The airport was dedicated by President John F. Kennedy in 1962 and named after former Secretary of State (under Eisenhower) John Foster Dulles. It is one of two operated in the continental United States by the Federal Aviation Agency, the other being Washington National Airport. The number of passengers using Dulles in FY 1964 was 698,609; in FY 1975, 2,324,055. Aircraft numbered 28,167 in FY 1964 and 54,314 in FY 1975. Dulles has operated at a deficit since it opened. Revenue in FY 1964 was $2,560,000, operating expenses $3,741,000; in FY 1975 revenue was $7,186,239, operating expenses $8,529,139.

Air France and British Airways began flying their supersonic transport plane, the Concorde, into Dulles on a regular basis on 24 May 1976. They were granted a sixteen-month trial period by Secretary of Transportation William T. Coleman for up to fourteen flights per week. This action was opposed by the board of supervisors and environmentalists who argued that the additional noise and air pollution could not be justified by the economic considerations.[28]

28. Interview, Anne Wilkins, 20 May 1974, Virginiana Collection, Fairfax County Library; William B. O'Neal, *Architecture in Virginia* (New York: Walker & Co., Inc., 1968), p. 129; Hugh Newell Jacobsen, *The Architecture of Washington, D.C.* (New York: Praeger, 1965), p. 129; Dulles Airport Operations Statistics, Public Affairs Office, FAA Headquarters, Washington, D.C., 23 July 1976.

V

In a Rural Setting
The Board's Business

An analysis of the varied and often voluminous deliberations recorded in the board of supervisors' minute books since the first meeting of that august county administrative body on 25 July 1870 tells a very interesting story about the growing complexity of county problems and the evolution of county government in the past 106 years. All of the recorded activities of the board were covered in 290 12- by 18-inch pages of manuscript for the fourteen years between 1870 and 1884. The January 1924 record book was the first in which typescript completely replaced manuscript. In this, 514 closely-typed 12- by 18-inch pages were required to record the actions of the board in the mere six years which followed, until December 1929. The calendar year 1974 required three 12- by 18-inch books totaling more than 1,000 pages to enter the official records of the board hearings and deliberations.[1]

With the advent of the automobile and truck as primary means of transportation, about 1925, and the unlimited mobility they gave the entire country's population, the rural county of Fairfax began to undergo dramatic changes which were a reflection of rapidly advancing world industrial technology.

Supervisors D. W. Buckley (Centreville), C. Norman Stewart (Lee), W. F. P. Reid (Mount Vernon), F. L. Ballenger (Falls Church), H. V. Leigh (Providence), and George F. Harrison (Dranesville) had been elected from the six magisterial districts; on 2 January 1924, they were duly sworn in by the clerk of the board of supervisors, F. W. Richardson, who was also county court clerk. Each district also had a school board, a district road board, district road bond issues, and an overseer of the poor

1. BOSMB, No. 1, pp. 1-290; BOSMB No. 5, pp. 1-514; BOSMB No. 75, 76. 77.

board. Salaries and accounts had to be paid out of the annual county levy and a steady stream of individual citizens and county organizations with requests, suggestions, claims, and complaints appeared for their separate hearings. The variety of subjects brought to the board's attention in the months to follow is intriguing. United States authorities requested permission to have their phone lines strung along county roads, a Confederate veteran and his wife wanted a letter of recommendation for their application to enter the Confederate home in Richmond, and a committee was appointed to install a new septic tank on the courthouse lot. A group of citizens complimented the board on the bounty law which had been adopted and proven very effective in ridding the county of hawks, owls, and crows, thus protecting poultry, farm crops, song and game birds, and small game animals. Over many years, thousands of dollars were paid out in bounties of fifteen cents to $1.00 by the county for scalps of owls, hawks, crows, grey and red fox, mink, and weasel. The wolves on which bounties had been paid in the eighteenth century had long since disappeared.[2]

R. E. Thornton, an attorney, was appointed tie-breaker for the board of supervisors in 1926. Since there was an even number of districts, an occasional tie vote of 3-3 would occur. This meant that on issues where the elected board was equally divided, the tie-breaker appointed by the circuit court judge would cast the deciding voice. The great power that this appointment gave to one man in the tie breaker position was of deep concern to William F. Carne, editor and publisher of the *Fairfax Herald*. In editorial after editorial he urged the formation of a seven-member board in order to avoid ties and to elect from six districts an additional supervisor-at-large by having an act of the legislature change the laws so that there could be seven members on the board of supervisors.[3]

Annexation: The Greenback Raid

When Alexandria proposed annexation of portions of Fairfax and Arlington counties to which it was providing or was capable of furnishing services, the board of supervisors strongly opposed it on the grounds that a successful attempt would cause a loss to the county of some of the most densely populated and best revenue-producing territory then within county boundaries. Active opposition to the board's view was expressed in the *Herndon News-Observer* which ran an editorial with the headline "Let Alexandria Expand." The *Fairfax Herald* sided with the board and opposed the annexation. Carne did not think the court would uphold the Alexandria landgrabbing effort. However, the

2. BOSMB No. 1, pp. 2-5; 113, 135, 173.
3. BOSMB No. 5, p. 163; *Fairfax Herald*, 13 August 1926; 11 February 1927; 14 December 1928.

court rule in favor of Alexandria on 15 November 1928 because the requested territory was "a compact body of land and is adaptable to city improvements . . . ."[4]

The Quality of Mercy . . .

At the December 1927 meeting, two actions came before the board which had far-reaching effects. One was the approval of the circuit court appointment of Carl McIntosh as a special officer. He later became the first chief of police when the separate department was created in 1940. The second was the proposal for a trial justice, in response to a citizen's petition signed by Robert Stump and others asking the board to adopt the judicial position which had been authorized for counties of 6,000 inhabitants or more by the General Assembly.

In an effort to relieve the county's overcrowded criminal docket due to prohibition violation cases, Paul Brown was appointed in 1932 to the position of trial justice. He served well. By October, he could report that the circuit court had been relieved of a major portion of its work on prohibition and other misdemeanors, saving compensation of trial jurors, and that the county had actually made a net gain as the accompanying fees were averaging over $300 per month while the judges' salary amounted to $225 per month.[5] Judge Paul Brown eventually became the senior circuit court justice of Fairfax County and served until his death in November 1966.

Civil rights came up for consideration by the board, which made a direct response to a letter of complaint received by Judge W. T. McCarthy from a resident of Ashland, Virginia. The citizen complained of the mistreatment of two young men from his area who had been subjected to a kangaroo court in the Fairfax County jail. Although the sheriff was unable to find proof of the charges, on advice of the commonwealth attorney, the board immediately adopted for the first time regulations for the protection of civil rights (property and health) of prisoners in the Fairfax County jail.[6]

For the Common Good: Power and Light

The accuracy of descriptions of roads had not improved substantially since the overseers had been ordered to improve the road between Mr. Thrift's turnip patch and the corner of John Jackson's fence in 1797, as witness the granting of permission to the Alexandria Light and

4. BOSMB No. 5, pp. 279-80; *Fairfax Herald*, 30 September, 21 October 1927.

5. BOSMB No. 5, p. 295; *Acts of Assembly*, 1926, p. 862; BOSMB No. 6, pp. 217, 241, 293; *Fairfax Herald*, 25 September 1931.

6. BOSMB No. 6, p. 217.

Power Company in 1924 to extend their electric line along Telegraph Road from Pullman's Store at Cameron Run to Mr. Charlie Sullivan's gate. The company was also given permission to erect poles and wires on the county road through Franklin Park "in order to convey electric current" to residents of that subdivision, as well as along Sleepy Hollow Road and from Falls Church to McLean.[7]

Rapid extension of electrical service to homes and business establishments in the county led to the advertising and passage of an ordinance providing for licensing and inspection of electrical wiring and for a county electrical inspector. The construction and maintenance of roads along which the wires were being strung on new poles needed more expert supervision, and F. Norvell Larkin, who was to serve the board and the county in many capacities, was employed as the county's road and bridge engineer in 1926. Larkin was a former employee of the Engineering Department of the State Highway Commission. His responsibilities included monthly accounting of the road contingency funds and also the six separate magisterial district road accounts. Beginning in March 1927, all requests for placing of telephone, telegraph, and electric lines and poles on public roads were to be made to Larkin.[8]

Alexandria Light and Power was not the only source of electricity in the county. James. V. Kincheloe, Howard Myers, C. H. Wine, Richard Hynson, and Bowie Doak organized an electrification project beginning in 1925. They constructed a crib dam of logs and stones across Bull Run above Yates Ford creating a seven-acre pond. In concrete housing at the east end of the dam were the overshot wheel and turbine for the manufacture of electricity to provide power and light for the towns of Clifton and Manassas. When among others, the Doak family's home "Woodburn" near Bull Run had been wired for electricity and the turbines were put into operation in October 1928, the family turned on every light in the house on the first evening and then went to a hill nearby to look down on the beautiful sight. The house sparkled like a jewel in the night!

The Rural Electrification Administration had loaned the Bull Run Power Company $86,000 to build the dam and plant. In the early 1930s it merged with the Prince William Electric Cooperative. The log structure was abandoned in 1940 in favor of more modern techniques, but it received favorable attention in *The National Farm News*, which noted that it had been an engineering feat, having produced the greatest amount of power for the smallest capital outlay in the entire country.[9]

7. BOSMB No. 5, pp. 12, 20, 86.

8. BOSMB No. 5, pp. 181, 229.

9. B. Franklin Cooling, *Historical Highlights of Bull Run Regional Park* (Fairfax: Fairfax County Office of Comprehensive Planning, 1970), pp. 79-81; *National Farm News*, 12 March 1927.

Dr. M. E. Church of Falls Church has been credited with having built the first electric light system in Arlington and Fairfax counties. It was sold to the Alexandria Lighting Company in 1914. During the depression of the 1930s, the efforts of the Rural Electrification Administration resulted in the remarkable achievement of electrification whereby Fairfax County led the State of Virginia in 1935 with 270 miles of lines in operation for 2,382 customers, an average of 8.8 customers per mile. During this year alone, community meetings were held at Lewis Chapel community house, Vale community house, and Fairfax courthouse to map out thirty additional routes to supply electricity from Virginia Public Service and Bull Run Power Company lines to farms and homes.

Virginia Public Service Company later merged with the Virginia Electric and Power Company as the result of proceedings brought by the Securities and Exchange Commission. In 1947, VEPCO became an independent, publicly owned utility with 450,000 customers in the state. The roots of VEPCO's corporate family tree date back to a General Assembly charter granted in 1787 which established the Appomattox Trustees, a canal company. As time went on, its corporate ancestry eventually included 235 companies founded for such diverse enterprises as water power, real estate, horseshoe manufacturing, icemaking, coal mining, laundry, railway, ferry service and street lighting.[10]

Sanitation, Water Supply, and Roads

The provision of sewer service to the eastern and more densely settled portion of the county was initially implemented through the General Assembly's Sanitary District Law of 1926. This statute enabled counties with both rural and urban areas to establish higher levels of services for which residents would pay additional taxes within the established districts. The rural citizens who were content with more traditional types of services would thus have neither the extra services nor the additional tax burden. Fairfax County did not inaugurate this system until 1943.

As more and more suburbanites moved into the county, some to farm but most to enjoy life in the country while being employed in government or military service, the board acted to provide better sanitary conditions throughout the county. An ordinance was passed unanimously in 1928 providing regulations for the disposal of human excreta. No longer could such waste be disposed on the surface of the ground where it would be exposed to flies, fowl, and animals. The

10. Steadman, *Falls Church*, pp. 284-85; CA Annual Report, 1935; Edwin H. Will, "The Past-Interesting; the Present-Intriguing; the Future-Bright, A Story of the Virginia Electric and Power Company," (New York: The Newcomen Society in North America, 1965), pp. 9, 17.

purpose was to eliminate this nuisance injurious to the public health, "to prevent and control the further spread of Typhoid Fever, Dysentary, Colotis [sic], Flux, Hook Worm and other bowel born diseases." No raw sewage was to be deposited into a water supply, stream, spring, or well which might be used for domestic purposes, drinking, or bathing. The ordinance also stipulated that each citizen had to provide his designs for sewerage disposal before obtaining a permit. The state enabling legislation had been passed four years before in 1924.

This new recognition of need which many years later led to the design of an integrated sewer system in the county was fostered in part by the tremendous promotional activities underway by Northern Virginia chambers of commerce, real estate and construction companies, and the Washington-Virginia Railway. These groups joined in an organization called the Northern Virginia Bureau which published a promotional pamphlet called *The Hills of Northern Virginia*. New highways were being built, including Lee (later renamed Arlington) Boulevard and the Mount Vernon Parkway. Francis Scott Key Bridge had just been completed, and Arlington Memorial Bridge and the George Washington National Masonic Memorial were under construction. Alexandria's water supply was praised as to quality, quantity, and reasonable cost. At this period, their water company's reservoir was Lake Barcroft, which had been formed by damming Holmes Run just north of both the old Barcroft Mill and Columbia Pike, near Bailey's Crossroads.[11]

"The modern method of measuring distance is by time, not by space." Figuring the elapsed time, the promotional booklet pronounced Arlington closer to the business center of Washington than other suburban towns in other directions from Washington. The bureau's attitude was very matter-of-fact: "the stability and growth of the Nation's Capital in population and beauty is more assured than is the future status of the average industrial metropolis. The prosperity of the District of Columbia is not dependent upon industrial circumstances. Of all the cities in the country, it is least affected by adverse commercial conditions." A patriotic note was sounded: "From the background of agricultural pursuits on Fairfax County estates came men who changed the map of the world by sword and pen and gave new meaning to the word Freedom. George Washington and George Mason, with a host of others, have made Fairfax County history a definite part of the nation's background . . . . Undoubtedly, no other section of the country is richer in historical traditions and romantic interest than Old Fairfax County . . . . "

Subdividers were characterized as being intelligent and conscientious, slowly moving toward the center of Fairfax County and into the

11. BOSMB No. 5, pp. 331, 332; *Acts of Assembly, 1924,* chapter 465; Northern Virginia Bureau, *The Hills of Northern Virginia,* (Alexandria, Va.: Newell-Cole Co., Inc., 1926).

northeastern and southeastern portions as a result of the expansion of both Alexandria and Washington. Alexandrians were establishing homes west of the city, and southward near the Belle Haven Golf and Country Club. Washingtonians were largely responsible for the increase in homebuilding near Falls Church, McLean, Langley, and the Chain Bridge area. In 1925 the average land value per acre in Fairfax County was $67.00, $15.47 higher than the average for the entire state. A steady rise in Fairfax County land values was predicted because of the future growth of Washington; land obtained in 1928 at very reasonable prices would prove to be an exceedingly profitable investment in years to come.[12]

The *Fairfax Herald* frequently printed humorous anecdotes and cartoons. A typical one, appropriate for the times, which probably produced mixed reactions among the government-employed suburbanites and certainly chuckles from the farmers was the following:

She: "Whats your brother doing now? He was trying to get a government job awhile ago."

He: "He's doing nothing, he got it!"

An advertisement in the *Herald* showed a growing interest in suburban life: "Owner of a high class apartment house in Washington desires to trade for country estate." Washington was definitely becoming interested in the Virginia suburbs. The *Herald* spoke in defense of county weekly newspapers and at the same time welcomed the big city papers "now being circulated in county districts."[13]

Fairfax was still basically a rural county. The few officers of the county were named as part of the official business at the January 1929 meeting: F. W. Richardson, county court clerk and board of supervisors clerk; Eppa P. Kirby, sheriff and jailer; W. M. Farr, commonwealth attorney (all three persons elected) M. D. Hall, superintendent of schools; H. B. Derr, county demonstrator; Miss Mary Lippard, county home demonstration agent; A. C. Ritchie, juvenile court judge; and John Pearson, janitor (these persons all appointed). Kyle A. Davis had been appointed Lee district supervisor on 27 June 1928 after the death of C. Norman Stewart. The future course of events was foreshadowed by the passing of an ordinance requiring that all subdivision plats be approved and endorsed by the county engineer before the clerk of the court could admit them to record. There were to be no duplicate names, streets were to have a minimum width of fifty feet, and all streets and alleys were to connect with adjacent subdivisions.[14]

Water shortage because of national drought conditions was critical in the summer of 1930. Virginia had only 60 percent of its normal

12. Northern Virginia Bureau, *Northern Virginia*; U.S. Census of Agriculture, 1925; Detwiler al al, *County of Fairfax*, 1925.
13. *Fairfax Herald*, 4 January 1929.
14. BOSMB No. 5, p. 432.

rainfall, and Harry Byrd, head of the Virginia Drought Relief Commission, demanded federal aid for relief in Virginia. He did not request that the State of Virginia provide funds. The *Fairfax Herald* urged its readers to pray for rain and reported that water in Salisbury Spring on Windover Heights in Vienna was being tested for use. The situation dramatized the need for a better water supply for Fairfax. State Delegate Edmund Allen was named chairman of a drought commission for Fairfax County to bring in tank cars and wagons for water distribution in case of emergency.[15]

Natural Gas

During 1930 and 1931, gas mains were laid along the county roads and cross-country. The board of supervisors granted franchises to the Alexandria and the Rosslyn Gas companies to install gas mains along the rights-of-way of public roads in Fairfax County. The board also granted permission to the Virginia Gas Transmission Corporation to transport natural and/or artificial gas in and through the county in twenty-inch steel pipelines, under and across public roads. The *Herald* reported that pipes to carry natural gas to Philadelphia were being unloaded in the county, providing employment for many.[16]

"Hello, Central"

When Dr. M. E. Church died in Falls Church in September 1931, it was said that he had done more for Northern Virginia than any other person. Church, a pharmacist whose birthplace was in Derby Line, Orleans County, Vermont, had operated drugstores first in Herndon and later in Falls Church. In 1888, he had established a telephone line from his drugstore in Falls Church to Washington and then provided a network of telephone companies and exchanges in Falls Church, Vienna, Herndon, Fairfax, Leesburg, and in Loudoun, Fauquier, and Prince William counties. During the Spanish-American War, he had furnished telephone and telegraph service for Camp Alger, near Merrifield. Dr. Church served as president, chief stockholder, and general manager of the company network and eventually sold his interests to the Chesapeake and Potomac Telephone Company in 1916.[17]

According to the Chesapeake and Potomac Telephone Company, the first Fairfax telephone office was located in the home of Walter Oliver, Sr. Early subscribers included R. C. L. Moncure, Walter Peyton, F. E. Smith, Louis E. Oliver (Andrew Chapel), Dr. Alfred Leigh (Colvin Run), Dr. Max Wiehle (Sunset Hills), Dr. Ed S. Detwiler, Dr. Ben Detwiler, W. Floyd Middleton, and Dr. Earnest Robey (Herndon).

15. Dabney, *Virginia,* p. 489; *Fairfax Herald,* 15 and 22 August 1930; 5, 12, 26 September 1930.
16. *Fairfax Herald,* 20 February 1931.
17. Steadman, *Falls Church,* pp. 284-85.

Manually operated switchboards were in use in Fairfax, Vienna, and Herndon until dial service was introduced in 1954.[18]

In 1935, Mrs. Lucy Madeira Wing, director of the private Madeira School for Girls at Greenway (moved from Washington, D. C. in 1932), and Mrs. Carl Swinson appeared before the board of supervisors as representatives of the Business and Professional Womens Club and asked that the board sponsor a Works Progress Administration project for making up a directory of the people of Fairfax County showing post office, location, telephone number, etc., which they stated could be done with federal aid and at no expense to the county. The supervisors voted unanimously to grant the request.[19]

Acute Depression: Taxes and Foreclosures

In April 1933, for the first time on record, the financial pinch of the depression stimulated lively and extensive participation by individuals and groups, discussing one by one the budget items proposed by the board for the coming fiscal year. Joseph Berry, representative for the Fairfax County Chamber of Commerce, and R. Colton Lewis who appeared for the Taxpayers League, asked for reductions in county salaries and elimination of several offices in the county government. R. E. Wagstaff spoke in favor of the state's paying for patrolling of the county roads now that it had responsibility for building and maintaining them. Others suggested that welfare items and the county health unit be eliminated. The Honorable R. Walton Moore was present through the entire hearing and supported the board on almost every item. With minor changes, the budget for the year 1933-34 was adopted.

The economic crunch of this period in the depression was emphasized by T. Mason Hirst, prominent local realtor. Hirst appeared before the board asking that the wholesale foreclosure of deeds of trust and of mortgaged property be stopped by the courts by a moratorium declared for at least two years. Help was on the way in the form of, first, a presidential order in 1933, and secondly, federal legislation. The National Housing Act of 1934 assured cautious, conservative bankers of federal backing for loans, and encouraged them to lower requirements for down payments, lower interest rates, reduce sizes of payments, and extend mortgage loan periods. This enabled more people to purchase and retain their own homes.[20]

Additional serious problems faced Fairfax. It was estimated that of the 5,000 heads of families in Fairfax, 1,000 were out of work. A public works program to improve streets, the jail, and buildings and grounds of

18. Chesapeake & Potomac Telephone Company, "Twentieth Anniversary of Dial Service in Fairfax," (Fairfax, Va.: Chesapeake & Potomac Telephone Co., 1974.)

19. BOSMB No. 7, p. 175.

20. BOSMB No. 6, pp. 368-85, 389; National Housing Act, 48 Stat, 1246, 27 June 1934.

sixteen white and colored schools was determined to be worthwhile. In November 1933, the board entered into an agreement with the federal government to provide a salary for a relief director to administer Federal Emergency Relief and the State Civil Works Administration program. E. W. Aud and F. N. Larkin were appointed director and assistant. The members of the Federal Reemployment Committee which was appointed to pass on applications and to determine which persons were to be given employment on various projects were W. J. Cleveland (Seminary Hill), Mrs. Lena G. Stuntz (Vienna), James V. Kincheloe, Mrs. Elizabeth Chilcott, and C. L. Rosamond (Fairfax), W. F. P. Reid (Groveton), Mrs. George C. Van Dornes (Clifton Station), and Mrs. Eleanore W. Aud, superintendent of public welfare.[21]

Recreational Pursuits

Even in hard times, people occasionally indulge in recreational pursuits. A trend which was widely represented throughout the United States at the time had local manifestations in the application of the formally constituted Green Forest Club for permission to establish a nudist colony, in the vicinity of "Sunset Hills", the A. Smith Bowman farm. The board of supervisors opposed it, the Order of Fraternal Americans, Kenmore, opposed it. So did Mr. Bowman, who had just applied for formal registration of the newly formed Fairfax Hunt with the Boston-based Masters of Foxhounds Association of America. A devotee of this time-honored Fairfax sport, Bowman obviously preferred to see foxes and hounds "streaking" through the wooded rolling plains.

Through the years, in addition to the nucleus of regular members, people from Washington rode with the hunt from time to time. These guests included General George Patton and his family, General Jonathan (Skinny) Wainwright, and Patrick Hurley, Secretary of War under Herbert Hoover. Randolph D. Rouse is the current Master of Foxhounds for the Fairfax Hunt, a position which he has held since 1964.[22]

Public Health

Early work in the county's health unit was performed by Dr. E. L. Flanagan, Dr. A. L. Carson, and Mrs. Fannie Lou Seamans, public health nurse, a well-loved and respected public servant. The Fairfax County Medical Society urged the board of supervisors in 1935 to abolish the health unit and recommended employment of "one or more county nurses who will work in cooperation with the physicians of the county in

21. BOSMB No. 6, pp. 453, 490, 513.

22. BOSMB No. 6, pp. 439, 465; Donald O. Opstad, *The History of the Fairfax Hunt, 1929-1972* (Fairfax, Va.: The Fairfax Hunt, 1972).

maintaining the public health, and in the control of contagious diseases in the homes and school." However, the society later supported the health programs of the unit, headed from 1937-1939 by Dr. Edward M. Holmes, Jr. By 1940, many other volunteer and public agencies and organizations were helping to provide encouragement and funding for a variety of health programs under the department's leadership. They included the county chapter of the American Red Cross, the Fairfax County Chamber of Commerce, the Community Chest Association, the Tuberculosis Association, and the Ladies Health League of Fairfax County. Tuberculin testing, eye and tonsil clinics, restaurant sanitation, venereal disease, maternity and infancy care, and advisory work regarding the disposal of sewage and protection of water supplies were just a few of the active programs.[23]

Retirements and Replacements

F. W. Richardson, who had been county court clerk as well as the clerk of the board of supervisors for fifty-five years, announced his retirement in 1934, and was succeeded by John W. Whalen. It was Whalen who observed the following January that during the year 1935, approximately 700 more deeds and trusts had been recorded than in any previous year. The influx of new residents was showing up in the courthouse: new office equipment was needed for filing and storage, and a wooden ladder was needed for access to the tops of cabinets.[24]

Later that year, when William H. Elmore, a member of the board of supervisors from the Dranesville district died in office, the circuit court judge appointed Miss Edith Rogers to succeed him. Miss Rogers, a former school teacher, dairy farmer, and member of the grange, was the first woman to serve as a supervisor, and she was eventually elected to the board. Miss Rogers was the supervisor who later made the motion to hire Joseph Beard as Fairfax County agricultural agent. At the same meeting, the board of supervisors adopted a resolution commending Dr. F. W. Huddleson, treasurer of Fairfax County from 1 January 1916 to 31 December 1937. At the time of Huddleson's resignation for reasons of health, he was "the senior county officer, both in years and in length of service" . . . and his daughter, Mrs. Elizabeth H. Chilcott, who "has served with great distinction as his Deputy . . . [is] a real wizard at figures . . ." The resolution went on to say that father and daughter, in preparation of the budget of the county, had used sound judgement and enabled the county to operate on a generally sound financial basis and rating.

23. BOSMB No. 7, p. 49; Joseph C. Muzyca, Sr., ed., *Historic Account, 1917-1976*, (Fairfax, Va.: Fairfax County Health Department, 1976), pp. 4-12 (hereinafter cited as Muzyca, *Historic Account*).

24. *Fairfax Herald*, 4 January 1935; BOSMB No. 7, p. 195.

Thus, in a little more than two years' time, three key men—Richardson, Derr and Huddleson—with combined service to the county of ninety-seven years, retired and left the running of county affairs to successors who would have to cope with an increasing number of new problems.[25]

Public Services

Demand grew for public services, the need for which had not been widely felt by the native rural population. The demand came mostly from the new suburbanites. The services desired (health, schools, sewers, water, police, and fire protection) were becoming more expensive, and farmers felt the pain of increased taxes needed to provide and maintain them. A more accurate assessment of the county's real estate had been urged for some time. In November 1939, Ronald Blake, representing the granges, stated that farmers "were bearing more than a fair part of the tax burden." The grange members favored reforms recommended by the Citizens Advisory Committee on Reassessment of Real Estate. Implementation began when supervisor Rogers moved to authorize the county purchasing agent, R. M. Loughborough, to obtain the United States Department of Agriculture aerial photos of the county plus index maps and office supplies for assessment and permanent records. The measure was approved unanimously.[26]

The board which was to experience the period of World War II—rationing, the influx of war workers, and the shortages of civilian supplies—was sworn in on 3 January 1940. Andrew W. Clarke of the Mount Vernon district replaced W. F. P. Reid, who had been chairman of the board. Maurice Fox of the Dranesville district replaced Miss Edith Rogers. All other supervisors were reelected, and G. Wallace Carper of Providence was elected chairman. In his opening remarks, he spoke of the board's great responsibility during the next few years in view of the rapid development of real estate in the county and the increasing amount of work coming before the board. He asked the cooperation of members of the board in handling these matters in the best interests of the citizens. Here was, indeed, a forward-looking statement, and yet the slow, charming, folksy ways of doing business persisted. Supervisor Fox had to be excused for part of this first meeting in office because he and his wife had previously been chosen to represent "the ideal farm family" on the National Farm and Home Hour. Miss Florence Jodzies thoughtfully brought her portable radio into the board room so that all present would hear the Foxes broadcast at 12:34 p.m. over radio station WMAL.[27]

25. BOSMB No. 7, pp. 597, 599-600.
26. BOSMB No. 8, p. 511.
27. BOSMB No. 8, pp. 552-53.

Burke Volunteer Fire Department, typical of many such structures of the period financed and constructed by the local communities, their volunteer firemen and the women's auxiliaries. Photo in 1948 by Porter.

Carl R. McIntosh was the first chief of police, appointed prior to the official establishment of the police department on 1 July 1940. He had first come to work as a deputy under sheriff J. R. Allison and continued to serve under sheriff Eppa Kirby. It was Kirby, known as the "no-gun sheriff" because he didn't like violence and refused to carry a pistol, who went before the board of supervisors and requested that a separate police department be set up. McIntosh appointed Henry T. Magarity as detective sergeant. Soon after, Magarity became coordinator of civil defense. The police department initially had a staff of eight on 12-hour shifts, with a county population in 1940 of 98,557. Thirty-five years later, the department had an authorized strength of 626 sworn officers and 282 civilians, a headquarters building, five district stations, and a criminal investigation division for a county population of over a half-million.[28]

28. BOSMB No. 8, p. 602; *Fairfax County Police Department Newsletter*, (Fairfax, Va.: 1975), 3(5): 1-8.

Fire protection services had a long history in the county before the police department came into existence. Falls Church established a volunteer fire department about 1898 after the town's old-fashioned "bucket brigade" failed to save the Kerr Mill. The town council ordered its first three chemical engines in 1899. Vienna purchased an engine around 1919 and for many years stored it under the large back porch of the Freeman house on Church Street, next to the Washington and Old Dominion Railroad track. These and other volunteer fire services existed for many years without applying for formal charters of incorporation. McLean, Number 1, had the first formally chartered company in 1923, giving it official status, bylaws, and a board of directors. The charter also protected individual volunteers from legal liability. Incorporated fire services were later established in Falls Church (1925), Fairfax (1928), Vienna and Herndon (1929), and Franconia (1935). In all, six companies were chartered in twelve years. Beginning in 1940, seven were chartered in three years. Each department bought its own land, firehouse, and equipment, and services were provided by volunteers. Later, the county began making payments on the expensive pieces of large equipment after individual companies made the initial downpayment.[29]

A County Library

The volunteer movement in library services was evident in Fairfax County history. It is a matter of record that John S. Mehler was selected as county librarian in June 1940, with a collection of 19,500 books housed in a new cinderblock building (fourteen feet by twenty-four feet) erected for that purpose behind the county courthouse. What is not so well known is that four Fairfax County towns had public libraries of their own which had been in use for many years and had been operated mostly by volunteers before the central public library system was established. Vienna townspeople formed a library association, acquired land, and built a facility on Library Lane in 1897. Herndon's Fortnightly Club established a library in 1889, and for many years this facility and the county's bookmobiles were the only library services available in the northwestern part of the county. The Falls Church community library was established in 1899, sponsored by the woman's club. The library in the town of Fairfax was established in the early 1900s and was later named for Dr. Huddleson.

In 1938, the Fairfax County Chamber of Commerce proposed to the board of supervisors a consolidation of the various library activities in

29. *Fairfax Herald*, 28 July 1899; Steadman, *Falls Church*, pp. 153-54; Marvin Cranshaw, "History of Fairfax County Fire Departments," (manuscript, 1976); "Fire Stations Charter or Operational Dates and Locations," information sheet (Fairfax: Fairfax County Fire Service, 1976).

Fairfax County Library Bookmobile, 1940. Fairfax County Library.

order to include both urban and rural areas of the county. Branches were to be established in heavily-populated areas, and bookmobiles were to serve the rest. The board of supervisors initially appropriated $250, and the newly organized library board of trustees contacted state and federal agencies for additional funds. The state library board and the Federal Emergency Works Progress Administration cooperated in the establishment and operation of a countywide system in conjunction with the existing libraries and funds from local sponsors.

A blue panel truck, which carried about 600 volumes, was loaned to the county in 1940 and served as the first bookmobile. Individual community libraries maintained their own identity, but acted in cooperation with the county librarian and central facility, which was only large enough to serve as a storage area and distribution point.[30]

30. John Sloan, "A History of the Fairfax County Public Library, Virginia: Its Growth and Service," master's thesis, University of Maryland, College Park, 1969) hereinafter cited as Sloan, Fairfax County Library); Historic American Building Survey Inventory, *Vienna Library* (Fairfax, Va.: Office of Comprehensive Planning, 1971); Steadman, *Falls Church*, pp. 155-6; "The History of the Fortnightly Club and Library Association of Herndon, Virginia, 1972", mimeographed report; Eleanor Lee Templeman and Nan Netherton, *Northern Virginia Heritage* (Arlington, Va.: 1966; reprint ed., New York: Avenel Books, 1976), p. 97.

VI

The War and Its Aftermath

A comparison of January issues of the *Fairfax Herald* of 1940 and the *Fairfax Standard* of 1949 shows drastic changes brought about by events connected with World War II and its aftermath, a ten-year period during which the lifestyle of county residents changed dramatically.[1]

The 1940 issue of the *Herald* was filled with reports of domestic, rural, and political activities, personal notes, and information about coming events. Settlement of the estate of William F. Carne, long-time publisher and editor of the *Fairfax Herald* was announced. News from New York City and abroad was featured. Local church and school news items appeared throughout the paper. An article entitled "Drys to Meet" told of the state conference of the Anti-Saloon League in Richmond. Fiction articles had moralistic overtones.

Comparative prices of some ordinary grocery items provide a glimpse into economic changes.

	Fairfax Herald 1940 Fairfax Market	*Fairfax Standard* [2] 1949 Safeway
pork sausage	19c per lb.	39c per lb
prime roast	25c per lb	69c per lb
cooking apples	10c for 3 lbs	25c for 3 lbs
yellow onions	10c for 3 lbs	5c per lb
kale	10c for 3 lbs	17c for 2 lb

1. *Fairfax Herald,* 5 January 1940; 6 January 1950.
2. *Fairfax Herald,* 5 January 1940; *Fairfax Standard,* 7 January 1949.

Advertisements in the 1950 issues of the *Herald* were indicators of changing patterns of life and work. Stenographic services and office supplies were offered, Christmas savings plans were available at the local bank, children's furniture, family recreation room construction, and art classes were offered. Local news was still featured, although fewer communities were represented. The fiction offered did not have the moralistic tone of the 1940 issue. Fairfax Service Garage was introducing the 1950 Chevrolet with power glide automatic transmission. Frozen foods were advertised, a forecast of a major future development in the convenience foods industry, although this modern trend was nicely balanced with an old-fashioned sleighing party in Falls Church and a taffy-pull in Herndon.[3]

The County Zoning Ordinance, 1941

> No one is enthusiastic about zoning except the people. The non-people—the professionals—hope it gets lost. The judges find zoning a monumental bore, most lawyers consider it a nuisance and the planners treat it as a cretinous member of the planning family about whom the less said, the better. Yet, thousands of local officials regard zoning as the greatest municipal achievement since the perfection of public sanitary systems. Zoning is the urban renewal (or more accurately, the urban reversal) of the village, the answer to the suburban maiden's prayer.[4]

In March 1941, Fairfax County enacted its first countywide zoning ordinance. This modern era of land planning and land-use control had been inaugurated by the General Assembly's passage of enabling legislation in 1936 and 1938.[5] The growth of the New Deal bureaucracy in Washington, D.C., and its accompanying multiplicity of federal agencies was generating an unprecedented demand for building in Fairfax County. People came from all over the country to take advantage of employment opportunities. The population figures had grown from 40,929 in 1930 to 98,557 in 1940.

The Fairfax ordinance provided that the county be zoned into districts, that permits be obtained for building, altering, or repairing structures; it regulated the use and size of yards and other open spaces and provided penalties for failure to comply. The avowed purpose was to promote the health, safety, morals, and general welfare of the community.[6]

3. *Fairfax Herald*, 6 January 1950.
4. Richard F. Babcock, *The Zoning Game* (Madison: University of Wisconsin Press, 1966), p. 17.
5. *Acts of Assembly*, 1 April 1938, Ch. 415, p. 777, (Richmond, Va.: Division of Purchase and Printing, 1938).
6. BOSMB No. 9, p. 464.

Spring Bank Trailer Camp, located on U.S. Route 1 south of Alexandria and occupied mostly by torpedo plant workers. The "Spring Bank" mansion in the background was once the home of a George Mason, grandson of George Mason of Gunston Hall. Photo in 1941 by Martha McMillan. Library of Congress.

Other Ordinances

Ordinances are an extemely accurate portrayal of conditions just prior to their time of passage, as William Waller Hening so accurately stated when he collected and published his *Statutes*. A picture of relative domestic tranquility appeared in 1940 and 1941, for example, when the following ordinances were brought up for consideration by the board of supervisors: regulation of dumping; dogs running at large; licensing of carnivals; regulation of restaurants and dance halls; regulation of building permits; and restriction of the burning of trash to certain hours of the day (this last because all the fire companies were manned by volunteers, most of whom had regular jobs elsewhere during the day).[7]

However, the picture soon changed, as one immediately can see by two ordinances passed in 1942 when the country was at war and a sudden influx of population had begun. One provision required compliance with blackout procedures in case of air raids, and other ordinances were passed regulating trailer camps and trailers. The ordinance on blackouts became necessary when some citizens refused to comply voluntarily during air raid drills. The trailer camps and trailers provided housing for government workers who were immigrating to take the jobs which were being generated by the country's gearing up for war.[8]

7. BOSMB No. 9, p. 111.

8. BOSMB 10, pp. 509-10.

"Frozen" cars and trucks were stored on a farm near Vienna, Virginia for the duration of World War II, due to rationing of parts and fuel. Photo in 1942 by John Collier. Library of Congress.

Virginia Governor James Price appointed the Virginia Defense Council in May 1940, only hours after President Franklin D. Roosevelt named the National Defense Commission. Because of Adolph Hitler's invasion of Poland, France, and the Low Countries, the European war buildup became a real threat to the United States. The Virginia aircraft warning system was set up with a statewide network of more than 1,000 stations for observation. The Selective Training and Service Act was approved by Congress in September 1940, the first peacetime program of compulsory military service in the United States. The Northern Virginia Regional Defense Council established communications centers, and three days after the attack on Pearl Harbor, the board ordered that a telephone line be installed to Washington, "such phone being necessary for direct warning in case of air raids . . . the United States having been at war with the Empire of Japan since the morning of December 7, 1941."[9] A United States Rationing Board was set up in the county to administer regulations of the Office of Price Administration on rationing of automobiles, processed foods, meat, butter, tires, sugar, coffee, gasoline, fuel oil, kerosene, shoes, liquor, cigarettes, stockings, etc. Ration books were issued. Along with rationing went salvaging, and like the rest of the country, the citizens of Fairfax County collected waste paper, scrap iron and other metals, rubber, and clothing to be recycled for the war effort. Civilians took Red Cross first aid courses, donated blood for the Red

9. Dabney, *Virginia*, p. 509; BOSMB No. 10, p. 399.

Green Spring Farm, the old Moss house, built about 1760, was, like many other colonial period homes, in a deteriorated condition in 1936. Photo by Delos Smith. Historic American Buildings Survey. Library of Congress.

Green Spring Farm in 1975, is now owned by the Fairfax County Park Authority. Headquarters of the Fairfax County Council of the Arts. Photo courtesy of McLean Providence Journal.

Cross program, and accepted designations as civil defense air raid wardens and spotters.[10]

As the rural nature of most county life had meant a minimal impact on residents during the depression of the 1930s ("we were poor but so was everyone else so we didn't know it") the advent, duration, and aftermath of World War II little affected day-to-day life outside the immediate proximity of Arlington, Falls Church, and Alexandria. There, population buildup of government workers was concentrated. Help for farming was hard to get, and sometimes conscientious objectors or German war prisoners were used as hired hands. It was true that gasoline, sugar, and other commodities were rationed and this caused inconvenience; the farmers, however, generally received a sufficient supply of gasoline for their needs. Relatives and friends enlisted in or were drafted for military service, resulted in daily fears "down on the farm" for the safety and lives of loved ones in military service. For the first time in history, the radio and its war correspondents made it possible for rural and isolated people to hear news of major events immediately after their occurence or sometimes occasional live broadcasts from the actual scenes of battle and bombing. This rapid communication of news from all sectors of the global conflict caused constant apprehension, for although the war was being carried on in Europe and Asia and the Pacific, many Fairfax County citizens feared that if France and England fell, the enemy would immediately attack the United States.

Fairfax men and women continued to go to war—people with surnames which dated back to the earliest families who settled in the county. At least ninety-eight of the men did not return from the battlefields.[11]

A few families connected with the government and war effort were attracted to the rural life away from close-in communities. A love for old houses drew Walter Thurston, a career member of the American diplomatic corps, and his mother Beatrice to Sully just before the war. She spent a great deal of time and money during the period of acute building material shortages to refurbish and preserve the 1794 structure near Herndon. The same attachment for old houses brought Michael Straight, editor of the *New Republic*, and his wife Belinda to Annandale and Green Spring Farm, the old Moss place dating from about 1760 and by 1942 in a desperately rundown condition.[12]

10. BOSMB No. 11, pp. 107, 187, 279, 397-98; Interview: Holden S. Harrison, Herndon, Va., 21 July 1976; Interview, Mrs. Mark S. Turner, Sr., Great Falls, Va., 21 July 1976.

11. Interview, Holden S. Harrison; W. Edwin Hemphill, *Gold Star Honor Roll of Virginians in the Second World War* (Charlottesville, Va. World War II History Commission, 1947), pp. 71-73.

12. Robert S. Gamble, *Sully: The Biography of a House* (Chantilly, Va.: Sully Foundation, Ltd., 1973), p. 130; Ross and Nan Netherton, *Green Spring Farm* (Fairfax, Virginia: Office of Comprehensive Planning, 1970), pp. 31-35 (hereinafter cited as Netherton, *Green Spring Farm*).

626 Fairfax County, Virginia—1925-1976

The government, both civilian and military, worked long hours in the interest of national defense. Early in World War II, just after the Japanese attack on Pearl Harbor, General Dwight D. Eisenhower was called to Washington, and while waiting for his family to join him, stayed in Falls Church with his youngest brother Milton and his wife Helen who were living at "Tallwood" on East Broad Street. At the time, the General was working eighteen-hour days, and later wrote: "I cannot remember ever seeing their house in daylight during all the months I served in Washington."[13]

Two army installations within the county engaged in intensive activity during World War II. Tens of thousands of draftees went through the training programs at Fort Belvoir on the Potomac preparatory to being sent overseas. North of Mount Vernon, Fort Hunt had been in use as a Civilian Conservation Corps camp and laboratory for the National Park Service prior to the declaration of war; it was transferred back to the Department of the Army by the Department of the Interior in 1942 for the war's duration plus one year. During the war peirod, 150 buildings were constructed to house troops engaged in secret joint war and navy intelligence operations under the Military District of Washington.[14]

The county librarian, Dorothea Asher, worked closely with the civilian population and the local military camps. Captain John F. Bethune was chairman of the library board of trustees in wartime, and he acknowledged the importance of preparation against invasion and for military preparedness. "But," he reported to the board of supervisors, "failure to provide for the maintenance of the cultural and intellectual development of the people of the county . . . would be a step backward in the whole problem of county development." In 1943, the County purchased a bookmobile which was well used; the circulation figure that year was approximately 75,800 volumes. The library was one of the first countywide community efforts, and citizens and the local newspapers enthusiastically supported the expansion of the program.[15]

Beginning in 1943, the county began to provide public works services through the creation of sanitary districts. The close concentration of population made it necessary for the circuit court to establish the first two sanitary districts, one in the vicinity of Falls Church, the other near Alexandria. The purpose for the two districts was to insure the general health, safety, and welfare of the residents and to provide sewer and water services within the districts.[16]

13. Dwight D. Eisenhower, *Crusade in Europe* (New York: Doubleday & Co., Inc., 1948), p. 24.

14. Robert T. Nelson, "Fort Hunt," Historical Society *Yearbook*, 9: 59-64. Maj. Gen. Robert F. Seedlock, "Ft. Belvoir Humming with 25,000 People," *Fairfax County Sun-Echo*, 16 May 1967, p. B-8.

15. Sloan, "Fairfax County Library," p. 4.

16. "History of Sanitary Districts in Fairfax County," (Fairfax, Va.: Office of Research and Statistics, 1975).

The Pentagon, a five-sided, five-ring office building for the armed forces, and the first phase of Shirley Highway were completed in 1943, both located in Arlington but having a profound effect on Fairfax County. Construction experts like Marcus J. Bles came to work on these projects and on construction projects like Fort Belvoir, National Airport, and sewer and water lines. Bles, originally from the Cape Girardeau, Missouri, area brought his family to Washington, D.C., in 1939 with less than $100 cash. Within a year they had purchased a home in McLean, and by 1946 he had become the biggest construction contractor in Northern Virginia.[17]

The military effort was beginning to cause some serious problems on the civilian front by the end of 1943. Even occupations which had been exempt were being reconsidered for the conscription. An excellent example of this situation was provided by the 1-A draft status of James J. Corbalis, county sanitary engineer. The board of supervisors asked for a deferment, passing a resolution "reciting the fact that Mr. Corbalis is about the most indispensable employee of the County, that the trunk line sewer is the first project of its kind in the County . . . and it is impossible to replace him at the present time."[18] He was deferred, but only for six months.

As did many of the rural native residents of the county, Mrs. Mark Turner, Sr., of Great Falls went to work at the Pentagon. Her husband was a dairy farmer, active in grange work at both county and state levels. Two sons were in military service, one a bomber pilot who served in both the European and Pacific theaters. The job she held during the war was in the locator office, from which contacts were made to servicemen all over the world when emergency situations arose at home. The success of the office operation worldwide was generally good; the attempts of some of her co-workers, however, to find their way back to their offices in the Pentagon once they had left for lunch, a coffee break, or even coming to work in the morning, were less than satisfactory, and in some cases, actually resulted in dismissals.

During the war, the Turners provided a summer home for two refugee girls of their acquaintance who had been evacuated from their home in Glasgow and sent to Canada to boarding school. The girls enjoyed six summer holidays in Fairfax County before it was safe for them to return to Scotland. In wartime community work, Mrs. Turner was influential in establishing the cannery in Herndon which provided facilities for farmers and householders to can their produce from their

---

17. Nan Netherton, "Three 'Northern Virginians,'" *Northern Virginia Country* (Middleburg: Enterprise Productions, 1976), pp. 26-27.

18. BOSMB No. 12, pp. 241-42.

Sledding on Church Street in Vienna, about 1946. Sketch courtesy of Vienna Presbyterian Church.

"victory gardens." The cannery operation continued as a service to county residents after the cessation of the war.[19]

During the war, a vast difference of experiences existed between the county residents in the outlaying areas (actually the majority of the county's land area) and those of the new suburbanites. Except for a scattering of articles and items on wartime subjects like rationing, and "What to Do With Defeated Germany," life as represented in the *Fairfax Herald* seemed to go on pretty much as usual. College students came home for vacations, people got engaged, married, divorced, attended meetings, and made New Year's resolutions. The school board met and the county agent suggested planting seeds for plants to provide cover for game birds. Just as Fairfax County's most famous citizen George Washington had been fond of doing, so rural residents in 1945 still enjoyed sitting "under their vine and fig tree."[20]

19. Interview, Mrs. Mark Turner, 21 July 1976.
20. *Fairfax Herald*, 5 January 1945.

The suburbanites, mostly located in the Falls Church and Alexandria environs, were well aware that the agriculturally-oriented officials of the county government were not responding to the growing pains in the eastern edge of the county resulting from the influx of new residents desiring sophisticated services and responsive government administration. In a request to the United State Civil Service Commission in 1949, Harold A. Ward, chairman of the federation of citizen's associations' Hatch Act Exception Committee, spelled out a list of grievances dating back to wartime, which his committee felt were in need of correction. The recommended solution was to permit federal employees residing in Fairfax County to take a more active part in local politics, in a controlled transition of the county from rural to urban status. From 1940 to 1943, an average of 4,200 people per year had moved into the county. Between 1943 and 1949, the annual increase was about 8,000. Arlington was almost fully developed, and a completely planned development to be built in Springfield by Edward R. Carr was going through established development schedules.

Some issues which needed special attention on behalf of the suburbanites were provision of public utilities at fair rates; provision of an adequate transportation system for federal government employees, who formed a high proportion of the county's population in 1949; and upgrading of the public school system and its administration. Ward concluded by expressing the opinion that the greatest concentration of highly specialized people in any area in the world resided in the District of Columbia and its environs. He pointed out that a brand new group of federal employees moving into the county to buy their own homes, pay taxes, and raise their children, was the young veterans of World War II.[21]

21. Harold A. Ward, "Report on Special or Unusual Circumstances Effecting [sic] Federal Employees Residing in Fairfax County, Virginia," Hatch Act Exemption Committee, Fairfax County Federation of Citizens Associations, 1940.

VII

A Place to Live: A Place to Grow

As the nation's veterans came home and wartime energies shifted to peacetime tasks, Fairfax County became the site of a major boom in the construction of small, low-cost, single-family houses. These houses were built for the most part on the edges of Falls Church in subdivisions such as Anna Lee Heights and Westlawn, North and South Woodley, and to the north of the city on the east side of Route 7, Pimmit Hills. A new Veterans Administration loan-guarantee program, geared more toward builders than veterans, took few amenities into consideration. The idea was to provide housing for a new market, the ex-GI and his new family who wanted a yard for the children to play in and "breathing and elbow room" which apartment living, also in short supply, did not provide. Author John Keats stated his views of the consequence of giving unconditional priority to this type of housing: "today's housing developments . . . [are] conceived in error, nurtured by greed, corroding everything they touch. They destroy established cities and trade patterns, pose dangerous problems for the areas they invade, and actually drive mad myriads of housewives shut up in them . . . ."[1]

The typical early VA-insured housing such as Pimmit Hills offered a builder-designed house with a "picture window" which usually looked across a narrow street into another picture window exactly like it. It was located on a quarter-acre lot for the small price of $10,500, with a $500 down payment, and twenty-five or thirty years to pay off the loan at $65 per month, including principal, interest, taxes, and insurance. This was a very attractive price when compared with the low rental cost of available apartments in the area such as Shirley-Duke near Shirley Highway, North and South Willston at Seven Corners, and Park-Fairfax,

1. John Keats, *The Crack in the Picture Window* (Boston: Houghton Mifflin, 1956), p. 178.

Fairlington, and Claremont, in nearby Arlington, to name a few. For a comparable cost, while the apartment dweller built a stack of rent receipts, the home mortgage owner could build an equity, month by month, as he paid off his loan. The latter was an attractive alternative which sold postwar houses by the thousands, with little thought on the part of the proud new purchasers of the effects of lack of community identity, schools, libraries, shopping and recreational facilities, and public transportation. The physical monotony of design and enforced intimacy with the homogeneous inhabitants who were similar in age, income, and background, caused a virtual segregation into a matriarchal society resulting from wage earners' (usually husbands and fathers) long commuting hours and "moonlight" jobs which often resulted in limited interrelationship between parents and children.[2]

One outstanding exception to this monotonous pattern was the Hollin Hills subdivision in the vicinity of Mount Vernon south of Alexandria. The original group was developed slowly and carefully between 1949 and 1954 by Charles M. Goodman Associates. It was the first major moderately-priced subdivision of architect-designed single-family dwellings, with only a few homes built at a time and with care taken to design streets and lots. The lots, from one-half to one acre in size were arranged to fit the rolling, wooded land contours, disturbing the natural amenities as little as possible. Choice of a variety of quality designs was offered to the home buyers. This collaboration between developer, architect, and owner was all too seldom experienced in the development of postwar housing.[3]

Another interesting exception in moderately priced homes was the Holmes Run Acres subdivision between Falls Church and Annandale. Here, two modest basic architectural designs, a single level and a two-level house, located on contour-designed streets and quarter-acre lots, were offered to the purchaser, with design potential for future expansion.[4]

In all, approximately 1,650 homes were eventually built in Pimmit Hills, 463 homes in Hollin Hills, and 350 in Holmes Run Acres.

In a Suburban Setting: The People's Businesss

Postwar expansion of job opportunities brought thousands of new residents to the Washington area, and with them came what seemed to be

2. Ibid., pp. 143-45.

3. Hugh Newell Jacobsen, *A Guide to the Architecture of Washington, D.C.* (New York: Praeger, 1965), p. 185 (hereinafter cited as Jacobsen, *Guide*); William B. O'Neal, *Architecture in Virginia* (New York: Walker & Co., Inc., 1968) p. 137.

4. Ben H. Badkikian, "The Rape of the Land," *Saturday Evening Post* (Philadelphia: Curtis Publishing Co., 18 June 1966); *Architectural Forum* (New York: Lawrence W. Mester, August 1951); *House Beautiful* (New York: Hearst Corporation, September 1951); *Family Circle* (New York: New York Times Media Company, November 1955).

a bumper crop of school-age and younger children. The parents first requested and then demanded many services of such a nature which the county government could only provide slowly if at all. This lack of response to the citizens' needs led to the development of two powerful groups who often spoke with one voice at the regular meetings of the Fairfax County board of supervisors at the Fairfax County courthouse.

The first organization was the Fairfax County Federation of Citizens Associations, first organized in 1940, with Dr. Thomas P. Martin of Dunn Loring as president. With increasing regularity, the federation communicated with the supervisors regarding such citizen concerns as unreasonable bus fares.

The League of Women Voters of the Fairfax area was organized in 1946; its first president was Jane Wellemeyer of Tauxemont, near Mount Vernon. The first task was to canvass all the county voters' registrars' lists and compare them with the poll tax lists, sending cards to everyone not registered, advising them to check on individual voting status. This action led directly to a revision of registration procedure in Fairfax County. Because of the lack of information on boundaries of voting precincts, Mrs. Lee Park, president of the League of Women Voters in 1947, spent many hours at the courthouse drawing up the county's first voting precinct map. She often had to go into the old court order books to get original descriptions, then mark them on a large county map. When completed, the map was offered to and accepted by the county planning office as the county's official precinct map. Other features were added and the board directed that the map then be reproduced and made available to the public for $1.00 per copy.[5]

In 1949, the league and the federation joined forces to petition and then fight for a referendum on a proposed county manager form of government. Instead, a compromise which appealed to both rural and suburban factions was arrived at in the more moderate changes represented by the county executive form, the voters approving a referendum for the latter on 7 November 1950, effective 1 January 1952. The board of supervisors appointed a Centreville resident, David Lawrence, publisher of *U.S. News and World Report*, as chairman of a research project to study transition to the new form of government and investigate the many questions arising in connection with the changeover. The existing system operated under an executive secretary subject to general laws applicable to counties in the State of Virginia. There were no departments of public works or assessments, no official purchasing agent, and no mechanism for regular monthly reports to the board of supervisors regarding administrative matters and the financial

5. *20 Years!* (Fairfax County, Va.: League of Women Voters of the Fairfax Area, 1968), pp. 14, 17 (hereinafter cited as *20 Years!*); BOSMB No. 14, p. 347; No. 15 p. 111; No. 16, p. 111.

condition of the county. The new system provided for regular examination of the books and papers of every office and department of the county. The general purpose of the research project was to provide separate reports for each of the major departments of the county government, a separate report on the duties and functions of the county executive, and a separate report on the functions and duties of the board of supervisors. The ultimate result was a document, *Guide to County Executive Form of Government, Fairfax County, Virginia*, released 7 November 1951.[6]

The board of supervisors meeting was called to order on 1 January 1952 by Thomas P. Chapman, Jr., clerk of the county court, the first meeting under the new county executive form of government. As a result of the November election, there were some former members of the board and some new faces: G. Wallace Carper, (Providence), Maurice W. Fox (Dranesville), Stuart T. DeBell (Centreville), Arthur I. Shaffer (Mount Vernon), Mrs. Anne Wilkins (Falls Church), and C.B. Jett (Lee). Two months later, the March 1952 issue of *Virginia and the Virginia County* featured Fairfax County and its new executive form of government, with a special article by David Lawrence, a brief history of the county written by former executive secretary R.M. Loughborough, and features about the county's agricultural extension, home demonstration, and 4-H club programs, the Fairfax Hunt, and Sunset Hills farm and bourbon distillery. There were biographies of Thomas P. Chapman, Jr., clerk, John E. Taylor, sheriff, David Lawrence, publisher, John Ferguson, supervisor of assessments, and Carlton C. Massey, manager of Henrico County (surrounding Richmond) for more than eight years prior to accepting the position as Fairfax's new county executive.

The federation recognized the great amount of effort put forth during the changing of the county's form of government and awarded the *Washington Evening Star* Fairfax County "Man of the Year" cup to David Lawrence in 1952 for his participation in the successful project.[7]

As more people moved to the county, needs for goods as well as services grew. Initially, small local shopping centers were built, each designed with parking lots for the automobiles required in the suburban residential pattern which, in its uneconomical use of land, scattered the residences of most patrons far and wide and too far from the shopping facility to enable shoppers to walk and carry purchases home. Beginning in 1953, the smaller centers were augmented by regional shopping malls designed to serve up to 50,000 persons. It was then that the thirty-four acre Frederick Foote tract at Fort Buffalo, Seven Corners, was rezoned from suburban residence to general business. Frederick Foote, a black

6. *20 Years!*, p. 12; BOSMB No. 18, pp. 31-32.
7. FCFCA *Bulletin*, February 1956.

Seven Corners, the intersection "where seven roads meet in a tangle." Photo in 1948 by Porter.

man with white and Indian blood, had purchased thirty-three acres of this land for $500 in 1864. In his will, he directed that the land must remain in the family and never be sold. The annual taxes on the property grew to tremendous proportions, however, and his descendants obtained a release from the will's provision and sold the acreage for $750,000.[8]

Kass-Berger, Inc., contractors in Washington, developed the Seven Corners shopping center. This new type of shopping center revolutionized the shopping habits, social life, youth culture, pattern of political campaigning, and relationship of county residents to the central city of Washington. Because residents could now do their shopping for major purchases within the county, there was a new orientation to the local community emphasizing a lifestyle which was gradually changing the relationship of Fairfax County from a solely suburban "bedroom" community satellite of the capital city. Two major Washington stores, Woodward & Lothrop and Garfinckel's, opened up branches in the center, as well as national chains including Brentano's bookstore, and Woolworth's five and ten cent store. There were specialty shops of many descriptions on the two shopping levels served by escalators.[9]

The board of supervisors requested in 1953 that the circuit court establish seven magisterial districts, calling for the election of a seventh

8. Steadman, *Falls Church*, p. 209.

9. BOSMB No. 20, pp. 221-26; Frederick Gutheim, *A History Program for Fairfax County* (Annandale, Va.: Fairfax County Park Authority, 1973), p. 37.

member of the board and eliminating the need for an appointed tie-breaker under the old even-number district division. This was a step which had been urged by *Fairfax Herald* publisher William Carne in the late 1920s and with ever greater frequency by citizens' groups since that time.[10]

·'Need for periodical dispensing of information on public issues of concern to county residents was met in part by the initiation of the important monthly *Bulletin* published by the Fairfax County Federation of Citizens Associations. Federation president Bernard Mullady of Springfield appointed Benton Bray of Columbia Pines as the first editor. Mullady pointed out in the first issue (October 1953) that Fairfax County was rapidly reaching critical stages in its development with pressing needs for water and sewer systems, schools, an integrated system of roads, streets and numbering, a broader and stronger financial base, fire and police protection, a more comprehensive health program, and a master plan for the county. This first issue pointed out one of the major problems the county had faced for decades: the county's expenditures for fiscal year 1953 had been $7,376,128, 71.4 percent of which was for schools. Revenues had amounted to $7,535,933, of which real and personal property taxes had only accounted for 64.9 percent.[11]

The League of Women Voters, as part of its public education program, presented the supervisors with copies of its first annual edition of "A Guide to Fairfax County Government." The publication was designed to assist citizens in finding their way around the increasingly complicated labyrinth of county regulations and local government departments providing many kinds of public services.

Several of the ordinances of that year were clear indications of new trends: zoning requirements for research laboratories on major highways; regulation of BB gun use (indicating more crowded living conditions); regulation of gravel pits; and regulation of private nursery schools.[12]

The board of supervisors heard from the Freeholders Protective Association at the 2 December 1953 meeting when its president Manning Gasch of Old Georgetown Pike urged that taxes be cut. The new courthouse building addition under construction was going to cost more than the funding raised by the bond issue passed for its construction. Gasch suggested that savings could be effected by using standard school plans instead of hiring architects; school children in first and second grades should be put on half days; and building codes should be tightened.[13]

10. BOSMB No. 20, p. 361.
11. FCFCA *Bulletin* October 1953, 1(1).
12. BOSMB No. 20, p. 111.
13. BOSMB No. 20, p. 511.

The development of the Seven Corners shopping center again drew the board's attention in 1954 when supervisor Wilkins urged that letters be sent immediately to General James A. Anderson, Commissioner of the Virginia Department of Highways, Congressman Joel T. Broyhill, state Senator John A.K. Donovan, and state Senator Charles R. Fenwick. The problem was explained: "Fort Buffalo intersection is one of the most dangerous and most frustrating situations to the motorists in Virginia and should have first priority in any major primary highway improvements to be made in the Northern Virginia area."[14]

The Korean war was a remote rumble and affected the county most in the civil defense concerns including nuclear attack defense training for the schools, the influx of military personnel to the Washington area, and the establishment of ten Nike missile bases for defense circling Washington. The three located in Fairfax County were on Pope's Head Road next to "Hope Park," on Magarity Road next to Pimmit Hills, and on Utterback Road near Great Falls. Mundane concerns were paramount: the county transferred Sanitary District Number 1 to the newly inaugurated countywide, integrated sewerage system. The inevitable happened: with the proliferation of ordinances, there had to be an ordinance adopted to codify all county ordinances advertised for public hearing.[15]

The Fairfax County Federation of Citizens Associations made its wishes known on 7 April 1955. In a comprehensive statement made by president John C. Shover, the organization approved the board of supervisors' increased annual budget for fiscal year 1955-56 totaling $14,054,662. The federation regretted the projected necessity of raising the tax rate per $100 evaluation from the existing $2.70 to the proposed $2.95 but after budget summary analysis, "It would appear that in many of the most important aspects of county services, to the public—in education, in police protection, in building inspection, in public health, and in some other fields—we are at last approaching a minimum acceptable standard. In some other fields, such as recreation and libraries, we are not yet in sight of an acceptable level, but the new budget does represent progressive forward movement in those fields. In still other fields—regional detention home, driver training in high school, water drainage to alleviate health hazards—the budget proposes pioneering moves which show a heartening recognition of the need for broadening the scope of public services in this county."[16]

---

14. BOSMB No. 21, p. 109.

15. Rick Beaudette, "Parks, Schools Are Nike Fallout," (Fairfax, Va.: MORKAP *Virginia Sentinel*, Publ. Co. 22 August 1973), p. A-12; BOSMB No. 21, p. 234; BOSMB No. 22. 111 [ordinance regulating ordinances].

16. FCFCA *Bulletin*, April 1955.

The federation and the League of Women Voters urged residents to register and vote in the fall election for members of the board of supervisors. Some of the reasons for desiring a change in county administration were spelled out in detail by Bernard Mullady in an article in the May 1955 federation bulletin. He explained that there had been far too little planning in the county in the 1940-1950 decade as the population mushroomed from 40,000 to 100,000. Its affairs were handled as if it were still a rural county. With a fairer reapportionment to seven magisterial districts, an opportunity now existed for election of supervisor candidates whose qualifications and viewpoints would best serve the needs of the entire county, and a majority of at least four such supervisors would implement the county executive government reorganization which had been approved by the voters in 1950 and had taken effect on 1 January 1952. Mullady urged the board to devote time and thought to plans and policies, to adopt criteria and principles, and then to direct county executive Carlton Massey to do the job. He urged the adoption of and adherence to a master plan. Voters were advised to check on voting records on zoning changes, many of which had been a gold mine for speculative builders and often not in the short- or long-range interest of Fairfax County taxpayers. Getting out the vote for the primary election was urged. A Washington *Post* editorial in April pointed out the board of supervisors' commercial spot-rezoning for supervisor C. B. Runyon. This was typical of the disregard shown for homeowners' pleas for zoning conformance in residential areas. The *Post* suggested two cures: The election by county residents of officials with broad public interest rather than narrow private interest, and the adoption by the supervisors of the upcoming master plan.[17]

When the newly-elected board first met on 4 January of the next year, five supervisors with a total of fifty-eight years in public office had been replaced. Chairman G. Wallace Carper of Dranesville was succeeded by Republican A. Claiborne Leigh; vice chairman Maurice Fox, redistricted out of his home territory, had been defeated in the Democratic primary by Stuart DeBell of Centreville; Arthur Shaffer was redistricted out of Mount Vernon and defeated in the Democratic primary by C. B. Jett, who was in turn defeated in the general election by Republican (General) Richard P. Ovenshine; Republican William H. Moss was elected in Lee district. C. B. Runyon, supervisor-at-large the previous two years, did not seek reelection. Anne Wilkins of Mason district, Joseph Freehill, of Falls Church district, and James Keith of Providence district, Democrats, were also elected. Freehill was elected to the chair which had been occupied by Carper for the previous sixteen

17. *Guide to County Executive Form of Government, Fairfax County, Virginia,* (Charlottesville, Va.: University of Virginia, 1951); FCFCA *Bulletin* May 1955; "Favoritism in Fairfax," *Washington Post and Times Herald,* 25 April 1955.

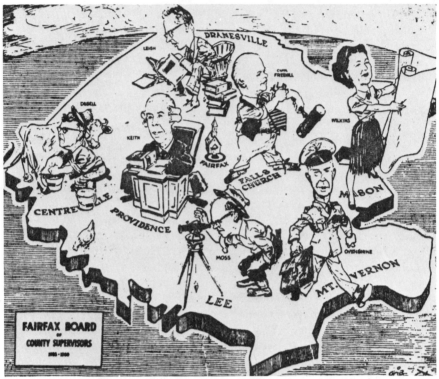

A View of Fairfax, seen through the eyes of Gib Crockett, a political cartoonist
for the Washington Star. The seven supervisors are shown in 1956 in
characteristic poses on a map of the county. Used with permission.

years, nominated by Mrs. Wilkins, seconded by General Ovenshine.
Keith was nominated by Leigh and seconded by DeBell. Moss's pivotal
vote supported Freehill. This close election crossing party lines was a
forecast of things to come.[18]

"What Fairfax County Offers"

In the fall of 1956, the Fairfax County Chamber of Commerce
published a public relations promotion booklet, *What Fairfax County
Offers . . . on the Virginia Side of Washington*, funded by an appropriation from the board of supervisors. Unabashedly, the point was
made that Fairfax County had more sites suitable for laboratories and
light industry within thirty minutes of the White House than all the rest
of the Washington metropolitan area combined. As had been the case in
the 1920s, time rather than distance was reckoned: the system of

18. Betsy Hinkle, ed., *Fairfax Newsletter* (Springfield, Va.: 7 January 1956), p. 1 (hereinafter cited
as Hinkle, *Fairfax Newsletter*).

expressways and overpasses had "no equivalents in the north, east or west of the city . . . . All this means you can choose a plant site in a parklike semi-rural Fairfax County setting and be within 20-25 minutes of the heart of Washington." Water supplies from the District of Columbia (Potomac River) and the Occoquan reservoir were praised as were new superhighways under construction or planned, plus rail and air service. One section of the booklet featured planning as a preservation technique for natural assets and protection of the environment. Builder Henry Rolfs' national award from *The American Home Magazine* for good design in his Rolfs Heights subdivision in Annandale was highlighted. Electric power, transcontinental phone dialing, natural gas, population growth statistics, and the county's problems, solutions, and progress were detailed. Schools, police, courts, records, taxation, health facilities, recreational opportunities, historic sites, farming as a hobby and an occupation—all were depicted and described. Each supervisor made a statement about his or her magisterial district. Five industrialists explained why they had chosen Fairfax County for location. They were Dr. Lloyd W. Hazleton, Hazleton Laboratories; Thomas Meloy, president of Westinghouse-Melpar, Inc.; M. E. St. Aubin, director, Service Section, General Motors; Dr. Arthur W. Sloan, vice president, Atlantic Research Corporation; and Carlyle Bogness, president, Southern Iron Works. The booklet closed with an offer from the chamber to help firms find the right sites for location in the County.

In the early 1950s, the combination of pressures from an expanding population, a number of septic tank failures, and water shortages had forced the county to hire a consultant. Francis Dodd McHugh, who had done a master plan for Westchester County, New York, was retained in September 1952 to direct the planning commission's technical staff in comprehensive studies in order to prepare a countywide master plan. A consultant study done for the master plan staff in 1953 by Homer Hoyt noted that 90 percent of county workers were federal employees and that the population growth had crested and would level off to a population of about 320,000 by 1980. The McHugh plan, rewritten once after the supervisors rejected it in 1954, was presented in 1956 to the new board, which declared a six-month zoning moratorium and approved the "Freehill amendment," a residential zoning map based on McHugh's master plan with reduction to two acres from his three-to-five-acre minimum lot sizes suggested for the western two-thirds of the county. This last-described portion of the master plan was later struck down by the Virginia Supreme Court of Appeals in an appeal by the county of a lower court decision on a case brought by former chairman of the board of supervisors G. Wallace Carper, an owner of considerable land in the county. Thus, an attempt to encourage concentration of building inside the integrated sewer district failed.

The leapfrogging growth of subdivisions beyond the existing suburban fringe began to escalate, and with it an increased per capita tax burden to provide duplicate urban facilities (schools, libraries, parks, police, and fire protection) in outlying areas of a county encompassing more than 400 square miles of land. After the failure of the Freehill amendment, the county adopted a zoning ordinance based on the comprehensive plan and studies of zoning prepared by consultant Hugh Pomeroy in 1958. The ordinance has been followed since and is presently in effect, although there is little resemblance between the 1959 zoning maps and the current maps because thousands of exceptions in the form of approved rezoning cases having been made during the intervening years. This *ad hoc* rezoning, usually considered at the request of an owner or developer of property, has created a situation where there is presently no county comprehensive plan being followed, zoning categories are inappropriate, applications for amendments to the zoning ordinance are backlogged, the circuit court spends an exorbitant amount of time considering the actions of the board on specific cases, and the board and staff spend an inordinate amount of time on evaluation of zoning cases while the level of services diminishes countywide.

As a result of a major study on the part of the board of supervisors, thousands of interested citizens, and the county's staff, the PLUS program (Planned Land Use System) evolved a new countywide master plan. This plan was adopted on 8 September 1975 after several years of innumerable hearings and work sessions, and following the prior adoption of four separate area plans. The new zoning ordinance, a primary tool to implement this new master plan, was developed by ZOSC (the Zoning Ordinance Study Committee) and adopted in principle by the board on 4 November 1974. It is scheduled to go into effect when the entire county has been completely remapped, tentatively in the fall of 1977.[19]

Some of the problems in land utilization which this plan hoped to address were anticipated almost twenty years prior to its adoption. A survey report made by the *New York Times* in 1957 expressed great concern over "suburban sprawl" already being experienced on the periphery of all large cities in the United States. Analyst Charles Grutzner predicted that problems which were large then would become even more serious from vertical New York City to horizontal Los Angeles. He reminded readers that Sir Patrick Geddes, British biologist and sociologist, had predicted before the turn of the century that the

19. *Board of County Supervisors v. Carper*, 107 S.E. 2nd 390 (1959); "Suburban Growth: A Case Study," *Population Bulletin*, (Washington: Population Reference Bureau, Inc., 1972), 28(1) 13; Office of the County Attorney, *A Brief History of Planning, Zoning, and Environmental Constraints in Fairfax County, Virginia*, PLUS Program Research Paper 1 (Fairfax: Fairfax County Government, 1974), pp. 2-6.

entire eastern seaboard of the United States would one day become one continuous city. "Fantastic as that seemed, the nation has come so far along the way that, today for the first time in this hemisphere, more than 27,000,000 people are living under urban conditions in a continuous area stretching more than 600 miles from Boston to the far tip of Fairfax county, Virginia. This is a 1950 census figure; estimates of the current population reach 32,000,000."[20] "This vast urbanized area, unique in the entire world and deserving in our opinion the name of megalopolis, extends over most of the Northern Piedmont in Virginia."[21]

The report of an administrative survey of Fairfax County, Virginia, was presented to Carlton Massey for transmittal to the board of supervisors in 1957. It was the result of a study conducted by Weldon Cooper, director of the Bureau of Public Administration at the University of Virginia. Taking into account the fact that the county executive form of government had been established in 1952, he offered recommendations after observing the recent functioning of various departments in the government under that system. Expressing the conviction that Fairfax County had much to be proud of about the operation of its government, he urged that the board concern itself more with long-range policy issues rather than administrative details. He stated that there was an unnecessarily wide dispersal of "independent" agencies (authorities, commissions, and boards), many of which needed to be integrated into a hierarchical structure; that there was a need to clarify functions, powers, and duties of each agency which would ideally recognize the board of supervisors as the ultimate authority in the government (although a board-administrator system could be established). He judged that coordination of the various agencies was an almost impossible task with the small staff in the county executive's office, and noted a lack of formalized procedures such as written reports and communications. Cooper's suggestion was that an administrative code be developed for the county by setting each agency to the task of coming up with a description of its role and functions and the procedures for discharging its duties.[22]

With leisure time available and the inconvenient distance from city cultural and recreational opportunities, the provision of facilities and programs by the county was far below the need felt by the suburbanites of the 1950s. The void was filled in part by the establishment of many private corporations which appointed or elected boards of directors, sold a set number of shares of stock, and built membership recreational facilities on private corporation-owned property. They then charged stockholders (members) annual dues to maintain and manage the

20. Charles Grutzner, "Urban Complexes Fostered by Auto," (New York: New York Times reprint of summary report, 27 January to 3 February 1957).

21. Gottmann, Virginia, p. 174.

22. Weldon Cooper, An Administrative Survey of Fairfax County, Virginia, (Charlottesville, Va.: University of Virginia, 1957), pp. 57-61.

Olympic Gold Medalist, Melissa Belote, who learned to swim at the age of three at a community swimming pool in Springfield. She won three gold medals swimming backstroke at Munich, Germany, in the 1972 Olympics.

swimming pool, tennis and/or basketball courts, and/or community centers provided by the corporations. This activity had the effect of syphoning off a great deal of initiative and energy which might otherwise have been devoted to working for expanded public-supported programs available to greater numbers of citizens.[23]

Other private initiative in the county resulted in the local government's acquisition of a map linen which was purchased from the Federation of Citizens Associations. The federation published a civic-government directory in 1957 together with the first countywide street map carefully prepared by Carpenter and Cobbs, surveyors of Fairfax, on an eight-foot-long linen. The county purchased this linen after the first 6,000 prints had been made by the federation for the directory project, and it was thereafter used for prints to sell to the public and for use by government departments.[24]

The local towns and cities were literally nibbling away at Fairfax County during 1957. Vienna began a suit in January to annex 1,400 acres adjoining the town boundaries. Although Fairfax County had successfully defended itself against a suit by Falls Church in 1950, it had shortly thereafter lost a sizable land area to Alexandria. In March, the board

23. Hinkle, *Fairfax Newsletter*, 1 January 1957.
24. Hinkle, *Fairfax Newsletter*, 23 March 1957.

appointed a legislative committee to try to effect changes in state legislation which would slow down or halt the trend toward incorporation and annexation within the county. The town of Fairfax engaged consultants in May to determine if the town should seek to annex a portion of the county and become a city of the second class. Vienna won a court decision for annexation in June, and the county did not appeal. In December, the town of Fairfax decided to annex 6,000 acres and 11,300 persons, providing water, sewer, and other facilities. The annexation also provided for an anticipated surge of growth in residential building.[25]

The business community was taking on new responsibilities and stimulating new activities. The board of supervisors created an economic and industrial development committee, and its first project was to commission a study by Arthur D. Little Company, Inc., of Cambridge, Massachusetts, to furnish a basis for presenting factual information to industrial prospects on facilities available and operation costs in Fairfax County. The Little report recommended, among other things, that the county consider industrial parks (a suggestion favored by the committee) and a nonprofit landholding corporation to option or purchase land to deter price increases. The Northern Virginia Builders' Association reported in December that it had a current membership of 589, having gained 119 new members in the previous twelve months and lost only eight, a growth percentage far exceeding that of any similar organization in the metropolitan area during 1957. Large construction projects were underway within the county in 1958. Not only had General E. R. Quesada, chairman of a national airport study committee, selected the Chantilly area for the 12,500-acre site for a second metropolitan Washington airport, but the Central Intelligence Agency (CIA) had decided on the Langley site near McLean for its new headquarters office building. The construction of the Virginia portion of the interstate circumferential highway Route 88 (later designated I-495) had begun, and so had the construction of the first unit of Fairfax Hospital on Gallows Road near Merrifield.[26]

An Attempt at Incorporation

In an effort to protect the county against further annexation, a committee was formed in 1958 to organize a county incorporation plan for proposal to the General Assembly. On the committee were state Senator John A. K. Donovan, delegates John Webb and Omer Hirst, the seven members of the board of supervisors, plus eleven other citizens from the county at large. As Betsy Hinkle twinkled in her *Fairfax*

25. Hinkle, *Fairfax Newsletter*, 26 January, 30 March, 8 June, 13 July 1957.
26. Hinkle, *Fairfax Newsletter*, 8 June, 7 September, 28 December 1957; 10 January 1959.

Lake Anne Village, Reston. In addition to single family dwellings, a wide variety of housing has been built in the "new town", first conceived by Robert E. Simon, whose initials form the name. Shown are clustered townhouses, condominiums, high-rise apartments and a medium-rise building with apartments for senior citizens overlooking Lake Anne. Gulf Reston, Inc.

Newsletter, "This is viewed by the more waggish as calling for one man, one woman, one Republican, one Democrat and eleven others who are none of these."[27]

The sudden death of Joseph Freehill immediately following a heart attack suffered during a board meeting in January 1959 was a loss felt deeply by many in the county. He had been a liberal and had worked unceasingly to try to bring about changes he felt were called for by the popular mandate of the recent election. The event raised serious questions about intolerable demands on mental and physical endurance of those on the board dedicated to serving more than fulltime on supposedly part-time jobs as supervisors.[28]

The Federation of Citizens Associations was as nervous as county government officials concerning the annexation suits being openly contemplated by both the cities of Alexandria and Falls Church in June 1959.

27. Hinkle, *Fairfax Newsletter*, 12 July 1958.
28. Hinkle, *Fairfax Newsletter*, 24 January 1976.

Their membership urged action on a metropolitan county system with a charter which would protect the county's borders. The newly created industrial development authority declared its support for the board to "institute whatsoever form of government that will preserve the territorial integrity and stability of Fairfax County."[29]

The pressure of the influx of population was recognized as an opportunity by the building and development industry. In October applications for the largest apartment-zoned acreage in the history of the county were made for 300 acres of the Bristow tract in Annandale, a part of the ancient Ravensworth estate. A minimum of 4,250 apartments was planned. One year later the Bristow apartments were approved.

Efforts continued to protect the best revenue-producing county territory from annexation by the towns and cities within and abutting its borders. In the spring of 1961, Frederick A. Babson, coordinator of the county's defenses against annexation, stated that incorporation was the only answer for Fairfax County, and the proposal was made that Fairfax County and the town of Clifton consolidate into a newly formed government. One feature of this plan was strenuously objected to by the existing towns within the borders which would either cease to exist or have to become cities. Activity was intense. In June, Robert E. Simon outlined his plans for a "new town" development called Reston in Sunset Hills. The city of Falls Church lost its second county annexation suit. Alexandria filed a petition for more than twenty-one square miles of Fairfax County (which it dropped in December). The town of Fairfax obtained court permission to become a city of the second class in order to avoid being abolished in the event the Clifton-county consolidation attempt proved successful. The attempt failed in the legislature.[30]

Steps Toward Urbanization

Evidence of the impact of both urbanization and advancing technology was amply represented by these and other events in late 1961 and 1962. Jet test flights were flown over the Dulles Airport construction site; supervisor Stuart DeBell proposed a committee to study for the first time the cultural needs of the county; Research Analysis Corporation announced its intention to establish a "think factory" at Westgate Industrial Park near Tysons Corner; county planner Rosser Payne told the board that mass transit would be a necessity in the future because it would not be possible to plan sufficient highway lanes to take care of anticipated traffic needs. Warren Quenstedt added emphasis to this view when he outlined mass transit alternatives to the Federation of Citizens Associations.[31]

29. FCFCA *Bulletin*, June 1969; Hinkle, *Fairfax Newsletter*, 27 June 1959.

30. Hinkle, *Fairfax Newsletter*, 1 July, 9 December 1961.

31. FCFCA *Bulletin*, February 1962.

On 1 April 1965 a massive street renaming and house renumbering program based on a countywide map grid system took effect. This procedure had been in the planning stages for years, and when it took place, 80 percent of all homes in Fairfax County were affected by the approximately 75,000 changes. Many confusing duplicate street names were eliminated, although the towns and cities elected not to conform, but retained their own existing systems within their boundaries.[32]

In September, the county's first crime commission was established with a membership of seven.

The obvious connection between the county government's power to regulate land development and the ability of land developers to make profits in their ventures created an atmosphere of temptation which, in 1966, severely tested the integrity of the county's planning and zoning functions. A Federal grand jury sitting in Alexandria on 20 September 1966 handed down fifty-six separate counts indicting a former state senator, a former planning director of Fairfax County, two supervisors, three former supervisors, a deputy director of county planning, a zoning attorney, and several builders. The cases involved bribery in rezoning cases for a trailer park, a shopping center, an apartment development, and a subdivision. The pressure of growth and development and accompanying temptation had had their effect in a very significant way. In October, circuit court judge Paul Brown appointed Frank F. Everest, Jr., to replace John P. Parrish of the Mount Vernon district who had voluntarily suspended himself from the board; in November, the judge appointed C. Meade Stull to replace Stuart DeBell of Centreville who had done the same. A number of the indicted were convicted and served time in a federal penitentiary. They included former supervisors John Parrish, A. Claiborne Leigh, and Robert C. Cotten, Jr., as well as several private developers. The Federation of Citizens Associations took immediate positive action in the form of resolutions to restore public confidence in the county government by strengthening the code of conduct and ethics for all county officers and employees. This was later augmented by a request for state-enabling legislation making conflict-of-interest violations misdemeanors.[33]

The complexity of dealing with a multiplicity of problems both from the standpoint of the governing body of the county and of an involved and concerned electorate were well demonstrated by the change to the urban county form of government approved by referendum in November 1966 and effective in January 1968. It provided, among other things, powers to the board of supervisors to redistrict the county from

32. Hinkle, *Fairfax Newsletter*, 18 April 1964; 5 April 1965.
33. FCFCA *Bulletin*, 20 October, 17 November 1966; 12 September 1968; *Northern Virginia Sun*, 25 February 1967; *Gazette*, 5 April 1967; *Washington Post*, 5 April 1967.

time to time, to create or alter service districts, to call for a referendum to decide the question of responsibility for the county's road system, and to elect a county chairman-at-large.[34]

A new county office building designed by Vosbeck and Vosbeck of Alexandria was under construction as the largest board of supervisors in the history of Fairfax County took office in January 1968. The supervisors had been elected in November from eight newly organized magisterial districts. Fred Babson, who had served on the board of supervisors since 1964, was elected the first county chairman-at-large; the other members were Martha Pennino (Centreville) Joseph Alexander (reelected from Lee); Donald R. Bowman (Springfield); Harriet Bradley (reelected from Dranesville); Herbert E. Harris, II (Mount Vernon); Charles Majer (Annandale); Harold O. Miller (Mason); and Thomas B. Wright (Providence).

Implementation of the new urban county government was aided by a study made for Fairfax County by the firm of Cresap, McCormick and Paget, management consultants. A senior associate in the firm, Dr. George J. Kelley, Jr., had the major responsibility for conducting the study. In June 1968, Dr. Kelley was appointed by the board of supervisors, at the recommendation of county executive Carlton Massey, to the new position of deputy county executive for planning and financial management. Many separate departments in the county government were consolidated at this time under three deputy county executives. The division of information was renamed Public Affairs and expanded its service to increase the flow of information about the county government to citizens and to handle citizen complaints and requests for information.[35]

In the November 1968 election, the electorate, under a local option proposition, voted yes on a liquor-by-the-drink resolution. This had a far-reaching economic effect on restaurant and luxury motor inn construction within the county, because for the first time, at least in recent history, drinks of higher alcoholic content than beer and wine could be served, a near necessity for attraction of hotel and motel chains, convention business, and the satellite commercial developments which usually follow.[36]

In November 1969, a three-judge annexation court ruled unanimously in Fairfax County's favor in denying a suit brought by the city of Alexandria to annex 8.3 square miles of the county. The county's case was coordinated by J. Hamilton Lambert who, with photographs

34. Urban county form, 1967 *Annual Report*; 1968 *Annual Report*, (Fairfax County, Va.: Division of Information).

35. 1969 *Annual Report* (Fairfax County, Va.: Division of Public Affairs, 1969).

36. FCFCA *Bulletin*, October 1968.

and detailed statistical information concerning the level of services being successfully provided, demonstrated to the court that Fairfax County was able to respond satisfactorily to its citizens' needs in an urban situation.[37]

The year 1969 had set a new record. It had taken five full minute books and parts of two others to contain the record of the deliberations (largely zoning cases) of the board of supervisors. Chairman Babson resigned from this time-consuming position on the board because of his private law practice. Dr. William S. Hoofnagle, chairman of the school board, was appointed to replace Babson. He stood for and won a special election, and won again for a four-year term in the 1971 general election. Dr. Hoofnagle assumed his new responsibilities in a year when national organizations were looking favorably at Fairfax County as a desirable location, near Dulles Airport and the nation's capital, in which to establish facilities for key operations or headquarters. The American Automobile Association, the American Newspaper Publishers Association, and the National Education Association all announced building plans in 1970. A pleasant living environment and financial considerations, an available supply of professionals and skilled personnel, and a base of support services were also deciding factors for these organizations. By 1974, 81 of the 1,200 trade and professional association headquarters in metropolitan Washington had been located in Fairfax County. The Washington area had become the primary location for these headquarters by 1974, accommodating 27 percent of the nation's total number.[38]

After almost nineteen years of service to the county, county executive Carlton Massey retired in January 1971. He had been active in 4-H Club work while in high school, had graduated from Virginia Poly-technical Institute with a degree in civil engineering, had worked for the city of Fredericksburg, and been town manager of Salem, Virginia, and county manager of Henrico. He praised the increasing interest of the public in community affairs during his tenure. For a long time, very few people had attended board and civic association meetings. In 1968 he commented on the great change: "The public takes so much interest in what is going on that it becomes difficult to get things done." The new county office building was named "Massey" in appreciation of his years of dedicated service during a time when the county's population grew more than 1,000 percent.[39] Dr. Kelley was appointed by the board in

37. 1970 *Annual Report.*

38. BOSMB No. 51-58; *The Fairfax Prospectus,* (Fairfax, Va.: Fairfax County Industrial Authority, December 1970), 1(4); *The Fairfax Prospectus,* (Fairfax, Va.: Fairfax County Economic Development Authority, April 1976), 7(2).

39. Anthony Sterago, "Carlton Massey: Top Man in Fairfax County Government," (Annandale, Va.: *Annandale Free Press,* 1 February 1968), p. 6.

March 1971 to succeed Massey. He assumed his responsibilities during a fiscal year when the voters approved $88,620,000 in separate bond issues for schools, libraries, health, transit, parks, and sewers. Two growing social problems were recognized with the establishment of a drug abuse study program and a "roving leader" program to curb juvenile delinquency.[40]

Growth and planning became major issues of the 1971 county election for the board of supervisors. The newly elected board, which included three former members, Martha Pennino, Herbert Harris, and Joseph Alexander, had five new members, most elected on a controlled-growth mandate of the electorate. They were Audrey Moore (Annandale), Rufus Phillips (Dranesville), Alan Magazine (Mason), James Scott (Providence), and John Herrity (Springfield). Sewer permit moratoria had been imposed, but the board's "pause for planning" had been overturned and moratoria were modified by the courts. Building increased during the first year of this board's tenure as developers rushed to get work initiated before new moratoria and restrictions were imposed.[41]

After two years of work to implement the urban county reorganization in conformance with the major features of the original management study, Dr. Kelley, in a policy dispute with the board of supervisors, resigned as county executive, effective 20 December 1972. His training at the University of Virginia in commerce and at George Washington University in business administration, as well as his consulting experience, had enable him to institute necessary procedures for conservative financial management of the county's budget, which in fiscal year 1971 had authorized the spending of $247.2 million, including $145.8 million for the Fairfax County public schools.

The board was not alone in its efforts to cope with major problems. With the funding of the public school system requiring approximately three-fifths of the annual budget, plus the increasing problems of overpopulation and resultant demands on natural resources and rising pollution of air, water, and land, it was appropriate that the federation concerned itself with a study of techniques of population control, abortion laws, limiting of fertility, and provision of family planning services. Many of these subjects were also the concerns of the Metropolitan Council of Governments (COG), the voluntary association of the local governments of the region.[42]

40. 1971 *Annual Report.*
41. Hinkle, *Fairfax Newsletter,* 1 January 1972; Thomas R. Williams and James L. McIlwaine v. Board of Supervisors of Fairfax County, Virginia, Re: "Rezoning Pause," At Law No. 26399. Opened 31 January 1972.
42. FCFCA *Bulletin,* January 1972.

Board business was lengthy and very time-consuming. Chairman Hoofnagle resigned in September 1972 and Jean Packard was elected to succeed him in the November general election. She remained in office for the full term elected, holding the post longer than her predecessors. Later, Warren Cikins of the Mount Vernon district was the first supervisor to be chosen in a separate special election under the new statutory requirement which finally supplanted the time-honored system of interim appointments by the circuit court judges. Mr. Cikins was elected and in January 1975 began to complete the remaining term of supervisor Herbert Harris, II, who had been elected to Congress from the eighth congressional district.[43]

The county's citizens were eager to do something about planning, controlling, and slowing down growth of population and the accompanying demand for services and increase in taxes for all county residents. The cost of running the county government had risen to an all-time high; expenditures of $328,677,383 were itemized in the 1972-1973 proposed budget. The level of fiscal activity stimulated the establishment of a department of budget and financial management in 1973, and James P. McDonald was appointed its first director. A five-year comprehensive plan requested by the county executive was prepared in 1972. It did not make recommendations, but presented costs of alternative plans. Because the plan ignored pressing transportation and environmental issues, public reaction was unfavorble, and the board abandoned this plan and created a task force to develop an acceptable program. Composed of three members of the board and the new county executive, Robert W. Wilson, the task force presented a work program which was approved by the board in July and funded with a $1.5 million appropriation of revenue-sharing funds. For the first time, the proposal was that zoning should no longer be the only land use planning and control system in the county. Dubbed PLUS, the new program was designed as a multifaceted process to make a comprehensive approach to land planning and land development management, a viewpoint which builders and developers did not appreciate. Later, the courts handed down some adverse decisions particularly regarding moratoria and tax assessments.[44]

The national press commented at length on the attempt to stimulate active citizen participation in bringing about change. Citizens were finally questioning the American theory that bigger is always better. The change meant a new look at American theories about property ownership: buying, selling, and making a profit from it. It was a nationwide

43. Hinkle, *Fairfax Newsletter*, 30 January 1975.

44. James Reid and Robert Jentsch, *AIP Newsletter*, (Washington, D.C.: American Institute of Planners, April 1975), pp. 11-13.

The Fairfax County Board of Supervisors in 1976. From left to right: Marie B.
Travesky, civic leader, former school board member; James M. Scott, civic
leader, consultant; Martha V. Pennino, civic leader, former member Vienna
Town Council; Audrey Moore, civic leader, member, Board of Directors of
Council of Governments; John F. Herrity, Chairman, of the board of
Supervisors, pension and financial planner; John P. Shacochis, civic leader,
retired Federal government employee; Joseph Alexander, merchant, savings
and loan company officer; Warren I. Cikins, consultant, lecturer; and Alan H.
Magazine, deputy assistant director, Commission on Federal Paperwork.
Photo by Bernie Boston.

problem. *Time Magazine* called it "The New American Land Rush" and
viewed the insistence of Americans on clustering in cities and suburbs
when actually the country has a vast amount of open land as one of the
major aspects of the national problem. *Time* quoted supervisor Rufus
Phillips of the task force as saying, "What we are trying to do is
orchestrate growth. We want to balance such things as transportation,
housing and schools with the quality of life." Because of the diversity of
citizenry, the large area of 399 square miles involved, and a land-use
range from urban to rural, the PLUS plan implementation will be
difficult, partly because of adverse court decisions and restrictive state
legislation.[45]

In the November 1975 elections, liberal Democrats Jean Packard and
Rufus Phillips were defeated at the polls by conservative Republicans
John Herrity, chairman-at-large, and John Shacochis. Republican Marie
Travesky won Herrity's Springfield supervisor position. In January 1976
Wilson resigned his position as county executive and J. Hamilton
Lambert was acting county executive for a few months. After extensive
advertising and interviewing, the board of supervisors selected Leonard
Whorton to assume the duties of county executive as of 1 August 1976. A
graduate of Wharton School of Finance, he previously had held positions
in Salem, Oregon, and Richmond, Virginia.[46]

45. Kenneth Bredemeier, "The Boom Fades as Area Weighs Value of Growth," *Washington Post*, 30
December 1973; *Time Magazine* (Chicago, Ill.: Time, Inc. 1 October 1973), pp. 80-99, 96; Jean R.
Packard, "PLUS, An Innovative County Planning Program," *Journal of Soil and Water Conservation,*
May-June 1975). (Ankeny, Iowa: The Soil Conservation Society of America.)

46. Hinkle, *Fairfax Newsletter*, January 1976; August 1976.

VIII

A Sense of Community

Builders

Some of the builders who had the greatest impact on Fairfax County were those who set their sights on developing entire communities: homes, shopping centers, recreational facilities, and open space. The first to implement a large development plan following World War II was Washington realtor Edward R. Carr, who conceived his own master plan for the Springfield area in 1946. He had studied maps of Northern Virginia and discovered that Springfield had the last sizable accessible tract of undeveloped land within a 12-mile zone around Washington. It was 1952 before sewer and water lines were in and plans were approved to build the first houses; 2,000 houses were completed by 1955. Schools, churches, shopping centers, and parks were part of the Carr plan. Residents of this new community recognized the need and desire for a local newspaper in the large, unincorporated area, and in 1953 five people, including Mr. and Mrs. Arthur Hughes, furnished a unifying influence for community indentity by publishing a bi-weekly tabloid, *The Springfield Independent*. It later became a weekly and was purchased in 1959 by Betsy and the late Harry Hinkle. Betsy still publishes it.[1] Edward R. Carr Inc. and many other builders continue to develop the land for commercial and residential purposes in the Springfield-Franconia-Burke area.

George C. Yeonas built his first house in 1946, and founded the organization which eventually became the Yeonas Company. He built Vienna Woods homes beginning in 1953. By 1973 his company was the largest builder of new homes in the metropolitan Washington area,

---

1. George Flynn, "Springfield Growth Surprises Planner," *The Sunday Star*, (Washington, D.C.), 24 April 1955, p. A-14.

having completed over 8,000 houses in forty-nine communities.[2] Vienna was an incorporated town and thus had a community identity. This was further augmented in 1961 when John R. Harris and Robert Hennessee began what became the *Globe* weekly community newspapers, published in Vienna with several editions for various areas of the county. Eventually the *Globe* bought out the weekly *Free Press* newspapers and Roosevelt der Tatevasion's *Fairfax County Sun-Echo*, which had been begun as the *Falls Church Echo* in 1940 by Carol and Charles Manly.[3]

The Fairfax County landscape is heavily settled with residents living in housing constructed by Carr, Yeonas, and many other builders. A distinguishing characteristic which has preserved much natural beauty in the county has been the care taken in contour street planning, and additional care taken to preserve the native trees. It is greatly to the credit of the majority of the county's builders that in their development of home sites they have left much of the existing forest for future enjoyment. Viewed from tall buildings or aircraft, the gently rolling terrain of Fairfax County still appears to be heavily forested, even though it is extensively developed.

In a county like Fairfax where population growth has been rapid, particularly in the past twenty-five years, it is difficult to examine every trend and change, and to select the most important movers and shakers for a given period. One indicator of interest and involvement of citizens with civic affairs is the annual selection of an outstanding citizen. On a countywide basis, the major civic organizations have assisted the Federation of Citizens Associations with this selection for the recipient to be honored with the *Evening Star* citizen-of-the-year award. The twenty-six Fairfax Countians so honored since 1950 reflect the unusually deep and sustained interest of county residents not only in the operation of their local government but also in voter registration, public schools, conservation, community services and programs, and human rights.[4]

But what of everyday life? The county is one of the most affluent political jurisdictions in the world, whose citizens have an extremely high average level of academic achievement. An average of seven to fourteen trips per day are made in motor vehicles in and out of private driveways, taking Fairfax Countians to work, to shop, to educational, recreational, and travel experiences. The private automobile is important; public transportation is inadequate. Cultural opportunities abound in Washington, and thousands cross the Potomac River bridges to attend

2. *Yeonas No. 1*, pamphlet (Vienna: The Yeonas Company, 1973).

3. Anne Bradford Cadman, "A Study of Washington's Suburban Virginia Newpapers" (Master's thesis, American University, Washington, D.C., 1967).

4. *Evening Star* cup, Citizen-of-the-year award programs, 1950-1976, file, Virginiana Collection Fairfax County Central Library.

Wolf Trap Park, the first national park dedicated to the performing arts was a gift from Mrs. Jouett Shouse in 1966, who also donated the Filene Center, an outdoor theater within the park, where public performances by local and international artists are given each year. National Park Service.

events at the John F. Kennedy Center for the Performing Arts, and to visit the Smithsonian Institution museums, the National Gallery of Art, the Robert F. Kennedy Stadium, the zoo, historic sites, and numerous other centers for the arts and for recreation. The sights in the county, particularly Mount Vernon, have also been seen and shown by Fairfax Countians to millions of visiting friends and relatives over the years. Dulles Airport, Reston, Wolf Trap Farm Park for the Performing Arts, Gunston Hall, Woodlawn, Sully Plantation, Colvin Run Mill, and Turkey Run and Frying Pan farms are some of the favorite local sites visited for novel experiences in the space age and for remembrance of things past. The Skyline Drive in the Blue Ridge Mountains has long been a favorite destination for driving, hiking, and camping since its first development in the 1930s. Great Falls Park is still a choice spot for rock climbing, hiking, and picnicking, although the old merry-go-round is no longer there. It was a feature at the park for many years with its carved and painted wooden animals to ride, real brass rings to catch, and a six-foot black snake who lived under it and occasionally emerged to better enjoy the caliope music and the visitors. Hurricane Agnes and her floods in 1972 precipitated the removal of the carousel.

The high per capita income in the county is reflected in the lifestyles and numerous material possessions of its residents. National and international travel has been common for government, military, and business purposes, as well as for the personal recreation. Foreign visitors to Fairfax County often write of their experiences in official reports or for the media after returning home. [5]

Leisure time is filled with a variety of activities. Within the home, television and radio have been important influences both in providing communication from the outside world and for entertainment. Brisk bookstore and recordshop sales continually attest to the popular hobbies of reading and stereo phonograph listening. Bridge, canasta, poker, cribbage and other card games are popular, as well as Monopoly and other board games; ping-pong, billiards, mah jong, and sex all have their devotees.

A House Becomes a Home

The designation of Fairfax County by the media in the 1950s as a Washington "Bedroom suburb" where the majority of wage earners was employed by either the federal government or the military establishment was appropriate at the time. Most employment, cultural, and shopping needs were meet by offices, programs, and stores within the District of Columbia. However, as families grew, many adults became interested in their local community association activities and needs, and particularly in the local county government which could supply some of the answers to those needs. Children attended the local public schools and became involved in after-hours recreation programs. Frequently, the parents became interested in the parent-teachers associations. Residents served on boards of directors of swimming-and-tennis clubs (dubbed "The poor man's country clubs") and in baseball, football, and scouting organizations. Literally hundreds of civic and social groups have flourished in Fairfax County from the 1950s to the present day. All these organizations have memberships and officers to support their activities. [6]

Recreational opportunities have varied. Before the community swimming pool era and home air conditioning, hot summers were made more bearable when families swam in the Potomac, at River Bend, or drove to public swimming pools at Middleburg or Purcellville in Loudoun County, or journeyed to the Chesapeake Bay, Eastern Shore, or the beaches of North Carolina's Outer Banks. Model cars and planes have been raced, minibikes have left their trail marks in many a pasture. Little League baseball for boys, Pony Tail leagues for girls, soccer, and both duckpin and tenpin bowling have provided active team sports in most county communities. The county's recreation department has had

5. Netherton, *Green Spring Farm* pp. 77-80.

6. Nan and Ross Netherton, eds., *Civic-Government Directory, 1956* (Annandale, Va.: Fairfax County Federation of Citizens Associations, 1956); Nan Netherton, ed., *Fairfax County Directory* (Falls Church, Va.: Fairfax County Cultural Association, 1965).

an increasing role in providing a diversified program of leisure-time activities for county residents of all ages. Private and public swimming, tennis, and ice skating facilities are well patronized.[7]

Three Communities: Hollin Hills, Holmes Run Acres, and Pimmit Hills

In general, the smallest community unit in Fairfax County is the residential subdivision, usually developed by more than one builder if it is sizable, and built over a period of several years. Hollin Hills, Holmes Run Acres, and Pimmit Hills have been chosen as examples in design, location, and growth.

The Hollin Hills subdivision was begun in 1949, south of the city of Alexandria, on the west side of Fort Hunt Road. The houses were designed in a contemporary style by architect Charles Goodman; the first builder was Robert Davenport. One of the goals of the project was to encourage the homeowner to collaborate with the developer and landscape architects Bernard Voight, Eric Paepcke, and Dan Kiley to make the community look as though it were a large park and not a collection of individual lots. The first buyers had a choice of three basic floor plans, a one-level, a two-level, and a split-level of brick and wood, with options available. No curbs and gutters were included in the street design in order to retain the park-like appearance of the heavily wooded, rolling terrain. Lot sizes varied, with the minimum about one-quarter acre; costs of house and lot in the first sections ran from $14,000 to $24,000. In 1976, the subdivision consisted of 463 homes, and the resale prices ranged from $60,000 to $114,000, depending on a variety of factors such as landscaping, location, house design, and additions to the buildings.[8]

Holmes Run Acres, on the east side of Gallows Road, and south of Route 50, (Arlington Boulevard), was begun in 1950 by Gerald and Eli Luria, who had recently completed several groups of colonial-style houses elsewhere. The developers wanted contemporary, efficient, economical dwellings which did not take on the appearance of rows of monotonous suburban tract houses. They engaged architects Nicholas Satterlee and Francis Lethbridge who designed a one-level and a two-level house, with several options. The structures were of wood and brick and placed on approximately one-quarter-acre lots; the original prices ranged from $13,750 to $17,450. Brick fireplace walls, exposed beams and extensive use of glass captured an indoor-outdoor feeling, and the lots and curbed and guttered contour streets were planned to make the most of gently rolling hillsides of woods and farm fields. The

7. Interview, Ilah T. Osborn, Falls Church, May 1975, Virginiana Collection, Fairfax County Public library.

8. *Architectural Forum*, December 1949; *Life Magazine*, 10 September 1951; *Parents Magazine*, February 1952; O'Neal, *Architecture in Virginia*, 1968, pp. 136-37.

architects urged homeowners not to fence yards. In 1976, resales of Holmes Run Acres houses, now numbering approximately 340, were bringing between $45,000 and $80,000, depending on lot, house style, and additions.[9]

Pimmit Hills, west of Falls Church and Pimmit Run, on the south side of Route 7, the Leesburg Pike, was a subdivision of small, simple, one-story rectangular frame houses built of either asbestos shingles or brick on concrete slabs. The first few sections were constructed by builder George Offutt of Warrenton, Virginia, who was followed later by other builders. The houses were all the same floor plan, some with a picture window looking out on the street, and some without. Most were built on quarter-acre lots and cost between $10,000 and $11,000, with Veterans Administration (VA) guaranteed loans when first offered for sale between 1949 and 1952. There were no curbs and gutters installed in the first sections developed. Part of the land was open pasture, and another part wooded; the builders saved most of the existing trees. When the subdivision was completed, approximately 1,650 houses had been built. In 1976, the houses were selling for between $43,000 and $53,000, depending on the lot and types of additions to the original structure.[10]

These three subdivisions present interesting examples of varying design concepts, architectural styles, community life and economic growth between the 1950s and 1970s. Each community—Hollin Hills, Holmes Run Acres, and Pimmit Hills,—has had an active civic association which has published a monthly newsletter for the past twenty-five years. The newsletters furnish detailed documentation of how each community developed a "root system" for the highly mobile society that came to live in the area of Northern Virginia near the nation's capital. They record problems and solutions, joys and sorrows, and achievements and frustrations of the county's public and private life. They reveal the social and business changes that occurred over two-and-a-half decades of the accelerated evolution that turned Fairfax County into one of America's leading urban-suburban centers. Historians, sociologists, and anthropologists of the future will find in these newsletters a wealth of information on the changing attitudes, values and circumstances of the resourceful and well-informed citizenry of Fairfax County.[11]

9. *Architectural Forum*, August 1951; *House and Home*, May 1952; Ben Bagdikian, "The Rape of the Land," (Philadelphia: *Saturday Evening Post*, 18 June 1966); Dena Leep, Rae Parmenter, and Vivian Smith, eds., *Holmes Run Acres: The Story of a Community* (Falls Church: Holmes Run Acres Civic Association, 1976); In 1953 Holmes Run Acres built the first community pool in Northern Virginia financed by the sale of stocks and operated on annual dues. Florence Sticker, ed., *The Big Splash: A History of Our Pool* (Annandale, Va.: Holmes Run Acres Recreation Association, 1963).

10. Interview, Carl and Anne Zimmer, Falls Church, Va., 6 August 1976.

11. *Hollins Hills Bulletin* (Alexandria: Hollin Hills Civic Association, monthly series 1951-present); *Holmes Runner* (Falls Church, Va.: Holmes Run Acres Civic Association, monthly series 1952-present);

IX

Woman's Place

Since the rapid growth in population in Fairfax County necessitated a corresponding growth in government services, women have slowly assumed roles with increasing responsibilities in government. The first woman to be a member of the Fairfax County board of supervisors was Edith Rogers, a teacher and dairy farmer from Herndon who was appointed in 1935 to fill the vacancy left by the death of W.H. Elmore of the Dranesville district. She was later elected for a full term from 1936 to 1940. Anne Wilkins was elected supervisor from Mason district in 1951 and served until 1964. In 1958 she was the first woman in the county's history to be elected chairman of the board of supervisors. In the same year, "M. K." Henderson of Mason district was elected the first woman chairman of the board of zoning appeals.[1] Edna Bicksler was appointed clerk to the board of supervisors and served from 1952 to 1971, in an office which had always, until that time, been filled by men. She was first succeeded by Helen Morisen and then by Ethel Wilcox Register, who presently serves in that capacity. Harriet Bradley represented the Dranesville district on the board for two terms, from 1964 to 1972. Martha Pennino has served as Centreville supervisor since her first term which began in 1968. Virginia McEnearney was appointed to complete the unexpired term of Donald Bowman of Springfield in 1971 and she served until 1972. Audrey Moore first assumed her position as supervisor from Annandale district in 1972 and was reelected in 1975.

Pimmit Hills Dispatch (Falls Church: Pimmit Hills Citizens Association, monthly series, 1952-present). A full series of each newsletter is available in the community civic association files and in the county's Virginiana collection, central library, Fairfax.

1. Hinkle, *Fairfax Newsletter*, 23 November 1957; 11 January, 15 March 1958; 21 June 1958.

TABLE II

DETAILED OCCUPATIONAL COMPOSITION OF EMPLOYED WOMEN

FAIRFAX COUNTY, 1960 and 1970

	1960		1970		Index of Occupational Shift, 1960-1970	
	Percent of Total Employed Female Labor Force	Females as % of Total Employed	Percent of Total Employed Female Labor Force	Females as % of Total Employed	Male	Female
White Collar	77.5	24.5	83.5	42.4	139.9	113.2
Professional	18.2	24.1	23.2	29.6	162.9	146.6
Managers	4.2	11.1	5.2	14.2	153.0	137.2
Sales	8.9	35.7	8.8	41.6	107.2	97.9
Clerical	46.2	68.4	46.3	76.0	82.3	100.7
Blue Collar	4.4	5.9	4.2	10.0	56.1	97.9
Craftsmen	0.7	1.4	0.9	3.7	41.0	173.5
Operatives	3.6	18.1	3.0	23.9	53.6	71.7
Laborers	0.1	0.9	0.3	7.2	50.4	759.6
Agriculture	0.1	7.1	0.1	13.3	-45.2	16.4
Service	8.0	44.5	9.9	56.0	156.9	139.2
Private House-hold	6.7	93.9	2.3	94.4	-28.8	-10.9
Not Reported	3.3			34.0		
Totals	100.0	26.4	100.0			

Number of Fairfax County Women in Labor Force 1960 = 25,209   1970 = 62,484

Sources: U.S. Bureau of the Census, *1960 Census of Population, Detailed Characteristics*, Series PC(1)-48D, Table 121. U.S. Bureau of the Census, *1970 Census of Population, General Social and Economic Characteristics*, Series PC (1)-C48, Table 122.

Prepared by David Sheatsley, Office of Research and Statistics, 1976

Marie Travesky, the supervisor representing the Springfield district, was elected in 1975.

Jean Packard, who had been the first woman president of the Federation of Citizens Associations, 1969-1970, was elected the first woman chairman-at-large of the Fairfax County board of supervisors in 1972 and served until January 1976.

In recent years, several women have been promoted or selected for top staff positions in various departments of the county government. Ilah Osborn headed the county's part-time recreation department from 1949 to 1957, operating a growing playground and activities program with funds provided by the county, Community Chest, and many private organizations and individuals. Mary K. McCulloch was director of Libraries from 1953 to 1969, and Frances Duffey served as director of the Department of Welfare from 1958 to 1970. After having served as deputy or chief deputy under the commissioner of revenue and supervisor of assessments since 1950, in 1969 Marion Earle was appointed director of the personal property, state income and license division of the office of assessment. She retired in 1976 as deputy supervisor of the assessments division.

Two women have been chairmen of the Fairfax County Park Authority board. Ella May Doyle served in that capacity from 1965 to 1968 and Nancy Brown for the year 1973. The Fairfax County History Commission has had three women chairmen: Joyce Wilkinson (1969-1970), Mary Fahringer (1972-1974), and Edith Sprouse (1976-1978). Mary Anne Lecos was school board chairman frim 1973 to 1976; Audrey Capone headed up the civil service commission in 1974. Ilene Blake was appointed director of the county's office of management and budget in 1973, a position in which she continues to serve. In the year 1973, women headed the county's board of supervisors, school board, park authority, history commission, and office of management and budget, possibly the only such combination in the country.[3]

Because of a concern about full participation by women in community, business, and government life, the Fairfax County Commission on Women, the first local commission for women in the state, was established in September 1971 by the Fairfax County board of supervisors. The initial directive was to prepare a report on the problems of the status of women in the county, particularly some of the major concerns relating to sex discrimination in employment, housing, and credit. The initial study, *First Report on the Fairfax County Commission on Women*, was published by the county in November 1972. It was an evaluation by which to measure future progress.

2. History Commission Minutes, January 1969; January 1972; January 1975.

3. County personnel records, under biographee's names; Board of Supervisors Minute Books; School Board minutes; Park Authority Board minutes, 1973.

X

The Brotherhood of Man

Fairfax County's history of relations between the races is complicated partly because its geographical location assured that the experiences of both North and South would influence its own response to the challenge of achieving harmony among residents belonging to different races. At times, this has meant that the county's black community suffered from forms of discrimination that were present in both North and South. At other times, the particular politics, society, and economy of Northern Virginia have provided opportunities for the black community that were not available elsewhere in Virginia.

A 1929 editorial in the *Fairfax Herald* warned that Republican victories could put white supremacy "which we have fought to preserve since the war" in grave danger. Editor Carne deplored the entertainment by President Hoover of a Negro in the White House and the appointment of a Negro postmaster in Albemarle County as efforts "to put the negro on social equality with white people." He feared that further Republican victories in local and state elections would "put shackles on the white people of Virginia," and "it is not beyond the realm of possibility that mixed schools might come as a result of Republican victory. The average white voter in Virginia does not care to take any chances of the lessening of white supremacy in any degree, and to vote with a party that has always represented the dark element in Virginia, will not be done."[1]

---

1. *Fairfax Herald*, 14 June, 21 June, 28 June, 5 July 1929; 4 April 1930.

The NAACP in Fairfax County

It was because of a discriminatory court case over residential segregation that the Falls Church Branch, predecessor to The Fairfax County Branch, of the National Association for the Advancement of Colored People was organized. The Virginia General Assembly had passed legislation in 1912 enabling cities and towns to adopt ordinances to permit segregation of the races. In 1915, the Falls Church town council proposed such an ordinance which would have restricted blacks to residence in a small section of town and prevented them from living in restricted districts even though they already had homes in those districts.

Edwin Bancroft Henderson, a graduate of Howard and Columbia universities and a descendant of the Foote family in Falls Church called a meeting to discuss the proposal. A temporary name for the action group was "The Colored Citizens Protective League" and the officers were: Joseph B. Tinner, president; the Rev. Mr. John Colbert, vice-president; E.B. Henderson, secretary; and the Rev. Mr. George Powell, treasurer. Others on the executive committee were Melvin Tinner, Robert J. Evans, George W. Simmons, and William Carpenter. Letters of protest were sent to the mayor and town councilmen, and eventually, the council announced on 15 May 1915 that a referendum on the question of the segregation ordinance would be submitted to the voters. Two lawyers from Washington, James A. Cobb and George E. C. Hayes, were engaged by the protective league, which had now become "The Falls Church and Vicinity—branch" of the National Association for the Advancement of Colored People. A brief was submitted to the town council pointing out the unconstitutionality of the plan, and the council dropped the matter.[2]

The NAACP began to take a very active part in the county's human relations activities, investigating complaints about unjust treatment of blacks, especially by the police. The organization mailed books and pamphlets to the whites to foster a better understanding of the problems of the blacks. There was a vigorous and continuing effort to get blacks to pay poll taxes and vote. "The poll tax had been enacted by the General Assembly to prevent negroes from registering. But about 50 percent of the County's negroes have continued to pay poll taxes, register and vote."[3]

Negroes were required by law to sit in the rear of the bus in Virginia, although not in the District of Columbia. Key Bridge was the place where the blacks had to move to the back of the bus, and sometimes whites would argue to attempt to have them sit in the back in the District as

2. Henderson, NAACP, p. 2,
3. Ibid., p. 3.

well. This "Jim Crow" law was set aside in the federal court in 1946 when the Lottee Taylor case was decided, ruling that the law was unconstitutional in interstate commerce. The case itself arose in Fairfax County when Mrs. Taylor was traveling from a town beyond Washington to a town in Virginia and was ejected from the bus. Lawyers were called in on the case, including Martin A. Martin of the state NAACP legal staff. "The court's decision, on the constitutional issue, was the basis for similar court victories elsewhere."[4]

The NAACP in Fairfax County was the first rural branch organized in the country. When the 1947 national convention was held in the District of Columbia, Fairfax County was honored as the best county branch in the nation. The branch president, the Rev. Mr. Milton Sheppard, was given a seat of honor at the Lincoln Memorial Meeting.[5]

In 1956-57, the Virginia legislature considered a group of bills, popularly known as the "anti-NAACP bills", in an attempt to curtail the functioning of various civil rights organizations. During the several hearings which were held in Northern Virginia by the Assembly's Thomson Committee at this time the question was asked, "Dr. Henderson, what is your race?" To which he replied, "This calls for some consideration. One of my great grandfathers was an Indian. My father's father was Portuguese and my mother's father was one of the highly respected white citizens in Williamsburg, Virginia. Her mother was this gentleman's slave. Now, which race shall I subscribe to?" No further questions were asked of E.B. Henderson.[6]

Black Students and Teachers

School desegregation in Fairfax County came about six years after the Supreme Court desegregation ruling as a result of concerted effort on the part of many individuals and groups. The NAACP played a major role. The first twenty-six black students who applied to be admitted to all-white schools in 1959 were denied enrollment as a result of the state's "massive resistance" policy then in force. The next year, after the policy was declared unconstitutional, twenty-seven black pupils enrolled in all-white schools for the first year of integrated education in the county. Each year, the integrated enrollment increased, due in part to litigation. In the spring of 1965, the school board announced that in the fall it would commence conversion to a fully desegregated system for both students

4. Ibid., p. 5.
5. Ibid., p. 15.
6. Ibid., p. 11. E. B. Henderson had once begun the study of medicine, but was unable to finish it for financial reasons.

and faculty. This policy was put into effect during the 1965-66 school year.[7]

Teachers had been segregated by race as well as students, and not just in schools. Even the Fairfax Education Association, the professional teachers' organization, specifically spelled out in their handbook that membership was open to "any white person engaged in the public schools of Fairfax County." The purpose of the F.E.A. was set forth: "to promote the educational work of the public schools of the county; to foster a cooperative and professional spirit among those engaged in educational work; and in cooperation with the Virginia Education Association, to strive to improve the standard of Public Education in the State of Virginia."[8]

Eventually, this unjust exclusion of black teachers from the organization had a positive effect on the leadership of the F.E.A., which was aware that the Arlington Education Association had been expelled from Virginia Education Association membership in 1961 when Arlington membership requirement was changed to admit blacks. Because the F.E.A. desired to retain membership in the state organization, the V.E.A. convention in Richmond in November 1962 granted local option rights to the F.E.A., resulting in a special mail ballot on an amendment to drop the word "white" from the membership regulations. When the ballots were counted, the vote of 2,495 to 405 favored the amendment.[9]

Jobs and Votes

There were other encouraging signs of changing attitudes. The county's recreation department had twenty-one black recreation workers in eight different locations in 1964. It became difficult to determine black personnel percentages after 1963 because race designation was dropped from the county records in that year. After years of effort by many civic and government groups, the Virginia poll tax was abolished in 1963, and the following year, the League of Women Voters conducted a massive voter registration drive. Every organization was invited to submit its membership list; it was then checked against the list of registered voters and returned indicating nonregistered members. The individual organizations then contacted members and urged them to register and vote. Over the next decade the changes in registration and voting patterns were so drastic that by the time a study was conducted in 1975 on voter registration rates in Virginia, race no longer seemed to be a

7. Fairfax County School Board, *Annual Report to the County* (Fairfax, Va.: Fairfax County Public Schools) 1964-1965; 1965-1966. Henderson, *NAACP*, pp. 9-10.

8. *Yearbook* (Fairfax: Fairfax Education Association, 1947-1948).

9. *Fairfax County Sun-Echo*, 16 August 1962; *Northern Virginia Sun*, 15 February 1963.

barrier on this basic level of political participation. Still another encouraging sign was reported by the county's personnel director when he stated at a monthly Federation of Citizens Associations meeting that the library system and health department had been the first Fairfax County units of government to hire blacks in white collar and professional positions. At that time, most positions held by blacks were in laboring, custodial, and allied duties.

In a November 1964 report on civil rights in the county, the League of Women Voters reported that the county government, many chain stores, and some large independent concerns were adopting policies of equal opportunity employment at all levels. Small businesses were finding it more difficult to liberalize their hiring policies. Public recreation facilities were open to all, but no private swimming pools. There were restrictions to team competition at some bowling alleys. The YWCA and YMCA and scouts had open participation policies. Large restaurants and motels were available to all, and only one theater was not open to blacks in 1963. Banks and financing were available to qualified blacks although many blacks had not had an opportunity to establish credit ratings. The most difficult problem was housing for blacks. The number of blacks in the county had remained almost constant for twenty years, but relative to the total population during that period, blacks had composed 16.6 percent in 1940 and only 5.4 percent in 1960.[10]

The League of Women Voters credited black churches for providing a focal point for the civil rights movement and fund raising by supporting civil rights organizations which included the Chamber of Commerce, Federation of Citizens Associations, the Congress of Racial Equality (CORE), the Fairfax County Council on Human Relations, the Fairfax Housing Council, Inc., Northern Virginia Fair Housing, Inc., the Young Women's Christian Association, and the National Association for the Advancement of Colored People.[11]

The Ku Klux Klan

The race riots of the 1960s were brought on by both the blacks and the whites and their respective leaders, fighting for justice, freedom, and a share for blacks in the administration of government antipoverty

---

10. "Civil Rights in Fairfax County," Fairfax County League of Women Voters report, November 1964; Carol Griffee, "Fairfax Zoners Approve Housing for Negroes," *Evening Star* Washington, D.C., 30 July 1964; "Race Relations in Fairfax County," Fairfax County League of Women Voters report, April 1964 (hereinafter cited as League of Women Voters, "Race Relations"); Michael Digby, "Explaining Voter Registration Rates in Virginia," *Newsletter of the Institute of Government* (Charlottesville, Va.: University of Virginia, 1975), 52(4).

11. League of Women Voters, "Race Relations," pp. 2-4.

programs. The Ku Klux Klan still existed as an active racist organization of 381 klan units in at least fifteen states. The klan had been founded in 1865 by six Confederate army veterans for social and amusement purposes. By 1867, however, at a convention in Nashville, the klan's main objective was stated as being "the maintenance and supremacy of the white race." The House Un-American Activities Committee revealed in 1966 a decrease in klan activity since its height in the 1920s, when Fairfax County's klan was sizable and apparently respected by the community. Klan-oriented activities were regularly featured for a number of years on a special day at Fairfax County's week-long county fair. The county's klan activities gradually died out after a resurgence in 1954 during the schools controversy, largely because of the civil rights movement fostering new legislation and the establishment of the Human Rights Commission in 1974.[12]

It was obvious from feature stories in the newspapers that increasing efforts toward cooperation and understanding were being made on the local community level. William A. West of Vienna, who observed his 100th birthday in 1974, has been an active participant and a keen observor of the passing scene and is frequently interviewed and quoted. During "Negro History Week" in 1970, the Fairfax County branch of the Young Women's Christian Association sponsored a program called "The Black Woman Speaks" which highlighted contributions made by black women in the fields of law, politics, music, poetry, and the armed services. John Gott, librarian at Langley High School, sponsored a project featuring a portrait gallery of black educators and, with student assistance, traced the historical development of education for blacks in Virginia. Hollie West wrote about John Jackson, a black recording artist from Fairfax Station. Jackson was planning his third European concert tour the following fall to "sing music that cuts across centuries, racial lines and regional differences . . . . His storehouse of songs includes blues, ballads, country dance tunes and rags, all of which he sings in a rich, craggy voice that ranges from tenor to baritone."[13]

Research by the Washington Center for Metropolitan Studies revealed in 1971 that the Capital Beltway was the major boundary line for integration and that 87.5 percent of blacks who lived in Fairfax and Montgomery counties were living in areas that were more than 80 percent white.[14]

12. Sandy Eubank, "Racial Discrimination and Extremism: A National Overview," (manuscript, Fairfax County, Va.: Virginiana Collection, 1975), pp. 2-12.

13. The Globe Newspapers, 12 February 1970, p. 15; Washington Post, 28 February 1971, p. F-1.

14. Kirk Scharfenburg, "Beltway is Now Boundary Line for Integration," Washington Post, 13 June 1971, p. D-1.

Gum Springs
The Saunders B. Moon Community Action Association

An outstanding example of county blacks working in a sustained and successful effort to improve their standard of living is illustrated by the Gum Springs community near Mount Vernon. In 1963, the Saunders B. Moon Community Action Association was established and named after the former principal of Gum Springs' Drew-Smith Elementary School. The purpose of the organization was to alleviate economic and social problems. One of the major problems was replacing substandard housing with better accommodations. Initially, both blacks and whites served together, but after five years of discussion and dissension, the black group voted to exclude all nonresidents of Gum Springs from leadership positions.

Since 1963, with funding provided from many government and private sources, the association, representing about 1,200 community residents, established a manpower training program, a day-care center and child development program, and a teen center. Martin Luther King, Jr. Park was established, and within its boundaries was constructed the first county-built community swimming pool. New, low-cost homes were built, as well as a large apartment project. Streets have been paved and storm drainage provided. [15]

Community Problems and Community Acceptance

A black neighborhood in Herndon called Cooktown caused concern among its residents and town and county officials because substandard streets and public services were below the level of those in surrounding white neighborhoods. Other county civic associations joined forces with the Cooktown civic association to bring action against the local governments to remedy the situation. [16]

There were also racial problems at Herndon High School, largest in the county, resulting in a melee between black and white students in October 1974. In discussions which followed the incident, students expressed their desire to have more participation in school decisions and more interest shown from the teachers. [17]

In 1976, the Rocky Run Citizens Association, a group of about 200 member-families living in the Rocky Run watershed near McLean,

15. *Virginia Sentinel*, 21 June 1973, p. 1; *Gum Springs Newsletter* (Fairfax County Central Library, Virginiana Collection), *Washington Post*, 9 June 1975, p. C-2.

16. *Reston Times*, 9 September 1971, p. 3.

17. Allen Frank, "Main Issues at Herndon: Discipline, Public Voice," *Evening Star*, (Washington, D.C.), 25 October 1974.

Taylor M. Williams was for many
years an administrator in the Fairfax
County public school system, and was
the first principal of the county's first
black high school, Luther Jackson, at
Merrifield. A graduate of Tuskegee
and American Universities, he retired
from the school system in 1975.

Mona Blake was the first black
member of the Fairfax County School
Board. She taught history in the
Washington, D.C. public schools
before moving to Reston. A graduate of
Howard University, she served on the
School Board from 1972-1974.

recommended to the Fairfax County board of supervisors that a stream
tributary to Rocky Run be named Sharper's Run and be so marked on all
local and United States Geological Survey maps. The purpose was to
honor a former slave, Daniel Sharper, who had earned his freedom in the
midnineteenth century, and as a free and family man had been an early
landholder and respected member of the Rocky Run community. The
board officially designated the stream Sharper's Run and so it will appear
on all future County and United States Geological Survey maps.[18]

A gradual community acceptance of blacks into the mainstream of
acitivities could be illustrated by hundreds of examples of cooperative
efforts and mutual consideration. One case in point was the awarding of
the *Washington Star* trophy to J. Sidney Holland as Fairfax County's
Citizen of the Year in May 1975. He was the first black to be so honored.
The selection committee for the 25th annual award was composed of
representatives from the Federation of Citizens Associations, the League

18. Fairfax County Office of Public Affairs, *News Release*, no. 144/75, 27 May 1975.

J. Sidney Holland. Fairfax County Citizen of the Year in 1975 was the first black to receive the award given by the Washington Evening Star annually since 1950.

of Women Voters, Chamber of Commerce, the Countywide Citizens Association, the Council of PTAs, and the United Way. They were honoring a man with a long record of participation in civic, religious, political, and fraternal activites in a predominantly white county. Mr. Holland, a native-born Virginian, moved from Fluvanna County to Fairfax in 1926. His concern and efforts on behalf of voter registration, fair housing, health, and education are illustrated by his membership on the Democratic Committee, his charter membership in the Human Relations Council, the Fairfax Hospital Association, the Higher Horizons board of directors, and other such activities. The deep involvement of this man in his community was succinctly summarized in the award citation: "Through these years of activity and service J. Sidney Holland's interests have been directed toward people rather than abstracts—How can citizens best be heard? What can we do to solve our neighbor's problem? These have been his concerns in the past and he will continue to pursue them in the future. Such persistence and dedication are the hallmarks of citizen participation and are the essence of a Citizen of the Year—this and every other year."[19]

19. Program, 25th Annual Awards Dinner, Fairfax County Federation of Citizens Associations, 9 May 1975.

XI

Suburban Life Support Systems

Water and Sewer Service

In March 1950, because water needs far exceeded capacity and because of increasing pollution from upstream development, the Alexandria Water Company sold its Lake Barcroft reservoir on Holmes Run and 680 acres of adjoining land to a group of developers from Massachusetts. They set about immediately developing a community of "miniature country estates." The group had searched the eastern seaboard and as far west as Texas for suitable property, and had found this Virginia land and its beautiful lake, within seven miles of the White House. The maintenance of the lake was a major concern of the property owners as homes were built and the community grew.

To replace Lake Barcroft as a reservoir, the Alexandria Water Company constructed a long concrete dam thirty feet high on the Occoquan River in 1950 to impound approximately 55 million gallons of water in the Occoquan Reservoir to provide water for its customers. Three years of drought caused shortages and water rationing in many areas of Fairfax County, and even the Occoquan Reservoir water level dropped so low that the water company had to pump 25 percent of its supply the summer of 1954 from tidewater at the town of Occoquan.[1]

The water problems of the county obviously required serious attention. Supervisor Anne Wilkins spoke to the Fairfax County Federation of Citizens Associations membership at a meeting on 15 September 1955 urging support of the proposed $30,000,000 water bond issue, a revenue bond which would not be considered a.debt against the county. The problem of pollution of the Potomac River was one which Mrs. Wilkins described in detail, claiming that Fairfax County's sewer

---

1 *Lake Barcroft Directory* (Falls Church, Va.: Lake Barcroft Community Association, Inc., 1960), pp. 2-6; *Sunday Star* (Washington, D.C.), 30 October 1955, A-14.

program of $20,000,000 funding had probably done more than any other jurisdiction in the area to clean up its share of Potomac River pollution, and that care had been taken to avoid installing any county sewage treatment plans above the District of Columbia water supply intake. She spoke of Lake Barcroft resident Stuart Finley's "Our Beautiful Potomac" television documentary and recent editorials and news stories as having done "an excellent job of stirring up public interest in cleaning up the Potomac River." Until 1950, despite the county's sanitation ordinance passed in 1928, practically all county sewage had entered the Potomac untreated either through the one existing trunk sewer in the Holmes Run watershed or into the streams of the county and thence to the river. The 1950 $3,000,000 sewer bond passed in the county's Sanitary District 1 had provided for construction of a treatment plant at Belle View to service the Holmes Run sewer. Plants on upper Pimmit Run, Little Hunting Creek, and Dogue Creek were later approved by the state health authorities and the water control board as primary treatment plants at their planned capacity.[2]

Despite the facts that wells were going dry and that there were very real prospects of insufficient water for minimum needs, the county voters defeated the water bond issue in November 1955. The consulting firm of Alexander Potter Associates made a survey of projected water needs to the year 2000, including existing company customers and adjacent areas to be served by line extensions except for Mason Neck and Herndon. At the time, Potter reported that there were fifteen private and four publicly owned companies supplying 45 percent of the county's population with water, the smallest company serving forty families, the largest, 15,000 people.[3]

Following the defeat of the bond issue, almost a year of exensive discussions ensured between board members, citizens groups, and individuals regarding the pros and cons of establishing a private corporation or an authority to solve the increasingly serious water shortage problem in the county. The town of Fairfax made a decision to undertake its own Loudoun County Goose Creek water supply project, including the building of a concrete dam for reservoir impoundment, a treatment plant, and twenty-two miles of pipeline mainly following the old Washington & Old Dominion right-of-way to deliver the water to Fairfax. Fall Church City was already buying water from the District of Columbia and contemplating the purchase of the Annandale Water Company. Since the Annandale company was considered an important key to a county integrated water system to insure quantity, quality, and

2. FCFCA *Bulletin*, October 1955.
3. Alexander Potter Associates, *Fairfax County, Virginia Comprehensive Water Supply Plan, Preliminary Report*, 16 March 1955, Alexander Potter Associates, Consulting Engineers, New York, N.Y.

economy, the board of supervisors moved with deliberate speed. The board voted unanimously in September 1957 to establish the Fairfax County Water Authority and appointed five persons for initial terms on the authority's board. Lytton H. Gibson, representing the Northern Virginia Builders Association at the hearing, asked that regulations be made flexible enough to allow reimbursement to developers for installation of mains. Douglas Tepper, president of the Federation of Citizens Associations, reported that his organization had met, thoroughly discussed the alternatives, and wholeheartedly agreed with the board's establishment of the authority.[4]

A second dam was constructed by the Alexandria Water Company in 1957 on the Occoquan River approximately 3,000 feet upstream from the existing dam. The resulting reservoir contains about 9.6 billion gallons of water, or 17,000 acres of water surface, which is presently used as a source of water supply. The Northern Virginia Regional Park Authority has the responsibility for administering the use of the reservoir for recreation by the public. Hydroelectric generating facilities utilize surplus stream flows to generate a portion of the power requirements of the water treatment plant. Principal chemicals used in the process include active carbon, alum, lime, potassium permanganate, chlorine and fluoride. According to the authority's 1974 *Annual Report*, the system was serving a population of 554,000 with 84,965 retail customers in Fairfax County. It was wholesaling 25 percent of all of the water it sold to the city of Alexandria and to Prince William County. The authority acquired all of the Alexandria Water Company's holdings outside the city limits in 1967. As was the case with the Lake Barcroft reservoir, Occoquan is subject to pollution from upstream development.[5]

At a meeting of the Fairfax County Republican Committee on Tuesday, 13 September 1960, Congressman Joel T. Broyhill presented supervisor William Moss with the pen which President Dwight D. Eisenhower had used to sign H. R. 1263 into law authorizing the Dulles International Airport interceptor sewer construction through Fairfax County.

At the time Broyhill was defending his congressional seat against Ralph Kaul of McLean, a Democrat who was running against what he declared to be Broyhill's do-nothing policy toward potential pollution problems the new airport would present. The incumbent Republican declared that Potomac pollution was being cleared up, and predicted that "within five years we'll be able to use the Potomac River for swimming as well as other recreational activities."[6]

4. W. M. Zollman, Jr., "Provide for Growth Before It Comes," (New York: *The American City*, June 1962); FCFCA *Bulletin*, September 1957; Hinkle, *Fairfax Newsletter*, 21 September 1957.

5. *Your Water Supply Facilities*, (Annandale, Va.: Fairfax County Water Authority, 1973).

6. *Northern Virginia Sun*, 14 September 1960; Cadman, "Virginia Newspapers," p. 47.

Generally, when countywide demand for a particular type of service has become sufficient, economics have made it advantageous to provide the service on a countywide scale. In the early 1960s, sewer and water services including those provided through sanitary districts were transferred to a countywide service. A bond issue for sewering the Pohick Creek watershed was approved by the voters in April 1965, opening up a large area for intensive development.[7]

Local problems sometimes became big problems. Lily pads, erosion, muddy water, pollution, and siltation from upstream runoff have required constant attention through the years. The tremendous volume of rainfall which deluged the metropolitan area during tropical storm Agnes in 1972 caused major erosion around one end of the Lake Barcroft dam, which had been built in 1915, and drained the lake down to an ugly mud flat. The time, thought, work, and money required from local residents and a Federal Small Business Administration loan of $500,000 to repair the damage and restore the lake would be a book in itself.[8]

In an article called "An Anatomy of Suburban Growth," Jeff Stansbury expressed strong personal views when he wrote of what he considered to be the most important single determinant for high density suburban development: sewerage. "In the dimensions of suburban sewers, the capacity of the treatment plants at the ends of the lines, the high-density rezonings which trunk sewers inspire, and the political-economic-legal forces which bear on sewerage, we can find more to reckon our demographic fate than in all the contraceptives, abortion law repeals, and family planning clinics we will ever bring forth." He used Fairfax County as a case study in an attempt to determine how the national suburban sprawl pattern was dropping the average density of U. S. urban areas from 6,580 persons per square mile a little over fifty years ago to a projected 3,000 persons in 1985. In the process, land was being gobbled up, pavement was covering top soil which might be needed later, gasoline and other forms of energy were being wasted, the costs of public services and taxes to pay for them were inflating, and economic barriers were being erected against low-income families. The net immigration contributing to almost two-thirds of Fairfax County's growth since 1960 had as of 1971 largely been housed in single-family dwellings which consumed more open space and were more expensive to supply with sewerage, police, libraries, and other services than row houses or apartment buildings.[9]

7. *History of Sanitary Districts in Fairfax County* (Fairfax, Va.: Office of Research and Statistics, 2 October 1975); *Public Law 566.*

8. *Lake Barcroft Directory* (Falls Church, Va.: Lake Barcroft Community Association, Inc., 1960); Ron Shaffer, "Loan to Repair Dam at Lake Barcroft Approved by Small Business Administration," *Washington Post,* 28 November 1972, p. C-1.

9. *Equilibrium* (Palo Alto, Ca.: Zero Population Growth, 1971), 1(1):9-11.

Sometimes inferior materials create problems in the system. Bituminous fiber pipes used in construction to provide sewer service to tens of thousands of homes in Fairfax County and many other parts of the country since the 1950s, even though they met code specifications, are collapsing in subdivisions like Waynewood and must be replaced at added cost.[10]

Through a complex and largely interconnecting network of gravity sewers and forced mains, sewage is conveyed to a number of treatment plants. At present these plants are either in the process of upgrading and expansion, or soon will be eliminated from the system. The largest of the county's plants is Lower Potomac, south of Ft. Belvoir, which is being expanded to handle flows now treated at Dogue Creek, Little Hunting Creek, Fort Belvoir, and Blue Plains. The Westgate Plant, near Bellehaven, will soon be eliminated and flows diverted to an enlarged and improved Alexandria plant. A small amount of treated wastewater flows into the Occoquan River from several small plants in Fairfax and Prince William counties. The Upper Occoquan Sewage Authority is constructing an advanced waste treatment plant to replace these.[11]

Health and Hospitals
The County Health Department

In 1954, the Fairfax County Health Department, serving a population of over 157,000, moved into new quarters in the Joseph Willard health Center, with a staff of twenty-four and a budget of $138,994. The many polio cases in the county in 1952 caused deep concern, and in 1954 and 1955, Dr. Harold Kennedy, county health officer, directed a program of Salk polio vaccine field trials with children in the first three grades of school, the first such expirament by a county in the United States.

Additional health programs through the years have included sanitary land fills, water fluoridation, rabies control, sewer bonds, countywide soils survey of 1954 and 1955 to help determine suitability for septic tank sewage disposal systems, the swimming pool ordinance of 1957, septic tank inspection ordinances in 1956, 1959, 1960, and 1973, and physical examinations and dental clinics for indigent school children. In 1959 annual tuberculin testing was begun using purified protein derivative (PPD), the first such testing conducted in the state. Maternal and child health clinics were established. The first air pollution ordinance in the state was passed in 1962. In that same year, Fairfax was the first county in the United States to participate in a mass vaccination trial program for measles, again under the direction of Dr. Kennedy.

10. Athelia Knight, "Defective Sewer Pipes Plague Fairfax Homeowners," *Washington Post,* 4 January 1976, p. B-1.

11. Fairfax County Office of Comprehensive Planning, *Fairfax County Virginia Plan,* Barbara M. Halpern and Stephen H. Lopez, eds: (Fairfax, Va.: 1975), pp. 1-PF-4 to 6; 11-PF-4.

Virginia's first well ordinance was passed to assure pure and adequate rural water supplies. Home care programs were inaugurated.

A daytime development center for retarded children opened at the health center in 1967, an addition to the speech and hearing center established there in 1963. A mobile health unit was operational by 1969, and a new health department building next to the Massey Building was occupied in the same year, complete with a public health laboratory. Between 1969 and 1971, a countywide immunization program against German measles (rubella) was conducted.

In 1971, Dr. Kennedy retired and was succeeded as director by Richard K. Miller, M.D., M.P.H. The health department's total operating budget for fiscal year 1975-76 was $5,455,807 and included a four-part alcohol abuse program not in the previous budget. School testing for hearing, vision, and speech has been a regular part of the county program. For economic reasons, a fee system for speech and hearing services had to be established in July 1975, and it significantly decreased the number of those seeking evaluation services. In 1976, the staff consisted of 443 employees implementing a many-faceted program in the public health field in Fairfax County.[12]

The Fairfax Hospital

In April 1955, Mrs. A. L. Caperton, chairman of the federation's health and hospitals committee, reported that efforts had been begun by the Fairfax County health council to establish a Fairfax County hospital. The prospect was bright because the county had already been determined eligible for federal-state aid under the Federal Hill-Burton Act, with the potential of 50 to 55 percent of the total cost supplied on a matching formula. Dr. Harold Kennedy urged the raising of half the million dollar cost anticipated for the proposed fifty-bed facility before an all-out fund-raising campaign was conducted.

In September, federation past-president Donald Wilkins reported the results of a survey of 239 county medical doctors regarding the proposed hospital: of the 187 who replied, 141 favored it. But instead of a fifty-bed facility, a minimum of 225 beds and a maximum of 325 operating at a maximum efficiency of 70 percent of capacity were in the desirable range, based on statistics available as of May 1955. The federation membership voted to support the efforts of the Fairfax County hospital and health center commission to obtain a nonpolitical, nonprofit facility as soon as possible, endorsing the board of supervisors' three-million-dollar bond issue referendum for this purpose which was approved on 2 November 1955.[13]

12. Muzyka, *Historic Account*, pp. 14-50.
13. FCFCA *Bulletin*, November 1955.

Members of the Board of Trustees of the Fairfax Hospital Association in 1961.
Seated left to right: Col. Raymond F. Rickard U.S. Army retired, banker, Chamber
of Commerce; Donald E. Ball, retired building contractor, bank director, and
president of the Hospital Association; Hon. Jouett Shouse, former assistant
Secretary of the Treasury, former chairman executive committee, National
Democratic Committee, former congressman from Kansas; G. Wallace Carper,
retired farmer and former chairman, Board of Supervisors. Standing, left to
right: William C. Crossman, Jr., dairy farmer; Mrs. Euan G. Davis, civic leader
and member, Hospital and Health Center Commission; Dr. Lloyd Hazleton,
pharmacologist and founder of research laboratory; Mandley T. Rust, merchant,
land developer and motel owner; Mrs. John S. Lucas, civic leader, retired
registered nurse, and member Hospital and Health Center Commission; John W.
Koons, automobile dealer and motel owner; Carl D. Soresi, editor and land
consultant; Walter L. Phillips, civil engineer and land developer. Not present at
the meeting were A. Smith Bowman, Jr., architect, and vice-president and
treasurer of the bourbon distillery; G. Norman Cobb, banker and insurance
agent; Col. Davis F. Condon, Jr., Marine Corps retired, Commissioner, U. S. Court
of Military Appeals; Robert C. Hunt, M.D., pediatrician and member Fairfax
County Medical Society; and Carl B. Fritsche, retired chemical manufacturer
and research consultant. Photo by Charles Baptie.

The benefit of the expertise of highly qualified citizens who lived in
the county and worked for the federal government and private industry
was typically available among the following board of supervisors'
appointees to the hospital's building subcommittee: Donald Wilkins,
chairman; Thomas Knott of the Building Trades Council of Northern
Virginia; Brandon Marsh, formerly of the Washington Post & Times
Herald, but at the time an administrative officer with Melpar; Maury
Odoroff, deputy director of hospital services, U.S. Department of
Health, Education and Welfare; and Pierre Palmer, deputy director of
the hospital construction section, Bureau of the Budget.[14]

The State Corporation Commission chartered the Fairfax Hospital
Association, the operating agency for the hospital, on 13 February 1956,
and a nineteen-member board of trustees was elected at a countywide
public meeting. The five-story brick building was funded with
$3,000,000 from Fairfax County bonds, $3,000,000 from Hill-Burton
funds, and $750,000 raised by hospital association fund drives. It was

14. Hinkle, Fairfax Newsletter, 7 January 1956.

under construction in December 1958 in a wooded area just off narrow, high-crowned Gallows Road near Route 50.[15]

Fairfax Hospital officially opened its doors at 8:30 A.M. on 6 February 1961, but actually one-half hour ahead of schedule. The first patient was admitted because arrival of baby number one was imminent. Since then, more than 40,000 babies have been born at the Fairfax Hospital.

As new needs arise, the hospital establishes new facilities. In 1971, an alcohol detoxification unit and a psychiatric section opened. Obstetric and gynecological units have been enlarged and several additions have been made to the original building. Over 688,000 persons have received treatment at Fairfax Hospital. Gallows Road is now a divided four-lane highway, and the completed Capital Beltway overpasses Route 50 only half a mile away.[16] The spectacular view from the tenth floor of the 700-bed complex reveals a wooded Virginia countryside dotted with single-family residences, townhouses, and apartment buildings in a network of roads and highways. Also close by are two mental health facilities.

Other Health Facilities

The Northern Virginia Mental Health Institute was established by the General Assembly in 1958 as a 120-bed, short-term, open-door hospital to provide intensive treatment for residents of the counties of Arlington, Fairfax, Loudoun, and Prince William, and the cities of Alexandria, Fairfax, and Falls Church. Outpatient and other services are available, and the institute is supervised and managed by the Department of Mental Health and Mental Retardation of the Commonwealth of Virginia. The first unit was built beside Fairfax Hospital, and opened in 1968. There are six twenty-bed units. Area residents who have episodes of acute psychiatric illness are eligible for treatment. The "milieu therapy" program is designed to provide early return of the patient to community life.[17]

About two blocks from Fairfax Hospital, on Woodburn Road, is the Woodburn Center for Community Mental Health. It had its beginnings in 1946 as the Fairfax County Child Consultation Service under community chest sponsorship. As more adults came with their own problems, the program expanded, and in 1960 the clinic was renamed the Fairfax-Falls Church Community Mental Health and Retardation Service with an annual budget in fiscal year 1975 of approximately $2 million and a monthly caseload of approximately 3,000 persons. There are three main branches: Mount Vernon Center to serve the Mount Vernon, Lee,

15. FCFCA *Bulletin*, December 1956.
16. Peggy Pond, "The Fairfax Hospital Story," (Vienna, Va.: *Virginia Cardinal*, May 1972).
17. *Information Booklet*, Northern Virginia Mental Health Institute, n. d. pp. 3, 4, 9.

and group psychotherapy, twenty-four-hour emergency service, partial hospitalization for adults, a therapeutic school for children, consultation, and medication. The operational control was transferred in 1974 from the Virginia Department of Mental Health and Retardation to the Fairfax-Falls Church Community Health and Retardation Service with an annual budget in fiscal year 1975 of approximately $2 million and a monthly caseload of approximately 3,000 persons. There are three main branches: Mount Vernon Center to serve the Mount Vernon, Lee, and and Springfield magisterial districts; Baileys to serve the Mason, Providence, and Annandale districts and the cities of Fairfax and Falls Church; and the Northwest Center for Community Health, serving the Centreville and Dranesville districts. [18]

The 1964 *Fact Sheet* issued by the National Association of Mental Health estimated that at least one person in every ten has some type of mental or emotional illness which needs psychiatric care. Factors which influence an increase in need include: an increase in certain groups vulnerable to emotional and mental stress, such as youth and the aging; an increase in socioeconomic problems; improved detection and early diagnosis; and an increase in awareness of need for help. [19]

In 1976, the Fairfax Hospital Association acquired the Commonwealth Doctors Hospital on Chain Bridge Road in Fairfax. It is a licensed 160-bed facility. The association opened the new Mount Vernon Hospital in October 1976. The Alexandria Hospital and Arlington Hospital served as the hospital facilities for the Northern Virginia area until Fairfax Hospital was built; they are still used by some county residents. Service personnel regularly use De Witt Army Hospital at Fort Belvoir, and other major hospitals in the metropolitan area also provide care for Fairfax County citizens. Fairfax House is a facility for troubled boys located on Woodburn Road. Girls' Probation House is located near Centreville on Route 29 and Route 211.

Police Department

Carl McIntosh, who had served as police chief since the department's inception in July 1940, retired in 1957 and was succeeded by Captain William L. Durrer who had joined the department in 1947. During Durrer's administration, a police headquarters building was opened at 10600 Page Avenue, Fairfax, in 1961; district stations were also established in McLean in 1963, Annandale in 1966, Chantilly in 1970; Franconia in 1973; and Reston and West Springfield in 1976. Groveton had opened the first substation in 1947.

When Chief Durrer retired in January 1975, the Fairfax County

---

18. *Woodburn Center for Community Mental Health Fact Sheet*, February 1975.
19. League of Women Voters of the Fairfax Area, *Mental Health Resources* (September 1965).

Board of Supervisors appointed a twenty-year veteran on the force, Colonel Richard A. King, as his successor. Chief King implemented a reorganization plan to decentralize the large department and to delegate a larger degree of authority to the district commanders at each substation. The 1975 department budget was $15 million and the officers are regularly given on-the-job training to keep pace with rapidly advancing technology.[20] The Northern Virginia regional police training center is a cooperative facility used by various local jurisdictions.

A study of serious crime reported during 1974 to the police department was released in April 1975, prepared under the direction of Colonel King. In a comparison between 1973 and 1974 figures, all offense category figures were higher, with the exception of homicide. Robbery was up over 44 percent, and rape over 37 percent. The former figure was explained by the worsening economic situation and reflected similar trends in other jurisdictions of the Washington metropolitan area. Out of the four suburban counties including Arlington, Prince Georges, Montgomery, and Fairfax, Fairfax crime ranked third, and Montgomery fourth. This ominous statement appeared: "In addition, while the tables show a worsening picture for serious crime rates, it is also clear Fairfax County has not yet experienced the full measure of problems facing some other jurisdictions and may have an opportunity to prepare." As of the end of 1975, the department was handling 140,000 to 145,000 crimes, accidents, and calls for service in a year's time.[21]

In 1976, construction of a larger jail facility was begun on land near the courthouse and Massey building.

Fire Services

Originally, the fire departments in Fairfax County were completely staffed and supported by volunteers. In order to keep the stations covered all hours of the day and night, the county board began to supply paid men at each station beginning in 1949. Training programs improved.

Storage space for archival records has always been at a premium in fire stations; therefore, many of the official records are no longer in existence since there was no convenient way of keeping them when they became "out-of-date." This is unfortunate, particularly since rescue squads, which are adjuncts to the fire departments, are important emergency services.

Because of the fact that the Potomac River is the county boundary on two sides, northeast and southeast, and also because of the existence

20. *Fairfax County Police Department Newsletter,* 1(5).
21. *News Release,* Fairfax County Public Affairs Office, 15 April 1975.

of several lakes within the county, water rescue equipment is kept in several departments; a scuba-diving unit is assigned to West Springfield for recovery of bodies and stolen property.

Recent additions to the rescue squads beginning in 1972 have been the specially trained emergency medical technicians (E.M.T.) and cardiac technician programs. These units are trained at the Fairfax County Fire Training Center and Fairfax Hospital and are able to act in situations where paramedical services actually can save lives. Not quite so dramatic and certainly not uncommon are births of babies in ambulances when expectant mothers are on the way to the hospital for delivery. In 1966, Fairfax Hospital began issuing plastic umbilical cord clamps free of charge to the county's rescue squads after one newborn infant was brought in with its umbilical cord tied off with a piece of electrician's tape. Members of rescue squads, always equal to this particular emergency, had previously come up with other ingenious solutions to the problem which included string and cord, as well as rubber bands and even an occasional shoelace.[22]

The initial expenditures required to construct buildings, acquire equipment, and train and maintain personnel for an urban fire protection program are substantial and the capital improvements are, in part, being funded by $5.6 million, part of a bond issue approved by the voters in 1971. The most recent stations built (companies 24-28) have been funded by the county and are paid stations rather than volunteer fire departments.[23]

22. *Northern Virginia Sun*, 4 March 1966. Martin Cranshaw, "History of Volunteer Fire Departments in Fairfax County, Virginia," (1976).

23 *Capital Improvements Program*, (CIP), Office of Comprehensive Planning, 1975; Interview, George Alexander, Director, Fire and Rescue Services, 15 October 1976;

XII

Quality of Life: The Amenities

The County Library

The first recorded effort made to establish a countywide library appeared in the board of supervisors' minutes of 6 November 1929, when Thomas R. Keith and Professor Armond Stone requested the use of a room in the old clerk's office building for the purpose. The board agreed, with the understanding that there was to be no further expense to the county. Volunteers publicized and worked for the library cause for a number of years and finally a regular, though small, budget was appropriated in 1940 when a full-time librarian was hired. A bookmobile and increasing demand during World War II stimulated public interest in the program.[1]

Because of the excessive demands for library service resulting in great part from the county's population growth from 25,000 in 1930 to 133,000 in 1953, the Fairfax County library board of trustees closed the library system in July 1953 for an inventory and reorganization. Two new branches of the county library were established at the Graham Road shopping center, west of Falls Church, and at the Belle View shopping center in the Mount Vernon district, both near heavy population concentrations. Mrs. Mary Katherine McCulloch was appointed library director with a budget of $57,949. On 1 January 1954, the library system opened its doors and resumed services. Within the next year, the library budget jumped to $75,000, with staunch citizen and press support.

One by one, branches were established throughout the county, each named for a man or woman of historical importance to the county, Virginia, or the area in which it was located. In 1959, a two-million-dollar bond referendum for the library system's building expansion was

1. BOSMB No. 6, pp. 20, 90, 575; No. 7, p. 407.

approved by county voters. The new central library building was officially opened in Fairfax in July 1962. The system's circulation figure of 1,118,838 was the highest in the state. Soon, the new headquarters housed a growing special collection of books and materials on Virginia and Fairfax County history. The interest of the patrons grew and diversified into all fields of knowledge. In 1966, the county's public affairs director wrote, "It has been said that our citizens consume more goods, read more books and have more babies than any other group...."[2]

After Mrs. McCulloch retired in 1969, William Whitesides, who had been with the system since 1966, was appointed director and still serves.

To find out what people were reading, a survey of the Holmes Run Acres' book club selections were studied for the years 1961-1971. The sampling produced a list of eighty-eight titles of widely varied subject matter. The club's selection process was very liberal: a book was chosen because someone had always wanted to read it, because it was on the best-seller list, because someone liked a particular author, or because the subject was of current interest. These reasons help to explain why *Exodus, The Prince, Zorba, the Greek,* and *Greek Plays* all appear on the list. *Let Us Now Praise Famous Men,* the Agee chronicle of the Depression, appears on the list along with *poems of e.e.cummings. Soul on Ice, Lady Chatterley's Lover, Catcher in the Rye, One Flew Over the Cuckoo's Nest, the Confessions of Nat Turner,* and *Dr. Zhivago* show a widely diversified selection among this one group of readers.

In 1974, the Fairfax County, Virginia, library system ranked first in Virginia and in the South, and fifteenth in the nation in circulation: 4,565,518 volumes for calendar year 1974. The budget ranked fourth at $4,533,608 among the ninety-four libraries with annual budgets of $200,000 or more which responded to questionnaires.[3]

Many services and programs are offered by the library: books, fiction and nonfiction; films; the Virginiana collection; a business and technical collection; financial services; a special music collection; newspapers; records; cassettes; foreign language collections; reference service for the Virginia legislature; and varied and numerous special programs and events for adults, families, young people, and the disadvantaged. As of 1 July 1976, the system had a central facility in Fairfax City, thirteen branches, three regional libraries, and two bookmobiles. In addition to the public libraries, each elementary, intermediate, and secondary school has a library operated by the school administration. Each college and university has library facilities, and there are numerous private professional and church libraries.

2. Sloan, *Fairfax County Library,* p. 10; Elliott G. Shaw, Jr., "The Consequences of Urban Growth: The Fairfax County Experience," *Newsletter of University of Virginia,* (Charlottesville, Va.: University of Virginia Press, 1966). 32:1.

3. "Rank of Southern Public Libraries," *Information Sheet of the Memphis [Tennessee] Public Library and Information Center, 1974.*

The Arts and Recreation

The Writer's Craft

The compulsion to write which was felt by George Mason and George Washington in the eighteenth century is still strong in twentieth-century Fairfax County. Skill and diversity of subjects are well exemplified by two of many local authors. Virgil Carrington "Pat" Jones of Centreville interested himself years ago in Civil War history and became an authority and writer on the Civil War guerrilla, John Singleton Mosby. Other talents emerged while Jones was working for the National Aeronautics and Space Administration (NASA). In 1972 he prepared *Log of Apollo 11,* the first official account of the first moon landing, written before the splashdown and published for the astronauts' official reception ceremony which followed.[4] Charlton Ogburn of Oakton following World War II wrote the history of his experiences during a major campaign of his U.S. Army unit in Asia, *The Marauders.* His intense interest in ecology and environmental matters subsequently led him to write many articles and books from this perspective, including *The Winter Beach* and *The Southern Appalachians.*

There are many other authors and journalists who find Fairfax County a place in which to live and work creatively. The younger set was well represented by Michael and David Straight of Green Spring Farm who, when they were schoolboys, published the *Green Spring-Menemsha Gazette* in imitation of their father's periodical, *The New Republic.* Their *Gazette* enjoyed the distinction of being prominently featured in an article written by Boris Kampov-Polevoy for the Soviet monthly *OKTYABR* in 1956. The Russian journalist had been intrigued with the youthful enterprise when he was a guest of the Straights at Green Spring Farm.[5]

Music Hath Charms.

In the school system and the community, music has played a continuing role of enrichment. Band and vocal music have been in the public school curriculum since the 1920s, and some groups have achieved a level of excellence which has enabled them to give concert tours both in this country and in Europe. The "Fairfax Jubilaires," the "Forefathers," and "Sweet Adelines" represent the Society for the Preservation and Encouragement of Barbershop Quartet Singing in America in the county. The Fairfax County Choral Society, the Fairfax Symphony Orchestra, the Northern Virginia Chamber Orchestra, the Northern

---

4. Office of Public Affairs, *Log of Apollo 11,* (Washington, D.C.: National Aeronautics and Space Administration, 1972).

5. Netherton, *Green Spring Farm,* pp. 78-80.

Virginia Youth Orchestra, and the Vienna Banjo Boys, have furnished hundreds of musicians and thousands of listeners with musical opportunities. Ensembles such as the Mount Vernon Chamber Orchestra, the McLean Chamber Group Orchestra, the Reston Chorale, and the Falls Church and Fairfax Civic Bands provide additional occasions for musicmaking and listening.[6]

The American Symphony Orchestra League

Because it was important for an eminent arts organization to be more effective and accessible, Mrs. Jouett Shouse made a gift of land and buildings on her Wolf Trap Farm outside Vienna to the American Symphony Orchestra League in 1962, and the organization's national headquarters were moved from Charleston, West Virginia, where it had first come into being in 1950.[7]

The Council of the Arts

The same year the orchestra league moved to "Symphony Hill" at Wolf Trap, the county's federation of women's clubs spearheaded a survey which encouraged the county board of supervisors to establish the Fairfax County Cultural Association in 1964. In 1971 the organization was renamed Fairfax County Council of the Arts. Although it initially suffered many growing pains, it has become a catalyst and coordinator for many community cultural programs and activities, including the annual International Children's Festival at Wolf Trap Farm Park, concerts in the public schools, and numerous exhibitions of local art and artists programs. Headquarters offices were moved from Willston to Green Spring Farm in 1975.[8]

In 1975, an advisory committee called FLAG, an acronym for Fairfax Legacy Action Group, was formed by the Fairfax County Park Authority to study the advisability of establishing a cultural center for the county. The group included representation from a cross section of county civic and cultural organizations and government agencies. A consultants' feasibility report is to form a basis for determination of need for a new county heritage and cultural facility.[9]

6. Fran Groover, "Bring Back that Melody," (Vienna, Va.: *Virginia Cardinal*, November 1973), pp. 14-16.

7. "American Symphony Group to Move Into Fairfax Headquarters Nov. 12," *Northern Virginia Sun*, 9 October 1962; *The Washington Post*, 13 June 1971; *Wall Street Journal*, 3 September 1971.

8. Mimi Pellettieri, "History of FCCA," 3 December 1975, memorandum, Fairfax County Council of the Arts; "County Has Esprit-de-Bore, Should Have Civic-Culture Center, Consultants Report," (McLean: *Providence Journal*, 18 April 1969).

9. *The Arts Newsletter* (Falls Church, Va.: FCCA, May 1974); *Globe Newspapers*, 10 July 1975.

Recreation

The Fairfax County Recreation Department, which now has numerous programs for the arts as well as extensive recreational programs, had its beginning in 1937 when the county's population was approximately 38,000. A few community-minded citizens, with private funds, set up three community centers that year for teenage dances, parties, picnics, and sports. In two years, the Fairfax County Recreation Association was formed as a policy guidance group for the community chest and other sponsoring and funding agencies, to operate summer playground programs, which for many years were under the direction of Ilah Osborn. The county began partial funding of this successful program in 1952, and by 1959 a year-round recreation department was established by the board of supervisors, which appointed Dr. William Dove Thompson director. He was succeeded in 1973 by J. Larry Fones, the present director.

With its multimillion-dollar annual program, the department provides organized leisure-time activities including operation of year-round community centers, adult and tot recreational and cultural tours and programs, fee classes on a variety of subjects and skills, senior citizen programs, and programs for the mentally and/or physically handicapped. Adult and youth athletic programs include such active team and individual sports as baseball, softball, soccer, hockey, basketball, volleyball, football, golf, tennis, horseshoes, archery, pool, swimming, ice skating, pingpong, and board games. The department assists local communities with formation of recreation councils and youth clubs, and in 1972 implemented the roving leader program established by the board of supervisors, which provides services for all youth with particular emphasis on the delinquent and potentially delinquent.[10]

Independent organizations such as little theater groups, as typified by the Oakton Hamsters, area churches, and individual clubs and organizations have provided a variety of opportunities in recent decades for both active participation in and appreciation for drama, music (both sacred and secular), and other art forms.

Historic Preservation in Fairfax County

Robert Stipe, a nationally recognized historical preservationist, has delineated the following reasons for preservation.

We seek to preserve because our historic resources are all that physically link us to our past. We strive to save our historic

---

10. Fairfax County Recreation Department, "About the Department: Its Origin," information sheet, 1976; J. Larry Fones, "FY1977 Budget Request to James P. McDonald, Director, Budget and Financial Management," 30 October 1975.

Young Archaeologists at Belvoir where the mansion of the Fairfax family once stood more than 200 years before. Fairfax County high school students learn techniques of archaeological excavation under the supervision of Lt. George Schott, on the grounds of Fort Belvoir. Fairfax County School Board.

and architectural heritage simply because we have lived with it and it has become a part of us. We preserve to maintain difference and uniqueness; we preserve historic sites and structures because of their relation to past events, eras, movements, and persons we feel are important to honor and understand. Nostalgia and patriotism are potential sources of imagination and creativity. We seek to preserve the architecture and landscape of the past simply because of their intrinsic values as art and because we believe in the right of our cities and countryside to be beautiful, enhancing the quality of human life.[11]

Belvoir

Belvoir was built about 1741 for William Fairfax, agent for his cousin Thomas, sixth Lord Fairfax. The mansion house burned in the late eighteenth century, and was demolished by British cannonballs fired from their ships in the Potomac River during the War of 1812. The ruins, which were placed on the National Register of Historic Places in 1973, have recently been excavated by high school students under the direction

11. Abstracted from Robert Stipe, "Why Preserve," *Preservation News* (Washington, D.C.: The National Trust for Historic Preservation, July 1972), 7(7).

of a professional archeaologist engaged by the United States Army Corps of Engineers. The national headquarters of the corps is located at Fort Belvoir on the former Fairfax family property, on the south side of Route 1, between Dogue and Accotink creeks.[12]

Mount Vernon

It was in 1853 that Ann Pamela Cunningham of South Carolina began what was to be one of the first major preservation efforts in the United States: George Washington's Mount Vernon, built about 1759. Dismayed at the unwillingness of the United States Congress to appropriate money for the purchase of the estate as a memorial, Miss Cunningham formed the Mount Vernon Ladies' Association of the Union and by 1858, having raised the necessary $200,000, the organization bought the Mount Vernon mansion and part of the original estate. The same organization still owns and operates Mount Vernon for the approximately one million domestic and foreign visitors who come to see it each year. Mount Vernon, located south of Alexandria on the George Washington Memorial Parkway, was designated a National Historic Landmark in 1960 and is on the National Register.[13]

Gunston Hall

Gunston Hall was built in 1758 by George Mason, a leading political thinker of the Revolution and author of the Virginia Constitution and Bill of Rights, the basis of the Federal Constitution's Bill of Rights. The mansion and a portion of the original estate were preserved and passed by bequest from the last private owner, Louis Hertle, in 1949, to the Commonwealth of Virginia, with the provision that a Board of Regents to administer the property be selected from the various State Societies of the National Society of Colonial Dames in America. Gunston Hall was designated a National Historic Landmark in 1960 and is on the National Register.[14] It is located on Mason Neck south of Route 1.

Pohick Church

Pohick Church, Truro Parish, was completed in 1774. George Washington, George Mason and George William Fairfax were on the vestry and building committee. The church fell into disrepair after the disestablishment in 1785, and was heavily damaged during the Civil War. It has undergone several restorations in the past 100 years. Pohick

12. George C. Shott, *The Belvoir Manor Project* (Fairfax, Va.: Department of Instructional Services, Division of Curriculum Service, Fairfax County Public Schools, 1974); Kenton Kilmer and Donald Sweig, *The Fairfax Family in Fairfax County* (Fairfax, Va.: Office of Comprehensive Planning, May 1975).

13. WPA Writers' Project, *Virginia: A Guide to the Old Dominion* (1940; reprinted., New York: Oxford University Press, 1965), pp 338-339 (herinafter cited as WPA, *Virginia*); O'Neal, *Architecture in Virginia*, pp. 125-27; Hugh Newell Jacobsen, *A Guide to the Architecture of Washington, D.C.* (New York: Praeger, 1965), p. 185 (hereinafter cited as Jacobsen, *Guide*).

14. WPA *Virginia*, p. 343; O'Neal, *Architecture in Virginia*, pp. 124-25; Jacobsen, *Guide*, p. 187.

Virginia's 200th Birthday was celebrated with a special ceremony at the Massey Building 29 June 1976. On that day 200 years earlier, Virginia had severed ties with Great Britain and adopted the first constitution of the Commonwealth. Speakers at the ceremony, held by the Board of Supervisors, were Virginia Governor Mills E. Godwin, Jr. and A.E. Dick Howard, a noted constitutional scholar from the University of Virginia. Board members signed a specially prepared document rededicating themselves to the principles of representative government as set forth by George Mason of Fairfax County in his Virginia Declaration of Rights. Photo by Bernie Boston.

Church, located on the south side of Route 1 at the south end of Telegraph Road, was placed on the National Register in 1969.[15]

Woodlawn

Woodlawn, built in 1805 as the home of George Washington's nephew, Lawrence Lewis, and Eleanor Custis, his wife, granddaughter of Martha Washington, has been preserved by the National Trust for Historic Preservation, as has the 1940 Frank Lloyd Wright-designed Pope-Leighey house, which was moved to a dense grove of trees on the Woodlawn estate to serve as an example of comparative architecture and social history. Woodlawn, a dwelling built in the grand manner for a culture dependent on abundant slave labor, is a marked contrast to the Pope-Leighey house, a modest dwelling built compactly and simply to minimize all household chores and free its inhabitants for intellectual and cultural pursuits in a modern era when servants of any sort are difficult to obtain.

15. WPA, *Virginia*, p. 343; O'Neal, *Architecture in Virginia*, pp. 126-28; Jacobsen, *Guide*, p. 187; *The Truro Parish Vestry Book*, (Lorton, Va.: Pohick Chruch, 1974).

Pope-Leighey House. Architect Frank Lloyd Wright designed this small unassuming house in 1940 at the request of Mr. and Mrs. Loren Pope of Falls Church. It was donated to the National Trust by its second owner, Mrs. Robert A. Leighey, and moved from its original site on Locust Street to Woodlawn when threatened by the building of Interstate Highway Route 66, in 1965. Photo by Jack E. Boucher.

Woodlawn Plantation. The land on which the mansion was built was originally part of George Washington's Mount Vernon estate. The structure was designed by Dr. William Thornton. National Trust photo taken at the 1975 horse and carriage meet by Charles Baptie.

Both Woodlawn and the Pope-Leighey house were placed on the National Register in 1970. They are located north of Route 1 at Dogue Creek and Mount Vernon Highway.[16]

Sully

Sully, a home built by Richard Bland Lee in 1798, has a particularly interesting preservation history, not only because of its age, but also because of the variety of means by which it came to be a museum house. The house was preserved in private hands by its several owners for almost 200 years, surviving the destruction of the Civil War because its owners stayed instead of leaving it vacant. When the Federal Aviation Agency purchased thousands of acres of land including Sully for the construction of Dulles International Airport, interested citizens, the Federal Aviation Agency, the United States Congress, and the Fairfax County Park Authority all cooperated to bring about the preservation of Sully for generations to come. Its continued existence will be substantially aided by the Sully Foundation, established and generously endowed, initially, by local historian and Sully curator, R. E. Wagstaff. The Foundation published *Sully: The Biography of a House*, written by Robert Gamble. Sully, on the east side of Route 28, north of Route 50, was placed on the National Register in 1970.

Fairfax County Courthouse

The first Fairfax County Courthouse, built at what is now called Tysons Corner around 1742, was apparently not preserved, nor was the second courthouse built in Alexandria on Market Square. The county's third courthouse was finished in 1800 and still exists at the site of the present county government complex as the oldest section of the court building. During the Civil War, the building was burned, so that only the exterior walls remained standing. Many of the county's original documents were destroyed or removed at that time. Shortly after the Civil War, the Fairfax County justices directed that the courthouse be restored. Still another restoration was made in 1967 by the Fairfax County Board of Supervisors at the instigation of the Fairfax County Bar Association, which requested that it be used as a courtroom and not as a museum. It was placed on the National Register in 1974.[17] It is located in Fairfax City, at the intersection of Chain Bridge Road and Little River Turnpike.

16. WPA, *Virginia*, p. 342; Helen Duprey Bullock and Terry Morton, eds., *Woodlawn Plantation* (Washington, D.C.: The National Trust for Historic Preservation, 1971); *The Pope-Leighey House* (Washington, D.C.: The National Trust for Historic Preservation, 1969); O'Neal, *Architecture in Virginia*, p. 129; Jacobsen, *Guide*, p. 186.

17. WPA, *Virginia*, p. 401; Ross Netherton and Ruby Waldeck, *The Fairfax County Courthouse* (Fairfax, Va.: Office of Comprehensive Planning, 1977).

Colvin Run Mill

The Fairfax County Park Authority now owns the Colvin Run Mill, extensively repaired, restored, and opened to the public for weekend tours beginning in July 1972. Stones grind cornmeal, and it is an unforgettable experience to hear the wooden wheels and gears creaking and groaning while they work. The brick mill was probably built by Philip Carper after 1811 on the site of an older mill, and is representative of many mills which once ground grain for commercial purposes and local home use. The miller's house is used as an arts and crafts center. A country store, post office, and blacksmith shop complete the complex, which was placed on the National Register in 1977 and is located on Leesburg Pike just west of Difficult Run. [18]

Dranesville Tavern

The Dranesville Tavern was built on the south side of Leesburg Pike and east of Sugarland Run about 1830. It served travelers and drovers taking livestock to the Georgetown, Washington, and Alexandria markets. It is owned and has been restored by the Fairfax County Park Authority, and was placed on the National Register in 1972. [19]

Saint Mary's Church

Saint Mary's Church was built in 1858 for Irish Catholic immigrant workers who built the Orange and Alexandria Railroad, now owned by the Southern Railway. After the battles of Second Manassas (Bull Run) and Chantilly (Ox Hill), the wounded from both Union and Confederate forces were brought here, cared for under Clara Barton's direction, and evacuated to nearby hospitals. Miss Barton later founded the American Red Cross. The church was placed on the National Register in 1976. [20] It is located on Ox Road, Route 123, at Fairfax Station.

Bull Run Stone Bridge

Bull Run Stone Bridge was originally constructed about 1820 during the turnpike era. The bridge was heavily damaged during the first and second battles of Manassas (Bull Run) in 1861 and 1862. It is owned by the National Park Service and is part of Manassas Battlefield Park on the north side of Lee Highway at Bull Run.

18. Ross D. Netherton, *The Colvin Run Mill* (Fairfax, Va.: Office of Comprehensive Planning, 1976).

19. E. Blaine Cliver and Tony P. Wrenn, *The Dranesville Tavern: An Architectural Analysis* (Fairfax, Va.: Fairfax County History Commission, 1970).

20. Jeanne Rodriques and William Hammond, *St. Mary's, Fairfax Station, Virginia: The Beginnings and Growth of a Community,* (Fairfax Station, Va.: St. Mary's Roman Catholic Church, 1975).

The Stone Bridge over Bull Run. Photo in 1972 by Bernie Boston.

Green Spring Farm

In October 1970, Michael and Belinda Crompton Straight gave the seventeen-acre estate and colonial home, Green Spring Farm, to the Fairfax County Park Authority for public use as a museum and arboretum. It is located on Green Spring Road south of Braddock Road and east of Little River Turnpike. The tract, valued at $400,000, includes two ponds, a two-and-one-half story brick house, and several out-buildings. In 1975, the Fairfax County Council of the Arts opened its headquarters there and currently conducts a continuing program of exhibits and events in the house and on the attractive grounds.[21]

Legato School

Legato School was built about 1877 and chosen in 1971 to represent the one-room schoolhouse for the centennial celebration of the public school system in Fairfax County. Next to the Fairfax County Courthouse on Chain Bridge Road, Fairfax City, it is the property of the Fairfax County School Board and is under restoration.[22]

Salona

Salona was probably built about 1810 for William Maffitt, a Presbyterian minister and teacher. President James Madison stayed here

21. Netherton, *Green Spring Farm.*
22. Wrenn, Peters, and Sprouse, *Legato School.*

the night the British burned the Capitol in 1814. Salona was placed on the National Register in 1973. The house is private, not open to the public, but has been preserved for the future through a perpetual easement agreement. Salona is south of Dolley Madison Boulevard on Buchanan Street in McLean.

Park Lands

Frying Pan Farm Park

Frying Pan Farm Park on West Ox Road, south of Centreville Road, was established by the Fairfax County Park Authority in 1973 to provide an educational experience for those who wish to understand American family farm life of the 1920s, prior to mechanization and conversion to large-scale farming methods. The complex includes livestock barns, a separator shed, a blacksmith shop, a chicken yard, pasture, and equipment.

Turkey Run Farm Park

Turkey Run Farm Park is a living-history presentation by the National Park Service, demonstrating the humble endeavor of a subsistence farmer of the Potomac Valley during the period of the American Revolution. Cultivation of crops, animal husbandry, and the preparation of food on an open hearth are demonstrated at this park located on the north side of Route 193 near Langley.

Great Falls Park

Great Falls Park is at the falls where the Potomac River plunges seventy-six feet over ancient rocks through a deep gorge. A canal and five locks were constructed around the falls at the end of the eighteenth century by the Patowmack Canal Company, whose first president was George Washington, to aid in commerce to and from the interior of the new country. The park is owned by the National Park Service. and located at the north end of Old Dominion Drive, north of Georgetown Pike.[23]

Carlyle House

The Carlyle House at the intersection of Fairfax and Cameron streets in Alexandria dates from 1752 and is associated with George Washington, British General Edward Braddock, and other pre-

---

23. Corra Bacon-Foster, *The Patomac Route to the West*, (Washington, D.C.: Columbia Historical Society, 1912); C. J. S. Durham, *Washington's Patowmack Canal Project at Great Falls*, (Fairfax County, Va.: The Nature Conservancy, Wildlife Management Institute and the Fairfax County Park Authority, 1957).

Revolutionary War figures. It is owned by the Northern Virginia Regional Park Authority and was placed on the National Register in 1969.

Additional National Register sites in other jurisdictions which hold a significant place in the history of Fairfax County are: The Falls Church and Cherry Hill, Falls Church; Arlington House, Arlington; and Christ Church, Gadsby's Tavern, the Lyceum, and the Bank of Alexandria, all in Alexandria.

The Marie Butler Leven Preserve was created as a bequest to the Fairfax County Park Authority by Maurice J. Leven, who died in 1962. It serves as a memorial to his wife. The eighteen-acre estate, originally called "Anoria," is used as an arboretum and nature preserve, and is located on Kirby Road above Pimmit Run. A botanical inventory taken in 1963 lists seventy-nine varieties of trees and shrubs on the estate.

The Ellanor C. Lawrence County Park, a strategically located square mile of land at Centreville, (possible the most valuable ever donated to a local government body in Virginia) was given to the Fairfax County Park Authority through the will of Mrs. David Lawrence, wife of the publisher of *U.S. News and World Report.* The tract, valued in 1971 at $4,946,000, contains several old houses and an old mill on Great Rocky Run, a major stream coursing through the property of 640 acres of fields, forests, and streams.[24]

On 20 June 1974, the Virginia State Highway Commission designated a twelve-mile segment of Old Georgetown Pike, between its junctions with Route 123 at Langley and Route 7 at Dranesville, as a "Virginia Byway." It was the first so designated in the state road system and was recommended by resolution from Virginia's Commission of Outdoor Recreation, under the 1966 Scenic Highways and Virginia Byways Act. The Highway Department's plans include acceptance of donations of scenic easements, and purchases of land it feels are necessary to maintain the scenic or historic character of the road as funds become available.[25]

Mason Neck has a combination of parks—county, regional, and state—plus large private holdings which will help keep it an attractive natural area. This situation has evolved through years of hard work, spearheaded in recent years by Elizabeth Hartwell. Mason Neck is a nesting place of the bald eagle.

---

24. *The Virginia Outdoors* (Richmond, Va.: March, 1971) 2(1); Anne Beresford, "The Three Lives of Walney," manuscript, Fairfax County Office of Comprehensive Planning, Fairfax, Va.: 1977.
25. *The Virginia Outdoors,* August 1974, 5(1).

The National Park Service

In an appraisal of the many parks within Fairfax County, county resident and author Charlton Ogburn has written: "Included in these are lake parks, stream-valley parks and river parks of outstanding natural beauty and among them Great Falls, which is perhaps unsurpassed for natural splendor in any metropolitan area in the world."

Besides owning and maintaining the George Washington Memorial Parkway, Bull Run Stone Bridge, Turkey Run Farm, and Great Falls Park, the National Park Service has a unique responsibility for developing and maintaining the nation's first national park for the performing arts. Wolf Trap Farm Park, northwest of Tysons Corner and south of Leesburg Pike, was a gift of ninety-five acres to the National Park Service in 1966 by Mrs. Jouett Shouse, who also donated several million dollars to build the Filene Center Amphitheater, with an opera-size stage and 3,500 seats. There is additional space for 4,000 more people on the gently sloping lawns outside.

The Fairfax County Park Authority

John Brookfield, chairman of the Fairfax County Park Authority at its inception in 1950, was successful in obtaining many gifts of park lands for public use. The growth of the program itself was demonstration of a need for an expanded program along with a salaried professional director to supplant the volunteer work which had been given until that time. Fred M. Packard was appointed the first Director of Parks for the Fairfax County Park Authority, effective 1 January 1959. He was followed by Fred Brown, James Bell, and the present executive director, Joseph Downs. The current chairman of the park authority is Fred Crabtree.

Man-made Burke Lake, with a large earthen dam holding back the waters of Opposum Creek and South Run, created a new facility in 1960 for what was then the largest camping site in the Washington area. The dam was built with funds from local, state, and federal sources.

A variety of acquisitions from Riverbend Park to the Moffett Blacksmith Shop, and from Lake Accotink, the Colvin Run Mill, to Dranesville Tavern have afforded unique opportunities for diversification of the park authority's extensive program to provide the public with a variety of opportunities for recreation and an appreciation for the preservation of local history. The 1974 acquisition of 1,262 federal government surplus acres in Hybla Valley was a welcome addition to the system, creating a park with natural woods and rolling countryside.

The Carlyle House. Alexandria. The stone house was originally built in 1753 by Scottish merchant John Carlyle, a founding trustee of Alexandria and commissary of the Virginia forces during the French and Indian War. Northern Virginia Regional Park Authority photo in 1976 by Wm. Edmund Barrett.

The Northern Virginia Regional Park Authority

In 1959, the same year the Fairfax County Park Authority hired its first director, the first official meeting of a body created by state legislation and named the Northern Virginia Regional Park Authority was held. The group had actually begun to meet informally eight years before at the Alexandria City Hall. Minutes of meetings from 1951 to 1954 were kept of this predecessor group called the Virginia National Capital Park Authority. The local governments in Northern Virginia decided to pool resources and buy parklands, particularly because the tremendous building boom was using up open land at an alarming rate. Moving into outlying areas, the new authority purchased parcels of land at approximately $300 per acre, in areas where recent purchases have averaged more than $4,000 per acre. Most purchases have been made on the basis of preserving the rich natural heritage of Northern Virginia's woods and meadows, lakes and streams, and to provide for outdoor recreation. The one purchase made for primarily historic preservation was the Carlyle House, built by John Carlyle, a merchant, an original trustee of the town of Alexandria, and son-in-law of William Fairfax of "Belvoir." Here it was that General Braddock met in 1755 with five colonial governors to discuss the funding and provisioning of the British regulars as they worked their way north and west to Fort Duquesne, during the French and Indian War. Also on the property is an early Bank of Alexandria building. The Carlyle House was officially opened in January 1976. The bank building is also to be restored when funds are available.

According to an auditor's statement of September 1975, the Northern Virginia Regional Park Authority owns over 8,000 acres of Northern Virginia land, which represent a public investment of almost $30 million—a fraction of what it would cost today. William Lightsey, who began as a part-time employee in an office shared with the Fairfax County Park Authority, was the first paid staff director of the Northern Virginia Regional Park Authority in 1963, and under his administration, the authority had as its goal the improvement of the quality of life through conservation, preservation, and recreation. The first chairman of the authority was Dr. Ira N. Gabrielson of Fairfax County; the present chairman is Walter L. Mess of Falls Church. Darrell Winslow is the staff director. Member jurisdictions are Alexandria, Falls Church, and Fairfax cities, and the counties of Loudoun, Arlington, and Fairfax. Annual appropriations from the member governments help the authority to participate in state and federal grant programs. Long-range plans are based on five-year acquisition and development schedules. Revenues from all sources including appropriations and grants for the 1974-75 fiscal year were projected at $6,345,476. Annual attendance in the regional parks is estimated at 400,000 visitors.

The Fairfax County History Commission

Speaking in February 1964 at the Annual Awards Dinner of the Fairfax County Federation of Citizens Associations, Secretary of the Interior Stewart Udall, a county resident, recommended that a landmarks commission be established which could "take an inventory of the historic landmarks of the county and provide a plan for their preservation." A little over a year later, the board of supervisors, upon the urging of members of the chamber of commerce, appointed a large citizens' landmarks preservation committee to serve on a new Fairfax County Landmarks Preservation Commission, for which the board immediately approved an initial appropriation. The Landmarks Preservation Commission was reconstituted by the board in April 1969 as the Fairfax County History Commission, and the number of members was reduced to nine.[26] Recently, the membership has been increased to twelve.

The purpose of the commission is to advise all county organizations regarding historic matters and to authenticate and document evidence leading to the identification and possible preservation, restoration, and conservation of historic and/or aesthetic landmarks and buildings. Implementation of the program is provided by the staff of the history

26. BOSMB No. 54, p. 7

branch in the county's Office of Comprehensive Planning, made up of an historic district planner, an historian, and a research historian. Since 1969, the history commission's inventory list has grown to more than 220 historic sites, each of which has been studied briefly. Some of the more important sites have been selected for in-depth study. Studies published by the history section of the Office of Comprehensive Planning include: Beginning at a White Oak . . . the Patents and Northern Neck Grants of Fairfax County, Virginia; Carlby; Centreville; Colchester; Colvin Run Mill; Dunbarton; Fairfax County in Virginia; Selections from Some Rare Sources; Fairfax County, Virginia, Tour Map; Fairfax County Courthouse; The Fairfax Family in Fairfax County; Green Spring Farm; Historical Highlights of Bull Run Regional Park; Huntley; Maplewood; Moorefield; Mount Air; Register of Free Blacks, 1822-1861; and Wakefield Chapel. The History Commission has published The Dranesville Tavern: An Architectural Analysis; The Legato School: A Centennial Souvenir; and Indices to the Hopkins Maps of 1879. An index of the early court minute books, from 1749, has been compiled and put on microfiche.

Special districts zoned to protect historic landmarks established to date by the board of supervisors include Pohick Church; Woodlawn; Sully; the Stone Bridge over Bull Run; Saint Mary's Church at Fairfax Station; Dranesville Tavern; Colvin Run Mill; and Huntley. An architectural review board serves in an advisory capacity to the board on matters relative to historic districts.

In 1974, the board of supervisors received an award for a decade of devotion to historic preservation from the American Association for State and Local History, Author Robert Gamble also received an award in 1974 from the AASLH for his book Sully: The Biography of a House which was written as an historical monograph for the Fairfax County, Virginia, Office of Comprehensive Planning. A certificate of commendation was presented by the AASLH in 1976 to Edith Moore Sprouse, chairman of the history commission, for her dedication to the advancement of local history in Northern Virginia.

The preserving of buildings and sites is an ongoing program, but so, too, is that of natural features and areas. Stewart Udall took note of reasons for this type of stewardship in his book, The Quiet Crisis:

> We are now a nomadic people. . . . Millions of Americans have no tie to the "natural habitat" that is their home. Yet the understanding of the grandeur and simplicity of the good earth is the umbilical cord that should never be cut. If the slow swing of the seasons has lost its magic for some of us, we are all diminished. If others have lost the path to the wellsprings of self-renewal, we are all the losers.

In 1963, "as a rebuke to the development-prone Fairfax County Board of Supervisors," Secretary of the Interior Stewart L. Udall successfully established a tight scenic easement on the Merrywood property. This land is on the Potomac Palisades two miles downstream from the 336-acre Burling Tract (now named Dranesville District Park), In 1971, through a great deal of citizen effort, fundraising, and self-assessment, the residents of the Dranesville district were able to acquire land for a wilderness park for the high cost of $3.9 million. This land had been planned for 309 luxury home sites. The fight to save Burling was described as a "Holy War . . . for the land" in which citizens had "squared off against land developers and public officials" and had won because of the intensity of their commitment and the inspiration of the beautiful land itself which brought out the best in community action. The Dranesville district citizens were reacting in a dynamic way to a new perspective which had been urged in 1965 by FitzGerald Bemiss in the forward-looking report to the Governor of Virginia and members of the General Assembly from his Virginia Outdoor Recreation Study Commission:

> If Virginia continues to grow and develop over the years to come at even the present rate, we can see plainly that individual citizens will have to give to the *quality of development* the same emphasis which over the past generation they have been giving to *quantity of development*. After all, the purpose of all our struggles is not just for more money, more goods and more impressive statistics—but for a good life, for an opportunity to enjoy the things we have acquired; a place of pleasure, dignity, and permanence which we can pass on to future generations with satisfaction and pride.[27]

27. John Barron, "The Merrywood Deal," *Sunday Star* (Washington, D.C.), 17 June 1962, p.1; Sharon Francis, The History of the Burling Tract, Unpublished report, 1972, pp. 1, 151-52; FitzGerald Bemiss, *Virginia's Common Wealth* (Richmond, Va.: 1965), p. 70.

XIII

The Way We Were: The Way We Are

The Fairfax County Office of Research and Statistics was organized in March 1973 by County Executive Robert W. Wilson. The need for the department was demonstrated by Samuel A. Finz, who served as its director from 1973 to 1976. The county data collection and economic and demographic analysis of county growth and development functions of the agency were gradually expanded to include analytical expertise in areas of program evaluation and management analysis.

The following statistical tables were compiled as part of the *Fairfax County Profile* publications of 1976 and 1977 by David Sheatsley, demographer of the Office of Research and Statistics.

TABLE III
PARENTAGE AND COUNTRY OF ORIGIN
FAIRFAX COUNTY, VIRGINIA
1960 and 1970

Country of Origin	1960*		1970*	
	Number	Percent	Number	Percent
Germany	3,943	14.1	7,551	12.8
United Kingdom	4,203	15.0	6,969	11.8
Canada	2,892	10.3	6,000	10.2
Italy	2,755	9.8	4,712	8.0
Ireland	1,455	5.2	2,766	4.7
U.S.S.R.	1,203	4.3	2,048	3.5
Austria	977	3.5	1,933	3.3
Poland	1,261	4.5	1,928	3.3
Sweden	595	2.1	1,275	2.2
Cuba	N/A	—	1,173	2.0
Czechoslovakia	665	2.4	1,090	1.8
Hungary	442	1.6	1,044	1.8
Mexico	187	0.7	680	1.2
All other and not reported	7,417	26.5	19,695	33.4
Total Foreign Stock	27,995	100.0	58,864	100.0
Percentage of Total Population		11.2		12.9

Sources: U.S. Bureau of the Census, *Census Tracts* Washington, D.C. - Maryland - Virginia Standard Metropolitan Statistical Area, 1960 and 1970.
*Excluding City of Fairfax

TABLE IV

RESIDENT BIRTHS AND DEATHS-RATES PER 1,000 POPULATION FOR

FAIRFAX COUNTY AND UNITED STATES, 1960—1974

	1960	1965	1966	1967	1968	1969	1970	1971	1972	1973	1974	1975
Live Births, Fairfax County	6,512	6,661	6,818	6,935	7,280	7,732	7,815	7,275	6,508	6,450	6,391	6,298
Deaths, Fairfax County	1,041	1,352	1,461	1,584	1,701	1,716	1,829	1,873	1,988	1,971	2,168	2,022
Natural Increase, Fairfax County	5,471	5,309	5,357	5,351	5,579	6,016	5,986	5,402	4,520	4,479	4,223	4,226
Birth Rate, Fairfax County	26.2	20.2	19.5	18.3	17.8	17.9	17.2	14.7	12.7	12.1	12.4	12.1
Birth Rate, United States	23.8	19.6	18.5	17.9	17.6	17.8	18.2	17.2	15.6	14.9	15.0	14.8
Death Rate, Fairfax County	4.2	4.1	4.2	4.2	4.2	4.0	4.0	3.8	3.9	3.7	4.2	3.9
Death Rate, United States	9.5	9.4	9.5	9.4	9.7	9.5	9.4	9.3	9.4	9.4	9.1	9.0

Sources: Virginia State Department of Health, Bureau of Vital Resources and Health Statistics.
U.S. Department of Commerce, Bureau of the Census. Series P-23, No. 49. May 1974.

Note: The Fairfax County birth and death rates shown above are based on estimated population figures supplied by Virginia State Department of Health, Bureau of Vital Records and Statistics, which differ from the population estimates of Fairfax County.

TABLE V

CHANGES IN ADULT AGE GROUPS 1960—1970—1975

Washington SMSA, Fairfax, Montgomery and Prince George's Counties

Age Group & Jurisdiction	1960 Number	1960 Percent of Total	1970 Number	1970 Percent of Total	1975 Number	1975 Percent of Total
25-34 Age Group						
Washington SMSA	301,560	15	438,050	15	516,000	17
Fairfax County	36,708	15	64,926	14	91,300	17
Montgomery County	45,128	13	69,402	13	81,300	14
Prince George's County	54,635	15	111,097	17	116,900	18
35-44 Age Group						
Washington SMSA	323,263	16	355,499	12	383,600	12
Fairfax County	47,981	19	69,648	15	73,100	14
Montgomery County	58,623	17	69,943	13	80,000	14
Prince George's County	55,028	15	79,252	12	80,300	12
45-54 Age Group						
Washington SMSA	240,956	12	330,198	12	322,500	10
Fairfax County	22,834	9	59,141	13	63,500	11
Montgomery County	39,669	12	69,331	13	73,700	13
Prince George's County	35,236	10	65,962	10	60,100	9
55-64 Age Group						
Washington SMSA	150,500	7	209.813	7	224,700	7
Fairfax County	9,686	4	23,412	5	33,300	6
Montgomery County	21,049	6	41,346	8	44,800	8
Prince George's County	19,757	6	36,947	6	36,800	6
65 + Age Group						
Washington SMSA	130,538	6	174,268	6	194,000	6
Fairfax County	7,260	3	13,674	3	16,100	3
Montgomery County	17,963	5	32,619	6	34,400	6
Prince George's County	14,977	4	26,669	4	31,900	5

Sources:

U.S. Bureau of the Census, *U.S. Census of Population: 1960 and 1970; General Population Characteristics*, PC(1)-B.

Washington Center for Metropolitan Studies, *Trends Alert*, 1975.

Fairfax County estimates are based on Office of Research and Statistics total population estimates distributed according to *Trends Alert* percentage distributions.

TABLE VI

POPULATION AGE DISTRIBUTION

FAIRFAX COUNTY, 1950—1975

	1950		1960		1970		1975 (est.)	
Age Group	Number	Percent	Number	Percent	Number	Percent	Number	Percent
Under 5	14,495	14.7	34,475	13.9	40,726	9.0	50,500	9.4
5 - 9	10,098	10.2	33,902	13.6	52,113	11.5	51,600	9.6
10 - 14	6,299	6.4	27,034	10.9	56,178	12.3	61,800	11.5
15 - 19	6,464	6.6	15,881	6.4	42,934	9.4	48,300	9.0
20 - 24	8,198	8.3	13,136	5.3	34,269	7.5	46,700	8.7
25 - 34	21,576	21.9	36,708	14.7	64,926	14.3	91,300	17.0
35 - 44	15,732	16.0	47,981	19.3	67,648	14.9	73,100	13.6
45 - 54	7,851	8.0	22,834	9.1	59,141	13.0	61,200	11.4
55 - 64	4,284	4.3	9,686	3.8	23,412	5.2	33,300	6.2
65 and Over	3,560	3.6	7,260	2.9	13,674	3.0	16,100	3.0
Not reported	NA	NA	NA	NA	NA	NA	3,300	0.6
Median Age		26.8		25.0		25.2		26.1

Sources:

U.S. Bureau of the Census, *U.S. Census of Population 1950, 1960, 1970; General Population Characteristics*, Virginia, PC(1)-B48. 1960 Census figures are corrected and *do not* include Fairfax City.

Office of Research and Statistics estimate based on Washington Center for Metropolitan Studies percentage distributions.

TABLE VII

SCHOOL MEMBERSHIP

Fairfax County, 1968 — 1976

School Year	Public Schools	George Mason University	All Campuses Northern Virginia Community College
1968 - 1969	122,077	1,445	5,271
1969 - 1970	129,979	1,890	7,629
1970 - 1971	133,362	2,390	9,718
1971 - 1972	135,948	3,110	12,047
1972 - 1973	135,780	4,125	13,974
1973 - 1974	135,839	4,926	17,261
1974 - 1975	136,508	6,124	21,439
1975 - 1976	136,944	8,022	27,198
1976 - 1977	134,784	8,470	26,557

Sources: Fairfax County Public Schools, Office of Statistical Support.
George Mason University, Office of the Registrar.
Northern Virginia Community College, Office of Institutional Research.

TABLE VIII

COMPARISONS OF SELECTED DEMOGRAPHIC CHARACTERISTICS, 1970
FAIRFAX COUNTY, VIRGINIA, UNITED STATES, AND REGIONS

Demographic Characteristic	Fairfax County	Virginia	U.S.A.	North-East	North Central	South	West
Education:							
Median School Years	12.9	11.7	12.1	12.1	12.1	11.3	12.4
%High School Graduates	78.8	47.8	52.4	53.0	53.7	45.1	62.3
% College Graduates	30.3	12.3	10.7	11.2	9.6	9.8	13.2
Employment:							
% in Civilian Labor Force	56.6	54.7	56.7	57.7	58.2	54.8	56.6
White Collar	75.2	49.0	48.2	51.3	45.8	45.4	52.7
Blue Collar	17.2	36.2	35.9	35.6	37.2	37.7	31.1
Agriculture	0.2	2.7	3.1	1.0	4.4	3.7	3.1
Service	7.4	12.1	12.8	12.2	12.7	13.1	13.2
Income:							
Median Income	$15,707	$ 9,049	$ 9,586	$10,537	$10,134	$ 8,075	$10,263
% Below Poverty	3.5	12.3	10.7	7.6	8.3	16.3	8.9
% Earning:							
Less than $2,000	2.2	6.6	5.9	4.1	4.7	8.9	4.8
Less than $5,000	6.2	22.0	20.3	15.6	17.3	27.9	17.9
Over $25,000	14.6	4.7	4.6	5.8	4.4	3.4	5.3
Per Capita Income							
1973	$ 6,488	$ 4,886	$ 5,041	$ 5,435	$ 5,263	$ 4,447	$ 5,225
1969	4,542	3,410	3,733	4,162	3,839	3,126	3,999
Housing:							
% Owner Occupied	62.0	62.0	62.9	57.6	68.0	64.7	59.0
Median Value	$35,400	$17,100	$17,000	$19,400	$16,700	$13,500	$20,500
Median Number of Rooms	6.3	5.2	5.0	5.1	5.1	4.9	4.7
% Over 1.01 Persons/ Room	3.6	8.0	8.2	6.5	7.3	10.3	8.4
Median Rent	$ 164	$ 92	$ 89	$ 92	$ 89	$ 71	$ 106

Sources: U.S. Bureau of the Census, *1970 Census of Population, General Social and Economic Characteristics*, Virginia, PC(1)-C48, *Characteristics of the Population, United States Summary*, Volume I, Part 1, Section 2, PC(1)-01. *1970 Census of Housing, General Housing Characteristics*, Virginia, HC(1)-A4S. *General Housing Characteristics, United States Summary*, HC(1)-A1. *Survey of Current Business*, August 1970.

Note: Regions of the United States are defined following standard Bureau of the Census definitions. For a detailed listing of states comprising each region, see Part 1, *1970 Census Users' Guide*, page 77.

TABLE IX

AGRICULTURAL AND NONAGRICULTURAL WAGE AND SALARY EMPLOYMENT
FAIRFAX COUNTY, 1950-1975*

	1950	1960	1970	1971	1972	1973	1974	1975
Nonagricultural Wage and Salary Employment	19,901	39,158	96,666	99,877	112,136	113,618	122,156	125,599
Manufacturing	272	628	3,815	3,999	3,563	4,469	5,064	6,096
Durable Goods	206	514	2,991	3,067	2,539	3,206	3,625	4,444
Nondurable Goods	66	114	824	838	1,024	1,263	1,439	1,652
Nonmanufacturing	16,112	29,888	78,686	82,540	95,134	109,149	117,092	119,503
Mining	26	138	139	133	140	184	163	121
Contract Construction	1,181	3,778	7,684	7,488	9,251	11,858	11,943	9,286
Transportation and Public Utilities	633	312	1,616	2,400	3,900	4,491	4,624	4,496
Wholesale and Retail Trade	1,637	5,815	18,877	20,749	23,667	29,249	30,220	32,770
Finance, Insurance, & Real Estate	571	1,064	5,002	5,333	6,501	7,759	7,952	6,402
Service	1,912	10,145	15,336	16,019	19,853	23,259	27,714	28,581
Government	9,931	8,474	29,646	30,032	31,349	31,711	33,715	37,302
Federal	NA	NA	12,798	11,888	11,872	11,260	11,979	14,034
State	NA	NA	1,404	1,531	2,085	1,928	2,367	2,823
Local	NA	NA	15,444	16,613	17,392	18,163	19,369	20,445
All Other Nonmanufacturing	221	162	386	386	473	638	761	545
All Other Nonagricultural Employment	3,517	8,642	14,165	13,338	13,439	NA	NA	NA
Agricultural Employment	1,506	800	540	522	510	NA	NA	NA
					Percent			
Manufacturing	1.3	1.6	3.9	4.0	3.2	3.9	4.1	4.9
Durable Goods	1.0	1.3	3.1	3.1	2.3	2.8	3.0	3.6
Nondurable Goods	0.3	0.3	0.9	0.8	0.9	1.1	1.2	1.3
Nonmanufacturing	81.0	76.3	81.4	82.6	84.8	96.1	95.9	95.1
Mining	0.1	0.4	0.1	0.1	0.1	0.2	0.1	0.1
Contract Construction	5.9	9.6	7.9	7.5	8.2	10.4	9.8	7.4
Transportation and Public Utilities	3.2	0.8	1.7	2.4	3.5	4.0	3.8	3.6
Wholesale and Retail Trade	8.2	14.9	19.5	20.8	21.1	25.7	24.7	26.1
Finance, Insurance, & Real Estate	2.9	2.7	5.2	5.3	5.8	6.8	6.5	5.1
Service	9.6	25.9	15.9	16.0	17.7	20.5	22.7	22.7
Government	49.9	21.6	30.7	30.1	28.0	27.9	27.6	29.7
Federal	—	—	13.2	11.9	10.6	9.9	9.8	11.2
State	—	—	1.5	1.5	1.9	1.7	1.9	2.2
Local	—	—	16.0	16.6	15.5	16.0	15.9	16.3
All Other Nonmanufacturing	1.2	0.4	0.4	0.4	0.4	0.6	0.7	0.5
All Other Nonagricultural Employment	17.7	22.1	14.7	13.3	12.0	—	—	—

SOURCE: Manpower Research, Virginia Employment Commission

NA: Not Available

* Data as of March of year shown.

TABLE X

FAMILY INCOME DISTRIBUTION, 1959--1975

Washington SMSA, Fairfax, Montgomery, and Prince George's Counties

Income Level and Jurisdiction	Number of Families					
	1959		1969		1975	
	No.	%	No.	%	No.	%
$15,000 and Over						
Washington SMSA	108,662	21.9	273,251	39.6	368,900	48.8
Fairfax County	15,227	25.8	60,111	52.7	93,300	64.4
Montgomery County	37,015	43.4	74,121	56.2	89,600	61.5
Prince George's County	12,861	14.7	56,173	34.4	76,000	45.6
$8,000--14,999						
Washington SMSA	196,688	39.7	252,112	36.5	193,600	25.6
Fairfax County	28,237	47.9	37,453	32.8	27,800	19.2
Montgomery County	28,733	33.7	40,369	30.6	29,500	20.2
Prince George's County	44,026	50.3	72,075	44.1	53,800	32.3
$4,000--7,999						
Washington SMSA	131,361	26.5	110,941	16.1	63,300	8.4
Fairfax County	10,966	18.6	11,410	10.0	6,100	4.2
Montgomery County	14,441	16.9	11,810	9.0	5,300	3.6
Prince George's County	23,627	27.0	25,332	15.5	13,300	8.0
Under $4,000						
Washington SMSA	59,159	11.9	53,805	7.8	31,100	4.1
Fairfax County	4,534	7.7	5,103	4.5	1,200	0.8
Montgomery County	5,083	6.0	5,631	4.2	1,600	1.1
Prince George's County	6,939	8.0	9,820	6.0	4,700	2.8
All Families						
Washington SMSA	495,870	100.0	690,109	100.0	656,900	86.9*
Fairfax County	58,964	100.0	114,077	100.0	128,400	88.6*
Montgomery County	85,272	100.0	131,931	100.0	126,000	86.4*
Prince George's County	87,453	100.0	163,400	100.0	147,800	88.7*

Sources:

U.S. Bureau of the Census, *U.S. Census of Population: 1960 and 1970; General Social and Economic Characteristics*, PC(1)-C.

Washington Center for Metropolitan Studies, *Population Factors Influencing Growth in Prince George's County*, July 1973, p. 40.

Washington Center for Metropolitan Studies, *Trends Alert*, 1975.

Notes:

1. 1959—1969 incomes adjusted to 1969 dollar levels.
2. 1975 estimates of income rounded to nearest hundred and not adjusted for inflation.
*   Total number of families shown for 1975 excludes "not reported" category.

TABLE XI

DIVORCES BY PLACE OF OCCURRENCE
Fairfax County and Virginia, 1967 to 1975

Year	Fairfax County Number	Annual Percent Change	Virginia Number	Annual Percent Change
1967	716	NA	9,682	NA
1968	804	+12.3	10,571	+ 9.2
1969	933	+16.0	11,417	+ 8.0
1970	1,019	+ 9.2	11,879	+ 4.0
1971	1,265	+24.1	13,261	+11.6
1972	1,397	+10.4	14,155	+ 6.7
1973	1,612	+15.4	16,078	+13.4
1974	1,818	+12.8	16,704	+ 3.9
1975	2,041	+12.3	19,311	+15.6

Source: Virginia Department of Health, Bureau of Vital Records and Health Statistics.

TABLE XII

COMMUTING DATA FOR RESIDENT LABOR FORCE

FAIRFAX COUNTY, 1970

Places of Work	White Resident Workers	Negro Resident Workers	Other Resident Workers	Total Resident Workers
Washington Central Business District	15,098	196	84	15,378
Remainder of Washington, DC	29,433	571	220	30,224
Montgomery County, Maryland	5,676	56	21	5,753
Prince George's County, Maryland	4,071	77	20	4,168
Arlington County, Virginia	28,277	581	165	29,023
City of Alexandria, Virginia	13,296	331	83	13,710
Fairfax City, Virginia	5,006	150	12	5,168
City of Falls Church, Virginia	3,688	197	7	3,892
Fairfax County, Virginia	59,658	2,681	477	62,816
Loudoun County, Virginia	1,061	23	0	1,084
Prince William County, Virginia	1,044	38	0	1,082
Baltimore City, Maryland	105	7	0	112
Baltimore County, Maryland	145	0	0	145
Anne Arundel County, Maryland	327	36	0	363
Howard County, Maryland	32	0	0	32
Remainder of Baltimore SMSA	6	0	0	6
Fauquier County, Virginia	141	0	0	141
Charles County, Maryland	139	0	0	139
Stafford County, Virginia	30	0	0	30
Calvert County, Maryland	36	0	0	36
Elsewhere	2,855	71	23	2,949
Not Reported	7,970	488	60	8,518
All Workers—TOTAL	178,094	5,503	1,172	184,769

Source: U.S. Bureau of Census, *U.S. Census Population: 1970.* Unpublished Tabulations.

TABLE XIII

VEHICLE TAG SALES

Fairfax County, 1960 to 1976

Year	Regular	TYPE OF TAG Motorcycle	Military	Other*	Total
1960	80,612	278	—	1,068	81,958
1961	87,928	299	—	1,115	89,342
1962	96,710	359	—	1,113	98,182
1963	107,633	452	—	1,202	109,287
1964	117,755	607	—	1,241	119,603
1965	129,348	975	—	1,352	131,675
1966	138,318	1,364	—	1,357	141,039
1967	142,092	1,516	16,605	2,926	163,139
1968	154,612	1,695	17,296'	3,333	176,936
1969	169,242	1,919	21,724	3,244	196,129
1970	181,193	2,307	21,678	3,627	208,805
1971	202,931	2,998	23,145	15,110	244,184
1972	227,497	3,550	25,211	15,486	271,744
1973	234,436	4,250	24,594	14,193	277,473
1974	258,829	5,766	24,599	15,445	304,639
1975	275,715	5,759	24,093	16,736	322,303
1976	293,253	5,465	25,203	19,512	343,433

Source: Fairfax County Office of Finance, Department of Budget and Financial Management.

* Other includes fire, duplicates, transfers, and free tags issued.

TABLE XIV

PRICE DISTRIBUTION OF OWNED HOUSING UNITS

FAIRFAX COUNTY, 1973—1976

	Year			
Price	1973	1974	1975	1976
	%	%	%	%
Under $30,000	7.7	7.2	5.9	3.5
30,000 - 34,999	5.4	3.9	3.4	3.1
35,000 - 39,999	7.7	6.2	5.4	4.5
40,000 - 44,999	11.1	9.1	6.3	5.6
45,000 - 49,999	12.1	11.1	8.9	7.7
50,000 - 54,999	13.8	12.4	10.6	9.8
55,000 - 59,999	11.2	12.0	11.5	10.4
60,000 - 69,999	15.8	18.0	18.9	20.4
70,000 - 79,999	7.3	9.3	13.1	14.8
80,000 - 89,999	3.3	4.6	7.7	9.1
90,000 - 99,999	1.6	2.2	3.6	4.9
$100,000 or More	3.0	3.7	4.7	6.2
Total	100.0	100.0	100.0	100.0
Median	$53,000	$55,000	$59,100	$62,600

Source: Fairfax County Office of Research and Statistics.

TABLE XV

FAIRFAX COUNTY OPERATING EXPENDITURES – FY1962 to FY1976[1]

	GENERAL GOVERNMENT EXPENSES (000's)											SCHOOL EXPENSES (000's)		
Fiscal Year	Total Gen. Govt. Expend.	County Admin.	Admin. of Justice	Crime Pre-vention	Fire Pre-vention	Public Welfare	Public Health	Public Works	County Devel.	Library	Other Oper. Expend.	Total School	Instruc-tion	Pupil Trans-port
1962	9,104	240	213	1,580	726	1,367	375	2,366	—	437	1,800	24,346[2]	17,472	788
1963	11,132	323	267	1,818	858	1,510	551	2,921	—	646	2,238	28,516	21,816	874
1964	12,384	363	286	1,972	957	1,696	589	3,141	—	765	2,615	34,268	26,513	1,067
1965	14,949	639	347	2,311	1,208	2,033	669	3,510	—	933	3,299	40,140	31,395	1,181
1966	17,467	820	395	2,620	1,411	2,371	824	3,901	—	1,123	4,002	47,614	37,533	1,224
1967	21,114	929	468	3,099	1,750	2,659	880	4,504	—	1,330	5,495	54,840	43,347	1,441
1968	25,815	1,124	585	3,756	2,200	3,336	1,001	5,631[4]	—	1,561	6,621	67,062	50,877	1,658
1969	31,191	1,452	699	4,606	2,764	4,120	1,198	4,657	1,612	1,667	8,416	84,538	63,585	2,139
1970	37,063	2,062	857	5,536	3,543	4,828	1,574	4,803	2,547	1,909	9,404	103,754	76,452	2,378
1971	48,285	2,418	1,159	6,008	4,239	6,408	1,612	6,265	2,816	2,813	14,547	118,422	86,541	2,129
1972	59,057	8,546[3]	1,569	7,433	5,252	8,354	1,965	8,680	3,289	3,192	10,777	130,207	94,770	1,844
1973	68,992	7,318	1,880	9,696	6,589	9,382	2,135	11,049	3,770	3,510	13,663	145,182	103,487	3,695
1974	79,105	10,360	2,462	11,398	7,638	11,095	2,827	12,132	4,471	3,950	12,772	162,128	112,155	4,577
1975	109,118	18,156	3,300	14,157	9,378	13,961	3,828	15,671	5,209	4,531	20,927	184,255	125,441	5,255
1976	126,851	21,270	3,840	16,017	11,034	16,386	4,389	21,783	2,258	4,828	20,208	212,580	142,202	5,347

Source: County of Fairfax, Virginia, Report on Audit. Schedules B-1 and B-2 for FY 1962 — FY 1967.
County of Fairfax, Virginia, Accountants' Report, Financial Statement and Supplementary Data, FY 1968 — FY 1976.

Notes: 1. Operating Expenditures do not include debt service or capital expenditures.
2. Fiscal Year 1962 school operating expenses were adjusted to reflect the removal of vehicle replacement costs.
3. County Administrative costs in FY1972 contain employee benefits in personnel costs for the first time. These costs were formerly in the other operating expenditures column.
4. Prior to 1969, some of the functions of the Department of Environmental Management were included within the Department of Public Works.

TABLE XVI

REVENUE SOURCES (000's) FOR ALL FUNDS

Fairfax County, FY 1962 — FY 1976

	Total	Local			State	Federal
Fiscal Year	Total Revenue[2] All Sources	Total Revenue From Local Sources	Revenue From Property[1] Taxes	Other Local Sources	Revenue From Common-wealth	Revenue From Federal Government
1962	$ 43,736	$ 30,213	$ 22,194	$ 8,019	$ 8,664	$ 4,859
1963	51,085	34,630	25,300	9,330	9,450	7,005
1964	59,982	42,275	31,292	10,983	10,412	7,295
1965	67,428	49,865	36,119	13,746	12,285	5,278
1966	83,842	59,720	44,442	15,278	13,550	10,572
1967	97,371	67,042	47,127	19,915	19,945	10,384
1968	120,051	81,875	53,399	28,476	25,802	12,374
1969	149,843	100,167	63,583	36,584	33,077	16,599
1970	173,068	119,763	74,073	45,690	38,391	14,914
1971	199,619	140,926	86,220	54,706	41,302	17,391
1972	238,014	174,429	97,500	76,929	47,469	16,116
1973	289,414	208,437	114,111	94,326	54,469	26,508
1974	331,500	239,458	130,970	108,488	60,998	31,044
1975	361,982	257,269	143,910	113,359	66,740	37,973
1976	413,111	285,362	160,742	124,620	74,664	53,085

Sources: County of Fairfax, Virginia; *Report on Audit* for the Fiscal Years 1962 to 1967.

County of Fairfax, Virginia; *Accountants' Report, Financial Statements and Supplementary Data* for the Fiscal Years 1968 to 1976.

Notes: 1.   Property Taxes include real and personal property.
2.   Revenue sources are not total income sources for the County; excluded are bond sales and other "non-revenue" items.

TABLE XVII

TAXABLE SALES BY BUSINESS CLASSIFICATION

FAIRFAX COUNTY, 1970—1975

Business Class	Taxable Sales						
	1970	1971	1972	1973	1974	1975	1976
Apparel	$ 52,365,154	$ 56,632,892	$ 59,824,481	$ 79,874,195	$ 87,682,458	$ 98,357,481	$ 115,003,988
Automotive	29,403,557	33,312,878	36,552,865	39,279,667	45,971,775	61,259,379	64,943,945
Food	229,010,106	242,657,729	267,343,184	312,723,499	396,509,255	451,867,956	496,666,952
Furniture Home Furnishings	39,737,872	35,848,849	53,187,753	60,250,362	70,953,908	67,674,280	72,542,669
General Merchandise	174,556,611	189,452,089	189,841,124	254,837,287	305,768,660	314,572,165	348,901,875
Lumber and Building Supplies	82,280,425	108,911,963	135,206,186	150,975,249	142,721,602	127,085,794	158,783,998
Fuel	5,756,570	6,308,053	6,252,986	6,830,604	11,244,999	13,462,864	13,614,360
Machinery, Equipment and Supplies	10,396,146	12,782,649	16,613,307	21,755,283	25,350,187	20,368,397	28,370,433
Miscellaneous	51,973,749	61,972,391	74,217,221	93,316,042	111,095,024	127,924,829	141,756,929
Hotels, Motels	6,494,458	7,047,712	8,324,538	9,264,181	12,213,969	14,388,241	21,075,723
Other, Not Identifiable	3,935,712	2,051,075	1,725,050	2,910,888	1,308,137	1,769,260	1,592,805
Total	$685,910,360	$756,978,280	$849,088,695	$1,032,017,257	$1,210,819,974	$1,298,730,646	$1,463,253,677

Source: Commonwealth of Virginia, Department of Taxation, *Taxable Sales*, for cited years.

TABLE XVIII

**COMPARISON OF ASSESSED VALUATION OF ALL
TAXABLE PROPERTY TO NET DEBT**

Fiscal Years 1962—1976

Fiscal Period	Total Assessed Valuation	Net Debt	Ratio of Assessed Valuation to Net Debt
1962	$ 709,789,496	$ 64,948,050	10.93
1963	725,761,562	68,023,920	10.67
1964	809,713,034	73,764,790	10.98
1965	932,197,088	80,680,460	11.55
1966	1,071,084,022	99,133,580	10.80
1967	1,153,857,711	118,256,850	9.76
1968	1,302,165,492	140,927,620	9.24
1969	1,543,724,600	163,015,140	9.47
1970	1,713,296,109	170,626,485	10.04
1971	1,973,746,124	215,461,680	9.16
1972	2,219,787,119	250,072,650	8.88
1973	2,620,998,827	264,713,455	9.90
1974	3,027,647,058	302,885,435	10.00
1975	3,477,553,643	314,825,415	11.05
1976	4,075,820,116	303,945,395	10.15

Source: County of Fairfax, Virginia, *Report on Audit*, for FY1962-FY1967.
County of Fairfax, Virginia, *Accountants' Report, Financial Statements, and
Supplementary Data* for FY 1968-FY 1976.

TABLE XIX

LONG TERM INDEBTEDNESS, FAIRFAX COUNTY

FY 1962—1976

Fiscal Year	Total Long Term Indebtedness	Self-Supporting Debt[1]	Net Debt[2]
1962	$83,933,050	$18,985,000	$ 64,948,050
1963	86,793,920	18,770,000	68,023,920
1964	102,279,790	28,515,000	73,764,790
1965	110,590,460	29,910,000	80,680,460
1966	128,483,580	29,350,000	99,133,580
1967	167,011,850	48,755,000	118,256,850
1968	189,397,620	48,470,000	140,927,620
1969	210,755,140	47,740,000	163,015,140
1970	217,601,485	46,975,000	170,626,485
1971	291,606,680	76,145,000	215,461,680
1972	325,342,650	75,270,000	250,072,650
1973	338,708,455	73,995,000	264,713,455
1974	374,575,435	71,690,000	302,885,435
1975	383,971,248	69,145,833	314,825,415
1976	370,475,395	66,530,000	303,945,395

Source:

County of Fairfax, Virginia, *Report on Audit,* Schedules A-2 for Fiscal Years 1962-1967. County of Fairfax, Virginia, *Accountants' Report, Financial Statements and Supplementary Data,* Schedule A-2 for Fiscal Years 1968-1976.

Note:

[1]*Self-Supporting Debt* is paid by means of service charges and not from the general fund. Included in this category are sanitary district sewer bonds and integrated sewer system sewer bonds.

[2]*Net Debt* is the difference between total long-term indebtedness and self-supporting debt. Net Debt is paid from the general fund.

TABLE XX
ROBBERY* IN THE WASHINGTON, D.C. SMSA BY VOLUME
1970—THIRD QUARTER 1975

Jurisdiction	Volume of Crime					
	1970	1971	1972	1973	1974	1975
District of Columbia	11,816	11,201	7,751	7,176	7,936	6,690
Prince George's County	929	1,738	1,391	1,434	1,818	1,540
Montgomery County	340	414	364	495	538	423
Alexandria City	518	490	435	472	550	367
Arlington County	211	245	181	180	329	181
Fairfax County	222	259	356	348	472	329
Town of Vienna	4	6	NA	9	6	5
Fairfax City	4	11	9	14	26	17
Falls Church City	24	14	27	25	41	28
Prince William County	9	33	43	50	41	65
Loudoun County	NA	NA	1	NA	NA	NA
Total SMSA	14,077	14,411	10,558	10,203	11,757	9,645

Source:
  Serious Crime in the Metropolitan Washington Area, Department of Public
  Safety, Metropolitan Washington Council of Governments.

  * Robbery is defined as larceny involving the use or threat of force or violence,
  including armed robbery, strongarm robbery (unarmed robbery), and attempted robbery.

TABLE XXI
INDEX CRIMES BY YEAR
Fairfax County*, 1974 to 1976

Index Crime	1974	1975	1976
Homicide	14	21	19
Rape	114	104	96
Robbery	493	433	385
Aggravated Assault	289	247	307
Burglary	5,648	5,624	5,551
Larceny	15,519	16,075	15,083
Auto Theft	2,399	2,013	1,753

* Excluding the population in Herndon, Vienna, Clifton, Lorton Reformatory, and
Fort Belvoir.

Source: Fairfax County Police Department

Appendix

THE POLL LIST FOR THE ELECTION OF THE BURGESSES FOR FAIRFAX COUNTY, VIRGINIA, IN THE YEAR 1744

Source: Fairfax County, Virginia Deed Book A-1, part I, p. 237.

This county was entitled to two members in the House of Burgesses. The names of the candidates were Col. John Colville, Capt. Lawrence Washington, Capt. Lewis Elzey, and John Sturman. Two candidates only were to be voted for by the same person. The names of the voters are recorded under the names of the candidates for whom they voted.

Col. John Colville	Col. Law. Washington	Capt. Lewis Elzey	Jno. Sturman
Esq. Fairfax	Esquire Fairfax	Magr Cock	Daniel Diskins
Catesby Cocke	John Grant	Chas Green	Thos Bosman
John Grant	James Scott	Daniel Diskin	Richard Carpenter
James Scott	James Keith	Jas Dixon	James Lane
James Keith	John Graham	Saml Harris Sr	John Hartley
John Graham	Thos John	Edward Norton	Edward Graham
Thomas John	Col Blackburn	John Hampton	Thos Brown
Col Blackburn	Daniel Hart	James Lane	Jas Roberts
Daniel Hart	John Hamilton	Amos Jenney	John Allen
Charles Green	Nimrod Hott	Wm Kitchen	Moses Linton
John Hamilton	Thos Beach	Jno Hartley	Geo Dunbarr
Nimrod Hott	Thos Lewis	Abel Jenney	Thomas Willis
Thomas Bosman	William Dodd	Samuel Stone	Wm Simpson
Thomas Beach	Amos Janney	Francis Hague	John Hartshorn
Joseph Dickson	John Shaddedin	Edmond Sands	John Roberts
Thomas Lewis	Abel Janney	Jacob Janney	Andrew Hutchinson
Samuel Harris, Sr	Samuel Stone	Jerh. Fairhurst	Rich'd Simpson
Edward Norton	Daniel French	Thos Brown	William Harle
William Dodd	Geo Harrison	Geo Simpson	John Roberts
Richard Carpenter	John West	Francis Wilks	John Keen
Jno Shadedin	Rich'd Sanford	James Roberts	John Canady
Daniel French Jr.	Thos Marshall	Henry Netherton	John Guest
George Harrison	Baldwin Dade	Jno Allen	Jas Wyatt
John West	Henry Peyton	Geo Dunbar	Thos Lewis Jr
Richard Sanford	Zeph Wade	Jno Grantham	James Grimsley
Thomas Marshall	Jereh Bronaugh	Wm Simpson	John Trammell
Baldwin Dade	Francis Hague	Ger'd Trammell	Michael Ashford
Henry Peyton	Edmond Sands	Danl Yount	Wm Roberts
Zeph. Wade	Jacob Janney	Jno Roberts	Thos Windsor
Jereh Bronaugh	Edw'd Grymes	Vincent Lewis	Wm Peake
Cornelius Eltinge	Col Eltinger	James Sanders	Jno Ferguson
Robert Sanford	Jerh Fairhurst	Andw Hutchinson	Wm Barer
Thos Monteith	Robert Sanford	Lewis Sanders	Wm Smith
Robert Baker	Thomas Monteith	Richd Simpson Sr	James Keen
Nathaniel Chapman	Jas Jacobs	Jas Smith	Thos Hicks
Vall Peyton	Francis Wilks	Abraham Lay	Christo Pritchett
Benjamin Adams	Robert Bates	Wm Harle	Thos Owsley
Nathaniel Popejoy	Nathaniel Chapman	Jno Roberts Sr	Wm Moore
Stephen Lewis	Val Pelton	Jno Canady	Wm Buckley
W.H. Terrett	Nathaniel Popejoy	Wm Barkley	Wm Hawling
Townsend Dade	Stephen Lewis	Fielding Turner	Fielding Turner
William Clifton	W H Terrett	Jacob Remey	Philip Noland
John Turley	Townsend Dade	Rich Omohundro	Richd Coleman
William Bartlett	Wm Clifton	Thos Pinson	Wm Ashford

Col. John Colville	Col. Law. Washington	Capt. Lewis Elzey	Jno. Sturman
John Grantham	Moses Linton	David Richardson	Wm Meckley
Owen Williams	John Turley	Job Carter	Thos Smith
William Stribling	Wm Stribling	Samuel Tillet	John Martin
Henry Watson	Henry Watson	Baxter Simpson	John Cockrell
John Mede	Garret Trammell	Jno Trammell	John Robinson
Cluthos Neale	Cluthos Neale	James Jeffery	Wm Trammell
William Gunnel	Daniel Young	Richard Wheelr	Abraham Lindsey
Moses Ball	Jno Hartshorn	Henry Gunnell	Jacob Smith
William Gunnell Jr	Wm Gunnell	Wm Grimes	Francis Summers
James Daniel	Moses Ball	Wm Boydstone	Jno Melton
James Saunders	Wm Gunnell Jr	Thos Wren	Henry Baggus
Gilbert Simpson	Jas Daniel	Wm Roberts	Robt Foster
Wm Williams Jr	Gilbert Simpson	Thos Winsor	Joseph Reid
Henry Brent	William Williams Sr	Rich Kirkland	Thos Standall
Thos Carney	Henry Brent	Blancr Duncan	Jas Murray
Abraham Lay	Thos Carney	Daniel Trammell	Samuel Conner
Gabriel Adams	Gabriel Adams	Jno Higgerson	Chas Griffin
Wm Saunders	Wm Saunders	Wm Barton	Bond Veale
Bryant Alliston	Jno Jenkins	Wm Wright	Jno Hampton
Jno Jenkins	Benj Adams	James Spurr	Wm Kitchen
Jno Keen	Owen Gilmore	Wm Barker	Jos Jacob
Daniel Thomas	Jacob Ramey	Wm Smith	Geo Simpson
Jno Musgrove	Richd Omohundro	Jno Bronaugh	Henry Netherton
Wm Davis	Jno Ashford	Thos Hall	Vincent Lewis
David Thomas	Daniel Thomas	Thos Ford	Lewis Sanders
Ezekiel Jenkins	Charles Broadwater	Rich'd Kirkland	James Smith
Jno Gust	Saml Conner	Benj Sebastian	Thos Penson
Gabriel Adams Jr	Wm Winsor	James Keen	Job Carter
David Richardson	Thos Moxley	James Turley	Baxter Simpson
William Hall Jr	James Waugh	Thos Hicks	Rich S Kirkland
Jno Ellett	Charles Griffin	Wm Moore	Thos Hall
Jno Manley	James Robinson	Jno Lucas	James Turley
Thomas Lewis Jr	Robert King	Wm Shortridge	Isaac Simmonds
George Taylor	Thos Whitford	Wm Buckley	Robert Thomas
Richard Wheeler	Jno Minor	Jno Hurst	John Robinson
Henry Gunnell	Wm Champneys	Edward Emms	John Gorham
Wm Grymes	Jno Musgrove	Wm Halling	Geo Adams
Wm Perkins	Wm Davis	Philip Noland	Geo Foster
Wm Boilston	David Thomas	Wm Rairdon	
Wm Bowling	Ezekiel Jenkins	Joseph Garrett	
Samuel Warner	Gabriel Adams Jr	Thos Smith	
Michael Ashford	James Wyatt	Jno Martin	
Wm Jenkins	Saml Tillett	Owen Williams	
Blancr Duncan	Jno Aylatt	Robert Thomas	
Robert Boggess	Jas Grymsley	James Halley	
Francis Triplet	George Taylor	Wm Kirkland	
Jno Taylor	James Jefferey	Wm Scutt	
Owen Gilmore	Wm Perkin	Jacob Smith	
Wm Peake	Thos Wren	Jno Goram	
Jno Farguson Sr	Wm Bowling	Francis Summers	
Guy Broadwater	Samuel Warner	Jno Melton	
James Spurr	Wm Jenkins	Josiah Clapham	
Daniel French Sr	Daniel Trammell	Geo Adams	
James Jenkins	John Hickerson	Geo Foster	
John Bronaugh	Wm Barton	Daniel Thomas	
John Baxter	Robert Boggess	Jno Ball	
Jacob Lucas	Francis Triplet	James Waugh	

Col. John Colville	Col Law. Washington	Capt. Lewis Elzey	Jno. Sturman
Thos Fford	Wm Wright		
Richard Kirkland	John Taylor		
Sampson Darrell	John Manley		
Lowell Jackson	Guy Broadwater		
John Lucas	Daniel French Sr		
Wm Shortridge	James Jenkins		
Hugh West	John Baxter		
John Husk	Jacob Lucas		
Garrat Alexander	Benj Sebastian		
Isaac Simmons	Christopher Pritchett		
John Summers	Thos Owsley		
Thos Falkner	Sampson Darrell		
Richd Coleman	Lovell Jackson		
William Ashford	Garrat Alexander		
Wm Reardon	Hugh West		
Francis Awbrey	Edward Emms		
Walter Williams	Jno Summers		
William McGee	Thos Falkner		
Thos Darns	Francis Awbrey		
Wm Trammell	Walter Williams		
Thos West	Thomas Darns		
Michael Valandigam	Josiah Garrett		
(Valandingham)	Thomas West		
Capt Chas Ewel	Michael Valandigam		
Jno Cockerill	(Valandingham)		
Wm Gladding	Chas Ewel		
Wm Kirkland	Wm Gladding		
Jno Gladding	John Gladding		
Thomas Ellet	Thos Ellett		
Bertram Ewell	Bertram Ewell		
John Straham	John Strahann		
William Stutt	John Meade		
John Diskins	John Diskins		
Robert Diskins	Abraham Linsey		
Christopher Neale	Josias Clapham		
Jadwin Crutcher	Henry Baugus		
Jacob Lawful	Christo Neale		
Jas Reid	George Platt		
Thos Scandall	Robert Foster		
Wm Hall Sr	Jadwin Crutcher		
James Murray	Bryant Alliston		
John Ashford	Jacob Lawful		
Chas Broadwater			
Wm Winsor			
Thomas Moxley			
John Ball			
James Robinson			
Robert King			
George Platt			
Thos Whitford			
John Minor			
Wm Champneys			

A copy Poll List for the House of Burgesses, recorded Liber A, No. 1, page 237, and examined.

Truly Recorded,

Test,   CATESBY COCKE, Cl. Cur.

FAIRFAX COUNTY CLERKS OF THE COURT
1742-1976

Sources: Frederick Johnston, *Memorials of Old Virginia Clerks;* Fairfax County Court
Order Books

Catesby Cocke	1742-46	William M. Fitzhugh	
John Graham	1746-52	(military)	1866-67
Peter Wagener	1752-72	F.D. Richardson, *pro tem*	1866-69
Peter Wagener, Jr.	1772-98	D. F. Dulany (military)	1869-70
George Deneale	1798-1801	F. D. Richardson	1870-80
William Moss	1801-33	F.W. Richardson, *pro tem*	1880-81
F.D. Richardson, *pro tem*	1833-35	F. W. Richardson	1881-87
Thomas Moss	1835-39	W. E. Graham	1887-1903
Alfred Moss, *pro tem*	Oct.-Nov., 1839	F. W. Richardson	1904-35
S. M. Ball	1839-52	John M. Whalen	1936-45
Alfred Moss	1852-61	Thomas P. Chapman, Jr.	1945-67
Henry T. Brooks (military)	1861-65	W. Franklin Gooding	1967-75
W. B. Gooding (military)	1865-66	James E. Hoofnagle	1976-

JUSTICES AND JUDGES OF CIRCUIT AND DISTRICT COURTS
FAIRFAX COUNTY, VIRGINIA
1742-1976

Sources: Fairfax County, Virginia, Court Order Books; Virginia State Library.
(Because of missing books and records, this listing is incomplete.)

Lists Compiled By E. Sprouse, P. Howe, V. Peters, A. Lewis, and N. Netherton

First Commission for
Fairfax County, *1742*

William Fairfax
John Colvill
Richard Osborne
Jeremiah Bronaugh
Lewis Elzey
William Payne
Thomas Pearson
John Minor
William Henry Terrett
John Gregg
Gerard Alexander
Edward Barry
Daniel Jennings
Thomas Arbuthnot

(1742-1748 Fairfax County
Court Order Books are
missing.)

1749

John Minor
William H. Terrett
Daniel Jennings
John Carlyle
William Ramsay
Charles Broadwater
Daniel McCarty
John Colvill
Moses Linton
Lewis Ellzey
William Payne
Richard Osborn
George W. Fairfax
Anthony Russell
Joseph Watkins
George Mason
Jeremiah Bronaugh
Thomas, sixth Lord Fairfax
    Chief Justice
Stephen Lewis

1750

John West
Lawrence Washington
Catesby Cocke

1752

Fielding Turner

1753

Thomas Colvill

1754

Hugh West

1755

John West, Jr.
Sampson Turley
Sampson Darrell
James Hamilton
Oneas Campbell

1757

Henry Gunnell

1758

John Hunter
Robert Adam
William Bronaugh
William Payne, Jr.

1759
Bryan Fairfax
Townshend Dade
Benjamin Grayson
Edward Blackburn
Lee Massey
William Adams

1762
Hector Ross

1764
George William Fairfax
William Ellzey
John West
George Mason
Daniel McCarty
John Carlyle
William Ramsay
Charles Broadwater
Thomas Colvill   dead
John West, Junior
Bryan Fairfax
Sampson Dorrell Sher.
Townshend Dade   Quo:
Henry Gunnell

1767
Marmaduke Beckwith
Robert Adam
John Hunter   dead
Richard Sanford
Wm. Payne
Benjamin Grayson
William Adams
Edward Blackburn
Hector Ross &
Alexander Henderson Gent.
George William Fairfax
Lewis Ellzey
John West
George Mason
Daniel McCarty
John Carlyle
Wm. Ramsay
Charles Broadwater
John West, Junr
Bryan Fairfax
Sampson Dorrell Quo:
Townshend Dade
Henry Gunnell
Wm. Adams
George Washington &
Daniel French Gent:

1768
George W Fairfax
Lewis Ellzey

John West
George Mason
Daniel McCarty
John Carlyle
Wm Ramsey
Charles Broadwater
John West Junior
Bryan Fairfax
Sampson Darrel
Townshend Dade Quorum
Henry Gunnell
Marmaduke Beckwith
Robert Adam
Richard Sanford
Wm Payne
Benjamin Grayson dead
Wm Adams
Hector Ross
Alexander Henderson
George Washington
Daniel French &
Edward Payne Gent:

1770
John West
George Mason
Daniel McCarty
John Carlyle
William Ramsay
Charles Broadwater
John West Junr
Bryan Fairfax
Sampson Darrell Quor.
Henry Gunnell
Robert Adam
William Payne
William Adams
Hector Ross
Alexander Henderson
George Washington and
Edward Payne Gent.

(1774-1782 Fairfax County
Court Order Books are
missing.)

1783
John Gibson
George Gilpin
Richard Chichester
Robert McCrea
Charles Little
James Hendricks
Josiah Watson
Henry Darne
Thomas Lewis
Robert T. Hooe

1784
James Wren
David Stuart
David Arell
Charles Alexander

1785
William Deneale
John Moss

1786
George Minor
William Herbert

1787
Roger West
Richard Conway
Thomas Gunnell
John Fitzgerald
William Brown
Benjamin Dulany
Thomas Pollard
James Waugh
John Potts

1788
Martin Cockburn
William Lyles

(1793-1796 Fairfax County
Court Order Books are
missing.)

1797
Thompson Mason
James Keith, Jr.

1798
Francis Adams
John Stewart Alexander
James Coleman
Elisha C. Dick
Charles Eskridge
John Gunnell
William Gunnell
John Jackson
William Lane, Jr.
Ludwell Lee
Richard Bland Lee
Samuel Love
John Potts, Jr.
Richad Ratcliff
William Stanhope
George Summers
William H. Washington

1801

Francis Adams
Charles Alexander
John S. Alexander
Charles Broadwater
James Coleman
Richard Conway
William Deneale
Elisha C. Dick
Benjamin Dulany
Charles Eskridge
John Fitzgerald
George Gilpin
John Gunnell
Thomas Gunnell
William Gunnell
William Herbert
Robert T. Hooe
John Jackson
William Lane, Jr.
Ludwell Lee
Richard B. Lee
Charles Little
Samuel Love
Daniel McCarty
Thompson Mason
George Minor
John Moss
William Payne
John Potts, Jr.
Richard Ratcliff
William Stanhope
David Stewart
George Summers
William H. Washington
James Waugh
John West
Roger West
James Wren
Now dead: Love, Fitzgerald,
    T. Gunnell, R. West,
    J. Gunnell, J. S.
    Alexander, D. McCarty
Now moved: Ludwell Lee
Now refuses to qualify:
    Summers
Now in D.C.: Gilpin, Hooe,
    Alexander, Conway,
    Herbert, Potts, Dick,
    Washington
Now disqualified: Adams

1802

Augustine J. Smith
Humphrey Peake
John Keene
James H. Blake

1803

Samuel Adams, Jr.

1804

Richard Coleman
Spencer Jackson
George Graham

1807

Present:
William Gunnell, Jr.
William Payne
Wm. Deneale
Augustine J. Smith
Hancock Lee
Humphrey Peake
Spencer Jackson
Absent:
George Summers, Gentleman
Persons to be recommended
    to the Governor as proper
    persons to be commission-
    ed by him as Justices of
    the Peace, or added to the
    Commission of the Peace
    for the County:
John C. Hunter
John C. Scott
Daniel McCarty Chichester
Joseph Powell
Edward Dulin
James L. Triplett
John Y. Ricketts
George Mason

1808

Present:
William Gunnell, Jr.
James Waugh
William Lane, Jr.
Thomson Mason
George Summers
Humphrey Peake
George Graham
James L. Triplett
Absent:
James Coleman
William Gunnell, Jr.
David Stuart
William Payne
William Deneale
Thompson Mason
Richard Ratcliffe
George Summers
Augustine I. Smith
James Waugh
Hancock Lee

Humphrey Peake
George Graham
John Coleman

Acting in 1816-17

James Coleman
Wm. Lane, Jr.
Thompson Mason
Rich. Ratcliffe
John Jackson
Augustine J. Smith
Rich. M. Scott
Humphrey Peake
Rich. Coleman
Spencer Jackson
John C. Hunter
James L. Triplett
John T. Ricketts
Lawrence Lewis
Wm. H. Terrett
Henry Gunnell, Jr.
Alex'r Waugh
Geo. Minor
Geo. Gunnell
Francis L. Lee
John W. Ashton
Dan'l M. Chichester
Geo. Taylor
Wm. H. Foote
James Waugh
James Sangster
Thomas Moss
Dan'l Dulany
Chas. G. Broadwater
Wm. H. Fitzhugh

1819-1826

William A. G. Dade

Acting in 1824

Rich. Ratcliffe
Rich. M. Scott
Lawrence Lewis
Spencer Jackson
John C. Hunter
James L. Triplett
Alex'r Waugh
Geo. Gunnell
Geo. Mason
Augst. J. Smith
John W. Ashton
Geo. Taylor
Wm. H. Foote
James Sangster
Thos. Moss
Dan'l Dulany
Chas. L. Broadwater
Wm. H. Fitzhugh

Chas. F. Ford
Benedict M. Lang
Eli Offutt
John Jackson
Robt. Ratcliffe
Chas. Ratcliffe
Wm. E. Beckwith
John Geanit
Mottrom Ball
Rich. C. Mason
Joshua Hutchison
Sam'l Summers

1831-1838

John Scott

Acting between 1825-42

Geo. Millan
Silas Burke
Rich. H. Cockerille
Rich. C. Mason
Dennis Johnston
John D. Bell
John Gunnell
Frederick Carper
Spencer M. Ball
Edward Sangster
James Millan
Thomas Nevett
John H. Halley
Wm. Ball
John Millan
Geo. Mason
John B. Hunter
Henry Fairfax
Wm. H. Alexander
Frederick A. Hunter
Wm. A. Chichester
Alfred Moss
Chas C. Stuart
James Hunter
Benj. F. Rose
James Cloud
Fred. M. Ford
Wm. R. Selectman
Nelson Conrad
W. W. Ball
Jno. Powell
Jno A. Washington
Wm. H. Wren

1839-52

John Scott
John W. Tyler

1852-55

Silas Burke
William Ball
Wm. R. Selecman
W. W. Ball
John Millan
Nelson Conrad
William H. Wrenn
James Hunter
Ira Williams
Thomas Suddath
George H. Padgett
James M. Benton
John R. Dale
Thos. A. Davis
S. T. Stuart
Levi Burke
James Fox
Robert M. Whaley
Abner Brush
John Cowling
F. W. Flood
Francis E. Johnston
John W. Hickey
R. C. Mason
R. McC. Throckmorton
W. W. Elzey
Willis B. McCormick
William Barker
F. M. Ford
Francis C. Davis
John W. Hickey
Spencer Jackson
John N. Taylor
John B. Farr
J. C. Gunnell
John R. Grigsby

1858-60

John C. Gunnell
Tenley S. Swink
Richard L. Nevitt
Daniel Kincheloe
Francis C. Davis
Richard Johnson
W. B. McCormick
F. C. Davis
Ira Williams
Francis E. Johnston
Geo. H. Padgett
George Burke
John Burke
John Dole
John A. Washington
Alfred Leigh
Francis C. Davis
James Hunter

W. B. McCormick
William L. Lee
Wm. W. Ellzey
John Cowling
Benjamin F. Shreve
William S. Seitz
James P. Machen
George Padgett
James Simpson
_____ Mann
W. W. Ball
Richard Johnston
B. D. Utterback
F. M. Ford
Cyrus Hickey
A. S. McKenzie
R. C. Mason
Henry Jenkins

1863-1867

Thomas P. Brown
James H. Rice
Wm. Terry
Andrew Sagar
Herain Cockrill
Samuel Pulman
Reuben Ives
Daniel W. Lewis
E. E. Mason
Levi Dening
Harry Bready
William A. Ferguson
William Walters
William T. Rumsey
Talmadge Thorne
Courtland Lukins
Metra Makely
John B. Troth
George B. Ives
Josiah B. Bowman
Job Hawxhurst
George F. M. Walters
J. W. Barcroft
George W. Millan
Cyrus Hickey
James C. Dentz
B. D. Utterback
Thomas E. Carper

1866

John Powell
Lewis George
Francis Davis

1867

T. Wm. Barcroft
W. B. Bowman
Thomas E. Carper
Francis C. Davis
James C. Dentz
M. E. Fora
Wm. E. Ford
John B. Troth
Job Hawxhurst
George B. Ives
Richard Johnson
William Lee
Alfred Leigh
Courtland Lukens
Metrah Makely
E. E. Mason
Samuel Pullman
James H. Rice
W. T. Rice
Jonathan Roberts
Silas Simpson
Daniel Sims
Cyrus Stickey
B. D. Utterback
Wm. F. McWalters

1868

T. Wm. Barcroft
W. B. Bowman
Thomas C. Carper
N. P. Dennison
Francis C. Davis
James C. Dentz
Wm. E. Ford
John B. Troth
Job Hawxhurst
Richard Johnson
George B. Ives
Alfred Leigh
Courtland Lukens
Metrah Makely
E. E. Mason
Sam Pullman
W. T. Rice
Silas Simpson
Daniel W. Sims
Cyrus Stickey
R. D. Utterback
Geo. F. M. Walters

1869

T. Wm. Barcroft
W. B. Bowman
Jacob Brooks
Carter Burton
John L. Detwiler

Wm. E. Ford
John B. Troth
George B. Ives
Job Hawxhurst
Richard Johnson
Alfred Leigh
Daniel W. M. Lewis
Courtland Lukens
E. E. Mason
Samuel Pullman
James H. Rice
T. W. Rice
Samuel Shaw
Silas Simpson
D. Sims
Cyrus Stickey
B. D. Utterback
E. W. Wakefield
Wm. Walters

1870

T. Wm. Barcroft
W. B. Bowman
Jacob Brooks
Carter Burton
George B. Ives
Job Hawxhurst
Courtland Lukens
Samuel Pullman
E. W. Wakefield
Geo. F. W. Walters

1870-1874

Richard H. Cockerille

1874-1885

James Sangster

1886-1899

D. M. Chichester

1897-1903

James M. Love

*Virginia Circuit
Court Judges*

John M. Tyler,
1852-1860

No record of a court held,
1861-1863

Edward K. Snead,
1864-1865

Henry W. Thomas,
1866-1868

W. Willoughby,
June 1869

Lysander Hill,
November 1869

James Keith,
1870-1894

C. E. Nicol,
1895-1907

Louis C. Barely,
1907

J.B.T. Thornton,
1908-1918

Samuel G. Brent,
1918-1928

Howard W. Smith,
1928-1930

Walter T. McCarthy,
1931-1944

Paul E. Brown,
1944-1966

Arthur W. Sinclair,
1950-1977

Harry L. Carrico,
1956-1961

Calvin Van Dyck,
1961-1967

Albert V. Bryan, Jr.,
1962-1971

Barnard F. Jennings,
1964-

James Keith,
1966-

William G. Plummer,
1967-

Lewis D. Morris,
1968-

Percy Thornton, Jr.,
1968-1977

Burch Millsap,
1968-

James C. Cacheris
1971-

Thomas J. Middleton,
1975-

Richard J. Jamborsky,
1976-

County General

District Court

Robert Fitzgerald,
1951-1955

John Corboy,
1954-1955

John A. Rothrock, Jr.
1955-

J. Mason Grove,
1955-

Martin E. Morris,
1965-

Donald C. Crounse,
1966-1974

Robert M. Hurst,
1972-

Lewis Hall Griffith,
1974-

G. William Hammer,
1976-

Juvenile Court Judges

Frank L. Deierhoi,
1965-

Richard J. Jamborsky,
1968-1976

Philip N. Brophy,
1973-

Arnold B. Kassabian,
1976-

Raymond O. Kellam,
1976-1977

MEMBERS, FAIRFAX COUNTY BOARD OF SUPERVISORS

Source of Information: Fairfax County, Virginia
Board of Supervisors Minute Books, 1870-1976

List Prepared by Virginia Peters, Anne Lewis and Nan Netherton

BOSMB No. 1, p. 1
25 July 1870

First meeting, Board of Supervisors
form of government

Jonathan H. Gray, President
W. M. Day (Dr.)
Courtland Lukins
John G. Worthington
Henry D. Rice
Richard Hirst

BOSMB No. 1, p. 23
7 August 1871

J.H. Gray, Chairman
J. G. Worthington
J. B. Coleman
Frank Sherman
H.D. Rice
C. Lukins

BOSMB No. 1, p. 46
5 August 1872

J.H. Gray
Frank Sherman
H.D. Rice

John B. Coleman
A.W. Pearson
John G. Worthington, Chairman

BOSMB No. 1, p. 52
10 March 1873

J.H. Gray
A.W. Pierson
John B. Coleman
C.F. Ford

BOSMB No. 1, p. 58
25 August 1873

J.H. Gray
A.W. Pierson
Ira Williams
John B. Coleman
James P. Machen, Chairman
Wm. M. Fitzhugh

BOSMB No. 1, p. 72
December 1874

A.W. Pierson, Chairman
O.E. Hine
Burdett Skinner
John B. Coleman
J.H. Gray

728 Fairfax County, Virginia

p. 76

E.F. Ford

BOSMB No. 1, p. 83
October 1875

J.B. Coleman, Chairman
Ira Williams
R.F. Roberts
R.S. Rotchford
C.F. Ford

BOSMB No. 1, p. 95
20 April 1876

J.B. Coleman
Ira Williams
R.L. Rotchford
R.F. Roberts
C.F. Ford
A.W. Pierson

BOSMB No. 1, p. 120
7 November 1877

J.B. Coleman, Chairman
Job Hawxhurst
R.L. Rotchford
C.F. Ford
George B. Ives
A.W. Pierson

BOSMB No. 1, p. 155
28 July 1879

Job Hawxhurst, Chairman
J.B. Coleman
J.J. Moran
Francis C. Davis
C.F. Ford
A.W. Pierson

BOSMB No. 1, p. 195
25 July 1881

F.C. Davis
J. B. Coleman, Chairman
C.F. Ford

p. 197

William Hunter
J.M. Thorne

p. 198

W.S. Smoot

BOSMB No. 1, p. 239
23 July 1883

J. B. Coleman

F.C. Davis
C.F. Ford
Job Hawxhurst
J.M. Thorne, Chairman

p. 242

S.H. Snowden

BOSMB No. 1, p. 268
30 June 1884

J.M. Thorne, Chairman
J.B. Coleman
F.C. Davis
C.F. Ford
S.H. Snowden
J.T. Ginnelly

BOSMB No. 2, p. 1
November 1884

J.M. Thorne, Chairman
J.B. Coleman
F.C. Davis
C.F. Ford
J.T. Ginnelly
S.H. Snowden

BOSMB No. 2, p. 16
27 July 1885

Capt. William P. Graham, President
S.H. Snowden
J.H. Hurst
E.S. Fairfax
C.F. Ford
J.T. Reynolds

BOSMB No. 2, p. 77
25 July 1887

J.T. Reynolds, President (Providence
  District)
Haywood Davis
C.F. Ford
J.H. Hurst
Walter Walton
George K. Pickett

BOSMB No. 2, p. 95
27 February 1888

J.T. Reynolds, Esq., Chairman
Walter Walton
J.H. Hurst
George K. Pickett
C.F. Ford
Haywood Davis

BOSMB No. 2, p. 138

Walter Walton, Chairman
Haywood Davis
C.F. Ford
J.H. Hurst
Benjamin Kenyon
_____ Payne

BOSMB No. 2, p. 194
27 July 1891

J.H. Hurst, Chairman
Benjamin Kenyon
G.K. Pickett
H.D. Rice
Benjamin Simpson
_____ Thomson

BOSMB No. 2, p. 209
28 March 1892

J. H. Hurst, Esq., Chairman
_____ Thompson
Benjamin Simpson
H.D. Rice
G.K. Pickett
Benjamin Kenyon

BOSMB No. 2, p. 240
24 July 1893

G.K. Pickett, Chairman
Haywood Davis
J.H. Hurst
Benjamin Simpson
Walter Walton
Franklin Williams

BOSMB No. 2, p. 251
4 December 1893

George Auld replaces Pickett
J.H. Hurst becomes Chairman

BOSMB No. 2, p. 254
1 January 1894

R.C. Triplett is appointed to fill vacancy
left by death of Walter Walton

BOSMB No. 2, p. 254
1 January 1894

J.H. Hurst, Chairman
George Auld
Haywood Davis
Benjamin Simpson
R.C. Triplett
Franklin Williams

BOSMB No. 2, p. 295
22 July 1895

John H. Hurst, Chairman
George Auld (Falls Church)
H.D. Rice (Lee)
Benjamin Simpson (Centreville)
R.C. Triplett (Mount Vernon)
Franklin Williams (Providence)

BOSMB No. 2, p. 311
6 April 1896

John H. Hurst, President
George Auld
H.D. Rice
Benjamin Simpson
R.C. Triplett
Franklin Williams

BOSMB No. 2, p. 354
26 July 1897

John H. Hurst, Chairman
A.L. Lukens
H.D. Rice
Benjamin Simpson
J.M. Thorne
F. Williams

BOSMB No. 2, p. 408
1 May 1899

George T. Harrison is appointed to fill
vacancy left by death of Benjamin
Simpson

BOSMB No. 2, p. 423
1899

H.D. Rice, Chairman
George Auld
George T. Harrison
J.S. Pearson
Richards C. Triplett
Franklin Williams

BOSMB No. 2, p. 438
2 January 1900

H.D. Rice, Esq., Chairman
George Auld
George T. Harrison
J. S. Pearson
R.C. Triplett
Franklin Williams

BOSMB No. 3, p. 10
22 July 1901

R.L. Spindle (Centreville)
H.D. Rice (Lee)
Richards C. Triplett (Mount Vernon)
J. George Auld (Falls Church)
J.S. Pearson (Dranesville)
Franklin Williams, Sr. (Providence)

BOSMB No. 3, p. 97
25 January 1904

George Auld, Chairman (Falls Church)
G.H. Burke (Lee)
J.S. Pearson (Dranesville)
R.S. Spindle (Centreville)
Richards C. Triplett (Mount Vernon)
Franklin Williams (Providence)

BOSMB No. 3, p. 191
6 January 1908

George Auld, Chairman (Falls Church)
R.R. Buckley (Centerville)
G.H. Burke (Lee)
J.S. Pearson (Dranesville)
F. Williams, Sr. (Providence)
R.C. Triplett (Mount Vernon)

BOSMB No. 3, p. 194
7 February 1908

W.F.P. Reid, Jr. (Mount Vernon) is appointed to fill vacancy left by death of R.C. Triplett.

BOSMB NO. 3, p. 382
1 January 1912

R.R. Buckley, Chairman (Centreville)
G.H. Burke (Lee)
John S. Pearson (Dranesville)
W.F.P. Reid (Mount Vernon)
F. Williams, Sr. (Providence)
Thomas A. Williams (Falls Church)

BOSMB No. 3, p. 503
6 May 1914

R.R. Buckley, Chairman (Centreville)
G.H. Burke (Lee)
John S. Pearson (Dranesville)
W.F.P. Reid (Mount Vernon)
Franklin Williams, Sr. (Providence)
Thomas A. Williams (Falls Church)

BOSMB No. 3, p. 505
3 June 1914

Franklin Williams, Sr. elected Chairman
D.Lee Sanders is appointed to fill vacancy left by R.R. Buckley's resignation.

BOSMB No. 3, p. 525
1 September 1914

Frank L. Ballenger is appointed to fill vacancy left by T.A. Williams' resignation.

BOSMB No. 4, p. 1
July 1915

Franklin Williams, Sr., Chairman
D. Lee Sanders
G.H. Burke
W.F.P. Reid
F.L. Ballenger
J.S. Pearson

BOSMB No. 4, p. 43
3 January 1916

J.R.M. Gheen (Centreville)
G.H. Burke (Lee)
W.F.P. Reid (Mount Vernon)
Frank L. Ballenger, Chairman (Falls Church)
Ronald Blake (Providence)
George F. Harrison (Dranesville)

BOSMB No. 4, p. 296
20 January 1920

D.W. Buckley, (Centreville)
Nathan C. Davis (Lee)
W.F.P. Reid (Mount Vernon)
Franklin L. Ballenger, Chairman (Falls Church)
Ronald Blake (Providence)
George F. Harrison (Dranesville)

BOSMB No. 4, p. 417
8 February 1922

C. Norman Stewart is appointed to fill vacancy left by death of Nathan C. Davis

BOSMB No. 5, p. 1
2 January 1924

D.W. Buckley (Centreville)
C.N. Stewart (Lee)
W.F.P. Reid (Mount Vernon)
F.L. Ballenger, Chairman (Falls Church)
Harry V. Leigh (Providence)
George F. Harrison (Dranesville)

BOSMB No. 5, p. 268
7 September 1927

W.F.P. Reid, Chairman (Mount
    Vernon)
D.W. Buckley (Centreville)
C.N. Stewart (Lee)
Harry V. Leigh (Providence)
George F. Harrison (Dranesville)
Victor C. Donaldson (Falls Church)

BOSMB No. 5, p. 303
2 January 1928

W.F.P. Reid, Chairman (Mount Vernon)
D.W. Buckley (Centreville)
C.N. Stewart (Lee)
C.H. Powell (Falls Church)
Harry V. Leigh (Providence)

p. 310

Mark Turner (Dranesville)
Kyle A. Davis is appointed to fill the
vacancy left by death of C. Norman
Stewart.

BOSMB No. 6, p. 1
6 January 1930

W.F. Reid, Chairman (Mount Vernon)
D.W. Buckley (Centreville)
C.H. Powell (Falls Church)
H.V. Leigh (Providence)
Mark Turner (Dranesville)
K.A. Davis (Lee)

BOSMB No. 6, p. 162
4 January 1932

W.F.P. Reid, Chairman (Mount
    Vernon)
D.W. Buckley (Centreville)
Kyle A. Davis (Lee)

p. 457

W.H. Ellmore (Dranesville)
G. Wallace Carper (Providence)
C.H. Powell (Falls Church)

BOSMB No. 7, p. 1
3 October 1934

W.F.P. Reid, Chairman (Mount
    Vernon)
G. Wallace Carper (Providence)
W.H. Ellmore (Dranesville)
D.W. Buckley (Centreville)
C.H. Powell (Falls Church)
Kyle A. Davis (Lee)

BOSMB No. 7, p. 75
6 March 1935

John T. Blincoe is appointed to fill
vacancy left by Kyle A. Davis' resignation.

BOSMB No. 7, p. 137
4 September 1935

Miss Edith Rogers is appointed to fill
vacancy left by death of W.H. Ellmore
(Dranesville)

BOSMB No. 7, p. 192
6 January 1936

W.F.P. Reid, Chairman (Mount
    Vernon)
D.W. Buckley (Centreville)
C.H. Powell (Falls Church)
John T. Blincoe (Lee)
G. Wallace Carper (Providence)
Edith Rogers (Dranesville)

BOSMB No. 8, p. 193
3 August 1938

W.F.P. Reid, Chairman (Mount
    Vernon)
Miss Edith Rogers (Dranesville)
D.W. Buckley (Centreville)
John T. Blincoe (Lee)
C.H. Powell (Falls Church)
G. Wallace Carper (Providence)

BOSMB No. 8, p. 552
January 1940

George Wallace Carper, Chairman
    (Providence)
Daniel W. Buckley (Centreville)
Maurice William Fox (Dranesville)
Charles H. Powell (Falls Church)
John T. Blincoe (Lee)
Andrew W. Clarke (Mount Vernon)

BOSMB No. 12, p. 264
10 January 1944

G. Wallace Carper, Chairman
    (Providence)
Daniel W. Buckley (Centreville)
Maurice W. Fox (Dranesville)
Burns N. Gibson (Falls Church) fills
    vacancy caused by the death of
    Charles H. Powell
John T. Blincoe (Lee)
Herbert Blunt (Mount Vernon) fills
    vacancy caused by election to the
    State Senate of Andrew W.
    Clarke

BOSMB No. 14, p. 196

E.C. Sheads (Lee) is appointed to fill vacancy left by death of John T. Blincoe.

BOSMB No. 15, p. 430-31
7 January 1948

G.W. Carper, Chairman (Providence)
Daniel W. Buckley (Centreville)
Maurice W. Fox (Dranesville)
C.B. Runyon (Falls Church)
E.C. Sheads (Lee)
Arthur I. Shaffer (Mount Vernon)

BOSMB No. 15, p. 549
19 May 1948

Robert R. Dye (Centreville) appointed to fill vacancy left by death of D.W. Buckley

BOSMB No. 19, p. 1
1 January 1952

G.W. Carper, Chairman (Providence)
Stuart T. DeBell (Centreville)
Maurice W. Fox (Dranesville)
Mrs. Anne Wilkins (Falls Church)
C.B. Jett (Lee)
Arthur I. Shaffer (Mount Vernon)

BOSMB No. 20, p. 389
7 January 1953

(Magisterial District lines redrawn)

G.W. Carper, Chairman (Dranesville)
Stuart T. DeBell (Centreville)
Maurice W. Fox (Centreville)
Anne A. Wilkins (Mason)
C.B. Jett (Lee)
Arthur I. Shaffer (Lee)

BOSMB No. 20, p. 460

Additional Supervisor elected, 3 November 1953

C. B. Runyon

BOSMB No. 24, p. 69
4 January 1956

Stuart T. DeBell
Joseph H. Freehill, Chairman
James Keith
A. Clayborne Leigh
William H. Moss
Richard P. Ovenshine
Anne A. Wilkins

BOSMB No. 25, p. 1
17 September 1956

Joseph H. Freehill, Chairman
Stuart T. DeBell
James Keith
William H. Moss
Richard P. Ovenshine
Anne A. Wilkins

BOSMB No. 25, pp. 215, 216, 370
2 January 1957

James Keith, Chairman (Providence)

BOSMB No. 26, p. 456-8
8 January 1958

Anne A. Wilkins, Chairman (Mason)

BOSMB No. 28, p. 79
7 January 1959

Stuart T. DeBell, Chairman (Centreville)

p. 137, 4 February 1959

Thomas S. Gray (Falls Church) appointed to fill vacancy left by death of Joseph H. Freehill.

BOSMB No. 30, p. 1-2
6 January 1960

Anne Wilkins, Chairman (Mason)
Stuart T. DeBell (Centreville)
A. Claiborne Leigh (Dranesville)
Robert C. Cotten (Falls Church)
William H. Moss (Lee)
George C. Landrith (Mount Vernon)
James Keith (Providence)

p. 458

John P. Parrish (Mount Vernon) appointed to fill unexpired term of George C. Landrith who resigned 8 June 1960.

BOSMB No. 33, p. 2

3 January 1962

William H. Moss (Lee) elected Chairman

p. 409

A. L. Brault (Providence) appointed to fill unexpired term of James Keith.

BOSMB No. 36, p. 1
12 June 1963

A. Claiborne Leigh (Dranesville) elected Chairman

BOSMB No. 37, p. 97
8 January 1964

Stuart T. DeBell, Chairman (Centreville)
Harriet Bradley (Dranesville)
Frederick A. Babson, Jr. (Falls Church)
Joseph Alexander (Lee)
Stanford E. Parris (Mason)
John P. Parrish (Mount Vernon)
John L. Beerman (Providence)

BOSMB No. 39, p. 232
6 January 1965

John P. Parrish, Chairman (Mount Vernon)

BOSMB No. 41, p. 432
5 January 1966

Frederick A. Babson, Jr., Chairman (Falls Church)

(Plan to have different Chairman and Vice-Chairman for 3 consecutive eight month terms.)

BOSMB No. 43, p. 196
7 September 1966

Joseph Alexander (Lee) elected Chairman

BOSMB No. 43, p. 393
18 October 1966

Frank F. Everest, Jr. (Mount Vernon) appointed to fill unexpired term of John P. Parrish.

BOSMB No. 43, p. 468
9 November 1966

C. Meade Stull (Centreville) appointed to fill unexpired term of Stuart T. DeBell.

BOSMB No. 45, p. 130
3 May 1967

John L. Beerman (Providence) elected Chairman

BOSMB No. 47, p. 218
3 January 1968

Frederick A. Babson, Chairman-at-Large
Joseph Alexander (Lee)
Donald R. Bowman (Springfield)
Harriet F. Bradley (Dranesville)
Herbert E. Harris, II (Mount Vernon)
Charles Majer (Annandale)
Harold O. Miller (Mason)
Martha V. Pennino (Centreville)
Thomas B. Wright (Providence)

BOSMB No. 58, p. 1-2

Dr. William S. Hoofnagle appointed to fill unexpired term of Frederick A. Babson

BOSMB No. 64, p. 53
19 May 1971

Virginia E. McEnearney (Springfield) appointed to fill unexpired term of Donald A. Bowman

BOSMB No. 68, p. 1
5 January 1972

William S. Hoofnagle, Chairman-at-Large
Joseph Alexander (Lee)
Herbert E. Harris II (Mount Vernon)
John Herrity (Springfield)
Alan H. Magazine (Mason)
Audrey Moore (Annandale)
Martha V. Pennino (Centreville)
Rufus Phillips (Dranesville)
James M. Scott (Providence)

BOSMB No. 70, p. 295
23 September 1972

Chairman Hoofnagle resigned.

BOSMB No. 71, p. 64
13 November 1972

Jean R. Packard, duly elected, sworn in as Chairman

Warren I. Cikins (Mount Vernon) after special election in January, 1975, replaced supervisor Herbert E. Harris, II, elected to Congress November, 1974.

BOSMB No. 82, p. 269
5 January 1976

John F. Herrity, Chairman
Joseph Alexander (Lee)
Audrey Moore (Annandale)
Martha V. Pennino (Centreville)
John P. Shacochis (Dranesville)
Marie B. Travesky (Springfield)
Warren I. Cikins (Mount Vernon)
Alan H. Magazine (Mason)
James M. Scott (Providence)

Bibliography

Introduction

Books

McCrary, Ben C. *Indians in Seventeenth Century Virginia.* Williamsburg, Va.: 350th Anniversary Celebration Corporation, 1957.

Rose, C. B., Jr. *Arlington County, Virginia: A History.* Arlington, Va.: Arlington Historical Society, 1976.

Smith, Captain John. *The Generall Historie of Virginia, New England and the Summer Isles.* London: printed by I. D. and I. H. for Michael Sparkes, 1624. Facsimile, World Publishing Co., 1966.

Stephenson, Robert L. *The Prehistoric People of Accokeek Creek.* Accokeek, Md.: Alice Ferguson Foundation, 1959.

Swanton, J. R. *The Indians of the Southeastern United States.* Bureau of American Ethnology Bulletin 137. Washington, D.C., 1946.

Articles

Gardner, William M.; Gluckman, Stephen J.; McDowell, Ellis E.; McNett, Charles W., Jr. "A Report of Excavation at the Stout Site," *Bulletin of the Archaeological Society of Virginia,* vol. 24. 1970.

Reynolds, E. R. "Ossuary at Accotink, Virginia." *Abstracts of Transactions of the Anthropological Society of Washington, D. C., 1880-1881.*

Section I   1649-1800

Books

Bailyn, Bernard. *The Ideological Origins of the American Revolution.* Cambridge: Harvard University Press, 1967.

Boyd, Julian P. *The Papers of Thomas Jefferson,* vol. 1. Princeton: Princeton University Press, 1950.

Colbourn, H. Trevor. *The Lamp of Experience.* Chapel Hill: University of North Carolina Press, 1965.

Commager, Henry Steele. *Documents of American History,* 6th ed. New York: Appleton-Century-Crofts, 1958.

Cresswell, Nicholas. *The Journal of Nicholas Cresswell, 1774-1777.* London: Jonathan Cape, Ltd., 1925.

Fitzpatrick, J. C., ed. *The Writings of George Washington from the Original Manuscript Sources, 1745-1799.* Washington, D. C.: United States Government Printing Office, 1932-1940.

Force, Peter, ed. *American Archives,* vols. 1 and 5. Washington, D. C.: M. St. Clair Clarke and Peter Force, 1837.

Freeman, Douglas Southall. *George Washington: A Biography.* New York: Charles Scribner's Sons, 1948.

Hamilton, Stanislaus Murray, ed. *Letters to Washington and Accompanying Papers,* vol. 5. Boston: Houghton, Mifflin and Company, 1901.

Harrison, Fairfax. *Landmarks of Old Prince William.* Berryville, Va.: Chesapeake Book Company, 1964.

Hening, William Waller. *The Statutes at Large: Being a Collection of all the Laws of Virginia. . .,* 13 vols. New York: R. & W. & G. Bartow, 1823.

Kilmer, Kenton, and Sweig, Donald. *The Fairfax Family in Fairfax County.* Fairfax, Va.: Fairfax County Office of Comprehensive Planning, 1975.

Labaree, Benjamin Woods. *The Boston Tea Party.* London: Oxford University Press, 1966.

Malone, Dumas. *Jefferson and the Rights of Man.* Boston: Little Brown and Co., 1951.

McIlwaine, H. R., ed. *Journals of the House of Burgesses of Virginia.* Richmond, Va.: 1909-1910.

Morgan, Edmund S., and Morgan, Helen M. *The Stamp Act Crises.* Chapel Hill: University of North Carolina Press, 1953.

Moxham, Robert M. *The Colonial Plantations of George Mason.* Springfield, Va.: Colonial Press, 1974.

Moxham, Robert M. *The Great Hunting Creek Land Grants.* Springfield, Va.: Colonial Press, 1974.

Rutland, Robert A., ed. *The Papers of George Mason,* vol. 1. Chapel Hill: University of North Carolina Press, 1970.

Sparks, Jared, ed. *Correspondence of the American Revolution being Letters of Eminent Men to George Washington. . .*, vol. 2. Boston: Little, Brown and Co., 1853.
Truro Parish, Virginia, Vestry. *Minutes of the Vestry, Truro Parish, Virginia, 1732-1785.* Lorton, Va.: Pohick Church, 1974.
Van Schreevan, William J., comp., and Scribner, Robert L., ed. *Revolutionary Virginia, the Road to Independence, Vol. I, Forming Thunderclouds and the First Convention, 1763-1774, A Documentary Record.* Charlottesville: University Press of Virginia, 1973.
Wood, Gordon S. *The Creation of the American Republic, 1776-1787.* Chapel Hill: University of North Carolina Press, 1969.

Articles and Periodicals

The Columbian Mirror and Alexandria Gazette, 1796.
Harrison, Fairfax. "A Map of Fairfax County in 1748." *Virginia Magazine of History and Biography* 36 (April 1928).
New Catholic Encyclopedia 10, 12 (1967).
Oxford English Dictionary 5.
Schlesinger, Arthur Meier, "Political Mobs and the American Revolution." *Proceedings of the American Philosophical Society* 99 (4).
"Test Acts," *Encyclopedia Britannica* 26 (1911).
Virginia Gazette (Purdie edition), 1775.
Virginia Gazette (Rind edition), 1774.
The Virginia Journal and Alexandria Advertiser, 1786, 1788, 1789; 1784-1789.
Virginia Magazine of History and Biography 3 (July 1895).

Collections, Unpublished Works, and Public Records

College of William and Mary. Earl Gregg Swem Library. Special Collections, Fairfax County Court Records.
Fairfax County (Virginia) Court Order Books: 1749-1763; 1772-1774; 1783-1793; 1797-1798; 1799-1800.
Fairfax County (Virginia) Deed Book B-1.
Fairfax Parish Vestry Book. Manuscript copy at Christ Church, Alexandria, Va. 1765-1770.
Library of Congress, Manuscript Division. Fairfax County List of Tithables for 1749.
Library of Congress, Manuscript Division. Peter Force Papers.
Library of Congress, Manuscript Division. Washington Papers.
Mitchell, Beth. "Tobacco Inspectors." Research Paper. Fairfax, Va.: 1975.
Mount Vernon Ladies Association of the Union Library, Washington Letters.
Stoessel, John. "The Port of Alexandria, Virginia in the Eighteenth Century." Master's thesis, Catholic University of America, 1969.
Sweig, Donald. "George Washington's Truro Parish Map." Research paper. Fairfax, Va.: Fairfax County Office of Comprehensive Planning, 1976.
Virginia State Library Archives, Alexandria City Legislative Petitions, 1779.
Virginia State Library Archives. Fairfax County Legislative Petitions, 1782; 1789.
Virginia State Library Archives. Fairfax County Personal Property Taxes, 1782.

Section II   1800-1840

Books

Adams, Henry. *History of the United States, 1801-1817,* vol. 8. Charles Scribner's Sons, 1904.
Affleck, Charles J. *The Obsolete Paper Money of Virginia.* 2d ed. Virginia Numismatic Association, 1968.
Asbury, Francis. *The Journal of the Rev. Francis Asbury.* New York: Bangs & Mason, 1821.
Bacon-Foster, Corra. *Patomac Route to the West.* Washington, D. C.: Columbia Historical Society, 1912.
Blanton, Wyndham B., M. D. *Medicine in Virginia in the Nineteenth Century.* Richmond, Va.: Garrett & Massie, 1933.
Board of Public Works. *Reports,* 1815-1816; 1818; 1826-1828. Richmond, Va.: Virginia State Library.
Calendar of Virginia State Papers, 8 and 9. Richmond, Va.
Caton, James R. *Legislative Chronicles of the City of Alexandria.* Alexandria, Va.: Newell Cole Co., 1933.
Corcoran Gallery of Art. *A Century of Alexandria, District of Columbia & Georgetown Silver, 1750-1850.* Exhibition Catalog, Washington, D.C.: Associates of the Corcoran Gallery of Art, January, 1966.
Craven, Avery O. *Soil Exhaustion as a Factor in the Agricultural History of Virginia and Maryland, 1606-1806.* Urbana: University of Illinois Press, 1925.

Cutton, George Barton. *Silversmiths of Virginia*. Richmond; Va.: The Dietz Press, 1952.

Dabney, Virginius. *Virginia: The New Dominion*. Garden City: Doubleday & Co., 1971.

Davis, John. *Travels in America, 1798-1802*. A condensation by Violet Davis Thatcher. Fairfax, Va., 1970.[?]

Davis, R. B. *Intellectual Life in Jefferson's Virginia*. Chapel Hill: University of North Carolina Press, 1964.

DiBacco, Thomas V. *Moorefield: Home of Early Baptist Preacher Jeremiah Moore*. Fairfax, Va.: Division of Planning, 1971.

Dunlap, William Cook. *Quaker Education in Baltimore and Virginia*. Philadelphia: 1936.

Ewell, James. *The Medical Companion*. Alexandria, Va.: Historic Alexandria Foundation, 1807.

Fordham, Elias Pym. *Personal Narrative of Travels in Virginia, Maryland. . . .* Cleveland: Arthur H. Clark Co., 1906.

Gamble, Robert S. *Sully: The Biography of a House*. Chantilly, Va.: Sully Foundation, Ltd., 1973.

Gutheim, Frederick. *The Potomac*. New York: Grosset & Dunlap, 1968.

Hallowell, Benjamin. *Autobiography* Philadelphia: Friend's Book Association, 1884.

Harlam, Alvin F. *Old Towpaths: The Story of the American Canal Era*. Port Washington, N.Y.: Kennikat Press, Inc., 1926.

Harrison, Fairfax. *Landmarks of Old Prince William*. Berryville, Va.: Chesapeake Book Company, 1964.

Hening, William Waller. *The Statutes at Large: Being a Collection of all the Laws of Virginia. . .,* 13 vols. New York: R. & W. & G. Bartow, 1823.

Jacobs, David, and Neville, Anthony. *Bridges, Canals & Tunnels*. New York: American Heritage Publishing Co. Inc. 1968.

Lord, Walter. *The Dawn's Early Light*. New York: W. W. Norton & Company, Inc., 1972.

Martin, Joseph. *A New and Comprehensive Gazetteer of Virginia and the District of Columbia*. Charlottesville, Va.: Joseph Martin, Mosely and Tompkins, Printers, 1836.

McIlwaine, H. R., ed. *Journals of the House of Burgesses, 1766-1769*. Williamsburg; Va.

Mitchell, Beth. *Beginning at a White Oak . . . Patents and Northern Neck Grants of Fairfax County, Virginia*. Fairfax, Va.: Fairfax County Office of Comprehensive Planning, 1977.

Moxham, Robert Morgan. *The Great Hunting Creek Land Grants*. North Springfield, Va.: Colonial Press, 1974.

Netherton, Ross D. *Colvin Run Mill*. Fairfax, Va.: Office of Comprehensive Planning, 1976.

Netherton, Ross, and Waldeck, Ruby W. *The Fairfax County Courthouse*. Fairfax, Va.: Office of Comprehensive Planning, 1977.

Netherton, Ross and Nan. *Green Spring Farm, Fairfax County, Virginia*. Fairfax, Va.: Office of Comprehensive Planning, 1970.

Packard, Joseph, D. D. *Recollections of a Long Life*. Washington, D. C.: Byron S. Adams, 1902.

Porter, Albert Ogden. *County Government in Virginia: A Legislative History, 1607-1904*. New York: Columbia University Press, 1947.

Rodrigues, Jeanne, with Hammond, William. *St. Mary's Fairfax Station, Virginia: The Beginnings and Growth of a Community*. Fairfax Station, Va.: St. Mary's Church, 1975.

Rose, Albert C. *Historic American Highways*. Washington, D. C.: American Association of State Highway Officials, 1953.

Royall, Anne Newport. *Sketches of History, Life and Manners in the United States*. Reprint. New York: Johnson Reprint Corp., 1970.

Ruffin, Edmund. *Essay on Calcareous Manures*. Petersburg, Va.: J. W. Campbell, 1832.

Russell, John H. *The Free Negro in Virginia*. Reprint. New York: Dover Publications, 1969.

Shepherd, Samuel. *Virginia Code of 1819*. Richmond, Va.: Thomas Ritchie, Printer to the Commonwealth, 1819.

Shepherd, Samuel. *Virginia Statutes at Large*, vols. 1 and 3. Reprint. New York: AMS Press, Inc., 1970.

Smith, Eugenia B. *Centreville, Virginia: Its History and Architecture*. Fairfax, Va.: Fairfax County Office of Comprehensive Planning, 1973.

Sprouse, Edith Moore. *Colchester: Colonial Port on the Potomac*. Fairfax, Va.: Fairfax County Office of Comprehensive Planning, 1975.

Starnes, George T. *Sixty Years of Branch Banking in Virginia*. New York: Macmillan Company, 1931.

Steadman, Melvin Lee, Jr. *Falls Church: By Fence and Fireside*. Falls Church, Va.: Falls Church Public Library, 1964.

Walling, H. C. *History of Dulin Chapel: 75th Anniversary History*. Falls Church, Va., 1944.

Watters, William, and Snowden, S. *A Short Account . . . .* Alexandria, Va., 1806. Library of Congress Rare Books Division.

Wiltse, Charles M. *The New Nation, 1800-1845*. New York: Hill and Wang, 1961.

Wrenn, Tony P. *Falls Church: History of a Virginia Village*. Falls Church, Va.: Historical Commission of the City of Falls Church, 1972.

Articles and Periodicals

Abbott, Richard H. "Yankee Farmers in Northern Virginia, 1840-1860." *Virginia Magazine of History and Biography*, January 1968.

Alexandria Advertiser and Gazette, 1798; 1800; 1801; 1803; 1805; 1806; 1808; 1809; 1810; 1811; 1812; 1815; 1816; 1835; 1842; 1876; 1962. (The *Alexandria Gazette* was published under several titles, including *Alexandria Advertiser*.)

"American Turf Register." February 1830.

Andrews, Marshall. "History of Railroads in Fairfax County." *Yearbook of the Historical Society of Fairfax County, Virginia* 3(1954).

Bailey, Worth. "Silversmiths of Alexandria." *Antiques Magazine*, February 1945.

Booth, Mordecai. National Archives Report on Removal of Powder from the Washington Navy Yard to Falls Church, 1814, Microcopy.

Brown, Brian. "Days of Sail in Alexandria." *Yearbook of the Alexandria Association*, 1957.

Clark, Allen C. "The Old Mills." *Records of the Columbia Historical Society* 31-32 (1930).

Curry, Mary E. "Theodore Roosevelt Island: A Broken Link to Early Washington, D.C. History." *Records of the Columbia Historical Society*, 48 (1971-72).

Daily National Intelligencer, 1809; 1821.

Davis, Courtland, and Alexander, Mrs. John. "Ravensworth." *Yearbook of the Historical Society of Fairfax County, Virginia, Inc.* 3 (1954).

Duhamel, James F. "Analostan Island." *Records of the Columbia Historical Society* 35-36 (1935).

Emery, Fred A. "Washington's Historic Bridges." *Records of the Columbia Historical Society* 39 (1938).

Howe, Charles E. "The Financial Institutions of Washington City in its Early Days." *Records of the Columbia Historical Society* 7-8 (1905).

Howrey, Edward F. "Foxhunting in Fairfax County." *Yearbook of the Historical Society of Fairfax County, Virginia, Inc.* 2 (1952-1953).

Johnson, Meredith, "A Day at Woodlawn with the Lewises." *Yearbook of the Historical Society of Fairfax County, Virginia, Inc.* 4 (1955).

Kabler, Dorothy Holcombe. "Early Cabinet Makers." *Yearbook of the Alexandria Association.* Alexandria, Va. 1957.

Lear, Tobias. "Observations on the River Potowmack and the Country Contiguous, &c." *New York Magazine or Literary Repository* 5 (1794).

"Letters of William Chamberlayne." *William and Mary Quarterly* 8(January 1928).

"The Medical Repository." 7-8(1797-1824). New York.

Mitchell, L.M. "Old Mills in the Centreville Area." *Yearbook of the Historical Society of Fairfax County, Virginia, Inc.* 6(1958-1959).

National Intelligence, 1825.

Peterson, Arthur G. "The Alexandria Market Prior to the Civil War." *William and Mary Quarterly,* Series 2, 12(April 1932).

Richmond Inquirer, 1809.

Stetson, Charles W. "George Washington's Woods on Four Mile Run." *Records of the Columbia Historical Society*, 1935.

Taylor, Robert L. "The History of the Potomac Bridges in the Washington Area." *The Arlington Historical Magazine* 1(October 1957).

True, Rodney H. "John Binns of Loudoun." *William and Mary Quarterly*, Series 2:1, January 1922.

Virginia Gazette and Weekly Advertiser. Richmond, Va.; 1783.

Wedderburn, Alex J. *Alexandria, Virginia, Souvenir Sesquicentennial, 1899.* Alexandria, Va.

Wyllie, John Cook, ed. "Observations Made during a Short Residence in Virginia." *Virginia Magazine of History and Biography*, October 1968.

Collections, Unpublished Works, and Public Records

Alexandria, Virginia, Will Book, 1811.

Anderson, Ellen. "Salona." Fairfax, Va.: Fairfax County Office of Comprehensive Planning, 1976.

Archives, Virginia State Library. Legislative Petitions, 1805.

Arlington County (Virginia) Deed Book, W-2.

Duke University, Broadside #3175, Alexandria, 1807.

Fairfax County [Virginia] Chancery Causes, Final #59 (198), Lee's Committee vs. Robertson.

Fairfax County [Virginia] Chancery Causes, Final #93 (4), Thompson vs. Swartwout.

Fairfax County [Virginia] Court Order Book, 1800; 1803; 1807-1810; 1817; 1820; 1822; 1825-1826; 1835; 1837-1838; 1840.

Fairfax County [Virginia] Deed Books, A-2, B-2, E-2, Q-1, D-3, C-4, R-4.

Fairfax County [Virginia] Will Books, G, J, K, L, M, N, Q, S, U.

Historical Society of Pennsylvania. Philadelphia, Pa: Society for Promoting the Abolition of Slavery Papers.
Historical Society of Pennsylvania. Philadelphia, Pa.: Drinker-Bringhurst Papers.
Historical Society of Pennsylvania. Philadelphia, Pa.: Parker Papers.
Library of Congress, Manuscripts Division. Collins Papers.
Library of Congress, Manuscripts Division. Richard Bland Lee Collection.
Library of Congress, Manuscripts Division. Force Collection, Charles Simms Papers.
Library of Congress, Manuscripts Division, Truro Vestry, List of Tithables, 1748/9, by Rev. Charles Green.
Marshall, J.B. Interview, Alexandria, Va., 1976.
Monk, Emily. Interview, Lyceum Exhibition on Silversmiths of Alexandria, June 1976.
"Mrs. Perry's Scrapbook." Alexandria, Va., Library.
Petersilia, Martin, and Wright, Russell. "Hope Park and Hope Park Mill." Fairfax, Va.: Office of Comprehensive Planning, 1972.
Richmond, Prince William County [Virginia]. Proceedings in Land Causes, Dumfries District Court.
Rothgeb, Roy Martin, Jr. "An Analysis of the Rise, Decline, and Possible Determinants of Redevelopment of the Seaport of Alexandria, Virginia." Master's thesis, College of the City of New York, 1957.
Slough, Donald. Interview, Stabler-Leadbeater Apothecary Museum, Alexandria, Va., May 1976.
Stuntz, Mrs. Mayo. Interview, Vienna, Va., 1976.
Sully Foundation, Ltd. Hunter Papers.
United States Decennial Census, 1790; 1810; 1820; 1830; 1840. National Archives, Washington, D.C.
Virginia Historical Society. Elizabeth Collins Lee Papers.
Virginia State Library Archives. Northern Neck Grant Book 2.

Section III   1840-1870

Books

Acts of the General Assembly of Virginia. 1831-1861.
Ambler, Charles H. *Francis H. Pierpont: Union War Governor of Virginia and Father of West Virginia.* Chapel Hill: University of North Carolina Press, 1937.
Bagby, George W. *The Old Virginia Gentleman and Other Sketches.* Edited by Ellen M. Bagby, Richmond, Va.: The Dietz Press, 1938.
Ballagh, James C. *A History of Slavery in Virginia.* Baltimore, Md.: Johns Hopkins University Press, 1902.
Boney, Francis N. *John Letcher of Virginia: The Story of Virginia's Civil War Governor.* University, Ala.: University of Alabama Press, 1966.
Buckingham, James Silk. *The Slave States of America,* Vol. 2. London: Fisher, Son & Co., 1842.
Cartmell, T. K. *An Historic Sketch of the Two Fairfax Families in Virginia.* New York: The Knickerbocker Press, 1913.
Catterall, Helen Tunnicliff, ed. *Cases From the Courts of England, Virginia, West Virginia and Kentucky.* Vol 1 of *Judicial Cases Concerning American Slavery and the Negro.* Washington, D.C.: Carnegie Institution of Washington, 1926-1927.
Channing, Steven A. *Crisis of Fear: Secession in South Carolina.* New York: Simon and Schuster, 1970.
Clark, Emmons. *History of the Seventh Regiment of New York.* 2 vols. New York: Published by the Seventh Regiment, 1890.
Clarke, James Freeman. *Autobiography, Diary and Correspondence.* Boston and New York: Houghton, Mifflin and Company, 1891.
Compendium of the Enumeration of the Inhabitants and Statistics of the United States, . . . Sixth Census. Washington, D.C.: Thomas Allen, 1841.
Cooling, Benjamin Franklin. *Historical Highlights of Bull Run Regional Park.* Fairfax, Va.: Fairfax County Division of Planning, 1971.
Cooling, Benjamin Franklin. *Symbol, Sword, and Shield: Defending Washington During the Civil War.* Hamden, Conn.: Archon Books, 1975.
Cornish, Dudley Taylor. *The Sable Arm: Negro Troops in the Union Army, 1861-1865.* 1956. Reprint. New York: W.W. Norton & Company, Inc., 1966.
Craven, Avery O. *Soil Exhaustion as a Factor in the Agricultural History of Virginia and Maryland, 1606-1860.* 1926. Reprint. Gloucester, Massachusetts: Peter Smith, 1965.
Crawford, J. Marshall. *Mosby and His Men: A Record of the Adventures of that Renowned Partisan Ranger, John S. Mosby.* New York: G.W. Carleton & Co., Publishers; London: S. Low, Son & Co., 1867.

The Debates and Proceedings of the Constitutional Convention of the State of Virginia, Assembled at Richmond, . . . December 3, 1867. Richmond, Va.: Office of the New Nation, 1867.

Debates and Proceedings of the First Constitutional Convention of West Virginia (1861-1863). 3 vols. Edited by Charles H. Ambler et al. Huntington, W. Va.: Gentry Brothers, Printers, n.d.

DeBow, J.D.B. *The Seventh Census of the United States: 1850.* [Book 1] Washington, D.C.: Robert Armstrong, Public Printer, 1853.

Dunlap, William C. *Quaker Education in Baltimore and Virginia Yearly Meetings.* [Philadelphia: The Science Printing Company, 1936].

Eckenrode, Hamilton James. *The Political History of Virginia During the Reconstruction.* Baltimore, Md.: Johns Hopkins University Press, 1904.

Elliott, Charles Winslow. *Winfield Scott: The Soldier and the Man.* New York: The Macmillan Company, 1937.

Epler, Percy H. *The Life of Clara Barton.* New York: The Macmillan Company, 1915.

Flers, Le Marquis de. *Le Comte de Paris.* London: W.H. Allen & Co., 1889.

Freeman, Douglas Southall. *Lee's Lieutenants: A Study in Command.* 3 vols. New York and London: Charles Scribner's Sons, 1942-1944.

Freeman, Douglas Southall. *R.E. Lee: A Biography.* 4 vols. New York and London: Charles Scribner's Sons, 1945.

Furnas, J.C. *The Road to Harper's Ferry.* New York: William Sloane Associates, 1959.

Gamble, Robert S. *Sully: The Biography of a House.* Chantilly, Va.: Sully Foundation, Limited, 1973.

Gates, Paul W. *The Farmer's Age: Agriculture, 1815-1860.* The Economic History of the United States, vol. 3. New York: Holt, Rinehart and Winston, 1962.

Genovese, Eugene D. *Roll, Jordan, Roll: The World the Slaves Made.* New York: Pantheon Books, [1974].

Gillette, William C. *Right to Vote: The Fifteenth Amendment.* Baltimore, Md.: Johns Hopkins University Press, 1965.

Goodwin, William Archer Rutherfoord, ed. *History of the Theological Seminary in Virginia and Its Historical Background.* 2 vols. New York: E.S. Gorham, 1923-1924.

Gray, Lewis Cecil. *History of Agriculture in the Southern United States to 1860.* 2 vols. 1933. Reprint. New York: Peter Smith, 1941.

Green, Constance McLaughlin. *Village and Capital, 1800-1878.* vol. 1 *Washington,* Princeton: Princeton University Press, 1962.

Hallowell, Benjamin. *Autobiography of Benjamin Hallowell.* Philadelphia: Friends' Book Association, 1883.

1871 Hand Book of the Baltimore Conference: Methodist Episcopal Church, South. Baltimore: King Brothers, 1871.

Hassler, Warren W., Jr. *General George B. McClellan: Shield of the Union.* Baton Rouge: Louisiana State University Press, 1957.

Howe, Julia Ward. *Reminiscences, 1819-1899.* Boston and New York: Houghton, Mifflin and Company, 1900.

Hurd, John Codman. *The Law of Freedom and Bondage in the United States,* Vol. 2. Boston: Little, Brown and Company, 1858.

Hurd, William B. *Alexandria, Virginia, 1861-1865.* Alexandria, Va.: City of Alexandria, 1970.

Jackson, Luther Porter. *Free Negro Labor and Property Holding in Virginia, 1830-1860.* New York and London: D. Appleton-Century Company, Inc., [1942].

James, Joseph B. *The Framing of the Fourteenth Amendment.* Urbana: University of Illinois Press, 1965.

Janney, Samuel M. *Memoirs of Samuel M. Janney.* Philadelphia: Friends' Book Association, 1881.

[Janney, Samuel M.]. *The Yankees in Fairfax County, Virginia.* Baltimore, Md.: Snodgrass & Wehrly, 1845.

Johnson, Allen, and Malone, Dumas, eds. *Dictionary of American Biography.* 20 vols. New York: Charles Scribner's Sons, 1928-1936.

Jones, Virgil C. *First Manassas: The Story of the Bull Run Campaign.* Gettysburg, Pa.: Historical Times, Inc., 1973.

Jones, Virgil Carrington. *Gray Ghosts and Rebel Raiders.* New York: Henry Holt and Company, 1956.

Jones, Virgil Carrington. *Ranger Mosby.* Chapel Hill: The University of North Carolina Press, 1944.

Journal of the House of Delegates of the [Restored] State of Virginia for the Extra Session, 1861. Wheeling, W. Va. Daily Press Book & Job Office, 1861.

Journal of the House of Delegates of the [Restored] State of Virginia for the Session of 1863-4. Alexandria, Va.: "State Journal" Print, 1864.

Journal of the House of Delegates of the State of Virginia for the Session of 1865-66. Richmond, Va.: Allegre & Goode, Printers, 1865.

Journal of the [Restored Virginia] Convention which Convened at Alexandria on the 13th Day of February, 1864. Alexandria, Va.: D. Turner, Printer to the State, 1864.

Journal of the Senate of the [Restored] Commonwealth of Virginia, (Extra Session) Begun and Held in the City of Wheeling, . . . July, 1861. Wheeling, W. Va.: "Daily Press" Book and Job Office, 1861.

Journal of the Senate of the [Restored] Commonwealth of Virginia, Extra Session, Held in the City of Wheeling, . . . December . . . , 1862. Wheeling, W. Va.: A.S. Trowbridge, State Printer, 1862.

Journal of the Senate of the State of Virginia Began and Held at the Capitol in Richmond . . . , 1865-66. Richmond, Va.: James E. Goode, 1866.

Journals and Papers of the Virginia State Convention of 1861, Vol. 1. Richmond, Va.: Virginia State Library, 1966.

Long, Armistead R. *The Constitution of Virginia: An Annotated Edition.* Lynchburg, Va.: J.P. Bell Company, 1901.

Lyell, Sir Charles. *A Second Visit to the United States*, Vol. 1. New York: Harper & Brothers, 1849.

Lyell, Sir Charles. *Travels in North America: With Geological Observations on the United States, Canada, and Nova Scotia*, Vol. 1. London: John Murray, Albermarle Street, 1845.

Machen, Arthur W., Jr., comp. *Letters of Arthur W. Machen with Biographical Sketches.* Baltimore, Md.: privately printed, 1913.

Mantell, Martin E. *Johnson, Grant, and the Politics of Reconstruction.* New York: Columbia University Press, 1973.

Mathews, Donald G. *Slavery and Methodism: A Chapter in American Morality, 1780-1845.* Princeton: Princeton University Press, 1965.

Maury, Matthew F. *Physical Survey of Virginia: Her Resources, Climate and Productions, Preliminary Report: No. 11.* Richmond, Va.: N.V. Randolph, 1878.

McKim, Randolph Harrison. *A Soldier's Recollections: Leaves from the Diary of a Young Confederate.* New York: Longmans, Green, and Co., 1910.

McKitrick, Eric. *Andrew Johnson and Reconstruction.* Chicago: The University of Chicago Press, 1960.

McPherson, James M. *The Struggle for Equality: Abolitionists and the Negro in the Civil War and Reconstruction.* Princeton: Princeton University Press, 1964.

Miller, Delavan S. *Drum Taps in Dixie: Memories of a Drummer Boy, 1861-1865.* Watertown, N.Y.: Hungerford-Holbrook Co., 1905.

Minutes of the Annual Conferences of the Methodist Episcopal Church, for the Year 1860. New York: Carlton & Porter, n.d.

Mitchell, Joseph B. *Decisive Battles of the Civil War.* New York: G.P. Putnam's Sons, 1955.

Moore, George Ellis. *A Banner in the Hills: West Virginia's Statehood.* New York: Appleton-Century Crofts, Division of Meredith Publishing Company, 1963.

Morgan, William H. *Personal Reminiscences of the War, 1861-5.* Lynchburg, Va.: J.P. Bell Company, Inc., 1911.

Morton, Richard L. *Virginia Since 1861.* History of Virginia, edited by Philip A. Bruce, vol. 3. Chicago and New York: The American Historical Society, 1924.

Mosby, John S. *The Memoirs of Colonel John S. Mosby.* Edited by Charles Wells Russell. Boston: Little, Brown, and Company, 1917.

Mosby, John S. *Mosby's War Reminiscences, and Stuart's Cavalry Campaigns.* New York: Dodd, Meade & Co., [1888].

Mott, James and Lucretia. *Life and Letters.* Edited by Anna Davis Hallowell. Boston: Houghton, Mifflin and Company, 1884.

Muir, Dorothy Troth. *Potomac Interlude: The Story of Woodlawn Mansion and the Mount Vernon Neighborhood, 1846-1943.* Washington, D.C.: Mount Vernon Print Shop, 1943.

Muir, Dorothy Troth. *Presence of a Lady: Mount Vernon, 1861-1868.* Washington, D.C.: Mount Vernon Publishing Company, 1946.

Murray, Charles Augustus. *Travels in North America During the Years 1834, 1835, & 1836*, Vol. 1. New York: Harper & Brothers, 1839.

My Ride to the Barbecue: Or, Revolutionary Reminiscences of the Old Dominion. By an Ex-Member of Congress. New York: S.A. Rollo, 1860.

Netherton, Ross D. *The Colvin Run Mill.* Fairfax, Va.: Fairfax County Office of Comprehensive Planning, 1976.

Nevins, Allan. *The War for the Union*, Vols. 1 and 2. New York: Charles Scribner's Sons, 1959-1960.

Oates, Stephen B. *To Purge This Land with Blood: A Biography of John Brown.* New York, Evanston, and London: Harper & Row, Publishers, 1970.

Olmsted, Frederick Law. *The Cotton Kingdom: A Traveller's Observations on Cotton and Slavery in the American Slave States.* New York: Mason Brothers, 1861.

Olmsted, Frederick Law. *A Journey in the Seaboard Slave States.* Vol. 1. New York: G.P. Putnam's Sons, 1904.

Porter, Albert Ogden. *County Government in Virginia: A Legislative History, 1607-1904.* New York: Columbia University Press, 1947.

Quarles, Benjamin. *Allies for Freedom: Blacks and John Brown.* New York: Oxford University Press, 1974.

Quarles, Benjamin. *The Negro in the Making of America.* New York: Collier Books, 1964.

Randall, James G. *Springfield to Gettysburg.* vol. 2. of *Lincoln the President.* New York: Dodd, Mead & Company, 1945.

Redford, A.H. *History of the Organization of the Methodist Episcopal Church, South.* Nashville: A.H. Redford, Agent for the Methodist Episcopal Church, South, 1871.

Report of the Joint Committee of the General Assembly of Virginia on the Harper's Ferry Outrages, January 26, 1860.

Virginia, North Carolina, South Carolina. Part II of *Report of the Joint Committee on Reconstruction at the First Session Thirty-Ninth Congress.* Washington, D.C.: Government Printing Office, 1866.

[Restored] *Virginia Constitution.* 1864.

Richards, Laura E., and Elliott, Maud Howe. *Julia Ward Howe.* Vol. I. Boston and New York: Houghton Mifflin Company, 1915.

Rose, Willie Lee, ed. *A Documentary History of Slavery in North America.* New York, London and Toronto: Oxford University Press, 1976.

Ruchames, Louis, ed. *John Brown: The Making of a Revolutionary.* New York: Grosset & Dunlap, 1969.

Russell, John H. *The Free Negro in Virginia, 1819-1865.* Baltimore, Md.: Johns Hopkins University Press, 1913.

Shanks, Henry T. *The Secession Movement in Virginia, 1847-1861.* Richmond, Va.: Garrett and Massie, 1934.

Shepherd, Samuel, comp. *The Statutes at Large of Virginia From October Session 1792, to December Session 1806. . . .* 3 vols. Richmond, Va.: Printed by Samuel Shepherd, 1835.

Simms, Henry Harrison. *The Rise of the Whigs in Virginia, 1824-1840.* Richmond, Va.: The William Byrd Press, Inc., 1929.

Snowden, William H. *Some Old Historic Landmarks of Virginia and Maryland, Described in a Handbook for Tourists. . . .* Philadelphia: J.B. Lippincott Company, 1894.

Spann, Barbara T. *Carlby.* Fairfax, Va.: Fairfax County Office of Comprehensive Planning, 1976.

Squires, William H.T. *Through Centuries Three: A Short History of the People of Virginia.* Portsmouth, Va.: Printcraft Press, Inc., 1929.

Squires, William H.T. *Unleashed at Long Last: Reconstruction in Virginia, April 9, 1865-January 26, 1870.* Portsmouth, Va.: Printcraft Press, Inc., 1939.

Statistics of the United States . . . in 1860; Compiled from the Original Returns of the Eighth Census. [Book 4]. Washington, D.C.: Government Printing Office, 1866.

Steadman, Melvin Lee, Jr. *Falls Church: By Fence and Fireside.* Falls Church, Va.: Falls Church Public Library, 1964.

Stuart, Alexander, H.H. *A Narrative of the Leading Incidents of the Organization of the First Popular Movement in Virginia in 1865 . . . and of the Subsequent Efforts . . . to Secure the Restoration of Virginia to the Union.* Richmond, Va.: William Ellis Jones, 1888.

Tharp, Louise Hall. *Three Saints and a Sinner: Julia Ward Howe, Louisa, Annie, and Dam Ward.* Boston and Toronto: Little, Brown and Company, 1956.

Thayne, Elswyth. *Mount Vernon is Ours: The Story of the Preservation and Restoration of Washington's Home.* New York: Duell, Sloan and Pearce, 1966.

Thomason, John W. *Jeb Stuart.* New York: Charles Scribner's Sons, 1930.

Trefousse, Hans L. *The Radical Republicans: Lincoln's Vanguard for Racial Justice.* New York: Alfred A. Knopf, 1969.

United States vs. The Great Falls Manufacturing Company. Deposition of Witnesses. Washington, D.C.: United States Government Printing Office, 1862.

Van Shreeven, William J. *The Conventions and Constitutions of Virginia, 1776-1966.* Richmond, Va.: Virginia State Library, 1967.

Villard, Oswald Garrison. *John Brown, 1800-1859: A Biography Fifty Years After.* Boston and New York: Houghton Mifflin Company, 1911.

Virginia Board of Public Works. *Annual Reports.* 1840-1860.

Virginia Constitution. 1830.

Virginia Constitution. 1851.

Virginia House of Delegates. Annual Message of the Governor of the Commonwealth and Accompanying Documents (title varies). 1840-1861.

Walker, Francis A., [comp.]. *A Compendium of the Ninth Census (June 1, 1870) Compiled Pursuant to a Concurrent Resolution of Congress. . . .* Washington, D.C.: Government Printing Office, 1872.

Walker, Francis A., [comp.]. *The Statistics of the Population of the United States . . . Compiled from the Original Returns of the Ninth Census (June 1, 1870).* Vol. I. Washington, D.C.: Government Printing Office, 1872.

---*The Statistics of the Wealth and Industry of the United States . . . Compiled from Original Returns of the Ninth Census (June 1, 1870).* Washington, D.C.: Government Printing Office, 1872.

Wallace, Lee A., Jr., comp. *A Guide to Virginia Military Organizations, 1861-1865.* Richmond: Virginia Civil War Commission, 1964.

War of the Rebellion: A Compilation of the Official Records of the Union and Confederate Armies. Series I. Washington, D.C.: Government Printing Office, 1880-1901.

Whitt, Jane Chapman. *Elephants and Quaker Guns: A History of Civil War and Circus Days.* New York: Vantage Press, 1966.

Williams, Kenneth P. *Lincoln Finds a General: A Military Study of the Civil War.* Vol. I. New York: Macmillan Company, 1949.

Williams, T. Harry. *Lincoln and His Generals.* New York: Alfred A. Knopf, 1952.

Williams, T. Harry. *P. G. T. Beauregard: Napoleon in Gray.* Baton Rouge: Louisiana State University Press, 1954.

Williamson, James J. *Mosby's Rangers: A Record of the Operation of the Forty-Third Battalion of Virginia Cavalry from Its Organization to the Surrender.* New York: Sturgis & Walton, Company, 1909.

Wills, Mary Alice. *The Confederate Blockade of Washington, D.C., 1861-1862.* Parsons, W.Va.: The McClain Printing Co., 1975.

Articles and Periodicals

Abbott, Richard H. "Yankee Farmers in Northern Virginia, 1840-1860." *Virginia Magazine of History and Biography* 66 (January 1968): 56-63.

Alexandria Boarding School. *Circular of Alexandria Boarding School, February 19, 1851.* Leaflet in Virginia Historical Society, Richmond, Virginia.

Alexandria Gazette. 1840; 1844-1846; 1850-1852; 1854-1856; 1858-1870.

American Agriculturist 6-10 (1847-1851).

Buckley, Richard Randolph. "A History of Clifton." *Yearbook of the Historical Society of Fairfax County* 4(1955).

Chapman, Thomas P., Jr. "The Secession Election in Fairfax County: May 23, 1861." *Yearbook of the Historical Society of Fairfax County* 4(1955).

Coates, Alice M., ed. "The Civil War Experiences of a Northern Family Settled in Virginia." *Yearbook of the Historical Society of Fairfax County* 8(1962-1963).

Country Gentleman 6-9 (1855-1857).

Cultivator (new series) 4 (1847).

DeBow's Review 12 (1857).

Farmers' Register 10 (1842).

Goss, Warren Lee. "Campaigning to No Purpose." *Battles and Leaders of the Civil War.* Edited by Robert Underwood Johnson and Clarence Clough Beel. Vol. 2 New York: Century Co., 1887.

Harpers Magazine 18 (1859).

Harper's Weekly 5 (1861).

Hickin, Patricia. "Gentle Agitator: Samuel M. Janney and the Antislavery Movement in Virginia, 1842-1851." *Journal of Southern History* 38(May 1971): 159-90.

Janney, Samuel M. "Virginia: Her Past, Present, and Future" in *Report of the Commissioners of Agriculture for the Year 1864.* Washington, D.C.: Government Printing Office, 1865.

Jones, Virgil Carrington. "General Stoughton's Capture." *Yearbook of the Historical Society of Fairfax County* 4(1955).

Lyon, Joan Gibbs. "The [Gibbs'] Home Place." *Yearbook of the Historical Society Fairfax County,* 9(1964-1965).

McDonald, John W. "Longstreet at Blackburn's Ford, July 18, 1861." *Yearbook of the Historical Society of Fairfax County* 3(1952-1953).

McDonald, John W. "Skirmishes near Bailey's Cross Roads, Fairfax County, Virginia, August 25 to September 1, 1861." *Yearbook of the Historical Society of Fairfax County* 2(1952-1953).

McDonald, John W. "Stuart's Burke Station Raid: 26-31 December." *Yearbook of the Historical Society of Fairfax County* 4(1955): 66

Milliken, Ralph LeRoy. "Then We Came to California: A Biography of Sarah Summers Clarke . . . ." *Yearbook of the Historical Society of Fairfax County* 8(1962-1963).

Monthly Journal of Agriculture 2(1846-1847).

Moore, Hannah M. Letter to Mrs. Jacob Walton Morris, 6 June 1861 In *Yearbook of the Historical Society of Fairfax County* 1(1951), 50-51.

New York, N.Y. *Times* 12 February 1862.

Philippe, Comte de Paris. "McClellan Organizing the Grand Army." from *Battles and Leaders of the Civil War*. Edited by Robert Underwood Johnson and Clarence Clough Beel, vol. 2. New York: Century Co., 1887.

Quenzel, Carroll H. "The Manufacture of Locomotives and Cars in Alexandria in the 1850's." *Virginia Magazine of History and Biography* 62 (April 1954): 181-89.

"Ravensworth." *Yearbook of the Historical Society of Fairfax County* 3(1954): 15-29.

Richmond, Virginia. *Whig.* 1845.

Smith, George Winston. "Ante-Bellum Attempts of Northern Business Interests to 'Redeem' the Upper South." *Journal of Southern History*, 11(May 1945), 177-213.

The Southern Methodist Pulpit 1-5 (1848-1852).

Southern Planter 2-19 (1841-1859).

Thompson, Pearl. "Woodlawn." *Yearbook of the Historical Society of Fairfax County*, 9(1964-1965).

U.S. House of Representatives, Committee of Elections. "S. Ferguson Beach: Report." Report No. 42. *Reports of Committees of the House of Representatives.* 37th cong., 2d. sess., 1862.

U.S. House of Representatives, Committee of Elections. Lewis McKenzie: Report." Report No. 33. *Reports of Committees of the House of Representatives.* 37th Cong., 3d. sess., 1863.

U.S. House of Representatives, Committee of Elections. "Charles Upton: Report." Report No. 17. *Reports of Committees of the House of Representatives.* 37th Cong., 2d. sess., 1862.

Washington, D.C. *National Era.* 1847-1860.

Washington, D.C. *National Intelligencer.* 1 June 1858.

Collections, Unpublished Works and Public Records

Alexandria County. Legislative Petitions, 1847-1860. Richmond, Va.: Archives Division, Virginia State Library.

Alexandria Female Seminary. Specimens of Composition of Pupils of the Alexandria Female Seminary Selected and Written by Themselves, 1853, 1858. Richmond, Va.: Virginia HIstorical Society.

Alexandria Town. Legislative Petitions. 1847. Richmond, Va.: Archives Division Virginia State Library.

Ball, William Selwyn. "Reminiscences of an Old Rebel." Xerox copy. Richmond, Va.: Virginia Historical Society, 1929-1931.

Bureau of Refugees, Freedmen, and Abandoned Lands. Fairfax County Virginia. Record Group 105, National Archives, Washington, D.C., 1865-1868.

Burrill, John Henry, Letters, 1861-1865. Xerox copy. *Civil War Times Illustrated* Collection. Carlisle Barracks, Pa.: U.S. Army Military History Research Collection.

Byrd Family Papers, 1791-1867. Richmond, Va.: Virginia Historical Society.

Caldwell, Alexander. Letters. 1863. Caldwell Family Letters. Xerox copy. *Civil War Times Illustrated* Collection. Carlisle Barracks, Pa.: U.S. Army Military History Research Collection.

Chamberlayne Family Papers, 1821-1938. Richmond, Va.: Virginia Historical Society.

Court Minute Books, 1839-1869. Originals in Fairfax County Courthouse, Fairfax, Virginia. Microfilm. Richmond, Va.: Archives Division, Virginia State Library.

Day, William Benjamin. Account Books, 1853-1889. Vol. 1 Richmond, Va.: Virginia Historical Society.

Deed Books. Libers D3-H3. Fairfax County Microfilm. Richmond, Va.: Archives Division, Virginia State Library.

Drane, S.C. Account Book, 1841-1842. Richmond, Va.: Virginia Historical Society.

Fairfax, Wilson Miles Cary. Diary, 1834-1857. Richmond, Va.: Virginia Historical Society.

Gerrish, Henry. Memoirs. 1909. Xerox Copy. *Civil War Times Illustrated* Collection. Carlisle Barracks, Pa.: U.S. Army Military History Research Collection.

Gillette, James. Letters. 1863. Xerox copy. *Civil War Times Illustrated* Collection. Carlisle Barracks, Pa.: U.S. Army Military History Research Collection.

Griscom, Manuscripts. Swarthmore, Pa.: Friends Historical Library, Swarthmore College.

Hall, Margery A. "History of Saint Paul's Church, Fairfax Parish, Alexandria, Virginia, 1810-1932." Mimeographed. Richmond, Va.: Virginia Historical Society, 1932-1933.

Heffelfinger, Jacob. Diary, April 1861-July 1865. Xerox copy. *Civil War Times Illustrated* Collection. Carlisle Barracks, Pa.: U.S. Army Military History Research Collection.

Hickin, Patricia. "Antislavery in Virginia, 1831-1861." Ph.D. dissertation, University of Virginia, 1968.

Hickin, Patricia. "John Curtis Underwood and the Antislavery Crusade, 1809-1860." Master's thesis, University of Virginia, 1961.

Samuel M. Janney Papers. Swarthmore, Pa.: Friends Historical Library, Swarthmore College.

Land Tax Books, 1840-1860. Fairfax County. Microfilm. Richmond, Va.: Archives Division, Virginia State Library.

Lee Family Papers, 1824-1918. Richmond, Va.: Virginia Historical Society.

George Bolling Lee Papers, 1813-1924. George Bolling Lee Papers, 1732-1870. Richmond, Va.: Virginia Historical Society.

Lee, Mary Custis. Letter to Mildred Lee, 19 June, [1861]. In *Yearbook of the Historical Society of Fairfax County* 1(1951):52-56.

Legislative Petitions, 1830-1860. Fairfax County. Richmond, Va.: Archives Division, Virginia State Library.

Letters of George Mason of Hollin Hall. Charlottesville, Va.: Alderman Library, University of Virginia.

[McNicol, Flossie C., comp. and ed.] Records of Frying Pan Springs Baptist Church. 1946. Richmond, Va.: Virginia Historical Society.

Moore, Hannah M. Letter to Mrs. Jacob Walton Morris, 6 June 1861. In *Yearbook of the Historical Society of Fairfax County* 1(1951), 50-51.

Muster Roll of Ball's Company, Co. I of the Northern Virginia Cavalry, 11th Regiment, 1861. Richmond, Va.: Virginia Historical Society.

Personal Property Tax Books, 1840, 1860. Fairfax County. Microfilm. Richmond, Va.: Archives Division, Virginia State Library.

Peyton Family Papers, 1770-1913. Richmond, Va.: Virginia Historical Society.

Pierpoint [sic], Francis H. Executive Journal, 22 June 1861-20 February 1865. In Papers of Francis H. Pierpoint [sic] and "Restored" Government of Virginia. Richmond, Va.: Archives Division, Virginia State Library.

Pierpoint [sic], Francis H. Miscellaneous Papers, January 1861-January 1868. Papers of Francis H. Pierpoint [sic] anc "Restored" Government of Virginia. Richmond, Va.: Archives Division, Virginia State Library.

Pierpoint, [sic], Francis H. Record Book of Proclamations and Messages, 1861-1863. RG-55. Executive Papers of Francis H. Pierpoint and "Restored" Government of Virginia. Richmond, Va.: Archives Division, Virginia State Library.

Record of the 1861 Virginia Convention. Precinct returns, 23 May 1861, referendum. Fairfax County. Richmond, Va.: Archives Division, Virginia State Library.

Records of the United States General Accounting Office. Records of the Third Auditor, 1794-1919. Southern Claims Commission, Fairfax County, 1871-1890. Record Group 217. Washington, D.C.: National Archives.

"Restored" Virginia Senate. Journal, July 1, 1861-May 15, 1862. In Papers of Francis H. Pierpoint and the "Restored" Government of Virginia. Richmond, Va.: Archives Division, Virginia State Library.

"Restored" Virginia Convention. "An Ordinance for the Reorganization of the State Government," n.d. In Ordinances of the Convention of West Virginia, 1861. Manuscript journal in Papers of Francis H. Pierpoint and the "Restored" Government of Virginia. Richmond, Va.: Archives Division, Virginia State Library.

Schubert, Joseph. "How I was Captured and My life in different Rebel Prisons [and] Penns." Xerox copy, n.d. Carlisle Barracks, Pa.: U.S. Army Military History Research Collection.

Gerrit Smith Papers. Syracuse, N.Y.: Syracuse University Library.

Smith, Elbert. "The Coming of the Civil War." Paper read at the Southern Historical Association Convention, 9 November 1975, Washington, D.C.

Society of Friends. Alexandria Men's Monthly Meeting. 1846-1849. Microfilm. Swarthmore, Pa.: Friends Historical Library, Swarthmore College.

Society of Friends. Alexandria Monthly Meeting. Minutes. Microfilm. Swarthmore, Pa.: Friends Historical Library, Swarthmore College.

Society of Friends. Alexandria Preparative Meeting. Minutes. 1833-1862. Microfilm. Friends Historical Library, Swarthmore, College. Swarthmore, Pa.:

Society of Friends. Cherry Street, Philadelphia, Pennsylvania, Monthly Meeting. Minutes. 1847. Microfilm. Swarthmore, Pa.: Friends Historical Library, Swarthmore College.

Society of Friends. Chester [Moorestown, New Jersey] Monthly Meeting. Minutes. 1847. Microfilm. Swarthmore, Pa.: Friends Historical Library, Swarthmore College.

Society of Friends. Darby, Pennsylvania, Monthly Meeting. Minutes. 1847. Microfilm. Swarthmore, Pa.: Friends Historical Library, Swarthmore College.

Society of Friends. Evesham, New Jersey, Monthly Meeting. Minutes. 1847. Microfilm. Swarthmore, Pa.: Friends Historical Library, Swarthmore College.

Society of Friends. Fairfax [Waterford, Virginia] Monthly Meeting. Minutes. 1839-1869. Microfilm. Swarthmore, Pa.: Friends Historical Library, Swarthmore College.

Society of Friends. Fairfax Quarterly Meeting. Minutes. 1847-1848. Microfilm. Swarthmore, Pa.: Friends Historical Library, Swarthmore College.

Society of Friends. New York, New York Monthly Meeting. Minutes. 1847.

Society of Friends. Nine Partners, New York, Monthly Meeting. Minutes. 1847.

Society of Friends. Saratoga, New York, Monthly Meeting. Minutes. 1847. Microfilm. Swarthmore, Pa.: Friends Historical Library, Swarthmore College.

Society of Friends. Troy, New York, Monthly Meeting. Minutes. 1847. Microfilm. Swarthmore, Pa.: Friends Historical Library, Swarthmore College.

Society of Friends. Upper Evesham, New Jersey, Monthly Meeting. Minutes. 1847. Microfilm. Swarthmore, Pa.: Friends Historical Library, Swarthmore College.

Society of Friends. Westbury, New Jersey, Monthly Meeting. Minutes. 1847. Microfilm. Swarthmore, Pa.: Friends Historical Library, Swarthmore College.

Society of Friends. Woodlawn Preparative Meeting. Minutes. 1860-1870. Microfilm. Swarthmore, Pa.: Friends Historical Library, Swarthmore College.

Stuart Family Papers. Charlottesville, Va.: Alderman Library, University of Virginia.

Tayloe Family of Richmond County, Virginia, Papers, 1650-1970. Richmond, Va.: Virginia Historical Society.

Thom, E.C. to mother, 25 January 1848. [Miscellaneous Papers.] Richmond, Va.: Virginia Historical Society.

Turner Papers. Record Groups. Swarthmore, Pa.: Friends Historical Library, Swarthmore College.

John C. Underwood Papers. Washington, D.C.: Manuscript Division, Library of Congress.

U.S. Census Office. Virginia Census Schedules. Agriculture. Fairfax County, 1850, 1860, 1870. Microfilm. Richmond, Va.: Archives Division, Virginia State Library.

U.S. Census Office. Virginia Census Schedules. Industry. Fairfax County, 1870. Microfilm. Richmond, Va.: Archives Division, Virginia State Library.

U.S. Census Office. Virginia Census Schedules. List of Inhabitants. Fairfax County, 1850, 1860, 1870. Originals in National Archives, Washington, D.C. Microfilm. Richmond, Va.: Archives Division, Virginia State Library.

U.S. Census Office. Virginia Census Schedules. Slave Schedules. Fairfax County, 1850, 1860. Originals in National Archives, Washington, D.C. Microfilm. Richmond, Va.: Archives Division, Virginia State Library.

Walker and McCollam. Alexandria, Virginia, Records, 1858-1859, Concerning Construction of the Customs House, Alexandria, Virginia. Richmond, Va.: Virginia Historical Society.

William Overton Winston Papers, 1858-1860. Richmond, Va.: Virginia Historical Society.

Wolf, Andrew M.D. "Black Settlement in Fairfax County, Virginia, During Reconstruction." Research paper. Washington, D.C.: St. Albans School for Boys, 1975.

Section IV   1870-1925

Books

Andrus, Virginia. *Selected Phases of Early Public Elementary Schools in Fairfax County, Virginia.* Master's thesis, George Washington University, 1947.

Chataigne's Virginia Gazetteer and Classified Business Directory. Richmond, Va.: J.H. Chataigne, 1877-78; 1884-85; 1897.

Collins, William G., ed. *Fairfax County, Va., Directory, 1906.* Falls Church, Va., 1906.

Curran, Louise C., and Curran, William J. *McLean Remembers.* McLean Scene, Inc., 1967.

Dabney, Virginius. *Virginia: The New Dominion.* Garden City: Doubleday, 1971.

Fairfax County Board of Supervisors, *Industrial and Historical Sketch of Fairfax County, Virginia.* Falls Church, Va.: Newell, 1907.

Fairfax County Chamber of Commerce. *Historic, Progressive Fairfax County in Old Virginia.* Alexandria, Va.: Newell-Cole Co., 1928.

Gamble, Robert S. *Sully: The Biography of a House.* Sully Foundation, 1973.

Geddes, Jean. *Fairfax County: Historical Highlights from 1607.* Middleburg, Va.: Denlinger's 1967.

Gutheim, Frederick. *A History Program for Fairfax County, Virginia.* Fairfax County Park Authority, 1973.

Henderson, E.B. (as told to Edith Hussey). *History of the Fairfax County Branch of the NAACP.* Fairfax, Va.: 1965.

Hinkle, Lonnie J. *A History of Public Secondary Education in Fairfax County, Virginia.* Ph.D. dissertation, George Washington University, 1971.

Hopkins, G.M. *Atlas of Fifteen Miles Around Washington Including the Counties of Fairfax and Alexandria, Virginia.* Philadelphia: G.M. Hopkins, 1879.

Loring Land and Improvement Company. *Town of Dunn Loring.* Judd & Detwiler, 1887.

Muir, Dorothy Troth. *Potomac Interlude: The Story of Woodlawn Mansion and the Mount Vernon Neighborhood, 1846-1943.* Washington, D.C.: Mount Vernon Print Shop, 1943.

Nickell, Lehman Patton, and Randolph, Cary J. *An Economic and Social Survey of Fairfax County.* University of Virginia Record Extension Series. Charlottesville, Va.: Michie, 1924.

Rust, Jeanne Johnson. *All-American Crossroads.* Fairfax, Va., 1970.

Rust, Jeanne Johnson. *A History of the Town of Fairfax.* Washington, D.C.: Moore & Moore, 1960.
Sandburg, Carl. *Abraham Lincoln: The War Years,* vol. 1. New York: Charles Scribner's Sons, 1939.
Schneider, Lottie Dyer. *Memories of Herndon, Virginia.* Marion, Va., 1962.
Snowden, William H. *Some Old Historic Landmarks of Virginia and Maryland, Described in a Handbook for the Tourist Over the Washington, Alexandria and Mt. Vernon Electric Railway.* Alexandria, Va.: G.H. Ramsay & Son, 1901.
Steadman, Melvin Lee, Jr. *Falls Church: By Fence and Fireside.* Falls Church, Va.: Falls Church Public ·Library, 1964.
Stewart, Charles Alexander. *A Virginia Village: Historical Sketch of Falls Church and the Old Colonial Church.* Falls Church, Virginia: J.H. Newell, 1904.
Trowbridge, John F. *The South: A Tour of its Battlefields and Ruined Cities.* Hartford, Connecticut: L. Stebbins, 1866.
United States Bureau of Census, Ninth Census, I. *The Statistics of the Population of the United States.* Washington, D.C.: Government Printing Office, 1872.
United States Bureau of Census. *Compendium of the Tenth Census of the United States, 1880,* Part I. Washington, D.C.: Government Printing Office, 1883.
United States Bureau of Census. *Twelfth Census of the United States, 1900,* Part I. Washington, D.C.: Government Printing Office, 1902.
United States Bureau of Census. *Thirteenth Census of the United States Taken in the Year 1910, Part III, Population 1910.* Washington, D.C.: Government Printing Office, 1913.
United States Bureau of Census. *Fourteenth Census of the United States Taken in the Year 1920, Part III, Population 1920.* Washington, D.C.: Government Printing Office, 1922.
United States Bureau of Census. *Fourteenth Census of the United States Taken in the Year 1920, Part II. Agriculture.* Washington, D.C.: Government Printing Office, 1922.
United States Bureau of Census. *United States Census of Agriculture, 1925, Part II, The Southern States.* Washington, D.C.: Government Printing Office, 1927.
United States *Report of the Commissioner of Agriculture, 1870.* "Status of Virginia Agriculture in 1870." Washington, D.C.: Government Printing Office, 1871.
Virginia Commissioner of Agriculture. *A Handbook of Virginia.* Richmond, Va.: Superintendent of Public Printing, 1879.
Virginia Education Commission and Virginia Survey Staff. *Virginia Public Schools,* Part I, Educational Survey Series, vol. 7. New York: World Book Co., 1920.
Virginia State Health Department. *Report of the Bureau of Vital Statistics for the Year.* Richmond, Va.: 1919.
Virginia State Health Department. *Report of the Bureau of Vital Statistics for the Year.* Richmond, Va.: 1920.
Walker, Ada. *Memories of Old Jefferson Institute.* Falls Church, Va.: 1964.
Whitehead, Thomas. *Virginia: A Hand-book.* Richmond, Va.: Everett Waddey Co., 1893.
Whitt, Jane Chapman. *Elephants and Quaker Guns: A History of Civil War and Circus Days.* New York: Vantage, 1966.
Williams, Ames W. *The Washington and Old Dominion Railroad.* Springfield, Va.: Capital Traction Quarterly, 1970.
Wrenn, Tony P. *Falls Church: History of a Virginia Village.* Falls Church, Va.: 1972.
Wrenn, Tony P. *Huntley: A Mason Family Country House.* Fairfax, Va.: Office of Comprehensive Planning, 1971.

Articles and Periodicals

Alden, Robert A. "Fairfax County and Constitutional Conventions: 1774-1956." *Yearbook of the Historical Society of Fairfax County, Virginia* 7(1960-61).
Alexandria Gazette, 1882.
Ball, Frank L. "Electric Railways of Arlington." *Arlington Historical Magazine* 3 (1966).
Bowman, A. Smith, Jr. "A History of Sunset Hills Farm." *Yearbook of the Historical Society of Fairfax County, Virginia* 6 (1958-59).
Buckley, Richard R. "A History of Clifton." *Yearbook of the Historical Society of Fairfax County, Virginia* 4 (1955).
Buckman, Horace D. 'The Quakers Come to Woodlawn." *Yearbook of the Historical Society of Fairfax County, Virginia* 9 (1964-65).
Burke, Elizabeth C. "History of Fairfax County." *Yearbook of the Historical Society of Fairfax County, Virginia* 5 (1956-57).
Butler, Susan Collet. "Windy Hill Farm." *Yearbook of the Historical Society of Fairfax County, Virginia* 11(1970-71).

Fairfax Herald, Fairfax, Virginia, 1872-1874; 1886-1889; 1891-1893; 1900-1901; 1904-1912; 1914-1918; 1921; 1923-1925.

Fairfax News, 1875.

Funk, W.C. "An Economic History of Small Farms Near Washington, D.C." *U.S. Department of Agriculture Bulletin 848*. Washington, D.C.: Government Printing Office, 1920.

Gott, John K., and Hogan, Katherine S. "Fairfax County Public Schools: A Brief History." *Legato School: A Centennial Sourvenir*. Fairfax; Va.: Fairfax County History Commission, 1976.

Herndon Observer, 1925; 1926; 1928.

Jones, Helen Rector. "A History of the Oakton School." *Yearbook of the Historical Society of Fairfax County, Virginia* 7 (1960-61).

Lyon, Harry B. "Wellington Villa and Vicinity." *Yearbook of the Historical Society of Fairfax County, Virginia* 9 (1964-65).

Lyon, Joan Gibbs. "The Home Place." *Yearbook of the Historical Society of Fairfax County, Virginia* 9 (1964-65).

Macgill, Mrs. Winfield Scott. "Hollin Hall." *Yearbook of the Historical Society of Fairfax County, Virginia* 9 (1964-65).

Mackall, John C. "McLean, Fairfax County, Virginia." *Yearbook of the Historical Society of Fairfax County, Virginia* 4(1955).

Marigold, Marguerite. "Hayfield." *Yearbook of the Historical Society of Fairfax County, Virginia* 9 (1964-65).

The McLean Scene, August 1965.

Parker, Mayme. "Along the River Front." *Yearbook of the Historical Society of Fairfax County, Virginia* 9 (1964-65).

Peters, Virginia B. "History of the Legato School." *Legato School: A Centennial Souvenir*, Fairfax, Va.: 1976.

Phillips, Clayton Beverly. "Education in Virginia Under Superintendent Richard Radcliffe Farr, 1882-1886." Master's thesis, University of Virginia, 1932.

Richmond State, 1882.

Richmond Times Dispatch, 1905.

Sheris, Candace Jo. "Truro Rectory." *Yearbook of the Historical Society of Fairfax County, Virginia* 11 (1971).

Shreve, Edgar. "Reminiscences of Mr. Edgar Shreve." *History of Dunn Loring and Vicinity*. Dunn Loring Volunteer Fire Department and the Ladies Auxiliary, Souvenir Program, 1954.

Shreve, Prentiss A. "A Short History and Some Anecdotes of Dunn Loring, Virginia, and Neighboring Towns." *History of Dunn Loring and Vicinity*. Dunn Loring Volunteer Fire Department and the Ladies Auxiliary, Souvenir Program, 1954.

Smith, Louise L. "St. John's Episcopal Church in McLean." *Yearbook of the Historical Society of Fairfax County, Virginia* 5 (1956-57).

Snowden, Kate. "The Passing of a Landmark." *Yearbook of the Historical Society of Fairfax County, Virginia* 9 (1964-65).

Wilkinson, Charles Kirk. "Sherwood Farm and Surrounding Area." *Yearbook of the Historical Society of Fairfax County, Virginia* 9 (1964-65).

Collections, Unpublished Works and Public Records

Corner, Charlotte, Interview, by Stephen L. Matthews, McLean, Va.; 12 August 1971.

Dunn, Pearl, Interview, by Stephen L. Matthews, Fairfax, Va.; 20 August 1971.

Fairfax County Board of Supervisors Minute Book, vol. 1.

Fowler, C.L. Fairfax County Agricultural Agent, Annual Reports, 1916.

Hebert, John, and Hebert, Celeste. "The History of the Town of Clifton, Virginia." Research paper Fairfax, Va.: Fairfax County Office of Comprehensive Planning, 1975.

Schug, Rita F. "The Town of Herndon " Research paper, George Mason University, 1973.

Steptoe, Lucy. Fairfax County Home Demonstration Agent, Annual Reports, 1924; 1925.

Stuntz, Mayo S. "Development of Postal Services in Fairfax County, Virginia, 1750-1890." Research paper, George Mason University, 1975.

Van Patten, Frances, Interview, by Stephen L. Matthews, Great Falls, Va.: 19 August 1971.

Wolf, Andrew M.D. "Black Settlement in Fairfax County, Virginia During Reconstruction." Research paper, Washington, D.C.: St. Albans School for Boys, 1975.

Section V   1925-1976

Books

Babcock, Richard F. *The Zoning Game.* Madison: University of Wisconsin Press, 1966.
Bacon-Foster, Corra. *The Patomac Route to the West.* Washington, D.C.: Columbia Historical Society, 1912.
Bemiss, FitzGerald. *Virginia's Common Wealth.* Richmond, Va.: 1965.
Bullock, Helen Duprey, and Morton, Terry, eds. *The Pope-Leighey House.* Washington, D.C.: The National Trust for Historic Preservation, 1969.
Bullock, Helen Duprey, and Morton, Terry, eds. *Woodlawn Plantation.* Washington, D.C.: The National Trust for Historic Preservation, 1971.
Burton, Robert C., and Knapp, Frederick D. *Socio-Economic Change in the Vicinity of the Capital Beltway in Virginia.* Highway Research Record Number 75. Washington, D.C.: Highway Research Board, 1965.
Cliver, E. Blaine, and Wrenn, Tony P. *The Dranesville Tavern: An Architectural Analysis.* Fairfax, Va.: Fairfax County History Commission, 1970.
Coates, Albert W., Jr. . . . *the most convenient wayes* . . . Richmond, Va.: Virginia Department of Highways, 1972.
Cooling, B. Franklin. *Historical Highlights of Bull Run Regional Park.* Fairfax, Va.: Fairfax County Office of Planning, 1970.
Cooper, Weldon. *Guide to County Executive Form of Government, Fairfax County, Virginia.* Charlottesville: University of Virginia, 1951.
Cron, F.W. *Pentagon Area Transportation Study.* Appendix A. Washington, D.C.: Bureau of Public Roads, 1960.
Dabney, Virginius. *Virginia: The New Dominion.* Garden City, N.Y.: Doubleday & Co., 1971.
Detwiler, Sadie C.; Nickell, Hollie; and Harrison, Katherine. *The County of Fairfax.* Charlottesville: University of Virginia; Fairfax County School Board, 1925.
Durham, C.J.S. *Washington's Potowmack Canal Project at Great Falls.* Fairfax County, Va.: The Nature Conservancy, Wildlife Management Institute and the Fairfax County Park Authority, 1957.
Eisenhower, Dwight D. *Crusade in Europe.* New York: Doubleday & Co., Inc., 1948.
Fairfax County Chamber of Commerce. *Historic, Progressive Fairfax County in Old Virginia.* Alexandria, Va.: Newell-Cole Co., Inc., 1928.
Fairfax County League of Women Voters. *Civil Rights in Fairfax County.* November 1964.
Fairfax County League of Women Voters of the Fairfax Area. *Mental Health Resources.* Fairfax, Va., September 1965.
Fairfax County League of Women Voters. *Race Relations in Fairfax County.* April 1964.
Fairfax County League of Women Voters. *Twenty Years!* Fairfax County, Va., 1966.
Fairfax County Office of Comprehensive Planning. *Fairfax County, Virginia Plan.* Fairfax, Va.: 1975.
Fairfax County Office of the County Attorney. *A Brief History of Planning, Zoning, and Environmental Constraints in Fairfax County, Virginia.* PLUS Program Research Paper 1. Fairfax, 1974.
Fairfax County Department of County Development. *Rainfall in Fairfax County.* Fairfax, Va.: Division of Design Review, 1972.
Fairfax County Farm Statistics, 1910-1966. Richmond, Va.: Virginia Cooperative Crop Reporting Service, August 1967.
Fairfax County, Virginia, Division of Public Affairs. *Annual Report,* Fairfax, 1967-1971.
Fairfax County, Virginia, Office of Research and Statistics. *History of Sanitary Districts in Fairfax County.* Fairfax: Office of Research and Statistics, 1975.
Fairfax County School Board. *Annual Report to the County.* Fairfax, Va.: Fairfax County Public Schools, 1964-1965; 1965-1966.
Fairfax County School Board. *Growing Up in Schools.* Fairfax: The Virginia Press, 1953.
Fairfax County School Board, Department of Instruction. *A Guide to Intergroup Education.* Fairfax, Va., 1965.
Fairfax County, Virginia, Public Schools. *Information for Parents.* Fairfax, 1975-1976.
Fairfax County Water Authority. *Your Water Supply Facilities.* Annandale, Va.: Fairfax County Water Authority, 1973.
Fairfax Education Association. *Yearbook.* Fairfax, Va., 1947-1948.
Fones, J. Larry. *FY 1977 Budget Request to James P. McDonald, Director, Budget and Financial Management,* 1975.
Gamble, Robert S. *Sully: The Biography of a House.* Chantilly, Va.: Sully Foundation, Ltd., 1973.
Gates, Robbins L. *The Making of Massive Resistance.* Chapel Hill: University of North Carolina Press, 1964.

The Gazetteer of the County of Cornwall. Truro, England: John Heard, 1817. British Museum, London.

George Mason University. *George Mason University Institutional Analysis Report.* Fairfax, Va.: 1975.

Gottmann, Jean. *Virginia In Our Century.* Charlottesville: 2nd ed; rev., The University Press of Virginia, 1969.

Gutheim, Frederick. *A History Program for Fairfax County.* Annandale, Va.: Fairfax County Park Authority, 1973.

Harwood, H.H., Jr. *Rails to the Blue Ridge.* Falls Church, Va.: Pioneer America Society, Inc. 1969.

Hemphill, W. Edwin. *Gold Star Honor Roll of Virginians in the Second World War.* Charlottesville: World War II History Commission, 1947.

Henderson, E.B. *The History of the Fairfax County Branch of the NAACP.* Annandale, Va.: The Turnpike Press, 1965.

Hilton, G.W., and Due, John F. *The Electric Interurban Railways in America.* Stanford: Stanford University Press, 1964.

Jacobsen, Hugh Newell. *A Guide to the Architecture of Washington, D.C.* New York: Frederick A. Praeger, 1965.

Johnson, Hugh A. *The Role of Commercial Agriculture in Land Use Planning for Fairfax County.* PLUS Working Paper No. 6. Fairfax, Va.: Office of Comprehensive Planning, 1974.

Keats, John. *The Crack in the Picture Window.* Boston: Houghton Mifflin, 1956.

Kilmer, Kenton, and Sweig, Donald. *The Fairfax Family in Fairfax County.* Fairfax, Va.: Office of Comprehensive Planning, 1975.

Lake Barcroft Community Association, Inc. *Lake Barcroft Directory.* Falls Church, Va., 1960.

Leep, Dena; Parmenter, Rae; and Smith, Vivian, eds. *Holmes Run Acres: The Story of a Community.* Falls Church, Va.: Holmes Run Acres Civic Association, 1976.

Muzyca, Joseph C., Sr., ed. *Historic Account, 1917-1976.* Fairfax, Va.: Fairfax County Health Department, 1976.

National Aeronautics and Space Administration, Office of Public Affairs. *Log of Apollo II.* Washington, D.C., 1972.

Netherton, Nan and Ross, eds. *Civic-Government Directory, 1956.* Annandale, Va.: Fairfax County Federation of Citizens Associations, 1956.

Netherton, Nan, ed. *Fairfax County Directory.* Falls Church, Va.: Fairfax County Cultural Association, 1965.

Netherton, Ross D. *The Colvin Run Mill.* Fairfax, Va.: Office of Comprehensive Planning, 1976.

Netherton, Ross D., *Control of Highway Access.* Madison, Wis.: University of Wisconsin Press, 1963.

Netherton, Ross and Nan. *Green Spring Farm.* Fairfax: Office of Planning, 1970.

Netherton, Ross, and Waldeck, Ruby. *The Fairfax County Courthouse.* Fairfax, Va.: Office of Comprehensive Planning, 1977.

Nickell, Lehman P., and Randolph, Cary J. *An Economic and Social Survey of Fairfax County.* Charlottesville: University of Virginia, 1924.

Northern Virginia Bureau. *The Hills of Northern Virginia.* Alexandria, Va.: Newell-Cole Co., Inc., 1926.

Northern Virginia Community College. *A Decade of Service, 1974-1975.* Annandale, Va.: NVCC Office of Planning Research and Management Services, 1976.

Northern Virginia Mental Health Institute. *Information Booklet.* n.d. (c. 1975)

O'Neal, William B. *Architecture in Virginia.* New York: Walker & Co., Inc., for the Virginia Museum, 1968.

Opstad, Donald O. *The History of the Fairfax Hunt, 1929-1972.* Fairfax, Va.: The Fairfax Hunt, 1972.

Rae, John B. *The American Automobile.* Chicago: University of Chicago Press, 1965.

Rodrigues, Jeanne, and Hammond, William. *St. Mary's, Fairfax Station, Virginia: The Beginnings and Growth of a Community.* Fairfax Station: St. Mary's Roman Catholic Church, 1975.

Sheatsley, David W., comp. *Fairfax County Profile.* Fairfax, Va.: Office of Research and Statistics, 1976.

Shott, George C. *The Belvoir Manor Project.* Fairfax, Va.: Department of Instructional Services, Division of Curriculum Service, Fairfax County Public Schools, 1974.

Steadman, Melvin Lee, Jr. *Falls Church: By Fence and Fireside.* Falls Church, Va.: Falls Church Public Library, 1964.

Stricker, Florence, ed. *The Big Splash: A History of Our Pool.* Annandale, Va.: Holmes Run Acres Recreation Association, 1963.

Templeman, Eleanor Lee, and Netherton, Nan. 1966 Reprint. *Northern Virginia Heritage.* New York: Avenel Books, 1976.

Truro Parish, Virginia, Vestry. *Minutes of the Vestry, Truro Parish, Virginia, 1732-1785.* Lorton, Va.: Pohick Church, 1974.

United States Bureau of the Census. *The Statistical Abstract of the U.S., The American Almanac.* New York: Grosset & Dunlap, 1973.
United States Department of Commerce, Bureau of the Census. *Statistical Abstract.* Washington, D.C.: U.S. Government Printing Office, 1960.
United States Department of Commerce. *1969 Census of Agriculture. County Data Book.* Washington, D.C.: U.S. Government Printing Office, 1972.
United States Department of Commerce, Bureau of the Census. *Statistical Abstract of Virginia. County and City Data Book.* Washington, D.C.: U.S. Government Printing Office, 1952, 1953; 1962.
University of Virginia. *An Administrative Survey of Fairfax County, Virginia.* Charlottesville, Va., 1957.
University of Virginia, Bureau of Population and Economic Research. *The Socio-Economic Impact of the Capital Beltway on Northern Virginia.* Charlottesville: University of Virginia, 1968.
University of Virginia, Thomas Jefferson Center for Political Economy. *Statistical Abstract of Virginia.* vols. 1 and 2. Charlottesville, Va., 1966.
Virginia Department of Highways. *Proceedings of the Fourth Annual Virginia Highway Conference.* Lexington, Va.,
Virginia Department of Highways. *Thirty-Seventh Report of the State Highway Commissioner to the Governor of Virginia.* Richmond, Va.: Division of Purchase and Printing, 1944.
Virginia Lives: The Old Dominion Who's Who. Hopkinsville, Ky.: Historical Record Association, 1964.
Who's Who in American Education. Nashville, Tenn.: Who's Who in American Education, Inc., 1955-1956.
Who's Who in the South and Southwest. Chicago: Marquis Who's Who, 1954.
Woodson, W.T. *Three Decades of Growth and Progress in Public Education.* Superintendent's Report, Fairfax, Va.: Fairfax County Public Schools, 1960-1961.
WPA Writers' Project. *Virginia: A Guide to the Old Dominion.* Reprint. New York: Oxford University Press, 1965.
Wrenn, Tony P.; Peters, Virginia B.; and Sprouse, Edith Moore, eds. *Legato School: A Centennial Souvenir.* Fairfax, Va.: Fairfax County History Commission, 1976.
The Yeonas Company. *Yeonas No. 1.* Vienna, Va.: 1973.

Articles and Periodicals

Alexandria Gazette. 10 January 1969.
Architectural Forum. December 1949; August 1951.
Bagdikian, Ben. "The Rape of the Land." *The Saturday Evening Post* 18 June 1966.
Barret, Mildred L. "Federal Aid in the Beginning." *Virginia Highway Bulletin.* Richmond: Virginia Highway Department, January, 1948.
Barron, John. "The Merrywood Deal." Washington *Sunday Star* 17 June 1962.
Beaudette, Rick. "Parks, Schools Are Nike Fallout." *Virginia Sentinel* 22 August 1973.
Bowman, A. Smith, Jr. "A History of Sunset Hills Farm." Vienna, Va.: *Yearbook of the Historical Society of Fairfax County* 6(1958-1959).
Bredemeier, Kenneth. "The Boom Fades as Area Weighs Value of Growth." *Washington Post* 30 December 1973.
Congregational Christian Church of Fairfax County. *Newsletter.* Annandale, Va.: Congregational Christian Church of Fairfax County, 13 February 1957.
Davis, S. John. "Humanizing the System Pays Dividends." *Fairfax Schools Bulletin.* Fairfax, Virginia: Department of School-Community Relations, June 1975.
Digby, Michael. "Explaining Voter Registration Rates in Virginia." *Institute of Government Newsletter.* Charlottesville: University of Virginia, 1975.
Equilibrium, 1(1). Palo Alto: Zero Population Growth, 1971.
Fairfax County Council of the Arts. *The Arts Newsletter.* Falls Church, Va.: May 1974.
Fairfax County Economic Development Authority. *The Fairfax Prospectus* 7 April 1976.
Fairfax County Federation of Citizens Associations Bulletin October 1853; November 1955; May 1956; November 1956; September 1957; February 1962; October 1966; November 1966; September 1968; June 1969; January 1972.
Fairfax County Industrial Authority. *The Fairfax Prospectus* vol. 1, no. 4 December 1970.
Fairfax County Police Department. *Newsletter.* vol. 1 no. 5 1975.
Fairfax County Office of Public Affairs. "How to Buy Firewood." *Weekly Agenda* 12(18 September 1974).
The Fairfax County Sun-Echo. 7 March 1957; 28 August 1958; 16 August 1962; 30 November 1964; 16 May 1967.
Fairfax Herald. 1925-1973.

Fairfax Journal. 10 July 1975.

Family Circle. November 1955.

Flynn, George. "Springfield Growth Surprises Planner." Washington: *The Sunday Star,* 24 April 1955.

Frank, Allen. "Main Issues at Herndon: Discipline, Public Voice." *Washington Evening Star* 25 October 1974.

Fugate, Douglas B. "Changing Highway Concepts." *Traffic Quarterly.* Saugatuck, Conn.: Eno Foundation, April 1970.

The Globe Newspapers, 12 February 1970; 10 July 1975; 25 September 1975.

Griffee, Carol. "Fairfax Zoners Approve Housing for Negroes." *Washington Evening Star,* 30 July 1964.

Groover, Fran. "Bring Back that Melody." *Virginia Cardinal* November 1973.

Grutzner, Charles. "Urban Complexes Fostered by Auto." *New York Times* reprint of summary report, 27 January-3 February 1957.

Hinkle. Betsy, ed. *Fairfax Newsletter.* 1956-1976.

"History of George Mason University." *George Mason University Catalog* 1973. Fairfax, Va.

Hollin Hills Civic Association. *Hollin Hills Bulletin.* 1951-1976.

Holmes Run Acres Civic Association. *Holmes Runner.* 1952-1976.

House and Home May 1952.

House Beautiful September 1951.

Knight, Athelia. "Defective Sewer Pipes Plague Fairfax Homeowners." *Washington Post* 4 January 1976.

Life Magazine 10 September 1951.

Neiley, Adelaide. *Fairfax Schools Bulletin,* 12(no.3, 1975).

Nelson, Robert T. "Ft. Hunt." *Yearbook of the Historical Society of Fairfax County, Virginia, Inc.* 9(1964-1965).

Netherton, Nan. "Three 'Northern Virginians.'" *Northern Virginia Country Yearbook* 1976.

Northern Virginia Sun. 22 August 1958; 14 September 1960; 9 October 1962; 15 February 1963; 4 March 1966; 12 May 1975; 11 June 1975.

Packard, Jean R. "PLUS, an innovative county planning program." *Journal of Soil and Water Conservation.* Ankeny, Iowa: The Soil Conservation Society of America, May-June, 1975.

Parents Magazine. February 1952.

Pimmit Hills Citizens Association. *Pimmit Hills Dispatch.* 1952-1976.

Pond, Peggy. "The Fairfax Hospital Story." *Virginia Cardinal* May 1972.

Population Reference Bureau, Inc. *Population Bulletin* 28:1(1972).

Providence Journal. 18 April 1969.

Reid, James, and Jentsch, Robert. *AIP Newsletter* April 1975.

The Reston Times. 18 June 1970; 9 September 1971.

Scharfenburg, Kirk. "Beltway is Now Boundary Line for Integration." *Washington Post.* 13 June 1971.

Seedlock, Maj. Gen. Robert F. "Ft. Belvoir Humming with 25,000 People." *Fairfax County Sun Echo.* 16 May 1967.

Shaffer, Ron. "Loan to Repair Dam at Lake Barcroft Approved by Small Business Administration." *Washington Post* 28 November 1972.

Shaw, Elliott G., Jr. "The Consequences of Urban Growth: The Fairfax County Experience." University of Virginia 23(1966). *Newsletter.*

Soil Conservation Service, United States Department of Agriculture. *Soil Conservation* October, 1957.

Sterago, Anthony. "Carlton Massey: Top Man in Fairfax County Government." *Annandale Free Press* 1 February 1968.

Stipe, Robert. "Why Preserve?" *Preservation News,* 12(July 1972).

Time Magazine 1 October 1973.

Virginia Department of Highways. *The Virginia Road Builder* 11(3).

The Virginia Outdoors. 2, No. 1, March 1971; 5, No. 1, August 1974.

Virginia Sentinel 21 June 1973.

Wall Street Journal 3 September 1971.

Washington Evening Star 23 August 1958.

Washington Evening Star, Citizen-of-the-Year Award Dinner *Programs.* Fairfax, 1950-1976. Fairfax, Va.: Fairfax County Public Library, Virginiana Collection.

Washington Post. 25 April 1955; 23 August 1958; 28 February 1971; 13 June 1971; 26 March 1975; 9 June 1975.

Washington Sunday Star, 30 October 1955.

Will, Edwin H. "The Past-Interesting; the Present-Intriguing; the Future-Bright: A Story of the Virginia Electric and Power Company." New York: The Newcomen Society in North America, 1965.

Wranek, William H., Jr. "The University Extension Center." *The Commonwealth Magazine* November 1955.
Zollman, W.M., Jr. "Provide for Growth Before It Comes." *The American City* June 1962.

Collections, Unpublished Works and Public Records

Beard, Joseph. Interview, Fairfax, Va., 9 August 1975; 23 November 1975.
Beresford, Anne. "The Three Lives of Walney." Manuscript, Fairfax County Office of Comprehensive Planning. Fairfax, Va.: 1977.
Cadman, Anne Bradford. "Washington Suburban Newspapers in Northern Virginia." Master's thesis, American University, 1967.
Cranshaw, Marvin. "History of Fairfax County Fire Departments." Fairfax County Public Library, Virginiana Collection, Fairfax, Va. 1976.
Davis, John. Interview, Northern Virginia Regional Park Authority, Fairfax, Va.: 17 December 1975.
Eubank, Sandy. "Racial Discrimination and Extremism: A National Overview." Fairfax County Public Library, Virginiana Collection, Fairfax, Va.: 1975.
Fairfax County Agricultural Extension County Agent. "Annual Reports." Mimeographed. Fairfax, Virginia, 1925-1971.
Fairfax City Board of Supervisors Minute Books: 5-12; 14-16; 18; 20-22; 47; 51-58; 75-77.
Fairfax County Deed Book, 3095.
Fairfax County Fire Service. "Fire Stations Charter or Operational Dates and Locations." Photocopied. 1976.
Fairfax County History Commission Minutes: 1969-1976.
Fairfax County personnel records.
Fairfax County Office of Public Affairs. "News Release," 15 April 1975; 27 May 1975.
Fairfax County Recreation Department. "About the Department: Its Origin." 1976.
Fairfax County School Board. Annual School Report to State Department of Education, 1928-1929; 1945.
Fairfax County School-Community Relations Office. Earl C. Funderburk Biography. Mimeographed. Fairfax, 1967.
Francis, Sharon. "The History of the Burling Tract." Photocopy. Fairfax County Public Library, Virginiana Collection, Fairfax, Va. 1972.
Hall, Charles L. Letter to Benjamin H. Weddle, Virginia Polytechnic Institute, 6 June 1973.
Harrison, Holden S. Interview, Herndon, Va., 21 July 1976.
Herndon Fortnightly Club, "The History of the Fortnightly Club and Library Association of Herndon, Virginia, 1972."
Memphis [Tennessee] Public Library and Information Center. "Rank of Southern Public Libraries." 1974.
Miller, Dr. K. Bruce. Interview, Luther Rice College, Alexandria, Va., 19 July 1976.
Pellettieri, Mimi. "History of FCCA." Photocopy. Fairfax County Council of the Arts, Fairfax, Va.: 1975.
Sloan, John. "A History of the Fairfax County Public Library, Virginia: Its Growth and Service." Master's thesis, University of Maryland, 1969.
Turner, Mrs. Mark S., Sr. Interview, Great Falls, Va., 21 July 1976.
Ward, Harold A. "Report on Special or Unusual Circumstances Effecting [sic] Federal Employees Residing in Fairfax County, Virginia." Hatch Act Exemption Committee, Fairfax County Federation of Citizens Associations, 1949.
Wilkins, Anne. Interview, Falls Church, Va.: 20 May 1974. Fairfax County Public Library, Virginiana Collection.
Woodburn Center for Community Mental Health. "Fact Sheet." Fairfax, 1975.
Zimmer, Carl and Anne. Interview, Pimmit Hills, Falls Church, Virginia, 6 August 1976.

Index